TOURISM

TOURISM

Principles,

Practices,

Philosophies

Tenth Edition

Charles R. Goeldner
J. R. Brent Ritchie

JOHN WILEY & SONS, INC.

Published by John Wiley & Sons, Inc., Hoboken, New Jersey
Published simultaneously in Canada

Library of Congress Cataloging-in-Publication Data

Goeldner, Charles R.
  Tourism : principles, practices, philosophies / Charles R. Goeldner, J.R.
Brent Ritchie.—10th ed.
      p.   cm.
  Includes bibliographical references and index.
  ISBN-13: 978-0-471-45038-2 (cloth)
  ISBN-10: 0-471-45038-3 (cloth)
1.   Tourism.   I. Ritchie, J. R. Brent.   II. Title.
  G155.A1M386   2006
  338.4′791—dc22
                                                            2005005944

Printed in the United States of America

10 9 8 7 6 5 4

CONTENTS

CHAPTER 10 • CULTURAL AND INTERNATIONAL TOURISM FOR LIFE'S ENRICHMENT 263

CHAPTER 11 • SOCIOLOGY OF TOURISM   297

PART FOUR   TOURISM SUPPLY, DEMAND, POLICY, PLANNING, AND DEVELOPMENT   325

CHAPTER 15 • TOURISM POLICY: STRUCTURE, CONTENT, AND PROCESS   403

CHAPTER 16 • TOURISM PLANNING, DEVELOPMENT, AND SOCIAL CONSIDERATIONS   435

PREFACE

Tourism can be defined as the science, art, and business of attracting visitors, transporting them, accommodating them, and graciously catering to their needs and wants (see additional definitions in Chapter 1).

In recent years, virtually every country throughout the world has taken steps to increase its number of visitors. The decrease in the cost of air travel and the continued development of technological resources such as the Internet have provided new opportunities for countries and individual tourism firms to promote tourism, both within and outside their borders. Political and industrial leaders have almost universally recognized the economic advantages that tourism can bring. However, what these countries have done to make tourism a viable, growing segment of their economy varies widely—from virtually nothing to the creating of superbly organized, highly productive tourism facilities. While the economic benefits of tourism have long been recognized, today greater attention is being paid to its social impact, which can be positive or negative, depending on how tourism is planned and managed.

This book is intended to be used primarily as a textbook for college and university courses in tourism. However, the book also provides valuable information and guidance for national, state, provincial, and local tourism offices, convention and visitors bureaus, chambers of commerce, tourism planning and development organizations, tourism promoters, tourist accommodations, attractions and other businesses, transportation carriers, oil and automotive companies, and any other organization that is interested or involved in the movement of people from their homes or business destinations.

NEW TO THIS EDITION

The tenth edition has been revised and updated to explore new trends in travel and tourism and discusses changes to the industry since the publication of the previous edition. New elements in the tenth edition include the following:

- New interior design
- Updated full-color insert featuring top tourist destinations
- Extensive treatment of the changing world of travel distribution
- Discussion of crisis management
- A new look at the future of travel
- Discussion of the use of the Internet in tourism research, marketing, and promotion
- Updated Internet Exercises at the end of each chapter
- Updated Internet Sites at the end of each chapter to provide an additional resource for students

ORGANIZATION AND CONTENT

This book explores major concepts in tourism, what makes tourism possible, and how tourism can become an important factor in the wealth of any nation. It is written in broad, global terms, discussing the principles, practices, and philosophies of tourism that have been found to bring about success. In this tenth edition of *Tourism,* even greater attention has been paid to the global impact of tourism, both economically and socially.

For tourism to be successful, a great variety of components must work together seamlessly to create a positive travel experience. This book is divided into six parts, which examine the various components of tourism, their function, and their significance.

Part 1 provides a broad overview of tourism, with chapters devoted specifically to the global impact of tourism, a history of travel, and career opportunities.

Part 2 looks at the governmental and private-sector organizations that provide services, products, and destinations for travelers. Individual chapters discuss tourist organizations, passenger transportation, lodging and food service providers, travel agents and wholesalers, and tourism attractions.

In **Part 3,** students learn about travel motivation, travel behavior, and the sociology of tourism.

Part 4 is devoted to tourism planning and a further examination of the components of tourism. A chapter on formulating tourism policy is included in this part. Other chapters cover topics such as tourism supply, forecasting demand, the economic impact of tourism, tourism planning, and environmental issues. In light of the growing importance of the environment, a particular effort has been made to explore fully the managerial issues at the tourism/environment interface—a point at which there is much potential for conflict.

Part 5 examines the important fields of tourism research and tourism marketing.

Part 6 looks at projections for tourism into the twenty-first century and suggests how today's

industry can prepare itself to accommodate future growth and meet tomorrow's challenges.

FEATURES

To help students better understand and process the information presented, a number of pedagogical features have been integrated into this textbook.

The **Learning Objectives** at the beginning of each chapter alert students to the important concepts that will be covered. The chapter Introduction sets the scene and provides some context for what students are about to read. When appropriate, boxes, tables, illustrations, photos, and Internet sites have been included to help illustrate important topics and ideas. The chapter discussion concludes with a written **Summary** to help students reinforce what they have read.

The authors have a number of **Readings** that follow some chapters. Excerpted from journals, government reports, and industry publications, the readings provide concrete examples of how the concepts discussed in the chapter are being put into practice. The list of **Key Concepts** serves as a valuable checkpoint for understanding the chapter topics. An updated directory of **Internet Sites** lists any Web sites referred to in the chapter, as well as additional sites to which students can turn for more information.

Three types of exercises have been provided to gauge student understanding of the subject matter. The **Questions for Review and Discussion** test students' recall of important chapter concepts and include some critical thinking questions. The **Case Problems** present hypothetical situations that require students to apply what they have learned. They can be used for written assignments or as the catalyst for class discussions. Also included are a series of **Internet Exercises**, designed to increase students' familiarity with technology by having them visit important travel industry Web sites and answer questions based on their investigation.

An *Instructor's Manual* (ISBN 0-471-78132-0) is available to professors who have adopted this book. The *Instructor's Manual* contains teaching suggestions, sample syllabi, and test questions and answers. A companion Web site, at **http://www.wiley.com/college** is also available with this text. It includes the *Instructor's Manual* and **PowerPoint slides**.

ACKNOWLEDGMENTS

As this tenth edition goes to press, we celebrate the thousands of students who have already begun their education in travel and tourism with previous editions of this book. We acknowledge their participation through their letters to us and to our publisher.

We are grateful for the help of all of the educators who have contributed to this and previous editions through their constructive comments and feedback at conferences, via telephone, and written correspondence.

Many thanks go to the current reviewers of the manuscript for their helpful comments. They include:

Denis Auger, University of Ottawa

David Baker, Eastern Illinois University

Bridget Bordelon, University of New Orleans

Jerusha M. Bloyer, North Carolina State University

John Bullaro, California Polytechnic State University

Liping Cai, Purdue University

Joseph Chen, Eastern Michigan University

Larkin Franks, Mount Hood Community College

Zaher Hallab, University of Southern Mississippi

M.J. Linney, El Paso Community College

Nancy Gard McGehee, Virginia Polytechnic University

Tony Psyck, State University of New York – Morrisville

Robert Robertson, Miami-Dade Community College

Roberta Sebo, Johnson & Wales University

Patty Silfies, Western Kentucky University

Dallen Timothy, Arizona State University

Muzzo Uysal, Virginia Polytechnic Institute and State University

We especially wish to thank Philip L. Pearce, Department of Tourism, James Cook University, Townsville, Queensland, Australia, for his contribution of Chapter 9, "Motivation for Pleasure Travel." A special word of thanks must also go to Dr. Richard F. Patterson, Associate Professor of Hotel, Restaurant, and Tourism Management, Western Kentucky University, who developed many of the Internet exercises for this textbook, and Cindy DiPersio, University of Colorado, and Jacqui Goeldner who proofread the manuscript.

We also acknowledge the support of the staff at John Wiley & Sons, especially JoAnna Turtletaub, Melissa Oliver, Tzviya Siegman, and Scott Amerman. Special recognition must go to Deb Angus at the University of Calgary, who tirelessly prepared the manuscript, artwork, index, and *Instructor's Manual*.

Charles R. Goeldner
University of Colorado

J. R. Brent Ritchie
University of Calgary

Tourism Overview

Florence, Italy, is a favorite destination in Europe for travelers around the world.
Copyright © Corbis Digital Stock.

TOURISM IN PERSPECTIVE

Learning Objectives

- Understand what tourism is and its many definitions.
- Learn the components of tourism and tourism management.
- Examine the various approaches to studying tourism and determine which is of greatest interest to you.
- Appreciate how important this industry is to the economy of the world and of many countries.
- Know the benefits and costs of tourism.

In Hong Kong, the eye moves quickly from boats in the harbor to the skyscrapers of the commercial center. *Copyright © Corbis Digital Stock.*

CHAPTER 1

INTRODUCTION

Bon Voyage!

You are setting off on a voyage to learn about the subject of **tourism.** Assuming that the forecasters and futurists are correct, you are studying the world's largest industry. Tourism is alive with dynamic growth, new activities, new destinations, new technology, new markets, and rapid changes. Record numbers of tourists are traveling the globe, attracted by an increased variety of tour packages, cruises, adventure experiences, and independent itineraries. All of these visitors and the activities they generate change local communities. They have an economic and social impact that cannot be ignored. In today's society, attention must be paid to environmental issues, cultural issues, economic issues, the way landscapes are created to appeal to tourists, and how tourists behave.

The tourism industry is global. It is big business and will continue to grow. Meeting this growth with well-planned environmentally sound development is a challenge for planning all over the world, whether it is Indonesia, Nepal, the United States, Australia, Thailand, or France. The goal of this chapter and the book is to raise issues, provide frameworks, and generate your thoughtful consideration of the issues and changes facing this complex field as it operates in an increasingly technological and global age.

WHAT IS TOURISM?

When we think of tourism, we think primarily of people who are visiting a particular place for sightseeing, visiting friends and relatives, taking a vacation, and having a good time. They may spend their leisure time engaging in various sports, sunbathing, talking, singing, taking rides, touring, reading, or simply enjoying the environment. If we consider the subject further, we may include in our definition of tourism people who are participating in a convention, a business conference, or some other kind of business or professional activity, as well as those who are taking a study tour under an expert guide or doing some kind of scientific research or study.

These visitors use all forms of transportation, from hiking in a wilderness park to flying in a jet to an exciting city. Transportation can include taking a chairlift up a Colorado mountainside or standing at the rail of a cruise ship looking across the blue Caribbean. Whether

Tourism is sightseeing in New York and other world-class cities, along with enjoying the museums, theater, food, architecture, and other activities urban settings provide.
Photo courtesy of NYC & Company.

people travel by one of these means or by car, motorcoach, camper, train, taxi, motorbike, or bicycle, they are taking a trip and thus are engaging in tourism. That is what this book is all about—why people travel (and why some don't) and the socioeconomic effects that their presence and expenditures have on a society.

Any attempt to define tourism and to describe its scope fully must consider the various groups that participate in and are affected by this industry. Their perspectives are vital to the development of a comprehensive definition. Four different perspectives of tourism can be identified:

1. **The tourist.** The tourist seeks various psychic and physical experiences and satisfactions. The nature of these will largely determine the destinations chosen and the activities enjoyed.
2. **The businesses providing tourist goods and services.** Businesspeople see tourism as an opportunity to make a profit by supplying the goods and services that the tourist market demands.
3. **The government of the host community or area.** Politicians view tourism as a wealth factor in the economy of their jurisdictions. Their perspective is related to the incomes their citizens can earn from this business. Politicians also consider the foreign exchange receipts from international tourism as well as the tax receipts collected from tourist expenditures, either directly or indirectly. The government can play an important role in tourism policy, development, promotion, and implementation (see Chapter 15).
4. **The host community.** Local people usually see tourism as a cultural and employment factor. Of importance to this group, for example, is the effect of the interaction between large numbers of international visitors and residents. This effect may be beneficial or harmful, or both.

Thus, tourism may be defined as the processes, activities, and outcomes arising from the relationships and the interactions among tourists, tourism suppliers, host governments, host communities, and surrounding environments that are involved in the attracting and hosting of visitors. (See the Glossary for definitions of **tourist** and **excursionist**.)

Tourism is a composite of activities, services, and industries that deliver a travel experience: transportation, accommodations, eating and drinking establishments, shops, entertainment, activity facilities, and other hospitality services available for individuals or groups that are traveling away from home. It encompasses all providers of visitor and visitor-related services. Tourism is the entire world industry of travel, hotels, transportation, and all other components that, including promotion, serve the needs and wants of travelers. Finally, tourism is the sum total of **tourist expenditures** within the borders of a nation or a political subdivision or a transportation-centered economic area of contiguous states or nations. This economic concept also considers the income multiplier of these tourist expenditures (discussed in Chapter 14).

One has only to consider the multidimensional aspects of tourism and its interactions with other activities to understand why it is difficult to come up with a meaningful definition that will be universally accepted. Each of the many definitions

Tourism is relaxing and enjoying a beautiful beach. The tranquility of St. Martin offers a quiet escape from the complexities of the modern world. *Photo courtesy of the Le Meridian Le Domaine, St. Martin.*

that have arisen is aimed at fitting a special situation and solving an immediate problem, and the lack of uniform definitions has hampered the study of tourism as a discipline. Development of a field depends on: (1) uniform definitions, (2) description, (3) analysis, (4) prediction, and (5) control.

Modern tourism is a discipline that has only recently attracted the attention of scholars from many fields. The majority of studies have been conducted for special purposes and have used narrow operational definitions to suit particular needs of researchers or government officials; these studies have not encompassed a systems approach. Consequently, many definitions of tourism and the tourist are based on distance traveled, the length of time spent, and the purpose of the trip. This makes it difficult to gather statistical information that scholars can use to develop a database, describe the tourism phenomenon, and do analyses.

The problem is not trivial. It has been tackled by a number of august bodies over the years, including the League of Nations, the United Nations, the World Tourism Organization (WTO), the Organization for Economic Cooperation and Development (OECD), the National Tourism Resources Review Commission, and the U.S. Senate's National Tourism Policy Study.

The following review of various definitions illustrates the problems of arriving at a consensus. We examine the concept of the movement of people and the terminology and definitions applied by the World Tourism Organization and those of the United States, Canada, the United Kingdom, and Australia. Later, a comprehensive classification of travelers is provided that endeavors to reflect a consensus of current thought and practice.

World Tourism Organization Definitions

The International Conference on Travel and Tourism Statistics convened by the World Tourism Organization (WTO) in Ottawa, Canada, in 1991 reviewed, updated, and expanded on the work of earlier international groups. The Ottawa Conference made some fundamental recommendations on definitions of tourism, travelers, and tourists. The United Nations Statistical Commission adopted the WTO's recommendations on tourism statistics on March 4, 1993.

Tourism

The WTO has taken the concept of tourism beyond a stereotypical image of "holiday making." The officially accepted definition is: "Tourism comprises the activities of persons traveling to and staying in places outside their **usual environment** for not more than one consecutive year for leisure, business, and other purposes." The term *usual environment* is intended to exclude trips within the area of usual residence, frequent and regular trips between the domicile and the workplace, and other community trips of a routine character.

1. **International tourism**
   a. **Inbound tourism:** Visits to a country by nonresidents
   b. **Outbound tourism:** Visits by residents of a country to another country
2. **Internal tourism:** Visits by residents and nonresidents of the country of reference
3. **Domestic tourism:** Visits by residents of a country to their own country
4. **National tourism:** Internal tourism plus outbound tourism (the resident tourism market for travel agents, airlines, and other suppliers)

Traveler Terminology for International Tourism

Underlying the foregoing conceptualization of tourism is the overall concept of traveler, defined as "any person on a trip between two or more countries or between two or more localities within his/her country of usual residence." All types of travelers engaged in tourism are described as **visitors,** a term that constitutes the basic concept of the entire system of tourism statistics. International visitors are persons who travel for a period not exceeding twelve months to a country other than the one in which they generally reside and whose main purpose is other than the exercise of an activity remunerated from within the place visited. Internal visitors are persons who travel to a destination within their own country, that is outside their usual environment, for a period not exceeding twelve months.

All visitors are subdivided into two further categories:

1. **Same-day visitors:** Visitors who do not spend the night in a collective or private accommodation in the country visited—for example, a cruise ship passenger spending four hours in a port—or day-trippers visiting an attraction

2. **Tourists:** Visitors who stay in the country visited for at least one night—for example, a visitor on a two-week vacation

There are many purposes for a visit—notably pleasure, business, and other purposes, such as family reasons, health, and transit.

United States

The Western Council for Travel Research in 1963 employed the term **visitor** and defined a **visit** as occurring every time a visitor entered an area under study. The definition of **tourist** used by the National Tourism Resources Review Commission in 1973 was: "A tourist is one who travels away from home for a distance of at least 50 miles (one way) for business, pleasure, personal affairs, or any other purpose except to commute to work, whether he stays overnight or returns the same day."

The Travelscope survey of the Travel Industry Association of America (TIA) research department defines a person trip as one person traveling 50 miles (one way) or more away from home or staying overnight, regardless of distance. Trips are included regardless of purpose, excluding only crews, students, military personnel on active duty, and commuters.

Canada

In a series of quarterly household sample surveys known as the Canadian Travel Survey that began in 1978, trips qualifying for inclusion are similar to those covered in Travelscope in the United States. The 50-mile figure was a compromise to satisfy concerns regarding the accuracy of recall for shorter trips and the possibility of the inclusion of trips completed entirely within the boundaries of a large metropolitan area such as Toronto.

The determination of which length of trip to include in surveys of domestic travel has varied according to the purpose of the survey methodology employed. Whereas there is general agreement that commuting journeys and one-way trips should be excluded, qualifying distances vary. The province of Ontario favors 25 miles.

In Canada's international travel surveys, the primary groups of travelers identified are nonresident travelers, resident travelers, and other travelers. Both nonresident and resident travelers include both same-day and business travelers. Other travelers consist of immigrants, former residents, military personnel, and crews.

United Kingdom

The National Tourist Boards of England, Scotland, and Northern Ireland sponsor a continuous survey of internal tourism, the United Kingdom Tourism Survey (UKTS). It measures all trips away from home lasting one night or more; these include: (1) trips taken by residents for holidays, (2) visits to friends and relatives (nonholiday), or (3) trips taken for business, conferences, and most other

Tourism is enjoying magical moments at Walt Disney World, where children of all ages delight in the parade that rolls down Main Street each day and in fantasies that come true. Guests discover worlds of fun at the 47-square-mile central Florida resort. *Photo courtesy of Walt Disney Parks and Resorts.*

purposes. In its findings, the UKTS distinguishes between holiday trips of short (one to three nights) and long (four-plus nights) duration.

The International Passenger Survey collects information on both overseas visitors to the United Kingdom and travel abroad by U.K. residents. It distinguishes five different types of visits: holiday independent, holiday inclusive, business, visits to friends and relatives, and miscellaneous.

Australia

The Australian Bureau of Industry Economics in 1979 placed length of stay and distance traveled constraints in its definition of *tourist* as follows: "A person visiting a location at least 40 kilometers from his usual place of residence, for a period of at least 24 hours and not exceeding 12 months."

In supporting the use of the WTO definitions, the Australian Bureau of Statistics notes that the term "usual environment is somewhat vague." It states that "visits to tourist attractions by local residents should not be included" and that visits to second homes should be included only "where they are clearly for temporary recreational purposes."

Comprehensive Classification of Travelers

The main types of travelers are indicated in Figure 1.1. Shown is the fundamental distinction between residents and visitors and the interest of travel and tourism practitioners in the characteristics of nontravelers as well as travelers. It also reflects the apparent consensus that business and same-day travel both fall within the scope of travel and tourism.

Placed to one side are some other types of travelers generally regarded as being outside the area of interest, although included in some travel surveys. Foremost among these exclusions are commuters, who seem to fall outside the area of interest to all in the travel and tourism community. Other travelers generally excluded from studies on travel and tourism are those who undertake trips within the community, which for convenience are described arbitrarily as trips involving less than a specific one-way distance, such as 50 miles. These "other travelers" have been focused on in the Nationwide Personal Transportation Surveys conducted by the U.S. Department of Transportation. The broad class of travelers categorized as migrants, both international and domestic, is also commonly excluded from tourism or travel research, on the grounds that their movement is not temporary, although they use the same facilities as other travelers, albeit in one direction, and frequently require temporary accommodation on reaching their destination. The real significance of migration to travel and tourism, however, is not in the one-way trip in itself, but in the long-run implications of a transplanted demand for travel and the creation of a new travel destination for separated friends and relatives.

Other groups of travelers are commonly excluded from travel and tourism studies because their travel is not affected by travel promotion, although they tend to compete for the same types of facilities and services. Students and temporary

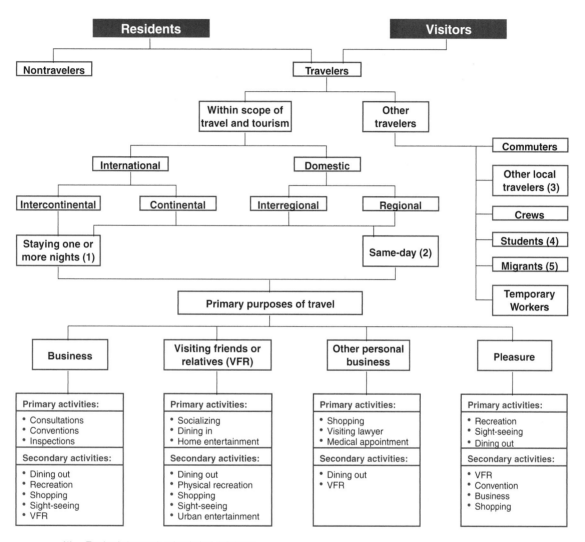

Primary purposes of travel			
Business	**Visiting friends or relatives (VFR)**	**Other personal business**	**Pleasure**
Primary activities:	Primary activities:	Primary activities:	Primary activities:
• Consultations • Conventions • Inspections	• Socializing • Dining in • Home entertainment	• Shopping • Visiting lawyer • Medical appointment	• Recreation • Sight-seeing • Dining out
Secondary activities:	Secondary activities:	Secondary activities:	Secondary activities:
• Dining out • Recreation • Shopping • Sight-seeing • VFR	• Dining out • Physical recreation • Shopping • Sight-seeing • Urban entertainment	• Dining out • VFR	• VFR • Convention • Business • Shopping

(1) *Tourists* in international technical definitions.
(2) *Excursionists* in international technical definitions.
(3) Travelers whose trips are shorter than those that qualify for travel and tourism: e.g., under 50 miles (80 km) from home.
(4) Students traveling between home and school only—other travel of students is within scope of travel and tourism.
(5) All persons moving to a new place of residence, including all one-way travelers, such as emigrants, immigrants, refugees, domestic migrants, and nomads.

Figure 1.1 Classification of travelers.

workers traveling purely for reasons of education or temporary employment are two leading examples. Another frequently excluded group consists of crews, although they can be regarded as special subsets of tourists.

Of those travelers directly within the scope of travel and tourism, basic distinctions are made among those whose trips are completed within one day. The same-day visitors are also called day-trippers and **excursionists** because they stay less than twenty-four hours. While they are important travelers, their economic significance pales in comparison to travelers who stay one or more nights. An additional meaningful division may also be made between those international travelers whose travel is between continents and those whose international travel is confined to countries within the same continent. In the case of the United States, the distinction is between (1) trips to or from the neighboring countries of Canada and Mexico or elsewhere

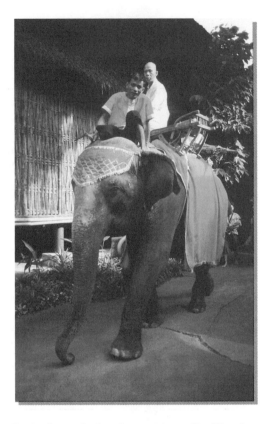

Tourism is engaging in unique experiences like riding elephants in interesting destinations such as Thailand.
Photographs Copyright © 2003 IMS Communications Ltd. www.picture-gallery.com.

in the Americas and (2) trips made to or from countries in Europe or on other continents.

The purposes of travel identified in Figure 1.1 go beyond those traditionally accepted because of the growing evidence that "visits to friends and relatives" (VFR) is a basic travel motivation and a distinctive factor in marketing, accounting for a major proportion of travel. In any event, "primary purpose" is an arbitrary concept because many journeys are undertaken for a combination of reasons, such as "business and vacation."

COMPONENTS OF TOURISM AND TOURISM MANAGEMENT

Tourism is a complex phenomenon, one that is extremely difficult to describe succinctly. Any "model" of tourism must "capture" the composition—or components—of the tourism system, as well as the key processes and outcomes that occur

The ability of Las Vegas to amaze and entertain seems unlimited. Its re-creation of many of the world's best-known destinations and icons offers visitors an exciting experience. *Photo courtesy of the Las Vegas News Bureau.*

within tourism. These processes and outcomes include the very essence of tourism, the travel experience, and the supporting means by which tourism is made possible. Figure 1.2 attempts to describe the complexity of the relationships among the many components of the tourism phenomenon.

The Tourist

The very heart of the tourism phenomenon model is unequivocally the **tourist,** and the travel experiences that he or she seeks when visiting a tourism destination. In order for a destination to provide stimulating, high-quality experiences, it is critical

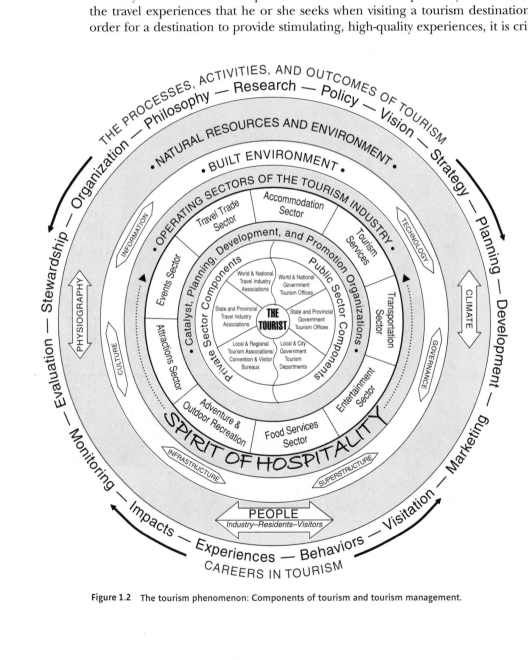

Figure 1.2   The tourism phenomenon: Components of tourism and tourism management.

that both policy makers and managers are able to understand tourists' motivation for pleasure travel, as well as the multiple factors that influence their selection of a destination, their mode of travel, and their ultimate choice among the myriad activities that may fulfill their travel needs. It is only when we understand the tourist as fully as possible that we can proceed to develop the facilities, events, activities, and programs that will distinguish a given destination, thus making it uniquely attractive to the tourist.

Natural Resources and Environment

A fundamental dimension of the model—indeed, the very basis of much tourism— is the Natural Resources and Environment component. Any given destination is primarily and unchangeably characterized by its **physiography** (the nature and appearance of its landscape) and its **climate** (the kind of weather it has over a period of years; i.e., the conditions of heat and cold, moisture and dryness, and wind). Finally, the third component of the natural environment is people. In the case of people, we must distinguish between two very important categories of individuals: (1) those who "belong" to the destination (its residents), and (2) those who are current or potential visitors to the destination (the tourism market).

Tourism is visiting the Indian Peaks Wilderness Area near Denver, Colorado, and marveling at all that nature has to offer. Outdoor recreationists recognize their responsibility to maintain the environmental integrity of the areas they explore. *Photo by Richard Grant, courtesy of Denver Metro Convention and Visitors Bureau.*

The Built Environment

Another dimension of the tourism phenomenon is the built environment that has been created by humans. This built environment first includes the culture of the residents of the host region. As discussed in Chapter 10, the **culture** of a people reflects many dimensions of its past development and its current way of life. Culture is relatively a very permanent characteristic of a destination, and one that cannot (and should not) be changed simply to enhance tourism development.

The **infrastructure** of a tourism destination is yet another dimension that has not been put in place mainly to serve tourism. Such basic things as roads, sewage systems, communication networks, and many commercial facilities (supermarkets and retail stores) have been put in place to meet the needs of local residents. While these components of the infrastructure can also be important to visitors, their primary functions are related to the ongoing daily needs of residents. In contrast, a destination's **tourism superstructure** includes those facilities that have been developed especially to respond to the demands of visitors. The most obvious examples include hotels, restaurants, conference centers, car rentals, and major attractions. Because of their special tourism orientation, the characteristics of components of the superstructure are essentially determined by visitor wishes rather than resident desires, even though residents often desire many benefits from certain elements of the tourism superstructure.

Technology is one of the most recent, and still increasingly influential, dimensions of the built environment that is shaping the nature of both tourism products/services and travel experiences. In many ways, technology can be viewed as one of the most distinctive and most powerful characteristics of the built environment since the dawn of modern tourism following World War II. The advent of jet aircraft and the massive invasion of telecommunications technology, linked closely with computer technology, have had a dramatic impact on the very essence of the tourism phenomenon. Indeed, each of these aspects of technology has become so pervasive and so important that they, in fact, represent very specialized elements of both the tourism infrastructure and superstructure. However, because of their unique identification with the modern era of the built environment, each merits specific identification.

A recent addition to the built environment of a destination is that of **information.** Increasingly, the success of a destination is determined by its ability to assemble, interpret, and utilize information in an effective manner. Information is of several types: information concerning the potential tourism market, which is essential for destination design and development; information on the level of satisfaction of current visitors regarding the quality, or enjoyment, of their visitation experience; information regarding competitors and their activities; information concerning the functioning or performance of the destination in its efforts to profitably provide attractive experiences to visitors; and information concerning the extent to which residents of the host region understand and support tourism as a long-term component of the socioeconomic system.

Finally, a dimension of tourism that often receives inadequate attention is the overall system of **governance** within which the tourism system functions. This topic is discussed in greater detail in Chapter 15. For present purposes, it should be noted that the system of governance surrounding tourism (the legal, political, and fiscal systems regulating its functioning) has a profound impact on the ability of a destination to compete in the international marketplace and subsequently plays a major role in determining the profitability of individual firms. While the system of governance of a country or region may be viewed as an evolutionary dimension of overall culture, it is subject to influence and change within an observable time frame. Sometimes these changes can be quite dramatic and can occur in a relatively short period of time in cultural terms. Recent high-profile examples include the worldwide phenomenon of deregulation and privatization and the more focused process of economic (and eventually social) integration brought about by the formation of regional trade blocs such as the European Union (EU) and the North American Free Trade Agreement (NAFTA). Parallel initiatives in Asia are Asia Pacific Economic Cooperation (APEC) and the Association of SouthEast Asia Nations (ASEAN). Even more recently, the events of September 11, 2001, have incited many governments to introduce new regulations concerning airline travel and entry to countries that impact on both domestic and international travel.

Operating Sectors of the Tourism Industry

The operating sectors of the tourism industry represent what many of the general public perceive as "tourism." First and foremost, the **transportation** sector (see Figure 1.2), comprising of airlines, bus companies, and so on, tends to typify the movement of people and travel (see Chapter 5). The **accommodation** sector, which includes many well-known "brands" such as Hilton, Marriott, Howard Johnson, Best Western, and so on, is highly visible to the public. Similarly, the **food services** sector also contains a broad spectrum of brands and logos that have become part of everyday life in many communities. Examples include the world-famous fast-food chains (McDonald's, Pizza Hut, Burger King, KFC) and internationally known gourmet restaurants such as Maxim's in Paris and Alfredo's in Rome. The accommodations and food service sectors are covered in Chapter 6.

The **attractions** sector also contains many well-known icons in the tourism industry. The undisputed leader of the attraction world is Disneyland/Walt Disney World. Other world-famous attractions include the upscale Louvre museum in Paris, France; the Hermitage in St. Petersburg, Russia; Marineland and Knott's Berry Farm in the United States; the pyramids in Egypt; Stonehenge in the United Kingdom; the Acropolis in Athens, Greece; and Niagara Falls, Canada. Attractions are the primary focus of Chapter 8.

Closely related to attractions is the **events** sector. Its icons include the Oktoberfest in Munich, Germany; the Calgary Stampede in Canada; the Mardi Gras of New Orleans and Rio de Janeiro, Brazil; the Boston Marathon; and the Super Bowl in the United States; as well as such transient events as World Cup Soccer and the International Summer and Winter Olympic Games.

The **adventure and outdoor recreation** sector is one of the most rapidly growing components of modern tourism. Changes in demographics, values, and lifestyles are creating increasing demand for activities such as golfing, skiing, snow-boarding, white-water rafting, parasailing, hang gliding, mountain biking, and mountaineering. Most of these activities are characterized by both an element of thrill seeking and an element of being outdoors. A closely related desire for close-ness to nature has given rise to the phenomenon of ecotourism, an ill-defined and often abused term for any type of travel activity in a natural setting (see Chapters 8 and 17).

At the other end of the "natural-manufactured" spectrum is the equally fast-growing component of **entertainment.** Certain destinations, most notably Las Vegas, Nashville, and Branson, Missouri, have grown up on a heavy diet of world-famous entertainers. More traditionally, New York/Broadway and Los Angeles/Hollywood have used various aspects of the entertainment industry to consolidate their worldwide reputations as "must see" destinations.

Less glamorous, but still essential to the success and well-being of the tourism industry, are the travel **trade sector** and **tourism services** (see Chapter 7). The travel trade is composed of the retail travel agent and the wholesale tour operator. Both of these entities are critical to linking "experience suppliers" and the tourist. The multifaceted travel industry services sector provides yet another type of critical support for successful tourism. Computer support services, retail services, financial services, specialized consulting services, and tourism educators all make an impor-tant and usually unique contribution to the effective and efficient functioning of the complex tourism system. While the public (and even many firms themselves) do not identify themselves as part of the tourism juggernaut, the fact remains that, as soon as any one of these services becomes deficient, tourism suffers.

Spirit of Hospitality

As discussed above, the operating sectors of tourism are responsible for delivering high-quality, memorable experiences. Care must be taken, however, to wrap these experiences in a warm spirit of hospitality. Quite simply, it is not enough to deliver all the attributes of an experience in a cold or detached manner. Each individual visitor must feel that he or she is more than a source of cold cash revenue for the business or destination. Rather, visitors have a natural human desire for warm ac-ceptance as they seek to enjoy the range of experiences the destination has to of-fer. As such, the challenge facing destinations is to deliver their experiences in a way that enables the visitors to believe they are welcome, that they truly are guests.

While tourists naturally recognize that they are transient visitors, destinations must first train industry personnel to treat the tourist with fairness, respect, and a level of politeness. Second, the destination must encourage its permanent resi-dents to behave as friendly hosts to visitors who are in unfamiliar surroundings. They should convey a friendly attitude and, when required, offer basic information and a helpful hand. These small but important gestures will do much to foster a destination spirit of hospitality that will, in turn, greatly enhance the perceived value of all the other aspects of the visitation experience.

The Anchorage Welcome Sign is but one means that communities use to convey to visitors the warm hospitality that local residents wish to offer to all tourists as they arrive at the destination. *Photo courtesy of Travel Alaska.*

Planning, Development, Promotion, and Catalyst Organizations

It is widely acknowledged that the success of tourism ultimately depends on the competence and ability of all of the operating sectors discussed above (i.e., the front line of tourism) to deliver a quality experience to each tourist—one person at a time. There is another hidden component of tourism that is equally important in determining the success of a tourism destination. It is known by the unwieldy name of **planning, development, promotion, and catalyst organizations** (PDPCO). It is the visionaries, policy makers, strategic planners, and individuals and groups who "make the right things happen" that are increasingly a determinant of successful tourism. In effect, in tourism it is as critical that we "do the right things" as that we "do things right." This means simply that policy makers need to ensure that their destination offers the kinds of travel experiences that are most appropriate to the visitor, always keeping in mind any limitations imposed by the resources of the destination.

Once the appropriate experiences have been identified through effective planning, it is essential to ensure that plans are translated into the facilities, events, and programs that are necessary to provide the visitor with the given experience "on the ground."

The organization responsible for providing the insight and leadership necessary to envisage and bring policies and plans into reality is increasingly referred to as the destination management organization (DMO). The specific identity of this organization depends on the "level" of the destination. In most countries, policy and planning involve two very important categories of stakeholders, namely, the public sector (governments) and the private sector (see Figure 1.2). At the **national** level, governments are usually represented by a national government tourism office (such as a department of tourism or a national tourism corporation). A national travel/tourism industry association typically represents the private sector.

At the **state/provincial** level, the public/private sector organizations are usually known respectively as the state/provincial government tourism office and the state/provincial travel industry association. The parallel equivalent at the **city/municipal** or **regional** level are local and city government tourism departments and local and city tourism associations or, more commonly, a convention and visitor bureau (CVB) (see Chapter 4).

The Importance of Integrated/Collaborative Planning and Development

One dimension of Figure 1.2 that is essential to note is the "wavy line" that forms the interface between the public and private sectors at all levels. This line is intended to convey the importance of integrated or collaborative planning and development efforts. Because both the public and private sectors each control (and often operate) an important percentage of tourism facilities, events, and programs, it is critical that policy, planning, and development efforts be continuously carried out within a joint, cooperative, collaborative organizational framework. Failure to acknowledge the importance of this reality leads only to antagonism, strife, and disjointed strategic planning and development. As such, each destination must strive to create DMOs where collaboration is built into the design. The actual name of the organization (be it a tourism authority, a tourism council, or a tourism partnership) matters little. What is important is the quality of the collaboration that occurs.

The Processes, Activities, and Outcomes of Tourism

Another dimension of Figure 1.2 that needs to be understood is the nature of the processes and activities that both surround and occur within the tourism system and that in the end create the outcomes that are the essence of the phenomenon we call tourism.

We have previously addressed the issue of organizing the components of tourism so that they work together effectively. As indicated, a common result of these organizational efforts is the creation of a DMO. For successful tourism, the DMO, in collaboration with all stakeholders, must define the tourism **philosophy** of the destination and formulate a supportive **policy, vision,** and **strategy** (see Chapter 15). These, in turn, provide direction and guidance for the detailed **planning** and **development** initiatives that will ultimately determine the nature and quality of the **experiences** the destination is capable of offering (see Chapter 16).

The availability of these "experience offerings" must be made known to potential visitors through effective **marketing,** defined in the broadest sense (see

Chapter 19). Such marketing includes highly visible promotional efforts as well as the less glamorous dimensions of pricing and distribution of the travel products/ experiences.

Successful marketing will attract a broad range of **visitors** whose **behaviors** provide them with enjoyment and the memorable experiences associated with these behaviors. These behaviors can give rise to both positive and negative **impacts.** The positive impacts pertain largely to the economic benefits (income and employment) that tourism provides. The negative impacts largely concern the ecological, social, cultural, and commemorative integrity of the destination.

The success of marketing efforts requires two subsequent activities. The first is a systematic **monitoring** of the levels and quality of visitation as well as visitor satisfaction regarding experiences and the destination (see Chapter 18). The second is a comprehensive program of **stewardship** to ensure that the success of tourism does not destroy the natural resources on which tourism depends so heavily (see Chapter 17).

The final activity that is essential to long-term success of tourism is an ongoing process of **evaluation.** Evaluation is simply an attempt to carefully assess the appropriateness, the effectiveness, the efficiency, and the overall performance of all components and processes in the tourism system. The results of the evaluation provide a critical source of information for the next ongoing stages of policy formulation, visioning, and strategic planning and development.

Careers in Tourism

All of the foregoing segments, sectors, and organizations require people to make the various processes work and to make the broad range of activities and experiences available to travelers. It is these "experiences" that are the tourism product, the intended outcome of the tourism phenomenon. The people in the tourism industry who provide these experiences, as in any industry, must perform a vast number of organizational functions. These functions range from relatively simple jobs to highly sophisticated and demanding tasks (see Chapter 3). All are important in providing a truly memorable vacation experience or efficient business travel.

The tourism industry is often characterized by the large number of frontline service jobs that must be performed for tourism to function effectively. For example, the accommodation sector requires bell staff, front desk staff, and room maintenance staff. The food services sector requires cooks, waitstaff, bartenders, and kitchen maintenance staff. The attractions sector requires facilitation and equipment operators, as do the entertainment, event, and transportation sectors. The adventure and outdoor recreation sector needs guides and group leaders. The travel trade and tourism services sectors must have the personnel to assist travelers as they plan their trips, and then to meet their many needs for information and assistance throughout their travel experiences. As can be surmised, the performance of the many tasks identified above requires many thousands of individuals who are trained to perform each specialized task in an effective and friendly manner.

But this is only the "face of tourism" that encompasses the many service jobs for which tourism is sometimes criticized, and even ridiculed. Behind this face (that incidentally provides many essential part-time and first-time jobs for students and less-skilled members of our society) are an extremely large number of highly attractive career positions that require sophisticated technical skills and/or managerial training. These career positions are attractive in two very different ways. First, they provide challenges equal to those in virtually any other industry. Second, the nature of tourism means that many of these careers are pursued in very attractive physical settings and among people who generally like to see others enjoy life. The career path of the manager of a large vacation resort, while just as challenging as those in many other sectors, offers both an attractive income and a lifestyle that is simply not available in many other sectors or professions.

BASIC APPROACHES TO THE STUDY OF TOURISM

Tourism commonly is approached through a variety of methods. However, there is little or no agreement on how the study of tourism should be undertaken. The following are several methods that have been used.

Institutional Approach

The institutional **approach to the study of tourism** considers the various intermediaries and institutions that perform tourism activities. It emphasizes institutions such as the travel agency. This approach requires an investigation of the organization, operating methods, problems, costs, and economic place of travel agents who act on behalf of the customer, purchasing services from airlines, rental car companies, hotels, and so on. An advantage of this approach is that the U.S. Census Bureau conducts a survey every five years on selected services that includes travel agents and lodging places, thus providing a database for further study.

Product Approach

The product approach involves the study of various tourism products and how they are produced, marketed, and consumed. For example, one might study an airline seat—how it is created, the people who are engaged in buying and selling it, how it is financed, how it is advertised, and so on. Repeating this procedure for rental cars, hotel rooms, meals, and other tourist services gives a full picture of the field. Unfortunately, the product approach tends to be too time-consuming; it does not allow the student to grasp the fundamentals of tourism quickly.

Historical Approach

The historical approach is not widely used. It involves an analysis of tourism activities and institutions from an evolutionary angle. It searches for the cause of innovations, their growth or decline, and shifts in interest. Because mass tourism is a fairly recent phenomenon, this approach has limited usefulness.

Managerial Approach

The managerial approach is firm-oriented (microeconomic), focusing on the management activities necessary to operate a tourist enterprise, such as planning, research, pricing, advertising, control, and the like. It is a popular approach, using insights gleaned from other approaches and disciplines. Although a major focus of this book is managerial, readers will recognize that other perspectives are also being used. Regardless of which approach is used to study tourism, it is important to know the managerial approach. Products change, institutions change, and society changes; this means that managerial objectives and procedures must be geared to change to meet shifts in the tourism environment. The *Journal of Travel Research* and *Tourism Management,* leading journals in the field, both feature this approach.

Economic Approach

Because of its importance to both domestic and world economies, tourism has been examined closely by economists, who focus on supply, demand, balance of payments, foreign exchange, employment, expenditures, development, multipliers, and other economic factors. This approach is useful in providing a framework for analyzing tourism and its contributions to a country's economy and economic development. The disadvantage of the economic approach is that whereas tourism is an important economic phenomenon, it has noneconomic impacts as well. The economic approach does not usually pay adequate attention to the environmental, cultural, psychological, sociological, and anthropological approaches. *Tourism Economics* is a journal utilizing the economic approach.

Sociological Approach

Tourism tends to be a social activity. Consequently, it has attracted the attention of sociologists, who have studied the tourism behavior of individuals and groups of people and the impact of tourism on society. This approach examines social classes, habits, and customs of both hosts and guests. The sociology of leisure is a relatively undeveloped field, but it shows promise of progressing rapidly and becoming more widely used. As tourism continues to make a massive impact on society, it will be studied more and more from a social point of view.

A prime reference in this area is *The Tourist: A New Theory of the Leisure Class,* by Dean MacCannell (Schocken Books, New York, 1976). Erik Cohen, of the Hebrew University of Jerusalem, has made many contributions in this area. Graham M. S. Dann, of the University of Luton, United Kingdom, has been a major contributor to the tourism sociology literature as well.

Geographical Approach

Geography is a wide-ranging discipline, so it is natural that geographers should be interested in tourism and its spatial aspects. The geographer specializes in the study of location, environment, climate, landscape, and economic aspects. The geographer's approach to tourism sheds light on the location of tourist areas, the movements of people created by tourism locales, the changes that tourism brings to the landscape in the form of tourism facilities, dispersion of tourism development, physical planning, and economic, social, and cultural problems. Because tourism touches geography at so many points, geographers have investigated the area more thoroughly than have scholars in many other disciplines. Because the geographers' approach is so encompassing—dealing with land use, economic aspects, demographic impacts, and cultural problems—a study of their contributions is highly recommended. Recreational geography is a common course title used by geographers studying this specialty. Because tourism, leisure, and recreation are so closely related, it is necessary to search for literature under all these titles to discover the contributions of various fields. Geographers were instrumental in starting both the *Journal of Leisure Research* and *Leisure Sciences.* Another journal, *Tourism Geographies,* was launched in February 1999 with the aim of providing a forum for the presentation and discussion of geographic perspectives on tourism and tourism-related areas of recreation and leisure studies.

Interdisciplinary Approaches

Tourism embraces virtually all aspects of our society. We have cultural and heritage tourism, which calls for an anthropological approach. Because people behave in different ways and travel for different reasons, it is necessary to use a psychological approach to determine the best way to promote and market tourism products. Because tourists cross borders and require passports and visas from government offices, and because most countries have government-operated tourism development departments, we find that political institutions are involved and are calling for a political science approach. Any industry that becomes an economic giant affecting the lives of many people attracts the attention of legislative bodies (along with that of the sociologists, geographers, economists, and anthropologists), which create the laws, regulations, and legal environment in which the tourist industry must operate; so we also have a legal approach. The great importance of transportation suggests passenger transportation as another approach. The fact simply is that tourism is so vast, so complex, and so multifaceted that it is necessary to have a number of approaches to studying the field, each geared to a somewhat different task or objective. Figure 1.3 illustrates the interdisciplinary nature of tourism studies and their reciprocity and mutuality. The *Annals of Tourism Research,* an interdisciplinary social sciences journal, is another publication that should be on the serious tourism student's reading list.

The Systems Approach

What is really needed to study tourism is a systems approach. A system is a set of interrelated groups coordinated to form a unified whole and organized to accomplish a set of goals. It integrates the other approaches into a comprehensive

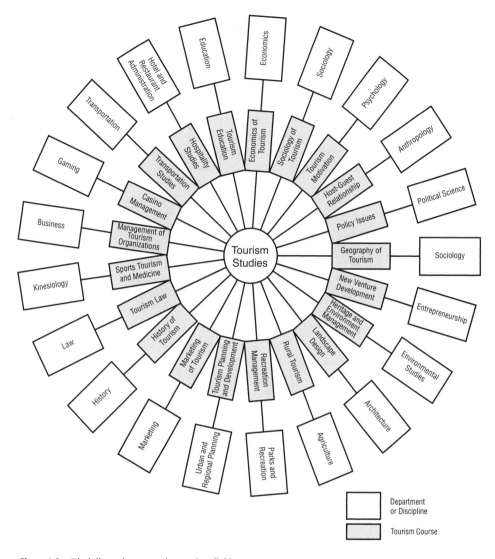

Figure 1.3 Disciplinary inputs to the tourism field. *Adapted from Jafar Jafari, University of Wisconsin-Stout,* Study of Tourism: Choices of Discipline and Approach.

method dealing with both micro and macro issues. It can examine the tourist firm's competitive environment, its market, its results, its linkages with other institutions, the consumer, and the interaction of the firm with the consumer. In addition, a system can take a macro viewpoint and examine the entire tourism system of a country, state, or area and how it operates within and relates to other systems, such as legal, political, economic, and social systems.

ECONOMIC IMPORTANCE

The World Travel and Tourism Council (WTTC) has been measuring the economic impact of travel and tourism for the world, regions, and OECD countries since 1991. In 1992 they released their first estimates indicating that travel and tourism is one of the world's largest industries and a generator of quality jobs. They continue their measurement efforts, and Table 1.1 shows their most recent world estimates for 2005 and forecasts for 2015. In 2005 the global travel and tourism industry was expected to generate $4.7 trillion of economic activity and over 221 million jobs (direct and indirect). Travel and tourism is projected to grow to $7.8 trillion of economic activity and over 269 million jobs by 2015.

Globally in 2005, the travel and tourism economy (direct and indirect) employment is estimated at 221,568,000 jobs, 8.3 percent of total employment, or 1 in every 12.0 jobs. By 2015, this should total 269,556,000 jobs, 8.9 percent of total employment or 1 in every 11.2 jobs. The world travel and tourism economy's contribution to gross domestic product is expected to total 10.6 percent ($4.7 trillion) in 2005 and rise to 11.3 percent ($7.8 trillion) in 2015.

The economic figures cited show that tourism has grown to be an activity of worldwide **importance** and **significance.** For a number of countries, tourism is the largest commodity in international trade. In many others, it ranks among the top three industries. Tourism has grown rapidly to become a major social and economic force in the world.

The 2005 WTTC estimates for the world is the fifth set of Tourism Satellite Accounting (TSA) that Oxford Economic Forecasting has prepared for WTTC. The first, commissioned in 2001, reengineered the models previously developed during the 1990s. The second, prepared in 2002, served an important role in helping to quantify the tragic events of September 11, 2001, on tourism. The third in 2003, significantly upgraded and enhanced the quality, sophistication, and precision of the

TABLE 1.1	**WORLD ECONOMIC IMPACT: ESTIMATES AND FORECASTS**			
	2005		**2015**	
WORLD	US$ BILLION	% OF TOT	US$ BILLION	% OF TOT
Personal Travel & Tourism	2,833.1	10.4	4,602.0	11.0
Business Travel	652.9	—	962.7	—
Government Expenditures	285.3	—	417.4	—
Capital Investment	918.0	9.4	1,673.0	10.0
Visitor Exports and Other Exports	1,512.5	12.0	3,023.5	11.0
Travel & Tourism Demand	6,201.5	—	10,678.5	—
T&T Industry GDP	1,712.4	3.8	2,660.6	3.9
T&T Economy GDP	4,745.7	10.6	7,798.7	11.3
T&T Industry Employment (000)	74,223.0	2.8	85,521	2.8
T&T Economy Employment (000)	221,568.0	8.3	269,556	8.9

Source: World Travel and Tourism Council.

STATISTICAL DATA AVAILABILITY

One of the problems in collecting and reporting statistical data for a book is the data lag. As this book was being revised, 2003 data were just becoming available. Unfortunately, data lags are increasing rather than decreasing. This disturbing reality is especially upsetting when one considers that travel is a dynamic and changing industry. The data in this book provide a perspective on the size and importance of the industry and its sectors. Users are encouraged to access the sources provided to update the information and determine if trends are continuing or changing. One of the best ways to do that is to get on the Internet. Web site addresses are provided in many cases to enable you to locate the latest information available.

TSA research and presented a second (worst-case) scenario for the Iraq war. The 2004 research increased the world coverage by adding thirteen countries not previously included in the TSA research, bringing the total number of countries included to 174. The 2005 research is now firmly anchored in the international standard for tourism satellite accounting that was developed by WTO, OECD, and Eurostat, and approved by the United Nations Statistical Commission in 2000 (see Chapter 14 for further discussion of tourism satellite accounting). Visit the WTTC Web site (**http://www.wttc.org**) for the latest estimates and forecasts for 174 countries.

As tourism has grown, it has moved from being the province of the rich to being accessible to the masses, involving millions of people. The WTO attempts to document tourism's growth in their annual publications entitled *Tourism Highlights* and *Compendium of Tourism Statistics*. Table 1.2 shows WTO international tourist arrival data up to 2004 and the strong rates of growth for the last several decades marred

TABLE 1.2	INTERNATIONAL TOURIST ARRIVALS: 1950, 1960, 1970, AND 1980–2004				
YEAR	ARRIVALS (MILLIONS)	PERCENT OF GROWTH	YEAR	ARRIVALS (MILLIONS)	PERCENT OF GROWTH
1950	25	—	1991	461	1
1960	69	176	1992	503	9
1970	166	141	1993	516	3
1980	288	73	1994	538	4
1981	290	1	1995	550	2
1982	290	0	1996	581	6
1983	293	1	1997	603	4
1984	320	9	1998	623	3
1985	330	3	1999	645	4
1986	341	3	2000	688	7
1987	367	8	2001	684	−0.6
1988	394	7	2002	704	3
1989	425	8	2003	695	−1
1990	456	8	2004	760	10

Source: World Tourism Organization (WTO).

by slight downturns in 2001 and 2003. WTO states that tourism is the world's largest growth industry with long-term signs being very positive. Their study, *Tourism 2020 Vision,* forecasts that international arrivals will exceed 1 billion by 2010, and 1.6 billion by 2020. Whether it is WTO or WTTC, dramatic growth appears to be in the future forecasts.

WTO's 2003 estimate of 695 million tourist arrivals was a result of an exceptionally difficult year in which negative factors came together (the Iraq war, terrorism fears, the Severe Acute Respiratory Syndrome [SARS], and a persistently weak world economy), causing a 1.2 percent decline in arrivals compared to 2002.

Preliminary arrival data from WTO for 2004 shows that after three years of stagnant growth, international arrivals rebounded sharply to a new record of 760 million for an increase of 10 percent. All regions recorded growth and produced the best results in twenty years.

While 2004 was a record tourism year, the entire world tourism community was shocked and saddened by the tsunami that struck the Indian Ocean on December 26, causing unprecedented loss of life and damage. In spite of the huge number of victims and destruction, the tsunami will have only a limited impact on world tourism in 2005. Reasons for this are that the six most affected Asian countries are estimated to possess less than 1 percent of the global market share. Also, most of the damage occurred along limited parts of coastal areas. The vast majority of tourist destinations in the affected countries remain untouched and fully operational, such as Bangkok and Chiangmai in Thailand, Goa and most of India, and the Indonesian island of Bali. The present expansion of tourism in Asia and the Pacific is at a record pace. In 2004 the region enjoyed the greatest expansion of both its economy and its tourism, and this growth is continuing. Finally, it should be remembered that the tourism industry is resilient. Experience with past disasters indicated that tourism has a remarkable capacity for recovery.

Top Ten

The world's top ten tourism destinations are shown in Table 1.3. France ranks number one in tourism arrivals, with 75.0 million, followed by Spain, the United States, Italy, and China. These five leading destinations account for 34.7 percent of the world volume of tourism flows. The top ten countries account for about 50 percent of the flows. While this is a heavy geographical concentration, the trend is toward a gradual diversification with the emergence of new destinations in the Asia-Pacific regions. In the ranking by international tourist arrivals the most significant modification is experienced by Canada, moving from the seventh to the tenth position as a result of the 13 percent decrease suffered in 2003 due to SARS. The benefiting destinations were Austria, climbing two positions to seventh, and Germany, climbing one to ninth.

A similar concentration pattern emerges if countries are classified according to their tourism receipts. Table 1.4 shows the rank of countries by international tourism receipts, with the United States leading, followed by Spain, France, Italy, Germany, United Kingdom, China, Austria, Turkey, and Greece. The order of tourism earners reflects the impact of SARS and the exchange rate fluctuations experienced in 2003, with European destinations moving up and Asian destinations

TABLE 1.3 **WORLD'S TOP TEN TOURISM DESTINATIONS, 2003**

RANK	COUNTRY	International Tourist Arrivals (million)		% Change	
		2002	2003*	02/01	03*/02
1	France	77.0	75.0	2.4	−2.6
2	Spain	52.3	52.5	4.5	0.3
3	United States	41.9	40.4	−6.7	−3.6
4	Italy	39.8	39.6	0.6	−0.5
5	China	36.8	33.0	11.0	−10.3
6	United Kingdom	24.2	24.8	5.9	2.6
7	Austria	18.6	19.1	2.4	2.6
8	Mexico	19.7	18.7	4.6	−4.9
9	Germany	18.0	18.4	0.6	2.4
10	Canada	20.1	17.5	1.9	−12.7

*Data as collected in WTO database June 2004.

Source: World Tourism Organization (WTO).

moving down. Germany and the United Kingdom each gained one position, while Greece entered the list. China lost two ranks and Hong Kong (China) disappeared from the first ten. For world tourism statistics, a visit to the World Tourism Organization's Web site is a must: **http://www.world-tourism.org.**

Canada
Canada was the world's tenth most popular tourism destination in 2003, with 17.5 million international visitors, dropping from seventh in 2002, according to the WTO. Provisional estimates show that Canada had a 2.5 percent share of the world total.

TABLE 1.4 **WORLD'S TOP TEN TOURISM EARNERS, 2003**

RANK	COUNTRY	International Tourist Receipts (US$ billion)		% Change	
		2002	2003*	02/01	03*/02
1	United States	66.5	65.1	−7.4	−2.2
2	Spain	33.6	41.7	2.2	24.1
3	France	32.3	36.6	7.8	13.2
4	Italy	26.9	31.3	4.3	16.2
5	Germany	19.2	23.0	4.0	20.0
6	United Kingdom	17.6	19.4	8.1	10.5
7	China	20.4	17.4	14.6	−14.6
8	Austria	11.2	13.6	11.1	21.0
9	Turkey	11.9	13.2	18.2	10.9
10	Greece	9.7	10.7	3.1	9.9

*Data as collected in WTO database June 2004.

Source: World Tourism Organization (WTO).

Results from Canada National Tourism Indicators (NTI) show that tourism spending in Canada for 2003 reached $50.0 billion, a 1.8 percent decrease from 2002. Foreign visitors spent an estimated $15.8 billion in Canada, while domestic travelers spent the remainder, $35.1 billion. The foreign tourism spending had a sharp decline at 11.5 percent from 2002. The NTI numbers also show that employment generated by tourism totaled 572,800 full- and part-time jobs in 2003, down 1.2 percent from 2002.

Canadians love to travel, and they recorded the highest level travel deficit in 10 years, increasing from $1.9 billion in 2002 to an estimated $4.3 billion in 2003 (up 132 percent). This was caused by a sharp decline in spending by nonresident travelers in Canada and a slight increase in travel spending by residents. While the Iraq war and the SARS crisis were the main reasons for foreign travelers to travel less and spend less in Canada, the stronger Canadian dollar may have contributed to an increase in travel and spending by Canadians abroad.

United States

In the United States, tourism is ranked as the third largest retail industry behind automobile and food sales. In employment, it is second to health services. Although tourism is often thought of as leisure travel, it also encompasses business and convention travel, meetings, seminars, recreation, student travel (if less than a year), transportation services, and accommodations. According to the Travel Industry Association of America (TIA) research department, travel and tourism generated $601.5 billion in spending in 2000, a record that has not yet been equaled. This total includes expenditures by foreign travelers, domestic travelers, and international passenger fares. The U.S. travel industry, already a leading employer, will continue its role as a job creator for Americans as it recovers from the impacts of September 11 and the Iraq war.

In 2003, the U.S. travel industry received more than $570.2 billion from domestic and international travelers (including international passenger fares). These travel expenditures, in turn, generated nearly 7.2 million jobs for Americans, with $158.4 billion in payroll income. Approximately one out of every eighteen U.S. residents in the civilian labor force was employed due to direct travel spending in the U.S. during 2003.

Traveler spending in the United States is projected to total $624.1 billion in 2005 and $652.9 billion in 2006, according to TIA's forecasts. Readers are encouraged to examine the TIA Travel Forecast, which is based on TIA's Travel Forecast Model. It also includes inbound travel data from the U.S. Commerce Department's International Trade Administration. It is the opinion of the authors that TIA is the most authoritative source of information on the U.S. travel industry, and you should visit their extensive Web site (**http://www.tia.org).**

Directly or indirectly, tourism is part of the fabric of most of the world's industries, including transportation, retailing, advertising, sports, sporting goods and equipment, clothing, the food industry, and health care. Tourism also plays a part in most communication media, particularly in the travel sections of newspapers. There are many print and visual media of direct interest to tourism. Media is also important to those engaged in marketing tourism, such as airlines, cruise lines, motorcoach and rail lines, tour companies, travel agencies, auto rental companies, accommodations, attractions, and tourism educational organizations.

Politicians at all levels are typically very concerned with tourism. They look increasingly at tourism as a tool for economic development. In development, they have enacted laws requiring land-use plans with subsequent zoning and building codes to control location, number, and manner of construction of tourist facilities. Parks and recreation programs are enjoyed by tourists as well as local residents. Many governments impose taxes, all or part of which are paid directly or indirectly by tourists and their suppliers. The power of tourism politically is sometimes manifested in unusual ways. An example was the threat of a travel boycott of Alaska by environmental groups protesting the state's planned aerial shooting of three hundred wolves. The plan was canceled.

Many industry analysts project a doubling of tourism by the year 2020, with constructive government policies. We believe that such policies will indeed be forthcoming if tourism leaders will convey their message effectively. It is in all our interests to achieve this growth, provided that it is accomplished in an intelligent, planned, and thoughtful manner by developers and the public alike. There is an unequivocal responsibility to review the social and environmental factors vigilantly in order to preserve and enhance those qualities that give any destination its special appeal and character. These comprise its culture, natural resources, host population, and the spirit of the place. We hope that you will strive to assist in the achievement of these ultimate worthy goals.

BENEFITS AND COSTS OF TOURISM

Tourism brings both economic and noneconomic **benefits** and **costs** to host communities. Some of the considerable economic impact and benefits were described in the preceding section. There are additional areas of benefit that have not received much research attention. These relate to the benefits occurring to the traveler, such as the contribution of pleasure travel to rest and relaxation, the educational benefit, the understanding of other people and cultures, and the physical and mental well-being of the traveler.

There is no question that tourism delivers benefits, but tourism is not perfect. Even advocates for tourism such as your authors (we have been accused of being cheerleaders for tourism) acknowledge that tourism is not an unqualified blessing. There are costs and benefits, and they do not accrue equally. Many of the social costs incurred are difficult or impossible to measure. Books such as *The Golden Hordes, Tourism: Blessing or Blight,* and *The Holiday Makers* (see the Selected References) point out some of the unpleasant aspects of tourism. Improperly planned and developed tourism can create problems. The demands of tourism may come into conflict with the needs and wishes of local residents. Thoughtless development, inappropriate development, overdevelopment, or unfinished development can easily damage the environment.

Tourism has been blamed for polluting beaches; raising the price of labor, land, goods, and so on; spoiling the countryside; contaminating the values of native people; crowding; congestion; noise; litter; crime; loss of privacy; creating social tensions; environmental deterioration; lack of control over a destination's future; and low-paid seasonal employment. These problems are common to many forms of development and in many cases represent dissatisfaction with the status quo or overdevelopment. They emphasize the need for a coordinated overall economic development plan, of which tourism will be one part.

We must accept that tourism is neither a blessing nor a blight, neither poison nor panacea. Tourism can bring great benefits, but it can also bring social problems. The world has experience in how to increase the benefits of tourism, and at least some experience in how to lessen social problems. What has to be done is to balance the benefits and costs to come up with the best cost/benefit result.

Tourism students and executives must have a clear understanding of both the positive and negative impacts of tourism on the quality of life of a nation, a province or state, or a community. What are the positive aspects? The negative aspects? We need a balance sheet. First we look at the plus side of the ledger; tourism:

- Provides employment opportunities, both skilled and unskilled, because it is a labor-intensive industry

- Generates a supply of needed foreign exchange

- Increases incomes

- Creates increased gross national product

- Can be built on existing infrastructure

- Develops an infrastructure that will also help stimulate local commerce and industry

- Can be developed with local products and resources

- Helps to diversify the economy

- Tends to be one of the most compatible economic development activities available to an area, complementing other economic activities

- Spreads development

- Has a high multiplier impact

- Increases governmental revenues

- Broadens educational and cultural horizons and improves feelings of self-worth

- Improves the quality of life related to a higher level of income and improved standards of living

- Reinforces preservation of heritage and tradition

- Justifies environmental protection and improvement

- Provides employment for artists, musicians, and other performing artists because of visitor interest in local culture, thereby enhancing the cultural heritage

- Provides tourist and recreational facilities that may be used by a local population

- Breaks down language barriers, sociocultural barriers, class barriers, racial barriers, political barriers, and religious barriers

- Creates a favorable worldwide image for a destination

- Promotes a global community

- Promotes international understanding and peace

On the minus side of the ledger we find a number of problems that can be created by tourism, especially by its overdevelopment:

- Develops excess demand for resources

- Creates the difficulties of seasonality

- Causes inflation

- Can result in unbalanced economic development

- Creates social problems

- Degrades the natural physical environment and creates pollution

- Degrades the cultural environment

- Increases the incidence of crime, prostitution, and gambling

- Increases vulnerability to economic and political changes

- Threatens family structure

- Commercializes culture, religion, and the arts

- Creates misunderstanding

- Creates conflicts in the host society

- Contributes to disease, economic fluctuation, and transportation problems

Like all change, tourism exacts a price. However, it is here, it is huge, and it needs to be planned and managed. The challenge is to get the right balance, which is to have the benefits outweigh the costs and take steps to lessen the unfavorable impacts that are a part of change. Tourism development must be a part of overall economic development and must be done in a manner that is sustainable.

SUMMARY

In this chapter we have examined the subject of tourism. The rapid growth in the movement of people, both domestically and internationally, has brought about an industry of vast proportions and diversity. Also, it is universal—found in all countries of the world, but in greatly varied qualities and proportions.

The economic importance and future prospects are also worthy of careful study. These considerations lead to the ways in which the study of tourism can be undertaken. There are a number of basic approaches to the study of tourism, and in this book we include all of them in the various chapters. By the time you complete the book you will know a great deal about the social and economic implications of tourism, and you will have developed a keen interest in our world and the fascinating panorama of places, peoples, cultures, beauty, and learning that travel provides in such abundance.

KEY CONCEPTS

accommodation	expenditures	same-day visitors
adventure and outdoor recreation	food services	study approaches to tourism
attractions	host community	tourism
benefits of tourism	host community government	tourist
built environment	importance of tourism	tourist industry
catalyst organizations	inbound tourism	transportation
costs of tourism	internal tourism	travel
culture	international tourism	travel trade
domestic tourism	marketing	traveler
economic impact	national resources	trip
entertainment	national tourism	usual environment
events	operating sectors	visit
excursionist	outbound tourism	visitor

Internet Sites

The Internet sites mentioned in this chapter are repeated here for convenience, plus some selected additional sites. For more information, visit these sites. Be aware that Internet addresses change frequently, so if a site cannot be accessed, use a search engine. Also use a search engine to locate many additional relevant sites.

American Society of Travel Agents
http://www.astanet.com

Annals of Tourism Research
http://www.elsevier.com/wps/find/
journaldescription.cws_home/689/
description#description

Tourism Australia
http://www.atc.net.au

CAB International
http://www.cabi.org

Canadian Tourism Commission
http://www.canadatourism.com

International Air Transport Association
http://www.iata.org

International Association of
Amusement Parks and Attractions
http://www.iaapa.org

International Association of
Convention and Visitor Bureaus
http://www.iacvb.org

International Council of Tourism
Partners
http://www.tourismpartners.org

International Council on Hotel,
Restaurant and Institutional
Education
http://www.chrie.org

International Festival and Events
Association
http://www.ifea.com

International Hotel and Restaurant
Association
http://www.ih-ra.com

International Society of Travel and
Tourism Educators (ISTTE)
http://www.istte.org

Journal of Travel Research
http://jtr.sagepub.com

Office of Travel and Tourism
Industries
http://tinet.ita.doc.gov

National Tourism Foundation
http://www.ntfonline.com

René Waksberg Tourism Research
Links
http://www.waksberg.com

Tourism Education Web Site
http://www.tourismeducation.org

Tourism Cares for Tomorrow
http://www.tourismcaresfortomor-
row.com

Tourism Management
http://www.elsevier.com/wps/find/
journaldescription.cws_home/30472/
description#description

Travel and Tourism Research
Association
http://www.ttra.com

Travel Industry Association of America
http://www.tia.org

Travel Trade
http://www.traveltrade.com

Travel Weekly
http://www.travelweekly.com

University of Waterloo Recreation and
Leisure Studies Electronic Library
http://www.lib.uwaterloo.ca/
discipline/recreation/index.html

World Tourism Organization
http://www.world-tourism.org

World Travel and Tourism Council
http://www.wttc.org

Yahoo! Directory for Recreation &
Travel
http://www.yahoo.com/recreation/
travel

Internet Exercise

Site Name: World Travel and Tourism Council
URL: http://www.wttc.org
Background Information: The World Travel and Tourism Council (WTTC) is the global business leaders' forum for travel and tourism. Its members are chief executives from all sectors of the travel and tourism industry, including accommodations, catering, cruises, entertainment, recreation, transportation, and travel-related services. Its central goal is to work with governments to realize the full economic impact of the world's largest generator of wealth and jobs, namely, travel and tourism.

Exercise
1. Visit the WTTC site and identify the organization's strategic priorities.

QUESTIONS FOR REVIEW AND DISCUSSION

1. Identify and describe the four perspectives contained in the definition of tourism, in terms of your home community.
2. Why do bodies such as the United States need specific tourism definitions? Why does a state or country need them? A county? A city?
3. What approach to tourism study does this course take? Which approach interests you most?
4. What are the components of tourism?
5. How important are tourist attractions?
6. Why are geographers, sociologists, anthropologists, and economists interested in tourism?
7. What will the tourism industry be like in the year 2020?
8. What are the benefits of tourism?
9. What are some negative aspects of tourism?
10. Why is tourism so popular?

CASE PROBLEMS

1. Suppose that you are a high school economics teacher. You plan to visit your principal's office and convince her that tourism should be included as part of one of your courses. What arguments would you use?

2. You are the minister of tourism of Jamaica, an island country. Identify the instructions you would issue to your statistics department concerning collecting data on tourist arrivals and expenditures.

SELECTED REFERENCES

Boniface, Brian G., and Chris Cooper. *Worldwide Destinations: The Geography of Travel and Tourism,* 3d ed. Oxford, UK: Butterworth-Heinemann, 2001.

Brown, F. *Tourism Reassessed: Blight or Blessing?* Oxford, UK: Butterworth-Heinemann, 1998.

Cook, Roy, Laura Yale, and Joseph Marqua. *Tourism: The Business of Travel.* Upper Saddle River, NJ: Prentice Hall, 2002.

Cooper, C., J. Fletcher, D. Gilbert, R. Shepherd, and S. Wanhill (eds). *Tourism: Principles and Practice.* Essex, UK: Longman, 1998.

Degg, Richard (ed). *Leisure, Recreation, and Tourism Abstracts,* quarterly. Wallingford, Oxfordshire, UK: CAB International.

Franklin, Adrian. *Tourism: An Introduction.* London: Sage Publications, 2003.

Fridgen, Joseph D. *Dimensions of Tourism.* Lansing, MI: Educational Institute of the American Hotel and Lodging Association, 1991.

Gee, Chuck, James Makens, and Dexter Choy. *The Travel Industry,* 3d ed. New York: Van Nostrand Reinhold, 1997.

Hunt, John, and Donlynne Layne. "Evaluation of Travel and Tourism Terminology and Definitions." *Journal of Travel Research,* Vol. 29, No. 4, pp. 7–11, Spring 1991.

Jackson, Ian. *An Introduction to Tourism.* Victoria, Australia: Hospitality Press, 1997.

Jafari, Jafar. "Anatomy of the Travel Industry." *Cornell Hotel and Restaurant Administration Quarterly,* Vol. 24, No. 1, pp. 71–77, May 1983.

Khan, Mahmood, Michael Olsen, and Turgut Var (eds). *VNR's Encyclopedia of Hospitality and Tourism.* New York: Van Nostrand Reinhold, 1993.

Krippendorf, Jost. *The Holiday Makers.* London: Butterworth-Heinemann, 1989.

Laws, Eric (ed). *The ATTT Tourism Education Handbook.* London: Tourism Society, 1997.

Leiper, Neil. "The Framework of Tourism: Towards a Definition of Tourism, Tourist, and the Tourism Industry." *Annals of Tourism Research,* Vol. 6, No. 4, pp. 390–407, October–December 1979.

Lickorish, Leonard J., and Carson L. Jenkins. *An Introduction to Tourism.* Oxford, UK: Butterworth-Heinemann, 1997.

Lockwood, Andrew, and S. Medlik (eds). *Tourism and Hospitality in the 21st Century.* Oxford, UK: Butterworth-Heinemann, 2001.

Medlik, S. *Dictionary of Travel, Tourism, and Hospitality,* 2d ed. Oxford, UK: Butterworth-Heinemann, 1996.

Medlik, S. *Understanding Tourism.* Oxford, UK: Butterworth-Heinemann, 1997.

Mill, Robert Christie, and Alastair M. Morrison. *The Tourism System,* 4th ed. Dubuque, IA: Kendall/Hunt, 2002.

Milman, Allen I. *Travel Industry World Yearbook: The Big Picture.* Spencertown, NY: Travel Industry Publishing Company, annual.

Morley, Clive L. "What Is Tourism: Definitions, Concepts, and Characteristics." *Journal of Tourism Studies,* Vol. 1, No. 1, pp 3–8, May 1990.

Nickerson, Norma P. *Foundations of Tourism.* Englewood Cliffs, NJ: Prentice Hall, 1996.

Powers, Tom, and Clayton W. Barrows. *Introduction to Management in the Hospitality Industry,* 6th ed. New York: Wiley, 1999.

Richardson, John I., and Martin Fluker. *Understanding and Managing Tourism.* Frenchs Forest, NSW: Pearson Education Australia, 2004.

Smith, Stephen L. J. "Defining Tourism: A Supply-Side View." *Annals of Tourism Research,* Vol. 15, No. 2, pp. 179–190, 1998.

Starr, Nona. *Viewpoint: An Introduction to Travel, Tourism, and Hospitality.* Upper Saddle River, NJ: Prentice Hall, 2003.

Travel Industry Association of America. *Domestic Travel Market Report.* Washington, DC: TIA, 2004.

Travel Industry Association of America. *Tourism Works for America,* annual. Washington, DC: TIA.

Turner, Louis, and John Ash. *The Golden Hordes.* London: Constable, 1975.

Van Harssel, Jan. *Tourism: An Exploration,* 3d ed. Englewood Cliffs, NJ: Prentice Hall Career and Technology, 1994.

Walker, John. *Introduction to Hospitality,* 3d ed. Upper Saddle River, NJ: Prentice Hall, 2002.

World Tourism Organization. *Yearbook of Tourism Statistics.* Madrid: WTO, 2004.

World Tourism Organization. *Compendium of Tourism Statistics.* Madrid: WTO, 2004.

World Tourism Organization. *Tourism in a Globalized Society.* Madrid: WTO, 2003.

World Tourism Organization. *Thesaurus on Tourism and Leisure Activities.* Madrid: WTO, 2001.

World Tourism Organization. *Educating the Educators in Tourism.* Madrid: WTO, 1996.

World Tourism Organization. *Concepts, Definitions, and Classifications for Tourism Statistics.* Madrid: WTO, 1995.

World Tourism Organization. *Implications of the WTO/UN Tourism Definitions.* Madrid: WTO, 1995.

World Tourism Organization. *Recommendations on Tourism Statistics.* Madrid: WTO, 1994.

Wyllie, Robert W. *Tourism and Society.* State College, PA: Venture Publishing, 2000.

Youell, R. *Tourism: An Introduction.* Essex, UK: Longman, 1998.

Young, George. *Tourism: Blessing or Blight?* Baltimore: Penguin Books, 1973.

CHAPTER 2

TOURISM
THE AG

Learning Objectives

- Recognize the ant
  man travel over va
  both sea and land

- Understand how
  have evolved from
  were difficult and
  ous, to mass trave
  today.

- Learn about som

For generations, travelers have flocked to the Great Wall of China. At least 2600 years old and some 3946 miles long, it is the only man-made structure on earth visible to the naked eye from the moon. *Photo courtesy of the China National Tourist Office.*

INTRODUCTION

> We travel long roads and cross the water to see what we disregard when it is under our eyes. This is either because nature has so arranged things that we go after what is far off and remain indifferent to what is nearby, or because any desire loses its intensity by being easily satisfied, or because we postpone whatever we can see whenever we want, feeling sure we will often get around to it. Whatever the reason, there are numbers of things in this city of ours and its environs which we have not even heard of, much less seen; yet, if they were in Greece or Egypt or Asia . . . we would have heard all about them, read all about them, looked over all there was to see.
>
> The Younger Pliny, second century C.E.[1]

Twenty-first-century travelers, tiredly pulling their carry-on bags from the overhead bin and waiting to walk down the jetway to a foreign destination, may think their experience is uniquely modern. But they are the latest in a long line of travelers reaching back to antiquity. From earliest times, "all modes of carriage (from animal to the sonic jet) and accommodations (from the meanest hovel to the five-star luxury hotel) have given a livelihood to countless legions."[2] Like today's travelers, these travelers did not do it alone. "Guiding, counseling, and harboring the traveler is among the world's earliest vocations."[3]

Typically, modern travelers enlist a travel agent to make plane reservations, book some hotels, and make recommendations for special tours upon arrival in Athens or Madrid. Despite specialized help, they frequently arrive feeling dirty and tired, complain about the crowded flight, and hope to clear customs without waiting in a long line. A middle-aged couple ruefully recall that the travel agent was not able to book a hotel that she could recommend. (An automobile festival or a visit by the pope had filled major hotels, and there was little choice.) Also, the local bank was out of pesetas or zlotys or won, or whatever the name of the destination country's currency. So the couple has to exchange money before getting a cab to that unpromising hotel and are sure that the driver won't speak English, will spot them as greenhorns, and will drive them all over—with the meter running on and on.

---

[1]Lionel Casson, *Travel in the Ancient World,* (London: Allen and Unwin, 1974), p. 253. A note on style: B.C.E. (Before the Common Era) and C.E. (Common Era), used by some authors and often used in scholarly literature, are the alternative designations corresponding to B.C. and A.D.

[2]Eric Friedheim, *Travel Agents: From Caravans and Clippers to the Concorde,* New York: Travel Agent Magazine Books, 1992, pp. 27–28.

[3]Ibid., p. 5.

EARLY BEGINNINGS

The invention of money by the **Sumerians** (Babylonians) and the development of trade beginning about 4000 B.C.E. mark the beginning of the modern era of travel. Not only were the Sumerians the first to grasp the idea of money and use it in business transactions, but they were also the first to invent cuneiform writing and the wheel, so they should be credited as the founders of the travel business. People could now pay for transportation and accommodations with money or by barter.

Five thousand years ago, cruises were organized and conducted from Egypt. Probably the first journey ever made for purposes of peace and tourism was made by Queen Hatshepsut to the land of Punt (believed to be on the east coast of Africa) in 1480 B.C.E. Descriptions of this tour have been recorded on the walls of the temple of Deir el-Bahri at Luxor. These texts and bas-reliefs are among the world's rarest artworks and are universally admired for their wondrous beauty and artistic qualities. The Colossi of Memnon at Thebes have on their pedestals the names of Greek tourists of the fifth century B.C.E.

Beginning in 2700 B.C.E. the pharaohs began to take advantage of the abundance of good building stone in the Nile valley to build their elaborate burial tombs. They included the Step Pyramid of Djoser, the Sphinx, the three great pyramids at Giza, and the pyramid complex at Abusir. These great outdoor wonders began attracting large numbers as early as the New Kingdom from 1600 to 1200 B.C.E. "Each monument was a hallowed spot, so the visitors always spent some moments in prayer, yet their prime motivation was curiosity or disinterested enjoyment, not religion."[4]

They left evidence of their visits in inscriptions such as the following: "Hadnakhte, scribe of the treasury, came to make an excursion and amuse himself on the west of Memphis together with his brother, Panakhti, scribe of the Vizier."[5] Like tourists through the ages, they felt the need to leave evidence of their visits. Some hastily painted their names; others scratched their names in the soft stone with a sharp point. The latter method was so common that the technical term we give to such scribblings is graffiti, Italian for "scratching."

A second recognizable tourist trait was the urge to acquire souvenirs. Harkhuf, an envoy of the pharaoh to the Sudan, brought home a pygmy trained in native dances to present to his ruler! Early **Egyptians** also purchased bargains or specialties abroad for their friends and relatives. In 1800 B.C.E. young Uzalum received this request: "I have never before written to you for something precious I wanted. But if you want to be like a father to me, get me a fine string full of beads, to be worn around the head."[6]

---

[4]Casson, *Travel in the Ancient World*, p. 32.
[5]Ibid., p. 32.
[6]Ibid., p. 34.

Ancient Egyptian pyramids and the Sphinx were some of the world's first tourist attractions.
Photo courtesy of Air France.

Herodotus reported:

The Egyptians meet to celebrate festivals not once a year but a number of times. The biggest and most popular is at Bubastis . . . the next at Busiris . . . the third at Saïs . . . the fourth at Heliopolis . . . the fifth at Buto . . . the sixth at Papremis. . . . They go there on the river, men and women together, a big crowd of each in each boat. As they sail, some of the women keep clicking castanets and some of the men playing on the pipes, and the rest, both men and women, sing and beat time with their hands. . . . And when they arrive at Bubastis, they celebrate the occasion with great sacrifices, and more wine is consumed at this one festival than during the whole rest of the year.[7]

When this holiday throng arrived at its sites, there were no commercial facilities offering food and lodging. Like modern attendees at a Grateful Dead concert, they

---

[7]Ibid., p. 31.

had to sleep in the open and feed themselves as best they could.[8] In contrast, government officials such as Harkhuf, the provider of the dancing pygmy, enjoyed the comforts of temples and government depots in their travels.

Early Roads

The wheel led to the development of a heavy wagon that could be drawn by teams of oxen or onagers, a type of wild ass. "A walker or animal needs only a track,"[9] but a vehicle needs a road. There were not many **early roads** that could take wheeled traffic. A king of Ur bragged that he went from Nippur to Ur, a distance of some 100 miles, and back in a day. This boast, sometime around 2050 B.C.E., implies the existence of a carriage road.[10] Even the best of the highways, however, were minimal. Paving was almost nonexistent until the time of the Hittites, who paved a mile and a third of road between their capital and a nearby sanctuary to carry heavily loaded wagons on festal days. Even then their war chariots, light horse-drawn carts invented for war, rolled over the countryside on dirt roads. Also, bridges were rare in a land that experienced frequent flooding. A hymn tells of King Shulgi exulting, "'I enlarged the footpaths, straightened the highways of the land' . . . but not every Mesopotamian monarch was a Shulgi, and there must have been long periods with nobody to 'straighten' the roads.'"[11]

Roads were better on the island of Crete, where the Minoans flourished from 2000 to 1500 B.C.E., and on the Greek peninsula of the Mycenaeans, who flourished from 1600 to 1200 B.C.E.[12] A two-lane road, 13½ feet wide, ran from the coast of Crete to the capital at Knossos. In Greece, roads were usually one lane, although some were as much as 11½ feet wide, making two-way traffic possible. Bridges and culverts kept them passable.

Who traveled? Mainly three groups: the military, government officials, and caravans. The warlike Assyrians, like the Romans after them, realized that roads were basic to moving their war chariots efficiently. As their empire expanded from the Mediterranean in the west to the Persian Gulf in the east, the Assyrians improved roads, largely for military use.

The Epic of Gilgamesh (c. 2000 B.C.E.) recounts the travels of a Sumerian king who is given directions by a deity. By only a slight stretch of the imagination, Gilgamesh's deity might be regarded as the first travel guide! This adds a fourth reason to credit the Sumerians with the beginnings of the travel industry.

The history of roads is thus related to the centralizing of populations in powerful cities. Alexander the Great found well-developed roads in India in 326 B.C.E. In Persia (now Iran) all the cities and provinces were connected to the capital, Susa, by roads built between 500 and 400 B.C.E. One of these roads was 1,500 miles long.

---

[8]Ibid., p. 35.
[9]Ibid., p. 25.
[10]Ibid., p. 25.
[11]Ibid., p. 27.
[12]Ibid., p. 27.

The **Romans** started building roads in about 150 B.C.E. These were quite elaborate in construction. The roadway was surveyed using a cross staff hung with plumb bobs. Soldiers and laborers dug the roadbed, and then stones and concrete were evenly placed. Paving stones were then laid on top, and the highway was edged with curbstones and contoured to a sloping crown to shed the rain. Some of these roads are still in use.

By the time of Emperor Trajan (ruled from 98 to 117 C.E.), the Roman roads comprised a network of some 50,000 miles. They girdled the Roman Empire, extending from near Scotland and Germany in the north to the south well within Egypt and along the southern shores of the Mediterranean Sea. To the east, roads extended to the Persian Gulf in what is now Iraq and Kuwait.

The Romans could travel as much as 100 miles a day using relays of horses furnished from rest posts 5 to 6 miles apart. Romans also journeyed to see famous temples in the Mediterranean area, particularly the pyramids and monuments of Egypt. Greece and Asia Minor were popular destinations, offering the Olympic Games, medicinal baths and seaside resorts, theatrical productions, festivals, athletic competitions, and other forms of amusement and entertainment. The Roman combination of empire, roads, the need for overseeing the empire, wealth, leisure, tourist attractions, and the desire for travel created a demand for accommodations and other tourist services that came into being as an early form of tourism.

Roman tourists went about sightseeing much as we do today. They used guidebooks, employed guides, left graffiti everywhere, and bought souvenirs. The examples are diverse and often amusing. The only guidebook to survive from ancient times is a guidebook of Greece, written by a Greek named Pausanias between 160 and 180 C.E. (during the reigns of emperors Hadrian, Antoninus Pius, and Marcus Aurelius). This guide "marks a milestone in the history of tourism. He [Pausanias] is the direct ancestor of the equally sober and unimaginative, painstakingly comprehensive and scrupulously accurate Karl Baedeker."[13]

The Silk Road

In 1889, Rudyard Kipling penned the oft-quoted line "East is East and West is West and never the twain shall meet." Actually, East and West had already met more than 2000 years earlier on the now-fabled Silk Road.

Indeed, it is a misnomer even to call it a road. From the beginning, some Silk Route sections were mere directions across trackless steppe or desert rather than visible paths: "the majority of states on the Silk Routes traded with their nearer neighbors, and travelers were like participants in a relay race stretching a third of the way around the world."[14]

Marco Polo, who traveled to China from Italy in the thirteenth century, became the first Western explorer to compose a popular and lasting account. Though his chronicle is probably more fiction than history, since it draws from the tales of

---

[13]Ibid., p. 299.
[14]Peter Neville-Hadley, *China: The Silk Routes*, Old Saybrook, CT: Globe Pequot Press, 1997.

many traders, his observations often ring true. In spite of omissions and exaggerations, his book has remained an international best seller.[15]

Just as the Silk Road was not a road, so silk was but a part of the trade. Westbound caravans carried furs, ceramics, spices, the day lily for its medicinal uses, peach, apricot, and even rhubarb.[16] Eastbound ones carried precious metals and gems, ivory, glass, perfumes, dyes, textiles, as well as the grapevine, alfalfa, chives, coriander, sesame, cucumber, fig, and safflower.[17]

For protection against marauders, merchants formed caravans of up to 1000 camels, protected by armed escorts. Each two-humped Bactrian camel could carry 400 to 500 pounds of merchandise. The long route was divided into areas of political and economic influence. "The Chinese traders escorted their merchandise as far as Dunhuang or beyond the Great Wall to Loulan where it was sold or bartered to Central Asian middlemen—Parthians, Sogdians, Indians, and Kushans—who carried the trade on to the cities of the Persian, Syrian, and Greek merchants. Each transaction increased the cost of the end product, which reached the Roman Empire in the hands of Greek and Jewish entrepreneurs."[18]

The Classical World

The lands of the Mediterranean Sea (2000 B.C.E. to 500 C.E.) produced a remarkable evolution in travel. In the cradle of Western civilization, travel for trade, commerce, religious purposes, festivals, medical treatment, or education developed at an early date. There are numerous references to caravans and traders in the Old Testament.

Beginning in 776 B.C.E., citizens of the city-states came together every four years to honor Zeus through athletic competition. Eventually, four of these national festivals emerged: the **Olympic Games,** Pythian Games, Isthmian Games, and Nemean Games. Each festival included sacrifice and prayer to a single god. They honored the deity by offering up a superlative athletic or artistic performance. Thus:

> the festivals furnished in one unique package the spectrum of **attractions** that have drawn tourists in all times and places: the feeling of being part of a great event and of enjoying a special experience; a gay festive mood punctuated by exalted religious moments; elaborate pageantry; the excitement of contests between performers of the highest calibre—and, on top of all this, a chance to wander among famous buildings and works of art. Imagine the modern Olympics taking place at Easter in Rome, with the religious services held at St. Peter's.[19]

---

[15]J. D. Brown, *Frommer's China: The 50 Most Memorable Trips,* New York: Simon & Schuster, 1998, p. 371.
[16]Neville-Hadley, *China,* p. 61.
[17]Stephen G. Haw, *A Traveller's History of China,* 2d ed., New York: N.W. Publishing Group, 1998, pp. 84–85.
[18]Judy Bonavia, *The Silk Road from Xi'an to Kashgar,* revised by William Lindesay and Wa Qi, 2d ed, New York: W.W. Norton & Co., 1999.
[19]Casson, *Travel in the Ancient World,* pp. 76–77.

The ruins of the Colosseum in Rome hold visitors spellbound; they see the pomp of emperors, the spectacle of gladiators and lions, as well as the shards of a great empire. *Copyright © Corbis Digital Stock.*

Greek inns provided little more than a night's shelter. A guest who wanted to wash had to carry his own towel down the street to the nearest public bath. Once there, he took off his clothes in a dressing room and put his clothes in someone's care, lest they be stolen while he bathed. "The bath itself . . . was a big basin over which he leaned while an attendant sloshed water over him."[20]

Everyday folk could also be found wending their way to the sanctuaries of the healing gods, especially Aesculapius. Such places were usually located in a beautiful setting that included pure air and water (often with mineral springs). The sanctuary at Epidaurus also included facilities for rest and diversion, including the temple with admired sculptures, colonnades for shaded walks, a stadium for athletic events, and the second-largest theater in Greece. The Greeks recognized rest and diversion as important elements in treatment of the sick.

People also traveled to seek advice of the oracles, especially those at Dodona and Delphi. Statesmen, generals, and other powerful figures sought advice before taking an important action. Socrates' disciple inquired about his master's wisdom at the temple of Delphi.[21]

---

[20]Ibid., p. 89.
[21]Ibid., pp. 84–85.

While festival visitors, businessmen, the sick, and advice seekers comprised the bulk of travelers in the fifth and fourth centuries B.C.E., there was also another small category, the tourist. Greece's "Father of History," Herodotus, would undoubtedly have qualified for the top category of frequent-traveler miles if such awards had been given. In addition to traveling all over Greece and the Aegean Islands, he sailed to Cyrene in North Africa, explored southern Italy and Sicily, and sailed from Ephesus on the west coast of Asia Minor to Sardis. He got as far east as Babylon by sailing to Syria, then striking east to the Euphrates and following a caravan track for weeks. There he looked upon the ancient city of Babylon:

> square in shape, with each side 14 miles long, a total of 56 miles. Babylon is not only of enormous size; it has a splendour such as no other city of all we have seen. . . . The city wall is 85½ feet wide and 342 high. . . . Its circuit is pierced by one hundred entrances, with gates, jambs, and lintels of bronze. . . . The town is full of three- and four-storey houses and is cut through with streets that are absolutely straight, not only the main ones but also the side streets going down to the river.[22]

His figures are inflated, probably because he got them from his guides. He loved doing the sights and, like most modern tourists, was dependent on guides for information. A Greek entering Asia Minor would encounter strange tongues and Oriental ways. Not until Alexander conquered the Persian Empire would the Greek ways spread into the ancient East.

Possibly, Herodotus's travel combined business and pleasure, as did that of Solon, who led Athens through a crisis, then took a trip abroad. Athens developed into a tourist attraction from the second half of the fifth century on, as people went to see the Parthenon and other new buildings atop the Acropolis.

Today's traveler who gets into trouble in a foreign city usually turns to his country's consul. The ancient Greek turned to his *proxenos* (from the Greek *pro*, before or for, and *xenos,* foreigner). The primary duty of the proxenos was to aid and assist in all ways possible any of his compatriots who turned up in the place of his residence, particularly those who had come in some official capacity.[23] His more mundane duties might include extending hospitality, obtaining theater tickets, or extending a loan for someone who had run short of funds while visiting. More complex duties included negotiating ransom for relatives of someone taken as a prisoner of war. The heirs of someone who died in the city might ask the proxenos to wind up essential financial matters there.[24]

As the fourth century B.C.E. came to a close in Greece, people traveled despite the discomfort and dangers. Traveling by sea, they worried about storms and pirates; by land, about bad roads, dismal inns, and highwaymen. Only the wealthy described by Homer could escape the worst pitfalls.

---

[22]Ibid., p. 99.
[23]Ibid., p. 93.
[24]Ibid., pp. 240–241.

Those who traveled for business, healing, or entertainment at festivals represented the majority. A small minority traveled for the sheer love of it—like Herodotus, the world's first great travel writer.

The museum, born in the ancient Near East, came of age with the Greeks. Sanctuaries such as Apollo's at Delphi and that of Zeus at Olympia gradually accumulated valuable objects donated either as thank-you offerings for services rendered or as bribes for acts the supplicant hoped would be rendered. Herodotus describes six gold mixing bowls dedicated by Gyges of Lydia and weighing some 1,730 pounds and a gold lion from Croesus weighing 375 pounds. While Herodotus singled these out because of their cost, others were notable for their aesthetic qualities. The Greeks had few precious metals, but hewed the plentiful marble with consummate skill. The temple of Hera exemplifies the scope and quality of sculpture acquired from the seventh through the third centuries B.C.E.:

> All over the Greek world through generous gifts of statues and paintings from the hopeful or the satisfied, temples became art galleries as well as houses of worship—exactly as Europe's cathedrals and churches were destined to become. . . . And they drew visitors the same way that art-laden churches do today to see the treasures and only incidentally, to say a prayer.[25]

In Asia Minor, beginning with the installation of a democratic government in Ephesus by Alexander the Great in 334 B.C.E., some 700,000 tourists would crowd in Ephesus (in what is now Turkey) in a single season to be entertained by the acrobats, animal acts, jugglers, magicians, and prostitutes who filled the streets. Ephesus also became an important trading center and, under Alexander, was one of the most important cities in the ancient world.

Early Ships

The Phoenicians were master shipwrights, building tubby wooden craft with a single square sail. By 800 B.C.E. they had built a network of trading posts around the Mediterranean emanating from their own thriving cities along the coast in what is now Lebanon. Acting as middlemen for their neighbors, they purveyed raw materials and also finished goods, such as linen and papyrus from Egypt, ivory and gold from Nubia, grain and copper from Sardinia, olive oil and wine from Sicily, cedar timbers from their homeland, and perfume and spices from the East. Presumably, they also occasionally carried a few passengers. They were the first creators of a maritime empire.

The Greeks followed the **Phoenicians** in becoming great sea traders. Improved ships accelerated a flourishing Mediterranean trade. Merchant ships also carried paying passengers (although Noah with his ark probably deserves credit for being

---

[25]Ibid., pp. 240–241.

the first cruise operator, even though his passengers were primarily animals). Unlike Noah's passengers, those sailing on Greek ships had to bring their own servants, food, and wine. Widely varying accommodations aboard, stormy seas, and pirate attacks were worrisome realities.

Chinese

Several tourism history scholars decry the eurocentricity of writings about the history of tourism. Most notable of these is Trevor Sofield, of the University of Tasmania, who states:

> The emperors of China had ministers for travel 4,000 years ago—well before imperial Rome and Herodotus. So, this is a plea to move beyond Chaucer's pilgrimage to Canterbury and Marco Polo's ventures from Venice, and go further back in time to explore other civilizations and their histories of travel besides (mainly western) Europe and North America. The history of pilgrimage travel in countries such as India, China, Nepal, Thailand, Iran, Vietnam, Sri Lanka, Myanmar and others pre-dates much European travel history. Inns and hospitality industries in these countries pre-date European examples.[26]

Sofield and Li in their article "Tourism Development and Cultural Policies in China" report that one of the main features of China's domestic tourism lies in the traditions about travel and heritage sites established over a 4,000 year period when ancestral gods and animistic spirits resided in mountains, rivers, lakes, and other natural features. They point out:

> Stretching in an unbroken chain from the beginnings of the Shang dynasty (ca 1350–1050 BC) to the final demise of the emperors in the fall of the Quing dynasty and the declaration of a Republic in 1912, each successive emperor and his court paid homage to a wide range of gods and goddesses. The sites multiplied over the centuries and as Buddhism became established, even more sacred sites were added. Much ancient travel was thus for pilgrimage, embedded in the beliefs of the god-kings.[27]

Polynesians

Among early voyages, those in Oceania were amazing. Small dugout canoes not over 40 feet in length were used for voyages from Southeast Asia southward and eastward through what is now called Micronesia across the Pacific to the Marquesas

---

[26]Internet correspondence.

[27]Trevor Sofield and Sarah Li, "Tourism Development and Cultural Policies in China," *Annals of Tourism Research*, Vol. 25, No. 2, pp. 362–392, 1998.

Islands, the Tuamotu Archipelago, and the Society Islands. About 500 C.E., **Polynesians** from the Society Islands traveled to Hawaii, a distance of over 2,000 miles. Navigation was accomplished by observing the position of the sun and stars, ocean swells, clouds, and bird flights. Considering the problems of fresh water and food supplies, such sea travel was astonishing. Later, navigation by the early explorers was facilitated by using a sandglass to measure time, a "log" line trailed behind the ship to measure distance, and a compass to gauge direction.

Europeans

The collapse of the Roman Empire in the fourth and fifth centuries spelled disaster for pleasure travel and tourism in Europe. During the Dark Ages (from the fall of the Western Roman Empire, 476 C.E., to the beginning of the modern era, 1450 C.E.), only the most adventurous persons would travel. A trip during this period in history was dangerous; no one associated travel with pleasure. The most notable exception to this in Europe during the period was the Crusades.

By the end of the Dark Ages, large numbers of pilgrims were traveling to such popular shrines as Canterbury in England (immortalized in Chaucer's *Canterbury Tales*) and St. James of Compostela. Fewer made the long, expensive, and often dangerous journey to the Holy Land. Beginning in 1388, King Richard II required pilgrims to carry permits, the forerunner of the modern passport. Despite hardship and dangers, they went by the thousands to pay reverence to hallowed sites, to atone for sins, or to fulfill promises they had made while ill.

A fourteenth-century travelers' guide gave pilgrims detailed directions about the regions through which they would pass and the types of inns they would encounter along the often inhospitable routes. Innkeeping had nearly disappeared except for local taverns, and a few inns were scattered throughout Europe. They typically were filthy, vermin-infested warrens. Inns in Spain and Italy provided a bed for each guest, but in Germany and other areas, guests commonly had to share beds. At the other end of the spectrum lay an inn of quality, such as the one described in Mandeville's guide. He quotes the mistress of the inn: "Jenette lyghte the candell, and lede them ther above in the solere [upper room], and bere them hoot watre for to wasshe their feet, and covere them with uysshons."

Travelers of any social distinction, however, were generally entertained in castles or private houses. Church monasteries or hospices offered accommodations for the majority. They offered services well beyond bed and board. They could provide a doctor and furnish medicines, replace worn garments, provide guides to show a visitor around the sights, or even grant a loan of money. They also offered opportunities for meditation and prayer.

The most famous stopover was the French Alpine hospice of Grand-Saint-Bernard, established in 962. (The Saint Bernard dogs that were sent to find and rescue travelers have been made famous by ads showing a little flask of wine appended to the dogs' collars.) St. Catherine's monastery at the foot of Mount Sinai still flourishes. Those who could afford to pay were expected to leave a generous donation.

Eventually, providing hospitality services for increasing numbers became burdensome to the religious houses. They could not turn the poor away, because Christian charity was an important element in the Church's mission; nor could they turn away the nobles, who made generous financial contributions. But they could, and increasingly did, refer the middle classes to taverns, inns, and wine shops. Thus, the church played an important role in the development of the hospitality industry during this period.

The Grand Tour

The **"Grand Tour"** of the seventeenth and eighteenth centuries was made by diplomats, businesspeople, and scholars who traveled to Europe, mainly to the cities of France and Italy. It became fashionable for scholars to study in Paris, Rome, Florence, and other cultural centers. While making the Grand Tour began as an educational experience, it has been criticized as eventually degenerating into the simple pursuit of pleasure. The following description from *A Geography of Tourism* describes the Grand Tour:

> One of the interesting aspects of the Grand Tour was its conventional and regular form. As early as 1678, Jean Gailhard, in his *Compleat Gentleman,* had prescribed a three-year tour as customary. A generally accepted itinerary was also laid down, which involved a long stay in France, especially in Paris, almost a year in Italy visiting Genoa, Milan, Florence, Rome, and Venice, and then a return by way of Germany and the Low Countries via Switzerland. Of course, there were variations to this itinerary, but this was the most popular route. It was generally believed that "there was little more to be seen in the rest of the civil world after Italy, France, and the Low Countries, but plain and prodigious barbarism."[28]

The term *Grand Tour* persists today, and the trip to Europe—the Continent— can be traced back to the early Grand Tour. Today's concept is far different, however: the tour is more likely to be three weeks, not three years.

Americans

The vast continent of North America, principally in what is now Florida and in the Southwest, was originally explored by the Spanish in the sixteenth century. Remarkably long journeys were made, often under severe conditions. The Spanish used horses, which were unknown to the American Indians until that time. In the East, Cape Cod was discovered by Gosnold in 1602, and the Plymouth Colony was established in 1620.

---

[28]H. Robinson, *A Geography of Tourism,* London: Macdonald and Evans, 1976, p. 13.

Nowhere in the United States can visitors experience so extensively life in the eighteenth century as in Colonial Williamsburg, with its mile-long Duke of Gloucester Street, horse-drawn carriages, and hundreds of restored colonial homes and gardens. *Photo Courtesy of Virginia Tourism Corporation.*

Early travel was on foot or on horseback, but travel by small boat or canoe provided access to the interior of the country. Generally, travel was from east to west. As roads were built, stagecoach travel became widespread, and "ordinaries" (small hotels) came into common use. Among the most remarkable journeys were those by covered wagon to the West across the Great Plains. This movement followed the Civil War (1861–1865). Construction of railroads across the country (the first transcontinental link was at Promontory, Utah, in 1869) popularized rail travel. The Wells Fargo Company organized the American Express Company in 1850. This pioneer company issued the first traveler's checks in 1891 and began other travel services, later becoming travel agents and arranging tours. Today, **American Express** is known throughout the world for its Traveler's Cheques, credit cards, and various travel and financial services.

One of the most significant events in America's travel history is the amount of travel done by servicemen and -women during World War II. Over 12 million Americans served in the armed forces from 1941 to 1945. Most were assigned to duty at places far removed from their homes, such as the European and Pacific theaters of war. Extensive domestic travel was commonplace, introducing the military traveler to different and often exotic places and bringing a broader perspective of what the North American continent and foreign countries had to offer visitors. Travel thus became a part of their experience. Following the war, a large increase in travel occurred when gasoline rationing was removed and automobiles were again being manufactured. Air, rail, and bus travel also expanded.

EARLY (AND LATER) TOURIST ATTRACTIONS

Sightseeing has always been a major activity of tourists; this has been true since ancient times. Most of us have heard of the Seven Wonders of the Ancient World, but few could win a trivia contest by naming them:

1. The Great Pyramids of Egypt, including the Sphinx
2. The Hanging Gardens of Babylon, sometimes including the Walls of Babylon and the Palace, in what is now Iraq
3. The Tomb of Mausolus at Halicarnassus, in what is now Turkey
4. The Statue of Zeus at Olympia in Greece
5. The Colossus of Rhodes in the Harbor at Rhodes, an island belonging to Greece
6. The Great Lighthouse (Pharos) in Alexandria, Egypt
7. The Temple of Artemis (also called the Temple of Diana) at Ephesus, at the time part of Greece, now in Turkey

The Great Pyramids of Egypt are the sole remaining wonder.

The Great Pyramids of Egypt are the sole remaining wonder of the Seven Wonders of the Ancient World.
Photo courtesy of United Nations.

Just as tourists in ancient times traveled to see these wonders, modern tourists travel to see such natural wonders as the Grand Canyon, Yosemite National Park, Yellowstone, Niagara Falls, the oceans, the Great Lakes, and human-built wonders such as great cities, museums, dams, and monuments.

Spas, Baths, Seaside Resorts

Another interesting aspect in the history of tourism was the development of spas, after their original use by the Romans, which took place in Britain and on the Continent. In the eighteenth century, spas became very fashionable among members of high society, not only for their curative aspects but also for the social events, games, dancing, and gambling that they offered. The spa at Bath, England, was one such successful health and social resort.

Sea bathing also became popular, and some believed that saltwater treatment was more beneficial than that at the inland spas. Well known in Britain were Brighton, Margate, Ramsgate, Worthing, Hastings, Weymouth, Blackpool, and Scarborough. By 1861 these successful seaside resorts indicated that there was a pent-up demand for vacation travel. Most visitors did not stay overnight but made one-day excursions to the seaside. Patronage of the hotels at these resorts was still limited to those with considerable means.

Thus, tourism owes a debt to medical practitioners who advocated the medicinal value of mineral waters and sent their patients to places where mineral springs were known to exist. Later, physicians also recommended sea bathing for its therapeutic value. While spas and seaside resorts were first visited for reasons of health, they soon became centers of entertainment, recreation, and gambling, attracting the rich and fashionable with or without ailments. This era of tourism illustrates that it is usually a combination of factors rather than one element that spells the success or failure of an enterprise. Today, one finds that hot springs, although they are not high on travelers' priority lists, are still tourist attractions. Examples in the United States are Hot Springs, Arkansas; French Lick, Indiana; and Glenwood Springs, Colorado. The sea, particularly in the Sun Belt, continues to have a powerful attraction and is one of the leading forces in tourism development, which is evident from the number of travelers to Hawaii, Florida, the Caribbean, and Mexico.

EARLY ECONOMIC REFERENCES

As tourists traveled to see pyramids, visit seaside resorts, and attend festivals and athletic events, they needed food and lodging, and they spent money for these services. Traders did the same. Then, as now, the economic impact of these expenditures was difficult to measure, as evidenced by the following quotation from Thomas Mun, who in 1620 wrote in England's *Treasure by Foreign Trade:* "There are yet some other petty things which seem to have a reference to this balance of which the said officers of His Majesty's Customs can take no notice to bring them into the account; as mainly, the expenses of the travelers."[29]

THE FIRST TRAVEL AGENTS

In 1822, **Robert Smart** of Bristol, England, announced himself as the first steamship agent. He began booking passengers on steamers to various Bristol Channel ports and to Dublin, Ireland.

In 1841, **Thomas Cook** began running a special excursion train from Leicester to Loughborough (in England), a trip of 12 miles. On July 5 of that year, Cook's train carried 570 passengers at a round-trip price of 1 shilling per passenger. This is believed to be the first publicly advertised excursion train. Thus, Cook can rightfully be recognized as the first rail excursion agent; his pioneering efforts were eventually copied widely in all parts of the world. Cook's company grew rapidly, providing escorted tours to the Continent and later to the United States and around the world. The company continues to be one of the world's largest travel organizations.

The first specialist in individual inclusive travel (the basic function of **travel agents**) was probably **Thomas Bennett** (1814–1898), an Englishman who served as secretary to the British consul general in Oslo, Norway. In this position, Bennett frequently arranged individual scenic tours in Norway for visiting British notables. Finally, in 1850 he set up a business as a "trip organizer" and provided individual tourists with itineraries, carriages, provisions, and a "traveling kit." He routinely made advance arrangements for horses and hotel rooms for his clients.

HISTORIC TRANSPORTATION

Another element in the tourism equation is transportation. The early tourists traveled on foot, on beasts of burden, by boat, and on wheeled vehicles.

Stagecoach Travel

Coaches were invented in Hungary in the fifteenth century and provided regular service there on prescribed routes. By the nineteenth century, stagecoach travel had become quite popular, especially in Great Britain. The development of the famous English tavern was brought about by the need for overnight lodging by stagecoach passengers.

---

[29]George Young, *Tourism: Blessing or Blight?* Middlesex, UK: Pelican Books, 1973, p. 1.

Water Travel

Market boats picked up passengers as well as goods on ship canals in England as early as 1772. The Duke of Bridgewater began such service between Manchester and London Bridge (near Warrington). Each boat had a coffee room from which refreshments were sold by the captain's wife. By 1815, steamboats were plying the Clyde, the Avon, and the Thames. A poster in 1833 announced steamboat excursion trips from London. By 1841, steamship excursions on the Thames were so well established that a publisher was bringing out a weekly Steamboat Excursion Guide.

Rail Travel

Railways were first built in England in 1825 and carried passengers beginning in 1830. The newly completed railway between Liverpool and Manchester featured special provisions for passengers. The railroad's directors did not expect much passenger business, but time proved them wrong. The typical charge of only 1 penny per mile created a sizable demand for rail travel—much to the delight of the rail companies. Because these fares were much lower than stagecoach fares, rail travel became widely accepted even for those with low incomes.

Early rail travel in Britain was not without its detractors, however. Writers in the most powerful organs of public opinion of that day seemed to consider the new form of rail locomotion a device of Satan. When a rail line was proposed from London to Woolrich to carry passengers at a speed of 18 miles per hour, one aghast contributor to the *Quarterly Review* wrote, "We should as soon expect the people of Woolrich to be fired off upon one of Congreve's ricochet rockets as trust them-

Older-style rail travel is still available in many places across the United States, so that tourists can experience this memorable mode of transportation. The steam train shown here carries visitors to the Grand Canyon National Park in Arizona. *Photo by James B. Winters.*

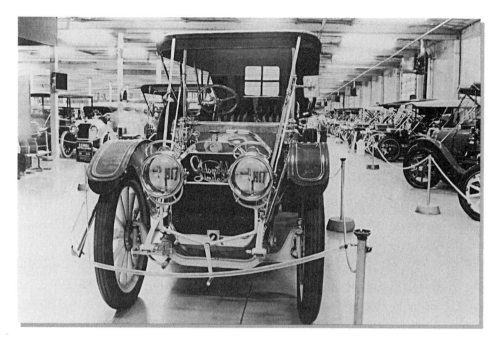

Automobiles dominate travel today, but visiting the National Automobile Museum (Harrah Collection) in Reno, Nevada, provides an appreciation of the old days, when cars were not quite so comfortable. *Photo courtesy of Reno News Bureau.*

selves to the mercy of such a machine going at such a rate." Another writer deemed the railroads for passenger transportation "visionary schemes unworthy of notice." Between 1826 and 1840 the first railroads were built in the United States.

Automobile and Motorcoach Travel

Automobiles entered the travel scene in the United States when Henry Ford introduced his famous Model T in 1908. The relatively cheap "tin lizzie" revolutionized travel in the country, creating a demand for better roads. By 1920 a road network became available, leading to the automobile's current dominance of the travel industry. Today, the automobile accounts for about 84 percent of intercity miles traveled and is the mode of travel for approximately 80 percent of all trips. The auto traveler brought about the early tourist courts in the 1920s and 1930s, which have evolved into the motels and motor hotels of today. Motorcoaches also came into use soon after the popularization of the automobile and remain a major mode of transportation.

Air Travel

Nearly 16 years after the airplane's first flight at Kitty Hawk, North Carolina, in 1903, regularly scheduled air service began in Germany. This was a Berlin-Leipzig-Weimar route, and the carrier later became known as Deutsche Lufthansa. Today,

Lufthansa is a major international airline. The first transatlantic passenger was Charles A. Levine, who flew with Clarence Chamberlin nonstop from New York to Germany. The plane made a forced landing 118 miles from Berlin, their destination, which they reached on June 7, 1927. This was shortly after Charles Lindbergh's historic solo flight from New York to Paris.

The first U.S. airline, Varney Airlines, was launched in 1926 and provided scheduled airmail service. However, this airline was formed only 11 days before Western Airlines, which began service on April 17, 1926. Varney Airlines later merged with three other lines to form United Air Lines. On April 1, 1987, Western merged with Delta Air Lines. At first, only one passenger was carried in addition to the mail, if the weight limitations permitted. The first international mail route was flown by **Pan American Airways** from Key West, Florida, to Havana, Cuba, on October 28, 1927. Pan Am flew the first passengers on the same route on January 16, 1928. The trip took 1 hour 10 minutes, and the fare was $50 each way.

The various U.S. airlines gradually expanded their services to more cities and international destinations. During World War II their equipment and most staff

Flight museums such as the Virginia Aviation Museum remind us what a short history the airplane has. *Photo by Cyane Lowdon, courtesy of the Science Museum of Virginia.*

were devoted to war service. Development of the DC-3 and the Boeing 314A transoceanic Clipper in the early 1940s established paying passenger traffic and brought about much wider acceptance of air travel. The jet engine, invented in England by Frank Whittle, was used on such military planes as the B-52. The first American commercial jet was the Boeing 707. The first U.S. transcontinental jet flight was operated by American Airlines on January 25, 1959, from Los Angeles to New York City, and the jumbo jet era began in January 1970 when Pan American World Airways flew 352 passengers from New York to London using the new Boeing 747 equipment.

The Concorde ushered in the era of supersonic flight. Concorde was a product of a joint British-French venture. A prototype was unveiled in 1967 and the jet made its first test flight in 1969. Concorde was a marvel of engineering and design. The white bird with its distinctive tilt needle nose and broad wingspan was an icon of the modern world. Concorde traveled at 1,350 miles per hour, twice the speed of sound. It flew at 60,000 feet, almost twice as high as other commercial jets. Probably no other civilian aircraft has captured the imagination of the traveling public as the Concorde.

The Concorde carried passengers for the last time on Friday, October 24, 2003, when British Airways retired their fleet. Air France retired its fleet of Concordes on May 31, 2003. Thus, after thirty-four years, ended a chapter in supersonic aviation. This marked the first time in aviation history that a major innovation was retired without a more advanced technological product replacing it.

British Airways has retired its fleet of Concordes and put them on display. They are to be found in the United States, the Museum of Flight in Seattle and the Intrepid Sea, Air and Space Museum in New York; in Britain, Airbus UK in Filton Bristol, Manchester Airport, Heathrow Airport, and the Museum of Flight near Edinburgh; and in Barbados, Grantly Adams Airport in Bridgetown.

Because of its speed, comfort, and safety, air travel is the leading mode of public transportation today, as measured in revenue passenger miles (one fare-paying passenger transported one mile).

ACCOMMODATIONS

The earliest guest rooms were parts of private dwellings, and travelers were hosted almost like members of the family. In the Middle East and in the Orient, caravansaries and inns date back to antiquity. In more modern times, first the stagecoach and then railroads, steamships, the automobile, motorcoach, and airplane expanded the need for adequate accommodations. The railroad brought the downtown city hotel, the automobile and motorcoach brought the motel, and the airplane led to the boom in accommodations within or near airports. Housing, feeding, and entertaining travelers is one of the world's most important industries.

CHRONOLOGIES OF TRAVEL

Herein are two chronologies of travel: (1) a chronology of ancient migrations, early explorers, and great travelers, and (2) a chronology of travel arrangers of their business and their suppliers. The selected travelers and explorers not only made remarkably long and arduous journeys to little-known (and often mistaken) places, but also wrote vivid descriptions or had scribes write for them. Their hardships were sometimes unbelievably difficult, often dangerous, and occasionally fatal.

The comfortable and pleasant (even sometimes inspiring) traveling facilities of today are truly a tribute to the development of modern technology, design, and engineering.

CHRONOLOGY OF ANCIENT MIGRATIONS, EARLY EXPLORERS, AND GREAT TRAVELERS

1 million years ago	*Homo erectus* originates in eastern and southern Africa; makes extensive migrations north to the Middle East and to Asia.
350,000 years ago	Early *Homo sapiens* evolves from *H. erectus;* dwells in Africa, Europe, and Asia.
50,000–30,000 years ago	Anatomically modern man, *H. sapiens,* evolves and expands into Australia from southeastern Asia and into northeastern Asia.
15,000 years ago	Upper Paleolithic people cross into northern latitudes of the New World from northeast Asia on a land bridge.

B.C.E.	
4000	Sumerians (Mesopotamia, Babylonia) invent money, cuneiform writing, and the wheel; also, the concept of a tour guide.
2000–332	Phoenicians begin maritime trading and navigating over the entire Mediterranean Sea area. They may possibly have sailed as far as the British Isles and probably along the coast of western Africa and to the Azores.
1501–1481	Queen Hatshepsut makes the journey from Egypt to the land of Punt, believed to be an area along the eastern coast of Africa.
336–323	Alexander the Great leads his army from Greece into Asia, crossing the Hindu Kush mountains (Afghanistan-Kashmir area), and to the Indus River.

C.E.	
500	Polynesians from the Society Islands sail to Hawaii, a distance of over 2,000 miles.
800–1100	Vikings establish trade and explore Iceland, Greenland, and the coast of North America.

1271–1295	Marco Polo, a Venetian merchant, travels to Persia, Tibet, Gobi Desert, Burma, Siam, Java, Sumatra, India, Ceylon, the Siberian arctic, and other places.
1325–1354	Ibn Battuwtah, the "Marco Polo of Islam," a Moroccan, makes six pilgrimages to Mecca; also visits India, China, Spain, and Timbuktu in Africa.
1492–1502	Christopher Columbus explores the New World, including the Bahamas, Cuba, Jamaica, Central America, and the northern coast of South America.
1497	John Cabot, an Italian navigator, sailing from Bristol, England, discovers North America at a point now known as Nova Scotia.
1513	Vasco Núñez de Balboa, a Spanish explorer, discovers the Pacific Ocean.
1519	Ferdinand Magellan sails west from Spain to circumnavigate the globe. He is killed in the Philippines, but some of his crew complete the circumnavigation.
1540–1541	Francisco Vásquez de Coronado, a Spanish explorer, seeks gold, silver, and precious jewels (without success) in what is now Arizona, New Mexico, Texas, Oklahoma, and other areas of the American Southwest.
1602	Bartholomew Gosnold, English explorer and colonizer, navigates the eastern coast of the (now) United States from Maine to Narragansett Bay; discovers and names Cape Cod. In 1606 his ship carries some of the first settlers to Virginia.
1768–1780	James Cook, an English naval officer, explores the northeastern coast of North America, and in the Pacific discovers New Caledonia, New Zealand, Australia, and Hawaii. He is killed in Hawaii.
1784–1808	Alexander Mackenzie, a Scot, makes the first overland exploration across North America north of Mexico; discovers the river now named for him, which flows into the Arctic Ocean, and the Fraser River, which discharges into the Pacific.
1804–1806	Meriwether Lewis and William Clark, Americans, lead an expedition that opens the American West, discovering the Columbia River and traveling to the Pacific coast.
1860–1863	John H. Speke, an Englishman, discovers the source of the Nile River to be the Victoria Nile flowing out of Ripon Falls, issuing from the north shore of Lake Victoria.
1925–1934	William Beebe, American underwater explorer and inventor, develops the bathysphere and dives to 3,034 feet offshore Bermuda.
1951–1955	Elizabeth Marshall Thomas, an American, explores the Kalahari Desert in central Africa.
1969	Neil Armstrong, Edwin Aldrin, Jr., and Michael Collins, American astronauts, make pioneer journey to the moon in the *Saturn V* space vehicle. First Armstrong and then Aldrin step out of the lunar module

onto the moon's surface. Collins continues to pilot the command and service module, which later joins with the lunar module for their return to Earth.

CHRONOLOGY OF TRAVEL ARRANGERS, THEIR BUSINESSES, FACILITIES, EQUIPMENT, AND SUPPLIERS

B.C.E.

2000 Caravansaries (inns) are established in the Near East and the Orient in ancient times. Located on caravan routes, they provide overnight rest needs for travelers and traders and for their donkeys and camels. These people travel in groups for mutual assistance and defense.

776 Greeks begin travels to the Olympic Games. Subsequently, the games are held every four years.

C.E.

500–1450 During Europe's Middle Ages, a royal party in unfamiliar territory sends out a harbinger to scout the best route, find accommodations and food, then return to the group as a guide.

1605 The hackney coach is introduced in London.

1801 Richard Trevithick, in England, perfects a steam locomotive capable of pulling heavy railcars.

1815 John L. McAdam and Thomas Telford, Britishers, invent all-weather roads, subsequently with a bituminous top.

1822 Robert Smart of Bristol, England, starts booking passengers on steamships sailing to Ireland.

1826–1840 Railroads begin service in the United States, first hauling minerals such as coal and, later, passengers.

1829 The Tremont House opens in Boston, the first "modern" hotel.

1830 First passengers are carried by rail in England.

1838 Stendhal, the pseudonym of Marie-Henri Beyle of France, authors *Mémoires d'un touriste,* believed to be the first disseminated printed use of the French word *tourist.*

1841 Thomas Cook organizes a special excursion train carrying 570 passengers from Leicester to Loughborough, England, a trip of 12 miles.

1850 Thomas Bennett, secretary to the British consul general in Oslo, Norway, sets up a "trip organizer" business as a sideline. He provides individual pleasure travel itineraries and other services.

1873 American Express Company is created by joining the original American Express Company formed in 1850 with the Wells Fargo Company, founded in 1852.

1902	The American Automobile Association (AAA) is founded in Chicago.
1903	Wilbur and Orville Wright make the first successful gasoline-powered airplane flight at Kitty Hawk, North Carolina.
1908	Henry Ford introduces the famous Model T automobile.
1918	Deutsche Lufthansa provides the first scheduled air passenger service from Berlin to Leipzig and Weimar.
1920	U.S. road system begins great improvement.
1926	Varney Airlines and Western Airlines become the first airlines in the United States.
1927	Charles A. Lindbergh flies solo from New York to Paris nonstop.
1927	Charles A. Levine becomes the first transatlantic passenger, flying from New York to within 118 miles of Berlin, his destination, because of a forced landing.
1927	Pan American Airways flies first international commercial mail flight from Key West, Florida, to Havana, Cuba.
1928	Pan Am flies first passenger flight on the same route.
1931	American Society of Steamship Agents is founded in New York.
1936	Air Transport Association (ATA) is formed in Chicago.
1939	Frank Whittle, an Englishman, develops the first jet engine capable of powering a full-size airplane.
1944	The American Society of Travel Agents (ASTA) is founded from the American Society of Steamship Agents.
1945	End of World War II and the beginning of the era of mass tourism.
1951	Founding of Pacific Asia Travel Association (PATA) in Honolulu, Hawaii.
1952	The U.S. Congress creates the National System of Interstate Highways.
1954	Great Britain produces the Comet, the first passenger jet plane.
1958	Boeing Commercial Airplane Company produces the B-707, first commercial jet plane built in the United States.
1959	American Airlines flies the first transcontinental B-707 flight from Los Angeles to New York.
1961	The U.S. Congress creates the U.S. Travel Service.
1964	American Airlines inaugurates the SABRE computerized reservation system (CRS).
1970	Pan American World Airways flies the first Boeing 747 "jumbo jet" plane with 352 passengers from New York to London.
1978	British Airways and Air France begin passenger service on the supersonic Concorde airplane. The U.S. Airline Deregulation Act is passed.
1990	Fall of the Berlin Wall.
1994	The "age of travel," wherein the most complex trip can be planned and arranged by a single phone call from the traveler; might involve

Prague, in the Czech Republic, has become one of the most popular destinations in Eastern Europe since the fall of the Iron Curtain in the early 1990s. *Copyright © Corbis Digital Stock.*

numerous airlines, a cruise ship, sightseeing tours, a local rental car, other ground services, and entertainment—all reserved by amazing computerized reservation systems worldwide, the entire trip, except for incidentals, paid for by a single credit card.

1994   The "Chunnel" undersea railway opens, providing rail travel under the English Channel between England and France.

1995   Delta Air Lines introduces commission caps, putting a ceiling on payments to travel agents for domestic tickets. Denver International Airport (DIA) opens as the first new U.S. airport in 20 years. The first White House Conference on Travel and Tourism is held.

1996   Alaska Airlines becomes the first carrier to accept online bookings and take payment through a Web site on the Internet.

1998   Hong Kong opens new $20 billion airport.
2001   Dennis Tito takes the world's first paid space vacation.
2003   The Concorde is retired.

SUMMARY

Early explorers, traders, and shippers laid the groundwork upon which our modern age of travel is based. Human needs to arrange trips and facilitate movements have not changed over the ages: Building roads, vehicles, and ships and providing overnight rest accommodations go back into antiquity. The brave explorers who went into the unknown made available to their contemporaries knowledge of what the world was really like.

Over the centuries, inventions such as the sandglass to measure time, the "log" line to measure distance, and the compass to gauge direction made possible successful sea exploration. The roads of early Persia and those of the Roman Empire were used for exploration, for military purposes, for transporting tribute, and for pleasure trips and recreation.

Subsequent inventions of better roads, stagecoaches, passenger railroads, passenger ships, automobiles, motorcoaches, and airplanes created an ever-speedier and more pleasant means of travel. Hotels and inns became more commodious and comfortable, with the added convenience of location, services, and appointments.

However, the conditions for an ever-expanding tourism market are little different now than from Roman times. Tourism will flourish if prospective travelers are convinced that they will be safe and comfortable and well rewarded by their trip. When the Roman Empire declined, tourism declined. The wealthy class was reduced, roads deteriorated, and the countryside was plagued by bandits and scoundrels. Today, wars, unrest, and terrorism are similarly detrimental to tourism. Peace, prosperity, effective marketing, and reasonable travel costs remain the essential ingredients needed for the universal growth of travel.

ABOUT THE READING

This reading presents a chart entitled "Some Past, Present, and Future Trends in the Travel Industry," which appeared in the 75th Anniversary Edition of *Travel Trade*.

READING 2.1

Some Past, Present, and Future Trends in the Travel Industry

Reprinted from the 75th Anniversary Edition of Travel Trade.

Travel Modes, Speeds, Times & Costs

	1929	1949	1969	1979
Travel Modes	**Air:** Ford, Fokker Trimoters **Rail:** first streamliners; 60-70 mph cruise **Auto:** Model T/A; ~35 mph; roads poor **Ship:** All overseas travel 25 mph.	DC-4; DC-6, Constellation; many DC-3s. **Railroads** near peak **Bus** travel growing **Cars** ~60 mph; roads good	707, DC-8, Electra, DC-9; 727 **Air** travel booming (Jets introduced end of 1950s) **Rail,** bus declining relatively **Cars** ~70 mph; Interstate hiway system 80% completed	747; various wide bodied craft. Limited Concorde service **Rail,** bus declining relatively; some technological & comfort improvements **Cars** (temporarily?) held to nominal 55 mph.

	1929	1949	1969	1979
Approx. Max. Travel Speeds	100-125 MPH	250-300 MPH	500-600 MPH	500-1300 MPH

Time Needed From NY To:	1929	1949	1969	1979
Sydney (10,000mi)	2 weeks	2 days	1 day	1 day
Moscow (4,700mi)	1 week	1 day	9 hours	9 hours
London (3,500mi)	5 days	18 hours	7 hours	4 hours

		Car	Rail	Air		Car	Rail	Air		Car	Rail	Air		Car	Rail	Air
LA (2,500mi)	Hrs.	120	70	25	Hrs.	80	65	12	Hrs.	60	55	5	Hrs.	70	—	5
Chicago (700mi)		25	16	9		15	14	5		13	13	3		15	13	2
Washington, DC (200mi)		9	5	3		6	4	3		4	4	1.5			4.5	3.5	1

Illustrative Minimum Travel Fares (1979 Dollars)	1929	1949	1969	1979
	NY-San Francisco: ~$725 one way (plane or train) ~28¢/mi	**1947** **NY-San Francisco** ~$470 or 19¢/mi **NY-London** ~$1,070 or 31¢/mi **NY-Sydney** ~$2,500 or 25¢/mi	**NY-San Francisco** ~$210 or 8¢/mi **NY-London** ~$280 or 8¢/mi **NY-Sydney** ~$833 or 8¢/mi	**NY-San Francisco** ~$125 or 5¢/mi **NY-London** ~$150 or 4.5¢/mi **NY-Sydney** ~$833 or 8¢/mi

Explanations: ALL prices have been computed in terms of 1979 U.S. dollars. Symbol: ~ = approximate.

Travel Modes, Speeds, Times & Costs

1989	1999	Present	2029
No real change in either subsonic or supersonic aircraft. Concorde routes unchanged: no second generation supersonic aircraft. 747-400 carries more people over longer range. ATC improvement just beginning. General aviation declined during decade. Fast rail expanded in Europe and Japan, but not U.S. No increase in car speed.	No real change in either subsonic or supersonic aircraft. Concorde routes unchanged. Development of second generation supersonic aircraft discontinued because of inability to balance economic and environmental factors. Boeing 747-400 carries more people over longer range. 50 passengers commuter airline jets growing in use. Crowded skies over U.S. and inability of ATC to keep up have lengthened travel time between major cities. No high-speed U.S. rail yet. 65-mph speed limit on interstate highways in open areas.	Supersonic air travel discontinued when Concorde is retired because of economic and environmental issues. Development of subsonic aircraft continues following introduction of 777. Terrorist attacks against U.S. in 2001 results in higher demand for corporate private jet travel. Turmoil in Middle East pushes jet fuel costs up. In the wake of "9/11," major air carriers were awash in red ink due to decline in air travel, higher fuel costs & debt accrued since 2001. A number of low-cost air carriers enter the market, including those started as subsidiaries by the majors. Rail service flags as ridership declines, except on East Coast. No high-speed rail available yet in the U.S.	Revolutionary new modes; e.g., "transplanetary tunnel." Many HSTs; still much subsonic air travel. Sub-orbital travel. Private space travel and tourism accommodations. Various fast automated private vehicles.

1989	1999	Present	2029
500-1300 MPH	500-1300 MPH	500-600 mph	500-6,000 MPH

1989	1999	Present	2029
1 day	1 day	1 day	3 hours
9 hours	9 hours	9 hours	2 hours
3 hours	3.5 hours (Concorde)	7 hours	2 hours

1989

	Car	Rail	Air
Hrs.	70	—	5
	15	13	2
	4.5	3.5	1

1999

	Car	Rail	Air
Hrs.	70	—	5.5
	15	13	2.5
	4.5	3.5	1

Present

	Car	Rail	Air
Hrs.	70	—	5.5
	15	13	2.5
	4.5	3.5	1

2029

1 hour
1 hour
.5

1989	1999	Present	2029
Increased competition lowered fares, especially as shown in terms of 1979 dollars (approximately 60% of 1989 dollars). **London** $118, 3.3 cents **San Francisco** $101, 4.0 cents **Sydney** $450, 4.5 cents	Increased competition lowered fares, especially as shown in terms of 1979 dollars (approximately 50% of 1989 dollars): **London** - 1999 winter fare $118, 3.3 cents; $59 (1.65 cents) in 1979 dollars **San Francisco** - 1999 sale fare $99, 4.0 cents; $49.50 (2.0 cents) in 1979 dollars **Sydney** - 1999 sale fare $450, (4.5 cents); $225 (2.25 cents) in 1979 dollars	Business fares at a six-year low (after being disproportionately higher than leisure fares) because of lowered post "9/11" demand and to competition and incursions by low-fare carriers. High jet fuel costs lead to surcharges on one-way air tickets ranging from $10-$15. Lowest fares as shown in 1979 dollars for one-way travel: **London** - $248.07 in 1979 dollars, 7 cents **San Francisco** - $123.00, .02 cents **Sydney** - 2004 $422.11, 4 cents	0-5¢ per miles Much transportation "free" as a public service

Progress in Technology

	1929	1949	1969	1979
Destinations/ Accessibility	Only nearby destinations practice for most tourists & many businesspersons.	Continental travel possible for many tourists. Overseas travel still limited.	Continental travel for most; overseas travel for many; growing rapidly.	Overseas travel possible for most people. New range of destinations opening up.
Conveniences	Very limited, but luxury and personal services available at high price.	Improving rapidly, e.g. car rentals, credit cards, handy motels.	"Convenience technology" e.g., moving sidewalks, improved baggage handling.	More frequent, shorter vacations, weekend commuting in some professional families.
Information and Reservations: Time Needed	By mail or office visits to carrier or travel agent; weeks to hours	Much by phone; hours to minutes	Phone/computer; minutes to seconds	Phone/computer; Improved, multi-enquiry computer; seconds.
Staying in Touch With Home	Mail; days Telegraph; hours	Mail/phone, days/minutes	Phone; direct-dialing credit cards; minutes/seconds.	Phone at widely acceptable-cost; seconds
Weather Prediction	Barely useful next day predictions in a few localities	Useful nationwide predictions	Some tourist planning on basis of weather	Good short-term predictions; days.

Economic & Social

	1929	1949	1969	1979
"Tourist Pollution" Issues	Practically none.	Negligible	Emerging	Frequent discussion; sometimes limiting
Role of Travel/Tourist Agent	Clerk—"Mom and Pop" store	Clerk, sometimes counselor; still "Mom and Pop"	More specialization; clerking aspects easier	Specialized "leisure counselor" Large agency chains grow
Travel/ Tourism/ Leisure	Some leisure, travel expensive; tourism for relative few	More leisure; travel cheaper; tourism available to many	$(\frac{Tourism}{Leisure} = \frac{T)}{L)}$ growing Booming business travel; Specialized tourism activity orientations and conventions	T/L still growing; new leisure options proliferate; Pleasure travel increasing relative for business travel.
	U.S. average work week ~48 hrs	Av. work week ~41 hrs.	Av. work week ~40 hrs.	Av. work week ~38 hrs.
Travel/Tourism and Economic Growth	Economy good (just before depression) Travel & tourism growing	End of two decades of depression and war Beginning of new economic growth & new era of travel and tourism. War-increased awareness of other places	Travel and tourism growth about double overall economic growth rate since 1949.	⟶ Rapid expansion of tourism as a way of life.

Progress in Technology

1989	1999	Present	2029
Very extensive, frequent worldwide travel. All destinations. Slumps when terrorist warnings elevated. State Department warnings keep Americans away from places with political, social or medical peril.	More frequent, shorter vacations. Growth of one-week to 10-day European trips. Weekend commuting in some professional families.	Very extensive, frequent worldwide travel. All destinctions. Slumps when terrorist warnings elevated. State Department warnings keep Americans away from places with political, social or medical peril.	Cheap, fast, convenient travel to everywhere (but space travel may be expensive).
Bank credit card and debit cards in wide use as America continues to move to a paperless society. Elec-tronic tickets pervasive with paper tickets being phase out, express check-in at airports reduce lines, express check-out by hand-held mobile pro-cess of car rental at the car. The Inter-net is used to check-in before airport departure, acquire drive maps, buy travel, research destination information.	Bank credit cards universal in working and middle-class America; electronic tickets made delivery of airline tickets easier; express check-out by hand-held mobile processor of car rental right at the car	Bank credit card and debit cards in wide use as America continues to move to a paperless society. Electronic tickets pervasive with paper tickets being phased out, express check-in at airports reduce lines, express checkout by hand-held mobile process of car rental at the car. The Internet is used to check-in before airport departure, acquire drive maps, buy travel, research destination information.	What is incremental convenience?
All data of interest and reservations available from home and wireless personal computers. Travelers have access to same information and booking capabilities as agents.	The Internet and World Wide Web, as well as fax and E-mail communication, vastly expand availability and speed of information. Travelers have access to same information sources as travel professionals.	All data of interest and reservations available from home computers and wireless personal computers. Travelers have access to same information and booking capabilities as agents.	Various formats e.g. holography in living room, for display, considerations of unlimited information.
Internet available globally, wireless phones with photo capabilities bring communications to new level, combining audio and video transmissions around the world.	Long-distance rates lowest ever, in both offices and homes, due to cut-throat competition; availability of fax and E-mail communication	Internet available globally, wireless phones with photo capabilities bring communications to new level, combining audio and video transmissions around the world.	Whole world videophone at negligible cost.
No significant change. Local conditions pinpointed by new generation of Doppler radar.	No real change. Local conditions pinpointed by Doppler radar.	No significant change. Local conditions pinpointed by new generation of Doppler radar.	Planning months ahead; cost discounts for bad weather periods.

Economic & Social

1989	1999	Present	2029
Receding as a controversial issue expect for extremely sensitive regions. Largely controlled by local option and improved management.	Some sites (Stonehenge, Roman Coliseum) limit tourists to fringe areas. Emergence of eco-tourism travel as a niche; expansion of pedestrian streets in tourist cities	Receding as a controversial issue except for extremely sensitive regions. Largely controlled by local option and improved management.	Not conceived as problem; fully managed; but various local limits are understood
Direct bookings increased via Internet travel sales. Agents refining role as destination/information specialists. Trend to cross-selling leisure/corporate. Shift to home-based and host agencies.	Increased market share of domestic tickets. Growth of home-based travel agents. Separation of commercial and leisure-oriented agencies. Use of Internet.	Direct bookings increased via Internet travel sales. Agents refining role as destination/information specialists. Trend to cross-selling leisure/corporate. Shift to home-based and host agencies.	Distinction between local and distant may have largely eroded—Every place is "next door"
Vast growth even though great increase in competition. Average work-week unchanged.	Business travel grew in the '80s and declined slightly in '90s. Continued growth of leisure travel.	Business travel falls as corporations contain costs. Travel reduced to areas in which economic, geopolitical or health issues prevail. Leisure travel leading a rebound.	Vast range of pleasant aesthetically satisfying, fulfilling activities (inc. travel); discretionaly choices among them
_____ Av. work week ~35 hrs.	Av. work week declined to 35 hrs in '80s and grew to more than 40 hrs in '90s due to downsizing and job re-engineering. More people working multiple jobs.	_____ Individual work week reflects choices; could be about 20 hours.	_____ Work time largely a matter of individual choices; could be slight; very many choices.
Both business and pleasure travel grew at rates well beyond the economic growth rate.	Leisure travel grew at rates well beyond the general economic growth rate. Corporate grew in the '80s and declined in the early '90s, becoming stable in the late '90s	Telecommunications still plays a relatively small role. Business community reduces all air travel to cut costs, migrate to low-cost carriers; reduced first-class travel. Leisure travel continues to grow; bookings typically last minute (90 days or less). Overall travel spending expected to rise 4.4% in 2004 to $568 billion.	"Steady state" for travel & leisure, but in overall slowly growing economy Many present categories (e.g., discretionary spending & leisure time) no longer meaningful

KEY CONCEPTS

accommodations
air travel
American Express
Americans
attractions
automotive travel
classical world
early beginnings
early roads
early ships

Egyptian
European
Grand Tour
Greeks
Olympic Games
Pan American Airways
Phoenicians
Polynesians
rail travel
Robert Smart

Romans
Silk Road
stagecoaches
Sumerians
Thomas Bennett
Thomas Cook
travel agents
water travel

Internet Sites

The Internet sites mentioned in this chapter are repeated here for convenience, plus some selected additional sites. For more information, visit these sites. Be aware that Internet addresses change frequently, so if a site cannot be accessed, use a search engine. Also use a search engine to locate many additional sites that are available.

H-Travel Network on History of Travel and Tourism
http://www.h-net.org/~travel

National Amusement Park Historical Association
http://www.napha.org

National Geographic
http://www.nationalgeographic.com

National Trust for Historic Preservation
http://www.nationaltrust.org

Smithsonian Institution
http://www.si.edu

Internet Exercises

Activity 1
Site Name: The National Amusement Park Historical Association
URL: http://www.napha.org
Background Information: The National Amusement Park Historical Association (NAPHA) is an international organization dedicated to the preservation and enjoyment of the amusement and theme park industry—past, present, and future.

Exercises
1. Trace the evolution of the amusement park from medieval Europe to the present day.
2. What is the prognosis for the amusement park industry in the United States today?

Activity 2
Site Name: National Trust for Historic Preservation
URL: http://www.nationaltrust.org
Background Information: The National Trust for Historic Preservation is a privately funded nonprofit organization that provides leadership, education, and advocacy to save America's diverse historic places and revitalize our communities.

Exercises
1. What are National Trust Historic Sites?
2. Where does the National Trust get its operating funds?
3. Does the National Trust decide which buildings are historic?

QUESTIONS FOR REVIEW AND DISCUSSION

1. Of what value is learning the fundamentals of tourism's long history?
2. Do today's travelers have motivations and concerns similar to those of travelers who lived during the Classical Era?
3. What were the principal travel impulses of such early sea explorers as Columbus, Cabot, Balboa, Magellan, and Gosnold?
4. Give some examples of how guides operated in early tourism. Why were they so important? Are their functions the same today? Their ethics? (When discussing, include tour escorts.)
5. Describe the parallels that exist between tourism in Roman times and that of today.
6. Why have the Olympic Games survived since 776 B.C.E.?
7. In the twenty-first century, how consequential for the international traveler is an ability in foreign languages?
8. Can one's money be converted to that of any other country?
9. What countries use the euro for currency?
10. Are museums, cathedrals, and art galleries really important to most visitors? Provide some outstanding examples.
11. How significant were religious motivations in early travel? Do these still exist? Examples?
12. Early religious houses such as churches and monasteries often accommodated travelers. Give reasons for this.
13. What, if any, were the impacts of Marco Polo's writings on the growth of travel by Europeans during the Renaissance (fourteenth through sixteenth centuries)?
14. Specifically, why did travel by rail supersede that by stagecoach?
15. Are medical and health travel motivations still important?
16. Describe ancient tourist attractions. How significant are they now?
17. Why has air travel become the primary mode for middle- and long-distance trips?
18. Who was the first travel agent, and what services did he provide? The first rail passenger agent? Tour operator? Steamship agent?
19. How have computerized reservations systems (CRSs) aided travel agencies and the traveler?
20. What will travel be like 20 years from now?

SELECTED REFERENCES

Belasco, Warren James. *Americans on the Road: From Autocamp to Motel, 1910–1945.* Cambridge, MA: MIT Press, 1979.

Burkart, A. J., and S. Medlik. *Historical Development of Tourism.* Aix-en-Provence, France: Centre des Hautes Studes Touristiques, 1990.

Casson, Lionel. *Travel in the Ancient World.* London: Allen and Unwin, 1974.

Cooper, Chris. *Classic Reviews in Tourism.* Clevedon, UK: Channel View Publications, 2003.

Douglas, Ngaire, and Norman Douglas. "P&O's Pacific." *Journal of Tourism Studies,* Vol. 7, No. 2, pp. 2–14, December 1996.

Evans, Michael R. "Newport, Rhode Island—America's First Resort: Lessons in Sustainable Tourism." *Journal of Travel Research,* Vol. 36, No. 2, pp. 63–67, Fall 1997.

Fagan, Brian M. *The Great Journey: The Peopling of Ancient America.* New York: Thames and Hudson, 1987.

Friedhiem, Eric. *Travel Agents: From Caravans and Clippers to the Concorde.* New York: Travel Agent Magazine Books, 1992.

Gee, Chuck Y., and Matt Lurie (eds). *The Story of the Pacific Asia Travel Association.* San Francisco: Pacific Asia Travel Association, 1993.

Gunn, Clare A. *Western Tourism: Can Paradise Be Reclaimed?* Elmsford, NY: Cognizant Communication Corporation, 2004.

Jakle, John A. *The Tourist: Travel in Twentieth-Century North America.* Lincoln: University of Nebraska Press, 1985.

Kreck, Lothar A. "Tourism in Former Eastern European Societies: Ideology in Conflict with Requisites." *Journal of Travel Research,* Vol. 36, No. 4, pp. 62–67, Spring 1998.

Lerner, Judith. "Traveling When the World Was Flat." *Travel Agent,* pp. 26–29, March 8, 1982.

McIntosh, Robert W. "Early Tourism Education in the United States." *Journal of Tourism Studies,* Vol. 3, No. 1, pp. 2–7, May 1992.

National Geographic. *Peoples and Places of the Past: The National Geographic Illustrated Cultural Atlas of the Ancient World.* Washington, DC: National Geographic Society, 1983.

Rae, W. Fraser. *The Business of Travel: A Fifty Years' Record of Progress.* London: Thomas Cook and Son, 1891.

Robinson, H. *A Geography of Tourism.* London: Macdonald and Evans, 1976.

Rugoff, Milton. *The Great Travelers.* New York: Simon and Schuster, 1960.

Shaw, Steve. *The Delicious History of the Holiday.* London: Routledge, 2000.

Sofield, Trevor, and Sarah Li. "Tourism Development and Cultural Policies in China." *Annals of Tourism Research,* Vol. 25, No. 2, pp. 362–392, 1998.

Sofield, Trevor, and Sarah Li. "Historical Methodology and Sustainability: An 800-year-old Festival from China." *Journal of Sustainable Tourism,* Vol. 6, No. 4, pp. 267–292, 1998.

Towner, John. "Approaches to Tourism History." *Annals of Tourism Research,* Vol. 15, No. 1, pp. 47–62, 1988.

Towner, John. "The Grand Tour: A Key Phase in the History of Tourism." *Annals of Tourism Research,* Vol. 12, No. 3, pp. 297–333, 1985.

Towner, John. "The Grand Tour: Sources and a Methodology for an Historical Study of Tourism." *Tourism Management,* Vol. 5, No. 3, pp. 215–222, September 1984.

Towner, John. "What Is Tourism's History?" *Tourism Management,* Vol. 16, No. 5, pp. 339–344, August 1995.

Towner, John, and Geoffrey Wall. "History and Tourism." *Annals of Tourism Research,* Vol. 18, No. 1, pp. 71–84, 1991.

Van Doren, Carlton S. "Pan Am's Legacy to World Tourism." *Journal of Travel Research,* Vol. 32, No. 1, pp. 3–12, Summer 1993.

CAREER OPPORTUNITIES

CHAPTER 3

Learning Objectives

- Evaluate future job opportunities in the tourism field.
- Learn about the careers available.
- Discover which careers might match your interests and abilities.
- Know additional sources of information on careers.

An airline employee checking in air travelers. *Copyright © Corbis Digital Stock.*

INTRODUCTION

Every student eventually must leave the college or university campus and seek a career-oriented job. This is a difficult decision-making time, often filled with doubt as to what goals or ambitions should be pursued. Coming face to face with the problem of getting a first major career-oriented job is a challenging task. You are marketing a product—yourself—and you will have to do a good job of communicating to convince a prospective employer that you have the abilities needed and that you will be an asset to the organization.

JOB FORECASTS

The World Travel and Tourism Council (WTTC) estimates that in 2005 there were over 221.5 million people worldwide, some 8.3 percent of the total workforce, employed in jobs that exist because of the demand generated by tourism. While tourism contributes to gross domestic product (GDP), capital investment, employment, foreign exchange, and export earnings, it is the job-creation capacity of tourism that is its most significant feature. By 2015, WTTC forecasts that there will be 269.5 million people around the globe having jobs created by tourism, accounting for 8.9 percent of total employment, or 1 in every 11.2 jobs.

JOB REQUIREMENTS

Are you suited to work in the tourism field? Do you like working with people? Can you provide leadership? Would you be genuinely concerned for a customer's comfort, needs, and well-being even if the customer might be rude and obnoxious? If you can answer in the affirmative, you can find a place in this industry. You have to like to do things for other people and work helpfully with them. If not, this is not the industry for you. Courtesy comes easily when customers are pleasant and gracious. But a great deal of self-discipline is required to serve every type of person, especially demanding or indecisive ones. In tourism, the customer might often change his or her mind. This requires patience and an unfailingly cheerful personality.

You must also ask if you have the physical stamina required to carry out many of the jobs available. It is difficult to work long hours on your feet or to work in a hot, humid, or cold environment. You might be involved in the pressure of a crush of people, such as at an airline ticket counter. A travel agency counselor must have keen vision, excellent hearing, and well-endowed nerves. A large-resort manager is constantly required to deal with sophisticated budgeting and investment decisions. The chief executive officer (CEO) of a major convention and visitors bureau must provide leadership to and coordinate the efforts of a very diverse membership. Try to evaluate your physical and mental attributes and skills to determine if you can perform.

To enhance your chances of getting a job and deciding if you would like it, visit several types of tourist-related organizations. Watch the activities being performed.

One of the best jobs in tourism is to serve as the head of a state/provincial tourism office. Shown here is Kim McNulty, Director of the Colorado State Tourism Office. *Photo by author.*

Talk to managers, supervisors, and employees. Try to obtain an internship. Work experience means a great deal. Once you have had that, these skills can be utilized in a wide variety of tourism enterprises in any number of locations.

CAREER POSSIBILITIES

Tourism today is one of the world's largest industries. It is made up of many segments, the principal ones being transportation, accommodations, food service, shopping, travel arrangements, and activities for tourists, such as history, culture, adventure, sports, recreation, entertainment, and other similar activities. The businesses that provide these services require knowledgeable business managers.

Familiarity with tourism, recreation, business, and leisure equips one to pursue a career in a number of tourism-related fields. Tourism skills are critically needed, and there are many opportunities available in a multitude of fields.

Because tourism is diverse and complex and each sector has many job opportunities and career paths, it is virtually impossible to list and describe all the jobs one might consider in this large field. However, as a student interested in tourism, you could examine the following areas, many of which are discussed in more detail in Chapters 5 to 8.

Airlines

The airlines are a major travel industry employer, offering a host of jobs at many levels, ranging from entry level to top management, including reservation agents, flight attendants, pilots, flight engineers, aircraft mechanics, maintenance staff, baggage handlers, airline food service jobs, sales representatives, sales jobs, computer specialists, training staff, office jobs, clerical positions, ticket agents, and research jobs. Because airlines have to meet safety and other requirements, opportunities also exist with the Federal Aviation Administration (FAA). The FAA hires air traffic controllers and various other specialists. Airports also use a wide range of personnel from parking attendants to airport managers. Other policy and air-safety-related jobs are available with associations such as the Air Transport Association.

People in tourism tend to enjoy their work. The opportunity to service visitors on vacation or on family outings is more satisfying than many other forms of employment.
Photo of Richard Nethaway by Dick Danielson of Dick Danielson Photography.

Bus Companies

Bus companies require management personnel, ticket agents, sales representatives, tour representatives, hostesses, information clerks, clerical positions, bus drivers, personnel people, and training employees.

Cruise Companies

The cruise industry is the fastest-growing segment of the tourism industry today. Job opportunities include those for sales representatives, clerical workers, market researchers, recreation directors, and CEOs. Because of its similarity in operations, the cruise industry has many of the same jobs as the lodging industry.

Railroads

Passenger rail service in the United States is dominated by Amtrak and in Canada by Via Rail. In Europe, Japan, and elsewhere rail passenger transportation is much more developed and widespread, offering greater opportunities than in North

America. Railroads hire managers, passenger service representatives, traffic analysts, marketing managers, sales representatives, reservations clerks, information specialists, conductors, engineers, coach and lounge car attendants, and station agents.

Rental Car Companies

With increased pleasure air travel and the growth of fly/drive programs, rental car companies are becoming an ever more important segment of the travel industry. This sector of tourism employs reservation agents, rental sales agents, clerks of various kinds, service agents, mechanics, and district and regional managers.

Hotels, Motels, and Resorts

The range of jobs in hotels and motels is extremely broad. The following list is representative: regional manager, general manager, resident manager, comptroller, accountants, management trainees, director of sales, director of convention sales, director of personnel, director of research, mail clerks, room clerks, reservation clerks, front-office manager, housekeepers, superintendent of service, bellhops, lobby porters, doormen, maids, chefs, cooks, kitchen helpers, storeroom employees,

Resorts provide a wide range of managerial job opportunities in attractive surroundings. *Photo courtesy of Holiday Inn Family Suites Resorts, Lake Buena Vista, Florida.*

dishwashers, waiters, bartenders, apprentice waiters, heating and air-conditioning personnel, maintenance workers, engineers, electricians, plumbers, carpenters, painters, and laundry workers.

Resorts tend to have the same jobs as those mentioned for hotels and motels; however, larger resorts will have greater job opportunities and require more assistants in all areas. Resorts also have a number of additional job opportunities in the areas of social events, entertainment, and recreation, such as for tennis and golf pros. At ski resorts there will be ski instructors, members of a safety patrol, and so on. The American Hotel and Lodging Association has launched the AH&LA Online Career Center, which lists open positions in the lodging industry. Visit their Web site at **http://ahla.new-jobs.com.**

Travel Agencies

Travel agencies range from very small to very large businesses. The smaller businesses are very much like any other small business. Very few people carry out all the business operations, and jobs include secretarial, travel counseling, and managerial activities. In large offices, job opportunities are more varied and include branch manager, commercial account specialists, domestic travel counselors, international travel counselors, research directors, and advertising managers. Trainee group sales consultants, accountants, file clerks, sales personnel, tour planners, tour guides, reservationists, group coordinators, trainees, operations employees, administrative assistants, advertising specialists, and computer specialists are other possibilities.

Tour Companies

Tour companies offer employment opportunities in such positions as tour manager or escort, tour coordinator, tour planner, publicist, reservations specialist, accountant, sales representative, group tour specialist, incentive tour coordinator, costing specialist, hotel coordinator, office supervisor, and managerial positions. Often, a graduate will begin employment as a management trainee, working in all the departments of the company before a permanent assignment is made.

Food Service

Many job opportunities are available in the rapidly growing food service industry, such as headwaiters, captains, waiters and waitresses, bus persons, chefs, cooks, bartenders, restaurant managers, assistant managers, personnel directors, dieticians, menu planners, cashiers, food service supervisors, purchasing agents, butchers, beverage workers, hostesses, kitchen helpers, and dishwashers. In addition, highly trained managers having a strong background in this sector are required to oversee the development and performance of large restaurant chains.

Professional chefs find great satisfaction in creating tasty, nutritious, and virtually irresistible food items. *Photo courtesy of Doral Golf Resort and Spa.*

Tourism Education

As global tourism continues to grow, the need for training and education grows. In recent years many colleges and universities have added travel and tourism programs, existing programs have expanded, vocational schools have launched programs, trade associations have introduced education and certification programs, and private firms have opened travel schools. There are job opportunities for administrators, teachers, professors, researchers, and support staff.

Tourism Research

Tourism research consists of the collection and analysis of data from both primary and secondary sources. The tourism researcher plans market studies, consumer surveys, and the implementation of research projects. Research jobs are available in national tourism offices, state/provincial travel offices, and so on.

Travel Communications

A number of opportunities are available in travel writing for editors, staff writers, and freelance writers. Most major travel firms need public relations people who write and edit, disseminate information, develop communication vehicles, obtain publicity, arrange special events, do public speaking, plan public relations campaigns, and so on. A travel photographer could find employment in either public relations or travel writing. Television is a medium with increasing opportunities.

Recreation and Leisure

Jobs in recreation and leisure are enormous. Some examples are activity director, aquatics specialist, ski instructor, park ranger, naturalist, museum guide, handicapped-program planner, forester, camping director, concert promoter, lifeguards, tennis and golf instructors, coaches for various athletic teams, and drama directors. Many recreation workers teach handicrafts. Resorts, parks, and recreation departments often employ recreation directors who hire specialists to work with senior citizens or youth groups, to serve as camp counselors, or to teach such skills as boating and sailing. Management, supervisory, and administrative positions are also available.

Attractions

Attractions such as amusement parks and theme parks are a major source of tourism employment. Large organizations such as Disney World, Disneyland, Six Flags, Europa-Park, Tivoli Gardens, and Sea World provide job opportunities ranging from top management jobs to clerical and maintenance jobs.

While tourism is generally a "people business," there are many important "behind-the-scenes" support careers that require individuals having well-developed technical expertise to ensure the delivery of a high-quality visitor experience. *Photo courtesy of U.S. Department of Agriculture.*

LEGOland® is a brand that draws shoppers from around the globe to their products and theme parks. In this case a sales associate happily displays the famous product at LEGOland® California located in Carlsbad. *LEGO, LEGOLAND, the LEGO, and LEGOLAND logos and the brick configuration are trademarks of the LEGO Group and are used here with special permission © 2005 The LEGO Group.*

Festivals and Events

Festivals and events are one of the fastest-growing segments of the tourism industry. Event management is emerging as a field, is becoming more professional, and is providing a new source of job opportunities. Events are creating offices and moving them to year-round operation. A study of the International Special Events Society showed that event managers earned between $25,000 and $75,000 per year and that the majority held baccalaureate degrees.

Sports Tourism

Sports are popular throughout the world, with many sports teams and enterprises becoming big businesses and offering job opportunities in the management and marketing areas.

Tourist Offices and Information Centers

Numerous jobs are available in tourist offices and information centers. Many chambers of commerce function as information centers and hire employees to provide this information. Many states operate welcome centers. Job titles found in state tourism offices are director, assistant director, deputy director, travel representative, economic development specialist, assistant director for travel promotion, statistical analyst, public information officer, assistant director for public relations, marketing coordinator, communications specialist, travel editor, media liaison, media specialist, photographer, administrative assistant, information specialist, media coordinator, manager of travel literature, writer, chief of news and information, marketing coordinator, market analyst, research analyst, economist, reference coordinator, secretary, package tour coordinator, and information clerk.

Convention and Visitors Bureaus (Destination Management Organizations)

As more and more cities enter the convention and visitor industry, employment opportunities in this segment grow. Many cities are devoting public funds to build convention centers to compete in this growing market. Convention and visitors bureaus require CEOs, managers, assistant managers, research directors, information specialists, marketing managers, public relations staff, sales personnel, secretaries, and clerks.

Meeting Planners

A growing profession is meeting planning. Many associations and corporations are hiring people whose job responsibilities are to arrange, plan, and conduct meetings.

Gaming

One of the fastest-growing sectors is gaming. Today, one is hard-pressed to find a state where gambling is not allowed or a gaming proposal is not in front of the state legislature. From riverboats to Indian reservations to land-based casinos, new destinations are being created. Casinos provide job opportunities ranging from managers to marketers to mechanics to clerical and maintenance jobs.

Other Opportunities

A fairly comprehensive list of career opportunities has been presented. Others that do not fit the general categories listed are club management, entertainment management, corporate travel departments, hotel representative companies, in-flight and trade magazines, and trade and professional associations.

CAREER PATHS IN TOURISM

In addition to considering one of the foregoing kinds of positions within a particular segment of the tourism sector, it is also useful to examine the various career paths that might be pursued. Because the tourism industry is so large and so diverse, it offers a broad range of challenging positions. While each of these positions offers its own unique opportunities and demands, people will find that the experience gained from working in a range of jobs in different subsectors of tourism can strengthen their understanding of the industry as a whole. Depending on one's career objectives, this broader understanding of tourism can be especially valuable when applying for certain types of positions. Examples include those in destination management organizations and national or provincial/state tourism offices.

To offer employees opportunities for growth and development, educators and personnel managers attempt continually to develop the concept of career paths in tourism. A schematic model illustrating the concept is shown in Figure 3.1. The fundamental premise of this general model is that people can pursue a variety of reasonably well defined alternative routes, first through the educational system and subsequently through the industry itself. Based on the training and experience gained, combined with high-quality performance, a person can pursue a career path starting at different levels, with the ultimate goal of achieving the position of senior executive. While not everyone will have the ability or will necessarily want to pass through all levels of the model, it does provide defined career paths for those who are interested. It also indicates what combination of training and experience is normally required to achieve various positions.

Although clearly an oversimplification, the career path model demonstrates that people may take a variety of routes in pursuing their careers at different levels within and across the various subsectors of tourism. The specific positions that will appeal to different people will, of course, vary according to their particular educational background and their occupational skills. The chosen career path will also reflect a person's values and interests. Just how the chosen occupation might

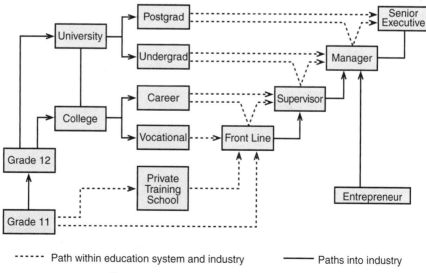

Figure 3.1 Career paths within the tourism industry.

A customer service representative is one of the many jobs available in the rental car field. *Photo by Tracy Brown, taken at Baltimore-Washington International Airport; Photo courtesy of the Cendant Car Rental Group.*

reflect individual values and interest is shown in Figure 3.2. As indicated, frontline staff (entry level and operations) must like dealing with people and possess a strong interest in providing them with high-quality service. Supervisors, managers, and entrepreneurs must possess additional values and interests that enable them to face the challenges of change as they attempt to meet the needs of a demanding and ever-shifting marketplace.

INTERNSHIPS

One of the best ways to get the job you want is to have internship (cooperative education) experience. Internship opportunities abound in the tourism area. Most internship programs are designed to provide students the opportunity to (1) acquire valuable, hands-on experience to supplement their academic learning; (2) learn potential practical skills; (3) develop professionalism; (4) interact with segments of the local business community and develop an appreciation for the daily operation and long-term strategic direction of a corporate or small business environment; and (5) develop a further understanding of their chosen field. Some examples of internship programs and sources of internships are Marriott, Hyatt, Disney, Universal Studios, the National Tourism Foundation, and the American

	Food & Beverage	Accommodations	Tour & Travel	Attractions Amusement Park
ENTREPRENEUR	**Restaurant Owner** • Independence • Flexible Work Hours • Financial & Personal Success • Control • Novelty/Change	**Hotel Owner** • Independence • Irregular Work Hours • Control • Money • People • Novelty/Change • Success	**Tour Bus Line Owner** • Quality • Commitment • Work Ethic • Optimism • People/Employees • Challenge • Growth • Humor • Flexibility • Organization • Working with Numbers	**General Manager** • Quality • Tourism & Tourists • Organization • Attention to Detail • Flexibility/ Diversity • People • Creativity • Business • Irregular Work Hours
MANAGER	**Restaurant Manager** • Quality • People • Leadership • Novelty/Change • Nutrition	**Hotel Manager** • Influencing People • Novelty/Change • Curiosity • Competition • People • Problem Solving • Status	**Tour Bus Line Manager** • Quality • Commitment • Work • People • Challenge • Flexibility • Growth • Humor • Organization • Innovation • Working with Numbers	**Director of Special Attractions** • Young People • Professionalism • Work Ethic • Creativity • Irregular Work Hours • Variable Work Environment • Challenge • Economic Value • Leisure/Fun • Analysis
SUPERVISOR	**Maître D'** • People • Quality • Challenge • Food Industry	**Assistant Executive Housekeeper** • Customers/ People • Quality • Cost Effectiveness • Team Efficiency • Problem Solving • Challenge	**Superintendent of Bus Maintenance** • People and Their Safety • Quality • Variety/Novelty • Machinery • Problems • Organization	**Amusement Park Supervisor** • People • Quality • Machinery • Challenge • Efficiency
	Bartender • People • Quality • Creativity • Flexible Work Hours	**Operations Chambermaid** • Customers/ People • Neatness • Fun • Variety • Cleaning	**Tour Bus Driver** • People • Esteem • Power/Control • Being Busy • Routine	**Operations Ride Operator** • People • Commitment • Initiative • Work • Teamwork • Being Busy
ENTRY LEVEL	**Food & Beverage Server** • People • Flexibility • Work Conditions	**Entry Chambermaid** • People • Cleanliness • Cultural Variety	**Ticket Agent** • People • Helpfulness • Challenge • Clerical Tasks • Math • Travel • Novelty/Variety	**Entry Ride Operator** • People • Fun
PRE-EMPLOYMENT	Personal Worth Work			

PREDOMINANT VALUES AND INTERESTS

PEOPLE
QUALITY
CHALLENGE
FLEXIBILITY
NOVELTY/CHANGE

PEOPLE

*NOTE
The values and interests listed here are samples. A small sample of experts was used in data collection.

* created for the INDUSTRY ANALYSIS and TRAINING INFORMATION BRANCH DEPARTMENT of CAREER DEVELOPMENT and EMPLOYMENT GOVERNMENT of ALBERTA by CAREER DEVELOPMENT INSTITUTE

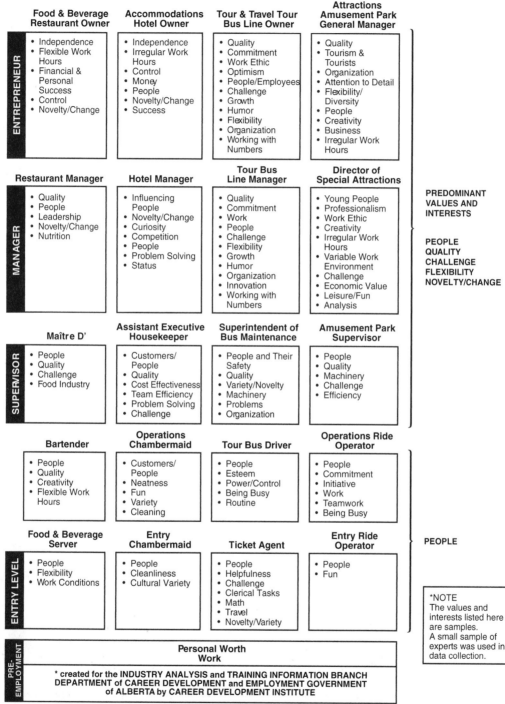

Figure 3.2   Career paths in tourism, sample occupations, values, and interests.

Hospitality Academy. The Marriott Lodging Internship Program is designed to stimulate student interest in hotel management and a career with Marriott International. Through the program, students gain practical work experience necessary to pursue a management career in the hospitality industry. In addition, it provides Marriott with an opportunity to make sound evaluations of potential management candidates. Internship opportunities are available in their Marriott Hotels, Resorts, and Suites; Renaissance Hotels; Residence Inn; Courtyard; and TownePlace Suites brands and their time-share business, Marriott Vacation Club International.

The Hyatt Hotels and Resorts Internship Program was created to generate student interest in hotel management and spark a desire to join a hospitality leader after graduation. Internships also give Hyatt the opportunity to recognize potential managers and continue developing relationships throughout the academic year. Structured internship opportunities are available in over ten of their hotel and resort locations.

Universal Studios Florida has internships in advertising, convention sales, food services, human resources, information systems, marketing, merchandise, park operations, production, public relations, technical entertainment, and technical services. Active juniors, seniors, and graduate students are eligible for the program.

Tourism Cares for Tomorrow, the nonprofit foundation that was created from combining the National Tourism Foundation (NTF) and the Travelers Conser-

Campus career fairs are places where students can learn about jobs, internships, and career paths. Here, college recruiters for Disney Worldwide Services, Inc., visit with students from the University of Colorado. *Photo by the author.*

vation Foundation(TCF) in January 2005, has announced the return of NTF's internship program. Tourism Cares for Tomorrow assembles dozens of internship offerings to benefit both students and the industry. Go to their Web site at **http://www.Tourismcaresfortomorrow.org/tourismcares/students** for information on internships and scholarships.

OTHER SOURCES OF CAREER INFORMATION

Most of the career opportunities available in the travel field have been listed. It is hoped that this overview will provide you with a guide and point out that these industries are so large that they are worthy of much further study by themselves. In considering career opportunities, it is important to gather information before you invest a great deal of time looking for a job. The following are good references on tourism jobs:

Riegel, Carl, and Melissa Dallas. *Hospitality and Tourism Careers.* Upper Saddle River, NJ: Prentice Hall, 1998.

Rubin, Karen. *Inside Secrets to Finding a Career in Travel.* Indianapolis, IN: JIST Works, 2001.

One book on how to get a job is particularly recommended:

Bolles, Richard. *What Color Is Your Parachute? A Practical Manual for Job-Hunters and Career-Changers.* Berkeley, CA: Ten Speed Press, 2005.

The information provided in this section should be an important starting point for you. However, it is really just the tip of the iceberg. It is up to you to explore the subject further and to gain additional information. You need to learn not only about careers in tourism and travel-related fields, but also about the task of marketing yourself—how to work up résumés and how to conduct yourself during interviews. General books on getting a job will help you in this task.

SUMMARY

A career in tourism offers many exciting and challenging employment opportunities. As indicated in Chapter 1, tourism is the largest industry in the world today. In the United States and throughout the rest of the world the travel industry is expected to be a growth industry. The labor-intensive tourism industry has a need for motivated people of all ages and backgrounds. Those who prepare themselves, maintain high energy, have a talent for working with people, and have a dedication to high-quality service will find themselves climbing the career ladder to success.

KEY CONCEPTS

accommodations
airlines
attractions
bus companies
career path
convention and visitors bureaus
cruise lines
employment forecasts

food service
internships
meeting planning
railroads
recreation
rental car companies
tour companies
tourism education

tourism job requirements
tourism research
tourist offices and information
    centers
travel agencies
travel communications

Internet Sites

The Internet sites mentioned in this chapter are repeated here for convenience, plus some selected additional sites. For more information, visit these sites. Be aware that Internet addresses change frequently, so if a site cannot be accessed, use a search engine. Also use a search engine to locate many additional relevant sites.

AH&LA Educational Institute
http://www.ei-ahla.org

American Hotel and Lodging
   Association
http://www.ahla.com

Canadian Tourism Human Resources
   Council
http://www.cthrc.ca/careerplanning

Career Women
http://www.careerwomen.com

Career Age.com
http://www.careerage.com/tourism

Cool Jobs Canada
http://www.cooljobscanada.com

Cool Works
http://www.coolworks.com

Destinations
http://www.destinations.ca

Hilton Hotels
http://www.hilton.com

Hospitality career net.com
http://www.hospitalitycareernet.com

Hospitality 1st
http://www.hospitality-1st.com

Hospitality Net
http://www.hospitalitynet.org

Hyatt Hotels and Resorts
http://www.hyatt.com

International Society of Travel and
   Tourism Educators
http://www.istte.org

Marriott International
http://www.careers.marriott.com

MGM Grand Hotel Casino
http://www.mgmgrand.com

National Restaurant Association
   Educational Foundation
http://www.nraef.org

National Tour Association
http://www.ntaonline.com

National Tourism Foundation
http://www.ntfonline.org

Ontario Hostelry Institute
http://www.ohischolarships.com

Tourism Cares for Tomorrow
http://www.tourismcaresfortomorrow.
    org

Total Jobs.com
http://www.totaljobs.com/
    travel-jobs.html

Travel Industry Association of America
http://www.tia.org

Travel Jobs
http://www.TravelJobs.com

World Travel and Tourism Council
http://www.wttc.org

Internet Exercises

Activity 1
Site Name: Hospitality Net
URL: http://www.hospitalitynet.org
Background Information: Hospitality Net is the leading hospitality industry resource on the Internet with information on employment opportunities, events, industry news, links to other sites, and so on.

Exercises
1. What are the categories for the job opportunities listed on this Web site?
2. Choose a category and find a job that would be of interest to you. Describe the job, where it is located, and why it appeals to you.

Activity 2
Site Name: World Travel and Tourism Council
URL: http://www.wttc.org
Background Information: The World Travel and Tourism Council (WTTC) is the global business leaders' forum for travel and tourism. Its members are chief executives from all sectors of the travel and tourism industry, including accommodations, catering, cruises, entertainment, recreation, transportation, and travel-related services. Its central goal is to work with governments to realize the full economic impact of the world's largest generator of wealth and jobs—travel and tourism.

Exercise
1. What is the WTTC's vision on jobs in the travel and tourism industry for the next decade?

QUESTIONS FOR REVIEW AND DISCUSSION

1. What is the growth potential for tourism jobs?
2. As a career in tourism, what position appeals to you at present?
3. What preparation will be needed for that position?
4. What are its probable rewards?
5. Identify the position's advancement opportunities.
6. Are your writing and speaking skills good enough to land a job?
7. What criteria would you use to choose a company for an interview?
8. How important is salary in your job choice?
9. Evaluate the job satisfaction in your chosen career.
10. What will tourism be like in the year 2020? What position might you visualize yourself to be in by that date?

CASE PROBLEMS

1. Donnell C. is graduating from a four-year travel and tourism curriculum. She has had several job offers. What type of organization would afford her the broadest range of experiences? How important is her beginning salary?

2. Jim B. is a successful resort manager. He is visited one day by a very bright high school senior who is most interested in becoming a resort manager. What educational preparation advice might Jim offer?

SELECTED REFERENCES

Altman, Lois A., and Linda R. Brothers. "Career Longevity of Hospitality Graduates." *FIU Hospitality Review,* Vol. 13, No. 2, pp. 77–83, Fall 1995.

Brownell, Judi. "Women in Hospitality Management: General Managers' Perception of Factors Related to Career Development." *International Journal of Hospitality Management,* Vol. 13, No. 2, pp. 101–118, June 1994.

Burns, Peter M. "Tourism's Workforce: Characteristics and Inter-Cultural Perspectives." *Tourism Recreation Research,* Vol. 22, No. 1, pp. 49–54, 1997.

Business Travel News. Travel Manager Salary and Attitude Survey. New York: *BTN—North America,* annual.

Choy, Dexter J. L. "The Quality of Tourism Employment." *Tourism Management,* Vol. 16, No. 2, pp. 129–137, March 1995.

Cook, Suzanne, and William Evans. *A Portrait of the Travel Industry Employment in the U.S. Economy.* Washington, DC: TIA Foundation, 1999.

LaLopa, Joseph M. "Commitment and Turnover in Resort Jobs." *Journal of Hospitality and Tourism Research,* Vol. 21, No. 2, pp. 11–26, 1997.

Langton, Bryan D. "High Quality Travel and Tourism Jobs." *Viewpoint,* Vol. 1, No. 2, pp. 26–33, no date.

Nebel, Eddystone C., III, Lee Ju-Soon, and Brani Vidakovic. "Hotel General Manager Career Paths in the United States." *International Journal of Hospitality Management,* Vol. 14, No. 3–4, pp. 245–260, September–December 1995.

Ninemeier, Jock, and Joe Perdue. *Hospitality Operations: Careers in the World's Greatest Industry.* Upper Saddle River, NJ: Prentice Hall, 2005.

Riegel, Carl, and Melissa Dallas. *Hospitality and Tourism Careers.* Upper Saddle River, NJ: Prentice Hall, 1998.

Rubin, Karen. *Inside Secrets to Finding a Career in Travel.* Indianapolis, IN: JIST Works, 2001.

Samuels, Jack, and Reginald Foucar-Szocki. *Guiding Your Entry into the Hospitality, Recreation, and Tourism Mega-Profession.* Upper Saddle River, NJ: Prentice Hall, 1999.

Sciarini, Michael P., Robert H. Woods, Ernest Boger, Philip Gardner, and G. Michael Harris. "College Freshmen Perceptions of Hospitality Careers: Gender and Ethnic Interest." *Journal of Hospitality and Tourism Education,* Vol. 9, No. 3, pp. 18–28, 1997.

U.S. Department of Labor. *Occupational Outlook Handbook.* Washington, DC: U.S. Government Printing Office, 2004.

Williams, Anna Graf, and Karen J. Hall. *Creating Your Career Portfolio: At-a-Glance Guide.* Upper Saddle River, NJ: Prentice Hall, 1997.

World Tourism Organization. *Human Resource Development in Asia and the Pacific.* Madrid: WTO, 2001.

World Travel and Tourism Council Human Resource Centre. *Steps to Success: Global Good Practices in Travel and Tourism Human Resource Development.* Vancouver: WTTCHRC, 1998.

PART 2

How Tourism Is Organized

The Dallas/Fort Worth Airport covers 17,500 acres. Purchasing facilities and an airport hotel can be seen in the center of the photograph. An automated shuttle train provides transportation to other terminals.

WORLD, NATIONAL, REGIONAL, AND OTHER ORGANIZATIONS

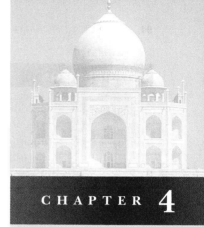

CHAPTER 4

Learning Objectives

- Understand the magnitude of world tourism in terms of the vast numbers of organizations that serve the needs of their diverse memberships.

- Recognize the variety of types and functions of tourism organizations.

- Know why states support official offices of tourism.

- Learn how national, regional, and trade organizations are structured and operated.

The Taj Mahal in Agra, India, is a favorite travel destination along the Asian Highway. The Asian Highway was initiated in 1958 and funded by the national governments in Asia. *Photo courtesy of the United Nations.*

INTRODUCTION

The complex organization of tourism involves literally thousands of units. This chapter focuses on some of the organizations that perform the catalyst, planning, development, and promotion functions within destinations. As Figure 4.1 stresses, all of these functions must be carried out with a high degree of cooperative interaction between the public and private sectors at all levels of the destination hierarchy. This destination hierarchy provides a geographical classification and subclassification of the world. The world is divided into nations, which in turn commonly consist of regions, states/provinces, and urban centers (cities/municipalities).

In addition to a geographic classification, tourism organizations can also be classified by ownership, such as government, quasi government, or private; by function or type of activity, such as regulators, suppliers, marketers, developers, consultants, researchers, educators, publishers, professional associations, trade organizations, and consumer organizations; by industry, such as transportation (air, bus, rail, auto, cruise), travel agents, tour wholesalers, lodging, attractions, and recreation; and by profit or nonprofit.

The purpose of Chapters 4 through 8 is to discuss the major types of tourist organizations and how they interrelate and operate, focusing on illustrative examples. The discussion begins with official international tourism groups in this chap-

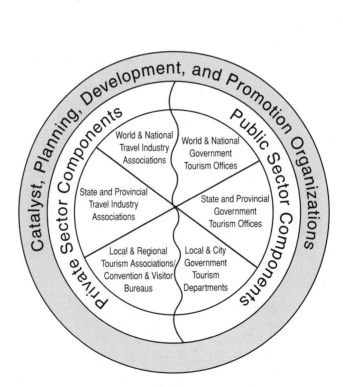

Figure 4.1   Tourism organizations.

ter and ends with the private organizations and firms that make up the tourism industry, covered in Chapters 5, 6, 7, and 8. Additional important supplemental areas that facilitate the tourism process, such as education, publishing, and marketing and publicity, are also included in Chapter 8.

INTERNATIONAL ORGANIZATIONS

World Tourism Organization

The World Tourism Organization (WTO) is the most widely recognized and the leading international organization in the field of travel and tourism today. It serves as a global forum for tourism policy issues and a practical source of tourism know-how. Its membership includes 145 countries and territories and more than 350 affiliate members representing local government, tourism associations, educational institutions, and private-sector companies, including airlines, hotel groups, and tour operators. With its headquarters in Madrid, WTO is a specialized agency of the United Nations (UN). UN specialized agency status entitles WTO to participate as a full member in the United Nations System Chief Executives Board for Coordination (CEB), which elaborates system-wide strategies in response to overall intergovernmental directives on economic cooperation and development. WTO's participation will enable it to highlight the role of tourism in support of socio-economic development and the achievement of the Millennium Development Goals.

The specialized agencies function on an autonomous basis, with their own charter, budget, governing boards, staff, and publishing operations. They make annual or biennial reports to the Economic and Social Council. The General Assembly can examine their budgets and make recommendations; however, each specialized agency exercises final control over its operations.

The World Tourism Organization is an official specialized agency of the United Nations and has the objective of promoting and developing tourism worldwide. *Photo by Ron Nelson.*

Thus, WTO is vested by the UN with a central and decisive role in promoting the development of responsible, sustainable, and universally accessible tourism, with the aim of contributing to economic development, international understanding, peace, prosperity, and universal respect for and observance of human rights and fundamental freedoms. In pursuing this aim, WTO pays particular attention to the interests of the developing countries in the field of tourism.

The World Tourism Organization had its beginnings as the International Union of Official Tourist Publicity Organizations set up in 1925 in The Hague. It was renamed the International Union for Official Tourism Organizations (IUOTO) after World War II and moved to Geneva. IUOTO was renamed the World Tourism Organization (WTO), and its first General Assembly was held in Madrid in May 1975. The Secretariat was installed in Madrid early the following year at the invitation of the Spanish government, which provides a building for the headquarters. In 1976, WTO became an executing agency of the United Nations Development Programme (UNDP); in 1977, a formal cooperation agreement was signed with the United Nations. In October 2003, WTO became a specialized agency of the United Nations.

WTO is engaged in many activities. The transfer of tourism know-how to developing countries is a major task. Here WTO contributes decades of experience in tourism to the sustainable development goals of nations throughout the world. WTO projects are based on the policy of sustainability, ensuring that the economic

The WTO works with the UNDP, which finances tourism planning projects and infrastructures, such as projects to improve transportation in southern Africa. *Photo courtesy of the United Nations.*

benefits of tourism development are not offset by damage to the environment or to local cultures.

WTO is well known for its statistics and market research. Research has been one of WTO's most important contributions. Their work here has set international standards for tourism measurement and reporting, measured the impact of tourism on national economies, produced forecasts, examined trends, and made the results available in publications.

Human resource development is another WTO goal. WTO sets standards for tourism education. The WTO Education Council—made up of leading tourism education, training, and research institutions—drives the education program of work, which includes the accreditation program for tourism education institutions (TedQual) and the Graduate Tourism Aptitude Test (GTAT). These are examples of their efforts to encourage standardization of curricula and to make degrees in tourism more internationally comparable. WTO also offers seminars, distance learning courses, and practicum courses for tourism officials from member countries.

WTO attempts to facilitate world travel through elimination or reduction of governmental measures for international travel as well as standardization of requirements for passports, visas, and so forth. They work to improve the quality of tourism through trade liberalization, access for travelers with disabilities, safety and security, and technical standards. They also work to improve the promotional efforts of member governments through effective media relations and serve as a clearinghouse for international tourism information.

In addition to these global activities, WTO engages in regional activities. Each region of the world—Africa, the Americas, East Asia and the Pacific, Europe, Middle East, and South Asia—receives special attention from that region's WTO representative. The representatives meet with top tourism officials from each of the countries in their region to analyze problems and help seek solutions, act as a liaison between tourism authorities and the UNDP to create specific development projects, organize national seminars of topics of particular relevance to an individual country, such as tourism promotion in Mexico or ecotourism in Kyrgyzstan, and hold regional conferences on problems that are shared by many countries so that members can exchange experiences and work toward common goals, such as safety and security in Eastern Europe or aviation and tourism policy in the Caribbean.

They are also involved in regional promotion projects. The Silk Road is a project being implemented in cooperation with the United Nations Educational, Scientific, and Cultural Organization (UNESCO). Launched in 1994, WTO's Silk Road project aims to revitalize through tourism the ancient highways used by Marco Polo and the caravan traders who came after him. The Silk Road stretches 12,000 kilometers from Asia to Europe. Sixteen Silk Road countries have joined forces for this project: Japan, Republic of Korea, Democratic People's Republic of Korea, China, Kazakhstan, Kyrgyzstan, Pakistan, Uzbekistan, Tajikistan, Turkmenistan, Iran, Azerbaijan, Turkey, Georgia, Greece, and Egypt. Joint promotional activities include a brochure and video, familiarization trips, and special events at major tourism trade fairs. Key projects that WTO is currently working on are poverty alleviation and elimination through sustainable tourism, protecting children from sexual exploitation in tourism, crisis management, ecotourism, and safety and security. Visit the WTO Web site at **http://www.world-tourism.org.**

World Travel and Tourism Council

The **World Travel and Tourism Council** (WTTC) is the forum for global business leaders in travel and tourism. It is comprised of the presidents, chairs, and chief executive officers of 100 of the world's foremost companies. These include accommodation, catering, cruises, entertainment, recreation, transportation, and travel-related services. WTTC is the only body representing the private sector in all parts of the industry worldwide. Established in 1990, WTTC is led by a nineteen-member executive committee, which meets twice a year and reports to an annual meeting of all members. Day-to-day operations are carried out by the president and a small staff based in London.

The mission of the council is to raise awareness of the economic and social contribution of travel and tourism and to work with governments on policies that unlock the industry's potential to create jobs and generate prosperity. Their vision of travel and tourism is that of a partnership among all stakeholders, delivering consistent results that match the needs of national economies, local and regional authorities and local communities with those of business, based on: (1) governments recognizing travel and tourism as a top priority; (2) business balancing economics with people, culture, and the environment; and (3) a shared pursuit of long-term growth and prosperity.

The activities of the council can be summarized under three broad themes:

Global Activities. WTTC addresses challenges and opportunities that affect all sectors of the global travel and tourism industry. It is empowered by its members to provide an effective voice for the industry in its dialogue with governments around the world. The council actively promotes public and private sector examples of best practices in tourism. A number of case studies from different parts of the world can be found on their Web site.

Regional Initiatives. Regional initiatives are set up in countries and regions that have huge potential for travel and tourism development, but that lack the framework or resources to achieve growth. The objective of these initiatives is to translate WTTC's Mission into action by working with governments, local leaders, and WTTC global members with a regional presence, to identify and eliminate barriers to growth.

Economic Research. WTTC now uses Oxford Economic Forecasting Ltd., to undertake extensive research to determine travel and tourism's total size and contribution to world, regional, and national economies. The WTTC forecast is the primary vehicle used to convey the message that tourism is the world's largest industry, that it has been growing faster than most other industries, that it will continue to grow strongly, and that it can create jobs and increase gross domestic product (GDP). WTTC plans to continue publishing this forecast and enhance its methodology. In fact, they continue to increase the number of economic impact reports, and under the auspices of the WTO they have developed proposals for an international standard Satellite Accounting System. Their latest 2005 forecast covers 174 national economies and shows that the tourism industry currently generates 221.5 million jobs and contributes over 10.6 percent of global GDP. WTTC has done more to create awareness of the economic importance of tourism than any other organization. Visit their Web site at **http://www.wttc.org.**

International Air Transport Association

The International Air Transport Association (IATA) is the global organization for virtually all the international air carriers. The principal function of IATA is to safely facilitate the movement of persons and goods from any point on the world air network to any other by any combination of routes. This can be accomplished by a single ticket bought at a single price in one currency and valid everywhere for the same amount and quality of service. The same principles apply to the movement of freight and mail.

Resolutions of IATA standardize not only tickets, but waybills, baggage checks, and other similar documents. These resolutions coordinate and unify handling and accounting procedures to permit rapid interline bookings and connections. They also create and maintain a stable pattern of international fares and rates. In effect, they permit the linking of many individual international airline routes into a single public service system.

While developing standards and procedures for the international airline industry to support interlining and enhance customer service continues to be a principal aim, IATA is involved in many other areas such as industry support, the environment, consumer issues, regulatory monitoring, legal support, corporate communications, scheduling, facilitation, safety, security, and services.

IATA is a valuable information source on the world airline industry. Their Airline Product Database provides a comparison of the product across 30 major carriers. Their annual publication, World Air Transport Statistics, is an authoritative source of international airline data. In addition, IATA makes passenger and freight forecasts. Their market research helps the industry develop its strategic and tactical marketing plans.

In summary, IATA's mission is to represent and serve the world airline industry. They serve four groups interested in the smooth operation of the world air transport system: (1) airlines, (2) the public, (3) governments, and (4) third parties such as suppliers and travel and cargo agents. IATA works closely with the International Civil Aviation Organization. IATA's head office is in Montreal; its executive office is in Geneva, Switzerland; and it has regional offices around the world. The IATA Web site is at **http://www.iata.org.**

International Civil Aviation Organization

The International Civil Aviation Organization (ICAO) is an organization of governments joined to promote civil aviation on a worldwide scale. This organization, established in 1944, has adopted a plan, "Guiding Civil Aviation into the 21st Century," to deal more effectively with the constantly evolving challenges facing civil aviation, particularly in the area of flight safety. The strategic action plan focuses on eight major objectives to further the safety, security, and efficiency of international civil aviation and identifies forty-three related activities. Visit the ICAO Web site at **http://www.icao.int.**

DEVELOPMENTAL ORGANIZATIONS (INTERNATIONAL AND NATIONAL)

Financing is always a major problem in tourism development. Large financial organizations are willing to make developmental loans. Examples include the **World Bank** (United States), International Finance Corporation (United States), the OPEC Fund for International Development (Austria), African Development Bank (Côite d'Ivoire), East African Development Bank (Uganda), Inter-American Development Bank (United States), Caribbean Development Bank (Barbados), Asian Development Bank (Philippines), European Investment Bank (Luxembourg), European Regional Development Fund (Belgium), European Bank for Reconstruction and Development (United Kingdom), Islamic Development Bank (Saudi Arabia), and the Arab Fund for Economic and Social Development (Kuwait). Examples of national organizations are FONATUR (Mexico) and Embratur (Brazil). Further sources include governments of countries that want additional hotel development or other supply components and are willing to make low-interest loans or grants or offer other financial inducements for such types of development.

Organization for Economic Cooperation and Development

The **Organization for Economic Cooperation and Development** (OECD) was set up under a convention, signed in Paris on December 14, 1960, that provides that the OECD shall promote policies designed to (1) achieve the highest sustainable economic growth and employment and a rising standard of living in member countries while maintaining financial stability, and thus to contribute to the development of the world economy; (2) contribute to sound economic expansion in member as well as nonmember countries in the process of economic development; and (3) contribute to the expansion of world trade on a multilateral, nondiscriminatory basis in accordance with international obligations.

Members of OECD are Australia, Austria, Belgium, Canada, Czech Republic, Denmark, European Union, Finland, France, Germany, Greece, Hungary, Iceland, Ireland, Italy, Japan, Korea, Luxembourg, Mexico, Netherlands, New Zealand, Norway, Poland, Portugal, Spain, Sweden, Switzerland, Turkey, the United Kingdom, and the United States. OECD's Tourism Committee acts as a forum of exchange for monitoring policies and structural changes affecting the development of international tourism. It encourages further liberalization of tourism activities, both within and outside the OECD area, and has undertaken the development of innovative statistics to improve the understanding of the role of tourism in the economy. Visit the OECD Web site at **http://www.oecd.org.**

REGIONAL INTERNATIONAL ORGANIZATIONS

Pacific Asia Travel Association

The Pacific Asia Travel Association (PATA) represents countries in the Pacific and Asia that have united to achieve a common goal, namely, excellence in travel and tourism growth in this vast region. Its work has been to promote tourism through programs of research, development, education, and marketing. PATA has gained a reputation for outstanding accomplishment among similar world organizations. Visit the PATA Web site at **http://www.pata.org.**

European Travel Commission

The European Travel Commission (ETC) is the strategic alliance that provides for the collaboration between thirty-three European national tourism organizations (NTOs). Founded in 1948, the ETC fills a unique role functioning as a "National Tourism Office of Europe." Its goal is to attract millions of potential and existing overseas customers from the major overseas markets to come to Europe. This is done through promotional campaigns and industry trade shows. The headquarters of the ETC is located in Brussels, Belgium. Visit their Web site at: **http://www.visiteurope.com.**

Asia is one of the fastest-growing travel destinations in the world. Kuala Lumpur, the capital of Malaysia, is one of the many locations in Asia that can provide rewarding experiences for visitors from Western cultures.
Photo courtesy of the Malaysia Tourism Board.

NATIONAL ORGANIZATIONS

Office of Travel and Tourism Industries (OTTI)

The United States is an example of how not to develop tourism. In April 1996 the United States Travel and

Tourism Administration (USTTA), which served as the nation's official government tourist office charged with developing tourism policy, promoting inbound tourism from abroad, and stimulating travel within the United States, was eliminated. Congress has made clear its intention that the federal government primarily rely on the private industry to market the United States as a destination, a primary function of the former USTTA.

While USTTA was eliminated, some of its functions and people were transferred to Trade Development, International Trade Administration (ITA), U.S. Department of Commerce, and a Tourism Industries (TI) office was established with its own deputy assistant secretary. In 2002, the office was renamed the **Office of Travel and Tourism Industries** (OTTI) and placed under the direction of the deputy assistant secretary for Service Industries, Tourism and Finance. The mission statement of OTTI reads: "The Office of Travel and Tourism Industries is dedicated to helping U.S. businesses gain access to and compete in the global marketplace." The goal of the office is to assist travel and tourism businesses by advancing policies and programs that strengthen economic development and export opportunities.

ITA was again reorganized in 2004. Now the OTTI initiative is operated by a director of the office who reports to the deputy assistant secretary for Service Industries, under Manufacturing and Services, ITA, the Department of Commerce, and has 11 employees. OTTI has three areas of responsibilities: (1) director for OTTI, (2) travel research and tourism development, and (3) tourism policy coordination, including the Tourism Policy Council. The organizational structure of OTTI is shown in Figure 4.2.

The office of the director is responsible for the following: fostering economic development through tourism trade development; representing the United States in tourism-related meetings with foreign government officials; serving as the principal point of contact in the U.S. government for the U.S. tourism industry on policy, international commercial diplomacy, and tourism trade development issues; furthering the recommendations for national tourism strategy from the White House Conference on Travel and Tourism (WHCTT); and interacting with the Foreign Commercial Service to advise and assist the tourism trade development officers on matters of policy, technical assistance, and research.

The Travel Research and Tourism Development responsibilities include collecting and disseminating baseline data for international travel, to and from the United States, incorporating eight comprehensive research programs and databases. Included are: (1) developing programs that provide a count of nonresident

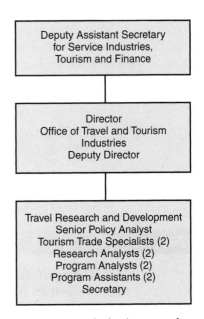

Figure 4.2 Organizational structure of the U.S. Office of Travel and Tourism Industries.

arrivals, estimates of U.S. outbound travel; (2) leading the development of a satellite account for travel and tourism; (3) forecasting on travel to the United States, forecasting for international travel to destinations in the United States, and U.S. outbound forecasting; (4) developing and managing the OTTI Web site, eventually providing an interactive data retrieval system on the Internet; (5) providing travel industry barometers and monitors; (6) providing technical assistance to communities and businesses to help match their tourism strengths with the most promising international markets and to help them bring their tourism products to the market; (7) surveying international air travelers (in-flight survey); and (8) maintaining the Canadian statistics program.

The Department of Commerce also provides tourism assistance by the U.S. Commercial Service. The service has staff in more than 100 U.S. cities and eighty countries abroad. The domestic and international staff work together to provide export counseling to U.S. businesses and destinations interested in entering or increasing their presence in international markets. Services include one-on-one counseling, market research, statistics, partner identification (i.e., outbound tour operators, travel agents, public relations firms), and assistance with international marketing efforts within the travel industry. There are about forty tourism specialists in the domestic offices and fifty in the international offices.

The Tourism Policy Coordination group is formed to (1) reinvigorate the Tourism Policy Council (TPC) dedicated to federal agency coordination for all tourism-related activities; (2) enhance communication with the industry, Congress, and state and local governments for travel and tourism information, data, and technical assistance available throughout the federal government; (3) coordinate interagency federal programs that affect tourism development, including facilitation issues such as support of the Visa Waiver Program; and (4) represent tourism industry needs and issue areas for international commercial diplomacy and in intergovernmental organizations and other relevant forums.

The Tourism Policy Council involves over fifteen federal agencies. The composition of the Tourism Policy Council is shown in Figure 4.3. Visit the Office of Travel and Tourism Industries Web site at **http://tinet.ita.doc.gov.**

Canadian Tourism Commission

The **Canadian Tourism Commission** (CTC) is a working partnership between tourism industry businesses and associations, provincial and territorial governments, and the government of Canada. CTC was one of the first public-private partnerships to be established. It is responsible for promoting and maintaining the orderly growth of tourism in Canada. CTC has one of the best and most comprehensive tourism programs in the world and serves as a model that many other nations strive to equal. Visit their Web site at **http://www.CanadaTourism.com.**

Tourism Australia

On July 1, 2004, a new body, Tourism Australia, was created that bought together the Australian Tourist Commission, See Australia, the Bureau of Tourism Research,

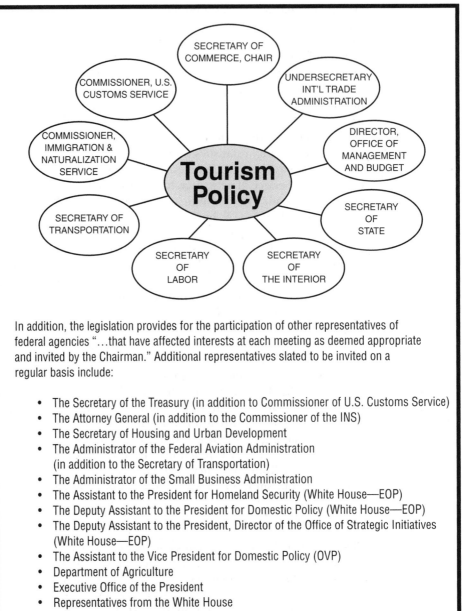

In addition, the legislation provides for the participation of other representatives of federal agencies "…that have affected interests at each meeting as deemed appropriate and invited by the Chairman." Additional representatives slated to be invited on a regular basis include:

- The Secretary of the Treasury (in addition to Commissioner of U.S. Customs Service)
- The Attorney General (in addition to the Commissioner of the INS)
- The Secretary of Housing and Urban Development
- The Administrator of the Federal Aviation Administration (in addition to the Secretary of Transportation)
- The Administrator of the Small Business Administration
- The Assistant to the President for Homeland Security (White House—EOP)
- The Deputy Assistant to the President for Domestic Policy (White House—EOP)
- The Deputy Assistant to the President, Director of the Office of Strategic Initiatives (White House—EOP)
- The Assistant to the Vice President for Domestic Policy (OVP)
- Department of Agriculture
- Executive Office of the President
- Representatives from the White House
- Council of Historic Preservation

Figure 4.3   Composition of the Tourism Policy Council.

and the Tourism Forecasting Council, harnessing the skills and knowledge of these organizations under one umbrella. Two new business units, Tourism Events Australia and Tourism Research Australia were also established to focus on industry and market needs. Tourism Research Australia incorporates a merger of the Bureau of Tourism Research and the Tourism Forecasting Council. Tourism Australia is now the federal government statutory authority responsible for international and domestic tourism marketing as well as the delivery of research and forecasts for the sector. It has a combined budget of $553 million over the next four years. Tourism Australia is another outstanding national tourism organization and would be a good model for others to follow. Visit their Web site at: **http://www.tourismaustralia.com.**

U.S. Federal Aviation Administration

Numerous responsibilities for efficient and safe air travel are assigned to the **Federal Aviation Administration** (FAA), which is illustrative of governmental regulating bodies. This U.S. government organization in the Department of Transportation formulates regulations and supervises or controls various aspects of airline and airport operations. Examples of these functions are air traffic control, air safety, flight standards, aviation engineering, airport administration districts,

The U.S. Federal Aviation Administration (FAA) provides air traffic control, air safety, and other vital aviation regulation and services. Shown here is the FAA control tower and Concourse C at the Denver International Airport. *Photo courtesy of Denver International Airport.*

airways facilities, and certification of new aircraft. The FAA also examines and licenses pilots and flight engineers. Their Web site is: **http://www.faa.gov.**

U.S. Department of Transportation

The **Department of Transportation** has the federal authority to protect air travelers and to police industry practices. It has responsibility for in-flight smoking rules, charters, denied boarding compensation, baggage liability, handicapped-traveler rules, passenger notices, computer reservations bias, and antitrust authority.

U.S. Department of Homeland Security

The events of September 11 brought another government agency that impacts tourism, the **Department of Homeland Security** (DHS). One primary reason for the establishment of the DHS was to provide the unifying core for the vast national network of organizations and institutions involved in efforts to secure the nation. The Transportation Security Administration (TSA) is responsible for protecting our nation's transportation systems and are the most visible at airports. Their screening is no easy task since 730 million people travel on commercial aircraft each year and there are now more than 700 million pieces of baggage being screened for explosives each year. A new tourism position has been established in the DHS to represent the interests of the tourism industry and work to meet security objectives while minimizing travel disruptions.

Other (U.S.) Government Agencies

Numerous other government agencies play an active role in tourism. The U.S. Department of State issues passports, the U.S. Customs Service monitors international travel, Statistics Canada and the U.S. Bureau of the Census compile travel statistics and data, the Interstate Commerce Commission regulates bus transportation, the National Maritime Commission deals with ships, the National Park Service and the Forest Service provide and administer many scenic attractions and facilities, the Bureau of Land Management is involved in several tourism initiatives (such as Back Country Byways, Adventures in the Past, and Watchable Wildlife), the Bureau of Reclamation administers over 300 recreation areas in seventeen western states, and the Federal Highway Administration is involved in the National Scenic Byways program, with the objective of increasing tourism while preserving the environment. Others are the National Trust for Historic Preservation, National Marine Sanctuary Program, Tennessee Valley Authority, Army Corps of Engineers, Fish and Wildlife Service, and the Immigration and Naturalization Service.

Travel Industry Association of America

The Washington, D.C.–based **Travel Industry Association of America** (TIA) is the leading private tourism organization in the United States. The nonprofit association serves as the unifying organization for all components of the U.S. travel industry. The business of travel and tourism in America is served by more than one-half million different organizations that offer a wide range of services to the traveler.

Originally founded in 1941, TIA has grown from a small association of travel officials into a national nonprofit organization with a membership that now represents all components of the travel industry: airlines, attractions, hotels and motels, travel agents, tour operators and brokers, convention and visitors bureaus, state government travel offices, area and regional tourism organizations, food service establishments, auto rental companies, intercity bus and rail lines, cruise lines, and other segments of what is known today as the travel industry.

TIA serves the U.S. travel and tourism industry through a number of programs that market and promote the U.S. travel experience, both abroad and at home; by furnishing research, publications, and reports for and about the industry as well as U.S. and international travelers; by providing strategic leadership for the industry in the U.S. business community and in matters of government at all levels; through its councils and committees that represent specific components of the industry; with its foundation, which finances research and scholarships in the area of travel and tourism; and through its nearly half-century-old awards program that honors achievements by both individuals and organizations within the travel and tourism industry.

The current mission of the TIA is to represent the whole of the U.S. travel industry to promote and facilitate increased travel to and within the United States. TIA fulfills this mission by accomplishing these objectives to: (1) promote a wider understanding of travel and tourism as a major industry that contributes to the economic, cultural, and social well-being of the nation; (2) develop, coordinate, and implement the industry's umbrella marketing efforts to promote travel to and within the United States; (3) pursue and influence policies, programs, and legislation that are responsive to the needs of the industry as a whole; (4) improve domestic and international travelers' experience, including gaining access to, arriving in, traveling within, and departing the United States; (5) enhance TIA's position as the authoritative source for travel industry information and research of the industry as a whole; (6) promote travel industry cohesion and provide communications forums for industry leaders; and (7) leverage resources to develop and execute programs that benefit the travel industry.

TIA has also taken a leadership role in organizing industry councils to provide a unified voice for segments of the industry that enables them to address legislative issues of mutual concern, carry out educational programs unique to their industry components, and offer guidance in the development of TIA policies and programs. Each of the councils is described briefly.

The National Council of State Tourism Directors (NCSTD), formed in 1969, was the first of the national councils to be established under the umbrella of TIA. Its purpose is to provide a forum for state tourism directors to exchange ideas and information on matters common to state and territorial tourism offices and to develop unified positions on industry issues at the national level. While there is great diversity among the states and territories in terms of specific needs and priorities, there are a number of common concerns in such areas as education, communication, marketing, research, and public affairs where NCSTD serves as a catalyst for developing programs that benefit all states and territories and, therefore, the entire U.S. travel industry. All fifty states, the five U.S. territories, and the District of Columbia are represented in NCSTD.

The National Council of Destination Organizations (NCDO) was originally established in 1976 as the National Council of Area and Regional Tourism Organizations (CARTO), and in 1999 as a result of a merger with the National Council of Urban Tourism Organizations (NCUTO), the NCDO was created. This council represents more than four hundred TIA member destination marketing organizations whose concern is the promotion and facilitation of travel to and within that specific area or region. NCDO provides a forum and communications network for professionals from these organizations to address matters common to their specific areas of interest and to develop consensus positions on national issues.

The National Council of Attractions (NCA) was formed in 1976 to unify the widely diverse travel attractions segment within TIA, which includes historic, cultural, scientific, scenic, natural, themed, and entertainment attractions, as well as attraction-related service organizations. NCA has over two hundred members.

TIA supports four major marketing programs: (1) the internationally acclaimed Discover America International Pow Wow, which brings together international tour operators and journalists from over sixty-five nations with U.S. travel suppliers, yielding the sale of over $3 billion worth of the U.S. travel product and invaluable media promotion of travel and tourism in America; (2) the Marketing Outlook Forum, an annual educational event, that in an intensive two-day series of seminars prepares travel industry leaders to understand and deal with travel issues and provides detailed projections concerning future travel patterns; (3) the See America National Domestic Travel Marketing Program, an ongoing, multifaceted, nationwide campaign designed to encourage U.S. consumers to see more of their country through themed promotions, electronic travel information, and widespread use of the title logo, which reinforces the urge to See America; and (4) the international marketing effort spearheaded by the See America brand campaign. Visit both the TIA and See America Web sites at **http://www.tia.org** and **http://www.seeamerica.org.**

REGIONAL ORGANIZATIONS

Regional tourism organizations have the goal of attracting tourists to their specific geographic region. There are several types of regional associations, such as multicountry, multistate, and multicounty. Examples range from PATA, which covers the Pacific region of the world, to groups such as Travel South USA, which promotes travel in the southern states, to the West Michigan Tourist Association, which promotes only one region in Michigan, the northwestern section. Another multistate organization is Foremost West, which promotes tourism in Colorado, Utah,

Arizona, New Mexico, Nevada, and Wyoming. Pennsylvania probably has more regional tourism organizations within its boundaries than any other state; fifty-nine tourist promotion agencies represent Pennsylvania's sixty-seven counties.

STATE AND COMMUNITY ORGANIZATIONS

State

Traditionally, states have promoted tourism as a tool for economic development. In most states, a tourism office has been established by statute and charged with the orderly growth and development of the travel and tourism industry in the state. These offices conduct programs of information, advertising, publicity, and research relating to the recreational, scenic, historic, highway, and tourist attractions in the state at large.

Each of the fifty states has a government agency responsible for travel development and promotion. Texas has two entities devoting funds and resources to tourism development. In Hawaii and Alaska, responsibility for travel development rests primarily with a privately operated nonprofit organization, the Hawaii Visitors

State governments have enacted many laws and regulations affecting tourism. Examples are organizations for promotion, transportation, food products, restaurant inspection, licensing boats, and many others. *Photo by South Dakota Tourism.*

and Convention Bureau, and the Alaska Travel Industry Association, which receive money from the state. The services performed and programs administered by the Hawaii Visitors and Convention Bureau and the Alaska Travel Industry Association are similar to those of the official state travel offices; thus all states are supporting tourism activity. The majority of states house their tourism offices in a Department of Economic Development (or Commerce).

Any review of **state travel offices** must start with TIA's annual Survey of U.S. State and Territory Tourism Offices. Their report covering the fiscal year 2003–2004, published in 2004, is the thirty-first annual report in the series and includes responses from forty-seven states. It shows that state travel offices are expected to spend more than $549.5 million on tourism development in fiscal year 2003–2004 or about $12 million average per state with forty-six states responding. This is less than 1 percent lower than the previous year's $551.8 million budget. Compared with the 1999–2000 fiscal year, the average state tourism budget has decreased 11 percent.

Hawaii remained the leader in tourism office spending with a budget of $56.3 million for 2003–2004. Number two is Illinois with a budget of $46.2 million. Rounding out the top five is Pennsylvania with $29.6 million, Texas with $29.5 million, and Florida with $25.6 million.

Public sector funds are the primary source of all tourism office funding, and indeed the sole source for thirty-two of the forty-six responding states. Of the $549.5 million combined total projected budget, public sector funds represent nearly 94.4 percent, or $518.9 million.

On average, more money was allocated in 2003–2004 than in 2002–2003 for domestic advertising, industry relations, international advertising, inquiry fulfillment, printing and production, press and public relations, research, welcome centers, and "other." Less money was allocated for cooperative marketing funds, film office, grant programs, other administrative costs, personnel services, sales promotion, and Web site development and maintenance.

Tourism offices reports collective 2003–2004 combined marketing and promotion-related budgets totaling $239,691,340. On average, states allocated $5,210,681, nearly 2 percent more than last year's average of $5,133,281. Overall, the portion of tourism office total budgets allocated in 2003–2004 for marketing and promotion-related activities increased slightly over 2002–2003, from 42.8 to 43.6 percent.

Besides advertising, states use a number of other means to promote travel to their destinations, including toll-free phone numbers for visitor inquiries, annual governors conferences on tourism, press tours, travel-related research, and for some, offices in international cities.

Internet Web sites have become the technology of choice for state tourism offices, although some use interactive kiosks and CD-ROM products. Other types of programs engaged in by state travel offices are product development, cultural heritage, rural development, transportation, sports authority development, regulatory, and environmental.

Community

Most communities have also recognized the importance of tourism and have established convention and visitors bureaus. In many smaller communities, the **chambers of commerce** or **resort associations** perform this function. Larger cities now own the central convention facilities. A great deal of promotion and sales effort is then devoted to backing these facilities.

Community tourism offices appear to have a long history. The first tourism office in France was created in 1875, in the town of Gerardmer, followed by Grenoble in 1889. In the Netherlands, the first office (in Dutch, Vereniging voor Vreendenverkeer, abbreviated VVV), was founded in the small city of Valkenburg in the Province of Limburg in the year 1885. They were meant to promote the city and to assist tourists. They are the predecessors of today's local tourist offices all over The Netherlands and are still called VVV.

City Convention and Visitors Bureaus

A **convention and visitors bureau** is a not-for-profit umbrella organization that represents a city or urban area in the solicitation and servicing of all types of travelers to that city or area, whether they visit for business, pleasure, or both. It is also frequently called a Destination Management Organization (DMO) or Destination Marketing Organization. It is the single entity that brings together the interests of city government, trade and civic associations, and individual "travel suppliers"—hotels, motels, restaurants, attractions, local transportation—in building outside visitor traffic to the area.

Urban tourism is an increasingly important source of income and employment in most metropolitan areas, and therefore it warrants a coordinated and concerted effort to make it grow. This growth is best nurtured by the role a convention and visitors bureau can play in continually improving the scope and caliber of services the city provides to corporate and association meeting planners, to individual business travelers, and to leisure travelers.

The bureau is the city's liaison between potential visitors to the area and the businesses that will host them when they come. It acts as an information clearinghouse, convention management consultant, and promotional agency for the city and often as a catalyst for urban development and renewal.

Typical services offered to meeting planners include orientation to the city, liaison between suppliers and meeting planners, and meeting management. The meetings and conventions market is huge. The Convention Industry Council estimates that meetings and conventions are a $102.3 billion-per-year industry (see Chapter 6).

International Association of Convention and Visitor Bureaus

Most of the city convention and visitors bureaus belong to the **International Association of Convention and Visitor Bureaus** (IACVB), 2025 M Street, NW, Suite 500, Washington, D.C. 20036. This group was founded in 1914 as the International

Tourists are provided with timely information and services at tourism information centers all over the world, such as this one in Torremolinos, Spain. *Photo courtesy of the author.*

Association of Convention Bureaus to promote sound professional practices in the solicitation and servicing of meetings and conventions. In 1974, the words "and Visitor" were added to IACB's name to reflect most bureaus' increasing involvement in the promotion of tourism. Since its inception, the association has taken a strong position of leadership in the travel industry. The organization has over twelve hundred members in approximately five hundred city destination management organizations in thirty countries. IACVB provides its members with numerous opportunities for professional dialogue and exchange of industry data on convention-holding organizations.

As the organization's board has recommended, IACVB has been renamed the Destination Marketing Association International (DMAI) with the tagline, Representing CVBs and Tourist Boards Worldwide. Members voted on the name change in the summer of 2005.

The IACVB Meeting Information Network (MINT) is the world's leading meetings and convention database, tracking historical and future records on more than twenty thousand meeting profiles of associations and corporations. The database provides marketing and sales direction to thousands of convention and visitor bureaus, hotels and motels, and other convention industry suppliers.

To encourage exchange between its members, IACVB holds an annual convention, organizes annual educational seminars leading to certificates in sales or bureau operations, organizes topical workshops and seminars, makes regular studies of convention industry trends, maintains a consulting service, and provides its members with government and industry liaison. Visit their Web site at **http://www.iacvb.org.**

SUMMARY

The World Tourism Organization represents governmental tourist interests and aids in world tourism development. Individual countries, states, and provinces have their own tourist promotion and development organizations that work to promote tourism in their area and coordinate tourism promotion with other groups. Most governments play a regulatory as well as developmental role in tourism through such agencies as civil aeronautics boards, federal aviation administrations, customs offices, passport bureaus, and so on. Government agencies typically compile research statistics and gather data. Governments also operate tourist enterprises such as airlines, national parks, and sometimes hotels and campgrounds.

ABOUT THE READING

The reading in this chapter discusses the Pacific Asia Travel Association (PATA). PATA is a regional association within the world group. It is unique in having a worldwide network of PATA chapters. It is also respected for its outstanding conferences and travel marts that are highly successful and valuable for the attendees.

READING 4.1

Pacific Asia Travel Association

Founded in Hawaii in 1951 to develop, promote, and facilitate travel to and among the destination areas in and bordering the Pacific Ocean, the Pacific Asia Travel Association (PATA) brings together governments, airline and steamship companies, hoteliers, tour operators, travel agents, and a wide range of other tourism-related organizations. Today, PATA is the global leader in Pacific Asian tourism. Members exchange ideas, seek solutions to problems, and participate in shaping the future of travel in Asia and the Pacific Area. Membership totals over two thousand organizations worldwide. Since its founding, the association has become an important source of accurate, up-to-date information for its members in the fields of marketing, development, information, education, sustainability, and other travel-related activities. PATA's activities and long-range plans are examined and adjusted each year at the association's annual conference. PATANET, the association's Web site, is at **http://www.pata.org.**

Marketing and Development

PATA'S marketing efforts are directed to influencing more individuals to travel to and within the Pacific area. The association also strives to improve marketing skills at the point of sale and in destination areas, to build profitable long-term business relationships, and to tap lucrative new markets. Development activities are geared toward improving and advancing facilities and services in new destinations, increasing the handling capacity of existing destinations, and preserving their heritage and quality.

Information

PATA keeps members up to date on relevant industry trends via the Strategic Information Centre, which provides members with timely research and market intelligence for business planning, product development, and marketing. In addition to its statistical reports and market research, PATA also produces the following periodic publications:

News@PATA Biweekly: E-mail newsletter highlights association events and activities.

Issues & Trends: Monthly research newsletter from PATA's Strategic Information Centre identifies and analyzes current trends impacting the travel industry.

PATA Compass: The association's bimonthly magazine covers PATA destinations, delivers practical business solutions, and offers wide-ranging perspectives from people within the industry.

PATA Conferences and Marts

Two of the more visible activities are the PATA Annual Conference and the PATA Travel Mart. The annual conference, held in a member country each year, brings together up to two thousand people, who join in discussions of the current needs and problems of Pacific tourism and participate in the association's annual business meeting. Sessions of the conference offer selected themes to assist members in gaining a better working knowledge of tourism. Regional conferences supply members with practical marketing ideas, new product information, and cost-saving management tips. Other seminars, organized to meet the specific needs of members, address pertinent topics such as heritage, technology, and human resources development.

The PATA Travel Marts bring to a single location the buyers and sellers of travel who meet to negotiate contracts for future business. An example would be a tour operator who meets with travel agents in countries that might supply travelers to participate in that company's tour offerings. Specifically, a tour operator in Australia would meet with travel agents from the United States who might send clients to Australia; or a tour operator in the United States who operates tours to Australia would meet with a ground operator (such as a local tour company) from Australia, who would supply a local tour for this tour group when it arrived in Sydney.

Sustainability

The future of the tourism industry depends on protecting the region's environmental, heritage, and cultural resources. PATA develops industrywide initiatives and sponsors conservation conferences to ensure sustainable growth. The association also honors significant accomplishments in this arena under its Gold Awards program.

The PATA Office of Environment and Culture (OEC) is a clearinghouse of information and initiatives relating to sustainable tourism. The office coordinates programs and submits policy recommendations to relevant government representatives. Members disseminate case studies on environmental issues in their own regions and learn how these have been addressed elsewhere.

The work of the official PATA organization is greatly augmented by an international network of over eighty PATA chapters. They comprise over seventeen thousand individual members worldwide. Chapter members meet regularly to learn about the various PATA destinations through educational presentations and out-of-country familiarization trips.

PATA moved its operational headquarters to Bangkok, Thailand, in September 1998; the association's administrative headquarters is located in Oakland, California. Other offices are located in Sydney and in Monaco.

Key Concepts

Canadian Tourism Commission
chambers of commerce
convention and visitors bureaus
Department of Homeland Security
Department of Transportation
European Travel Commission
Federal Aviation Administration

International Air Transport Association
International Association of Convention and Visitor Bureaus
Office of Travel and Tourism Industries
Organization for Economic Cooperation and Development

Pacific Asia Travel Association
state tourism offices
Tourism Australia
Travel Industry Association of America
World Bank
World Tourism Organization
World Travel and Tourism Council

Internet Sites

The Internet sites mentioned in this chapter are repeated here for convenience, plus some selected additional sites. For more information, visit these sites. Be aware that Internet addresses change frequently, so if a site cannot be accessed, use a search engine. Also use a search engine to locate many additional relevant sites.

Asia-Pacific Economic Cooperation
http://www.apecsec.org.sg

British Tourist Authority
http://www.britishtouristauthority.org

Canadian Tourism Commission
http://www.canadatourism.com

Caribbean Tourism Organisation
http://www.doitcaribbean.com

Convention Industry Council
http://www.conventionindustry.org

European Travel Commission
http://www.visiteurope.com

International Air Transport Association
http://www.iata.org

International Association of Convention and Visitor Bureaus
http://www.iacvb.org

International Civil Aviation Organization
http://www.icao.org

Irish Tourist Board
http://www.ireland.travel.ie

Office of Travel and Tourism Industries
http://tinet.ita.doc.gov

Organization for Economic Cooperation and Development
http://www.oecd.org

Organization of American States
http://www.oas.org

Pacific Asia Travel Association
http://www.pata.org

Tourism Australia
http://www.tourismaustralia.com

Travel Industry Association of America
http://www.tia.org

United Nations
http://www.un.org

World Bank
http://worldbank.org

World Tourism Organization
http://www.world-tourism.org

World Travel and Tourism Council
http://www.wttc.org

Internet Exercises

Site Name: World Tourism Organization
URL: http://www.world-tourism.org
Background Information: The World Tourism Organization is the leading international organization in the field of travel and tourism. It serves as a global forum for tourism policy issues and a practical source of tourism know-how.

Exercises
Explore the WTO Web site and find the following information:
1. How does the WTO communicate with its members and nonmembers?
2. As global competition in tourism becomes more intense, quality is the factor that can make the difference

between success and failure. WTO's section on Quality and Trade in Tourism aims to help member destinations improve quality to become more competitive and ensure sustainable development.

What are the basic components of WTO's quality program?

3. List five publications produced by the WTO and why they might be beneficial to a tourism professional.

QUESTIONS FOR REVIEW AND DISCUSSION

1. The World Tourism Organization (WTO) has made poverty alleviation through tourism one of its leading priorities. Do you believe this is feasible? What are the major problems you anticipate they will encounter in their efforts to develop and implement this priority?

2. If you were minister of tourism for Thailand, what types of assistance might you request from WTO?

3. Referring to question 1, what aid would probably be forthcoming from the Pacific Asia Travel Association?

4. Tourism is the largest export industry in American Samoa. How might its minister of tourism's office be organized?

5. Do you feel that education should be one of the principal functions of any tourism organization? Why or why not?

6. If you were the president of a large international development bank such as FONATUR, what interest would you have in the World Travel and Tourism Council (WTTC)?

7. Speaking philosophically, why should a national government transportation department have any authority to regulate or control passenger fares or cargo rates?

8. Referring to question 7, should a private international organization such as the International Air Transport Association (IATA) have any authority to govern passenger airfares? If so, why?

9. Explain how the OECD, headquartered in Paris, could help develop tourism in its European member countries.

10. What main points would you expound if you were supporting next year's Office of Travel and Tourism Industries (OTTI) budget on the floor of the U.S. House of Representatives?

11. Is there any need for a private national organization such as the Travel Industry Association of America (TIA)?

12. A state senator strongly opposes the budget for tourism promotion. "Let the hotels and transportation companies promote our state," he exclaims. "We need this money for better schools." As a member of the senate's tourism committee, what would your rebuttal be?

13. If you are a Canadian citizen, how do you feel about your tax dollars being spent on research jointly with the U.S. Tourism Industries Office?

14. Is there a relationship between the work of the Office of Travel and Tourism and the U.S. trade deficit?

15. In what ways does a city's convention and visitors bureau function? How is this organization usually financed?

16. As the manager of a fine resort lodge, what arguments would you use with your board of directors to obtain financial support for your local and regional tourism promotion organization?

17. If you, as manager of a hotel, had joined a tourist association and placed an ad in their publication, how would you ascertain if such investments were paying off?

CASE PROBLEMS

1. A quite popular tourist state has fallen on hard times. The state government can no longer provide adequate funds for their state park system. The governor has proposed a "group maintenance" policy for the parks. This means that all the parks in a given part of the state would be managed on a group basis. Eliminated would be all of the individual local park managers. Several million people visit these parks each year—an important part of the state's tourism. What might be some feasible solutions to the funding problems of the park system?

2. Two city council members are having an argument. A proposed budget item for tourist promotion for

the coming fiscal year is being considered. One member endorses this item enthusiastically. The other states, "We don't benefit much from tourists' spending here because of the high leakage. I won't vote for this item; let's forget it." You are attending this meeting as a representative of the convention and visitor bureau. How would you respond? If you felt that your declarations were not very convincing, what research should be conducted immediately to strengthen your pro-tourism position?

SELECTED REFERENCES

Bonham, Carl, and James Mak. "Private versus Public Financing of State Destination Promotion." *Journal of Travel Research*, Vol. 35, No. 2, pp. 3–10, Fall 1996.

Bramwell, Bill, and Liz Rawding. "Tourism Marketing Organizations in Industrial Cities: Organizations, Objectives, and Urban Governance." *Tourism Management*, Vol. 15, No. 6, pp. 425–434, 1994.

McKercher, Bob, and Megan Ritchie. "The Third Tier of Public Sector Tourism: A Profile of Local Government Tourism Officers in Australia." *Journal of Travel Research*, Vol. 36, No. 1, pp. 66–72, Summer 1997.

Organization for Economic Cooperation and Development. *Tourism Policy and International Tourism in OECD Member Countries*. Paris: OECD, 1996.

Pearce, Douglas G. "Regional Tourist Organizations in Spain: Emergence, Policies, and Consequences." *Tourism Economics*, Vol. 2, No. 2, pp. 119–136, June 1996.

Pearce, Douglas G. *Tourist Organizations*. Essex: Longman Scientific and Technical, 1992.

Pearce, Douglas G. "Tourist Organizations in Sweden." *Tourism Management*, Vol. 17, No. 6, pp. 413–424, September 1996.

Soteriou, Evi C., and Chris Roberts. "The Strategic Planning Process in National Tourism Organizations." *Journal of Travel Research*, Vol. 37, No. 1, pp. 21–29, August 1998.

Sussmann, Silvia, and Michael Baker. "Responding to the Electronic Marketplace: Lessons from Destination Management Systems." *International Journal of Hospitality Management*, Vol. 15, No. 2, pp. 99–112, June 1996.

Travel Industry Association of America. *Survey of U.S. State and Territory Tourism Offices: 2002–2003*. Washington, DC: TIA, 2004.

Wanhill, Stephen. "Encompassing the Social and Environmental Aspects of Tourism within an Institutional Context: A National Tourist Board Perspective." *Progress in Tourism and Hospitality Research*, Vol. 2, No. 3–4, pp. 321–335, September–December 1996.

World Tourism Organization. *Yearbook of Tourism Statistics*. Madrid: WTO, 2004.

World Tourism Organization. *Compendium of Tourism Statistics*. Madrid: WTO, 2003.

World Tourism Organization. *Tourism and Poverty Alleviation*. Madrid: WTO, 2002.

World Tourism Organization. *Public-Private Sector Cooperation*. Madrid: WTO, 2001.

World Tourism Organization. *Budgets of National Tourism Administration*. Madrid: WTO, 1996.

World Travel and Tourism Council. *Progress and Priorities, 2004/05*. London: WTTC, 2004.

PASSENGER TRANSPORTATION

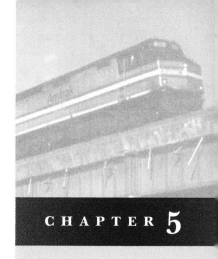

CHAPTER 5

Learning Objectives

- Comprehend the importance of transportation in tourism.
- Understand the airline industry and its role in travel.
- Examine the domination of the automobile in travel.
- Learn about the role of rail and motorcoach travel.
- Study the cruise industry.

An Amtrak intercity passenger train glides overhead, as vacationers fish and relax at Powells Creek, Virginia. *Photo courtesy of Matt Van Hattem.*

INTRODUCTION

Chapters 5, 6, 7, and 8 focus on the operating sectors of the tourism industry, starting with transportation. As shown in Figure 5.1, these sectors represent a critical segment of the tourism phenomenon shown in Figure 1.2. It is the operating sectors that deliver the tourism experience and tend to be viewed by the media, public, and visitors as the "tourism industry." It is the task of the operating sectors to develop and deliver tourism services and experiences with a spirit of hospitality so they will be truly memorable.

Turning our attention to the transportation sector, we find that since the beginning of time, people have been traveling by various modes, from on foot to riding in a supersonic aircraft. Tourism and **transportation** are inextricably linked. As world tourism increases, additional demands will be placed on the transportation sectors (see Figure 5.2). Looking at the position occupied by the various modes of passenger transportation, one finds that air travel dominates long-distance and middle-distance tourism. The private automobile dominates for shorter trips and is the most popular means of travel for most domestic journeys. The automobile is also very important in regional and international tourism. Rail travel now plays a more limited role than it did in the past. However, this mode could increase its market share, especially in Europe. The development of high-speed trains will increase rail traffic.

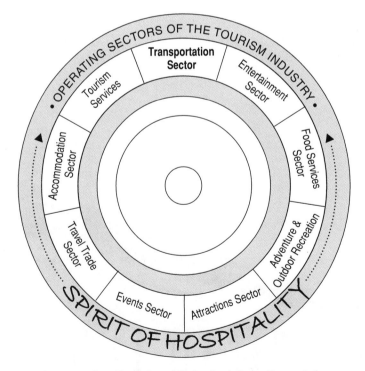

Figure 5.1   Operating sectors of the tourism industry: Transportation.

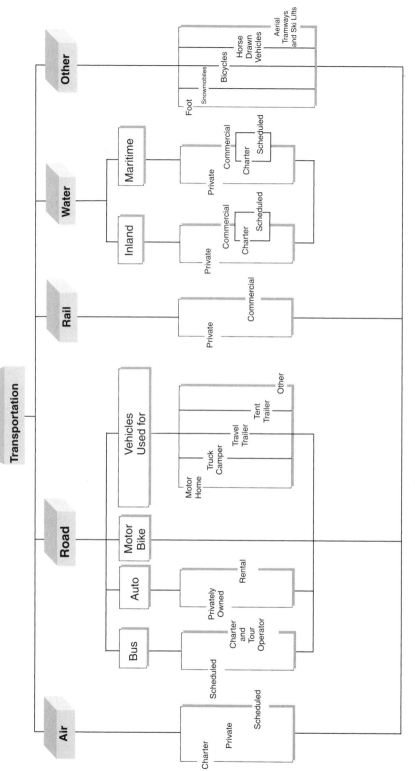

Figure 5.2   Passenger transportation structure.

Motorcoach transportation reaches many communities that are not served by any other public mode; but quantitatively, motorcoaches account for a very small percentage of vehicle miles. Cruises are becoming more popular and are the fastest-growing segment of tourism. However, this segment is still small quantitatively.

An increase in traffic due to world tourism growth puts pressure on transportation facilities, and this can have adverse effects. Situations in the world vary widely within regions, countries, states, and provinces. Also, variations exist between such areas. Even so, the problems seem to be the same all over the world. Those needing the urgent attention of policy makers are as follows:

1. **Congestion.** Serious congestion affects most passenger transportation modes, particularly on roads and at airports during peak periods. In major cities there is the danger of reaching gridlock. Congestion means delays that are a serious waste of time and energy.
2. **Safety and security.** Ensuring safety and security in transportation is a basic requirement for tourism. This was true before September 11 and is even more critical today.
3. **Environment.** An increase in traffic may harm the environment if an area does not have the carrying capacity for additional tourists. Transportation planning must take economic, social, cultural, and natural resources costs into account when designing expanded facilities.
4. **Seasonality.** Seasonal patterns of travel demand create overcrowding at certain times. Conversely, low occupancies and load factors will occur at other periods. At peak travel periods the problems of congestion, security, and the environment become much more severe.

All of these problems are challenges facing transportation planners. They have had and will continue to have an unfavorable impact on the perception that tourists have of their vacation experiences. Transportation problems have the potential of creating an unfavorable image of a tourist destination. As the modes of transportation are reviewed in this chapter, think about how they can be developed and integrated to serve the tourist in the best possible manner.

THE AIRLINE INDUSTRY

On December 17, 1903, at Kitty Hawk, North Carolina, Orville and Wilbur Wright launched the aviation age when Orville made the first controlled, sustained flight in a motorized, heavier-than-air craft. While that famous first flight lasted less than a minute, it changed the transportation world forever. Air travel has changed the way people view time and distance. As we celebrate 100 years of flight, we find the **airline industry** has grown from an infant to a giant. The world's airline industry now carries over 1.6 billion passengers per year. In the United States alone, commercial aviation generates more than $100 billion in annual revenue and employs about 600,000 people.

While the world airline industry is huge, it is facing many challenges. It was thought that 2004 was going to be the first profitable year for the air industry this century. In 2003, the world airline industry survived SARS, the conflict in Iraq, terrorism, and a sluggish economy, but with $2.8 billion in losses. In 2004, in spite of outstanding passenger gains, the price of oil denied profitability again. World airlines have reported three consecutive years of multibillion-dollar losses, and the 2004 figures may mean four consecutive years. U.S. airlines have fared even worse, suffering $3.6 billion in losses in 2003.

Low-cost carriers are growing, threatening the major carriers, and making a return to profitability a more difficult task. Brand names like Southwest, JetBlue, Ryanair, WestJet, and easyJet are growing and gaining ground against their larger competitors. They are also making a profit. They are being joined by new low-cost carriers in all parts of the world.

The bright spot in the global air industry is Asia and the Pacific. The dynamic economy of the region is making its own airlines profitable and helping carriers from outside the region with extensive Asia/Pacific operations. At present, the Orient is the number one growth center for air travel in the world.

The world's economy and the tourism industry need a healthy air transportation system. Without airline passengers, rental cars go unrented, hotel beds go unsold, and attractions go unvisited. The airlines have revolutionized travel, and the

A jet aircraft can carry hundreds of passengers in a minimum amount of time. Air travel is the most comfortable mode for mid- to long-distance trips. *Copyright © Corbis Digital Stock.*

range and speed of jet travel have greatly expanded what tourists or business travelers could once accomplish with the equivalent time and funds at their disposal. Today, for example, it is possible to fly around the globe in less time than it takes to drive across the United States. The system is also incredibly efficient: You need to make only one call to an airline or a travel agent to purchase a ticket to your desired destination; then all you have to do is go to the airport and check your bags through to the final destination. The logistics that make it happen are complex, but the system works well. For example, United Airlines (including United Express and Ted) offers over 3,500 flights a day to 193 domestic and international destinations. Other airlines have similar structures and combine to make a total system that blankets the world.

Although the major advantage of air travel is speed, which results in more time for other activities, there are negative aspects for those who wish to travel by air. These include some people's fear of flying, and a lack of geographic accessibility, since many communities in the country are not served by air transportation. An additional problem is the length of time spent getting to and from the airport. Frequently, this time exceeds that spent en route.

In the United States, air carriers are classified as major if they record over $1 billion in revenue annually. There are ten: Alaska, America West, American, ATA, Continental, Delta, Northwest, Southwest, United, and US Airways. National carriers are those recording annual revenues of $100 million to $1 billion and include Air Tran, Air Transport International, Air Wisconsin, Aloha, Astar, Atlantic Southeast, Atlas, Champion, Comair, Continental Micronesia, Evergreen, Executive, ExpressJet, Frontier, Gemini, Hawaiian, Horizon, JetBlue, Kitty Hawk, Mesa Air Group, Miami Air, Midwest, North American, Polar, Ryan International, Spirit, Trans States, and World. There are about 35 regional airlines with annual revenues under $100 million. The top ten U.S. airlines by revenue passenger miles are shown in Table 5.1. The table shows American was the largest carrier in 2003.

TABLE 5.1	**TOP TEN U.S. AIRLINES BY REVENUE PASSENGER MILES, 2003**
AIRLINE	**REVENUE PASSENGER MILES**
1 American	125,844,000,000
2 United	104,464,000,000
3 Delta	98,674,000,000
4 Northwest	68,476,151,000
5 Continental	64,934,000,000
6 Southwest	47,943,066,000
7 US Airways	37,740,584,000
8 America West	21,295,000,000
9 Alaska	16,194,000,000
10 ATA Airlines	12,079,271,000

Source: Business Travel News.

TABLE 5.2	TOP TWENTY WORLD AIRLINES BY REVENUE PASSENGER KILOMETERS, 2003

RANK AIRLINE	RPKs (000,000)
1 American	193,604
2 United	167,970
3 Delta	143,896
4 Northwest	110,637
5 Air France[a]	101,644
6 British Airways	100,850
7 JAL Group[a]	93,847
8 Continental	92,662
9 Lufthansa Group	90,708
10 Southwest	77,288
11 Qantas[a]	77,225
12 Singapore	63,940
13 US Airways	60,792
14 Air Canada	59,507
15 KLM	57,368
16 All Nippon[a]	50,182
17 Thai	44,934
18 Cathay Pacific	42,774
19 Iberia	41,983
20 Emirates	40,000

[a]Fiscal year.

Source: Air Transport World.

It is interesting to compare Table 5.1 and 5.2. Table 5.2 shows the top world airlines based on revenue passenger kilometers (RPKs), since that is the measurement used in most of the world. Note that U.S. airlines occupy six of the top ten spots.

A 1997–1998 survey of air travelers by the Gallup Organization revealed that a record 81 percent of the entire adult population in the United States had flown. Two out of every five U.S. citizens flew during 1997–1998. The survey found that 53 percent of airline trips during 1997–1998 were for pleasure or other personal reasons, and 47 percent were for business.

One of the best sources of data on the airline industry is an annual report published by the Air Transport Association of America, 1301 Pennsylvania Avenue NW, Suite 1100, Washington, D.C. 20004. The International Air Transport Association (see Chapter 4) makes forecasts and publishes financial and traffic statistics on the world airline industry. Their *World Air Transport Statistics* is in its forty-eighth year of publication and is reported to be the single most timely and authoritative source of international airline data.

Air Transport World (ATW) publishes an annual World Airline Report that typically appears in their July issue. The report is available from ATW at (202) 659-8500 or **http://www.atwonline.com.** The comprehensive report covers the world's top twenty-five airlines, world airline financial statistics, Africa, Asia/Pacific, Canada, Europe, Latin America/Caribbean, Middle East, U.S. Majors, U.S. Nationals, U.S. Cargo Carriers, U.S. Regional/Specialty Carriers, and World Airline Fleets. *Air Transport World* is published monthly by Penton Media, Inc.

Another useful source of information on the airline industry is the U.S. Federal Aviation Administration. Consumer protection is the responsibility of the Department of Transportation.

Deregulation and Alliances

Under deregulation, the airline industry has undergone dramatic change. It is hard to believe that almost thirty years have passed since U.S. airline deregulation was passed in October 1978. Looking back, we can see that it has led to significant consolidation, hub systems, low airfares in competitive situations, and high airfares where competition is lacking.

The future holds more concentration as consolidations and a wave of **alliances** have taken place and more are proposed. Alliances now involve the six largest carriers in the United States. The merger of Air France and KLM in 2004 makes it the world's largest airline in terms of passenger revenue, surpassing American Airlines. International alliances have been debated since KLM and Northwest linked in 1992. United has the Star Alliance (created in May 1997), which originally included Lufthansa, Air Canada, Thai Airways, and SAS. Since then, United has added Brazil's Varig, Air New Zealand, All Nippon Airways, Austrian Airlines, BMI British Midland, Asiania Airlines, LOT Polish Airlines, Spanair, U.S. Airways, Lauda Air, Singapore Airlines, and Austrain Arrows. Through membership in the Star Alliance, United provides connections to 700 destinations in 120 countries worldwide. United's nearly 63,000 employees reside in every state in the United States and in many countries around the world. SkyTeam is the global alliance partnering Aeromexico, Air France, Alitalia, CSA Czech Airlines, Delta Air Lines, Korean Air, Continental Airlines, KLM, and Northwest Airlines. Through one of the world's most extensive hub networks, SkyTeam offers its 341 million annual passengers a worldwide system of more than 14,320 daily flights covering all major destinations. American and British Airways have launched a global alliance with Qantas, Cathay Pacific Airways, Aer Lingus, Iberia, Lan, and Finnair called Oneworld. They also plan to expand the grouping. There are other alliances and partners too numerous to mention, but the above alliances indicate the high level of concentration present.

Are more alliances the wave of the future of the aviation industry? Will alliances benefit the consumer through greater choice, more seamless travel, lower fares, greater convenience, and frequent-flyer miles? Or will alliances create oligopoly and monopoly, higher fares, and a noncompetitive situation? Only time and government action will answer these questions. The expectation is that the alliance trend will continue for several years unless regulatory agencies stop it. Authorities in both the United States and the European Union are analyzing how to deal with major airline alliances. The decisions made will shape the future of airlines around the world.

New Planes

The world airline industry now has two new planes to choose from. One is the Airbus A380, which is the largest commercial airliner ever designed. It will have twin decks, seat 555 passengers, and enter airline service in 2006. The other is the Boeing 787 Dreamliner. This technologically advanced airplane will use 20 percent less fuel than today's airplanes of comparable size. It will hold 200 to 300 passengers, and operate on routes between 3,500 and 8,500 nautical miles. Production of the 787 Dreamliner will begin in 2006, with entry into service expected in 2008.

Growth

World and U.S. air transportation is expected to grow at a steady rate in the future now that the setbacks of September 11, the war in Iraq, SARS, and a weak economy are over. The stronger the world economy, the greater will be the rate of growth. An example of how the FAA expects U.S. carriers to grow is shown in Table 5.3, where forecasts are given to the year 2015. Air transport growth is an essential ingredient in tourism's future because the growth of tourism is linked to air transport performance. Without growth in airline passengers, there are fewer new customers to rent cars, stay in accommodations, and visit attractions.

Air Transport Association of America

The airline industry is supported by three major organizations. IATA and ICAO have already been discussed in Chapter 4 under international organizations; they

TABLE 5.3	FAA AVIATION FORECASTS: U.S. COMMERCIAL AIR CARRIERS[a], 2004–2015					
	REVENUE PASSENGER ENPLANEMENTS (IN MILLIONS)			REVENUE PASSENGER MILES (IN BILLIONS)		
FISCAL YEAR	DOMESTIC	INTERNATIONAL	SYSTEM	DOMESTIC	INTERNATIONAL	SYSTEM
2004	627.2	59.5	686.7	525.5	174.0	699.4
2005	668.5	63.3	731.8	560.1	186.7	746.8
2006	697.8	66.4	764.2	584.9	197.6	782.4
2007	724.1	69.6	793.8	607.5	208.1	815.6
2008	749.6	72.9	822.5	631.0	218.8	849.8
2009	776.8	76.2	853.0	655.9	229.6	885.6
2010	804.0	79.7	883.7	681.0	241.0	922.0
2011	831.5	83.3	914.8	705.8	252.7	958.5
2012	860.5	87.1	947.6	732.1	264.8	996.9
2013	891.2	91.0	982.1	761.8	277.3	1039.0
2014	924.2	95.0	1,019.2	795.3	290.1	1,085.4
2015	958.4	99.1	1,057.6	830.8	303.4	1,134.2

[a]Sum of large air carriers and regionals/commuters.

Source: U.S. Department of Transport.

are two key associations controlling air travel. The major U.S. organization is the **Air Transport Association of America.**

In 1936, fourteen fledgling airlines met in Chicago to form the Air Transport Association (ATA) "to do all things tending to promote the betterment of airline business, and in general, to do everything in its power to best serve the interest and welfare of the members of this association and the public at large."

Today, from its headquarters in Washington, D.C., the ATA is the nation's oldest and largest airline trade association. Its membership of twenty-two U.S. and four associate (non-U.S.) airlines carried about 95 percent of the passenger and cargo traffic carried by scheduled U.S. airlines.

ATA is the meeting place where the airlines cooperate in noncompetitive areas to improve airline service, safety, and efficiency. The mission of the ATA is to support and assist its member carriers by promoting aviation safety, advocating industry positions, conducting designated industrywide programs, and ensuring public understanding.

Thus, while the carriers are intensely competitive among themselves and with other forms of transportation in their individual promotion of airline service for the traveling and shipping public, they are equally intense in their mutual cooperation on matters of industrywide importance, such as safety, technological progress, and passenger service improvement.

While ATA's agenda of issues continuously changes, its major priorities remain unchanged. They include:

- Assisting the airline industry in continuing to provide the world's safest system of transportation

- Advocating the modernization of the Federal Aviation Administration's air traffic control system, in order to improve service for airline customers and to benefit the environment

- Increasing the security of airline passengers and cargo against threats directed at the United States

- Seeking to prevent legislative and regulatory actions that would penalize airlines and their customers by imposing rate, route, service, or schedule controls on the industry

- Endeavoring to reduce the disproportionate share of taxes and fees paid by airlines and their customers at the federal, state, and local levels

- Improving the industry's ability to attract capital

- Helping to shape international aviation policy, to ensure that U.S. and foreign carriers can compete on equal terms

During its more than sixty years of existence, the ATA has seen the airline industry grow from the small, pioneering companies of the 1930s into key players in the world's economy. ATA members continue to play a major role in shaping the future of air transportation.

ATA headquarters are located at 1301 Pennsylvania Avenue NW, Suite 1100, Washington, D.C. 20004; telephone (202) 626-4000; Web site: **http://www.airlines.org.**

THE RAIL INDUSTRY

Rail passenger transportation, once the major mode of travel in the United States, reached its peak volume in 1920. Major railroads wished to rid themselves of the passenger business, and today the survival of service (other than commuter service) depends largely on Amtrak. In Canada the situation has been similar and future rail travel depends on VIA Rail Canada.

Outside North America, where passenger rail service is more extensive, rail transportation assumes a more important role. Ultramodern railway systems with high-speed trains operate in many countries, handling passenger traffic in an economical and efficient manner and providing an alternative to air travel. France and Japan are well known for their high-speed trains. France has been willing to subsidize its rail system. The French government has taken responsibility for rail infrastructure of the state-owned SNCF rail company. Japan continues to improve and

Amtrak's Acela Express exemplifies the latest technology in rail service. Passengers in the Northeast Corridor can enjoy high-speed rail service traveling at 150 miles per hour in modern comfort. *Copyright ©2001 Amtrak. Photo provided as a courtesy by Amtrak.*

expand its famous "bullet train." Some of the largest railways in the world are found in the former Soviet Union, India, and China.

Australia made a significant step forward in rail travel in February 2004 when the new 882 miles of tracks from Alice Springs to Darwin opened. Now one can finally travel on the legendary Ghan Train across the country from Adelaide in the south to Darwin in the north.

Amtrak

Amtrak is the marketing name for the National Railroad Passenger Corporation, an operating railroad corporation, the controlling stock of which is owned by the U.S. government through the U.S. Department of Transportation. Amtrak's business is providing rail passenger transportation in the major intercity markets of the United States. The National Railroad Passenger Corporation was established by the Rail Passenger Service Act of 1970.

Although it receives financial support from the federal government, Amtrak is not a government agency. It is a corporation structured and managed like other large businesses in the United States and competes with all other modes in the transportation marketplace.

Serving forty-six states and 500 destinations on its 22,000-mile route system, Amtrak carried more than 24 million intercity passengers in fiscal 2003. Amtrak employs more than 20,000 people. Its employees are represented by fourteen different labor organizations.

Amtrak was launched as an experiment to identify the importance of rail passenger service to a balanced national transportation system. A key for continued support of Amtrak in the mid-1970s was the dramatic impact of the oil embargo and recognition of the need for alternative forms of transportation.

In various transportation corridors, Amtrak is the dominant public carrier. Amtrak provides energy-efficient and environmentally friendly service in some of the nation's most densely populated, congested, and polluted rail corridors,

Cable cars not only provide transportation but they also have become an essential part of the tourism experience in San Francisco. Their charm continues to draw visitors from around the world. *Photo by San Francisco Conventions and Visitors Bureau.*

including the Washington, D.C.–Boston Northeast Corridor and between San Diego and Los Angeles, San Francisco and Sacramento, St. Louis and Chicago, and Chicago and Detroit. Amtrak currently serves almost half of the combined air-rail market between the end points of New York and Washington, D.C.; when intermediate cities (such as Baltimore and Philadelphia) are included, Amtrak's share of the air-rail market rises to 70 percent.

Amtrak launched its new Acela Express service between Boston and Washington, D.C., in December 2000 to serve the Northeast Corridor. Passengers can enjoy high-speed rail service traveling at 150 miles per hour in modern comfort. This service promises to improve Amtrak's revenue stream. Acela Express will become the prototype for high-speed trains in the Pacific Northwest, the Midwest, and the South.

Because Amtrak is subsidized, suppliers of the other modes of transportation (especially bus) feel that Amtrak is attracting its customers with taxpayer assistance. However, even with the controversy, Congress is likely to see that Amtrak remains in business for the foreseeable future. Amtrak typically faces annual cuts in its funding, but is usually rescued by Congress.

THE MOTORCOACH INDUSTRY

The American Bus Association (ABA) reports that there are about 44,000 commercial motorcoaches in use for charters, tours, regular route service, and special operations in North America. The buses carry about 800 million passengers a year. Carriers involved in the regular-route part of the industry operate approximately 8,000 to 10,000 over-the-road intercity coaches. Buses perform a wide range of services, with half of industry mileage on scheduled intercity services, one-third on charters, and the rest on tours, private commutes, airport shuttles, and others.

In 1999, motorcoaches were driven about 2.6 billion miles, with the average bus traveling 50,600 miles. The industry consumed 498 million gallons of fuel, yielding a conservative performance of 160 passenger miles per gallon.

As reported at the 1993 White House Conference on Global Climate Change, intercity bus service is the most energy-efficient passenger transportation mode. In 1991, it was twice as efficient as Amtrak service, three times as efficient as automobiles and mass transit, and four times as efficient as commercial aviation. In comparing data from large bus companies, the carriers consume 997 Btu per passenger mile, compared to 1,995 for Amtrak, 3,325 for passenger cars, and 4,457 for certificated air carriers domestic operations.

The industry is composed largely of small entrepreneurial businesses. There are over 4,000 companies, 90 percent of which have fewer than twenty-five buses. These entrepreneurial companies operate about 19,000 motorcoaches, account for almost 40 percent of the total industry mileage, and carry one in five passengers. More than half of motorcoach jobs are with small businesses employing fewer than fifty people. The industry employs 200,000 workers, not including jobs in the bus manufacturing and supplier sector. Clearly, motorcoach travel contributes significantly to tourism revenues in local communities. In Washington, D.C., alone, 23.4 percent of 21 million annual visitors arrive by motorcoach. If only half of those visitors came as part of an overnight tour, $424 million would flow into those local businesses.

Motorcoaches are also the intermodal glue in America's often-disjointed transportation system. Motorcoaches link passengers arriving and departing through airports, train stations, and seaports with their final home, work, and tourism destinations.

Regular/Route/Scheduled Bus Service

There are about one hundred privately owned companies in the United States that offer regular route bus service. Greyhound Lines, Inc., the only nationwide bus carrier for regular intercity route service, serves more than 2,500 destinations with 17,000 daily departures. The Trailways Transportation System, a federation of independently owned bus companies that market intercity service under the Trailways name, covers a large portion of the United States. Other independent companies provide service on a regional basis and feed passengers into the Greyhound or Trailways systems, into the Amtrak rail system, and into airports. The approximate number of places in the United States served by intercity buses is 4,200. This compares to about 750 airports with scheduled airline service, and to

The motorcoach industry is the most pervasive form of intercity public transportation in the world. Motorcoaches provide both scheduled and charter service. This motorcoach carried passengers from Alice Springs, Australia, to Ayers Rock. *Photo by the author.*

about 600 Amtrak stations (108 of which are served only by contract bus service). Motorcoaches serve six times more destinations than airlines and nearly seven times more destinations than passenger rail.

Charters and Tours

Both domestic and international travelers are heavy users of motorcoaches because coach travel gives them time to see and experience sights with a group of friends without having to deal with traffic and road maps. About one-third of U.S. motorcoach and tour operators polled by ABA report an increase in overseas visitors. Sales of tours and charters are expected to grow in the 3 to 5 percent range. Because of the increasing popularity of motorcoach tours, tour operators nationwide now conduct trips to myriad destinations and drive there safely in state-of-the-art-equipped vehicles at an economical price.

The National Tour Association's NTA 2000 Packaged Travel in North America study provides information that enables tourism professionals to determine the economic impact of a motorcoach visiting a destination. The impact to the local economy is $192 per passenger per day, or $7,680 per day if the motorcoach has forty passengers. Expenditures include such items as meals, lodging, shopping, admission fees, souvenirs, and local taxes.

Trends

Do you expect to enjoy a full-length feature film on your next motorcoach trip? Or relax in a comfortable seat? If you think you can do these traveling only on an airline, think again. Leisure motorcoach travel is a popular way to see North America. The modern trip by motorcoach is nothing like you remember from your childhood days. Forget your preconceived ideas of crowded, stuffy buses. Today's luxury vehicles have reclining seats and air conditioning and are among the safest and cleanest modes of transportation available.

Motorcoach Organizations

The **American Bus Association** (ABA) is the national organization of the intercity bus industry and serves as the prime source of industry statistics. ABA represents approximately 950 motorcoach and tour companies in the United States and Canada. Its members operate charter, tour, regular route, airport express, special operations, and contract services (commuter, school, transit). Another 2,300 member organizations represent the travel and tourism industry and suppliers of bus products and services who work in partnership with the North American motorcoach industry. ABA has a total membership of about three thousand companies. ABA's headquarters are located in downtown Washington, D.C.: American Bus Association, 700 13th Street NW, Suite 575, Washington, D.C. 20005-5923; telephone (202) 842-1645; Fax (202) 842-0850; E-mail abainfo@buses.org; Web site is **http://www.buses.org.**

The **United Motorcoach Association** (UMA), founded as the United Bus Owners of America in 1971, is a trade association with about two thousand motorcoach company members and motorcoach industry manufacturers, suppliers, and vendors spread across North America. UMA member companies provide a broad variety of charter motorcoach services, much of it for preformed groups. Other member services include tours, schools, intercity transit, and shuttle or commuter lines. UMA serves the informational, legislative, regulatory, and business needs of its member companies. Within the membership, companies range from one and two vehicles to those with many hundreds of coaches; from small tour-specific companies to those performing intercity route service, charter operations, and tour operations on a coast-to-coast scale.

UMA's offices are located at 113 S. West Street, Alexandria, VA 22314-2824; telephone (800) 424-8262 or (703) 838-2929; E-mail info@uma.org; Web site **http://www.uma.org.**

THE AUTOMOBILE

Most of the travel in the world takes place in the **automobile.** In the United States, auto travel is an integral part of the travel industry with the vast majority, 79 percent, of U.S. domestic person-trips being taken by car, truck, camper/RV, or rental car. Affordability, flexibility, and convenience make auto travel the most popular mode of transportation all over the world. Because passenger car registrations continue to increase worldwide, motor vehicles will continue to be the dominant mode of transportation for decades to come.

All studies show the automobile's dominance, whether the study is from the Air Transport Association, the Highway Administration, the Census Bureau, or TIA's research department. There is no doubt that the great bulk of intercity transportation of passengers is by automobile. Data also indicate that this has been constant for several decades. The energy crisis that many have forgotten made some inroads into auto travel, causing some shifts to common carriers, but these inroads have been small. However, because of the great dominance of the automobile in travel, even a small shift in automobile travel to the common carriers can result in enormous increases in the carriers' business.

The automobile has played an even more important role in travel because of the tragedy of September 11, 2001. As with past incidents, the trend is to shift from air travel to auto travel and to take trips closer to home. After September 11, the share of auto person-trips increased 2 percent in just one year, and auto travelers stayed close to home. Future incidents will likely produce the same results.

The interstate highway system significantly encouraged vacation travel and especially encouraged long-distance travel. It made automobile travel much faster and more comfortable. A major concern of tourism groups today is the maintenance of the highway network. There is growing evidence that the highway system is in need of substantial repair to prevent it from suffering further deterioration. A poor road system costs the individual driver, the bus operator, and other users

Affordability, flexibility, and convenience make auto travel the most popular mode of transportation all over the world. *Photo by the author.*

additional funds in terms of increased fuel use and vehicle maintenance, and the knowledge that a highway is in poor condition may cause the traveler to select another destination to avoid the problem.

On the whole, people's attitudes are very favorable toward travel by automobile. The key feature of the automobile is immediate accessibility and convenience. The automobile owner can leave from his or her own doorstep at any hour of the day or night and travel to a chosen destination. When two or more persons travel by automobile, the per-person cost of travel is more favorable than it is with the other transportation modes. Air is the primary competitor to the automobile when it comes to travel, especially for long trips. The advantages of air travel—the quality of service, speed, and comfort—must be weighed by travelers against the automobile's advantages of price and accessibility.

Recreation Vehicles

The **recreation vehicle** (RV) segment deserves special mention because, according to the Recreation Vehicle Industry Association (RVIA), there are currently 7.2 million RVs on the road in the United States, enjoyed by some 30 million enthusiasts. One in twelve vehicle-owning households has an RV, with ownership predicted to increase 15 percent by the year 2010. RVers travel an average of 4,500 miles per year, spending some twenty-eight to thirty-five days in their vehicle. In Canada, estimates put privately owned RVs at 500,000 to 850,000. While the RV market has had its ups and downs because of events such as the energy crisis, the recession, and the Iraq war, the market for recreation vehicles is huge, with sales in 2004 totaling $12 billion.

Slide-out technology, introduced during the mid-1990s, has now advanced to become available in living rooms, dining rooms, bedrooms, and kitchens. At the touch of a button, this mechanism lets a portion of the room and the objects in it, such as a couch, table, or refrigerator, slide outward up to about 3½ feet. Slide-outs are available in a wide variety of RVs: motor homes, mini-motor homes, travel trailers, fifth-wheel trailers, and even folding camping trailers. Electronics have also come to RV travel, with direct broadcast satellite systems, computer hookups, onboard global positioning systems (GPS), and rearview monitors now popular options.

The typical U.S. RV owner is 49 years old, is married, owns a home, and has an annual income of $56,000. A University of Michigan study indicates that intentions to purchase an RV are strongest among baby boomers. Nearly 10 percent of those 55 and over own an RV, slightly exceeding the 8.9 percent ownership rates of 35-to 54-year-olds.

Of increasing economic significance is the steady rise in RV rentals. The Recreation Vehicle Rental Association (RVRA) reports that its members are experiencing significant growth, and strong demand has encouraged hundreds of businesses to enter the rental market, while others have expanded their operations. More than four hundred national RV rental chain outlets and local RV dealerships offer state-of-the-art, late-model-year vehicles for rent.

Travel agencies around the world are responding to the demand by including RV rental information in their customer brochures. Also available from some rental dealers are comprehensive tour packages that include services such as airline and railway connections for fly/drive and rail/drive plans, one-way packages, off-season rates, vacation planning, guided escort tours, and campground discounts. The recent surge of foreign visitors has helped increase the RV rental market. Arrivals from Japan, Australia, New Zealand, and the United Kingdom are major customers. An estimated half million overseas visitors a year rent RVs. Visit the Recreation Vehicle Industry Association Web site at **http://www.rvia.org.**

Highways and Scenic Byways

Automobile travel in the United States has received a boost from the **Highways and Scenic Byways program.** The Intermodal Surface Transportation Efficiency Act of 1991 (ISTEA) established the Scenic Byways program, which provided $80 million over six years for carrying out eligible programs on designated scenic byways. According to the Federal Highway Administration, the United States has four million miles of roads and approximately 51,500 have been designated as or are potential scenic byways. All fifty states have existing byways, with an average of nine routes per state. An ISTEA reauthorization bill, the Transportation Equity Act for the Twenty-first Century (TEA-21), became law on June 9, 1998, and will ensure continuation of the National Scenic Byways program. The act calls for $148 million for improvements to roads of scenic or historic value. TEA-21 provides 40 percent more funding for transportation than the 1991 law it replaced, authorizing a six-year expenditure of $216 billion. TEA-21 now needs to be reauthorized. The current proposal is called SAFETEA (Safe, Accountable, Flexible and Efficient Transportation Equity Act) and would make no significant changes to the National Scenic Byways, Transportation Enhancements, or Federal Lands Highways programs.

Rental Cars

An important aspect of automobile travel is the **rental car industry,** whose growth has been paralleling or exceeding the growth in air travel. While there is no question about the rental car business having heavy use by businesses, it also has substantial vacation use and frequent combination-trip use.

Air travel is critical to the car rental business as airport revenues account for approximately 88 percent of overall car rentals in the United States. Hertz is the airport market leader with about one-third of the airport rental business.

According to *Business Travel News* (BTN) in their *2004 Business Travel Survey,* the rental car industry grosses around $20 billion. The major companies are Hertz, Avis, Budget, National, Alamo, Dollar, Thrifty, Advantage, and Payless. Table 5.4 shows them ranked by their 2003 total revenue. BTN does not include Enterprise in its rankings.

A customer-oriented transportation system requires that the interface between different modes of travel be facilitated. Technology is increasingly used to ensure fast and convenient service. *Photo courtesy of Budget Rent-A-Car Company.*

TABLE 5.4	U.S. RENTAL CAR COMPANIES RANKED BY REVENUE, 2003
CAR COMPANY	REVENUE ($000)
1 Hertz	4,239,200
2 Avis	4,067,910
3 National	1,650,000
4 Budget	1,240,000
5 Alamo	970,000
6 Dollar	949,700
7 Thrifty	867,500
8 Advantage	155,000
9 Payless	82,700

Source: Business Travel News.

Recent years have witnessed a vast change in the ownership of the major rental car companies, and shifts continue to take place. Hertz has returned to private ownership. In October 2003, Worldwide Accelerated Leasing, Inc., purchased ANC Car Rental, the parent of Alamo and National, and renamed it Vanguard Car Rental USA. Cendant Car Rental Group now owns Avis and Budget.

Enterprise Rent-A-Car is one of the surprises in the rental car business. The privately held rental car firm has the largest revenues and one of the largest fleets of rental cars in the United States, with over 460,000. It was launched as an insurance replacement firm that supplies rental cars to people whose vehicles have been damaged or stolen or are undergoing mechanical repairs. In addition to this market segment Enterprise has now gone global and serves all rental markets. However, airport locations are dominated by the big four: Hertz, Avis, Budget, and National. Enterprise delivers its cars to customers who phone for service.

Computerized navigation systems have come to rental cars and are predicted to be a growing attraction. Bookings over the Internet are increasing.

Many of the auto rental systems are international and have services in virtually every tourist destination area in the world. These companies arrange for the purchase, lease, or rental of automobiles domestically and abroad. Companies representative of this type of organization are Americar Rental System; Auto Europe; Europcar International; Hertz International, Ltd.; the Kemwel Group, Inc.; and Inter Rent.

Taxi and Limousine Service

Taxi and limousine companies play an exceedingly important part in tourism. Local transportation companies perform vital services for bus, rail, and shipping lines. Businesspersons and tourists alike would have a difficult time getting from place to place if these services were not available. Inclines and aerial trams serve as a form of taxi service and are of a special interest to visitors in scenic tourist destination areas as a form of recreation and sightseeing.

At many destinations the visitors begin their journey in a taxi. Cab drivers represent the "first ambassador" of a destination and thus are critically important to visitor satisfaction. *Photo courtesy of Coach USA.*

The Taxicab, Limousine, and Paratransit Association (TLPA) in Kensington, Maryland, is the major taxicab association. It was formed in 1966 by a merger of the National Association of Taxicab Owners, the Cab Research Bureau, and the American Taxicab Association. TLPA has 1,100 members who are fleet owners operating thousands of passenger vehicles, including taxicabs, limousines, liveries, vans, airport shuttle fleets, and minibuses. The association sponsors an annual convention and trade show, is involved with political action, and publishes *Transportation Leader* quarterly.

The National Limousine Association, located in Marlton, New Jersey, was founded in 1985, has 2,000 members, and is made up of limousine owners and operators, and limousine manufacturers and suppliers to the industry. It seeks to promote and advance industry professionalism, the common interests of members, and the use of limousines. It monitors legislation; sponsors seminars on safety, regulatory issues, and management; compiles statistics; and offers insurance plans.

Oil Companies

Oil companies the world over have a very important stake in automobile tourism and thus are organized in many ways to serve the wants and needs of travelers. In the United States, many of the major oil companies publish road maps as a touring

Trams and cable cars can greatly enhance visitors' abilities to enjoy many different views of a destination. Here, the halfway point on the Palm Springs tram's journey from the 2,643-foot Valley Station to the 8,516-foot Mountain Station is reached when the two cars pass between towers two and three. At this point, the two cars are 34 feet apart. *Photo courtesy of the Palm Springs Aerial Tramway.*

service. Some companies have organized motor clubs, such as the Amoco Motor Club, which provides travel information and routing services for its members, among other services. An example of special travel services is the *Mobil Travel Guide,* which has eight regional editions and lists over 22,000 hotels, motels, and restaurants. They also cover more than 3,000 cities and towns and describe 11,000 points of interest. The accommodations are rated from one to five stars in quality and indicate the prices of typical meals and accommodations to suit every budget. Each guide also contains a variety of special sightseeing tours with easy-to-follow maps.

Automobile Clubs and Organizations

The **American Automobile Association** (AAA) is the world's largest single-membership travel group, with a membership of over 44 million people in the United States and Canada. This organization promotes travel in several different forms among its members, including auto travel as a primary form of transportation. It also operates worldwide travel services similar to those provided by a travel agency or tour company. The AAA Travel Agency also provides travel services for nonmembers and is thus competitive with other tour companies and retail travel agencies. This additional service gives the club a certain glamour and status in the community, and nonmembers who are brought into the club office through the travel service become prospects for new members in the automobile club.

AAA provides emergency road service to members. It also provides insurance protection to motorists through its various state and city affiliate organizations (such as AAA Michigan), publishes travel maps and tour books, and has a national touring board as well as a national touring bureau staff. The principal function of the tour books is to describe the history, attractions, points of interest, and accommodations in hotels, resorts, motels, and restaurants that have been inspected and approved by AAA field representatives. All accommodations listed have been selected on the basis of a satisfactory report submitted by the AAA field representative.

An organization of wider geographic membership is the World Touring and Automobile Organization, with headquarters in London, England. Other organizations of a similar nature are the International Road Federation of Washington, D.C.; the Pan American Highway Congress, Washington, D.C.; Inter-American Federation of Touring and Automobile Clubs, Buenos Aires; and the International Automobile Federation, with headquarters in Paris.

THE CRUISE INDUSTRY

Cruise Lines International Association (CLIA) states that cruising is currently the fastest-growing segment of the travel industry. It is experiencing a surge of growth in passengers, ships, and ship passenger capacity. **Cruise lines** are expanding their fleets and adding new amenities and new ports of call. As with other sectors of travel suppliers, a great deal of consolidation is taking place.

Since 1980, the industry has had an average annual growth rate of 8.1 percent. In 1980, 1.43 million passengers cruised; in 2003, a new record was set with 8.19 million passengers (see Table 5.5). The average length of a cruise in 2003 was 6.9 days. CLIA estimates that a record 10.5 million passengers took a cruise in 2004 and predicts 11.1 million will cruise in 2005.

Although ships have been a means of transportation since early times, the cruise industry is young. Its purpose is really to provide a resort experience rather than point-to-point transportation. Though the modern-day cruise industry is barely 25 years old, it has established itself as an important component of the United States travel and tourism industry. According to a study by Business Research and Economic Advisors (BREA), commissioned by International Council of Cruise Lines (ICCL), the North American cruise industry generated $12 billion in direct spending and $20.4 billion in total economic activity in 2002. An estimated 279,112 American jobs were created.

Historically, most of the cruise companies have focused their marketing efforts on North American clientele. However, with a marked increase in recent years of European, South American, and Asian vacationers taking American-style cruises, those companies have begun to pay more attention to the international markets. Additionally, some of these cruise companies have positioned ships in Europe for seasonal operations, thereby creating greater awareness among European clientele.

The cruise industry's performance and satisfaction are the pacesetter for the rest of the travel industry. No other vacation category can touch a cruise for product satisfaction and repeat business. Of those who have cruised in the last five years, the average number of cruises per person is 2.4, or one cruise every two years.

Growth has affected not only passenger and ship capacity, but the ports of embarkation as well.

TABLE 5.5	**NUMBER OF NORTH AMERICAN PASSENGERS**		
YEAR	PASSENGERS (IN MILLIONS)	YEAR	PASSENGERS (IN MILLIONS)
1980	1.43	1992	4.13
1981	1.45	1993	4.48
1982	1.47	1994	4.44
1983	1.75	1995	4.37
1984	1.85	1996	4.65
1985	2.15	1997	5.05
1986	2.62	1998	5.42
1987	2.89	1999	5.89
1988	3.17	2000	6.88
1989	3.28	2001	6.90
1990	3.64	2002	7.64
1991	3.97	2003	8.19

Source: Cruise Lines International Association, 2003 year-end Passenger Carryings Report.

The cruise industry is one of the most rapidly growing sectors of tourism. Its growth is expected to continue, and many new ships are scheduled to come on line in the next few years. *Copyright © Carnival Cruise Lines.*

Embarkation Ports

Ports within the state of Florida serve as home for the majority of the U.S.-based cruise industry. This is primarily due to the state's close proximity to the prime cruising waters of the Caribbean. Most of these cruises are three, four, or seven days in length, though there are some voyages of ten or fourteen days. Miami currently claims the title "Cruise Capital of the World." Ports in Fort Lauderdale, Tampa, and Port Canaveral also play host to a number of cruise ships. Several ships operating Caribbean cruises are also based in New Orleans.

New York City and Boston are popular embarkation points for cruises to New England, Bermuda, and Canada's maritime provinces. On the West Coast of the United States, both Los Angeles and San Diego are home ports for cruises of three, four, or seven days to Mexico. San Francisco and Seattle are also popular ports. San Juan, Puerto Rico, a U.S. territory, has also become a popular port of embarkation for seven-day cruises to the southern Caribbean.

One of the most popular summertime cruising areas in recent years is Alaska's Inside Passage. These cruises are frequently combined with land excursions into

Alaska's interior and the Yukon Territory. Most of these cruises depart from Vancouver, British Columbia, Canada.

One company, Delta Queen Steamboat Company, offers cruises on some of America's most famous rivers, including the Mississippi and Ohio, on riverboats styled after turn-of-the-century paddle-wheel steamers.

Cruise Itineraries Cover the Globe

Though the islands of the Caribbean continue to be the leading year-round destination, CLIA member cruise lines service cruising areas around the world. The Mediterranean Sea plays host to an increasing number of cruise ships during the summer season, and CLIA reports that the industry continues to show an increased emphasis on European and Southeast Asia itineraries. In 2003 the Caribbean share was over 45 percent, the Mediterranean 12.6 percent, Europe 9.8 percent, Alaska 7.7 percent, western Mexico 6.2 percent, TransCanal 3.8 percent, and Hawaii 3.4 percent.

And one of the world's greatest adventures—a transit of the Panama Canal—remains one of the industry's big attractions. These cruises usually either begin or end in San Francisco, Los Angeles, or Ft. Lauderdale.

New Ships and New Markets

The North American cruise industry has enjoyed tremendous success in the last decade and has continued to reinvest profits in new, modern cruise ships. Approximately eighty new ships have been introduced since 1990. Another twenty new ships are contracted or planned to be added to the North American fleet from 2005 through 2008. Berths have been expanding at a rapid rate. CLIA reported 206,423 berths in 142 ships in 2004. As the cruise industry continues to expand, industry observers predict that new markets outside North America will become of greater importance in the coming years.

Security

The cruise industry's highest priority is to ensure the security and safety of its passengers and crew. The International Council of Cruise Lines (ICCL) works closely with the Department of Homeland Security (DHS), which now houses the U.S. Coast Guard, Customs and Border Protection, Bureau of Immigration and Customs Enforcement, and the Transportation Security Administration. By working with these agencies, the industry ensures compliance with all U.S. and international maritime standards established to maintain shipboard security.

Consolidation

Consolidation that has been taking place in the travel industry is rampant in the cruise sector as well. Carnival Corporation, the world's largest cruise company, recently acquired Princess Cruises and already owned Cunard, Costa, Holland

CLIA MEMBER LINES (AS OF JUNE 18, 2004)

Carnival Cruise Lines
Celebrity Cruises
Costa Cruises
Crystal Cruises
Cunard Line
Disney Cruise Line
Holland America Line
MSC Cruises
Norwegian Coastal Voyage Inc.
Norwegian Cruise Line

Oceania Cruises
Orient Lines
Princess Cruises
Radisson Seven Seas Cruises
Royal Caribbean International
Seabourn Cruise Line
Silversea Cruises
Swan Hellenic
Windstar Cruises

America, Windstar, and Seabourn. Royal Caribbean International (RCI) is the second-largest player and recently acquired Celebrity Cruises. Competition is fierce, with these two companies adding new passenger ships and Disney now in the cruise business.

While CLIA members (see box) represent over 90 percent of the North American cruise market and over 80 percent of the ships, the world cruise fleet is supplemented by freighter cruises, river cruises, yachts, ferries, and charters. About eighty freighters provide accommodations for a limited number of passengers, such as six to twelve. Freighter cruises tend to last a long time, go to unknown parts, have schedules that can change rapidly, and be moderately priced. They appeal to the more adventurous traveler. River cruises are popular in the United States on the Mississippi River on the *Delta Queen* and *Mississippi Queen,* in Egypt on the Nile, in Brazil on the Amazon, and in Europe on the Danube and Rhine, just to mention a few. Riverboat gambling is a recent addition on the Mississippi. Barge and canal trips are also popular in many places.

Cruise Lines International Association

Cruise Lines International Association (CLIA) is a marketing and promotional trade organization made up of nineteen of the major cruise lines serving North America, representing over 142 ships (see box). CLIA was formed in 1975 out of a need for the cruise industry to develop a vehicle to promote the general concept of cruising. CLIA exists to educate, train, promote, and explain the value, desirability, and profitability of the cruise product.

When, in mid-1984, the Federal Maritime Commission consolidated other industry organizations into CLIA, it became the sole marketing organization of the cruise industry. CLIA represents almost 97 percent of the cruise industry, and more than 17,000 travel agents are affiliated with CLIA and display the CLIA seal, which identifies them as authorities on cruise vacations. The CLIA headquarters is located at 80 Broad Street, Suite 1800, New York, NY 10004; telephone (212) 921-0066; fax (212) 921-0549; Web site **http://www.cruising.org.**

OTHER MODES

While tourists use planes, trains, motorcoaches, taxis, shuttle buses, boats, and cruise ships to arrive at destinations, other modes of transportation are also an integral part of tourism. One of the most important and easily overlooked is pedestrian travel, or walking. Tourists and locals alike depend on their feet as a primary mode of travel. Tourists are great walkers, covering many miles sightseeing or using their feet to arrive at an attraction, sidewalk café, or gelato stand. Thus, it is imperative that pedestrian environments and the surface where tourists walk and the areas in which they move are welcoming and safe. Tourism planners must make pedestrian travel part of their development plans.

The walking paths by the river in Brisbane, Australia, are an outstanding example of good planning benefiting both tourist and locals with an attractive, safe, integrated transportation scheme. In contrast, walking in Cairo, Egypt, or Kuala Lumpur, Malaysia, is a challenge.

In addition, walking tours around the world have proven popular, as evidenced by the many itineraries offered by such firms as Country Walkers whose slogan is "Explore the world one step at a time."®

Cycling is another mode embraced by some travelers and tourist destinations. A number of companies feature biking tours. The Hoge Veluwe National Park in Holland is laced with paths for cars, bicycles, and walkers. There are more than 27 miles of paths specifically designed for bicycling. While most people visit the park for the Kroller-Muller Museum (famous for its Van Gogh paintings), the park also contains a magnificent sculpture garden, forests, and sand dunes. It is possible to cycle your way around the park thanks to a 1,000-plus fleet of free-to-use white bicycles. The fleet of bicycles reduces bus and auto traffic in the park and allows tourists a convenient way to see all the sights.

Trams, cable cars, gondolas, and ski lifts are all additional modes of tranportation that are important to specific resorts and destinations. They facilitate the flow of tourists and in many cases bring them to places that would otherwise be inaccessible. Also they can be tourist attractions themselves.

SUMMARY

Transportation services and facilities are an integral component of tourism. In fact, the success of practically all forms of travel depends on adequate transportation. Transportation services and facilities are the arteries through which the lifeblood of the travel industry flows. Travel by air dominates long- and middle-distance travel in the United States. But private automobiles carry the bulk (about 80 percent) of all travelers on short trips. Automobiles are also very important on long and international trips. Rental cars are popular, because they supplement air travel. Rail travel in the United States has declined substantially since the 1950s but is still important in commuting and longer-haul traffic. Motorcoach transportation is available at far more places than either air or rail, but it constitutes a rather small percentage of total vehicle miles. Vacationing on cruise ships has become the fastest-growing segment of the U.S. travel industry. New and refurbished cruise ships are appearing regularly.

Associations and groups of passenger carriers are important to their sectors' well-being and growth. Some of the most important are Air Transport Association of America; American Bus Association, United Motorcoach Association, American Automobile Association (affiliated with the Canadian Automobile Association); World Touring and Automobile Association; Recreation Vehicle Industry Association; Taxicab, Limousine, and Paratransit Association; National Limousine Association; and the Cruise Lines International Association.

Increases in almost all forms of tourism automatically boost passenger traffic, sometimes creating problems. Congestion can be especially bad on streets and roads and at airport terminals. Safety and security are basic requirements, and successful tourism depends on these factors. The environment will be affected by any form of transportation. Careful planning and increased awareness and preventative measures are needed to minimize such undesirable effects.

Long-term projections show increases in the demand for transportation. Increased taxes and fuel prices on this industry are having an adverse effect. It is hoped that these can be mitigated in time. Rail travel is increasing in Europe and Asia, where high-speed trains are being used.

ABOUT THE READING

The reading in this chapter discusses the Sydney, Australia, Olympic Park Station and rail link. This ground transportation facility served the crowds at the Olympics, and now transports visitors to this sporting and cultural center because it has been designed as an integral part of the Sydney metropolitan rail system. It is a good example of using a megaevent to improve infrastructure for local citizens.

READING 5.1

Australia's Olympic Park Station and Rail Link

When it was decided to develop Homebush Bay into Sydney's premier sporting and cultural facility, it was clear that to be a success, it had to be serviced by the best available public transport network.

The New South Wales (NSW) government decided the key to that network was a heavy rail link right into the heart of the Olympic and Showground facilities. As a result, the Olympic Coordination Authority (OCA) has overseen the development of the Olympic Park Station and rail link, which opened on March 8, 1998.

The new 5.3-kilometer rail link transports visitors to within a short walk of all the major facilities at Homebush Bay. The $95 million project moves tens of thousands of people an hour to and from Homebush Bay for concerts, exhibitions, and sports matches as well as major events such as the Royal Easter Show and the Olympic and Paralympic Games. It is an important supplement to Sydney's metropolitan rail service and provides an easy, fast, and comfortable alternative to driving.

Major Main Line Link

The Homebush Bay rail link is designed as an integral part of the Sydney metropolitan rail system. Trains traveling in either direction on the Main Western Line are able to enter the Homebush Bay loop. For major events the Olympic Park Station is serviced by eight-car double-deck suburban trains, which are designed for rapid embarking and disembarking of passengers. Country trains from places like the Blue Mountains and Newcastle are also able to drop off passengers directly into the heart of Homebush Bay.

The line is mostly above ground but goes below for one kilometer, allowing people to move freely around areas adjacent to the Olympic Park Station. Construction of the rail link began in August 1996, and track laying started in June 1997.

Capacity

The Homebush Bay rail link is designed for big crowds. During the Olympic and Paralympic Games, trains ran every two minutes. That's a total of fifty thousand people an hour, or about three times the number that use Sydney's busy Town Hall interchange in any morning peak period.

Design

Olympic Park Station and its surrounding public spaces are designed to reflect the excitement of the Olympic and Paralympic Games and to capture the atmosphere of the world's great transport terminals.

The station's design dramatically achieves this aim. The station is an imposing vaulted building that presents an exciting gateway to Homebush Bay and is a natural meeting place. It is situated next to the Showground and just 400 meters from the Olympic Stadium. The soaring 20-meter-high vaulted roof offers protection from the sun and the rain and creates a comfortable light and airy atmosphere for travelers.

Access

During the design of Olympic Park Station, OCA consulted with groups representing a wide range of people with disabilities and special needs to ensure that it would be accessible for everyone. The ground-level concourse is connected to the platforms below by a series of lifts, stairs, ramps, and escalators, which provide easy access into and out of the station.

Environment

The Homebush Bay rail link is a major environmental feature in its own right. A trainload of passengers can remove up to a thousand cars from the roads, helping improve Sydney's air quality. The design maximizes natural light and ventilation, thereby lowering energy consumption and reducing NSW's contribution to greenhouse gas emissions.

KEY CONCEPTS

airline industry	automobile	rail travel
Air Transport Association	cruise lines	recreation vehicles
alliances	Highways and Scenic Byways	rental cars
American Automobile Association	program	safety and security
American Bus Association	motorcoaches	taxi and limousine service
Amtrak	oil companies	transportation (importance of)

◢ Internet Sites

The Internet sites mentioned in this chapter are repeated here for convenience, plus some additional sites. For more information, visit these sites. Be aware that Internet addresses change frequently, so if a site cannot be accessed, use a search engine. Also use a search engine to locate many additional relevant sites.

Airports Council International–North America
http://www.aci-na.org

Air Transport Association of America
http://www.airlines.org

American Automobile Association
http://www.aaa.com

American Bus Association
http://www.buses.org

American Highway Users Alliance
http://www.highways.org

American Public Transportation Association
http://www.apta.com

Civil Aviation Authority, UK
http://www.caa.co.uk

Cruise Lines International Association
http://www.cruising.org

Europe by Eurail
http://www.railpass.com

Federal Aviation Administration
http://www.faa.gov

Florida-Caribbean Cruise Association
http://ww.f-cca.com

International Air Transport Association
http://www.iata.org

International Council of Cruise Lines
http://www.iccl.org

National Association of Railroad Passengers
http://www.narprail.org

National Limousine Association
http://www.limo.org

One World
http://www.oneworldalliance.com

Recreation Vehicle Industry Association
http://www.rvia.org

Regional Airline Association
http://www.raa.org

Skyteam
http://www.skyteam.com

Star Alliance
http://www.star-alliance.com

Taxicab, Limousine, and Paratransit Association
http://www.tlpa.org

Travel Industry Association of America
http://www.tia.org

United Motorcoach Association
http://www.uma.org

Internet Exercises

Site Name: Cruise Lines International Association (CLIA)

URL: http://www.cruising.org

Background Information: CLIA's primary objective is to help the over 16,500 CLIA-affiliated agencies become more successful at capitalizing on the booming and profitable cruise market. CLIA has 19 member lines, which represent virtually 100 percent of the cruise industry.

Exercises

1. You are working for a travel agency and have a family in your office. You realize early in the conversation that the wife is very interested in a cruise but the husband has some definite reservations. After probing for several minutes, the husband identifies the following concerns and questions he has about cruises: (1) I will get bored and feel confined. (2) I am afraid I will get seasick. (3) Cruises are only for rich people. (4) What can you do with kids on a ship? (5) What is there to do at night? How would you address these concerns/questions in order to sell this family a cruise?

2. Choose a cruise line and develop a summary of entertainment features the cruise line offers.

3. Choose a cruise line and identify what packages they offer for honeymooners and for families with children.

QUESTIONS FOR REVIEW AND DISCUSSION

1. Explain why air travel now dominates long- and middle-distance travel.
2. What were the main reasons that rail passenger transportation declined in the United States after 1920?
3. Identify the social and economic factors that would bring about a resurgence in motorcoach travel.
4. Describe the principal appeals of cruising.
5. Why is the cruise market expected to continue its extraordinary growth pattern?
6. What might be at least a partial solution to the problem of automobile congestion at major airports?
7. Similarly, make clear your ideas for alleviating flight arrival and departure congestion.
8. If you knew in advance that you would have a long drive through heavy traffic to reach the airport, followed by a wait in line for 30 minutes at the airline departure desk, 30 minutes at security, and that your plane would be remaining on the runway for 30 minutes before taking off, would you still make the pleasure trip?
9. Evaluate the importance of safety and security in all forms of travel. What is the safest mode of passenger transportation?
10. Taking each mode of transportation, what specifically can be done to minimize damage to the environment?
11. If you were vice president of marketing for an airline, what programs would you undertake to even out peaks and valleys in demand?

CASE PROBLEMS

1. The Rotary Club program chairman has asked you to give a talk on the advantages of cruises. He has also hinted that the club might be interested in taking a group cruise with their wives and children. What would you include in your talk?
2. Air transportation is truly a global industry. However, future growth in world demand is being impeded by many nations that have enacted various air regulations and restrictive laws. A beginning toward a "new world order" of global competition and interconnectedness has appeared. The first "open skies" agreement was established between the United States and the Netherlands. This agreement, dubbed Open Skies I, signals the beginning of what could become global. The agreement abolishes all legal and diplomatic environments as well as all other trade barriers that impede airline efficiency. It also encourages competition. The Open Skies I accord completely deregulates air services between the two countries. If such pacts were to become a reality on a much wider scale, how would this affect demand for travel on the world's airlines? Explain and give several examples.

SELECTED REFERENCES

Air Transport Association of America. *ATA Economic Report for the U.S. Airline Industry.* Washington, DC: ATA, 2004.

Dickinson, Bob, and Andy Vladimir. *Selling the Sea.* New York: Wiley, 1997.

Francis, Graham, Ian Humphreys, and Stephen Ison. "Airports' Perspectives on the Growth of Low-Cost Airlines and the Remodeling of the Airport-Airline Relationship." *Tourism Management,* Vol. 25, No. 4, pp. 507, 2004.

Graham, Anne. *Managing Airports: An International Perspective.* Oxford, UK: Butterworth-Heinemann, 2003.

Graham, B. *Geography and Air Transport.* New York: Wiley, 1995.

Hanlon, P. *Global Airline: Competition in a Transnational Industry.* Oxford, UK: Butterworth-Heinemann, 1996.

Heraty, Margaret J. "Tourism Transport: Implications for Developing Countries." *Tourism Management,* Vol. 10, No. 4, pp. 288–292, December 1989.

Marti, Bruce E. "The Cruise Ship Vessel Sanitation Program." *Journal of Travel Research,* Vol. 33, No. 4, pp. 29–38, Spring 1995.

Page, S. *Transport for Tourism.* London: Routledge, 1994.

Semer-Purzycki, Jeanne, and Robert Purzycki. *Sails for Profit: A Complete Guide to Selling and Booking Cruise Travel.* Upper Saddle River, NJ: Prentice Hall, 1999.

Tourism Industries. *In-Flight Survey of International Air Travelers.* Washington, DC: International Trade Administration, 2004.

Travel Industry Association of America. *Auto Travel in the U.S.* Washington, DC: TIA, 2003.

World Tourism Organization. *Tourism and Air Transport.* Madrid: WTO, 2001.

HOSPITALITY AND RELATED SERVICES

CHAPTER 6

Learning Objectives

- Study the lodging industry, its ancient origins, its associations, names of leading companies, and its vital role in the economy.
- Appreciate the immensity of the restaurant food service industry.

- Learn the current trends in resorts and timesharing modes of operation.
- Discover why meetings and conventions, as well as meeting planners, are so important to tourism.

There are numerous resorts on the Mexican coast, such as those found in Manzanillo. *Copyright © Corbis Digital Stock.*

INTRODUCTION

As noted in Chapter 2, providing overnight accommodations for travelers goes back into antiquity; it is the world's oldest commercial business. Guest rooms were first part of private dwellings. Then came caravansaries and guest quarters provided in monasteries. Today, lodging and food service activities are enormous in economic importance. Many lodging places provide meeting rooms, convention facilities and services, restaurants, bars, entertainment, gift shops, gaming, health clubs, and other activities and facilities. Figure 6.1 extracts the operating sectors from Figure 1.2 and shows that accommodations and food services are critical sectors of the tourism industry. See Figure 6.2 for the structure of the accommodations industry. In this chapter we examine this industry as well as the even larger food service business, meetings and conventions, and related services.

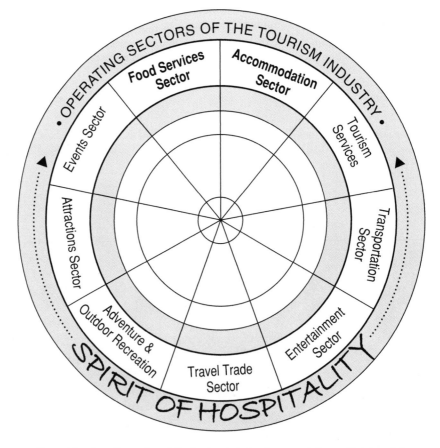

Figure 6.1   Operating sectors of the tourism industry: Accommodation and food services.

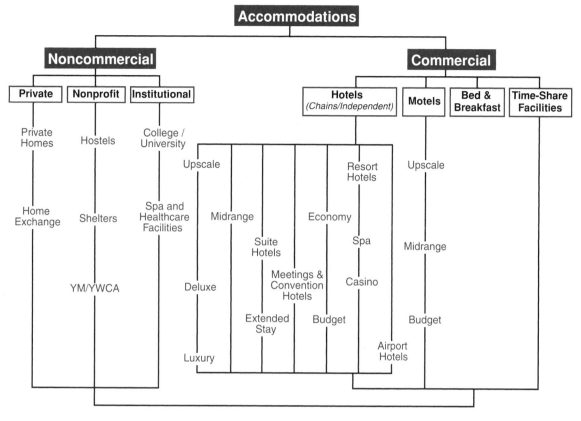

Figure 6.2 Accommodations structure.

THE LODGING INDUSTRY

The World Tourism Organization (WTO) estimates that the world hotel room inventory grows by about 2.5 percent a year. Occupancy rates vary, but they average about 65 percent overall. Such places as London, Beijing, New York, San Francisco, Hawaii, the Caribbean area, and the city of Las Vegas are noted for higher occupancy rates. During the 1980s there was a great deal of overbuilding, especially in North America. The supply of rooms outstripped demand, resulting in low occupancy and low room rates. For example, in the United States between 1986 and 1992 the hotel industry lost about $14 billion. Much of the problem was the result of overbuilding caused by tax laws that encouraged construction as a tax shelter. The law was changed in 1986, ending the tax shelter, but construction could not be ended in midstream. Currently, in most tourist destinations the creation of new lodging facilities is striking a better balance. After difficult years in the early 1990s, the remainder of the decade was extremely profitable.

In Eastern Europe, the former Soviet Union, and Asia there is now a considerable amount of new hotel construction to serve an anticipated growing demand.

Hotel accommodations are heavily concentrated in Europe and North America, with Europe accounting for 44.7 percent of the world's room supply and the United States accounting for 27 percent, for a total of over 71 percent. Asia and the Pacific region account for 13.9 percent, Africa 3.1 percent, and the Middle East 1.5 percent.

According to the American Hotel and Lodging Association (AH&LA), the lodging industry (which includes hotels, motels, suites, and resort properties) recorded a profitable year in 2003. The industry grossed $12.8 billion in pretax profits in 2003, down considerably from the record $24.0 billion in pretax profits in 2000. Total industry revenues in 2003 were $105.3 billion up from $102.6 billion in 2002, but short of the record set in 2000 of $108.6 billion. The lodging industry's performance reflects the difficult times the tourism industry has had since September 11, 2001.

The AH&LA 2004 Lodging Industry Profile shows the industry numbered 47,584 properties, 4.4 million rooms, $105.3 billion in sales, $12.8 billion in pretax profit, 61.1 percent average occupancy rate, and $50.42 revenue per available room (RevPAR, a combination of occupancy and average room rate). The average room rate was $82.52 in 2003, down from $83.54 in 2002. However, over the past ten years this number has increased significantly. The average room rate was $88.27 in 2001, $85.89 in 2000, $81.33 in 1999, $78.62 in 1998, $75.31 in 1997, $70.93 in 1996, $66.65 in 1995, $62.86 in 1994, and $60.53 in 1993. Forecasts for 2005 are continued recovery in the lodging sector as occupancy and room rates are expected to rise. Demand increases will exceed room supply growth.

Who is the typical lodging customer? According to the AH&LA, 24 percent are on vacation, 29 percent are transient business travelers, 25 percent are attending a conference or meeting, and 22 percent are traveling for other reasons such as a special event, family, or personal. The typical business room night is generated by a male (71 percent), age 35 to 54 (53 percent), employed with a professional or managerial position (50 percent), and earning an average yearly household income of $82,800. Typically, these guests travel alone (76 percent), make reservations (90 percent), and pay $91 per room night.

The typical leisure room night is generated by two adults (52 percent), ages 35 to 54 (45 percent), and earning an average yearly household income of $74,000. The typical leisure traveler also travels by auto (73 percent), makes reservations (84 percent), and pays $87 per room night.

For a hotel stay, 40 percent of all business travelers spend one night, 24 percent spend two nights, and 36 percent spend three or more nights. Of leisure travelers, 47 percent spend one night, 26 percent spend two nights, and 27 percent spend three or more nights.

The impact of international travelers on the hotel industry is considerable. In 2003, 13.9 million overseas travelers stayed in a hotel or motel. Their average length of stay in a hotel was 7.5 nights, with 1.7 people in the travel party. The main purposes of trips for overseas travelers who stayed in hotels and motels were leisure, recreation, and holiday at 53 percent, and business at 27 percent. These extremely mobile travelers visited 1.6 states while within the country. To move about the United States they rented cars (35 percent) and took taxis and limousines (46 percent).

Technology has had a profound influence on the lodging industry in recent years. Over 90 percent of hotel companies have Web sites and industry surveys show that business travelers want computers with Internet access and printers in their guest rooms. Many hotels are becoming wireless. Online expenditures for hotel bookings are increasing. The Cornell Center for Hospitality Research reports that

Elegance and comfort meet in this spacious double guest room at the Phoenician Resort in Scottsdale, Arizona, which also offers scenic views of the desert. *Photo courtesy of the Phoenician.*

by 2005, an estimated one in five hotel bookings will be made on an Internet site, up from one in twelve in 2002.

Self-service check-in and check-out took a step forward when Starwood Hotels and Resorts tested self-service kiosks at their Boston and New York properties. The kiosks are located in the lobby and allow the guests to check in or out of the hotel by simply swiping their credit card, eliminating the need to go to the front desk. The kiosks are similar to the ones used by the airlines. Hilton Hotels and Hyatt Hotels are adding similar technology. It is predicted kiosks will become common in hotel lobbies in the future.

Smith Travel Research and AH&LA provide valuable information on the lodging industry. In addition to the annual lodging profile, AH&LA has Smith Travel Research do a comprehensive study of the industry periodically. The AH&LA has just released their latest study that looks at the size, scope, and emerging trends of the lodging industry and makes comparisons with previous studies. The 2004 survey includes new categories on wireless technology and the latest menu options

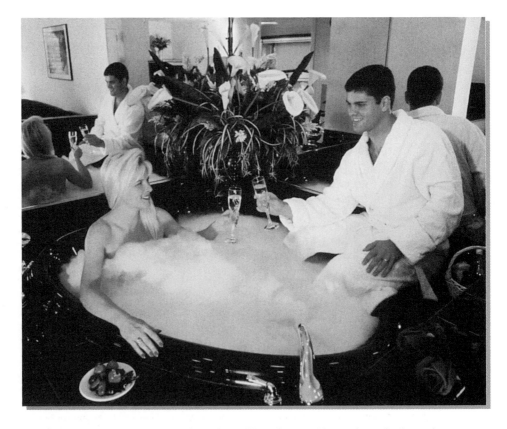

The hospitality industry creates many unique, pleasurable, and memorable experiences for the tourist.
Photo courtesy of Holiday Inn Family Suites Resort, Lake Buena Vista, Orlando, Florida.

for low-carbohydrate and low-calorie dietary needs. Popular and returning categories include meeting room high-speed Internet access, in-room safes, pet policies, the age of properties, energy management sensors, property Web sites, special discounted rate offers, nonsmoking rooms, air purifiers, and security cameras in lobbies.

Some of the highlights of the survey are that high-speed Internet access has increased from 7 percent in 1998 to 50 percent in 2004; linen/towel reuse programs continue to grow in popularity, rising from 14 percent 1994 to 57 percent in 2004; voice mail has grown from 4 percent in 1990 to more than 78 percent in 2004; hotels offering cable or satellite television has increased from 69 percent in 1998 to 98 percent in 2004; and only 8 percent offer DVD players in their guestrooms.

The lodging industry has practiced market segmentation in recent years. Many of the big chains offer products at almost every price level: full-service luxury hotels, luxury all-suite hotels, resort hotels, moderately priced full-service hotels, moderately priced all-suites, moderately priced limited-service, and economy or budget motels (see box). Hotels and motels are classified in a variety of ways. One

GLOSSARY

- Revenue per available room (RevPAR). Total guest-room revenue for a given period divided by the total number of occupied rooms during the same period (excluding public rooms). A simple way to calculate is to multiply the occupancy times the room rate.

- Average daily room rate for guest. Total guest-room revenue for a given period divided by the total number of guests accommodated for the same time period.

- Percentage of occupancy. The percentage of available rooms occupied for a given period. It is computed by dividing the number of rooms occupied for a period by the number of rooms available for the same period.

- Income before other fixed charges. Income after management fees, property taxes, and insurance does not include deductions for depreciation, rent, interest, amortization, and income taxes. Comparisons beyond income after property taxes and insurance are virtually meaningless due to wide variances in ownership, depreciation methods, financing bases, applicable income taxes, and so on.

- Full-service hotel. A hotel that provides a wide variety of facilities and amenities, including food and beverage outlets, meeting rooms, and recreational activities.

- Limited-service hotel. A hotel that provides only some of the facilities and amenities of a full-service property. This category includes properties commonly referred to as motels or motor hotels.

- Resort hotel. A hotel in which all rooms have separate, but not necessarily physically divided, sleeping and living areas.

- Convention hotel. A hotel that provides facilities and services geared to meet the needs of large group and association meetings and trade shows. Typically, these hotels have in excess of four hundred guest rooms and contain substantial amounts of function and banquet space flexibly designed for use by large meeting groups. They often work in concert with other convention hotels and convention centers to provide facilities for citywide conventions and trade shows.

of the most common is by location, such as resort, city center, airport, suburban, or highway.

Rank

There are a number of very large companies in the lodging industry, and many of the big chains are getting bigger. *Hotels* (published by Cahners Business Information, 2000 Clearwater Drive, Oak Brook, Illinois, 60544-8809) compiles an annual listing of the world's three hundred largest corporate hotel chains. The July 2004 issue reports the thirty-fourth annual listing of lodging's giant companies. The concentration of the lodging industry is clearly demonstrated by the ranking of the top twenty-five, which appears in Table 6.1. The ranking is based on the number of rooms. The top ten companies have 3.5 million rooms. The July 2004 issue of *Hotels* reports a new leader as the InterContinental Hotel Group moved to the top with the acquisition of the Candlewood branded hotels and a total room count of 536,318. Cendant fell to second as they completed a system-wide house-cleaning which reduced their room count to 518,747. Marriott International ranked third with 490,564 rooms, Accor was fourth with 453,403, and Choice Hotels rounded out the top five with 388,618.

While sixteen of the top twenty-five international franchised hotel chains are headquarted in the United States, the list is global. England has the top ranked InterContinental Hotel Group; Hilton Group, ranked tenth; and Le Méridien Hotels and Resorts ranked twenty-third. France has Accor, ranked fourth; Societé du Louvre, ranked fourteenth; and Club Méditerranée ranked twenty-second.

TABLE 6.1   **TOP TWENTY-FIVE HOTEL CHAINS**

Rank[a]	Company	Rooms	Hotels
2003		2003	2003
2002	Headquarters	2002	2002
1	**InterContinental Hotels Group**	536,318	3,520
2	Windsor, Berkshire, ENGLAND	514,873	3,333
2	**Cendant Corp.**	518,747	6,402
1	Parsippany, New Jersey, USA	536,097	6,513
3	**Marriott International**	490,564	2,718
3	Washington, DC, USA	463,429	2,557
4	**Accor**	453,403	3,894
4	Paris, FRANCE	440,807	3,829
5	**Choice Hotels International**	388,618	4,810
5	Silver Spring, Maryland, USA	373,722	4,664
6	**Hilton Hotels Corp.**	348,483	2,173
6	Beverly Hills, California, USA	337,116	2,084

TABLE 6.1 (*CONTINUED*)

RANK 2003 2002	COMPANY HEADQUARTERS	ROOMS 2003 2002	HOTELS 2003 2002
7	**Best Western International**	310,245	4,110
7	Phoenix, Arizona, USA	308,911	4,064
8	**Starwood Hotels & Resorts Worldwide**	229,247	738
8	White Plains, New York, USA	226,970	748
9	**Carlson Hospitality Worldwide**	147,624	881
9	Minneapolis, Minnesota, USA	141,923	847
10	**Hilton Group plc**	98,689	392
10	Watford, Herts, ENGLAND	96,380	384
11	**Hyatt Hotels/Hyatt International**	89,602	208
11	Chicago, Illiniois, USA	92,278	210
12	**Sol Meliá SA**	80,494	331
13	Palma de Mallorca, SPAIN	87,717	350
13	**TUI AG/TUI Hotels & Resorts**	76,000	290
14	Hannover, GERMANY	75,000	285
14	**Société du Louvre**	66,356	896
15	Paris, FRANCE	67,990	900
15	**Interstate Hotels & Resorts**	65,250	295
12	Arlington, Virginia, USA	83,456	390
16	**Wyndham International**	50,980	190
16	Dallas, Texas, USA	51,342	201
17	**Extended Stay America**	50,240	472
18	Spartanburg, South Carolina, USA	48,431	455
18	**FelCor Lodging Trust**	45,000	161
17	Irving, Texas, USA	48,857	183
19	**La Quinta Corp.**	43,457	363
19	Irving, Texas, USA	42,865	349
20	**Westmount Hospitality Group**	40,000	332
20	Houston, Texas, USA	40,000	332
21	**U.S. Franchise Systems**	36,633	470
21	Atlanta, Georgia, USA	39,317	494
22	**Club Méditerranée**	36,106	103
22	Paris, FRANCE	39,114	140
23	**Le Méridien Hotels & Resorts**	35,589	143
23	London, ENGLAND	36,479	141
24	**NH Hotelés SA**	34,458	239
24	Madrid, SPAIN	34,410	239
25	**Hospitality Properties Trust**	34,284	271
25	Newton, Massachusetts, USA	34,284	251

[a]Rankings are based on total rooms.

Source: Hotels, July 2004. *Hotels* magazine, a Cahners Publication, 2000 Clearwater Drive, Oak Brook, IL USA 60523.

Spain has Sol Meliá, ranked twelfth; and NH Hotelés, ranked twenty-fourth. Germany has TUI AG/TUI Hotels and Resorts, ranked thirteenth.

Trends

The trend in the lodging industry has been away from independently owned and operated properties toward chain and franchise affiliations, which get larger and larger. There are also referral groups or voluntary membership associations. Both independents and chains have found it profitable to join together to market their properties.

The trend toward consolidation and acquisition will continue because chains have the potential for improvement in productivity and because of the advantages that accrue to large size. Chains can most effectively use training programs, employee selection programs, major equipment with different layouts, prices, advertising, equipment, technology, marketing, and so on, and what works well in one property can be employed chainwide. One reason for the popularity of the referral groups is that members who are independent operators achieve the marketing benefits of chains without chain membership.

Franchising is also well known in the lodging industry and has made a rapid penetration into the marketplace. However, franchising generates mixed reports. Many managements believe that it is difficult to control the franchises and maintain the quality that the chain advertises and the standards that are supposed to be met. Thus, many chains are buying back franchises to ensure that management maintains the quality level desired. In other cases, firms are moving ahead rapidly with franchising because they can conserve cash and expand more rapidly by franchising. In addition, the franchisee, having invested his or her own capital, has great motivation to succeed.

Franchisees have the advantage that they receive a known "name," the knowledge, advice, and assistance of a proven operator. Franchising also spreads the costs of promotion, advertising, and reservation systems over all outlets, making the unit cost much lower. If the franchiser has an excellent reputation and image, the franchisee benefits greatly. Most of the companies with franchise operations also operate company-owned units. Industry predictions are that as the industry grows and matures, there will be less franchising, which will give the chains more control over their properties and operations so that they can maintain the desired quality control. Increased competitiveness and improved properties will necessitate having the ability to make these improvements.

A trend in the lodging industry appears to be that more large properties will be operated under management contracts. Investors, such as insurance companies, frequently purchase hotel properties and turn them over to chains or independents to manage—a process that has advantages to both parties. The owner has the financial resources and the manager has the reputation and experience to manage the property profitably. Starwood is experimenting with automatic check-in kiosks. Other trends are the increased use of central reservation systems, emphasis on service, and the use of yield management techniques.

One of the increasingly popular amenities offered by modern hotels is a fitness facility. These are provided in response to the changing lifestyles and demands of customers. *Photo courtesy of the Sheraton Russell Hotel.*

Bed and Breakfasts

Moving from the megacorporate chain to the **bed-and-breakfast** establishment demonstrates the diversity in lodging accommodations and the fact that many small businesses make up much of the tourism industry.

The growing bed-and-breakfast (B&B) segment is made up of over 20,000 privately owned homes, inns, and reservation services. B&Bs provide both luxury and economy accommodations and are found in resort areas as well as in many areas where major hotel and motel chains do not build. This brings tourism dollars into communities often neglected by most tourists.

Insight into the characteristics and operation of B&Bs is provided by their trade association, the Professional Association of Innkeepers International (PAII), who hired PKF Consulting to study the operations, marketing, and finances of B&Bs. The PAII *2002 Industry Study* shows the B&B industry is $3.1 billion in size. The average B&B had 8.5 rooms, an average daily rate of $136.70 and an average occupancy rate of 38 percent. The study found 32 percent were in rural locations, 18 percent were urban, and 50 percent were village; 87 percent were tourist destination/resort properties; 95 percent of rooms had a private bath; 74 percent of the larger inns (21-plus sleeping rooms) have meeting space; 53 percent handle weddings and do an average of 7 per year; 11 percent were new B&Bs; and 8 percent of B&Bs were sold with an average purchase price of $653,981.

B&B guests were 50 percent leisure travelers. Tourists and guests celebrating a special occasion such as a honeymoon, anniversary, or birthday accounted for 24 percent. International guests totaled 8 percent as did those on business. Guest registrations from the Internet were 45 percent up from 22 percent in 1998. Visit the PAII Web site at **http://www.paii.org.**

B&Bs provide the best possible avenue for travelers of all ages and locations to experience firsthand the lifestyles in areas of the country previously unknown to guests. The B&B host can become an area's best ambassador. In many cases around the nation, the institution of a B&B has saved a historic property that might otherwise have been destroyed.

B&B reservation services inspect and approve B&B homes and inns, maintain ongoing quality control, and provide one-stop shopping for the traveler. They can provide the traveler with a chain of recourse in case of a problem. Reservation services are privately owned corporations, partnerships, or single proprietorships, each representing from 35 to 100 host homes and inns.

Timeshare Resorts

In its book *Timeshare: The New Force in Tourism,* the World Tourism Organization (WTO) has named timeshare as one of the fastest-growing sectors of the travel and tourism industry. WTO states that timeshare has grown at an annual rate of more than 15 percent since the 1980s, compared to a growth rate of slightly over 2 percent for hotel accommodations and 4 percent for tourism overall. Timeshare—or vacation ownership, as it is also called—is worldwide.

The American Resort Development Association (ARDA) reports there are 5,425 resorts worldwide located in 95 countries. Figure 6.3 shows the locations of timeshare resorts. North America leads with over 1,700, of which 1,590 are in the United States. Europe hosts 25 percent led by Spain, Latin American has 16 percent led by Mexico, Asia has 14 percent led by Japan; Africa with 6 percent, the Caribbean with 5 percent, and the Pacific with 3 percent round out the locations.

These resorts provide about 325,000 accommodation units worldwide. Some 132,000 (41 percent) are in the U.S., where timeshare resorts tend to be largest, averaging more than 80 units each. On a global basis, the average timeshare resort offers about 60 units. Some 6.7 million households own the rights to about 10.7 million timeshare weeks. Timeshare owners reside in more than 270 countries. In the United States, 3 million consumers own 4.9 million timeshare weeks.

In 2002, worldwide timeshare volume was $9.4 billion. Sales of U.S. timeshares made up $5.5 billion of this total. Globally, the average price of a timeshare week was $10,600, while in the United States it was $14,500. The average maintenance fee worldwide is $325 per week of annual use and in the United States it is $385.

Timeshare is one of the fastest growing and most resilient segments of the U.S. tourism industry. In the period since September 11, 2001, unlike other sectors,

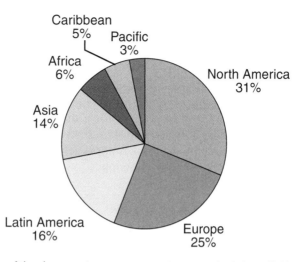

Figure 6.3 **Locations of timeshare resorts.** *Source: Ragatz Associates, Resort Timesharing Worldwide and in the United States: 2003 Edition, Summary Report.*

timeshare figures have shown strong growth. ARDA reports that U.S. sales grew by over 14 percent in 2002 and strong sales are continuing.

The median age of the U.S. timeshare owner is 53, 84 percent are married, 95 percent own their homes, median household income is $85,000, 46 percent attended college, and 30 percent hold a graduate or professional degree. Florida has the largest number of timeshare resorts with 366, followed by California with 125, South Carolina with 119, and Colorado with 75. Attraction and entertainment resort areas such as Orlando, Branson, Las Vegas, and Gatlinburg rank tops in sales. Ocean beach areas run a close second, followed by mountain, golf, lake, and history/culture locations. Satisfaction among timeshare owners has always been at a high level. The 2003 edition of *Resort Timesharing in the United States* indicates it remains high at 84 percent.

Since 1979, demand studies of the U.S. timeshare characteristics, motivations, satisfaction, and use patterns have been prepared by Ragatz Associates for ARDA. Other studies on financial impact and the economic impact of the timeshare industry have been conducted by PricewaterhouseCoopers and others for ARDA. Throughout its history ARDA has been the preeminent source of information about timesharing and vacation ownership. Visit their Web site at **http://www.arda.org.**

Timesharing is expected to increase in the United States because major companies such as Disney, Marriott, Hyatt, Four Seasons, Ramada, Accor, Starwood, and Hilton have become involved in bringing more respectability to the industry. Once considered to be a sleazy real estate proposition with unfulfilled promises, high pressure, and marketing hype, timesharing has evolved into a mainstream option. Today, timeshares are sold by some of the best names in the hotel industry. *Vacation ownership* or *internal ownership* is the terminology used. Major hotel chains are gaining a large share of the market.

An example is Marriott. They entered the vacation ownership industry in 1984 and began redefining the timeshare industry. Incorporating the signature quality, service, and hospitality expertise of Marriott, a new product was created that offered the ownership of a first-class luxury villa and the flexibility to experience great vacation destinations around the world. Marriott Vacation Club International has successfully combined the benefits of property ownership, Marriott quality management, and fixed costs for a lifetime of vacations. Marriott has about two thousand villas at beach and ski resorts across the country. Over the past ten years, Marriott has refined a low-key approach and sold "vacation ownership intervals" to more than sixty thousand people.

Camping and Campgrounds

Camping has a long history in many countries including the United States. Millions of campsites are available to the tourist, both public and private. At one time camping meant roughing it and involved setting up a tent or sleeping under the stars. Today travelers can still do that, or more likely they will park a recreational vehicle, or rent cabins, cottages, or lodges. RV parks and campgrounds offer a wide variety of amenities, activities, and services for the comfort of their camping customers. Many campgrounds offer electricity, cable TV hookups, computer connections, wireless Internet service, hot showers, and laundry facilities. The National Association of RV Parks and Campgrounds is the national association representing almost 3,700 parks and campgrounds in North America. The association is headquartered in Falls Church, Virginia. Visit their Web site at **http://www.arvc.org.**

Lodging Organizations

There are a large number of accommodation organizations: international, regional, state, and local. Of these, the American Hotel and Lodging Association (AH&LA) is the largest and most prominent in the United States. AH&LA now represents over 10,000 members. AH&LA works on programs such as guest and employee communications, information processing and related technology, international travel, external and internal marketing, quality assurance programs, industry research, safety and fire protection, and so on.

AH&LA has one of the best information centers in the United States. Their information center provides a collection of resources covering the lodging, hospitality, and travel and tourism fields; a professional staff of librarians/researchers; a wealth of industry-specific and related knowledge; a resource center of over 70,000 current articles on more than 2,500 topics, reference materials, books, reports, and surveys; and an access point to major domestic and international bibliographic and statistical databases. AH&LA has a commitment to technology and is dedicated to providing members and the media with up-to-date information, industry trends, and association news via the Internet. Visit their Web site: **http://www.ahla.com.**

The International Hotel and Restaurant Association (IH&RA), located in Paris, France, is a global network for the hotel and restaurant industry in over 150 countries. It represents, protects, promotes, and informs its members. IH&RA research reports provide members with valuable information on the global hospitality industry, careers, taxes, and technology. Visit their Web site at **http://www.ihra.com.**

Lodging Information Sources

Data on the lodging industry can be obtained from Smith Travel Research in Hendersonville, Tennessee. Smith is the leader in lodging industry tracking and analysis, providing regular industry reporting to all major U.S. hotel chains, many independent hotels, and a variety of management companies and hotel owners. The company also tracks lodging industry performance in Canada, Mexico, and other major world destinations. Visit their Web site at **http://www.str-online.com.**

PricewaterhouseCoopers, LLP (1301 Avenue of the Americas, New York, NY 10019), has Lodging Research Network (**http://www.lodgingresearch.com**), which contains econometric forecasts for the lodging industry, breaking lodging industry news, and an exclusive database of lodging industry real estate acquisitions, financial data of publicly traded lodging companies, hotel construction data, lodging census data from Smith Travel Research, and an extensive research library.

In late 1998, the PricewaterhouseCoopers lodging and gaming groups and Smith Travel Research signed an agreement to form a worldwide alliance for lodging industry research. The organizations will cooperate to collect and report hotel operating data in over twenty countries outside of North America. In addition, PKF Consulting, San Francisco, and the U.S. Census Bureau, Washington, D.C., provide lodging information.

THE FOOD SERVICE INDUSTRY

Early Food Services

Like the lodging industry, the **food service industry** is a very old business. Such service came out of the early inns and monasteries. In cities, small restaurants began serving simple dishes such as soups and breads. One such restaurant, *le restaurant divin* (the divine restorative) opened in Paris in 1765. (Like *tourist, restaurant* is a French word.) The famous English taverns provided food, drink, and lodging.

In the United States the early ordinaries, taverns, and inns typically provided food and lodging. Good examples of these can be found in Colonial Williamsburg, Virginia. Politics and other concerns of the day were often discussed in such taverns.

With the development of stagecoaches, taverns began providing food and lodging along the early roads and in small communities. Some believe that these roadside taverns were really the beginnings of the American hotel industry. As cities grew, so did eating establishments. Some names of historic restaurants in the 1820s in New York City were Niblo's Garden, the Sans Souci, and Delmonico's.

French service was often used in these early restaurants. In French service, some kinds of entrées are prepared by the dining room captain right at the guests' table, sometimes using heat from a small burner, then serving from larger dishes onto the guest's plate. The kinds and amounts of each food item are chosen individually. By contrast, in Russian service the entire plate, with predetermined portions, is served to each guest.

Menus can be of two types, à la carte and table d'hôte. The à la carte menu consists of a complete list of all the food items being offered on that day. The patron then chooses the individual items desired. In table d'hôte, a combination of items is chosen.

Eating and drinking places are big business. Although much of this activity is local, eating and drinking are favorite pastimes of travelers, and the food service industry would face difficult times without the tourist market. See Figure 6.4 for the structure of the food service industry.

The National Restaurant Association projected that food industry sales for 2005 would total $475.8 billion and equal 4 percent of U.S. gross domestic product. This level is 4.9 percent over 2004 sales and marks the fourteenth consecutive year of sales growth for the industry. The nation's 900,000 restaurants provide employment for 12.2 million people, over 9 percent of the U.S. workforce, making the industry the largest private sector employer in the nation. About 55 percent of all those in food service occupations are women, 13 percent are Hispanic, and 11 percent are African American. The food service industry employs more minority managers than any other retail industry. Travelers contribute about $130 billion to food service sales each year, whether for a coffee shop breakfast, a dinner on an airline, a sandwich from a bus station vending machine, or a ten-course dinner on a cruise

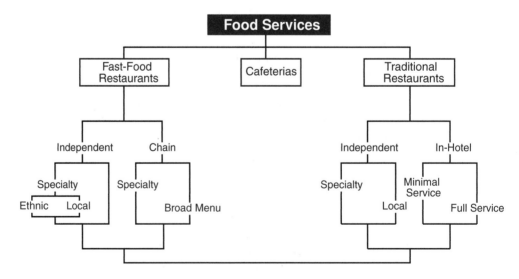

Figure 6.4   Food services structure.

ship. Travelers, including foreign visitors, spend more money on food than anything else except transportation, and travelers account for about one-third of the total sales in the food service industry.

The food service industry consists of restaurants, travel food service, and vending and contract institutional food service. Local restaurants are made up of establishments that include fast-food units, coffee shops, specialty restaurants, family restaurants, cafeterias, and full-service restaurants with carefully orchestrated "atmosphere." Travel food service consists of food operations in hotels and motels, roadside service to automobile travelers, and all food service on airplanes, trains, and ships. Institutional food service in companies, hospitals, nursing homes, and so on is not considered part of the tourism industry.

Over the past two decades, the food and beverage business has grown at a phenomenal rate. This has been especially true for the fast-food segment, with the franchising portion in the fast-food segment becoming the dominant growth sector. This remarkable increase has been gained at the expense of other food service operators and supermarkets. Franchisees control approximately three-fourths of

An unusual waiter indeed! This special breakfast dining experience at Disneyland delights children and can be the highlight of a family vacation. *Photo courtesy of the Disneyland Hotel.*

the fast-food outlets, whose hamburgers, chickens, steaks, and pizzas dominate the fast-food business.

Fast-food chains have enjoyed great success in part because they limit their menus, which gives them greater purchasing power, less waste, more portion control, and, of importance to the consumer, lower operating costs. They are leaders in labor productivity in the restaurant industry. Most fast-food operations use disposable paper and plastic; the expense for these materials is more than offset by the savings resulting from not providing regular service and from not employing the personnel required to wash the dinner service. Fast-food operations also enjoy the advantages of specialization; they have become specialists in menu items, job simplification, and operating systems. Franchising has been used extensively in both the restaurant field and the lodging field as a means of achieving rapid growth. Using the franchisee's capital, the entrepreneur can get much more rapid penetration of the marketplace.

As noted earlier, franchise units account for approximately three-fourths of the growing fast-food portion of the industry. Advantages of franchising accrue to both sides. The franchisee gets the start-up help, advice from experienced management, buying power, advertising, and low unit costs from spreading fixed costs over large numbers of units. The franchisor has the advantage of a lower capital investment, rapid growth, and royalty income. The fast-food franchise operators have a great

Fine dining is available to travelers throughout the world. Nowhere is this more of a reality than on cruise ships, where food is only one highlight of the memorable experience they offer. *Copyright of Carnival Cruise Lines.*

deal of concentration in their segment of the industry. The seven largest account for almost half of the fast-food units and almost half of the sales. Franchise firms are household words: McDonald's, KFC (Kentucky Fried Chicken), A&W, Wendy's, Dairy Queen, Burger King, Pizza Hut, Arby's, and Taco Bell.

Although the fast-food segment is the most rapidly growing segment, the high-quality segment of the restaurant industry must not be overlooked. Much of this business is based on customers seeking a special or different experience in dining out. Local entrepreneurs who emphasize special menus, varying atmospheres, and high-quality food and service have most effectively satisfied this demand. New concepts or trends include ethnic restaurants, especially those with an oriental or Mexican flavor; increased demand for health foods, fish, local produce, and regional dishes; and variety in portion sizes.

Restaurant Organizations

The National Restaurant Association (NRA), a full-service trade association with over sixty thousand members, is the most important trade association in the food service field. Membership is diverse, running the gamut from the New Jersey prison system to "21" Club and including white-tablecloth and fast-food members, institutional feeders, and vending machine operators.

Old Town Amusement Park in Kissimmee, Florida, features "All American Food." Here a family enjoys hamburgers, french fries, and root beer before taking a journey into a nostalgic past that captures the sights, sounds, and aromas of a simpler, more carefree time. *Photo Courtesy of Old Town.*

The goals and objectives of NRA are channeled in three directions: (1) political action, (2) information, and (3) promotion. Through their political action and political education committees, NRA promotes the political and legislative concerns of the industry and combats any potentially harmful attempts by government to regulate the operational aspects of the industry. Their educational foundation contributes to the current and future training and educational/informational needs of the food service industry.

NRA works to position the industry and its services before the public in a favorable light. The association regularly publishes surveys and reports on a wide variety of topics, ranging from employee management to consumer attitudes toward smoking in restaurants. Through its library's information service, NRA responds to thousands of requests for information. NRA is located at 1200 Seventeenth Street NW, Washington, DC 20036; telephone (202) 331-5900; Web site **http://www.restaurant.org.**

MEETING PLANNERS

Because of the growth in the meeting and conventions area, it is an area of interest to students of tourism. With the growth of more corporate and association meetings, there is a need for more meeting planners, meeting consultants, and suppliers of goods and services to meeting planners. Professional meeting planners are involved with such tasks as negotiating hotel contracts, negotiating with airlines, writing contracts, planning educational meetings and seminars, developing incentive meetings, negotiating with foreign countries and hotels for incentive travel, budgeting, promotion, public relations, and planning special events and postmeeting tours. Meeting planners are found in corporations, special-interest associations, educational institutions, trade shows, and government.

MEETINGS AND CONVENTIONS

The conventions and meeting business is huge and booms when the economy is growing and retrenches when economic growth slows. Meeting Professionals International (MPI) estimates that meetings and conventions are a $102.3-billion-a-year industry. For a city, the financial benefits of hosting a convention are substantial.

According to the International Association of Convention and Visitor Bureaus (IACVB) *2004 Convention Expenditure and Impact Study,* the average convention attendee spent $945 in the host city. Delegates spend $266 per day excluding registration fees and transportation to and from the city. They stay an average of 3.5 nights. Lodging at 48 percent and food and beverage at 29 percent account for 77 percent of visitor spending. In addition to the delegates, the host city also benefits from the organizers spending an average of $96 per delegate for the event and exhibitors who spend an average of $350 each for the event. Delegates attending international, national, and regional events spend more money than those attending state and local events.

The meetings and conventions business is important to local economies. *Courtesy of The Greater Minneapolis Convention & Visitors Association © Bob Perzel.*

There will probably be an oversupply of convention meeting facilities in the United States as the number of convention centers continues to grow. Many U.S. cities are building new convention centers or expanding their existing centers. Even though the United States leads the world in conventions, in terms of both numbers of attendees and the amount of exhibit and meeting space, the growth in facilities is outpacing the demand. There are more than 330 convention centers in the United States, 50 percent more than in 1980.

SUMMARY

Lodging and food services are major essential supply components of tourism. These services date back to antiquity. World hotel room inventory is growing about 2.5 percent yearly. Room occupancy averages about 65 percent. But such data vary considerably. The 1980s saw considerable overbuilding and losses, especially in North America. However, in the late '90s record profitability was achieved. In the new century lodging has been profitable but has suffered from the events of September 11, war, terrorism, and SARS. About 70 percent of the world's lodging establishments are located in Europe and North America. There is a trend toward more franchising, chain or system ownership, and growth in bed-and-breakfast lodging.

Resort and timesharing arrangements are also increasing worldwide. There are 5,425 timeshare resorts worldwide and 1,590 in the United States. Worldwide about 6.7 million consumers own timeshare and about 3 million U.S. households own timeshare intervals. The American Hotel and Lodging Association is the leading lodging trade association in the United States, but many others are active in North America and elsewhere. Eating and drinking places are big business. In the United States this industry is expected to gross $475.8 billion in 2005, and employ over 12 million persons, making the industry the largest private-sector employer in the nation. The National Restaurant Association is the industry's most important trade association.

Meetings and conventions constitute a major reason for business travel. Expenditure on these stimulates all segments of tourism. In the United States there will probably be an oversupply of convention centers within a few years, because many cities are currently building new centers or expanding existing ones.

The profession of meeting planner is an important and growing one. Those attending meetings and conventions expect a rewarding experience. Thus, expert planning is critical to the success of such events. Meeting planners provide all arrangements necessary for a successful meeting, from transportation services to special events. They are particularly adept at negotiating elements needed for the meeting. Some corporations, associations, government agencies, and others have created their own meeting-planning department, with their own employees handling this important function.

KEY CONCEPTS

American Hotel and Lodging
   Association
bed and breakfast
fast-food companies
food service industry

franchising
largest hotel companies
lodging industry
meeting planners
meetings and conventions

National Restaurant Association
timesharing resorts
trends in lodging industry

Internet Sites

The Internet sites mentioned in this chapter are repeated here for convenience, plus some selected additional sites. For more information, visit these sites. Be aware that Internet addresses change frequently, so if a site cannot be accessed, use a search engine. Also use a search engine to locate many additional relevant sites.

American Culinary Federation
http://www.acfchefs.org

American Hotel and Lodging
   Association
http://www.ahla.com

American Resort Development
  Association
http://www.arda.org

Club Managers Association of America
http://www.cmaa.org

Convention Industry Council
http://www.conventionindustry.org

Cornell University Hotel and
  Restaurant Administration Quarterly
http://www.hotelschool.cornell.edu/
  publications/hraq

Council on Hotel, Restaurant, and
  Institutional Education (CHRIE)
http://www.chrie.org

Disney Vacation Club
http://www.dvc.disney.go.com

The Educational Foundation of NRA
http://www.restaurant.org/careers

The Educational Institute of AH&LA
http://www.ei-ahla.org

Fairmont Hotels and Resorts
http://www.Fairmont.com

Hilton Grand Vacations Company
http://www.hgvc.com

Hilton Hotels
http://www.hilton.com

Hotel and Catering International
  Management Association
http://www.hcima.org.uk

HVS International
http://www.hvsinternational.com

Hyatt Hotels and Resorts
http://www.hyatt.com

Hyatt Vacation Club
http://www.hyattvacationclub.com

Inn and Travel Network
http://www.innandtravel.com

International Association of
  Convention and Visitor Bureaus
http://www.iacvb.org

International Culinary Tourism
  Association
http://www.culinarytourism.org

International Food Service Executives
  Association
http://ifsea.org

International Franchise Association
http://www.franchise.org

International Hotel and Restaurant
  Association
http://www.ih-ra.com

Interval International
http://www.intervalworld.com

Marriott International
http://www.marriott.com

Marriott Vacation Club
  International
http://www.marriott.com/vacationclub

McDonald's Restaurants
http://www.mcdonalds.com

Meeting News
http://www.meetingnews.com

Meeting Professionals International
http://www.mpiweb.org

Meetings and Conventions
http://www.mcmag.com

National Association of RV Parks and
  Campgrounds
http://www.arvc.org

National Restaurant Association
http://www.restaurant.org

Professional Association of Innkeepers
  International
http://www.paii.org

Professional Convention Management Association
http://www.pcma.org

Radisson Hotels and Resorts
http://www.radisson.com

Resort Condominiums International, Inc.
http://www.rci.com

Smith Travel Research
http://www.str-online.com

Starwood Hotels and Resorts Worldwide
http://www.starwoodhotels.com

Internet Exercises

Activity 1
Site Name: The National Restaurant Association (NRA)
URL: http://www.restaurant.org
Background Information: The NRA provides information on consumer studies, trends in restaurants, and press releases that identify trends and issues confronting the industry.

Exercises
1. Choose a state or region in the United States and describe the potential for growth in the restaurant industry for that state/region.
2. What impact do you think travel has on the growth of the restaurant industry in the state/region selected? Why?

Activity 2
Site Name: Directory of Hotel and Restaurant Homepages
URL: http://www.wku.edu/~hrtm/hotlrest.htm
Background Information: This is a directory of the major hotel and restaurant chains with a link to their home pages.

Exercise
1. Choose a hotel chain and determine their projected growth rate. How does this compare with the growth figures identified in the textbook?

QUESTIONS FOR REVIEW AND DISCUSSION

1. Why are the world's lodging businesses growing at the rate of 2.5 percent per year?
2. Identify the reasons why Las Vegas has a high hotel occupancy.
3. Explain the current trend in the United States for slow expansion in the construction of new lodging places.
4. How successful do you think future tourism will be in the countries of Eastern Europe and the former Soviet Union?
5. What reasons have brought about the concentration of lodging businesses in Europe and North America?
6. Why have chain and brand-identification hotels and motels continued to expand worldwide versus independent properties?
7. Define franchising. What are the trends and benefits of such groupings? Give examples.
8. List services provided to its members by the American Hotel and Lodging Association. Are state hotel and motel associations affiliated?
9. Similarly, what services do members obtain from the National Restaurant Association?
10. Are profit percentages on sales higher in fast-food places than in table-service types? If so, why?
11. Explain timesharing. Describe its advantages over owning one's own resort property.
12. What factors influence attendance at meetings and conventions?
13. Would you be interested in a career as a professional meeting planner? If so, where would you find out more about this field?

CASE PROBLEMS

1. You are the food and beverage manager of a resort hotel located in an interesting historical destination similar to Colonial Williamsburg, Virginia. Recently, you decided that all the guest servers in the dining room should wear authentic costumes typical of those when the area was at its peak as an early trading center. Some of the staff object to this plan, saying that it is a silly idea and also that the costumes look like they might be uncomfortable. What would your reaction be?

2. Angelo V. and his son Leonard are co-owners of a fine-quality 150-seat table-service restaurant. Leonard has been gradually acquiring more authority and responsibility for management. However, recently he and his father have had some sharp disagreements relating to becoming members of their state's restaurant association and the National Restaurant Association. Angelo feels that membership would be a waste of money. If you were Leonard, what would your arguments in favor be?

SELECTED REFERENCES

Angelo, Rocco M., and Andrew N. Vladimir. *Hospitality Today: An Introduction,* 5th ed. Orlando, FL: Educational Institute of the American Hotel and Lodging Association, 2004.

Brown, James R., and Chekitan S. Dev. "The Franchisor-Franchisee Relationship: A Key to Franchise Performance." *Cornell Hotel and Restaurant Administration Quarterly,* Vol. 38, No. 6, pp. 30–38, December 1997.

Callan, Roger J. "Attributional Analysis of Customers' Hotel Selection Criteria by U.K. Grading Scheme Categories." *Journal of Travel Research,* Vol. 36, No. 3, pp. 20–34, Winter 1998.

Crouch, Geoffrey I., and J. R. Brent Ritchie. "Convention Site Selection Research: A Review, Conceptual Model, and Propositional Framework." *Journal of Convention and Exhibition Management,* Vol. 1, No. 1, pp. 49–69, 1998.

Dwyer, Larry, and Peter Forsyth. "Impacts and Benefits of MICE Tourism: A Framework for Analysis." *Tourism Economics,* Vol. 3, No. 1, pp. 21–38, March 1997.

Emerick, Robert E., and Carol A. Emerick. "Profiling American Bed and Breakfast Accommodations." *Journal of Travel Research,* Vol. 32, No. 4, pp. 20–25, Spring 1994.

Getz, Donald, Don Anderson, and Lorn Sheehan. "Roles, Issues, and Strategies for Convention and Visitors' Bureaux in Destination Planning and Product Development: A Survey of Canadian Bureaux." *Tourism Management,* Vol. 19, No. 4, pp. 331–340, August 1998.

Gustin, Mary Elizabeth, and Pamela A. Weaver. "Are Hotels Prepared for the Environmental Consumer?" *Hospitality Research Journal,* Vol. 20, No. 2, pp. 1–14, 1996.

Kasavana, Michael L., and John J. Cahill. *Managing Technology in the Hospitality Industry,* 4th ed. Lansing, MI: Educational Institute of the American Hotel and Lodging Association, 2003.

Katz, Jeff B. *Restaurant Planning, Design, and Construction.* New York: Wiley, 1997.

Kaufman, Tammie J., Pamela A. Weaver, and Julia Poynter. "Success Attributes of B&B Operators." *Cornell Hotel and Restaurant Administration Quarterly,* Vol. 37, No. 4, pp. 29–33, August 1996.

Lattin, Gerald W. *The Lodging and Food Service Industry,* 5th ed. Lansing, MI: Educational Institute of the American Hotel and Lodging Association, 2002.

Lawton, Laura J., David Weaver, and Bill Faulkner. "Customer Satisfaction in the Australian Timeshare Industry." *Journal of Travel Research,* Vol. 37, No. 1, pp. 30–38, August 1998.

Meetings and Conventions. *2004 Meetings Market Report.* Secaucus, NJ: M&C, August 2004.

Manickas, Peter A., and Linda J. Shea. "Hotel Complaint Behavior and Resolution: A Content Analysis." *Journal of Travel Research,* Vol. 36, No. 2, pp. 68–73, Fall 1997.

O'Connor, Peter, and A. J. Frew. "An Evaluation Methodology for Hotel Electronic Channels of Distribution." *International Journal of Hospitality Management,* Vol. 23, No. 2, pp. 179–199, June 2004.

Olsen, Michael, Eliza Ching-Yick Tse, and Joseph West. *Strategic Management in the Hospitality Industry,* 2d ed. New York: Wiley, 1998.

PricewaterhouseCoopers. *Economic Impact of the Timeshare Industry on the U.S. Economy.* Washington, DC: ARDA International Foundation, 2004.

Ragatz Associates. *Resort Timesharing in the United States.* Carmel, IN: RCI, 2003.

Ragatz Associates. *Resort Timesharing Worldwide.* Carmel, IN: RCI, 2003.

Scanlon, Nancy Loman. *Quality Restaurant Service Guaranteed.* New York: Wiley, 1998.

Travel Industry Association of America. *Business & Convention Travelers.* Washington, DC: TIA, 2004.

Travel Industry Association of America. *The Domestic Hotel/Motel Traveler.* Washington, DC: TIA, 2000.

World Tourism Organization. *Timeshare: The New Force in Tourism.* Madrid: WTO, 1996.

ORGANIZATIONS IN THE DISTRIBUTION PROCESS

CHAPTER 7

Learning Objectives

- Become familiar with tourism distribution system organizations and their functions.

- Understand the role of travel agents and their dominance in the distribution system.

- Consider the growing impact of the Internet on the distribution system.

- Examine the role of the tour wholesaler.

- Recognize that travel suppliers can use a combination of all channels of distribution.

The Internet has made it easier for travel planning. Sites such as Expedia, Travelocity, and Orbitz have made it easy to compare costs for flights, hotels, and car rentals. © Ryan McVay/PhotoDisc.

INTRODUCTION

The tourism **channel of distribution** is an operating structure, system, or linkage of various combinations of organizations through which a producer of travel products describes, sells, or confirms travel arrangements to the buyer. For example, it would be impractical for a cruise line to have a sales office in every market city of five thousand or more people. The most efficient method is to market through over 20,000 retail travel agencies in the United States and pay them a commission for every cruise sold. The cruises could also be sold through such intermediaries as tour wholesalers (who would include a cruise in a package vacation), through corporate travel offices, via the Internet, or by an association such as an automobile club. Thus, the cruise line uses a combination of distribution channel organizations to sell cruises. Figure 7.1 extracts the operating sectors from Figure 1.2 and shows that travel trade is one of the important sectors of the tourism industry.

Tourism distribution channels are similar to those of other basic industries such as agriculture or manufacturing (see Figure 7.2). Their products flow to the

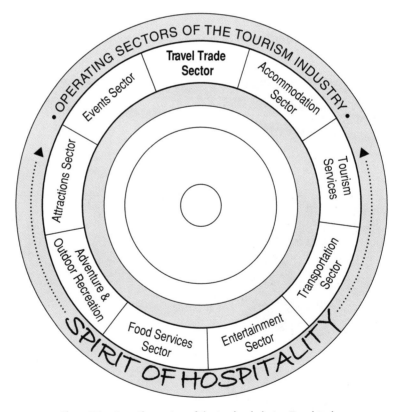

Figure 7.1 Operating sectors of the tourism industry: Travel trade.

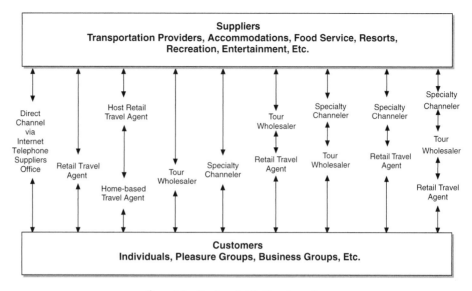

Figure 7.2 Tourism distribution channels.

ultimate consumer through wholesalers, distributors, and middlemen. While there are similarities with other industries, the tourism distribution system is unique. Tourism produces mainly services that are intangible. There is no physical product that can be held in inventory to flow from one sales intermediary to another. Instead, the "product" is, for example, a hotel room that is available on a certain day, which is very temporal. If the room is not sold, that revenue is lost forever.

The travel industry landscape is contantly changing and nowhere is this more true than in travel distribution. Powered by advances in technology and the growth of e-commerce, travel distribution has changed dramatically. The impact on travel agents and consumers brought about by the Internet and airline commission cuts are examined in this chapter.

TRAVEL AGENTS

Travel, whether for business or pleasure, requires arrangements. The traveler usually faces a variety of choices regarding transportation and accommodations; and if the trip is for pleasure, there are a variety of choices regarding destinations, attractions, and activities. The traveler may gather information on prices, value, schedules, characteristics of the destination, and available activities directly, investing a considerable amount of time on the Internet, or possibly money on long-distance telephone calls, to complete the trip arrangements. Alternatively, the traveler may use the services of a travel agency, obtaining all these arrangements for a fee.

What Is a Travel Agent?

A **travel agency** is a middleman—a business or person selling the travel industry's individual parts or a combination of the parts to the consumer. In marketing terms a travel agent is an agent middleman, acting on behalf of the client, making arrangements with suppliers of travel (airlines, hotels, tour operators), and receiving a commission from the suppliers and/or a fee from the client.

In legal terms, a travel agency is an agent of the principal—specifically, transportation companies. The agency operates as a legally appointed agent, representing the principal in a certain geographic area. The agency functions as a broker (bringing buyer and seller together) for the other suppliers, such as hotels, car rentals, ground operators, and tour companies.

A travel agent is thus an expert, knowledgeable in schedules, routing, lodging, currency, prices, regulations, destinations, and all other aspects of travel and travel opportunities. In short, the travel agent is a specialist and counselor who saves the client both time and money.

Airlines Reporting Corporation

When talking about travel agents it is necessary to talk about the Airlines Reporting Corporation (ARC) because travel agents are accredited by ARC, endorsed by the

Travel agents work with clients, saving them time and money with a personal touch. Using the latest computer reservation technologies, travel agents are able to access the most up-to-date information. *Photo by the author.*

International Airlines Travel Agency Network (IATAN), or appointed by Cruise Lines International Association (CLIA) to do business.

ARC is the premier provider of financial settlement solutions and data and analytical services for the travel industry. Airlines, travel agencies, corporate travel departments, railroads, and other travel suppliers process more than $60 billion annually through ARC's world-class settlement system, making it the financial backbone of travel distribution. ARC is an airline-owned company. The ARC Web site is **http://www.arccorp.com.**

The Changing World of the Travel Agent

While the travel industry has struggled through tough times in recent years because of September 11, SARS, terrorism, and war, the long-term expectation for all sectors except travel agents is recovery and growth. The travel agent sector reached its peak in numbers in September 1997 with 33,775 ARC-accredited retail agency locations. As of May 2004, there were 21,552 ARC-accredited agency locations. Agents sold $83.5 billion worth of air travel in 2000 (which was a record travel year), but this dropped by 16 percent to $69.9 billion in 2001, another 8 percent to $64.1 billion in 2002, and another 4 percent to $61.8 billion in 2003.

Very tangible factors contributed to this decline. The first was shrinking airline commissions, beginning in 1995 and continuing until 2002, when they were eliminated. A brief review of this scenario follows:

February 1995	Domestic commission cap of $50 roundtrip
September 1997	Domestic commissions cut from 10 percent to 8 percent
November 1998	International commission cap of $100 roundtrip
October 1999	Domestic base commissions cut to 5 percent
August 2001	Domestic commissions reduced from $50 to $20 roundtrip
March 2002	Domestic commissions cut to zero

So, after decades of offering travel agents a standard commission of 10 percent or more, with no cap, many of the larger carriers in the United States stopped paying base commissions to travel agents. These changes in the commission system driven by the airlines altered the distribution system fundamentally. Agents were no longer paid to process transactions, and the airlines lost a huge sales force that was not paid until a sale was made.

To offset the loss of commissions, agents had to develop new sources of income. The most readily available source was service fees. Today, over 96 percent of the travel agencies charge fees compared with 64 percent in 1998. On average, in 2003 ASTA travel agencies charged their customers $26.93 for issuing airline tickets. Service fees ranged from $50 to $200 depending on the service. Agents have also turned to selling nonairline tickets such as cruises and tour packages, and shifted to an emphasis on leisure travel.

Service fees put agents at a price disadvantage because when airlines sell directly to passengers, whether off-line or online, they do not add a separate fee to cover their own distribution costs. Therefore, an airline-direct fare for the same seat for the same journey is lower than a comparable ticket offered by an agent charging a fee. That provides an incentive for the customer to deal directly with the airline, and reduces the agents' share of the distribution pie.

A second major factor is the Internet, which has impacted travel purchase behavior. The Internet has changed the way commerce is conducted. Many businesses use the Internet as a way to bypass product and service intermediaries and deal directly with consumers. The airlines have been a leader in aggressively using e-commerce.

In 1995 low-fare carrier Southwest Airlines was the first to provide customers with schedule and fare information on the Internet. This marked a significant departure for the air industry that had been limited almost exclusively to CRSs (Central Reservation Systems) for the electronic distribution of information. The Internet and e-tickets became a natural combination as airlines added online booking in 1996. At first, airline booking site development was slower than that of the leading online travel agents, Expedia and Travelocity. Soon airlines realized they could reduce distribution costs and have direct contact with consumers. The major carriers built powerful Web sites where passengers could make reservations, review frequent flyer accounts, and check on the status of flights. As a result, airline online bookings increased, as did the depth of information airlines were able to collect on customers. Such information gave the airlines a marketing advantage in creating direct relationships with consumers. The relatively low cost of e-mail marketing enabled the airlines to contact customers more frequently and less expensively than through the mail.

The low-cost carriers in the United States and around the world have been leading the use of the Internet and will continue to do so to keep their distribution costs low. This means major carriers must follow. Southwest Airlines has stated that over 46 percent of its passenger revenue is booked from their Web site and Air Tran estimates over half.

In parallel with airline Web site development, online travel agencies invested large sums to improve their sites and presence. Since 1995 a number of online booking and fare search sites have appeared (and disappeared), disseminating almost unlimited information on any possible destination and thus creating more interest in travel. Consumers searched for information and booked online to make travel the most successful commercial sector on the Internet. Surveys show the public perceives that the lowest airfares are on the Internet. As the Internet's "easier and less expensive" reputation grows, market share will continue to shift away from traditional travel agents. Table 7.1 shows the estimates of PhoCusWright on how they predict shares will shift.

Another important factor is that airlines now attempt to bypass travel agents. As more people have Internet access and are willing to purchase over the Web, airlines have adopted the strategy of selling direct, diverting business away from travel agents and dealing directly with the passenger. This has two advantages: (1) reduced distribution costs, and (2) increased control over passenger information. Sale of travel over their own airline sites has not only reduced CRS booking fees and commission costs, it has also attracted passengers who have previously used

TABLE 7.1   **LEISURE AND UNMANAGED AIR SALES**[a]

	2001	2004
Travel Agents		
Traditional	49.6%	32.1%
Online	12.8	21.5
Airlines		
Web site	18.0	34.7
Call Center	19.6	11.7

[a]Note: Online travel agency sales includes sales by traditional travel agencies. While this figure was minimal in 2001, it could be up to 5% of online travel agency sales in 2005. Airline Web site sales also include sales made by travel agencies on airline Web sites.

Source: PhoCusWright Inc.

travel agents. In addition, the five largest U.S. airlines (American, Continental, Delta, Northwest, and United) launched Orbitz, an online agency to compete with Expedia and Travelocity. Orbitz has proven to be a viable competitor with its sales rising rapidly. In November 2004, Orbitz was sold to Cendant for $1.25 billion.

The Internet has become the distribution channel of choice for the airlines, and they are aggressively pushing sales on their own sites. Traditional travel agents will continue to lose sales to airlines sites and to online agencies.

While the above explains some major reasons why there has been a decrease in the number of travel agents, they have not gone away and are still the major distribution channel for travel. They will maintain that position as long as they continue to deliver valuable service.

The Travel Agent versus the Internet

Consumers now have a choice. They can make their own bookings on the Internet, or they can use the services of the travel agent. The particular situation will determine whether the Internet or the travel agency will provide the better solution.

The Internet can be a powerful tool. It can increase the scope and reach of a consumer's efforts and allow a person to check hundreds of options or research destinations in depth. But to make the Internet work effectively, a person has to understand where to look and what questions to ask, otherwise hours can be wasted surfing the Web and ultimately produce unsatisfactory results. This is where a travel agent can make a world of difference.

Because of the expertise of travel agents, customers may save time and achieve savings that more than cover the cost of service fees. Agents have superior knowledge of the industry and are aware of various alternatives that provide lower fares that the average consumer is unaware of. Agents are more likely to know enough to check alternative airports and departure times. Agents can search the Internet as well as their CRS for low fares, and they typically have specialized Web search tools that make searching more efficient. Perhaps the greatest advantage is that once a booking is made, travel agents continue to manage the customer's travel, serving as an alert system, trouble shooter, and customer advocate when supplier problems occur. The Internet can be a valuable resource, but it cannot replace a human being who will provide personalized service to help a client and offer a number of alternatives.

Dimension of the Travel Agency Business

Data are available on travel agencies from American Society of Travel Agents (ASTA), and highlights of their 2003 travel agency profile are shown below. Another good source of travel agent information is to look at the studies conducted by Harris Interactive for *Travel Weekly,* which started in 1970 and were conducted every two years until 2000. Today, *Travel Weekly* includes travel agent information in their annual *U.S. Travel Industry Survey.*

Top Ten Agencies
Table 7.2 shows the top ten travel agencies by sales volume. All ten recorded over a billion dollars in sales and their total sales volume was $60.5 billion.

Numbers
For years it was easy to track the number of travel agents because the Airlines Reporting Corporation (ARC) provided an accurate count of the travel agent market. However, since travel agencies became less reliant on selling airline tickets, ARC accreditation no longer gives a true picture of market size. The travel agency market is now made up of ARC and non-ARC sellers of travel. As of May 2004, there were 21,552 ARC-accredited agency locations. The number of non-ARC sellers, including home-based agents, has not been quantified, but is in the thousands. According to the Bureau of Labor Statistics (BLS), there were 103,840 travel agents

TABLE 7.2	TOP TEN TRAVEL AGENCIES	
RANK	COMPANY	2003 SALES
1	American Express Travel	$16.0 billion
2	Carlson Wagonlit Travel	12.7 billion
3	Interactivecorp	10.5 billion
4	Worldtravel BTI	4.2 billion
5	TQ3 Navigant	3.9 billion
6	Travelocity	4.0 billion
7	Orbitz	3.4 billion
8	AAA Travel	3.0 billion
9	Cendant Travel Distribution System	1.7 billion
10	Liberty Travel	1.5 billion

Source: Travel Weekly, June 14, 2004.

in 2003. The average ASTA travel agency has been in business for twenty-two years and has been an ASTA member for seventeen years.

Agency Size

The average ASTA agency has 5.7 full-time employees. This is up from 2002, when the average was 4.6. Also 89.8 percent of the agencies employ one or more part-time employees, and 86.9 percent work with at least one independent contractor. On average, agencies work with five independent agents.

Agency Locations

The majority of ASTA agencies are located in storefront offices. Just under 40 percent of survey respondents have main street locations. An additional 22.4 percent are located in strip mall offices. The percentage of agents working out of their homes is up to 9.4 percent from 4.6 percent in 2002. Locations are as follows: main street, 38.9 percent; strip mall, 22.4 percent; office complex, 21.0 percent; home-based, 9.4 percent; high rise, 3.5 percent; and other, 4.7 percent.

The phone continues to be the number one way for agents to conduct business. Agents report they conduct an average of 71.9 percent of total business over the phone. Customers visiting the office account for an average of 19.6 percent of business, and the remaining 8.5 percent is generated by Internet business. There are no major changes compared to 2002.

Business Practices

The vast majority of travel agencies (96.5 percent) now charge service fees because of the airlines move to zero base commissions. Service fees range from $5 to $200, depending on the service. The average charge for an airline ticket is $26.93. Agencies charge the most for trip planning and research. Agencies charge an average of $65 for this service. The average revenue generated by service fees is increasing. Agents reported that around 15 percent of their total revenue is now generated by service fees, compared to 10 percent in 2002.

A stable 84.5 percent of agencies belong to a consortia and/or franchise such as Ensemble Travel, Virtuoso, UNIGLOBE, Cruise One, or Cruise and Travel Stores. Travel agents are increasingly Internet savvy, with 98.3 percent reporting they have Internet access. Since 1995 Internet usage among agents has increased by 310 percent. E-mail has become an indispensable point of communication and is used by 94.7 percent of agents. The number of agencies using Global Distribution Systems (GDS) to make travel reservations remained stable at 93.8 percent. Sabre was the most popular GDS used by agencies. The majority of agencies (81.4 percent) used the Internet to compare online prices to those found in the GDS. ASTA agents book close to 90 percent of all air bookings through the GDS. Agents use the GDS much less frequently for booking cruises and tours. Only 28.3 percent of all cruises are booked through the GDS and 35.8 percent of all tours.

ASTA agencies report that an average of 73.7 percent of total sales are accounted for by leisure products. Corporate sales make up just over one-quarter of total sales. In 2000, the corporate share was 35.5 percent. The majority of trips booked concern travel within the United States. Agencies report that an average of 60.0 percent of total bookings concern domestic trips. The sales mix is the same as in 2002.

A trend is specialization. Agencies are specializing in leisure products and/or destinations. Over 38 percent of agents define their businesses as dedicated to one particular destination or type of travel. The remaining 61.3 percent run all-purpose agencies.

Types of Travel Arrangements Made

Table 7.3 shows travel agency sales by travel sector for selected years and shows the trends away from air travel arrangements. ASTA projected that 2004 air sales would fall to 27.2 percent of sales, while cruise sales would grow to 25.9 percent and tour packages would grow to 29.9 percent. Much smaller proportions of the total sales are attributable to lodging, car rentals, and miscellaneous arrangements; the activities account for 17.1 percent of sales.

Independent and Home-Based Travel Sellers

Many argue there has been a decline in the number of ARC agency locations but not in sellers of travel. Some of the decrease in agents has to do with consolidation with larger agencies buying smaller ones and large agencies merging.

Another large part of the decrease in ARC agents is people going independent and being home-based. Independents are the fastest growing segment of the industry. This is not only a trend in travel distribution, but other fields where it is possible to work from home by going into business for oneself. In the travel industry, technology has turned just about any location such as a home into a sophisticated office from which business can be conducted.

As independents started writing a considerable amount of business, suppliers that were once skeptical of working with independents have become increasingly eager for their business. This once maligned and misunderstood marketing force

TABLE 7.3	**AGENCY SALES BY TRAVEL SECTOR**						
	1996	1997	2000	2001	2002	2003	PROJECTED 2004
Airline	58%	58%	56.1%	54.0%	33.6%	32.1%	27.2%
Cruise	10	16	16.8	16.6	22.1	22.1	25.9
Hotel	5	11	14.7	16.0	8.1	8.5	8.4
Car Rental	5	9	8.1	8.8	5.0	4.7	4.6
Tour Packages	15	—	—	—	27.4	28.5	29.9
Other	6	6	4.3	4.6	3.8	4.1	4.0
	99.0	100.0	100.0	100.0	100.0	100.0	100.0

Source: ASTA.

that was once shunned by suppliers is now the fastest-growing segment of the industry and sought after by agencies and suppliers alike. While no figures are available on the numbers of agents who are either home-based or working in host agencies as independent contractors, organizations that serve them give an indication of growth and importance. The National Association of Commissioned Travel Agents (NACTA), which serves this group, reports their growth is dramatic, going from 1,000 to more than 2,300 members in the past three years. NACTA is the national trade association for independent travel agents, home-based travel agents, cruise-oriented agents, outside sales travel agents, and traditional ARC-appointed travel agencies that provide services and support to such professionals. NACTA is an affiliate of ASTA (American Society of Travel Agents). Visit the NACTA Web site at **http://www.nacta.com.**

Other recognition of the growth of this sector is that on January 19, 2003, *Travel Trade* started publishing *Home-Based Trade* to serve this market. In 2004, several other publishers created publications for this market. In August 2004, Orbitz took advantage of final GDS deregulation to expand its affiliate program and open its arms to home-based agents. The online travel agency has opened its Premier Affiliate Program to travel agents, providing them with a low-cost alternative to access most travel options and unbiased matrix displays. This low-cost booking tool is aimed at smaller home-based travel agents that find participating in a traditional GDS is too expensive.

In 2005, the travel agency industry survives in a form that would have been unrecognizable a decade or two ago. Successful agencies have shown a flexibility and adaptability to compete in a changing world.

The Future of Travel Agents

One of the problems of being an intermediary (wholesaler or retailer) is that someone is always trying to eliminate you. So-called experts have been predicting for years that **intermediaries** would disappear—that with the current level of education, technology, and communication, consumers could conduct business directly with suppliers, and middlemen would gradually disappear because they were no longer needed. The experts have been wrong; intermediaries are doing more business than ever before, while at the same time there has been an increase in direct selling.

Because of the Internet, commission caps, commission cuts, commission eliminations, and the changing world of travel, popular questions being raised today are: Will there be a travel agent in the future? Will travel agents survive the elimination of airline commissions? Will the Internet result in the demise of the travel agent? Ever since the Internet gave consumers the ability to plan and book their own travel, there has been speculation surrounding the viability of the traditional travel agent. Numerous articles have suggested the downfall of the travel agent channel of distribution.

Despite the many predictions that the travel agent would disappear, the species is alive and well and will adapt to the changing marketplace and survive. Travel

Travel agents love sending clients on cruise vacations because they come back as satisfied customers. Cruise vacations have one of the highest satisfaction ratings of all vacation types. *Copyright © Carnival Cruise Lines.*

agents offer a service that is valued by the majority of clients. The travel industry cannot get along without travel agents, and they will continue to save clients time and money far into the future, even with the fees they will be required to charge.

Travel agents are still the leading distributors of travel products and services. Agents (including online) book a majority of all air travel, 25 percent of hotel reservations, 95 percent of all cruise reservations, 40 percent of rental cars, and 90 percent of tour packages. Agents are the best professionals to sort through nearly a hundred thousand daily changes in airfares alone. Yesawich, Pepperdine, Brown & Russell (YPB&R) report in their September 2003 *eNewsletter* that travel agents are alive, well, and booking:

> Much has been written and spoken about the changing role of "off-line" travel agents in our increasingly wired world . . . most of which might lead you to conclude that their days as a viable channel for the distribution of travel services are numbered. Nothing could be further from the truth.

Although there are approximately 8,000 fewer ARC-appointed agency locations today than in 1999, the roughly 23,000 agency locations in business are booking approximately 140% more per year than they did four years ago. As in the lodging, cruise, and car rental businesses, consolidation is a strategy that has been pursued aggressively (and successfully) by a number of agency consortia as a way in which to build market share. And the strong have not only survived . . . they have flourished!

So who uses travel agents? Approximately one out of every three leisure travelers did so during the past twelve months (the figure rises to four out of ten for airline and hotel users).

It is also increasingly clear that agents will morph into sellers of more leisure than business travel services as demand for the latter continues to decline. Furthermore, their product mix will grow to favor more "complex" and "high risk" transactions like bookings for tours, cruises, honeymoons, and all-inclusives as the Internet becomes the preferred choice for "simple" and "low risk" transactions like point-to-point airline tickets or a hotel room for two nights. And, they will continue to be the preferred choice of international travelers because of the complexity associated with planning travel outside of the United States.

Another factor supporting travel agents is that the industry is one of America's relatively few businesses that have used computers for years and know the value of computer technology. John Naisbitt, in his best-selling book, *Megatrends,* said, "High tech requires high touch." In this day and age of the information superhighway, virtual reality, cyberspace, ticketless travel, e-mail, paging devices, and the Internet, it is the professional, knowledgeable travel agent who can provide both high tech and high touch. A knowledgeable travel agent can provide timesaving, cost-saving, pleasure-adding ingredients that cannot be achieved via computer technology.

Travel agents are adapting to new ways of doing business. In spite of the Internet, commission caps, commission cuts, and bypass strategies, agencies are continuing to achieve record travel sales volume. Travel agents are shifting their revenue sources from the airlines toward other suppliers; they are increasing in size; they are charging fees; and they are maintaining profitability in spite of cuts in their principal source of revenue. Travel agents are joining consortiums. They are creating their own Web sites. While the Internet looms as a threat, it also represents an opportunity to reach a much larger audience. Fees are gaining acceptance by both agents and their clients.

The consumer will continue to rely on agents for trip information, planning, and booking because they offer valuable professional services that save time and money. The travel industry's principal sales intermediary will adjust to changing conditions and survive.

Travel Agency Organizations

The American Society of Travel Agents (ASTA) is the largest association of travel and tourism professionals in the world, with over 20,000 members located in over

140 countries. Established in 1931, ASTA continues to serve the best interests of the travel industry and the traveling public. ASTA's purposes are:

- To promote and encourage travel among people of all nations

- To promote the image and encourage the use of professional travel agents worldwide

- To promote and represent the views and interests of travel agents to all levels of government and industry

- To promote professional and ethical conduct in the travel agency industry worldwide

- To serve as an information resource for the industry worldwide

- To promote consumer protection and safety for the traveling public

- To conduct educational programs for members on subjects related to the travel industry

- To encourage environmentally sound tourism worldwide

To be an active ASTA member, a travel agency must be currently accredited with the Airline Reporting Corporation (ARC) or endorsed by the International Airlines Travel Agent Network (IATAN). All ASTA members agree to comply with the Society's Principles of Professional Conduct and Ethics.

ASTA is managed by a board of directors elected by travel agency members. The categories of membership are agency, travel professional, supplier, supplier associate, international company, international company associate, travel school, and future travel professional. The association has both U.S. chapters and international chapters, each with its own elected officers and appointed committees. All officers of ASTA are working travel agents. They are elected every two years by the society's active members. Day-to-day activities are administered by a staff of more than fifty professionals located at ASTA's world headquarters in the Washington, D.C., metropolitan area.

ASTA provides a wide range of services to its members and the travel industry, including educational seminars, the annual World Travel Congress and Trade Show, legislative efforts, publication of an ASTA network magazine and e-newsletter, *Dateline Weekly,* a marketing services program, research and statistics programs, and a scholarship foundation. Visit the ASTA Web site at **http://www.astanet.com.**

A smaller organization of travel agents is the Association of Retail Travel Agents (ARTA). Their membership is 100 percent professional travel agents. The purpose of this organization is similar to that of ASTA, but ARTA does not supply the range of services provided to the members of ASTA. While ARTA addresses many travel agency issues at different levels, its two primary activities are to provide education and training to its members and to lobby on their behalf. Visit their Web site at **http://www.artaonline.com.**

For specialized travel agencies that sell only cruises, there is the National Association of Cruise Oriented Agencies (NACOA). This group provides promo-

Travel agents love to send their clients to relaxing and idyllic settings such as the Abaco Beach Resort and Boat Harbour in Abaco, Bahamas. *Photo courtesy of Abaco Beach Resort and Boat Harbour.*

tional and management assistance to its members. On a global scale, travel agent organizations include the United Federation of Travel Agents' Associations and the World Association of Travel Agencies.

Particularly in the British Commonwealth and in the United States, there are travel agents' organizations whose purpose is to raise business and professional competency and to award certification. In the United States, The Travel Institute, formerly the Institute of Certified Travel Agents (ICTA), provides an educational and certification program leading to the designation CTC (Certified Travel Counselor) and CTA (Certified Travel Associate). The CTC curriculum covers three core areas: business development, contemporary issues, and professional development. CTC candidates are required to complete two core courses and two electives from each area, for a total of twelve CTC courses. The CTA program covers four critical skill areas. The institute has developed thirteen unique destination specialist courses, which cover destinations such as North America, the Caribbean, Western Europe, and the South Pacific. In addition, they have developed the Travel Agent Proficiency Test (TAP).

INTERNET

In today's marketplace it is necessary to talk about the **Internet** as a channel of distribution. It makes direct selling from the supplier to the consumer more possible than ever before. There have always been direct sales in travel from suppliers to consumers via suppliers' offices or the telephone. Telephone sales received a huge boost with the advent of 800 numbers, and at the time, 800 numbers were considered to be state-of-the-art technology. We have witnessed the coming of computers, central reservation systems (CRS), faxes, smart cards, videos, CD-ROMS, and the impact they have had on the travel distribution process. However, the newest technology entrant is attracting more attention and has more potential than any of its predecessors. It's the Internet. As an evolving communications and booking tool, the Internet is delivering on its vast potential because travel is an information-based product. The Internet, that vast network of computer networks around the world, confronts us with a bewildering blizzard of data. The World Wide Web is estimated to have over 144 million users in the United States and millions of pages of information. The Web gives consumers the information and power to plan and book their own travel. The Web also gives travel agents and tour operators the opportunity to have their own sites and greatly expands their reach. The Web gives suppliers (airlines, hotels, rental car companies, cruise lines, attractions, and so on) a direct sales channel that can reduce distribution costs by having the consumer do the booking, thereby eliminating travel agency commissions and computer reservation system fees. The Internet is both an information source and transaction source. Consequently, the Internet is a relatively new marketing medium. It has the advantage that it can be used by virtually everyone in the tourism industry from the largest operator to the smallest. The airline giants and lodging giants have excellent Web sites, as do smaller-scale businesses such as bed and breakfasts, dude ranches, ski areas, tour operators, travel agents, tourism organizations, and even restaurants. These travel suppliers have a new promotional tool to work with and one that promises cost savings.

Electronic Commerce

The term *e-commerce* refers to the selling of goods and services via the Internet. Many studies indicate that travel is being swept into the Web economy. Tourism-related services are now the king of Internet sales. The Travel Industry Association of America (TIA), PhoCusWright, Forrester Research, and Jupiter Research all conduct studies that show online travel sales are increasing and are expected to continue to grow.

Some facts about e-travel consumers from these organizations and other sources follow:

- TIA's study, *Travelers' Use of the Internet,* estimates that travelers' use of the Internet to plan and book their trips remains stable as 63.8 million online travelers used the Internet in 2004 to get information on destinations or check prices or schedules. Of that group, 44.6 million or nearly three-fourths of all online travel planners booked travel using the Internet, up 6 percent from 2003. Airline tickets continued to be the most frequently purchased travel products online, reported by 82 percent of all online travel bookers up from 75 percent in 2003. This was followed closely by accommodations at 67 percent, down 4 percent from 2003. Rental cars were the third most popular travel service or product booked online (40 percent). Online travel bookers spend an average of $2,700 online in a year, up from $2,600 in 2003. The survey also shows that e-mail appears to be an effective means of marketing for travel suppliers. More than 35 million online travelers have signed up with a travel-supplier Web site or an online travel service to receive e-mail offers and promotions.

- Yesawich, Pepperdine, Brown & Russell report that more travelers are planning and booking online. According to their *2004 National Travel Monitor,* 69 percent of business travelers now use the Internet to plan some aspect of travel, up from 55 percent in 2002, and 51 percent now book travel services online, up from 33 percent in 2002. Among active leisure travelers, 63 percent use the Internet to plan some aspect of a vacation trip, up from 53 percent in 2002, and 45 percent book travel services online, up from 32 percent in 2002.

- A PhoCusWright report released in July 2004 reported that online travel revenues will increase by 34 percent to reach $52.8 billion in 2004, compared with $39.4 billion in 2003. This represents a huge increase from 1998, when online travel sales accounted for $3 billion in revenue. The percentage of travel booked on the Internet continues to rise and will comprise one-third of travel bookings by the end of 2006, compared to one-fifth in 2003 and 15 percent in 2002.

- Forrester Research reports that despite numerous economic and business challenges and slightly lower than expected Web adoption in 2003, U.S. online leisure travel is poised to surge forward. In 2004, online travelers will buy $53 billion worth of airline tickets, lodging, rental cars, vacation packages and tours, cruises, and Amtrak tickets on the Web. By 2009, U.S. online leisure travel spending will reach $110.5 billion on the Web.

- Chinese online travel service company, Ctrip.com International, Ltd., reported a sharp increase in revenues throughout 2003, owing to the rising enthusiasm to travel among Chinese people and higher usage of the Internet. Its annual revenues reached US $20.9 million in 2003 for a 73 percent increase.

- Visa EU (the credit card company) reports the travel and tourism sector is driving online sales in Europe, recording sales in 2003 over three times that in 2002.

Creating this growth are suppliers' Web sites and Internet booking services such as Expedia, Travelocity, Orbitz, GetThere.com, Vacation.com, Cheap Tickets, Cruises Only, Priceline, American Express, and Travel Web, which are full-service megasites. While most airlines have sophisticated Web sites for their own schedules and fares, these sites rarely show comparison rates. The consumer may find it easier to use services such as Expedia, Travelocity, or Orbitz to find helpful travel information and a comparison of fares and schedules among different airlines.

Small to medium-size firms are using the global reach of the Web. It serves as a great equalizer for small firms because travelers around the globe can seek out a small hotel or B&B just as easily as a five-star property. A small hotel in Amsterdam, unlisted in guidebooks, reported that 80 percent of its U.S. reservations came from the Web.

The easiest prediction of all to make is that Internet technology and growth will continue during the next five years, as will the number of people who buy and sell on the Internet. While the future appears bright for this new distribution channel, one needs to remember it has limitations.

Limitations

Despite its great potential, the Internet has limitations. While it is high tech, it is not high touch. It produces an overwhelming amount of information—in many cases, more than the consumer can digest. It is a challenge to get the user's attention long enough to deliver your message. A key to Web success is keeping information current, which is a formidable task. Nothing is worse than seeing outdated information on the Web. Speed and ease of use still need to be improved. Pop-up ads are also annoying. Consumers have two major concerns about the Web. One is their right to privacy, and the other is the security of the site. Consumers question if it is safe to use their credit cards on the Internet even though it is probably much more secure than other places they are used. Travel distribution uses technology, but travel is not about technology. Travel is a complex service industry where the customer requires value. In the final analysis, consumer value will prevail over technology.

Beyond the Internet

In the ever-changing technological environment, it is essential that all components of the tourism industry, whether large or small, public or private, have the best intelligence on which to base decisions. One of the ways to do that is to tap the Internet as an information source. The day will come when a large segment of the market will communicate and transact business on the Internet as routinely as we talk on the phone today.

Another way is to think beyond the Internet. How soon will the Internet be old technology? How soon will consumers be able to book travel from all sorts of devices, such as their television set or an appliance we don't know about yet in a networked home? Voice-recognition systems are improving, and the price of hardware and software required to support them is declining. How soon will they become a part of the automated system? The smart agent or digital robot is a computer application that can complete specific tasks without human intervention. Will this application become commonplace?

CONSOLIDATORS

Consolidators are travel agencies that sell airline tickets at sizeable discounts. They specialize in this area and have contracts with one or more airlines to distribute discount tickets. Airlines work with consolidators to help fill what would otherwise be empty seats.

Some consolidators act strictly as wholesalers, selling their tickets only through other travel agencies. Others also sell directly to the public, usually at higher than wholesale prices. Thus, they function as both a wholesaler and a retailer.

Discount agencies sell consolidator tickets or other discounted travel services to the public. Some act as their own consolidators, while others buy from wholesale consolidators. It is now relatively easy to find a discounter that sells consolidator tickets. Consumer travel publications list consolidators, and consumers can also buy consolidator tickets from most full-service travel agencies.

THE TOUR WHOLESALER

The **tour wholesaler** (also called tour operator) puts together a tour and all of its components and sells the tour through his or her own company, through retail outlets, and/or through approved retail travel agencies. Wholesalers can offer vacation packages to the traveling public at prices lower than an individual traveler can arrange because wholesalers can buy services such as transportation, hotel rooms, sightseeing services, airport transfers, and meals in large quantities at discounted prices.

Tour wholesaling became an important segment of the U.S. travel industry after World War II. It has expanded substantially since the 1960s, largely because air carriers wanted to fill the increasing numbers of aircraft seats. The tour wholesale business consists primarily of planning, preparing, and marketing a vacation tour, including making reservations and consolidating transportation and ground services into a tour assembled for a departure date to a specific destination. Tours are then sold to the public through retail outlets such as travel agents and airline ticket offices.

The number of independent tour operators has grown dramatically over the past decade and now numbers over two thousand. A large portion of the business, however, is concentrated in the hands of a small number of large operators.

Independent tour wholesalers provide significant revenue to transportation and ground service suppliers. They also provide the retailer and the public with a wide selection of tours to a large number of destinations at varying costs, for varying durations, and in various seasons. Furthermore, they supply advance notice and increased assurance of future passenger volumes to suppliers.

The independent tour wholesaler's business is characterized by relative ease of entry, high velocity of cash flow, low return on sales, and the potential for high return on equity because the investment necessary to start such a business is small.

Motorcoach tours, both one-day and multiday, are a significant component of the tour operator's business.
Photo courtesy of Globus & Cosmos.

Tour wholesaling businesses are usually one of four kinds: (1) the independent tour wholesaler, (2) the airline working in close cooperation with a tour wholesaling business, (3) the retail travel agent who packages tours for its clients, and (4) the operator of motorcoach tours. These four entities, along with incentive travel companies and travel clubs, comprise the industry.

Figure 7.3 illustrates the position of the tour wholesaler in the basic structure of the travel industry. The public or the consumer is the driving force and can purchase travel services from a retail travel agent or directly from the suppliers of travel services: the airlines, hotels, and other providers of destination services. The tour wholesaler's role is that of consolidating the services of airlines and other carriers with the ground services needed into one package, which can be sold through travel agents to the consuming public.

Tour operators have not been immune to the effects of online packaging and have been working to keep pace with this new distribution channel. The National Tour Association (NTA) *2003 Member Needs Survey* reports that 81 percent of NTA tour operators surveyed have a Web site, with 31 percent stating some level of online booking capability. Additionally, 9 percent of NTA tour operators currently have some partnership with an Internet travel company.

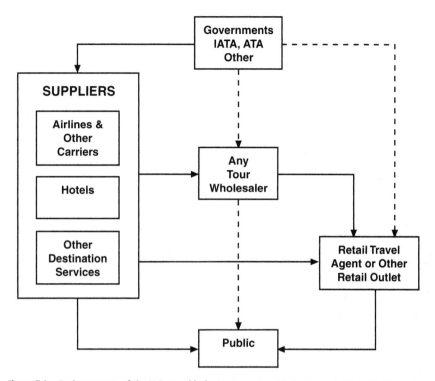

Figure 7.3   Basic structure of the U.S. travel industry. *Source: Tour Wholesaler Industry Study, Touche, Ross & Co.*

While the number of tour operator/Internet company partnerships is relatively low, it is meaningful for the packaged travel industry. As the Internet first emerged, its greatest function appeared to be online booking of hotel and air travel. As technology has developed and consumers' demand for value and ease of packaging travel components increased, online travel sites began to make dynamic packaging one of their top goals. The idea of dynamic packaging online is a new concept even among the online companies. The tour operators who have formed partnerships with Internet travel sites are on the cutting edge of this new travel technology.

Tour Wholesaler Organizations

The **National Tour Association** (NTA) is an association for travel professionals who have a keen interest in the packaged travel sector of the industry. Promoting partnering and networking among its members, the association brings together those who package travel with suppliers and destinations who represent the various components of a trip. NTA focuses on the development, promotion, and increased use of tour operator packaged travel. They also serve as a consumer

Touring the mountains of Queenstown, New Zealand, from a jet boat never fails to overwhelm visitors with the majesty of the surroundings and the thrill of coming close to rocks. *Copyright © PhotoDisc, Inc.*

advocate through their code of ethics, stringent membership requirements, and education.

The association provides marketing assistance, educational programs, governmental representation, and communications for its membership, and it annually produces the NTA Convention and Tour and Travel Exchange. This event is one of the largest travel industry gatherings held in North America, offering members the opportunity to conduct intensive business sessions and attend education seminars that increase professionalism in the industry. The association also produces the Tour Operator Spring Meet, which provides members with a second opportunity each year to conduct business and participate in educational programs.

NTA requires its members to adhere to a strict code of ethics that ensures proper business activity between individual members, for the ultimate good of the traveling public. The association acts as the primary advocate for consumers of the group tour product in North America and works to promote consumer awareness of that vacation alternative. NTA provides the traveling public protection through their Consumer Protection Plan. Visit their Web site at **http://www.ntaonline.com.**

The **United States U.S. Tour Operators Association** (USTOA) also represents wholesale tour operators. The goals of USTOA are to ensure consumer protection and education; to inform the travel industry, government agencies, and the public about tour operators' activities and objectives; to maintain a high level of professionalism within the industry; and to facilitate travel on a worldwide basis. USTOA's members must subscribe to the organization's strict code of ethics. Members are required to represent all information pertaining to tours, to maintain a high level of professionalism, and to state clearly all costs and facilities in advertising and promotional materials. Visit their Web site at **http://www.ustoa.com.**

Most tour operators and wholesalers belong to the American Society of Travel Agents. Many also belong to the various promotional groups such as PATA (Pacific Asia Travel Association), CTO (Caribbean Tourism Organization), and TIA (Travel Industry Association of America).

Local or short tours are conducted by sightseeing companies, and many of them are organized into American Sightseeing International and Gray Line. These organizations aid sightseeing companies by providing local sightseeing services and competent personnel. Many sightseeing tour companies are also affiliated with the organizations already mentioned.

SPECIALTY CHANNELERS

Specialty intermediaries include such organizations as incentive travel firms, business meeting and convention planners, corporate travel offices, association executives, hotel representatives, travel consultants, and supplier sales offices. While specialty intermediaries are a small force in distribution compared to travel agencies, they have considerable power to influence when, where, and how people travel. Such groups can represent either buyers or sellers, receiving either a commission or a salary from their employer. Specialty intermediaries are experts in

Tour operators plan and organize all elements of a trip. Viewing wild animals in their natural habitat is the mainstay of African safari tours. *Copyright © PhotoDisc, Inc.*

their particular aspect of travel. As tourism becomes more specialized, these types of channelers will become increasingly important.

Incentive Travel Firms

Incentive travel has been enjoying significant growth because travel rewards are one of the most powerful motivators for increased employee performance. Companies can reward distributors, customers, and their employees. In the United States there are about five hundred travel incentive planning firms selling their professional services of designing, promoting, and accomplishing incentive travel programs for buyers. They have a national trade association, the Society of Incentive Travel Executives (SITE).

Corporate Travel Departments

Just as many corporations have chosen to set up their own meeting planning departments, many also have travel sections. Growth in this area took place when the airline industry was deregulated in the late 1970s. Such in-house offices try to contain travel and entertainment costs by getting the best prices on travel. They typically provide the same services as those of travel agencies serving the corporate market.

Hotel Sales Representative Firms

Some companies specialize in representing hotels, motels, resorts, and destination areas. This type of firm provides an alternative to a property hiring its own sales force and is an economical way to be represented in foreign markets. These firms are also active in the convention and meetings field.

Automated Distribution

Using telephone lines, the satellite ticket printer (STP) enables a travel agency to print tickets electronically in an office of a corporation that the agency serves, thus eliminating the cost of delivering tickets. If this corporation wishes to use a particular agency's expertise, they can do so, regardless of the distance involved. Also, the corporation's travel expenses can be summarized into one periodic account—a beneficial arrangement. Automated ticketing machines (ATMs) are owned by airlines and located in major airports for passenger convenience. The customer inserts a credit card into the machine, which provides flight information, makes a reservation, and prints a ticket and boarding pass.

CHOOSING CHANNELS

Any marketing executive must decide on which combination of distribution channels would be most productive. One of his or her most important tasks is to research and identify distribution possibilities. Then the particular travel product can be integrated into the distributor's operation. Some channels are very evident, such as travel agencies. However, depending on the individual product, additional distributors, such as tour companies, specialty channelers, incentive travel firms, corporate travel departments, hotel sales reps, and associations, can be very sales-effective. Often, associations have huge numbers of members, which make them particularly good avenues for increasing sales.

SUMMARY

Tourism channels of distribution are organizational links in a travel product producer's system of describing, selling, and confirming travel arrangements to the buyer. Such channels are needed because it is impractical for any supplier to own sales outlets in every market city. It is much more feasible and productive to distribute the product through, for example, 22,000 retail travel agencies. There are specialty channelers of many kinds.

The Internet is a new force in the sale of travel today. It will grow in importance in the future and have an impact on the travel distribution system. Travel distribution channels are similar to those used in other industries. But tourism products are intangible. They cannot be stored and sold another time. An airplane seat, if not occupied for a trip, is revenue lost forever.

KEY CONCEPTS

American Society of Travel
  Agents
automated distribution
choosing channels
corporate travel departments
distribution channels

domination of travel agencies
electronic commerce
hotel sales representatives
incentive travel firms
intermediaries
Internet

National Tour Association
retail travel agencies
specialty channelers
tour wholesalers
United States Tour Operators
  Association

Internet Sites

The Internet sites mentioned in this chapter are repeated here for convenience plus some selected additional sites. For more information, visit these sites. Be aware that Internet addresses change frequently, so if a site cannot be accessed, use a search engine. Also use a search engine to locate many additional relevant sites.

Airline Reporting Corporation (ARC)
http://www.arccorp.com

American Society of Travel Agents
http://www.astanet.com

Association of Retail Travel Agents
http://www.artaonline.com

Canadian Institute of Travel Counsellors of Ontario
http://www.citcontario.com

Expedia Travel
http://www.expedia.com

Gray Line Worldwide
http://www.grayline.com

International Association of Internet Tour Operators
http://www.iaito.org

Jupiter Research Center
http://www.jup.com

National Association of Commissioned Travel Agents
http://www.nacta.com

National Association Cruise Oriented Agencies
http://www.nacoaonline.com

National Tour Association
http://www.ntaonline.com

Orbitz
http://www.orbitz.com

Rocky Mountain International
http://www.rmi-realamerica.com

Society of Government Travel Professionals
http://www.government-travel.org

The Travel Institute
http://www.thetravelinstitute.com

Tour Operators Initiative for Sustainable Development
http://www.toinitiative.org

Travel Agents and Tour Operators in Europe
http://www.ectaa.org

Travel Industry Association of America
http://www.tia.org

Travelocity
http://www.travelocity.com

Travel Web
http://www.travelweb.com

Travel Weekly
http://www.travelweekly.com

United Federation of Travel Agents'
Association
http://www.uftaa.org

United States Tour Operators
Association
http://www.ustoa.com

Internet Exercises

Activity 1
Site Name: Expedia Travel
URL: http://www.expedia.com
Background Information: This site features comprehensive destination information, timely and relevant travel news, expert advice, the lowdown on deals, and much more.
Site Name: Travelocity
URL: http://www.travelocity.com
Background Information: Travelocity, powered by the SABRE system, provides reservations capabilities for over 420 airlines, 40,000 hotels, and more than 50 car rental companies.
Site Name: Orbitz
URL: http://www.orbitz.com
Background Information: Orbitz is an online agency owned by Cendant. It is a major competitor to Expedia and Travelocity.

Exercise
1. Describe the features of these three sites and identify their role in the tourism distribution system.

Activity 2
Site Name: National Tour Association
URL: http://www.ntaonline.com
Background Information: The National Tour Association is an association for travel professionals who have a keen interest in the packaged travel sector of the industry. Their mission is to provide unsurpassed value for the global packaged travel industry.

Exercise
1. Go to the site and find the definition of "packaged travel."
2. Find the number and composition of members of the National Tour Association.
3. Outline the membership benefits.

QUESTIONS FOR REVIEW AND DISCUSSION

1. As a producer of travel products, why not just sell your services directly to the consumer?
2. For what reasons do retail travel agencies continue to be an important tourism distribution channel?
3. Give some examples of marketing aids that a supplier might provide to your travel agency.
4. Some counselors are not really good salespersons. As manager of your agency, what skill-building program would you inaugurate?
5. You are marketing director for a cruise line operating truly luxurious ships. These have superb service and cuisine. How would you proceed to identify the most promising distributors?
6. Air travel sales constitute the bulk of a travel agency's business. But auto travel makes up 80 percent of the intercity U.S. market. How could agencies increase their auto travel–related business?
7. As the president of a newly formed tour company, you must now decide if your tours are to be marketed through retail travel agencies or whether you should try to sell them directly to the consumer. Identify the advantages and disadvantages of each alternative. Would it be wise to do both? Discuss.
8. Why should an independently owned and operated travel agency become affiliated with one of the consortia, cooperatives, or franchise groups?
9. What do you see as the future of the travel agent?
10. List the advantages of a tour company becoming a member of USTOA.

11. Similarly, what advantages does a travel agency derive from its membership in ASTA?

12. A fairly large manufacturer of specialty electric products is located in your city. What steps would you take to sell this company on an incentive travel plan?

13. List the names of several prominent hotel rep firms. Explain how they function on behalf of an independently owned resort hotel. Would a Holiday Inn use such a firm? Why or why not?

CASE PROBLEMS

1. Joan S. and her husband are planning a vacation to a destination about which they know very little. They have seen an exciting ad for this area in a travel magazine. They respond to the ad, and subsequently they receive a group of fascinating brochures describing all the attractions, accommodations, shops, climate, and other allures. In the same magazine they saw an ad for an airline that serves this destination, including an 800 telephone number for reservations. Why should they seek the help of a travel agency?

2. A professor recently walked into a travel agency—his first visit there—and asked for a specific cruise brochure. The travel agent rose from her desk, found the promotional piece requested, and handed it to him. The professor thanked her and then asked, "How is the travel business these days?" She replied, "Business and corporate are OK but vacation travel is way off. Very few people are traveling now." She then sat down, looked into her CRS screen, and said, "Have a nice day." Can you believe such a scenario? What should the conversation have been?

3. A prominent national columnist recently advised his readers that they should bypass their local travel agencies and obtain their air tickets and arrange their cruise vacations directly from the suppliers by phone or Internet. This recommen-

dation was intended to save the public money because, he explained, air and ship lines pay commissions to travel agencies whenever a sale is made. What's wrong with such advice?

4. An international tour company partnership is owned by Bill and Jane W. Bill is a rather deliberate, cautious type; Jane tends to be more aggressive and promotional in her day-to-day business relationships. The company's volume of business has declined somewhat during the past two years. Considering the decline, they recently had an extended discussion as to possible steps that might increase tour sales. Jane finally proposed that they should contact some of the largest travel agency cooperatives, also known as co-ops, consortia, franchisers, joint marketing organizations, stockholder licensee groups, and individual and corporate-owned chains. Jane thought that perhaps if their company could become a so-called preferred supplier to one or several of these groups, they would then increase their business considerably. Almost all of their tours are sold through retail travel agencies. Bill listened to this suggestion and then said, "I doubt that this idea would do us any good. The co-op movement is not well established, and a lot of agencies are not members at all." Who's right? Why? Explain your position.

SELECTED REFERENCES

Appelman, Jaco H. *Governance of Global International Tourism Networks: Changing Forms of Co-ordination Between the Travel Agency and Aviation Sector.* Rotterdam: Erasmus University, 2004.

Cahners Travel Group. *Travel Weekly U.S. Travel Agency Survey 2000.* Secaucus, NJ: Cahners, 2001.

Duke, Charles R., and Margaret A. Persia. "Consumer-Defined Dimensions for the Escorted Tour Industry Segment: Expectations, Satisfactions, and Importance." *Journal of Travel and Tourism Marketing,* Vol. 5, No. 1–2, pp. 77–99, 1996.

Evans, Nigel G., and Mike J. Stabler. "A Future for the Package Tour Operator in the 25th Century?" *Tourism Economics,* Vol. 1, No. 3, pp. 245–264, September 1995.

(ABOVE) Hoover Dam near Las Vegas is not only an engineering marvel attracting tourists, but it also provides incredible water recreation, tours, and electrical power generation.
Photo courtesy of Las Vegas News Bureau.

(ABOVE) The Great Wall of China stretches into the horizon, undeterred by the most formidable topographical obstacles.
Copyright © Corbis Digital Stock.

(RIGHT) Whether trekking to the top, greeting the sun at dawn, or saluting its setting with champagne, the traveler leaves moved by the power and culture of the timeless Ayers Rock in Australia.
Copyright © PhotoDisc, Inc.

(**LEFT**) Speechless, travelers can only pay silent tribute to a love that inspired the ageless beauty and splendor of the Taj Mahal. *Copyright © Corbis Digital Stock.*
(**BELOW**) The opportunity to engage in new, exciting activities such as scuba diving is a prime travel motivator. Reef, wreck, and night dives in places such as the Florida Keys provide exhilarating experiences. *Copyright © PhotoDisc, Inc.*
(**BOTTOM**) The majestic beauty of the Iguassu Falls, on the border of Brazil and Argentina, is a travel motivator. *Copyright © Corbis Digital Stock.*

(ABOVE) Tourists are often drawn to the serenity and calm of Japanese temples and gardens.
Copyright © Corbis Digital Stock.
(RIGHT) The Space Needle in Seattle is a popular and unique site for tourists.
Copyright © Corbis Digital Stock.
(BOTTOM) The rugged beauty and haunting mystery of Stonehenge cause visitors to give pause and consider their place as a speck in the hourglass of time.
Copyright © Corbis Digital Stock.

(LEFT) The Tower Bridge in London is a favorite site of visitors.
Copyright © PhotoDisc, Inc.
(BELOW) Beautiful parks like Sioux Falls in South Dakota can encourage people to turn touring into healthy exercise.
Photo by South Dakota Tourism
(BOTTOM) The ancient city of Machu Picchu in Peru inspires respect for the Inca tribe who built the city in the 1400s. *Copyright © PhotoDisc, Inc.*

(ABOVE) Clouds gather around the top of Mount Kilamanjaro, an active volcano in Tanzania. *Copyright © Corbis Digital Stock.*
(RIGHT) The excitement of skiing at high speed is just the adrenaline rush that some vacationers are seeking. *Copyright © Corbis Digital Stock.*

The sunlight bouncing off the towers of the Catherine Palace in Pushkin, Russia, draws the attention of any passer-by. *Copyright © Corbis Digital Stock.*

(RIGHT) The expansive beauty of the Grand Canyon gives tourists an appreciation for the natural world that surrounds them. *Copyright © Corbis Digital Stock.*

(LEFT) Architectural beauty, history, and pop culture intertwine to lure tourists to visit the Arc de Triomphe in Paris in every season. *Copyright © Corbis Digital Stock.*

(RIGHT) A tourist in Madrid can see a bullfight, a sport unique to the region. *Copyright © Corbis Digital Stock.*

Many tourists prefer to experience scenery first hand instead of just viewing it.
Photo by South Dakota Tourism.

The unique experience of standing in a limestone cave
carved out over millions of years amazes tourists in
Wind Cave National Park in South Dakota
Photo by South Dakota Tourism.

Friedheim, Eric. *Travel Agents: From Caravans and Clippers to the Concorde.* New York: Travel Agent Magazine Books, 1992.

Goldsmith, Ronald E., Leisa Reinecke Flynn, and Mark Bonn. "An Empirical Study of Heavy Users of Travel Agencies." *Journal of Travel Research,* Vol. 33, No. 1, pp. 38–43, Summer 1994.

Hope, Christine, Robert Hope, and Lara Tavridou. "The Impact of Information Technology on Distribution Channels." *The Tourist Review,* No. 4, pp. 9–14, 1997.

Laws, Eric. *Managing Packaged Tourism.* Boston: International Thomson Business Press, 1997.

Morrell, Peter S. "Airline Sales and Distribution Channels: The Impact of New Technology." *Tourism Economics,* Vol. 4, No. 1, pp. 5–20, March 1998.

O'Connor, Peter, and A. J. Frew. "An Evaluation Methodology for Hotel Electronic Channels of Distribution." *International Journal of Hospitality Management,* Vol. 23, No. 2, pp. 179–199, June 2004.

Oppermann, Martin. "Service Attributes of Travel Agencies: A Comparative Perspective of Users and Providers." *Journal of Vacation Marketing,* Vol. 4, No. 3, pp. 265–281, 1998.

Rutledge, Joy L., and John F. Hunter. "Relation, by States, between Population and Number of Travel Agencies." *Journal of Travel Research,* Vol. 34, No. 4, pp. 73–76, Spring 1996.

Sheldon, P. J. *Tourism Information Technology.* Oxford, UK: CAB International, 1997.

Sheldon, Pauline, Karl Wöber, and Daniel Fesenmaier, eds. *Information and Communication Technologies in Tourism 2001.* Vienna: Springer-Verlag, 2001.

Travel Industry Association of America. *E-Travel Consumers: How They Plan and Buy Leisure Travel Online.* Washington, DC: TIA, 2001.

Travel Industry Association of America. *Travelers' Use of the Internet.* Washington, DC: TIA, 2004.

Attractions, Entertainment, Recreation, and Other

CHAPTER 8

Learning Objectives

- Examine the attractions sphere.
- Look at the role of theme parks.
- Understand the gaming industry.
- Describe public and commercial recreation facilities.
- Recognize shopping as a travel attraction.

Preserved castles, mansions, and gardens are a popular tourist attraction throughout Europe. Shown here is Egeskov Castle in Funen, Denmark. *Copyright © Corbis Digital Stock.*

INTRODUCTION

One can make the argument that attractions are the reason people travel. If so, attractions are the most important component in the tourism system; and a case could be made that because of their importance in the tourism system, they should be covered in Chapter 1 rather than Chapter 8. There is no doubt that attractions are the main motivators for travel. Without attractions drawing tourists to destinations, there would be little need for all other tourism services such as transportation, lodging, food, distribution, and so on. However, as important as attractions are in motivating the tourist to travel, the attraction frequently receives the smallest portion of the tourist's expenditure. An example is the ski resort that sells only the lift ticket providing uphill transportation. This expenditure is the smallest of the travel experience, with the most expenditures going for air transportation, lodging, and food.

The list of attractions is extensive, and in many cases it is a combination of attractions that brings the tourist to a destination area. The opportunities for sightseeing, shopping, entertainment, gaming, culture, and recreation play an important role in determining the competitiveness of a destination. Figure 8.1 extracts

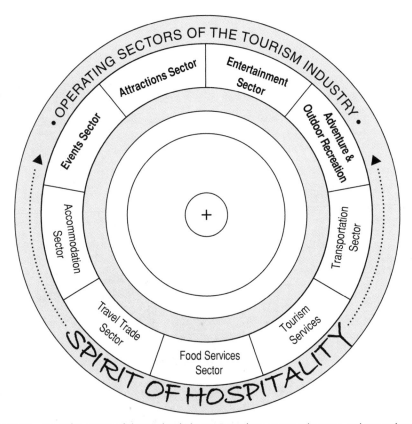

Figure 8.1   Operating sectors of the tourism industry: Attractions, events, adventure, and entertainment.

the operating sectors from Figure 1.2 and shows that attractions, events, adventure and outdoor recreation, entertainment are important supply components.

ATTRACTIONS

Attractions can be classified in a number of ways (see Figure 8.2). One of the categories that first comes to mind is theme or amusement parks. The roots of these attractions go back to medieval Europe, when pleasure gardens were created. These gardens were the forerunner of today's parks, featuring rides, fireworks, dancing, and games. Today, theme parks are high-profile attractions made famous by Disney, Universal Studios, Busch Gardens, and others. They represent multimillion-dollar investments.

Natural attractions are the "mainsprings" that drive many people to travel. The great national parks of the United States and other countries, such as those in Canada, India, Australia, and Japan, are examples. National forests in the United States attract millions of recreationists. State parks exist in many areas that have tourist appeal. The same is true for botanical, zoological, mountain, and seaside

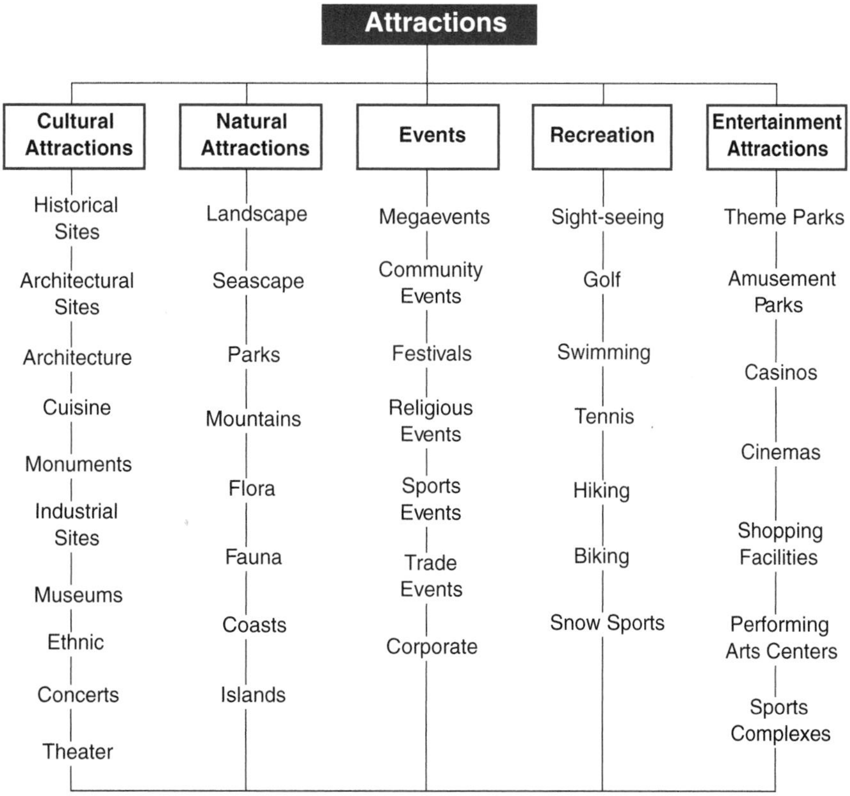

Attractions				
Cultural Attractions	**Natural Attractions**	**Events**	**Recreation**	**Entertainment Attractions**
Historical Sites	Landscape	Megaevents	Sight-seeing	Theme Parks
Architectural Sites	Seascape	Community Events	Golf	Amusement Parks
Architecture	Parks	Festivals	Swimming	Casinos
Cuisine	Mountains	Religious Events	Tennis	
Monuments	Flora	Sports Events	Hiking	Cinemas
Industrial Sites	Fauna	Trade Events	Biking	Shopping Facilities
Museums	Coasts	Corporate	Snow Sports	Performing Arts Centers
Ethnic	Islands			Sports Complexes
Concerts				
Theater				

Figure 8.2 Overview of attractions.

parks. Thus, these natural wonders lure travelers to enjoy the natural beauty, recreation, and inspiration that they provide.

Heritage attractions (such as historic sites) and prehistoric and archaeological sites (such as the ancient monuments of Egypt, Greece, Israel, Turkey, Indonesia, India, Mexico, and Peru) also have appeal for those inspired to learn more about contemporary and long-vanished civilizations.

Recreation attractions maintain and provide access to indoor and outdoor facilities where people can participate in sports and other recreational activities. Examples include swimming pools, bowling alleys, ice skating rinks, golf courses, ski resorts, hiking trails, bicycle paths, and marinas.

Commercial attractions are retail operations dealing in gifts, handcrafted goods, art, and souvenirs that attract tourists. Recent surveys show that shopping is the number-one activity participated in by both domestic and international visitors.

Industrial attractions cannot be overlooked. Wineries and breweries have long been tourist attractions. Factory tours are growing in number, and manufacturers have developed elaborate facilities to handle tourists. An example is the Waterford Crystal Factory in Ireland, which houses a world-class crystal museum.

Great modern cities with their cultural treasures of many sorts provide powerful attractions to millions of visitors each year. Sightseeing tours are provided in most cities, giving easy access to the city's attractions. Theaters, museums, special buildings, zoos, aquariums, cultural events, festivals, shopping, and dining are some of the appeals.

Entertainment has become a powerful magnet. Musical entertainment has put Nashville, Tennessee, and Branson, Missouri, on the map.

The Attractions Industry

The attractions industry consists of fixed-location amusement parks and attractions in the United States and forty other countries. They are primarily private businesses, although there are a number of publicly operated facilities. Amusement parks and attractions in the United States generate approximately $10.3 billion in annual revenues. Over 275,000 people are employed seasonally by the industry in the United States, and over 322 million people visited amusement parks and attractions, according to the International Association of Amusement Parks and Attractions (IAAPA).

The attractions industry is dominated by Disneyland and Walt Disney World, which have been two of the most successful attractions ever developed. However, while theme parks are a major tourist attraction, there are more than ten thousand natural scenic, historic, cultural, and entertainment attractions that appeal to travelers. Attractions include not only theme parks but also the entertainment park, amusement park, animal park, museum, scenic railway, historic village, preserved mansion, scenic cruise, natural wonder, restaurant, music festival, industry exhibit, cave, theater, historic farm, scenic overlook, resort complex, historic site, botanical garden, arboretum, plantation, hall of fame, water show, zoo, sports complex, cultural center, state park, national park, county park, outdoor theater, Native American reservation, and transportation exhibit.

Theme Parks

The **theme park business** has enjoyed spectacular expansion since the opening of Disneyland in 1955 in Anaheim, California. The opening of Disneyland changed the local amusement park business considerably because it expanded the concept of amusement parks from simply rides and carnival barkers to include shows, shops, and restaurants in theme settings with immaculate cleanliness, promising adventure, history, science fiction, and fantasy.

The success of Disneyland brought Walt Disney World, the largest and grandest theme park in the world, with its Magic Kingdom as the focal point of the resort complex. The Magic Kingdom attracts over 14.0 million visitors annually (see Table 8.1). The Orlando site also has a 7500-acre conservation project for the preservation of fauna and wildlife of the Everglades; an experimental prototype community of tomorrow (EPCOT); the Disney World Showcase, where

America's first theme park, Knott's Berry Farm, has 150 acres of rides, live shows, and family adventures, celebrating the lure and lore of the West. Snoopy is part of the magic at Knott's. Camp Snoopy is the official six-acre home of the Peanuts gang. *Photo courtesy of Knott's Berry Farm. Snoopy ®1958 United Features Syndicate, Inc.*

several nations feature exhibits of their country's attractions and culture; Disney-MGM Studios; and Pleasure Island. Their newest attraction is Animal Kingdom.

As in the past, the Walt Disney Company's six theme parks hold down the top five positions in Table 8.1, accounting for a total of 50.5 million visits. Disney's California Adventure ranks eighth and recorded another 5.3 million visits. Table 8.2 shows that Disneyland Paris also leads in European attendance, and shows attendance figures for leading European theme parks. Large theme parks are located around the world. Everland and Lotte World in South Korea draw 8.8 million and 8.5 million, respectively. Yokohama Hakkeijima Sea Paradise and Nagashima Spa Land in Japan attract 5.3 million and 2.4 million annually. Ocean Park in Hong Kong attracts 3.0 million. Tokyo Disneyland draws 13.2 million, and Tokyo Disney Sea draws 12.2 million.

As would be expected, the success of the Disney theme parks brought imitators and large corporations to the business. In addition to those listed in Table 8.1, other prominent theme parks in the United States are Sea World in San Antonio, Texas; Great America, Santa Clara, California; Canada's Wonderland, Toronto, Ontario; Busch Gardens, Williamsburg, Virginia; and Legoland, Carlsbad, California.

TABLE 8.1   **TOP U.S. THEME PARKS**

RANK, 2003	THEME PARK AND LOCATION	ATTENDANCE (IN MILLIONS)
1	**The Magic Kingdom,** *Orlando*	14.0
2	**Disneyland,** *Anaheim, California*	12.7
3	**Epcot,** *Orlando*	8.6
4	**Disney-MGM Studios,** *Orlando*	7.9
5	**Disney's Animal Kingdom,** *Orlando*	7.3
6	**Universal Studios,** *Orlando*	6.9
7	**Islands of Adventure at Universal,** *Orlando*	6.1
8	**Disney's California Adventure,** *Anaheim*	5.3
9	**Sea World,** *Orlando*	5.2
10	**Universal Studios,** *Los Angeles*	4.6

Source: Amusement Business.

TABLE 8.2   **TOP EUROPEAN AMUSEMENT/THEME PARK ADMISSIONS**

RANK, 2003	PARK AND LOCATION	ATTENDANCE (IN MILLIONS)
1	**Disneyland Paris** *Marne la Vallée, France*	10.2
2	**Blackpool Pleasure Beach** *Blackpool, England*	6.2
3	**Europa-Park** *Rust, Germany*	3.3
4	**Tivoli Gardens** *Copenhagen, Denmark*	3.2
5	**De Efteling** *Kaatsheuvel, the Netherlands*	3.2
6	**Universal Mediterranée** *Salou, Spain*	3.0
7	**Gardaland** *Castelnuovo del Garda, Italy*	2.9
8	**Liseberg** *Göteborg, Sweden*	2.7
9	**Bakken** *Klampenborg, Denmark*	2.7
10	**Alton Towers** *Staffordshire, England*	2.5

Source: Amusement Business.

The United States' major theme parks are concentrated in Florida and California. Disney has projects in both states, and the Orlando area has the largest number of theme parks and attractions in any single location. This concentration is likely to continue, because new attractions or expansions are still taking place in the area.

The Travel Industry Association of America (TIA) reports theme and amusement park trips are likely to be family vacations, as they are much more likely than the average trip to include children under age 19 (55 percent versus 24 percent). These trips also include longer overnight stays (5.3 nights) compared to the average U.S. trip (4.1 nights). One-fourth (25 percent) of theme park trips last seven nights or more. In addition, overnight trips including a theme park are more likely than the average U.S. trip to include a stay in a hotel/motel/B&B (67 percent vs. 55 percent) or a condo/timeshare (9 percent vs. 4 percent).

Theme park travelers are more likely than average to fly to their destination (19 percent vs. 16 percent) and rent a car once they arrive (8 percent vs. 5 percent). These travelers also engage in many other activities while on theme park trips. For example, many theme park trips also include shopping (40 percent), visits to historical places or museums (20 percent), and visits to the beach (20 percent).

Theme parks are popular all over the world. New parks and expanded parks are occurring in the United States, Latin America, Europe, Middle East, and Asia.

Sea World of San Antonio permits children to have a close personal encounter with the park's dolphins.
Photo courtesy of the San Antonio Convention & Visitor Bureau (SACVB)/Sea World San Antonio.

For example, Asia is one of the amusement industry's prime markets as home to five of the ten more visited theme parks in the world. They will soon have another park, with Disney opening a new park in Hong Kong. Dubai has announced a £3 billion "Dubailand" theme park. The mixed-use theme park spread over two billion square feet will be located ten minutes from Dubai International Airport and sixty minutes from Abu Dhabi. The development will include 45 main projects and 200 subprojects, creating six zones to form tourist attractions catering mainly to the family market. The main zones will include Adventure World, Sports World, Eco Tourism World, Theme Leisure & Vacation World, Shopping World, and Family World. The park is expected to be open by late 2006.

Theme parks have found that in order to grow attendance and revenue, they have to add new attractions on a regular basis. Some examples of new attractions are Six Flags properties launching Stargate SG 3000, an interactive simulation adventure that made its debut at Space Center Bremen in Germany. Hershey Park opened for the summer of 2004 with a new $12.5 million Storm Runner, a hydraulic roller coaster with corkscrew turns, and technology that takes riders from a stopped position to 72 miles per hour in two seconds. Disney's California Adventure new thrill ride is the Twilight Zone Tower of Terror. IAAPA estimates that more than 100 new park rides were added in 2004.

These are selected examples of the type of improvements that take place each year. The industry is constantly making annual improvements that range from fresh paint to multimillion-dollar rides to entire new parks.

International Association of Amusement Parks and Attractions

The world's largest amusement park and attractions association is the **International Association of Amusement Parks and Attractions (IAAPA).** The association, founded in 1918, has over five thousand members in seventy-two countries. It represents and serves operators of amusement parks, tourist attractions, water parks, miniature golf courses, family entertainment centers, and manufacturers and suppliers of amusement equipment and services. The association conducts research, compiles statistics, and publishes *FunWorld* and an annual *International Directory and Buyer's Guide.* They hold an annual convention and trade show. Located in Alexandria, Virginia, they can be reached at (703) 836-4800 or **http://www.iaapa.org.**

GAMING

The U.S. gaming-entertainment industry has seen tremendous change over the last decade. As recently as 1988, only two states—Nevada and New Jersey—permitted casino gaming, but now, in 2005, with Indian gaming included, twenty-eight states have casino gaming. Today, only two states—Hawaii and Utah—have no legalized gaming whatsoever.

Gambling, or the **gaming industry,** has become a major force in the tourism industry. The gaming industry has grown from a narrow Nevada base with limited ac-

Gaming as a recreational pursuit is becoming more popular, especially in the United States. It is often combined with other types of entertainment such as nightclub shows and sports activities. *Photo courtesy of Carnival Cruise Lines.*

ceptance in the financial and public sector to a recognized growth industry. While gaming has always been a popular form of recreation, it has also been controversial.

There is no question that gaming generates travel. Nevada has been the leader in gambling, which has made tourism the leading industry in the state. Las Vegas is considered the casino capital of the world. It is interesting to note the differences in the types of tourists and their modes of transportation when comparing Las Vegas and Atlantic City. Las Vegas attracts destination visitors from long distances who fly or drive, while Atlantic City is located in a densely populated area and attracts nearby residents (those within 150 miles). Atlantic City has successfully promoted short-duration motorcoach tours to increase its numbers. It is also now successfully promoting itself as a destination area.

Today, according to the American Gaming Association (AGA), the gaming industry is a $68.7 billion business that employs, directly and indirectly, more than one million men and women. This includes all forms of gaming, including casinos, Indian gaming, charitable organizations, the pari-mutuel industry, and lotteries. United States gaming revenue has grown an average of over 11 percent annually between 1992 and 2002, and the casino industry's revenues alone have almost tripled since 1992. In 2002, casinos alone generated upward of $26.5 billion in revenue.

The fact is that people enjoy gaming as an entertainment option in their lives. According to a 2004 AGA survey, over 80 percent of the American people view casino entertainment as acceptable for themselves or others. In 2003, there were 310 million visits made to casinos, up from 297 million in 2002—a 4.4 percent increase. As acceptance has grown, millions of Americans also understand the capital investment, tourism, public revenues, and employment impacts of casino gaming. According to the same survey, 76 percent of Americans see casino gaming as an important part of the community's entertainment and tourism offering.

In 1993, the casino industry reached a milestone when more Americans went to casinos than visited major league baseball parks. Today, more Americans visit casinos than zoos, aquariums, and wildlife parks. This entertainment trend is continuing as more and more people visit casinos.

The employment opportunities provided by the gaming-entertainment industry deserve special attention. In 2003 the commercial casino industry, which included 443 casinos nationwide, created 352,428 direct industry employees, who earned $11.8 billion in salaries, including benefits and tips.

In deciding whether to add casino gaming to a community or to the mix of gaming already in existence, it is important that voters and their elected representatives have the correct information, data, and statistics so that their decision, either pro or con, is an informed one. The National Gambling Impact Study Commission (NGISC), signed into law in August 1996 to conduct a comprehensive study of the social and economic impacts of gaming in the United States, released their report in 1999. The final report concluded the following: "As it has grown, [gambling] has become more than simply an entertainment past-time: the gambling industry has emerged as an economic mainstay in many communities and plays an increasingly prominent role in state and even regional economies."

Indian reservation gaming in the United States became a growth industry in the past decade when the U.S. Supreme Court in 1987 recognized Indian people's right to run gaming: It ruled that states had no authority to regulate gaming on Indian land if such gaming is permitted outside the reservation for any other purpose. Congress established the legal basis for this right when it passed the Indian Gaming Regulatory Act (IGRA) in 1988. In 2004 the National Indian Gaming Commission reported that there were 354 Indian gaming operations and 249 tribe/state compacts in twenty-eight states. More than one-third of the tribes in the United States have gaming operations. Indian gaming is 21 percent of the entire gaming industry. The IGRA mandates that tribal governments, not individuals, can have gaming operations. Thus, the entire proceeds of the industry go back to fund tribal government programs. Indian tribes are using gaming revenues to build houses, schools, roads, and sewer and water systems; to fund the health care and education of their people; and to develop a strong, diverse economic base for the future.

The Mashantucket Pequot Tribal Nation operates the Foxwoods Resort Casino, which is the largest casino in the United States. Foxwoods averages over 55,000 patrons each day and more than 20 million visitors each year. They employ over 13,000 people.

Gaming is available in many parts of the world, as well as on cruise ships. Well-known areas for casino gambling include Monaco, the Caribbean, London, Nice, Macau, and Rio de Janeiro.

As new casinos go up in Las Vegas, Atlantic City, New Orleans, Colorado, the Mississippi River, South Dakota, Indian reservations, and the Bahamas, one sees the impact of gaming on tourism and the local economy. Given the current growth in gaming, it is safe to predict that gaming will continue to play a role in tourism and economic development.

Gaming Organizations

The American Gaming Association (AGA) was formed in June 1995 after President Clinton proposed a 4 percent gross receipts tax on the gaming industry. Realizing that this would have monumental repercussions, casino industry leaders decided that it was time to form an association to represent them on Capitol Hill. Although the bill didn't materialize, the AGA thrived and today has more than one hundred member companies. Since the AGA's opening, when the first 14 members consisted exclusively of casino companies and gaming equipment manufacturers, the diversity of the association's members has expanded to include financial and professional services, suppliers and vendors, state associations, and publications.

The AGA's primary goal is to create a better understanding of gaming entertainment by bringing the facts about the industry to the general public, elected officials, other decision makers, and the media through education and advocacy. An integral part of AGA's mission is the commitment to address "problem" and underage gaming. The AGA is located in Washington, D.C.; phone (202) 637-6500; Web site **http://www.americangaming.org.**

The National Indian Gaming Association (NIGA) operates as a clearinghouse and educational, legislative, and public policy resource for tribes, policy makers, and the public on Indian gaming issues and tribal community development. They have statistics and economic studies on Indian gaming. They are located in Washington, D.C.; phone (202) 546-7711; fax (202) 546-1755; e-mail info@indian gaming.org; Web site **http://www.indiangaming.org.**

RECREATION

Recreation is a diverse industry, representing over $400 billion in expenditures each year. The industry generates millions of jobs in the manufacturing, sales, and service sectors. Nearly 50 percent of Americans describe themselves as "outdoor people." They enjoy a wide variety of activities to keep fit, to add excitement to their lives, to have fun with family and friends, to pursue solitary activities, and to experience nature firsthand.

The draw of recreation opportunities throughout the United States is one factor in the rise of domestic travel, as well as in the increase in international visits to the United States. Outdoor adventure travel is gaining in popularity, and travel professionals have better access to information on recreational travel options than they used to. People are seeking higher-quality services and amenities.

A family camping in Woodford State Park, near Bennington, Vermont. *Photo courtesy of Vermont Department of Tourism and Marketing.*

Illustrative of the range of businesses within the recreation industry are recreation vehicle (RV) manufacturers and dealers, boat manufacturers and dealers, full-line recreation product manufacturers, park concessionaires, campground owners, resorts, enthusiast groups, snowmobile manufacturers, recreation publications, motorcoach operators, bicycling interests, and others.

Companies manufacturing recreation products tend to be large. For example, the manufacturing of new RVs is a $12 billion-per-year industry, according to the Recreation Vehicle Dealers Association.

The **Recreation Vehicle Industry Association** (RVIA), located in Reston, Virginia, is a primary source of shipment statistics, market research, and technical data. The association also supplies campground directories, and publications covering RV maintenance, trip preparation, and safety issues (Web site: **http://www.rvia.org**).

In contrast to the large companies involved in manufacturing RVs, boats, pools, mountain bikes, skis, and so on, the private service sector is made up primarily of small businesses, ranging from campgrounds to marinas to wilderness guides. There is also the public sector, providing services through the National Park Service, Forest Service, and state and local agencies.

Parks

Both private and government enterprises operate various kinds of **parks,** including amusement parks. National parks are often very important parts of a nation's or state's tourism. In some countries (such as certain countries in Africa), national parks are their primary attractions. Typical are Kenya, Rwanda, Uganda, Tanzania, Botswana, and South Africa.

National and State Parks

The U.S. National Park System is one of the country's greatest tourist attractions, appealing to both domestic and international visitors. U.S. National Parks host over 266 million visitors a year. A recreation visit is the entry of one person for any part of a day on lands or waters administered by the **National Park Service (NPS)** for recreation purposes. The NPS administers 388 parks, recreation areas, preserves, battlefields, historical sites, lakeshores, monuments, memorials, seashores, and parkways (see Figure 8.3), which encompass 84.4 million acres. The Blue Ridge Parkway (at 18.3 million visits) continued as the most visited unit of the system, and Great Smoky Mountains National Park continued as the most visited national park (at 9.4 million).

Overnight stays in the concession lodges of the parks totaled 3.5 million, while campgrounds saw over 5.7 million overnight guests in 2003. Another 1.0 million stayed in a concession or campground. Another 1.8 million visitors spent the night in a park backcountry site that they hiked into. Most park visitors stay in facilities in "gateway communities" outside park boundaries or are simply day users.

While the most popular parks continue to experience a crowded peak summer season, the spring and fall are excellent times to visit the well-known areas, and

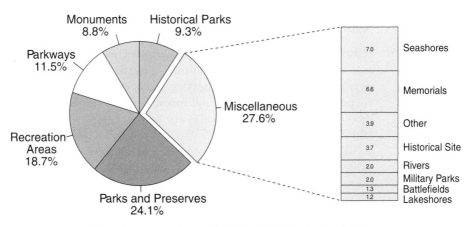

Figure 8.3   Types of areas administered by the National Park Service.

there are a great many units of the National Park System that are still underutilized. See the section entitled "Matching Supply with Demand" in Chapter 12.

Not wishing to limit visitation to the parks but needing to cope with the increasing number of cars attempting to enter the most popular parks in the peak season, the NPS has signed an important technical assistance agreement with the Federal Highway Administration. One of the first actions was to implement mass-transit plans within three major national parks—Yosemite, Grand Canyon, and Zion National Parks.

Visitors to NPS areas have a large economic impact on the surrounding communities, with estimated direct sales in 2003 of $7.6 billion. An additional $3.6 billion was generated indirectly from tourism expenditures, for a total economic impact of $11.2 billion. This spending by NPS visitors helped generate over two hundred and twenty thousand jobs.

The National Park Service publishes information on visits to national park areas in its annual report, *National Park Statistical Abstract*. They also publish biannually *The National Parks Index*, which contains brief descriptions, with acreages, of each area administered by the NPS.

In the United States many individual states operate park systems, some of the most outstanding being in New York, California, Tennessee, Oregon, Indiana, Kentucky, Florida, and Michigan. The National Association of State Park Directors (NASPD) compiles statistics for state parks. There are 5,616 state parks totaling 13 million acres and 3,963 trails encompassing 26,337 miles of trails. In 2001, state parks received 766 million visitors with 91.5 percent being daytime users. The parks employ 20,884 full-time personnel and 56,237 total personnel including part-time and seasonal staff.

Parks are also operated by other units of government, such as county or park districts like the Huron-Clinton Metropolitan Authority of the greater Detroit area in southeastern Michigan. This system has six parks within easy access of residents of the Detroit metropolitan area. Counties, townships, and cities also operate parks and often campgrounds as parts of parks.

National Forests

Visitors typically spend over 340 million recreation visitor days (12 visit-hours by one or more persons) in national forests. Part of the U.S. Department of Agriculture, the U.S. Forest Service maintains 192 million acres in the National Forest System, with 165 national forests and 22 grasslands in 42 states and Puerto Rico. Especially popular activities are hiking, camping, hunting, fishing, canoeing, and skiing.

The U.S. Forest Service reports that its developed recreation sites include 4,300 campgrounds; over 140 swimming areas; 1,496 picnic grounds; 1,222 boating sites; and 135 alpine ski areas. Other tourism assets are 4,418 miles of wild and scenic rivers, 136 scenic byways, 133,000 miles of trails, 277,000 heritage sites, and 403 wilderness areas.

The state of Arkansas contains over 200 scenic hiking trails covering 750 miles. Here, two hikers take in the view from a trail in the Ouachita National Forest. *Photo courtesy of Arkansas Department of Parks and Tourism.*

Other Recreational Lands

The Bureau of Land Management (BLM) oversees more than 264 million acres of public land located primarily in 12 western states. The BLM has nearly 2,400 day-use and 16,698 family camp units on 50,000 acres. It also has 3,179 miles of designated backcountry byways, 62,768 miles of roads suitable for highway vehicles, 90.8 acres open to off-highway vehicles, 54.4 million more acres open to limited off-highway vehicular use, and 19,000 miles of trails for motorized vehicles. The most popular recreational activities on BLM lands are camping and motorized travel.

The Corps of Engineers (COE) is the nation's largest provider of outdoor recreation, operating more than 2,500 recreation areas at 463 projects (mostly lakes) and leasing an additional 1,800 sites to state or local park and recreation authorities or private interests. The COE hosts about 360 million visits a year at its lakes, beaches, and other areas. They estimate that 25 million Americans visit a COE project at least once a year. Supporting visitors to these recreation areas generates 600,000 jobs. Some of the recreation facilities provided on the 11 million acres include 93,000 campsites, 55,000 picnic areas, 3,500 boat launching ramps, 990 swimming areas, and 1,900 miles of hiking trails.

The U.S. Fish and Wildlife Service (FWS) manages over 91 million acres of fish and wildlife habitats and provides recreation opportunities. According to the FWS, participants in hunting, fishing, birdwatching, and other wildlife-related recreation spent $96.9 billion enjoying these activities.

Adventure Travel

Many outdoor recreation activities are sports related and have been classified in the adventure travel area. The National Sporting Goods Association (NSGA) conducts an annual study of sports participation by Americans seven years of age and older. They report that the top outdoor recreation adventure activities were overnight vacation camping (51.4 million participants), bicycle riding (36.3 million), fishing (38.2 million), hiking (25.0 million), hunting with firearms (17.9 million), backpacking/wilderness camping (13.7 million), alpine skiing (6.8 million), off-road mountain biking (8.2 million), waterskiing (5.5 million), hunting with a bow and arrow (5.0 million), sailing (2.6 million), kayaking/rafting (4.7 million), cross-country skiing (1.9 million), and snowboarding (6.3 million).

The NSGA is the world's largest sporting goods trade association, representing more than 22,000 retail outlets and 3,000 product manufacturers, suppliers, and sales agents. They are located at 1601 Feehanville Drive, Suite 300, Mount Prospect, IL 60056; telephone (847) 296-6742; fax (847) 391-9827; e-mail info@nsga.org; Web site: **http://www.nsga.org.**

Another source of outdoor recreation information is the American Recreation Coalition (ARC). They conduct research on a regular basis, organize national conferences, and disseminate information on recreational needs, satisfaction, and initiatives. ARC monitors legislative proposals that influence recreation and works with government agencies. ARC is located at 1225 New York Avenue, N.W., Suite 450, Washington, D.C. 20005; telephone (202) 682-9530; fax (202) 682-9529; Web site: **http://www.funoutdoors.com.**

Winter Sports

Snow and winter sports tourism is an important component of the world tourism industry and is a key element for a better quality of life in many countries. Of the modern winter sports activities, skiing is by far the most popular. In the United States about five hundred ski resorts were operating in the 2003–2004 season. Skier/snowboarder visits are one of the key performance indicators in the U.S. ski industry. On a nationwide basis, the number of visits has been relatively flat for the last two decades, hovering around 54 million. The 2003–2004 season recorded 56.8 million visits for the third-best season on record. The ski industry has performed strongly in the past four seasons, including the record 57.6 million visits in 2002–2003, the second-best 57.3 million visits in the 2000–2001 season, and the relatively strong 54.4 million in the 2001–2002 season, which came despite September 11, economic recession, and poor snow conditions. A skier/snowboarder visit represents one person visiting a ski area for all or any part of a day or night and includes full-day, half-day, and night, and complimentary, adult, child, season, and any other ticket types that gives one the use of an area's facility. Snowboarding has been the growth portion of the ski industry, representing 30.8 percent of the total visits in 2003–2004.

Another trend is the emphasis on the multidimensional aspects of the snow resort experience. Today, ski areas appeal to all on-snow participants whether they are downhill skiers, snowboarders, telemarkers, cross-country skiers, snowshoers, or tubers. Vail Resorts has created Adventure Ridge, which is an example of this trend. This facility, located at the top of Vail Mountain, offers snowshoeing, tubing, ice skating, laser tag, snowmobile tours, and four dining experiences until ten o'clock every night.

Over the years, the U.S. ski industry has grown and evolved just like other industries. Consolidations continue to take place, and ski resorts have developed into major destination resorts. Today, four companies have emerged at the forefront to consolidate ski areas under corporate banners. Large operations have become even larger. The big four are the American Skiing Company, Vail Resorts, Inc., Booth Creek Ski Holdings, Inc., and Intrawest Corporation.

Ownership consolidation will lead to more innovative development and marketing. We will see more emphasis on real estate with core village developments that feature shopping, attractions, conference facilities, and other amenities that create a year-round destination resort. On the marketing scene we will see interchangeable lift tickets, frequent-skier programs, ski discount cards good at multiple resorts, and increased promotion. Increased size increases the opportunity to use media more effectively, especially television.

The National Ski Areas Association (NSAA) is the trade association for ski area owners and operators. It represents 326 alpine resorts that account for more than 90 percent of the skier/snowboarder visits nationwide. Additionally, it has 400 supplier members who provide equipment, goods, and services to the mountain resort industry. For more information visit **http://www.nsaa.org.**

Historic Sites

Historic sites have always been popular attractions for both domestic and international travelers. In 2003 TIA released a report on historic/cultural travelers. Over 81 percent of adults (118 million) who traveled in 2002 were considered historic/cultural travelers. While travelers tend to engage in multiple activities when they travel, 30 percent of the historic/cultural travelers said these activities were the primary motive for the trip.

The National Park Service maintains an estimated 66,757 historic sites, as noted in the National Register of Historic Places. Approximately 15 percent of these properties are historic districts, and about 1,015,434 historic properties are located within the sites.

The National Trust for Historic Preservation provides leadership, education, and advocacy to save America's diverse historic places and revitalize communities. They own and manage twenty historic sites that are open to the public, and they

A much-visited spot is the Mount Rushmore National Memorial in the Black Hills of South Dakota. The famous faces of four U.S. presidents measure 60 feet from forehead to chin and look over a setting of pine, spruce, birch, and aspen. *Photo by South Dakota Tourism.*

offer study tours—namely, the Historic Hotels of America Program and the Heritage Tourism Program—to destinations all over the world. The National Trust is a nonprofit organization chartered by Congress in 1949 and has over 250,000 members. Located in Washington, D.C., it can be reached by phone (202-588-6000) and by Web site **(http://www.nthp.org).**

Zoos, "Jungles," and Aquariums

The menageries and aviaries of China, Egypt, and Rome were famous in ancient times. Today, **zoological parks** and **aquariums** continue to be popular attractions. A recent development in the United States has been the creation of indoor rain forests. Notable are the Lied Jungle in the Henry Doorly Zoo in Omaha, Nebraska, and the RainForest within the Cleveland Metroparks Zoo. The Lied Jungle is the world's largest indoor rain forest, with its $15 million cost financed by the Lied Foundation. It re-creates rain forests as found in Asia, Africa, and South America. The "jungle" occupies 1.5 acres under one roof. It contains 2,000 species of tropical plants and 517 animal species, and it attracts over 1.3 million visitors annually. This has become the biggest tourist attraction in Nebraska.

ENTERTAINMENT

Another powerful tourism magnet is **entertainment.** Live entertainment is often the main attraction for a vacation trip. The Deadheads who followed the Grateful Dead concert tour are a prime example. Another is people traveling to Nashville, Tennessee, to hear country-and-western music at the Grand Ole Opry. Branson, Missouri, has put itself on the map as a music entertainment center and is now challenging Nashville. One of the centerpieces of the famous "I Love New York" advertising campaign was going to a Broadway play or musical. A theater tour to London is a powerful vacation lure. Large numbers of performing arts tours are offered.

Entertainment has risen to a new level in the vacation decision-making process. There is a growing influence of entertainment on vacation travel choices. Today the traveling public wants to have fun, to be entertained, to enjoy fantasy, and to escape from the realities of everyday life. Think about these facts: The top two North American vacation destinations—Walt Disney World and Las Vegas—are built around the appeal of entertainment. The growing cruise market features entertainment. Disney features "edutainment" (combining education and entertainment). The growing influence of entertainment and the marriage of gaming, live entertainment, themed resorts, and theme parks are creating new careers in entertainment management.

The development of super entertainment complexes is a trend in the tourism industry. It's happening not only in Las Vegas and Atlantic City but also in other markets. Las Vegas megaresorts appeal to the family vacation market as well as to gamblers. It is interesting to note that Las Vegas has most of the largest hotels in the world, and the majority are not only hotels but attractions and entertainment centers as well. The Luxor, New York New York, Excalibur, Paris Las Vegas, Bellagio, Mandalay Bay, Venetian, and Treasure Island are all examples of themed resort hotels.

FESTIVALS AND EVENTS

Among the fastest-growing segments of tourism in the world are festivals and events. Countries and cities compete vigorously for megaevents such as the Olympics, World Cup, and World's Fairs. **Festivals** and **events** are pervasive around the globe. Societies are always holding

"Fabulous" entertainment has become standard on cruises. *Photo courtesy of Carnival Cruise Lines.*

Events that re-create a colorful past are a major attraction to visitors from all over the world. Frontier Days in Cheyenne, Wyoming, is but one example of the contributions of Native Americans to the cultural richness of tourism. *Photo courtesy of Cheyenne Frontier Days.*

some kind of an event, whether it is a fair, festival, market, parade, celebration, anniversary, sports event, or a charitable endeavor.

Festivals and events are an important part of the tourism industry. They can serve as a powerful tool to attract tourists during the off-season and to create an image and awareness for an area.

Sponsorships have become an essential ingredient in festivals and events. Most events, whether local, national, or international, would have a difficult time existing without them. Sponsors provide funds or "in-kind" contributions to promoters of events. Sponsorships have become big business today and involve the right to use logos and identify with the event.

Volunteers are one of the key factors in the success of events. The International Festivals and Events Association (IFEA) reports that the average weekend attendance at an event is approximately 222,000. It takes the hard work and support from community volunteers to ensure that a festival or event runs smoothly. With the average weekend event requiring up to two thousand volunteers, most events would not be able to take place without them.

There is a movement toward professional management of events and year-round operation of event offices. Event management is emerging as a field, becoming more professional, and providing a new source of job opportunities. As the number of events has grown by expanding in size and complexity, the number of staff and volunteers has mushroomed. This has given rise to professional associations, books, formal education, and training programs. Classes are offered in event management in a number of tourism programs around the globe. George Washington University in Washington, D.C., offers a certificate program and a sequence in their master's degree program in event management.

Donald Getz, University of Calgary, wrote a book entitled *Festivals, Special Events, and Tourism.* He states that festivals and events appeal to a very broad audience. However, elements of these or specific themes can be effectively targeted to desired tourist market segments. Festivals and events also have the ability to spread tourism geographically and seasonally. Special events allow a region or community to celebrate its uniqueness, promote itself, develop local pride, and enhance its economic well-being.

Events produce sizeable economic and tourism benefits. For example, SunFest, an annual festival in Florida, has a year-round staff of nine and a budget of $3 million. The SunFest generates an economic impact of approximately $21.5 million in the local community. The National Western Stock Show held in Denver each January for twelve days has a permanent staff of about fifty year-round employees who plan, organize, and market the event. During the stock show, this grows to 950 employees. They serve some two thousand animals and six hundred thousand people attending the event. Considering both direct and indirect effects, it is estimated that the event provides a hefty $123 million boost to the Denver economy.

Even small communities can stage such events. Many local festivals originally designed to entertain local residents have grown to attract visitors from many miles away. Smaller communities that do not have convention bureaus and meeting space can turn to event tourism to seek tourism dollars by producing arts and craft shows, historical reenactments, music festivals, film festivals, food festivals, and the like. Consequently, events have shown tremendous growth as small and medium-size towns seek tourism dollars through short-term events. The International Festival and Events Association (IFEA) estimates that every year there are between fifty thousand and sixty thousand half-day to one-day events and five thousand or more festivals of two days or longer.

The IFEA has provided cutting-edge professional development and fund-raising ideas for the special events industry for forty-five years. Through publications, seminars, annual conventions, trade shows, and ongoing networking, IFEA is advancing festivals and events throughout the world. More than 2,700 professionals are currently members. The IFEA is located in Boise, Idaho; telephone (208) 433-0950; fax (208) 433-9812; Web site **http://ifea.com.**

SHOPPING

Shopping is an important part of any tourist's activities. Shopping leads as the number-one activity while traveling for both domestic and international travelers. The Travel Industry Association of America (TIA) reports that shopping continues to be the most popular of common activities for U.S. travelers. In 2000 about

Shopping leads as the number-one activity while traveling. Vacation shopping is one of the features of Old Town in Kissimmee, Florida. *Photo courtesy of Old Town.*

91 million people, or 63 percent of travelers, included shopping as an activity on a trip. The Office of Travel and Tourism Industries in the U.S. Department of Commerce reports that shopping was the top leisure activity participated in by overseas travelers in 2002 as 86.6 percent shopped in the United States as part of their vacation activities.

An example of shopping's importance is the Bayside Marketplace. Launched by the Rouse Company in April 1987, the Bayside Marketplace has become Miami–Dade County's number-one visitor attraction. It has attracted more than 120 million visitors from South Florida and around the world. The Greater Miami Convention and Visitors Bureau has repeatedly identified Bayside as Miami–Dade County's number-one visitor attraction, and *Florida Trend* magazine recently published a report naming Bayside as the fifth-most-visited attraction in the state of Florida.

Bayside has nearly 140 shops offering a variety of merchandise in both the North and South Pavilions and Pier 5 Marketplace. In addition, Hard Rock Cafe and nine additional full-service restaurants offer everything from Italian to Caribbean, Spanish, Nicaraguan, Cuban, and American cuisine. For visitors on the run, the International Food Court offers twenty fast-food eateries. Bayside is also the only entertainment venue in the city offering free concerts every day of the year.

The **Mall of America** in Bloomington, Minnesota, is the largest mall in the United States. It has proven to be a real tourist attraction. Excursion motorcoach tours in Minnesota and nearby states now feature packages with Mall of America as their destination. This mall is particularly attractive to children because it features Lego's gigantic space station, dinosaurs, a medieval castle, and other intricate creations. They can also enjoy Knott's Camp Snoopy and plenty of rides. There are fourteen theaters in the Upper East Side entertainment district, plus a comedy club, sports bars, and a variety of nightclubs. While shopping at the **West Edmonton Mall** in Alberta, Canada, one can view sharks from a submarine, live a Roman fantasy, or soak in a bubble-filled spa near a volcano. This mall is the largest in the world. It even contains a full-scale replica of Columbus's ship *Santa Maria*, roulette wheels, the Ice Palace, and, of course, hundreds of stores, plus some theme parks.

Factory **outlet shopping malls** have become major attractions for U.S. and international travelers. TIA reports that 37 percent of all leisure and business travelers visited a discount outlet mall in 1997. This translates to 55 million discount outlet travelers out of a total of 149 million adult travelers annually. The 55 million includes 25 million men (46 percent) and 29 million women (54 percent). The TIA survey includes trips of 100 miles or more, one way, away from home.

One in ten discount outlet mall travelers (10 percent) cited the outlet shopping experience as the primary reason for their trip. Most (79 percent) said it was a secondary reason, while the rest (11 percent) said it was not a reason. Men and women were the same on this assessment.

Manufacturer's outlets are the fastest-growing segment of retail trade. There are approximately 325 outlet centers scattered over the United States, occupying over 50 million square feet of space. Over 13,000 stores are open in factory outlets. An example of an outlet shopping mall is Sawgrass Mills, the 1.9-million-square-foot complex in Sunrise, Florida. It is the largest outlet mall combining retail and entertainment, and is second only to Walt Disney World as the most popular tourist attraction in the state, according to the Mills Corporation, which developed it. Over 25 million people annually tramp through the mile-long stretch of stores, from Bed Bath & Beyond to the Ann Taylor Loft; about seven million shoppers come from abroad.

To make shopping as convenient as possible, many resorts and hotels provide shops featuring gift items, particularly local handicrafts and artwork. In the shopping areas of each community that caters successfully to tourists, there are high-quality gift and souvenir shops featuring items of particular interest to visitors. The chain hotel and motel companies have also organized gift shops as part of their operations. Airports have virtually become shopping centers.

EDUCATION

Suppliers of the tourism product look to educational organizations as sources of talent for their industries. These include secondary schools, vocational schools, junior or community colleges, four-year colleges and universities, and trade association schools and institutes. Most high schools, which are known by various terms in different countries, offer curricula and subjects of value to travel firms. Examples are native and foreign languages, geography, history, writing, use of computers, secretarial skills, bookkeeping, and food preparation. Many vocational schools produce entry-level employees for travel agencies, tour companies, airlines, accommodations, food service, and others, and junior and community colleges offer education and training in various skills applicable to the travel industry.

Trade associations and professional societies are also active in education. Examples of these are the educational programs and home study courses of the American Society of Travel Agents, the Travel Institute, the Educational Institute of the American Hotel and Lodging Association, the National Restaurant Association Educational Foundation, and, in Great Britain, the Institute of Travel and Tourism. Most public carriers, especially the airlines, provide rigorous training and educational programs for their employees, as well as for those working for travel agencies and tour companies. The International Labour Organization (a U.N. affiliate in Geneva, Switzerland) has conducted numerous types of training programs in tourism-related vocations. Similarly, the World Tourism Organization conducts courses for those in official tourism departments.

Four-year colleges and universities provide instruction in similar skills and management education. In keeping with the diversity of the industry, courses are offered in schools of business, schools of hotel and restaurant administration, colleges of natural resources, commercial recreation departments, sociology departments, geography departments, and anthropology departments. A number of schools offer graduate programs in travel and tourism. In addition to courses and educational programs, universities and colleges conduct a great deal of research, which is available to the industry.

The Council on Hotel, Restaurant, and Institutional Education (CHRIE) lists 550 schools that offer two-year, four-year, and graduate study programs in the United States and abroad. The publication *A Guide to College Programs in Culinary Arts, Hospitality, and Tourism* provides a description of tourism programs and is available from CHRIE or John Wiley & Sons.

Finally, land-grant schools provide services through the Cooperative Extension Service, which operates in all fifty states. Educational services are available to managers of hotels, motels, restaurants, resorts, clubs, marinas, small service businesses, and similar enterprises from some state organizations. Short courses and conferences are sometimes held for managers of these businesses to make them more efficient and productive. These educational services are provided by the land-grant colleges and universities, and the Cooperative Extension Service, which is supported in part by the U.S. Department of Agriculture.

Educational Organizations

The Travel and Tourism Research Association (TTRA) has over 150 educational members. In addition, educators' sessions are held at the annual conference. The National Recreation and Park Association has a section called the Society of Park and Recreation Educators (SPRE). This group works on appropriate curriculum and features programs on education and research. Hotel and restaurant educators formed the Council on Hotel, Restaurant, and Institutional Education (CHRIE), which fosters improved teaching methods and aids in curriculum development for all educational levels, from high schools through four-year colleges and universities. The International Society of Travel and Tourism Educators (ISTTE) holds an annual conference and publishes a newsletter. The society strives to improve tourism teaching. Finally, there is the International Academy for the Study of Tourism, which seeks to improve tourism education and research.

PUBLISHING

Producers of printed news, feature articles, advertising, publicity, and electronic news constitute a very important type of business within tourism. Because the field is so fast-changing, such news and feature articles must be read in order to keep up to date, but also for current information needed for intelligent counseling and management.

Another vital group of publishers includes those that produce reference manuals, tariffs, guides, atlases, timetables, and operational handbooks both online and in hard copies. Without these, no travel organization could function. Counselors and others who contact travelers must be informed as to the nomenclature of their particular part of the business. They must also know rules and regulations, methods of operation, schedules, transit times, accommodations, equipment and service, tariffs, rates, commissions, and other information, such as details of any travel destination. The list of these is long and varies for each country. No single publication could possibly cover the needed information for any particular branch of the industry. References can be grouped as follows:

1. Independently published references for the travel industry, such as the *Official Airline Guide, Hotel and Travel Index, AH&LA Red Book,* and the *Official Steamship Guide*
2. Publications of the national tourism organizations and destination management organizations

3.   Hotel chain or hotel representatives references
4.   Guides published mainly for the public but used in the travel industry, such as Michelin, Fodor's, Rand McNally, and Frommer's
5.   Specialized guides such as *Castle Hotels of Europe*

MARKETING AND PUBLICITY ORGANIZATIONS

Travel marketing consultants provide valuable assistance to any organization needing specialized sales services. A travel marketing consultant organization will provide assistance in planning a publicity and sales campaign, selecting markets, selecting media, providing market research, discovering new markets, and overall conducting of a sales and marketing program.

Most state-level tourism promotion programs are conducted through established advertising agencies. To conduct this program successfully, these agencies must do market analysis of the travel industry, and many of these agencies have developed an expertise in this field. The names of the advertising agencies serving the various state tourism organizations can be obtained by writing to the state organization. A list of the state tourism organizations can be obtained from the Travel Industry Association of America, 1100 New York Avenue, N.W., Washington, D.C. 20005.

MISCELLANEOUS SERVICES

Many other organizations provide essential services to tourism. Examples are hospitals and medical services; police services; sanitary trash pickup and disposal services; laundry services; construction services; retail stores such as department stores, drugstores, and clothing stores; newspapers (including tourist newspapers and special travel editions); travel writers; and magazines.

SUMMARY

The businesses and organizations that provide attractions, recreation, entertainment, shopping, and others comprise major parts of tourism. For example, trips just for entertainment constitute about one-fourth of all travel in the United States. Tourists engage in many activities—a wealth of opportunities.

Theme parks such as Disneyland and Universal Studios also attract millions each year. Most of these are showing a steady rise in patronage. Gaming or gambling is also a growing industry. It has now been legalized in states other than Nevada and New Jersey, and attendance continues to rise. Parks come in all sizes and types. They serve both local and visitor recreational needs. National parks are of particular interest to both domestic and international visitors. National forests are very popular. Zoos, "jungles," and aquariums, usually located in parks, attract locals as well as millions of tourists. A new development is the re-creation of tropical rain forests within zoological parks. An outstanding example is the Lied Jungle in Omaha, Nebraska.

Shopping continues to be a major attraction. Spectacular malls such as the Mall of America in Minnesota and the West Edmonton Mall in Alberta, Canada, have become tourist destinations. They contain an amazing variety of recreational facilities as well as hundreds of shops. Festivals and events are attractions of great and growing importance. Megaevents such as the Olympics are sought-after awards to a city. Local festivals typically attract a wider audience once they become better publicized.

ABOUT THE READING

This fun reading gives a brief history of the amusement park industry and lists some great (and not so great) moments in amusement park history.

READING 8.1

History of Amusement Parks

by Jim Futrell, Historian,
National Amusement Park Historical Association

The roots of the amusement park industry go back to medieval Europe, when pleasure gardens began to spring up on the outskirts of major European cities. These gardens were a forerunner of today's amusement parks, featuring live entertainment, fireworks, dancing, games, and even primitive amusement rides. Pleasure gardens remained extremely popular until the 1700s, when political unrest caused many of these parks to close. However, one of these parks remains: Bakken, north of Copenhagen, opened in 1583 and now enjoys the status of the world's oldest operating amusement park.

In the late 1800s, the growth of the industry shifted to America. Following the American Civil War, increased urbanization gave rise to electric traction (trolley) companies. At that time, utility companies charged the trolley companies a flat fee for the use of their electricity. As a result, the transportation companies looked for a way to stimulate weekend ridership. This resulted in the amusement park. Typically built at the end of a trolley line, amusement parks initially were simple operations consisting of picnic facilities, dance halls, restaurants, games, and a few

amusement rides. These parks were immediately successful and soon opened across America.

The amusement park entered its golden era with the 1893 World's Colombian Exposition in Chicago. This World's Fair introduced the Ferris wheel and the amusement midway to the world. The midway, with its wide array of rides and concessions, was a huge success and dictated amusement park design for the next sixty years. The following year, Captain Paul Boynton borrowed the midway concept and opened the world's first modern amusement park: Paul Boynton's Water Chutes on Chicago's South Side. The success of his Chicago park inspired him to open a similar facility at the fledgling Coney Island resort in New York in 1895. The amusement park industry grew tremendously over the next three decades. The center of the industry was Coney Island in New York. Hundreds of new amusement parks opened around the world, while new innovations provided greater and more intense thrills to the growing crowds. By 1919, in the United States, over 1500 amusement parks were in operation. Unfortunately, this glory did not last.

In 1929, America entered the Depression; and by 1935, only four hundred amusement parks still remained, struggling to survive. The industry was further hurt by World War II, when many parks closed and others refrained from adding new attractions due to the rationing.

With the end of World War II, America and the amusement park industry enjoyed postwar prosperity. Attendance and revenues grew to new records as new parks opened across America. A new concept, the kiddieland, took advantage of the postwar baby boom, introducing a new generation to the joys of the amusement park. Unfortunately, this resurgence was short-lived.

As the 1950s dawned, television, urban decay, desegregation, and suburban growth began to take a heavy toll on the aging, urban amusement park. The industry was again in distress when the public turned elsewhere for entertainment. What was needed was a new concept, and that new concept was Disneyland.

When Disneyland first opened in 1955, many people were skeptical that an amusement park without any of the traditional attractions would succeed. But Disneyland was different. Instead of a midway, Disneyland offered five distinct themed areas, providing guests with the fantasy of travel to different lands and times. Disneyland was an immediate success; as a result, the theme park era was born. Over the next several years, there were many unsuccessful attempts to copy Disneyland's success. It wasn't until 1961, when Six Flags Over Texas opened, that another theme park was successful. Throughout the 1960s and 1970s, theme parks were built in many major cities across America. Unfortunately, while theme parks were opening across the country, many of the grand old traditional amusement parks continued to close in the face of increased competition and urban decay. However, some of the traditional parks were able to thrive during the theme park era because the renewed interest in amusement parks brought people back to their local park. In addition, many older traditional parks were able to borrow ideas from theme parks and introduce new rides and attractions to their longtime patrons.

As the 1980s dawned, the theme park boom began spreading around the world. Meanwhile, theme park growth slowed considerably in the United States because of the escalating costs and a lack of enough markets to support a theme park. During the 1990s, the amusement park remained an international favorite. Many developing nations experienced the joys of the amusement park for the first time, while the older, more established amusement parks continued to search for new and different ways to keep their customers happy.

Founded in 1978, the National Amusement Park Historical Association is an international organization dedicated to promoting the preservation and enjoyment of the amusement and theme park industry—past, present, and future.

Great (and Not So Great) Moments in Amusement Park History

1550–1700: Pleasure gardens begin to appear in Europe. These were the first permanent areas set aside specifically for outdoor entertainment. The attractions included fountains, flower gardens, bowling, games, music, dancing, staged spectacles, and a few primitive amusement rides.

1650: Large ice slides, supported by heavy timbers, become popular as a wintertime diversion in Russia. Small wooden sleds used iron runners to glide down hills in St. Petersburg and were quite elaborate. These simple amusements were the forerunner of today's roller coasters.

1846: The first looping gravity railway is exhibited at Frascati Gardens in Paris, France. The French called the device Chemin du Centrifuge.

1875: With the completion of the first railroad to Coney Island in Brooklyn, New York, it is fast becoming popular as a seaside resort. Coney's most popular attractions were located in pavilions built near the water. The attractions included cabaret entertainment, vaudeville acts, melodramas, fortune-tellers, games, and rides such as small carousels.

1884: LaMarcus A. Thompson introduces his Switchback Gravity Pleasure Railway at Coney Island. This device is recognized as the first true roller coaster in America.

1889: Lina Beecher of New York constructs America's first vertical looping roller coaster in Toledo. It is later relocated to New York's Coney Island.

1893: Chicago's Columbian Exposition introduces the famous George Ferris Giant Wheel. A true wonder of the then-modern world, the Ferris wheel weighed in at over 4 million pounds and was 264 feet high. Also introduced at the Columbian Exposition was the Midway Plaisance (or White City Midway). The ornate building facades and brilliant electric lights dictated amusement park design for the next sixty years.

1894: Chutes Park in Chicago opens. Built by Captain Paul Boynton, Chutes Park was the first amusement park to be enclosed and charge an admission. After relocating in 1896, Chutes Park closed in 1908. The park served as a model for Sea Lion Park at New York's Coney Island.

1895: Captain Paul Boynton's Sea Lion Park opens at Coney Island. Sea Lion Park inspired numerous amusement parks throughout the United States, including the three great Coney Island parks: Luna Park (1903–1947), Dreamland (1904–1911), and Steeplechase (1897–1964).

The Turn of the Twentieth Century: The late 1800s saw the beginning of a brand-new industry, public transportation. Electric traction (trolley) companies began to appear in the urban United States. Electric light and power companies charged the traction companies a flat monthly fee for electricity on which they ran their trolleys. It didn't matter how much or how little the trolleys were used. Naturally, the trolley magnates became frustrated because little need existed to operate trolleys during the weekends, although they still had to pay for the electricity to operate their systems. A solution was to get the general public to ride the trolleys on Saturdays and Sundays, thus creating more revenue for the traction companies. How did they do this? By building an amusement park at the end of the trolley line, hence the term *trolley park,* and a new era began. Soon hundreds of trolley parks were in operation throughout the United States. However, only 12 remain.

1903: Thompson and Dundy's Luna Park, Coney Island, opens on May 16. The electrical "Arabian Nights" style of architecture attracted over forty thousand patrons that first evening. Luna Park burned down in 1947.

1910: By this date, more than two thousand amusement parks are operating throughout the United States.

1912: John Miller patents his design for the underfriction roller coaster. This new method of holding the coaster to the tracks, while reducing drag, would revolutionize the roller coaster, safely allowing for higher, steeper drops and faster speeds.

1915–1920: Many parks close, because of: (1) the public's increased mobility caused by the invention of the automobile, and (2) interest in new attractions such as motion pictures.

1920s: This is the golden age of amusement parks. Many larger cities had as many as six. Competition spawns the Great Wild Ride building boom that lasts until the end of the decade. Many of the best roller coasters of all time are built during this period.

1929–1933: The Stock Market Crash and the Great Depression cause the closing of many more parks. The number of amusement parks in the United States decreases to less than five hundred from over two thousand in 1910.

1940s: Amusement parks offer a diversion from the Second World War. Rationing and scarcity of supplies hamper the wartime growth of amusement parks.

1950s: Baby boomers come of age and a new innovation, kiddielands, begins to spring up, near another postwar phenomenon, the shopping center. Due to rapidly rising property values, the boom in kiddieland building is short-lived.

1955: Disneyland opens. Generally considered the nation's first theme park and built at a cost of $17 million, Disneyland represents the largest investment for building an amusement park made up to that time. In spite of skepticism over such a new concept, the park is an instant success, drawing 3.8 million visitors to its five themed areas during its first season.

1959: The Matterhorn premiers at Disneyland. The first major tubular steel roller coaster, it forever changes the face of roller coaster development.

1961: The first Six Flags park opens in Texas, the first successful regional theme park. In its first full season of operation, 1.3 million visitors pass through the turnstiles.

1963: Arrow Development introduces the Log Flume ride at Six Flags over Texas. The ride quickly becomes the most popular ride at the park, and soon the Log Flume is being built at theme and traditional parks around the world.

Late 1960s to early 1970s: Large inner-city parks begin closing, reflecting changing times. As turmoil increases throughout large cities, parks feel similar pressures.

1970s: Large corporate-backed theme parks begin growing in numbers with such major corporations as Marriott, Penn Central, Anheuser-Busch, Taft Broadcasting, Mattel, and Harcourt Brace Jovanovich investing in theme parks. Many small family-owned traditional parks succumb to competitive pressures and go the way of the mom-and-pop grocery store. Still other traditional parks renovate and expand to compete with the new wave of theme parks. Examples include Kennywood, Pittsburgh, Pennsylvania; Cedar Point, Sandusky, Ohio; Dorney Park, Allentown, Pennsylvania; Geauga Lake, Aurora, Ohio; Lagoon, Farmington, Utah; and Hersheypark, Hershey, Pennsylvania.

1971: Walt Disney World opens on 27,500 acres of central Florida. Disney makes the biggest investment ever for an amusement resort, a whopping $250 million.

1972: Kings Island theme park near Cincinnati, Ohio, opens and is credited with the revival of the classic wooden roller coaster by building the Racer. Wooden coasters, once numbering near two thousand, have now dwindled to less than one hundred.

1981: Canada's Wonderland opens in Toronto, Ontario, and is widely considered to be the last theme park to be constructed in North America for several years. With costs up and all major markets apparently taken, experts considered the American theme park markets saturated.

1982: EPCOT Center opens at Walt Disney World in Florida. Considered a permanent World's Fair, EPCOT is the first theme park to surpass $1 billion in cost.

1983: Disneyland opens in Tokyo. Other corporations in the amusement business are now looking to the Far East and Europe to expand their operations.

1987: Kennywood in Pittsburgh, Pennsylvania and Playland in Rye, New York, are listed on the National Register of Historic Places, the first operating amusement parks to be honored. This is symbolic of the renewed appreciation of the heritage of the amusement park industry.

1988: Sea World San Antonio opens in Texas. The first major theme park to open in North America since 1981, it reinvigorates a slumbering industry. Soon several other new parks are under development, although not at the frenzied pace of the 1970s. Other new parks include:

- Fiesta Texas, San Antonio (1992)
- Knott's Camp Snoopy, Bloomington, Minnesota (1992)
- Bonfante Gardens, Gilroy, California (2001)
- Disney's Animal Kingdom, Walt Disney World, Florida (1998)
- Legoland, Carlsbad, California (1999)
- Universal's Islands of Adventure, Orlando, Florida (1999)
- Jazzland, New Orleans, Louisiana (2000).

1990: Boardwalk and Baseball in Florida closes. Opened in 1974 as Circus World, Boardwalk and Baseball was the first corporate theme park to close. Facing stiff competition from Walt Disney World, Busch Gardens, Cypress Gardens, and Sea World Orlando, the park never made a profit during its existence.

1992: Batman the Ride opens at Six Flags Great America in Gurnee, Illinois. The first inverted roller coaster, in which the cars travel underneath the structure, it is an immediate hit, and soon parks around the world are building them.

1997: Superman the Ride opens at Six Flags Magic Mountain, Valencia, California. This roller coaster breaks previously unthought-of records for height (415 feet tall) and speed (100 miles per hour).

1998: Disney's Animal Kingdom opens on April 22, 1998.

Source: National Amusement Park Historical Association. See their Web site at **http://www.napha.org.**

KEY CONCEPTS

activities
aquariums
attractions
entertainment
events
festivals
gaming or
    gambling

International Association of
    Amusement Parks and
    Attractions
"jungles" (rain forests)
national forests
National Park Service
outlet malls
parks

recreation
Recreation Vehicle Industry
    Association
shopping
theme parks
West Edmonton Mall
zoological parks

Internet Sites

The Internet sites mentioned in this chapter are repeated here for convenience, plus some selected additional sites. For more information, visit these sites. Be aware that Internet addresses change frequently, so if a site cannot be accessed, use a search engine. Also use a search engine to locate many additional relevant sites.

American Gaming Association
http://www.americangaming.org

American Recreation Coalition
http://www.funoutdoors.com

Amusement Business
http://www.amusementbusiness.com

Bureau of Land Management
http://www.blm.gov

Caesars Palace
http://www.caesars.com

Council on Hotel, Restaurant, and Institutional Education
http://www.chrie.org

Foxwoods Resort Casino
http://www.foxwoods.com

Great Outdoor Recreation Pages
http://www.gorp.com

International Association of Amusement Parks and Attractions
http://www.iaapa.org

International Festival and Events Association
http://ifea.com

International Society of Travel and Tourism Educators
http://www.istte.org

International SPA Association
http://www.experienceispa.com

International Special Events Society
http://www.ises.com

Multi-Federal Land Recreation Site
http://www.recreation.gov

National Amusement Park Historical Association
http://www.napha.org

National Indian Gaming Association
http://www.indiangaming.org

National Park Service
http://www.nps.gov

National Ski Areas Association
http://www.nsaa.org

National Sporting Goods Association
http://www.nsga.org

National Trust for Historic Preservation
http://www.nthp.org

Recreation Vehicle Industry Association
http://www.rvia.org

Travel and Tourism Research Association
http://www.ttra.com

U.S. Bureau of Reclamation
http://www.usbr.gov

U.S. Fish and Wildlife Service
http://www.fws.gov

USDA Forest Service—Recreation
http://www.fs.fed.us/recreation

Internet Exercises

Site Name: Walt Disney World
URL: http://disneyworld.disney.go.com
Background Information: Everything you need to plan your Walt Disney World Resort vacation is at this site. You can use this site to make all your Disney arrangements.

Site Name: Guide to Theme Parks
URL: http://themeparks.miningco.com
Background Information: Provides links to theme parks and amusement parks worldwide.

Site Name: Recreation.gov
URL: http://www.recreation.gov
Background Information: Recreation.gov is a one-stop resource for information about recreation on federal lands. The site offers information from all of the federal land management agencies and allows tourists to search for recreation sites by state, by agency, or by recreational activity.

Site Name: National Park Service
URL: http://www.nps.gov
Background Information: On August 25, 1916, President Woodrow Wilson signed the act creating the National Park Service, a new federal bureau in the Department of the Interior. The fundamental purpose of the National Park Service is to conserve the scenery, natural and historic objects, and wildlife in the parks, as well as to provide for the enjoyment of the national parks in such manner as to remain unimpaired for the enjoyment of future generations.

Exercises

1. What role do the above sites play in the tourism industry? How do these sites encourage people to travel?
2. Choose a commercial destination and a government-sponsored destination from the above sites and describe how they differ. To whom would these sites appeal?

QUESTIONS FOR REVIEW AND DISCUSSION

1. Give some of the main reasons that attractions and entertainment places are enjoying growing popularity.
2. How important are these factors as pleasure travel motivators?
3. If you were planning a destination-type resort, how much attention would you give to its recreation and entertainment features?
4. Why have theme parks changed the amusement park business so drastically?
5. Identify the principal appeals of theme parks. Explain their growth trends.
6. What are the directions being taken in the U.S. gambling industry?
7. Is the ownership of recreational vehicles a passing fad?
8. Where are the most famous national parks located? Select various countries.
9. Should the spectacular new shopping malls include a director of tourism?

10. Suppose that your firm was considering building a new theater or attraction in Branson, Missouri. Where would you seek information and data? What kind of data would be needed?

11. List the advantages to local people who sponsor a festival that subsequently becomes attractive to a wider market.

12. Evaluate the national forests as recreational resources.

CASE PROBLEM

Many of the states in the United States are experiencing budget problems. A number of legislatures are considering legalizing gaming (gambling). Some states have already done so. As a state representative, you have decided to introduce legislation legalizing gaming, to bolster your state's budget. What would be your arguments supporting this bill? What opposition would you expect?

SELECTED REFERENCES

Allen, Johnny, William O'Toole, Ian McDonnell, and Rob Harris. *Festival and Special Event Management,* New York: Wiley, 2002.

Braunlich, Carl G. "Lessons from the Atlantic City Casino Experience." *Journal of Travel Research,* Vol. 34, No. 3, pp. 46–56, Winter 1996.

Childress, Rebecca D., and John L. Crompton. "A Comparison of Alternative Direction and Discrepancy Approaches to Measuring Quality of Performance at a Festival." *Journal of Travel Research,* Vol. 36, No. 2, pp. 43–57, Fall 1997.

Choi, Hak. "Gambling in Hong Kong." *Journal of Travel Research,* Vol. 36, No. 2, pp. 23–28, Fall 1997.

Deply, Lisa. "An Overview of Sport Tourism: Building toward a Dimensional Framework." *Journal of Vacation Marketing,* Vol. 4, No. 1, pp. 23–28, January 1998.

Douglas, N., W. Douglas, and R. Derrett (eds). *Special Interest Tourism: Context and Cases.* Brisbane: Wiley, 2001.

Eadington, William R. "The Legalization of Casinos: Policy Objectives, Regulatory Alternatives, and Cost/Benefit Considerations." *Journal of Travel Research,* Vol. 34, No. 3, pp. 3–8, Winter 1996.

Fyall, Alan, Brian Garrod, and Anna Leask. *Managing Visitor Attractions: New Directions.* Oxford, UK: Butterworth Heinemann, 2003.

Getz, Donald. *Event Management and Event Tourism.* New York: Cognizant Communication Corporation, 1997.

Goldblatt, Joe. *The Dictionary of Event Management.* New York: Van Nostrand Reinhold, 1996.

Goldblatt, Joe. *Special Events,* 3d ed. New York: Wiley, 2002.

Grado, Stephen C., Charles H. Strauss, and Bruce E. Lord. "Antiquing as a Tourism Recreational Activity in Southwestern Pennsylvania." *Journal of Travel Research,* Vol. 35, No. 3, pp. 52–56, Winter 1997.

Hall, C. Michael, and Christopher Hamon. "Casinos and Urban Redevelopment in Australia." *Journal of Travel Research,* Vol. 34, No. 3, pp. 30–36, Winter 1996.

Heung, Vincent C. S., and Hailin Qu. "Tourism Shopping and Its Contributions to Hong Kong." *Tourism Management,* Vol. 19, No. 4, pp. 383–386, August 1998.

Hoyle, Leonard H. *Event Marketing.* New York: Wiley, 2002.

International Association of Scientific Experts in Tourism. *Sports and Tourism.* St. Gallen: AIEST, 2003.

Kilby, Jim, and Jim Fox. *Casino Operations Management.* New York: Wiley, 1998.

Lawson, Rob, Juergen Gnoth, and Kerry Paulin. "Tourists' Awareness of Prices for Attractions and Activities." *Journal of Travel Research,* Vol. 34, No. 1, pp. 52–58, Summer 1997.

Long, Patrick, Jo Clark, and Derek Liston. *Win, Lose, or Draw? Gambling with America's Small Towns.* Washington, DC: The Aspen Institute, 1994.

Smeral, Egon. "Economic Aspects of Casino Gaming in Austria." *Journal of Travel Research,* Vol. 36, No. 4, pp. 33–39, Spring 1998.

Stokowski, Patricia A. *Riches and Regrets: Betting on Gambling in Two Colorado Mountain Towns.* Niwot: University Press of Colorado, 1996.

Swarbrooke, John. *The Development and Management of Visitor Attractions,* 2d ed. Boston: Butterworth-Heinemann, 2001.

Tarlow, Peter E. *Event Risk Management and Safety.* New York: Wiley, 2002.

Travel Industry Association of America. *The National Parks Traveler.* Washington, DC: TIA, 2004.

Travel Industry Association of America. *The Historical/Cultural Traveler.* Washington, DC: TIA, 2003.

Travel Industry Association of America. *Domestic Travel Market Report.* Washington, DC: TIA, 2003.

Travel Industry Association of America. *Profile of Travelers Who Attend Sports Events.* Washington, DC: TIA, 2001.

Travel Industry Association of America. *Profile of Travelers Who Participate in Gambling.* Washington, DC: TIA, 2001.

Travel Industry Association of America. *The Shopping Traveler.* Washington, DC: TIA, 2001.

U.S. Bureau of the Census. *Statistical Abstract of the United States: 2004.* Washington, DC: U.S. Government Printing Office, 2004.

Watt, D. *Event Management in Leisure and Tourism.* Essex, UK: Longman, 1998.

PART 3

Understanding Travel Behavior

Travelers passing through an airport concourse. *Copyright © PhotoDisc, Inc.*

MOTIVATION FOR PLEASURE TRAVEL[1]

CHAPTER 9

Learning Objectives

- Adopt a professional approach to motivation and recognize differences in other people's motives.

- Appreciate the range of ideas on travel motivation, including historical accounts and psychological theories.

- Be aware of contemporary research practices in tourism that integrate motive and destination feature assessments.

- Be familiar with conceptual approaches to tourist motivation and recognize that there is continual development and enhancement of ideas in this field.

---

[1]This chapter was prepared by Philip L. Pearce, Tourism Program, James Cook University, Queensland, Australia.

For many, snow means skiing. Recreational pursuits are popular vacation choices. *Copyright © PhotoDisc, Inc.*

INTRODUCTION

To be successful, tourism practitioners must understand consumer motivation. **History** offers a glimpse of behaviors to study. Even the supposedly spiritually motivated medieval pilgrims were sometimes wont to succumb to temptations during the long journey! So, though crusaders' motivations might have been spiritual, they often succumbed to the need to increase immediate gratification. Thus, from ancient times until now, astute operators understand the importance of understanding the psychology of tourism. Such travel **motivation** studies include consumer motivation, decision making, product satisfaction, overall acceptability of holiday experiences, pleasure in the vacation environment, and interaction with the local inhabitants. In short, tourists travel for reasons including spirituality, social status, escape, and cultural enrichment. **Maslow**'s hierarchy of needs provides insight into ways in which a trip may satisfy disparate needs. If these concepts are studied within a context, they can provide information into how visitors select activities and experiences to suit their personal psychological and motivational profiles.

A FOCUS ON CUSTOMERS

Students and analysts of tourist behavior face a particular problem when attempting to assess tourist motivation. Many individuals with an enthusiasm for traveling and holidays are able to articulate their own motivation. The problem lies in then assuming that other people are also motivated by these same forces. This chapter introduces a range of ideas, concepts, and studies on pleasure travel motivation. Readers are encouraged to develop a professional view of motivation, constantly being mindful that other travelers may not be driven by the same social, cultural, and biological needs as themselves.

A professional understanding of the consumer is at the core of the successful business practice in the tourist industry. If the various facets of the tourism, travel, and hospitality world can meet the needs of the consumer, then some chance of business success is possible provided other financial and managerial inputs are appropriate. Thus, if a theme park can meet the needs of its customers, if a wilderness lodge can provide the kind of accommodation its users expect, and if an adventure tour operator can organize an exciting white-water rafting trip, then there is a basis for a successful tourism business. When consumer expectations are met or exceeded by the tourism operations, one can expect repeat business and positive word-of-mouth advertising as well as the ability to maintain or even increase the current level of charging for the existing tourism service. Clearly, consumers matter to tourism businesses.

The general issue of understanding consumer needs falls within the area of the **psychology** of tourists' behavior. This study area is concerned with what motivates tourists, how they make decisions, what tourists think of the products they buy, how much they enjoy and learn during their holiday experiences, how they interact with the local people and environment, and how satisfied they are with their holidays.

Asking the Question

The study of travel motivation is the fundamental starting point in studying the psychology of tourist behavior. The question is often expressed simply as: Why do tourists travel? One of the lessons of social science research is to learn to ask good questions—that is, questions that are stimulating and challenging to our understanding of the world but that can be answered with enough specificity and information to enhance our knowledge. "Why do tourists travel?" is not a good question. Instead we need to ask why certain groups of people choose certain holiday experiences, because this more specific question focuses attention on the similarities among groups of people and the kinds of experiences they seek. It should be noted that we are emphasizing people's desire for certain experiences and we are not assuming that destinations such as Las Vegas or central Africa offer only one kind of opportunity to fulfill travelers' motives. Instead it can be argued that destinations offer many kinds of holiday experiences, and to assume that areas as diverse as resort cities or countries are going to attract just one group of visitors with a certain narrow range of motivations would be simplistic. The title of this chapter is "Motivation for Pleasure Travel," an obvious indication of the focus of attention, but it is worth noting that rich research and practical opportunities exist to develop our understanding of the motivation of business, sports, and other travel groups (Moscardo et al., 2000).

Background

Three main sources of ideas assist in answering questions concerning travel motivation. Historical and literary accounts of travel and travelers provide one such source.

Seeing the rare bald eagle in its native natural environment is a thrill for visitors to national parks and wildlife preserves. *Copyright © PhotoDisc, Inc.*

Additionally, the discipline of psychology and its long history of trying to under-stand and explain human behavior is a rich vein of writing for travel motivation. And finally, the current practices of tourism industry researchers, particularly those involved in surveying visitors, offer some additional insights concerning how we might approach travel motivation.

History and Literature

Historians provide a range of accounts concerning why travelers have set about their journeys over the centuries. Casson (1974) and Wolfe (1967) point out that the wealthier members of Athenian and Roman society owned summer resorts and used to holiday there to avoid the heat of the cities and indulge in a social life char-acterized by much eating and drinking. The stability of the Roman world permit-ted its citizens to interest themselves in some long-distant travel; Anthony (1973) reports that visiting the Egyptian monuments and collecting souvenirs from these sites were well-accepted and socially prestigious practices. If motives such as escape, social interaction, and social comparison were popular in Roman times, then the emergence of the pilgrimage in the Middle Ages can be seen as adding a serious travel motive to our historical perspective. The original pilgrimages were essentially journeys to sacred places undertaken because of religious motives. Travelers sought the assistance or bounty of their god and journeyed long distances to revere the de-ity. Rowling (1971) has noted that later in the Middle Ages, revelry and feasting be-came important accompaniments to the journey and "licentious living" among the pilgrims was not unknown. The legacy of the pilgrimage for understanding mod-ern traveler motivation is not insignificant. The pilgrimage elevated the impor-tance of travel as an activity in one's life and created the idea that certain key sites or attractions were of long-lasting spiritual benefit to the sojourner. Good times and spiritual times were, however, often linked.

The seriousness of travel was further enhanced by the Grand Tour, an activity intended principally as a training ground for the young and wealthy members of the English courts in Tudor times. By the end of the eighteenth century, the Grand Tour had gained favor as an ideal finishing school for a youth's education, a theme consistent with the analysis of much contemporary youth travel (Hibbert, 1969).

The effects of industrialization, urbanization, and improved transportation possibilities brought travel to the middle classes in the mid-nineteenth century, and strong elements of social status and class consciousness characterize the fashions of the railway and spa resorts of nineteenth-century Europe (Swinglehurst, 1974).

One of the first tourism scholars, Pimlott, writing in 1947, noted, "In the pres-ent century holidays have become a cult. . . . For many they are the principal ob-jects for life—saved and planned for during the rest of the year and enjoyed in retrospect when they are over."

Tourism is now, of course, a worldwide phenomenon with enormous differen-tiation in its available environments, host cultures, and types of visitors. Nevertheless, some of the chief motivations noted in this brief historical review—such as travel for escape, cultural curiosity, spirituality, education, and social sta-tus—must be accounted for in any summary of contemporary travel.

Much of the contemporary travel scene is eloquently described by literary figures and professional travel writers. Their accounts of travel motivation, both of themselves and of others, are subjective rather than professional but can also be considered as a background for our understanding. The noted American writer John Steinbeck conceived of travel as an "itch," a disease or pseudomedical condition, "the travel bug," which periodically drove him to "be some place else." Additionally, the theme of traveling to discover oneself has a long literary tradition and is present in the early works of Ovid, Chaucer, Spenser, and Tennyson, as well as in twentieth-century fiction, including works by Kerouac, Forster, Lawrence, Hemingway, and Conrad. The professional travel writers of the last two decades, such as Paul Theroux, Jan Morris, and Eric Newby, have also emphasized discovery and curiosity in their analysis of the motives of travelers.

The rich tapestry of ideas about travel motivation from historical accounts and literary sources can be supplemented by theories of motivation from the discipline of psychology.

The Contribution of Psychological Theory

Psychology, as a separate area of inquiry, is often considered as originating in 1879 with the creation of the first laboratory for the scientific study of behavior by Wilhelm Wundt in Germany. In their own journey studying human behavior, psychology writers and researchers have frequently addressed the topic of human motivation. The scope of this research is impressive, as it embraces both detailed studies of human physiology and the nervous system as well as broad approaches with a more sociological and anthropological orientation.

Many well-known theories in psychology have a strong motivation component. In many instances the discussion or study of motivation is a part of a broader theory directed at understanding human personality or, more simply, what makes individuals different. A summary of some major theories in psychology that have been concerned in part with the topic of motivation is presented in Table 9.1. It must be noted that these psychology researchers and thinkers were not considering travel motivation directly when formulating these

The beauty of an unspoiled natural landscape is a strong travel motivator. These boys are on a rock overlooking Victoria Falls in Zimbabwe, one of southern Africa's most famous natural attractions.

TABLE 9.1	HUMAN MOTIVES AND NEEDS IN PSYCHOLOGY THEORY AND RESEARCH[a]	
THEORIST/RESEARCHER	THEORETICAL APPROACH	MOTIVES OR NEEDS EMPHASIZED
Sigmund Freud	Psychoanalytic theory	Need for sex, need for aggression. Emphasis on unconscious needs.
Carl Jung	Psychoanalytic approach	Need for arousal, need to create and self-actualize.
Alfred Adler	Modified psychoanalytic	Need for competence, need for mastery to overcome incompetence.
Harry Stack Sullivan	Modified psychoanalytic	Need for acceptance and love.
Karen Horney	Modified psychoanalytic	Need to control anxiety, need for love and security
Clark Hull	Learning theory	Need to reduce tension.
Gordon Allport	Trait theory	Need to repeat intrinsically satisfying behaviors.
Albert Bandura,	Social learning theory	Need for self-efficacy or personal mastery.
David McClelland,	Social approaches	Need for achievement.
John Atkinson		
Carl Rogers	Humanistic	Need for self-development.
Abraham Maslow	Humanistic	Hierarchy of needs from physiological needs to safety needs to love and relationship needs to self-esteem to self-actualization.
D. E. Berlyne	Cognitive approaches	Need to satisfy curiosity, seek mental stimulation.
Rom Harré	Ethogenic (social and philosophical)	Need to earn respect and avoid contempt of others.
Stanley Cohen and Laurie Taylor	Sociological theory	Need to escape, need for excitement and meaning.
George Kelly	Personal construct theory	Need to predict and explain the world.
Mihaly Csikszentmihalyi	Humanistic approach	Need for peak experiences.

[a]For clarity the terms *motives* and *needs* are used together in this summary table. Some writers prefer to see needs as more physiologically based and motives as more socially oriented.

approaches. Nevertheless the third column of the table lists a number of human needs and motives that might be usefully applied to the question of why certain groups of travelers seek particular kinds of holiday experiences.

A direct application of these psychological theories for tourist motivation adds some new motives to the list obtained from the historical and literary review. In particular, motives such as personal control, love, sex, competence, tension reduction, arousal, achievement, acceptance, self-development, respect, curiosity, security, understanding, and self-actualization can be identified.

Current Market Research Practices
An understanding of travel motivation can also be approached by examining the kinds of motivation questions asked in surveys of travelers. Basic passport questions

that are standardized around the world include only broad categories of motivation and are limited to such distinctions as "Are you traveling for business reasons, for holiday, to visit friends and relatives, for a convention, or for other reasons?"

More specific market research questions are typified in the studies of "travel benefits" or the rewards of travel. It can be argued that these travel benefits or rewards can be seen as the outcomes or satisfactions linked to tourists' motives for traveling.

Most parents are motivated to provide their children with wholesome and memorable vacation experiences, such as a visit to a Florida water park. *Photo courtesy of VISIT FLORIDA.*

In a typical study of travel benefits, Loker and Perdue (1992) studied visitors to North Carolina and factor-analyzed twelve benefit statements as a part of a survey of summer travelers to that state. Using the two statistical sorting procedures of factor analysis and cluster analysis, the researchers argued that there were six segments of the market receiving different kinds of benefits from their holidays: (1) those who emphasized excitement and escape, (2) pure adrenaline/excitement seekers, (3) a family- and friends-oriented group, (4) naturalists (those who enjoyed natural surroundings), (5) a group who emphasized the value of escape by itself, and (6) a group who enjoyed all benefits. This kind of research, which has been repeated by several other scholars with slightly different benefit groups emerging for different settings, represents a summary of travel satisfaction for a particular destination. It is thus not a pure or clean analysis of travel motivation but helps us to understand the importance of travel motivation in tourism studies by emphasizing that for travel motivation analysis to be useful and meaningful it must be put in a context. Thus, while the list of motives from psychology theories and the history/literature of travel provide a rich source of potential motives, an understanding of travel motivation makes sense only in a particular context—that is, when people are describing why they might seek certain holiday experiences.

Frequently market survey companies or firms provide potential travelers with lists of items that the researchers believe are relevant to the question of why people travel to particular destinations. In reviewing this kind of work Echtner and Ritchie (1991) provide a summary list of thirty-four attributes used in fourteen key studies of destination image. Of these thirty-four attributes, twenty-four were used in at least three studies. These lists are often a mixture of attributes of the destination and select motives of the traveler. An example of such a list is provided in Table 9.2. The items in Table 9.2 were derived from the Pleasure Travel Market Survey, a major survey conducted by United States and Canadian tourism authorities throughout the 1980s and 1990s. The survey contains a list of travel philosophies (parallel to travel motives) and trip-driven attributes (destination features). The travel motivation items are represented in bold.

TABLE 9.2   **TRIP-DRIVEN ATTRIBUTES FOR AUSTRALIAN OUTBOUND TRAVELERS**

(Bold items represent statements corresponding to motives. Items not in bold are destination characteristics.)

ITEM	MEAN IMPORTANCE RATING[a]
Going to places I haven't visited before	**3.26**
Outstanding scenery	3.16
Meeting new and different people	**3.11**
Opportunities to increase one's knowledge	**3.10**
Interesting rural countryside	3.10
Destinations that provide value for my holiday money	3.01
Personal safety	**3.01**
Arts and cultural attractions	2.98
Public transportation such as airlines	2.97
Experiencing new and different lifestyles	**2.97**
Having fun, being entertained	**2.92**
Standards of hygiene and cleanliness	2.89
Visiting friends and relatives	**2.86**
Historical, archaeological, or military sites, buildings, and places	2.85
Just relaxing	**2.85**
Escaping from the ordinary	**2.85**
Being together as a family	**2.84**
Inexpensive travel to the country	2.79
The best deal I could get	2.78
Availability of pretrip/in-country tourist information	2.78
Being able to communicate in English	2.72
Inexpensive travel within the country	2.71
Nice weather	2.69
Trying new food	**2.67**
Shopping	2.66
Ease of obtaining visa	2.61
Visits to appreciate natural ecological sites (forests, wetlands, etc.)	2.59
Talking about the trip after I returned home	**2.55**
Meeting people with similar interests	**2.55**
Getting a change from a busy job	**2.47**
Unique or different native cultural groups such as Eskimo and Indian	2.45
Ease of exchanging the currency	2.40
Getting away from the demands of home	2.36
Finding thrills and excitement	2.33
Exotic atmosphere	2.30
Unique or different immigrant culture	2.27
Ease of driving on my own	2.25
Advertised low-cost excursions	2.24
Environmental quality of the air, water, and soil	2.24
Indulging in luxury	**2.20**
Visiting places where my family came from	2.19

(continued)

TABLE 9.2   (*CONTINUED*)

(Bold items represent statements corresponding to motives. Items not in bold are destination characteristics.)

ITEM	MEAN IMPORTANCE RATING[a]
Activities for the whole family	2.16
Going places my friends have not been	1.97
Being able to communicate in the foreign language	1.96
Outdoor activity	1.92
Experiencing a simpler lifestyle	**1.91**
Doing nothing at all	**1.83**
Exercise and fitness opportunities	1.55
Roughing it	**1.50**

[a] 4 = very important; 1 = not at all important.

While such lists of motives and destination features mixed together are common in studies trying to explain the appeal of places, they have some limitations. In particular, the lists may not be comprehensive; they may reflect the biases of the researchers; they may not explore the relative importance of the various features or reasons for visiting and incorrectly assume that all reasons are equally important (although the data in Table 9.2 does indicate importance). Additionally, the way in which the attributes are interrelated is not often considered. For example, the characteristics of "seclusion" and "exciting nightlife" may be mutually exclusive.

THE NEED FOR A THEORY

This review of travel motivation has stressed that there are three sources of information that can provide a listing of motives concerning why people travel. The list of potential travel motivations is a long one and includes a range of needs from excitement and arousal to self-development and personal growth. Additionally, the brief review of contemporary market research practice concerning destination image indicated that there were further lists of destination features that might be thought of as a mix of travel motives and destination characteristics.

Theories or models in social science research typically summarize or reorganize knowledge in an area. Occasionally the theory will provide a new perspective and foster prediction or specifications of future directions for human action and research. The area of tourist motivation requires a theoretical approach. The lists of motives need to be summarized; connections need to be made with other areas of inquiry such as destination image studies; and our current understanding needs to be challenged and enhanced. Pearce (1992) has outlined seven features that are necessary for a good theory of tourist motivation. These are listed in Table 9.3.

TABLE 9.3	REQUIREMENTS OF A SOUND THEORY OF TOURIST MOTIVATION
ELEMENT	EXPLANATION
1. The role of the theory	Must be able to integrate existing tourist needs, reorganize the needs, and provide a new orientation for future research.
2. The ownership and appeal of the theory	Must be appealing to specialist researchers, useful in tourism industry settings, and credible to marketers and consumers.
3. Ease of communication	Must be relatively easy to explain to potential users and be universal (not country specific) in its application.
4. Ability to measure travel motivation	Must be amenable to empirical study. The ideas can be translated into questions and responses for assessment purposes.
5. A multimotive versus single-trait approach	Must consider the view that travelers may seek to satisfy several needs at once. Must be able to model the pattern of traveler needs, not just consider one need.
6. A dynamic versus snapshot approach	Must recognize that both individuals and societies change over time. Must be able to consider or model the changes that take place continuously in tourism.
7. The roles of extrinsic and intrinsic motivation	Must be able to consider that travelers are variously motivated by intrinsic, self-satisfying goals and at other times are motivated by extrinsic, socially controlled rewards (e.g., others' opinions).

One starting point in the conceptual approaches to motivation is the work of Stanley Plog (1974, 1987, 1991). This work, often uncritically accepted as the major approach to tourist motivation, stressed that travelers could be categorized on a psychocentric (nonadventurous, inward-looking) to allocentric (adventurous, outward-looking) scale. Plog claimed the U.S. population was normally distributed along a continuum between these two extreme types. The approach was historically important in providing one organizing theory of travel motivation. It does not, however, fulfill many of the criteria listed in Table 9.3 and was notably deficient, at least initially, in terms of offering only a single-trait, static, and extrinsic account of tourist motivation. In the 1991 version of the approach, a second dimension, energy versus lethargy, was added to the psychocentric-allocentric dimension, thus developing a four-part categorization scheme. Nevertheless, the approach is still limited because of its North American bias, and it does not consider the issues of multimotive behavior, nor does it provide measurement details or consider the dynamic nature of motives in the travelers' life span.

Some new emerging theories of tourist and leisure motivation fulfill more of the criteria described in Table 9.3. In particular the intrinsic-motivation—optimal-arousal perspective of Iso-Ahola (1982) and the travel needs model of Pearce (1988, 1992) both added new perspectives to the tourist-motivation field.

Iso-Ahola argues that tourist and leisure behavior takes place within a framework of optimal arousal and incongruity. That is, while individuals seek different

Traveling on a train with family members is a satisfying holiday experience. *Copyright ©2001 Amtrak. Photo provided as a courtesy by Amtrak.*

levels of stimulation, they share the need to avoid either overstimulation (mental and physical exhaustion) or boredom (too little stimulation). Leisure needs change during the life span and across places and social company. He advises researchers to keep the motivation questions for leisure close to the actual participation in time and emphasizes the importance of participants' feelings of self-determination and competence to ensure satisfaction.

The **travel-needs model** articulated by Pearce and coworkers is more explicitly concerned with tourists and their motives rather than with leisure, which is the focus of Iso-Ahola's work. The travel-needs model argues that people have a career in their travel behavior that reflects a hierarchy of their travel motives. A travel career is similar to a work career: People may start at different levels; they are likely

Sailing on the Nile River in a felucca combines recreational activity, cultural appreciation, and natural beauty.
Photo courtesy of the Egyptian Tourist Authority.

to change their levels during their life cycle; and they can be inhibited in their travel career by money, health, and other people.

The steps or levels on the travel-needs or career model was likened to a ladder, and this concept was built on Maslow's hierarchy of needs (Maslow, 1970). By expanding and extending the range of specific needs at each ladder level that fit with Maslow's original formulation, Pearce achieved a comprehensive and rich catalogue of the many different psychological needs and motives noted earlier in this chapter (see Figure 9.1). The earliest version of the travel-needs ladder retained Maslow's ideas that lower levels on the ladder have to be satisfied before the individual moves to higher levels of the ladder. In this approach, travelers concerned with developing and extending their **relationships** while traveling will also have needs in terms of **safety** and **physiological** level factors but may not yet be particularly concerned with **self-esteem** and **self-development needs.** Recent and ongoing revisions to this model place less emphasis on the strict hierarchy of needs and more on changing patterns of motives. Importantly, the travel-needs ladder approach emphasizes that people have a range of motives for seeking out holiday experiences. For example, a visitor to Canada who attends the Calgary Stampede might be motivated to do so by the pleasant, safe setting, to entertain a child and develop family experiences of togetherness, and to add to knowledge about Canadian culture. That is, several levels of a travel-needs pattern work together for a rich multimotive picture of travel motivation. This flexibility and variability rec-

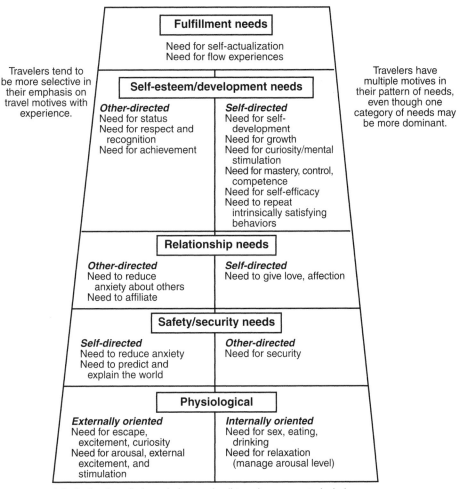

Figure 9.1 Travel-career needs.

ognizes that motivation may change over time and across situations so that the same individual visiting Great Britain might emphasize cultural understanding and curiosity motives more than relationship and family-development motives.

In the travel-needs model, destinations are seen as settings where vastly different holiday experiences are possible. Thus, travelers' motives influence what they seek from a destination, and destinations will vary in their capacity to provide a range of holiday experiences. In short, travelers do not visit a place with standard objective destination features but instead journey to a location where they select activities and holiday experiences from those on offer to suit their personal psychological and motivational profile.

The travel-needs model was formulated so that a dynamic, multimotive account of travel behavior could serve our understanding of tourism. It acts as a blueprint for the assessment of tourist motives and requires individual tailoring to specific situations. That is, the context or setting helps frame the way in which the travel-needs ladder questions are asked. Pearce and Dermott (1991), working in a theme-park setting, were able to use the travel-needs ladder to explain the motives of different consumers for that setting. This individual tailoring is done by taking sections of the travel-needs ladder (e.g., the physiological level and the need for stimulation) and asking questions about the importance of rides and adventure activities in the theme park. Similarly, questions about the importance of going with friends were asked. In this way a full range of theme-park motives is determined by linking travel motivation to other tourism studies.

THE DEVELOPMENT OF MOTIVATION MODELS

The proposals for travel motivation put forward by Plog, Iso-Ahola, and Pearce (and other researchers not listed in full in this chapter) are not static or "finished" products of social science research. The model developed by Plog in 1973 was updated in 1991 and is undoubtedly undergoing further modification in the tourism consultancy world where it is principally used. Similarly Ryan (1998) provided a commentary on the travel-needs ladder of Pearce, arguing that there was not yet solid evidence that the "ladder" component of the model was appropriate. It is important for the tourism student to understand the value of this kind of academic revision. Some commentary and criticisms of a theory or approach do not necessarily mean all of it is wrong or more simply that academics disagree. Instead it is more useful to see the comments as a part of a constructive process. For example, the travel-career ladder model is currently being enhanced by referring to the system as travel-career patterns, an approach that retains the multimotive focus but that accounts for some recent findings that inexperienced travelers emphasize all motives whereas experienced travelers are more selective in their ratings of motivation statements. Further, initial work suggests a core spine of motives (curiosity, relationships, relaxation) exists in everyone's motivation, and extensions to this core vary with experience (Pearce and Lee, in preparation). Tourism students have a rich opportunity to participate in the development of ideas in this field in graduate study as researchers develop this area of tourism analysis in the next decade.

SUMMARY

This chapter has argued that a theory of tourist motivation such as the travel-needs approach helps summarize existing statements and ideas about the motives of travelers. It can also be useful in answering the questions:

- Why do certain groups of travelers seek particular holiday experiences?

- Why do certain groups of travelers travel to destination X?

The chapter has stressed that these questions will not have one simple answer, but rather that different groups of individuals will place different weightings on a structured set of answers, producing shifting patterns of motivation. For example, young teenagers emphasize the motives of stimulation and relationships in visiting theme parks, while young couples emphasize developing relationships and the need for relaxation. For other travelers—for example, those exploring exotic locations and participating in more diverse forms of tourism—a wider range of motives including self-development, mastery, curiosity, escape, and self-fulfillment will be involved (Fielding, Pearce, and Hughes, 1992).

Travel motivation studies can be the basis of many consumer analyses in tourism. A good motivational profile of visitors should be of assistance in understanding how well the destination characteristics fit the needs of the travelers. The key to linking travel motivation studies to other tourism studies such as destination choice lies in analyzing the activities offered by the destination and the activities that fulfill the travelers' motives. Thus if visitors strongly motivated by the need to enhance their understanding of art and history visit well-managed, quality cultural attractions, then satisfaction is likely. A mismatch can also occur, such as the unfortunate visitor to a tropical island who is seeking peace and quiet but is instead assaulted by a tourism product that is set up for those seeking a "party lifestyle," that is, stimulation, excitement, and new relationships. As tourism grows into an increasingly sophisticated consumer industry, the value of understanding the needs of travelers will increase and the motivation of tourists will become a driving part of all tourism studies.

KEY CONCEPTS

consumers
destination attributes
discipline of psychology
Freud
fulfillment needs
Grand Tour

history
Maslow
motivation
needs
physiological needs
psychological theory

relationship needs
safety/security needs
self-esteem needs
travel motivation analysis
travel-needs model

Internet Exercise

Site Name: Seniors Search
URL: http://www.seniorssearch.com
Background Information: A search directory exclusively for the over-fifty age group.
Site Name: Accessible Journeys
URL: http://www.disabilitytravel.com
Background Information: Since 1985, Disability Travel has been designing accessible holidays and escorting groups on vacations exclusively for slow walkers, wheelchair travelers, and their families and friends.

Site Name: Grandtravel
URL: http://www.grandtrvl.com
Background Information: Grandparents and grandchildren make outstanding travel companions! On a Grandtravel tour, grandparents participate in the cultural enrichment of their grandchildren's lives, and everyone has a wonderful time.

Site Name: Kids Go Too
URL: http://www.kidsgotootravel.com
Background Information: Kids Go Too provides you with specific and meaningful information on lodging, activities, and restaurants that are perfectly suited to a unique and exciting vacation that is fun and satisfying to every member of the family.
Site Name: Eurocamp
URL: http://www.eurocamp.com

Background Information: Visit this Web site to find out more about self-drive camping holidays in Europe. You can search their campsite and regional databases.

Exercise

1. Choose at least two of the Web sites indicated above. Describe how they use travel psychology to motivate people to travel who may have barriers to travel.

Questions for Review and Discussion

1. Why is it important for tourism people to have a good understanding of travel motivation?
2. Explain the relationship of customer (tourist) satisfaction and travel motivation.
3. The author states that the question "Why do tourists travel?" is not a good starting point for research on this subject. Comment.
4. "Why do certain groups of people choose certain holiday experiences?" is a much better question. Why?
5. Identify five motivations for travel of Europeans during Roman times, the Middle Ages, and Tudor times. Do such motivations exist today?
6. How important are the motives of discovery and curiosity?
7. Are your travel benefits or rewards linked closely to your travel motives? Elucidate.
8. Provide a few examples of how a person's travel needs change over a life span.
9. Give an example of travel experience overstimulation (mental or physical exhaustion or both). Similarly, give an example of boredom (too little stimulation).
10. Consider Pearce's five-level travel-needs ladder and provide some examples of externally and in-

ternally oriented physiological needs. Why are these needs at the bottom of the ladder?
11. Referring to the preceding question, provide similar representations of safety/security needs, relationship needs, self-esteem/development needs, and fulfillment needs.
12. Assume that you are employed by a nature (ecotour) company and are planning a new tour to a newly established national park. Describe several ingredients of such a tour that meet most of these needs as shown in question 11.
13. How could a resort hotel's activities or social director help guests with their fulfillment needs? Give several cases in point.
14. Below is a short list of travel motivations. Suggest a travel experience or product that would match each motivation.
    a. Rest/relaxation
    b. Unspoiled natural environment enjoyment
    c. Interesting countryside and wildlife study opportunities
    d. Lots of nightlife and entertainment
    e. Adventure activities
    f. Good shopping and browsing
15. How important are a variety of available experiences at a destination?

Case Problems

1. You have been promoted to director of training of the Cruise Lines International Association. Reviewing the listed travel motivations in question 14, which would you select for a group of travel-marketing sales seminars that will be sponsored

by CLIA? (Attending would be travel agents and tour company reps.)
2. Referring to the preceding problem, after selecting the motivations, what kinds of instructional materials and teaching methods would you employ? Why?

3. Your first assignment after joining a tour company staff is to design a tour that would appeal to young singles. Obviously, you must create a tour that would probably motivate a market sufficiently large for your company to make a profit on it. Identify the motivation(s) selected, then describe briefly your tour concept and the specific marketing elements you would feature in its promotion to reach this very promising market.

4. Pleasure travel motivation is often added to a business trip, such as attending a convention. Give an example of such a combination. Identify the principal motivations involved. How would you sell this idea to the convention planning committee?

5. The holiday season is approaching. Jeff R. is trying to compose a direct-mail promotion letter to be sent to each person on his travel agency's mailing list. He's convinced that giving a gift of travel would be very appealing to many of his clients. What key phrases should he embody in this letter to motivate such giving?

SELECTED REFERENCES

Anthony, I. *Verulamium.* Hanley, UK: Wood Mitchell, 1973.

Awaritefe, Onome D. "Tourists Values, Activities and Motivation for Travel to Third World Destinations: Case Study of Nigeria." *Tourist Review,* Vol. 59, No. 1, pp. 34–43, 2004.

Casson, L. *Travel in the Ancient World.* London: Allen and Unwin, 1974.

Crouch, G. I., R. R. Perdue, H. Timmermans, and M. Uysal. *Consumer Psychology of Tourism, Hospitality and Leisure,* vol 3. Oxfordshire, UK: CABI Publishing, 2004.

Earl, P. E., and S. Kemp (eds.). *The Elgar Companion to Consumer Research and Economic Psychology.* Northampton, MA: Edward Elgar, 1999.

Echtner, Charlotte M., and J. R. Brent Ritchie. "The Meaning and Measurement of Destination Image." *Journal of Tourism Studies,* Vol. 2, No. 2, pp. 2–12, 1991.

Fielding, K., P. L. Pearce, and K. Hughes. "Climbing Ayers Rock: Relating Motivation, Time Perception, and Enjoyment." *Journal of Tourism Studies,* Vol. 3, No. 2, pp. 49–57, 1992.

Hibbert, C. *The Grand Tour.* London: Weidenfeld and Nicolson, 1969.

Iso-Ahola, S. "Toward a Social Psychological Theory of Tourism Motivation: A Rejoinder." *Annals of Tourism Research,* Vol. 9, No. 2, pp. 256–262, 1982.

Loker, L. E., and R. Perdue. "A Benefit-Based Segmentation of a Nonresident Summer Travel Market." *Journal of Travel Research,* Vol. 31, No. 1, pp. 30–35, 1992.

Maslow, A. H. *Motivation and Personality,* 2d ed. New York: Harper & Row, 1970.

Mazanec, Joseph A., Geoffrey I. Crouch, J. R. Brent Ritchie, and Arch G. Woodside (eds). *Consumer Psychology of Tourism, Hospitality, and Leisure,* vol. 2. Oxfordshire, UK: CABI Publishing, 2001.

Moscardo, G., P. Pearce, A. Morrison, D. Green, and J. T. O'Leary. "Developing a Typology for Understanding Visiting Friends and Relatives Markets." *Journal of Travel Research,* Vol. 38, No. 3, pp. 251–259, February 2000.

Pearce, P., and B. Dermott. *Dreamworld Report.* Queensland, Australia: Department of Tourism, James Cook University of North Queensland, 1991.

Pearce, P. L. "Fundamentals of Tourist Motivation." In D. G. Pearce and R. W. Butler (eds.) *Fundamentals of Tourist Motivation,* pp. 113–134. London: Routledge, 1992.

Pearce, P. L. *The Ulysses Factor: Evaluating Visitors in Tourist Settings.* New York: Springer-Verlag, 1988.

Pearce, P. L., and U. Lee. *Travel Career Patterns* (in preparation).

Pimlott, J. A. R. *The Englishman's Holiday.* London: Faber & Faber, 1947.

Plog, S. *Leisure Travel: Making It a Growth Market . . . Again!* New York: Wiley, 1991.

Plog, S. "Understanding Psychographics in Tourism Research." In J. R. B. Ritchie and C. Goeldner (eds), *Travel, Tourism, and Hospitality Research,* pp. 203–14. New York: Wiley, 1987.

Plog, S. "Why Destination Areas Rise and Fall in Popularity." *Cornell Hotel and Restaurant Quarterly,* pp. 55–58, 1974.

Rowling, M. *Everyday Life of Medieval Travellers.* London: B. T. Batsford, 1971.

Ryan, C. "The Travel Career Ladder: An Appraisal." *Annals of Tourism Research,* Vol. 25, No. 4, pp. 936–957, October 1998.

Swinglehurst, E. *The Romantic Journey.* London: Pica Editions, 1974.

Wolfe, R. I. "Recreational Travel: The New Migration." *Geographical Bulletin,* Vol. 2, pp. 159–167, 1967.

Woodside, Arch G., Geoffrey I. Crouch, Joseph A. Mazanec, Martin Oppermann, and Marcia Y. Sakai (eds). *Consumer Psychology of Tourism, Hospitality, and Leisure,* vol. 1. Oxfordshire, UK: CABI Publishing, 1999.

CULTURAL AND INTERNATIONAL TOURISM FOR LIFE'S ENRICHMENT

CHAPTER 10

Learning Objectives

- Recognize that travel experiences are the best way to learn about other cultures.

- Identify the cultural factors in tourism.

- Appreciate the rewards of participation in life-seeing tourism.

- Become aware of the most effective promotional measures involving an area's cultural resources.

- Realize the importance of cultural attractions to any area promoting itself as a tourist destination.

- Evaluate the contributions that international tourism can make toward world peace.

The Hermitage Museum in St. Petersburg, Russia. *Copyright © Corbis Digital Stock.*

INTRODUCTION

The highest purpose of tourism is to become better acquainted with people in other places and countries, because this furthers the understanding and appreciation that builds a better world for all. International travel also involves the exchange of knowledge and ideas, another worthy objective. Travel raises levels of human experience, recognition, and achievements in many areas of learning, research, and artistic activity. Tourism goes beyond dependable transportation and comfortable hotels; it necessitates enhancing all the avenues through which a country presents itself. They include educational, cultural, media, science, and meeting/congress activities. To increase accessibility, cultural institutions need to adapt to meet visitors' needs, sometimes providing multilingual guides and signage. Tourists can then more easily choose the purposeful activities that will match their interests.

Travel experiences vary according to the varieties of humankind and their geographical distribution. To classify destinations so that a systematic discussion of tourism motivation can be undertaken, Valene L. Smith has identified six categories of tourism: (1) ethnic tourism, (2) cultural tourism, (3) historical tourism, (4) environmental tourism, (5) recreational tourism, and (6) business tourism. Obviously, destinations can, and usually do, provide more than one type of tourism experience.

IMPORTANCE

While **culture** is only one factor that determines the overall attractiveness of a tourism region (see Figure 10.1, Stage 1), it is a very rich and diverse one. The elements of a society's culture are a complex reflection of the way its people live, work, and play (Figure 10.1, Stage 2).

Cultural tourism covers all aspects of travel whereby people learn about each other's ways of life and thought. Tourism is thus an important means of promoting cultural relations and international cooperation. Conversely, development of cultural factors within a nation is a means of enhancing resources to attract visitors. In many countries, tourism can be linked with a "cultural relations" policy. It is used to promote not only knowledge and understanding but also a favorable image of the nation among foreigners in the travel market.

The channels through which a country presents itself to tourists can be considered its cultural factors. These are the entertainment, food, drink, hospitality, architecture, manufactured and handcrafted products of a country, and all other characteristics of a nation's way of life.

Successful tourism is not simply a matter of having better transportation and hotels but of adding a particular national flavor in keeping with traditional ways of life and projecting a favorable image of the benefits to tourists of such goods and services. A nation's cultural attractions must be presented intelligently and creatively. In this age of uniformity, the products of one nation are almost in-

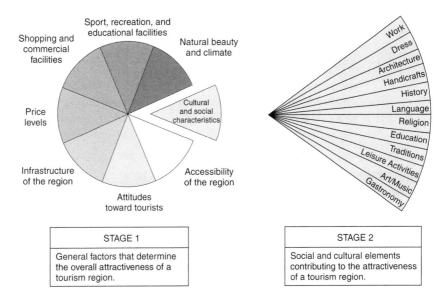

Figure 10.1   Variables influencing the attractiveness of a tourism region. *Source: J. R. Brent Ritchie and Michel Zins, "Culture as Determinant of the Attractiveness of a Tourism Region,"* Annals of Tourism Research, *April–June 1978, p. 256.*

distinguishable from those of another. There is a great need for encouraging cultural diversity. Improved techniques of architectural design and artistic presentation can be used to create an expression of originality in every part of the world.

Taken in their narrower sense, cultural factors in tourism play a dominant role chiefly in activities that are specifically intended to promote the transmission or sharing of knowledge and ideas. Consider the following factors:

1. Libraries, museums, exhibitions
2. Musical, dramatic, or film performances
3. Radio and television programs, recordings
4. Study tours or short courses
5. Schools and universities for longer-term study and research
6. Scientific and archaeological expeditions, schools at sea
7. Joint production of films
8. Conferences, congresses, meetings, seminars

In addition, many activities that are not educational or cultural in a narrow sense provide opportunities for peoples of different nations to get to know each other.

A study from the Travel Industry Association of America (TIA) and *Smithsonian* magazine shows continued and growing interest in travelers' desire to experience cultural, arts, historic, and heritage activities. Study results, as reported in *The Historic/Cultural Traveler,* 2003 edition, show that a remarkable 81 percent of the U.S. adults, or 118 million, are considered historic/cultural travelers. These travelers included historical or cultural activities on almost 217 million person-trips last year, up 13 percent from 192 million in 1996. (A person-trip is one person on one trip traveling 50 miles or more from home, one way.)

These travelers also spend more money on historic/cultural trips compared to the average U.S. trip (average $623 versus $457, excluding cost of transportation), making historic/cultural travelers a lucrative market for destinations and attractions. In fact, for 30 percent of historic/cultural travelers, their destination choice was influenced by a specific historic or cultural event or activity.

LIFE-SEEING TOURISM

Traditionally, a person "sees the high points" of a given location and thus feels that he or she has "seen" this area. However, there is a growing belief among tourism specialists that such an approach, although traditionally valid, is by no means the best approach. Purposeful activities that match the travelers' interests are becoming more commonly accepted and recognized. (In popular tourist areas, such arrangements may have to be limited to the off-season periods of the year.) For example, a physician on a vacation might be interested in talking with local physicians and viewing interesting or progressive medical installations or facilities. He or she may wish to participate in a symposium or some type of educational endeavor there or have lunch with a group of physicians interested in the same particular specialty or in public health or medical practices in general. This visitor may also wish to visit the home of a well-known physician to exchange ideas.

Suggestions made by the travel agent and machinery provided to make such experiences come about are of growing importance to successful tourism. Any place that wishes to become a successful tourist destination must have more activities for visitors than the traditional recreational activities such as lying on the beach or patronizing a nightclub or visiting popular tourist attractions.

Experiencing new cultures, along with their architecture, food, and dress, is a strong travel motivation. This mosque in the Arab community of Singapore presents striking architecture. *Photo by the author.*

Axel Dessau, former director of the Danish Tourist Board, is credited with this concept of **"life-seeing tourism."** In Denmark, for example, the visitor is met by a graduate student or other person who is technically familiar with the field of interest that a visitor may have. This guide then arranges for purposeful visits in a schedule suited to the visitor.

The plan is usually set up on a half-day basis, with the visitor spending afternoons visiting tourist highlights, shopping, and pursuing other traditional recreational activities. The mornings would be devoted to visiting organizations and establishments with programs planned by a special expert guide. A travel agent can make these arrangements.

For example, the visitor might be interested in reviewing social problems and city government. The expert guide would make arrangements for the visitor to visit city planning offices, schools, social welfare establishments, and rehabilitation centers; to attend meetings or seminars at which problems of this nature are discussed; and to participate in other opportunities to learn firsthand what is happening in his or her field in Denmark.

Another aspect of life-seeing tourism is the opportunity to have social intercourse with families. These families host the visitor or the visitor's family in the evening after dinner for conversation and sociability. Or the visitor can stay in a private home—an excellent way in which to become acquainted with the culture and lifestyle of persons in a different locality. In the Bahamas, visitors can discover the island group's people and culture in a very personal way through their People-to-People Programme. This stimulating and exciting program is organized by the Ministry of Tourism. It matches Bahamian volunteers with visitors having similar professions or interests. The Bahamian host or host family may choose to take guests to a local theater performance or a Sunday church service or may invite them to a home-cooked Bahamian dinner. A wide variety of other activities may be included, depending on the interests of the visitor(s). Such opportunities substantially increase visitor appreciation and understanding of the culture they are visiting, and often bring about lasting friendships.

THE ROMANCE OF PLEASURE TRAVEL

Perhaps the strongest of all individual travel motivations is simply that of satisfying a need for pleasure. Travel has the unique quality of being able to satisfy this desire to an extremely high degree. Not all trips are pleasurable, but some are more pleasurable than anticipated. The planning and anticipation period prior to the trip can be as enjoyable as the trip itself. Discussing prospects of the trip with friends and pursuing research, educational, and shopping activities relating to the trip and the area to be visited are important parts of the total pleasure travel experience. In the formulation of marketing programs and advertising, in particular, the pleasurable aspects of the trip need to be emphasized. The prospective traveler should be told how much fun it is to go to the popular, as well as some of the more uncommon, destinations.

The romance of the trip is also a strong motivation, particularly in relation to honeymoon travel and for those who are thrilled with the romantic aspects of seeing, experiencing, and enjoying the culture of strange and attractive places. Thus, the romance and pleasure of the trip are primary attributes of the travel experience and need to be emphasized far more than they have been in the past. Sharing experiences with members of the family or friends is another integral part of the enjoyment of the trip. A trip can become a fine medium through which additional pleasure, appreciation, and romance are experienced.

DEVELOPMENTAL AND PROMOTIONAL MEASURES

Measures taken to develop and promote the cultural elements in tourism through special activities can be considered from several different points of view.

Development of Methods and Techniques

The examples just listed involve specialized methods, techniques, and skills, all of which can be developed in their own right, without any direct reference to the promotion of tourism. Theaters, libraries, museums, and other such national institutions are not usually created with tourism in mind, but they are a great asset in attracting the interest of visitors. Museums and monuments, especially, are among the expected features of a tourist itinerary. These and other activities that can assist in the development of tourism may also be desirable elements in the cultural development of the nation. The methods and techniques associated with each of the examples listed constitute a whole field of specialized knowledge. As in most other fields of expert knowledge, information and ideas can be acquired from abroad and adapted to national situations.

Even when the necessary facilities exist, it may be desirable to adapt them to the needs of tourism. Special courses will often have to be created for foreigners. Multilingual guides must be trained. Captions and instructions in museums and cinemas should be provided in at least two languages. Special arrangements may be made for tourists to be given free or inexpensive access to institutions of interest to them. Life-seeing arrangements can also be made.

Improvement in Educational and Cultural Content of Tourism

There is always room for improvement in what a tourist may learn abroad. This applies chiefly to books, pamphlets, films, and all types of illustrated information material. The services of experts are greatly needed in such matters, not only in assembling material on the history or geography of a country, but also in the attractive and accurate presentation of the material in several languages.

Heritage interpretation as an academic discipline can be very useful in tourism. Courses can be developed to enable local citizens to become authentic interpreters of their area's cultural, historical, and natural heritage. Achievement of such

The Terra Cotta Warriors and Horses at the Qin Shi Huang's Mausoleum, Lintong County, Shaanxi province, are an important archeological excavation that attracts many tourists. *Copyright © Corbis Digital Stock.*

knowledge builds a person's ability to become a fully qualified interpreter. One example might be a forty-hour course entitled "Tourism: Keeper of the Culture." Those who successfully complete the course would be fully aware of their area's resources and thus would be capable of providing guide services or other services in which their knowledge can be useful. All forms of tourism, from group to individual, can in various ways benefit from the assistance of such informed, enthusiastic individuals.

Such an educational effort, when publicized, also creates a new self-awareness and pride in the community and a resulting improvement in the quality of life. Local art events, for example, can be organized to be attractive to the community and tourists alike. "Heritage Trails" or "Cultural Highways" can be designated. "Art in the Park" and festivals with various cultural themes help show off the area's resources and help to lengthen the season or fill in low spots in visitor demand. From the tourist's standpoint, engaging in such culturally oriented activities builds a heightened appreciation and respect for the qualities and abilities of their hosts.

Concentration of Activities around Important Themes

In recent years, much has been done to link tourist-related activities with themes or events of widespread interest, as in the case of festivals that bring together a variety of dramatic, musical, or cinema performances. An example is the successful Winter Carnival in Quebec, Canada. Another way is to focus attention on large exhibitions or fairs. Events such as these give an opportunity for the combined sponsorship of many different types of activity. International congresses or meetings can be held at the same time as the exhibitions or festivals. Youth festivals or jamborees can take place to coincide with important sporting events or large conventions.

Another way of stimulating interest is through **"twinning,"** whereby towns, communities, or regions in different countries establish relations with each other and send delegations to events arranged by their partners. Special attractions such as Epcot at Walt Disney World in Florida bring together in one location large-scale cultural exhibits and entertainment of several countries. Another example is the Polynesian Cultural Center in Hawaii. A map of the center is shown in Figure 10.2.

Uses of Mass Media

Mass media are always important in the development of tourism. Whether for use outside a country as a means of attracting tourists or to inform and entertain them after their arrival, high-quality products created by journalists, film producers, and artists can fill a great need. Many countries have some who already specialize in the field of tourism whose services can be used to advantage. The Society of American Travel Writers is one professional group dedicated to good travel journalism.

Development of Out-of-Season Tourism

Educational and cultural activities are particularly well adapted to out-of-season tourism development. International meetings and study courses do not depend on good weather and entertainment. Often, their sponsors are glad to take advantage of off-season rates in hotels. Efforts should therefore be made to develop facilities and publicity to attract suitable activities and events. Theater tours are a good example.

ANTHROPOGRAPHY (GEOGRAPHY OF HUMANKIND)

Anthropography is defined as the branch of anthropology that describes the varieties of humankind and its geographical distribution. One of the most important motivations for travel is interest in the culture of other peoples. The Mexicans are not like the Swiss, and the Balinese are not like the Eskimos. Our natural curiosity about our world and its peoples constitutes one of the most powerful travel-motivating influences. A travel agent or other travel counselor must be familiar with the basic differences in culture among the peoples of the world, where accessible examples of such cultures are located, and which of these cultures (or groups of cultures) would be most interesting to a particular would-be traveler.

Most of the earth's 5 billion people are concentrated in a limited number of geographical areas. These population concentrations provide attractions in themselves. On the other hand, areas of the earth that are largely empty—such as

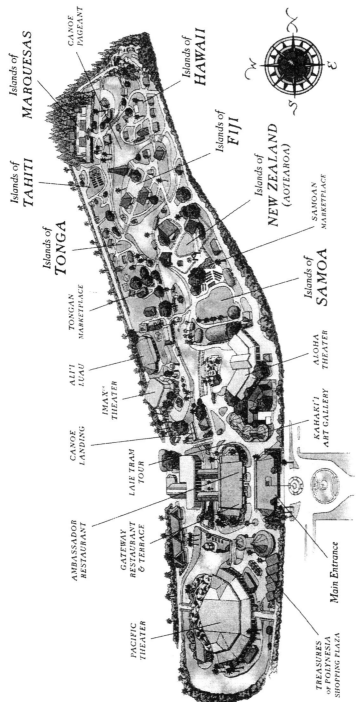

Figure 10.2 Polynesian Cultural Center, Hawaii. There are many different villages at the Polynesian Cultural Center. Each is a combination of buildings, gardens, activities, and people as you would find them if you were to travel to the various island groups represented.

Canada, parts of the western United States, Siberia, western China, Australia, most of Africa, and much of South America—have appeal because of the absence of humans. The landscape, with its towns and villages and rural (and perhaps nomadic) cultures, provides interesting contrasts to urban centers. Visits to primitive cultures are enriching and exciting travel experiences. In the United States, such cultural groups as the Amish in Pennsylvania or the American Indian have tourist appeal.

TYPES OF DESTINATIONS AS TRAVEL EXPERIENCES

The spatial and characteristic diversity among destinations has become so great that it is important to classify destinations so that a systematic discussion of tourism psychology and motivation can be undertaken. One way to do this is to build on Valene L. Smith's identification of several types of tourism.[1] That is, a classification of destinations can be developed on the basis of the types of travel experience provided at the various destinations.

Smith identified six categories of tourism:

1. **Ethnic tourism** is travel for the purpose of observing the cultural expressions and lifestyles of truly exotic peoples. Such tourism is exemplified by travel to Panama to study the San Blas Indians or to India to observe the isolated hill tribes of Assam. Typical destination activities would include visiting native homes, attending dances and ceremonies, and possibly participating in religious rituals.

2. **Cultural tourism** is travel to experience and, in some cases, participate in a vanishing lifestyle that lies within human memory (see Figure 10.3). The picturesque setting or "local color" in the destination area is the main attraction. Destination activities typically include meals in rustic inns, costume festivals, folk dance performances, and arts and crafts demonstrations in "old-style" fashion. Visits to Colonial Williamsburg, Virginia, and Greenfield Village in Dearborn, Michigan, or to Mystic Seaport, Connecticut, are examples of cultural tourism.

3. **Historical tourism** is the museum-cathedral tour that stresses the glories of the past—Rome, Egypt, and Greece. Civil War sites in the United States such

---

[1] Valene L. Smith, *Hosts and Guests*. Philadephia: University of Pennsylvania Press, 1997, pp. 2–3.

Figure 10.3   The Maya Route is a proposed system of paved roads, dirt roads, and trails connecting archeological sites of the magnificent culture shaped by people called the Maya. Between c.e. 250 and 900 "the Maya created one of the most distinguished civilizations of all antiquity" according to *National Geographic* author George Stuart. How the Maya raised their enormous pyramids and stone temples is one of the many mysteries confronting investigators. The Maya Route plan would also introduce visitors to Spanish Colonial architecture, marvelous tropical forests teeming with wildlife, miles of pristine beaches, excellent snorkeling, and villages of great charm. Preliminary work is now underway for creating and promoting this four-nation ecocultural tourism circuit. *Map courtesy of National Geographic magazine.*

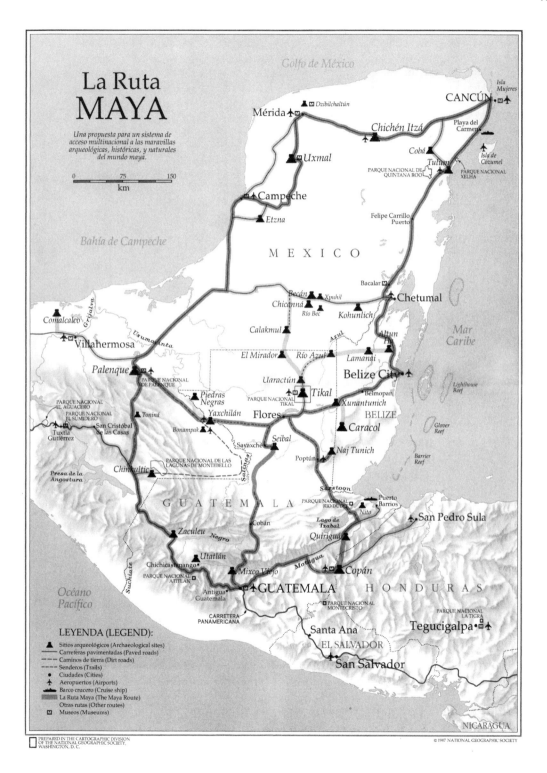

La Ruta MAYA

Una propuesta para un sistema de
acceso multinacional a las maravillas
arqueológicas, históricas, y naturales
del mundo maya.

0   75   150
km

LEYENDA (LEGEND):

- Sitios arqueológicos (Archaeological sites)
- Carreteras pavimentadas (Paved roads)
- Caminos de tierra (Dirt roads)
- Senderos (Trails)
- Ciudades (Cities)
- Aeropuertos (Airports)
- Barco crucero (Cruise ship)
- La Ruta Maya (The Maya Route)
- Otras rutas (Other routes)
- Museos (Museums)

PREPARED IN THE CARTOGRAPHIC DIVISION
OF THE NATIONAL GEOGRAPHIC SOCIETY,
WASHINGTON, D. C.

© 1987 NATIONAL GEOGRAPHIC SOCIETY

A pyramid on the "Ruta Maya" at Chichén Itzá in Mexico is a constant source of amazement to visitors and offers a unique challenge to those who wish to climb to the top. *Copyright © PhotoDisc, Inc.*

as Gettysburg, Pennsylvania, and Chancellorsville, Virginia, are other examples. Guided tours of monuments, visits to churches and cathedrals, and sound and light performances that encapsulate the lifestyle of important events of a bygone era are favored destination activities. Such tourism is facilitated because the attractions are either in or are readily accessible from large cities. Typically, such attractions seem particularly adaptable to organized mass tourism.

4. **Environmental tourism** is similar to ethnic tourism, drawing tourists to remote areas. But the emphasis here is on natural and environmental attractions, rather than ethnic ones. Travel for the purposes of "getting back to nature" and to appreciate (or become sensitive to) people-land relationships falls in this category. Environmental tourism is primarily geographic and includes such destinations and natural wonders as the Galápagos, Antarctic, Victoria Falls, Niagara Falls, the Grand Canyon, and Yellowstone National Park. Typical destination activities include photography, hiking, mountain climbing, canoeing, and camping.

5. **Recreational tourism** centers on participation in sports, curative spas, sunbathing, and social contacts in a relaxed environment. Such areas often promote sand, sea, and sex through beautiful color photographs that make you want to be there on the ski slopes, on palm-fringed beaches, on championship golf courses, or on tennis courts. Such promotion is designed to attract tourists whose essential purpose is to relax. Las Vegas epitomizes

another type of recreational travel—gambling, spectacular floor shows, and away-from-home freedom.

6. **Business tourism** as characterized by conventions, meetings, and seminars is another important form of travel. (The United Nations includes the business traveler in its definition of a tourist.) Business travel is frequently combined with one or more of the types of tourism already identified.

This classification system is by no means unassailable. Destination areas can, and in most cases do, provide more than one type of tourism experience. For example, Las Vegas, which essentially provides recreational tourism, is also a popular convention destination. Resorts in Hawaii provide recreational, environmental, and cultural tourism, depending on what types of activities the tourist desires. A tourist vacationing in India, in addition to recreational tourism on one of the spectacular beaches in that country, has the opportunity for ethnic tourist experiences. Visits can be made to the villages to observe the lifestyles of remote populations.

Conversely, a tourist can select from myriad destinations that provide the same basic type of tourism. For instance, a tourist with an interest in historical tourism may travel to any country that has historical appeal.

OTHER TOURIST APPEALS

Other representative expressions of a people provide powerful attractions for travel. Art, music, architecture, engineering achievements, and many other areas of activity have tourist appeal.

Fine Arts

Such **cultural** media as painting, sculpture, graphic arts, architecture, and landscape architecture constitute an important motivation for travel. As a specific example, recall the beauty of art forms such as cloisonné or scroll paintings.

A recent trend in resort hotel operations has been the display of local art and craft objects within the hotel or in the immediate vicinity so that the guests may become acquainted with the art of the local people. These objects may be for sale and thus

Feeding the Flamingos by Louis Comfort Tiffany is just one of the works of art visitors can view at the Charles Hosmer Morse Museum of American Art in Winter Park, Florida. *From the collection of the Charles Hosmer Morse Museum of American Art, Winter Park, Florida.*

become valued souvenirs. Art festivals often include various types of fine arts together with other cultural expressions to make them more broadly appealing. There are many examples of these, such as the Edinburgh Festival in Scotland. This festival features not only displays of art, but also other forms of craftwork, music, pageants, ceremonial military formations, and other cultural attractions.

Music and Dance

The **musical** expression and resources of a country are among its most appealing and enjoyable aspects. In fact, in some countries or states the music is a major source of enjoyment and satisfaction to visitors. Hawaii, Mexico, Haiti, Spain, various sections of the continental United States, and the Balkans are examples.

Resort hotels, particularly, can bring to the guests opportunities for enjoyment of local music at its best. Evening entertainment programs,

Ancient Malaysian craftsmen lovingly carved and painted temple statuary that commands our respect and admiration. *Copyright © Corbis Digital Stock.*

concerts, recordings, and sound reproduction systems all aid in presenting this aspect of the art of the country. Community concerts, parades, and welcoming ceremonies are appreciated by visitors. Digital or tape recordings that the visitor can purchase provide another effective means of keeping in touch with the culture of a particular area.

Ethnic dancing is another exciting and appealing aspect of a country's culture. The color, costumes, music, setting, and skill of forms and execution add to the appeal. Almost all countries have native or ethnic dancing. Local shows, nightclubs, and community programs present additional opportunities.

Notable examples of dance as a cultural expression are those of Polynesian dancers, the Ballet Folklorico of Mexico, the Russian ballet, folk dances of the Eastern European countries, dances of many African nations, Thai dancing, the Kabuki dancers of Japan, and Philippine country dancing.

Handicraft

To satisfy tourists, gifts and souvenirs offered for sale should be **handcrafted** or manufactured in the country or region where the purchase is made. There is much

The hills and "hollers" of the southern Appalachian Mountains have long been known as a source of quality, traditional handmade crafts. Here Kevin Riddle creates chairs and hayforks using only hand tools.
Photo by Tom Myers/Copyright © Kevin Riddle.

dissatisfaction in purchasing a craft article that you later discover was made in another country thousands of miles away. There is no substitute for genuineness. If the locally produced article is useful and appealing, it should be made available in conveniently located shops. A visit to shops where handicraft products for sale are actually being made is another effective form of guest entertainment.

Industry and Business

The **industrial** aspects of an area provide important motivation for travel. A large proportion of travelers, particularly international travelers, are intellectually curious about the economy of any state or country. They are interested in the country's industry, commerce, manufactured products, and economic base.

Industry tours are a good way to develop an interest in the culture of the area and provide a potential market for the product being made. Tourist organizations should encourage tours to factories or processing plants when such visits are appropriate and pleasant experiences. Lists of such industrial installations can be maintained by tourist promotional organizations, chambers of commerce, resort hotels, motels, restaurants, or other establishments or service organizations where tourist contacts are made.

Industrialists from one country are often interested in the industry of another. Group tours can be organized for manufacturers of a particular product who visit another country to see how the manufacture of that or a similar product is accomplished. Such visits are mutually beneficial because each country's representatives learn from the others.

Chambers of commerce or other business or industrial groups often conduct tours to become acquainted with markets and processors in other countries in an effort to develop more interest in their products and to increase sales in various market areas. Business establishments, particularly retail stores, are of considerable interest to visitors. Excellent examples are shopping centers near resort areas, where a wide variety of stores are concentrated so that the visitor can readily find the products or services desired.

Shopping is one of the most important elements in tourism. Attractiveness, cleanliness, courtesy, and variety of products are among the most significant elements of the success of any shopping area. In fact, much goodwill can be created by courteous and devoted store clerks who assist the visitor in finding just what is being sought. Probably the world's most notable example of businesses that cater to the tourist is in Hong Kong, where shopping and business activity are most likely the most important aspects of any visitor's experience.

Souvenirs that bring back memories of a travel experience can be a lifelong treasure. Those based on authentic craftsmanship from a local artisan can be especially valuable. *Photo courtesy of the Malaysia Tourism Promotion Board.*

Agriculture

The **agriculture** of an area may be of interest to visitors. The type of farming conducted—livestock, poultry, dairy, crops, vineyards and wine production, fresh fruits and vegetables—is an interesting aspect of the culture. Farmers markets such as the well-known Los Angeles Farmers Market or roadside stands that offer local agriculture products are also an important part of tourist services in many areas. This is particularly true of stands selling fresh fruits, vegetables, honey, wine, cider and other drinks, and products from nearby farms readily enjoyed by the traveler.

Exemplary agricultural systems provide a point of interest for farm groups who may wish to visit a particular industry from another part of the country. Denmark, with its outstanding pork industry, is of great interest to hog farmers in many parts of the world.

Local tours should include agricultural developments and services so that visitors can see the agricultural products and operations within the country and perhaps try some of the products. On a one-day tour of Oahu in Hawaii, visitors have a chance to sample field-ripened pineapple at a stand adjacent to a great pineapple plantation. State and country fairs and livestock shows also have interesting tourist attractions. Other examples are cheese tours in Austria and Holland, wine tours in many parts of the world, the Peach Festival in Grand Junction, Colorado, and the fresh food farm tour on the Mornington Peninsula, Australia.

Education

Citizens of one country are often concerned with **education systems** of another. The college and university campuses of any country provide important attractions to tourists. Many of these are beautifully landscaped and attractively situated for a pleasant and enlightening visit. Well-known universities in England such as Oxford or Cambridge are in themselves important tourist attractions.

The operation of high schools and grade schools as well as private schools and other types of vocational training institutions are features of the culture of the area that can be utilized to a considerable degree as attractions for visitors. International education centers provide still another dimension of the relationship between tourism and education. Many universities conduct adult education programs within the university's continuing education service. Such educational opportunities attract learners from other areas within their own country or from many countries around the world. This provides an incentive for travel. International conferences of business and industrial groups as well as scientific and educational organizations are often held on the campuses of colleges, universities, or other educational institutions.

Outstanding examples of this type of operation are two adult education centers, the Kellogg Center at Michigan State University and the East-West Center at the University of Hawaii. These centers attract thousands of adults each year for continuing education courses, conferences, and meetings of an educational nature. "Elderhostel" educational programs for senior citizens are held at many colleges and universities around the world. These are short programs embracing a wide range of subject matter.

Literature and Language

The **literary** achievements of a state or country, though having more limited appeal than some cultural aspects, still constitute a significant element of travel motivation. Books, magazines, newspapers, booklets, pamphlets, and other printed literary works are among the most important expressions of the culture of the country. Interestingly, the availability or absence of certain literature is indicative of the political system of the area. Consider the restriction on distribution of literature from various areas of the world practiced by some countries.

Libraries are favorite cultural institutions for the visitor. Many have well-appointed reading lounges and comfortable, attractive surroundings. Particularly on rainy days, the visitor can enjoy reading about the history, culture, arts, and folkways of the host area. Often guest entertainment programs will feature the reading of poetry or the discussion of various books or other literary works as a cultural enrichment opportunity for visitors.

A well-educated person is likely to speak or at least have studied more than one language. Interest in the language of another nation or state is a motivating force for travel. This is particularly true of students traveling to a particular area to practice the language and to become better acquainted with its colloquial usage.

Travel-study programs are particularly valuable learning experiences. Receiving instruction in a foreign language abroad might well be integrated into any comprehensive travel-study curriculum. Language study institutes flourish all over the world. They can be private or associated with universities. Some examples of the latter are the University of Geneva, Switzerland; the University of Grenoble, France; and the University of California at Berkeley in the United States. Sophomore or Junior Year Abroad programs for college students provide excellent opportunities to learn a different language. Such programs are numerous in Europe and in other parts of the world. Elderhostel learning opportunities for senior citizens provide another example of travel-study programs in which a foreign laguage can be pursued.

Most travelers like to learn at least some of the language to use while they are in a foreign country. Usually, this is in the form of expressions related to ordering food in a restaurant or in talking with hotel or other tourism employees. Classes in language could be included in an entertainment or activities program within a tourist area.

Science

The **scientific** activities of a country constitute an interest to visitors, particularly those in technical industries, education, or scientific research. Organizations responsible for tourist promotion can serve the scientific community by offering facilities for the exchange of scientific information, organization of scientific seminars, visits to scientific installations, and other activities that provide access to scientific information by visitors.

The most popular scientific appeals include museums of science and industry, planetariums, and visits to unusual scientific installations such as atomic power plants and space exploration centers. Zoos and aquariums are also popular. An outstanding example is the Kennedy Space Center in northeastern Florida. This installation attracts substantial numbers of visitors each year and provides educational and scientific knowledge for even the most unsophisticated visitor. Another is the Smithsonian National Air and Space Museum in Washington, D.C.

Government

Systems of **government** vary throughout the world. Persons interested in political science and government find visits to centers of government, such as capitals, particularly valuable and highly motivating. Whenever a person visits another area, he or she is made aware of the type of government system in effect and notes the differences between this and the home country. Persons from Western countries are particularly aware of the differences between their form of government and that of Eastern Europe or the former Soviet Union, for example. Probably the world's best example of this was the city of Berlin, which was divided between a Western democratic government and an Eastern totalitarian government before the wall came down.

Persons interested in politics and the ways in which other countries and areas solve their political problems represent another part of the market. Lawmakers often visit another state or country to observe the procedures developed to solve social or economic problems.

A visit to Washington, D.C., can show visitors the lawmaking process in the House of Representatives and in the Senate. Hearings on various proposed regulations or statutes are often open to visitors. As the center of the government of the United States, this city provides educational opportunities in many areas to both American and foreign travelers.

Religion

Another motivation for travel through all of recorded history is the **religious** pilgrimage. As noted in Chapter 2, pilgrimages are one of the oldest reasons for travel. Many inns and taverns developed to support pilgrimage travelers. Probably the best known are pilgrimages to Mecca. Large numbers of people go to the headquarters of their church organizations and to areas well known in their religious literature. Often these are group trips, for example, a group of Protestants visiting magnificent churches and headquarters of various church denominations in different parts of the world. Similarly, missionaries travel with a religious mission. The large amount of travel to Israel is in part based on religious motivation, as are travels to the Catholic centers at Vatican City within Rome; Oberammergau, in Bavaria, Germany; Lourdes, France; and Mexico City, Mexico. Visits to prominent houses of worship of all forms of religious doctrine are an

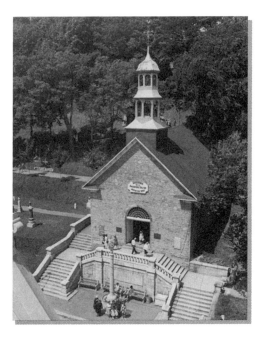

The renowned pilgrim center at Sainte-Anne-de-Beaupré in Quebec, Canada, has attracted millions of people for over three centuries. A sign on the chapel commemorates the first church to be built at Sainte-Anne in 1662.

important motivation for travel. Notre Dame cathedral in Paris, Saint Peter's Basilica in Rome, and the Great Mosque at Mecca are examples.

Food and Drink

Food and **drink** of a country are among its most important cultural expressions. The tourist enjoys native foods, particularly items of a local or ethnic nature. When traveling, trying out local dishes is part of the fun.

Restaurants and hotels can make a favorable impression on the tourist if they feature local dishes and also perhaps an explanation on the menu about what the dish consists of and how it is prepared. Of particular appeal is the type of restaurant in which the atmosphere complements the type of food being served, such as seafood restaurants on the wharf.

The purchase of local food and drink is another source of tourist revenue. Advertising messages that include reference to local food are highly effective. The tourist considers eating and drinking important aspects of a vacation. How these foods and drinks are prepared and presented are of great importance. Among the happiest memories may be the experience of dining in a particularly attractive or

Top hotels in the world seek to serve their guests a wide range of internationally famous dishes. In this case, guests are offered a regional specialty in Brittany—a bowl of cider and mussels steamed or boiled in a white wine sauce or cream. Moules et Frites are a common lunch menu in many parts of France. *Photo courtesy of Robert Pierce.*

unusual eating place where local foods were prepared and served. Encouragement from tourist organizations for restaurants and hotels to feature local food is highly recommended.

History and Prehistory

The cultural heritage of an area is expressed in its **historical** resources (see Figure 10.3). Some tourist destination areas are devoted to history, such as the Mackinaw City area of northern Michigan; St. Augustine, Florida; the Alamo and San Juan Mission in San Antonio, Texas; old gold-mining tours in many western states; Machu Picchu in Peru; and the spectacular archaeological find at Xian in east-central China.

The preservation of history and the quality and management of museums is of utmost importance for successful tourism. Becoming familiar with the history and prehistory (archaeology) of an area can be one of the most compelling of all travel motivations. One of the principal weaknesses observed in historical museums is that the explanations of the exhibits are provided in only one language. This is a serious limitation to many tourists' enjoyment of such historical exhibits.

The Clinton Library in Little Rock, Arkansas, which opened on November 18, 2004, is the most recent of a series of presidential libraries to honor past presidents. Because of the extent of text and visual documents, each library has become a significant attraction for tourists from all over the world. *Courtesy of Cranford Johnson Robinson Woods, Little Rock, Arkansas.*

The hours of operation of historical points of interest and museums are significant and should be arranged to provide access for visitors at convenient times. Admittance fees to museums and points of historical interest should be kept as low as possible to encourage maximum attendance. Promotion is necessary, and tourist contact organizations such as chambers of commerce, tourist information offices, hotels, resorts, restaurants, and other businesses should have available literature that describes the point of interest, hours, admittance fees, special events, and any other information needed by the tourist to visit this historical attraction.

Some notable examples of museums include the National Museum of Anthropology at Mexico City, the American Museum of Natural History of New York City, the various branches of the British Museum in London, the Hermitage in St. Petersburg, and the various museums of the Smithsonian in Washington, D.C.

Other types of historical preservation are national historic parks and monuments and national parks with a history or prehistory theme, such as Mesa Verde National Park, Colorado. Another type is the "living history" farms in Iowa and Illinois.

Among the most outstanding innovations in the presentation of history are the "sound and light" programs found mainly in Europe, the Mediterranean countries, and Mexico. A series of loudspeakers, broadcasting recorded voices in several languages with sound effects, tell the history of an unusually significant structure or place. Varying lights intensify the effect and focus the attention of the audience on various parts of the location.

At the Forum in Rome, the history of Rome is presented at night in half a dozen languages. Visitors can hear the voices of the emperors and hear the crackling flames as Rome burns. At the pyramids of Teotihuacán, about 30 miles northeast of Mexico City, famous actors relate the history of the area in another sound-and-light presentation given in Spanish- and English-language versions. Egypt offers similar programs at its ancient monuments.

TOURISM AND PEACE

Tourism is believed to have a positive effect on world **peace.** When people travel from place to place with a sincere desire to learn more about their global neighbors, knowledge and understanding grow. Then at least a start has been made in improving world communication, which seems so important in building bridges of mutual appreciation, respect, and friendship.

Tourism: A Vital Force for Peace

Since its founding in 1986, the International Institute for Peace Through Tourism (IIPT) has sponsored a series of global conferences, summits, round tables, and seminars that seek to "build a culture of peace through tourism." In October 1988, the inaugural conference on the theme "Tourism: A Vital Force for Peace" was held in Vancouver, British Columbia, Canada. Some five hundred delegates from sixty-five countries attended. The purpose of the conference was to explore ways in which the world's hundreds of millions of international travelers could, by increasing interests, improving attitudes, and engaging in various social and other activities, contribute to better mutual **understanding and appreciation**—an important contribution toward world peace.

The conference provided a forum to examine tourism and its many dimensions as a force for peace. It brought recognition that tourism has the potential to be the largest peacetime movement in the history of humankind because tourism involves people: their culture, economy, traditions, heritage, and religion. Tourism provides the contacts that make understanding possible among peoples and cultures. The conference clearly demonstrated that tourism has the potential to make the world a better place in which to live.

One of the outcomes of the conference was distribution of the following.

Credo of the Peaceful Traveler

Grateful for the opportunity to travel and experience the world and because peace begins with the individual, I affirm my personal responsibility and commitment to:

- Journey with an open mind and gentle heart
- Accept with grace and gratitude the diversity I encounter
- Revere and protect the natural environment which sustains all life
- Appreciate all cultures I discover
- Respect and thank my hosts for their welcome
- Offer my hand in friendship to everyone I meet
- Support travel services that share these views and act upon them and,
- By my spirit, words and actions, encourage others to travel the world in peace

Subsequently, two more conferences have been held in Montreal, Quebec, Canada, in 1994; in Glasgow, Scotland, in 1999. Then the first Global Summit on Peace Through Tourism was held in Amman, Jordan, in 2000. Following is the declaration that emanated from the Jordan conference.

Amman Declaration on Peace Through Tourism

We the representatives and participants at the Global Summit on Peace Through Tourism, assembled in Amman, Jordan, from 8–11 November 2000 . . .

. . . *recognize* that travel and tourism is a worldwide social and cultural phenomenon, engaging people of all nations as hosts and guests, and as such is one of humanity's truly global activities.

. . . and that travel and tourism is one of the world's largest and fastest growing industries, creating one in eleven jobs, contributing to international and regional economic growth, bridging disparities between developed and developing countries, and bringing prosperity which fosters peace.

. . . and that peace is an essential precondition for travel and tourism and all aspects of human growth and development.

. . . and the development of tourism as a global vehicle for promoting understanding, trust and goodwill among peoples of the world requires an appropriate political and economic framework.

. . . Do hereby *declare* our commitment to building a Culture of Peace Through Tourism, and support for the following principles:

1. That tourism is a fundamental human activity engaging social, cultural, religious, economic, educational, environmental, and political values and responsibilities.
2. That the right of people to travel is a fundamental human right which should be exercised without undue restriction including the facilitation of travel for those with disabilities and special needs.
3. That community livelihood should be enhanced and local cohesion encouraged and that all peoples and communities be recognized as being manifestations of a heritage.
4. That human differences be respected and cultural diversity celebrated, as a precious human asset and that peaceful relationships among all people be promoted and nurtured through sustainable tourism.
5. That historical monuments and land-marks be protected and where necessary restored and rehabilitated and made accessible to everyone as valuable assets for humanity and legacies for future generations.
6. That the preservation and wise use of the environment, and ecological balance, are essential to the future of tourism, and that ancient wisdoms of Indigenous Peoples and care for the Earth be acknowledged and respected.
7. That the global reach of the tourist industry be utilized in promoting "dialogues on peace" and in bridging the have and have-not societies of the various regions of the world.

. . . and *acknowledge* the legacy of His Majesty The Late King Hussein of Jordan in laying the foundations of peace in the region and for his effort to make the Hashemite Kingdom of Jordan "a land of peace" and a place of welcome for the peaceful traveler; the commitment of His Majesty King Abdullah II to strengthen and expand King Hussein's Legacy of peace; and to the Government and people of Jordan, for their hospitality and support and their generous contributions to the success of the conference.

. . . and *commend* the IIPT for giving scope to the vision of peace through tourism and for its untiring effort toward that end, and to the title spon-

sor and other sponsors and contributors, for advancing the cause of
Peace through Tourism.

. . . and *welcome* the declaration by the United Nations of the
International Year for the Culture of Peace (2000) and the International
Decade for a Culture of Peace and Non-Violence for the Children of the
World (2001–2010).

. . . and *commit* ourselves to the realization of the goals and objectives as
enshrined in the United Nations Declaration of Program of Action on a
Culture of Peace through our activities and initiatives.

Adopted at Amman November 11, 2000
May Peace prevail on Earth

The Third Global Summit on Peace Through Tourism has been announced for
Pattaga, Thailand, October 2–5, 2005. In addition to peace, this summit will also address the areas of culture, environment, sport, poverty reduction, and sustainable
development. The Third Global Summit on Peace Through Tourism builds on
these foundations: three global conferences, in Vancouver, 1988; Montreal, 1999;
and Glasgow, 1999; two African conferences in Nelspruit, Mpumalanga Province,
South Africa, 2001, and Dar es Salaam, Tanzania, 2003; two previous global summits,
in Amman, 2000, and Geneva, 2003; and a series of smaller conferences and sym-
posia in Turkey, Greece, Italy, Pakistan, Israel, Caribbean, United Kingdom, Australia, and the United States.

The International Institute for Peace Through Tourism (IIPT) is a nonprofit
organization dedicated to fostering and facilitating tourism initiatives that contribute to international understanding and cooperation, an improved quality of environment, the preservation of heritage, and through these initiatives, helping to
bring about a peaceful and sustainable world. It is based on a vision of the world's
largest industry, travel and tourism, becoming the world's first global peace industry, and the belief that every traveler is potentially an "ambassador for peace." Visit
the IIPT Web site at **http://www.iipt.org.**

A Philosophy of Tourism and Peace

Great leaders in many fields have extolled the social benefits to humanity that result from travel. Travel is one of the noblest human occupations. In 550 B.C.E. the
famous Greek statesman Solon recommended that we travel "in order to see." To
see is to increase understanding and appreciation of other peoples, other cultures,
and other lands. Jason, leader of the Argonauts—those incessant sailors in Greek
mythology who were searching for the Golden Fleece—said, "The essential thing is
not to live, the essential thing is to navigate."

Marco Polo became a prince of merchants, papal envoy, governor of a Chinese
city, favorite of Kublai Khan, master of exotic languages, war correspondent, and
the first travel writer. His book describing his adventures, written in C.E. 1298, established the first bond between East and West. Polo was wonderstruck at splendors

that he saw and of which he heard. During the Renaissance, his book was the chief and almost the sole Western source of information on the East.

This brief dip into history and mythology has but one purpose: to emphasize that travel—and written accounts of it in later years—have often done more to create bonds and mutual understanding between various peoples of the world than any other single force throughout civilization's long existence.

There's no better way in which to gain a panoramic view of civilization than making a trip around the world. Being a guest for dinner is probably the best way to sense the unity that exists among peoples throughout the world. Here, people joined by blood or friendly spirit gather to break bread under the same roof. A few examples might include a dinner with a Japanese family, marveling at the swift movement of chopsticks gracefully picking rice from small snow-white porcelain

Meeting people from other parts of the world and partaking in their culture and customs can be one of the most rewarding aspects of travel. Enjoying a coffee in Morocco is one example. *Photo by the author.*

bowls. Or a meal with Thais in the floating markets of Bangkok, where sampans loaded with pyramids of tropical fruits, vegetables, and fish ply the klongs (canals) in search of buyers. With Arabs in Tunisia, it may be having a delicious lunch in the shade of a tent out on the Sahara desert, in a landscape of stark, wild beauty, enriched by the lively warm hospitality of these friendly people.

Whatever happens in any home—be it a modest wooden house furnished with straw mats and rice-paper windows in Kyoto, a solemn British mansion on Victoria Hill, a mud hut on the banks of the Nile, a Cape Cod bungalow, or a Rio de Janeiro apartment—being born, living, eating, drinking, resting, and dying are the same the world over. These similarities reflect the basic unity of people. This unity is really well understood by people, but, alas, is too often forgotten by nations and their rulers and leaders.

There are many ways in which a traveling family can meet and become acquainted with families in other lands. One of the best known of these plans is the "people-to-people" program. Arrangements can be made by a travel agent through a local contractor, say, in Copenhagen, to provide a program of social contacts and other activities to enrich the visitor's acquaintanceship and understanding of the Danish people. Arrangements can be made to stay in a private home or to attend a seminar or similar program. Such opportunities can be and are operating in hundreds of places, in many parts of the world. A greater awareness of such possibilities and more widespread use of this type of program would increase understanding, friendship, and appreciation of other people.

A tourist standing on the balcony of a $100 to $200-per-day hotel room looking at the passersby below obtains little real knowledge of the people in the country being visited. However, if opportunities are readily available for social contacts with locals of that country, increased understanding and appreciation for the people of that area will take place.

Can tourism contribute to peace? If understanding and increased appreciation for other people's way of life, mores, culture, and language make us more a part of a world community, then the answer must be yes. This is especially so if at least casual acquaintance can be made with residents of the host country. Tourism provides a vehicle whereby people from one area become acquainted with people of another. Efforts to build that acquaintance will contribute to understanding, and understanding is at least the first step in creating and maintaining friendly national relationships.

Countries whose leaders understand and encourage tourism are making an effort to improve the personal relationship between their citizens and those of other countries. Although economic considerations may be uppermost, the importance of social contacts is also recognized.

Tourism flourishes in a climate of peace and prosperity. Political unrest, terrorism, wars, depressions, recessions, and civil strife discourage tourism.

Tourism, if properly planned, organized, and managed, can bring understanding, appreciation, prosperity, and a better life to all who are involved. Let it grow and its positive effects increase. Tourism, if not a passport to peace, is at least a worthy effort toward building peace. Wherever and whenever visitor and host meet and greet each other with mutual appreciation, respect, and friendship, a movement toward peace has been made.

The following statement, from a Holiday Inn publication, reflects the goals of tourism:

> In today's shrinking world, neighbors are across the ocean, down the continent, and in every corner of the world. Time is different. So is dress, language, even food. But for all to live as neighbors, mankind must understand each other.
>
> Understanding is impossible without communication. That which is unknown often seems forbidding, even wrong. People must learn other ways of life besides their own.
>
> Only travel and communication closes this gap of knowledge. By world tourism it is possible to discover distant neighbors, how they live and think as human beings.

In Malaysia, visitors can observe local carvers creating works of art. Such opportunities for interaction increase understanding and awareness. *Photo courtesy of the Malaysia Tourism Promotion Board.*

World tourism and understanding go hand in hand. For travel is the way to knowledge. So let everyone do his part, traveling about the earth, keeping his mind and heart open. And the world will become a better place for all.

SUMMARY

The cultural expressions of a people are of great interest to most travelers. These include fine arts, music and dance, handicrafts, food and drink, industry and business, agriculture, education, literature and language, science, government, religion, history, and prehistory. Tourists' experiences are enriched when they make a sincere effort to become better acquainted with local people.

Any country or area that seeks to attract tourists must plan and develop facilities and promote programs that invite access to such cultural expressions. A useful concept is "life-seeing tourism," a structured local program that arranges evening visits to local homes by tourists or, alternatively, a plan whereby interested tourists are accommodated for a few days in local homes.

Cultural interpretation in any area that hosts foreign tourists requires bilingual provisions. These include foreign language ability by guides, bilingual signs, labels, and literature.

Examination of the interrelationships of the cultural backgrounds of visitors and cultural expressions of the host society as provided by this chapter should provide useful guidance to hosts.

Because tourism can lead to better understanding among people, it has the potential to contribute to a more peaceful and better world.

ABOUT THE READING

The reading in this chapter presents a list of the many tourism experiences one may have. It was compiled by J. R. Brent Ritchie.

──────── READING 10.1 ────────

Examples of Tourism Experiences

- **The "Get Away from It All" Relaxation Experience**
  The typical "sun, sand, and sea" or other type of holiday experience vacation where visitors are seeking a period of rest and renewal.

- **The Exploration Experience**
  The experience in which the visitor is seeking to expand his/her visitation horizons. The newness of the experience depends on the individual. For novice travelers, virtually any different locale may be "new." For the experienced traveler, it may be difficult to find new travel horizons.

- **The Adventure Experience**
  In these experiences, the visitor is seeking the so-called adrenaline high that may come from whitewater rafting, heli-skiing, jungle exploration, mountaineering, Antarctic expeditions, or even visitation to insecure, war-torn areas.

- **The Social Experience**
  These experiences provide an opportunity for the visitor either to share the travel experience with old friends or to make new ones. To some extent, the actual destination may be unimportant.

- **The Family Travel Experience**
  The family travel experience is a special subset of the social travel experience in which the social network involved is very special to the visitor—especially in relation to the stage of the family cycle for the visitors. Clearly "young" families are seeking quite different experiences from more mature families. Nevertheless, underlying the motivation to visit a destination is the desire to create and retain a very special experience for the given stage of the family life cycle.

- **The Educational or Learning Experience**
  This type of travel experience has grown in significance lately, and often reflects the desire of a more mature, more sophisticated travelers to enhance their depth of understanding of a destination, its culture, or some special characteristic it may possess.

- **The "Quick Getaway" Experience**
  This is again a subset of a broader type of experience, the "Getaway from It All" relaxation experience. In this case, however, the emphasis is more on the getting away from it all, than on total relaxation and renewal. These experiences are often as short as a weekend, and as such may not be all that distant from the individual's place of residence.

- **The VFR (Visit Friends and Family) Experience**
  For many, the VFR experience is by far the most valued, and may be the only type of experience they seek for most of their lifetime. For a destination manager, the challenge is to discuss how the destination in question can benefit most from this popular form of travel.

- **The "Return to a Single Destination" Experience**

  As Plog pointed out many years ago, a certain segment of the travel market eschews all the glamour of international travel and simply wishes to return to a "comfortable" destination repeatedly. This comfortable destination may be a privately owned recreation facility, or it may just as well be a public destination site to which the visitor has become attached for a whole range of reasons.

- **The Special Event Experience**

  Many destinations have come to appreciate the appeal that a special event may have in attracting visitors who might otherwise have little or no interest in visiting the destination. Destinations that host such one-time megaevents as the Olympic Games or World Cup Finals can increase visitation both during the event and following it as a result of their enhanced awareness, reputation, and image. Alternatively, the successful repeat event, such as the Boston Marathon, Oberammergau, the Master's Golf Tournament, the New Orlean's Mardi Gras, the Calgary Stampede, and the Superbowl attract what are often one-time visitors. This market, however, is large, and it can be a major source of reputation and of visitation as part of total destination marketing strategy.

- **The Participation Event Experience**

  In contrast to events that draw visitors to observe the event, other events can draw visitors who are seeking to participate actively in the event, or who wish to watch a close friend or family member perform in the event. Examples include amateur sporting events (softball, hockey, soccer, football, races), music festivals, beauty festivals, and children's festivals.

- **The Nature-Based Experience**

  The concern for and interest in the environment has grown, the appeal of destinations that provide the opportunity for visitors to "commune with nature" is also growing in significance. Destinations that contain areas such as national parks are often viewed as the epitome of the nature-based experience. Here the opportunity to explore environmentally sensitive yet protected regions and to view wildlife in close proximity are becoming increasingly valued.

- **The Spiritual Experience**

  Destinations that for historical reasons have a particular spiritual attraction to individuals around the world have a special advantage in their ability to provide a spiritual experience. Cities such as Mecca and Rome that are the seat of major religions, as well as those that are the home to recognized religious structures, can focus on their ability to provide spiritually related experiences. But not all spiritual experiences are related to traditional religions. Other destinations, such as Nepal, have over time gained a special spiritual reputation in many parts.

- **The Entertainment Experience**

  While broad in concept, a destination may focus on the provision of various types of entertainment on the basis of its primary market appeal. While the previously cited examples of London, New York, Las Vegas, Nashville, and Branson, Missouri, have become classic examples of the providers of entertainment experiences, they are certainly not alone. The essence of this experience is the opportunity for the destination visitor to observe performances that are either well known in themselves or presented by well-known "stars." To the extent that a destination can develop a critical mass of these entertainment experiences, it can position itself as an entertainment-based destination.

- **The Attractions Experience**

  Certain attractions can become so well known that they can provide the basis of the appeal of an entire destination, and indeed may almost become the totality of the destination. Disney World in Florida is undoubtedly the classic example of an attraction that many families feel they must "experience" at least once in the lifetime of the family. Indeed, this attraction experience has become so pervasive that it forms the foundation for most of the tourism industry in the city of Orlando, Florida. It has proven popular in other parts of the world with Disney Parks being developed in Japan, France, and Hong Kong.

- **The "Take a Chance" Experience**

  More commonly referred to as gaming or gambling, the "Take a Chance" experience is designed to appeal to those whose adrenalin is stimulated by the risk taking associated with a broad range of "games of chance." Many well-known destinations owe their origin and often their continuing existence to the legalization of activities that fifty years ago were considered both illegal and immoral. Times have changed, so much that just about every destination wants to add a gaming component to its array of attractions. In the meantime, Las Vegas, Atlantic City, and Monte Carlo continue to maintain their pinnacle positions as providers of this type of experience. The first two, located in North America, combine gaming with entertainment. In contrast, Monte Carlo's European location emphasizes class and eliteness in appealing to a select market segment.

- **The "No Holds Barred" Experience**
This experience often has names that are much less socially acceptable. "Sex tourism" was in the past a popular but disguised travel experience that the World Tourism Organization and some governments have now explicitly declared undesirable, and even illegal. The Club Méditerranée for many years implied that visitors to certain of its many resorts around the globe could expect a vacation free of normal social constraints. The piles of broken glass around night spots in Spanish seaside resorts following all-night festivities gives evidence to behaviors not normally engaged in by many of their U.K. (and other) guests. And from what seems to be the beginning of time, Mardi Gras in both Rio de Janeiro and New Orleans have attracted both residents and visitors seeking experiences in very specific segments of the market.

- **The "Get to Know Your Global Friends" Experience**
This type of experience represents what many feel tourism should be all about—visitation experiences that encourage the visitor to get to know members of the host destination. There are many ways to attempt to achieve this goal, but Ireland has been offering an approach that many consider to be par excellence. For years, the Irish Tourist Board has worked with residents to develop a comprehensive network of homes that are willing to welcome visitors from around the world to visit not only the house but also, to a certain degree, household members. While admittedly (and necessarily) having multiple dimensions that can be difficult to manage in terms of quality control, it is a "risk" that many visitors consider very worthwhile.
Visit their Web site at: **http://www. irishfarmholidays.com.**

- **The "Understand the Real World" Experience**
While some may interpret this kind of experience as a version of the adventure experience, it depends on the travelers. What this experience implies is visitation to a destination in which the traveler is not artificially protected from some of the realities of living that many of the world's residents experience every day. Visits to many regions of Africa, India, China, and Asia in which the visitor does not stay in high-quality hotels, eats the food of the common people, and travels using the local modes of transportation are not for everyone, but they can provide memorable lifetime experiences for those in good physical condition with the right mindset.

KEY CONCEPTS

agriculture	fine arts	literature and language
anthropography	food and drink	music and dance
appreciation	government	peace
appropriate tourism	handicraft	religion
community interpretation	heritage interpretation	science
cultural attractions	history and prehistory	twinning principle
cultural tourism	industry and business	understanding
education	life-seeing tourism	

Internet Sites

The Internet sites mentioned in this chapter are repeated here for convenience, plus some selected additional sites. For more information, visit these sites. Be aware that Internet addresses change frequently, so if a site cannot be accessed, use a search engine. Also use a search engine to locate many additional relevant sites.

Compendium Cultural Policies in Europe
http://www.culturalpolicies.net

Council of Europe
http://www.coe.int

Ethnologue Database
http://www.ethnologue.com

International Institute for Peace Through Tourism (IIPT)
http://www.iipt.org

National Geographic Society
http://www.nationalgeographic.com

National Park Service
http://www.nps.gov

National Trust for Historic Preservation
http://www.nthp.org

Organization of World Heritage Cities
http://www.ovpm.org/main.asp

Smithsonian Institution
http://www.si.edu

World Heritage
http://www.unesco.org/whc

Internet Exercise

Site Name: National Geographic Society
URL: http://www.nationalgeographic.com
Background Information: The National Geographic Society is propelled by new concerns: the alarming lack of geographic knowledge among our nation's young people and the pressing need to protect the planet's natural resources. The society continues to develop new and exciting vehicles for broadening their reach and enhancing their ability to get people in touch with the world around them.

Exercise
1. Visit the National Geographic Society and search its database for two destinations you think would have a cultural tourism attraction. Collect data on these destinations and design an advertisement that would appeal to individuals who have cultural tourism in mind.

QUESTIONS FOR REVIEW AND DISCUSSION

1. Evaluate culture as a travel motivator.
2. What do you see as the appeal of cultural simularities and cultural differences as motivation to travel to various destinations?
3. Give an example of a cultural experience that would be most satisfying to a visitor in a country much different from his or her own.
4. Create a life-seeing tourism program in your community.
5. What type of life-seeing experience would you particularly enjoy?
6. How much cultural difference can most tourists tolerate? Give examples.
7. Identify some of the rewards that international travel can bring to a perceptive, sensitive traveler.
8. For what reasons did the minister of tourism for the Bahamas promote their People-to-People Program?

9. Referring to question 8, identify some other countries where a similar program would be equally successful.

10. A philosopher states that culture is what we know. Research changes our viewpoint. Thus new discoveries make us change. Do you agree?

11. Does your community possess some distinctive cultural attraction?

12. In what way can world peace be enhanced by tourism?

Case Problems

1. An attractive lakeside community of five thousand persons is presently a popular tourist center, primarily because of its appeal to sports enthusiasts and its proximity to a magnificent state park. However, tourist expenditures are low, principally because of the lack of entertainment in the community. The movie theater closed three years ago, and there is virtually no entertainment except that to be found in a couple of beer taverns. The town and surrounding countryside are rich in history, but the only museum is a small one in the front part of a bar. How could a museum and other entertainment be provided?

2. As the director of an area tourism organization, you have been approached by a fine arts group to consider the feasibility of promoting a Shakespearean festival in your community similar to the long-established festival at Stratford, Ontario, Canada. What factors would you consider in evaluating this request, and how would you work with your state and national tourism organizations to determine how this cultural event could be publicized?

Selected References

Ashworth, G. J., and J. E. Tunbridge. *The Tourist-Historic City: Retrospect and Prospect of Managing the Heritage City.* New York: Pergamon, 2000.

Azmier, Jason J. *Culture and Economic Competitiveness: Emerging Role for Arts in Canada.* Calgary, Alberta: Canada West Foundation, 2002.

Boniface, P. *Managing Quality Cultural Tourism.* London: Routledge, 1995.

Chambers, Erve (ed). *Tourism and Culture: An Applied Perspective.* Albany: State University of New York Press, 1997.

Clift, Stephen, and Simon Carter (eds). *Tourism and Sex: Culture, Commerce, and Coercion.* London: Pinter, 1999.

Cronin, Michael, and Barbara O'Connor. *Irish Tourism: Image, Culture and Identity.* Clevedon, UK: Channel View Publications, 2003.

Crotts, John, and Abrahm Pizam. "The Effect of National Culture on Consumers' Evaluation of Travel Services." *Tourism, Culture and Communication,* Vol. 4, No. 1, pp. 17–28, 2003.

Graburn, Nelson H. H. "The Anthropology of Tourism." *Annals of Tourism Research,* Vol. 10, No. 1, pp. 9–33. Special Issue on the Anthropology of Tourism, 1983.

Graburn, Nelson H. H. (ed). *Ethnic and Tourist Arts.* Berkeley: University of California Press, 1976.

International Association of Scientific Experts in Tourism. *Tourism and Culture.* St. Gallen, Switzerland: AIEST, 2000.

Kerstetter, Deborah, John Confer, and Kelly Bricker. "Industrial Heritage Attractions: Types and Tourists." *Journal of Travel and Tourism Marketing,* Vol. 7, No. 2, pp. 91–104, 1998.

Litvin, Stephen W. "Tourism: The World's Peace Industry?" *Journal of Travel Research,* Vol. 37, No. 1, pp. 63–66, August 1998.

Master, Hoda, and Bruce Prideaux. "Culture and Vacation Satisfaction: A Study of Taiwanese Tourists in South East Queensland," *Tourism Management,* Vol. 21, No. 5, pp. 445–449, October 2000.

McCool, S. F., and R. N. Moisey (eds). *Tourism, Recreation, and Sustainability: Linking Culture and the Environment.* New York: CABI Publishing, 2001.

Nash, Dennison. *Anthropology of Tourism.* Kidlington, Oxford, UK: Pergamon Press, 1996.

Plog, Stanley C. *Leisure Travel: Making It a Growth Market . . . Again!* New York: Wiley, 1991.

Reisinger, Yvette, and Lindsay Turner. *Cross-Cultural Behaviour in Tourism: Concepts and Analysis.* Oxford, UK: Butterworth-Heinemann, 2003.

Richards, Greg. *Cultural Attractions and European Tourism.* Oxfordshire, UK: CABI Publishing, 2001.

Rudd, Michelle Andreadakis, and James A. Davis. "Industrial Heritage Tourism at the Bingham Canyon Copper Mine." *Journal of Travel Research,* Vol. 36, No. 3, pp. 85–89, Winter 1998.

Shackley, Myra. *Managing Sacred Sites.* London: The Continuum International Publishing Group, 2001.

Smith, Valene L. *Hosts and Guests: The Anthropology of Tourism,* 2d ed. Philadelphia: University of Pennsylvania Press, 1989.

Smith, Valene, and Maryann Brent. *Hosts and Guest Revisited: Tourism Issues of the 21st Century.* Elmsford, NY: Cognizant Communication Corporation, 2001.

Travel Industry Association of America. *Emerging International Tourism Markets: Trends & Insights.* Washington, DC: TIA, 2004.

Travel Industry Association of America. *International Outlook for Travel and Tourism.* Washington, DC: TIA, 2005.

Travel Industry Association of America. *The Historic/Cultural Traveler.* Washington, DC: TIA, 2003.

Travel Industry Association of America. *Profile of Travelers Who Participate in Historic and Cultural Activities: Results from the TravelScope Survey.* Washington, DC: TIA, August 1997.

Walle, Alf H. *Cultural Tourism: A Strategic Focus.* Boulder, CO: Westview Press, 1998.

World Tourism Organization. *Handbook on Tourism Congestion Management at Natural and Cultural Sites.* Madrid: WTO, 2003.

Zeppel, Heather. "Cultural Tourism at the Cowichan Native Village, British Columbia." *Journal of Travel Research.* Vol. 41, No. 1, pp. 92–100, 2002.

SOCIOLOGY OF TOURISM

Learning Objectives

- Appreciate the inordinate social impact that travel experiences make on the individual, the family or group, and society as a whole—especially the host society.

- Recognize that a country's indigenous population may resent the presence of visitors, especially in large numbers. Also recognize

that the influence of these visitors may be considered detrimental, both socially and economically.

- Discover that travel patterns change with changing life characteristics and social class.

- Become familiar with the concept of social tourism and its importance in various countries.

Travel experiences have an impact on people, whether it is a visit to a bustling city or a climb to the top of a remote mountain. *Photo courtesy of Arkansas Department of Parks and Tourism.*

CHAPTER 11

INTRODUCTION

Sociology is the science of society, social institutions, and social relationships. Visitors to a community or area create social relationships that typically differ greatly from the affiliations among the indigenous population. In this chapter we identify and evaluate tourist-host relationships and prescribe methods of managing these to create significant advantages for both groups. The ultimate effects of travel experiences on the population in areas of origin as well as in places of destination should determine to what extent societies encourage or discourage tourism.

EFFECTS ON THE INDIVIDUAL

Someone who travels, particularly to a strange location, finds an environment that is unfamiliar, not only geographically but also personally, socially, and culturally. Thus the traveler faces problems for which a solution must be found if the trip is to be fully enjoyable and rewarding. Travelers must manage their resources of money and time in situations much different from those at home. They also must manage their social interactions and social relations to obtain sustenance, shelter, and other needs and possibly to find companionship. Determining the extent of the **cultural distance,** they may wish to maintain results in decisions as to just how unfamiliar the traveler wants his or her environment away from home base to be. People who travel do so with different degrees of contact with the new cultures in which they may find themselves. Life-seeing tourism, for example, is a structured method for those who wish deeper immersion in local ways of life to acquire such enrichment. Some travelers prefer a more selective contact experience as might be arranged by a tour company. Tours designed around cultural subjects and experiences such as an anthropological study tour or participation in an arts and crafts festival are examples. Regardless of the degree of local participation, the individual traveler must at least superficially study the country to be visited and reach some level of decision on how these problems in environmental differences are to be resolved. Advance preparation is an intelligent approach. Travel experiences have a profound effect on the traveler as well as on society, because travel experiences often are among the most outstanding memories in the traveler's life.

Family vacation fun is provided by a beach vacation in Florida. *Photo courtesy of VISIT FLORIDA.*

EFFECTS ON THE FAMILY

As a **family** is growing and the children are maturing, the trips taken as a family are highlights of any year. The excitement of preparation and anticipation and the actual travel experience are memorable occasions of family life. Travels with a measure of adventure are likely to be the most memorable. Family travel may also be educational. The more purposeful and educational a trip becomes, the more beneficial it is. Study before taking the trip and expert travel counseling greatly add to a maximization of the trip's benefits.

EFFECTS ON SOCIETY

Travel has a significant influence on national understanding and appreciation of other people. Government policies in progressive and enlightened nations encourage travel, particularly domestic travel, as a means of acquainting citizens with other parts of their country and building appreciation for the homeland.

The presence of visitors in a country affects the living patterns of indigenous peoples. The way visitors conduct themselves and their personal relationships with citizens of the host country often has a profound effect on the mode of life and attitudes of local people. Probably the most pronounced effects of this phenomenon are noted when visitors from North America or Western Europe travel in an emerging country that has a primitive culture or a culture characterized by a low (economic) standard of living and an unsophisticated population. Conversely, the visitor is influenced by the contrast in culture. Generally, however, this brings about an increased appreciation for qualities of life in the society visited that may not be present at home.

A favorable situation exists when visitors and residents of the host country mingle socially and become better acquainted. This greatly increases the awareness of one another's character and qualities, building appreciation and respect in both groups.

Tourism: Security and Crime

Unfortunately, tourists can be easy prey for criminals. Tourists do not know about dangerous areas or local situations in which they might be very vulnerable to violent crimes. They become easy marks for robbers and other offenders because they are readily identified and are usually not very well equipped to ward off an attack.

Sometimes popular tourist attractions such as parks or beaches are within walking distance from hotel areas. However, a walking tour from the hotel may bring the tourist into a high-crime area lying directly in the path taken to reach this attraction. If such high-crime areas exist, active efforts must be made to inform visitors and guests. Hotels and others that publish maps of walking tours should route such tours into safe areas only. Also, they should warn guests of the danger that could arise if the visitor undertakes certain activities.

Crimes against tourists result in bad publicity and create a negative image in the minds of prospective visitors. Thus, tour companies tend to avoid destinations that have the reputation for crimes against tourists. Eventually, no matter how much effort is applied to publicize the area's benefits and visitor rewards, decreasing popularity will result in failure.

Pizam, Reichel, and Shieh found that tourism expenditures had a negligible effect on crime.[1] However, they suggested that tourism could be considered a potential determinant of crime, negatively affecting the quality of the environment. The tourist industry cannot be held responsible for the occurrence of crime. But one must be aware that tourists are a potential target of crime. Protecting them from offenders is essential to the survival and growth of the industry.

Resentments

Resentment by local people toward the tourist can be generated by the apparent gap in economic circumstances, behavioral patterns, appearance, and economic effects. Resentment of visitors is not uncommon in areas where there is conflict of interests because of tourists. For example, in North America, local people may resent visiting sports enthusiasts because they are "shooting our deer" or "catching our fish." The demand by tourists for goods may tend to increase prices and cause bad feelings.

Another form of resentment may result in a feeling of inferiority among indigenous groups because of unfavorable contrasts with foreign visitors. Local persons employed in the service industries catering to visitors may be better paid and thus exhibit feelings of superiority toward their less fortunate fellow citizens. This creates a poor attitude toward the entire visitor industry.

Financial dislocations can also occur. While a tourist may give a young bellhop a dollar tip for delivering bags, the bellhop's father may be working out in the fields as a farm laborer for a total daily wage of only a dollar or a dollar and a half.

As a rule, both hosts and guests in any society can learn from one another. Beneficial social contact and planned visits to observe local life and culture do much to build appreciation for the indigenous culture. At the same time, the visitors' interest in their ways of life increases the local people's respect for these visitors and gives them a feeling of pride in their own accomplishments.

Tourism often facilitates a transition from rigid authoritarian social structure to one that is more sensitive to the individual's needs. When societies are "closed" from outside influences, they tend to become rigid. By encouraging visitors, this policy is changed to a more moderate one, for the benefit of hosts and guests. The preservation of wildlife sanctuaries and parks as well as national monuments and other cultural resources is often encouraged when tourism begins to be a force in the society.

One-to-one interaction between hosts and guests can break down stereotypes, or the act of categorizing groups of people based upon a single dimension. By "labeling" people, often erroneously, individualism is lost. When a visitor gets to know people personally and is aware of their problems, hopes, and ways in which they are making life more pleasant, this visitor becomes much more sensitive to the uni-

---

[1]Abraham Pizam, Arie Reichel, and Chia Fian Shieh, "Tourism and Crime: Is There a Relationship?" *Journal of Travel Research*, Vol. 20, No. 3, pp. 7–10, Winter 1982.

versality of humankind. It is much easier to distrust and dislike indistinguishable groups of people than to distrust and dislike individuals one has come to know personally.

Some problems are often rooted in economic problems, such as unemployment or underemployment. The economic contributions of tourism can help to moderate such social difficulties. **Negative social effects on a host society** have been identified as follows:

1. Introduction of undesirable activities such as gambling, prostitution, drunkenness, and other excesses
2. The so-called demonstration effect of local people wanting the same luxuries and imported goods as those indulged in by tourists
3. Racial tension, particularly where there are very obvious racial differences between tourists and their hosts
4. Development of a servile attitude on the part of tourist business employees
5. "Trinketization" of crafts and art to produce volumes of souvenirs for the tourist trade
6. Standardization of employee roles such as the international waiter—same type of person in every country
7. Loss of cultural pride, if the culture is viewed by the visitor as a quaint custom or as entertainment
8. Too-rapid change in local ways of life because of being overwhelmed by too many tourists
9. Disproportionate numbers of workers in low-paid, menial jobs characteristic of much hotel and restaurant employment

Many, if not all, of these negative effects can be moderated or eliminated by intelligent planning and progressive management methods. Tourism can be developed in ways that will not impose such a heavy social cost. Strict control of land use by zoning and building codes, enlightened policies on the part of the minister of tourism or similar official organization, and proper phasing of supply components such as infrastructure and superstructure to match supply with demand for orderly development are some of the measures needed. Education and good public relations programs can accomplish much. Enforcing proper standards of quality in the marketing of local arts and crafts can actually enhance and "rescue" such skills from oblivion. As cited in the book *Hosts and Guests*,[2] the creative skills of America's Indians of the Southwest were kept alive, enhanced, encouraged, and ultimately expanded to provide tourists with authentic Indian rugs and turquoise jewelry particularly, but other crafts as well. Fred Harvey, founder of the Fred Harvey Company, is credited with encouraging Indians to continue these attractive crafts so that he could market them in his hotels, restaurants, and gift shops.

---

[2]Valene L. Smith (ed.), *Hosts and Guests,* Philadelphia: University of Pennsylvania Press, 1977, p. 176.

Changing Population and Travel Interests

People change, group attitudes change, and populations change. All these factors affect travel interests. Travel interests also change. Some countries grow in travel popularity; others wane. World events tend to focus public attention on particular countries or regions of the world. Examples are the emergence of Japan and Korea as travel destinations following World War II and the Korean War, and interest in visiting the Caribbean area, as well as Israel, Spain, Morocco, and east Africa. Currently, travel to China and Australia is of great interest. There is an old saying among travel promoters that "mass follows class." This has been proven beyond a doubt. Travel-page publicity concerning prominent persons visiting a particular area inevitably produces a growth of interest in the area and subsequent increases in demand for travel to such well-publicized areas.

The growth of communication systems, particularly network and cable television, has broadened the scope of peoples' interests in other lands and other peoples. To be able to see, as well as hear, has a powerful impact on the viewer's mind and provides acquaintanceship with conditions in another country, and this viewer may develop a desire for a visit. As communications resources grow, awareness and interest also grow.

LIFE CHARACTERISTICS AND TRAVEL

Rising standards of living, changes in the population age composition, the increasing levels of educational attainment, better communication, increased social consciousness of people relating to the welfare and activities of other people throughout the world, and the psychological shrinking of the world by the jet plane have combined to produce an interest among nations in all other nations.

Travel Patterns Related to Age

With age (late sixties and upward) the traveler may become more passive. Family recreation patterns are associated with life stages of the family. The presence of young children tends to reduce the number of trips taken, whereas married couples with no children are among the best travel prospects. As the children mature, however, families increase their travel activities, and families with children between the ages of 15 and 17 have a much higher family travel pattern than do those with younger children. As the children grow up and leave home, the married couple (again without children) renews interest in travel. Also, couples in this life stage are more likely to have more discretionary income and are financially able to afford more travel. Persons living in urban centers are more travel inclined than are those in rural areas.

Senior Citizen Market

A major trend is the growth of the over-65 senior citizen market and the semi-senior citizen market—that is, those over 55 years old. Many have dubbed this the

To reflect the travel patterns of different age groups, some cruise lines offer special cruises and trips for those with specific interests. *Photo courtesy of Carnival Cruise Lines.*

mature market, senior market, retirement market, or elderly market. Others look at it as the 50-plus market because 50 is the age for membership in AARP (formerly the American Association of Retired Persons).

Whatever this market is called, it is an important and growing market. The over-65 group totaled 25.5 million in 1980, 31.2 million in 1990, and 34.8 million in 2000. Then, because of the small number of births during the Great Depression, the group will grow more slowly to 39.7 million in 2010. After that, it is expected to grow rapidly to 70.3 million in 2030 as the baby boomers reach this age (see Figure 11.1).

Income

Buying power is another factor for the tourism manager to consider. People must have buying power to create a market. There is no question that a large and increasing percentage of the population today has sufficient discretionary **income** to finance business and pleasure travel, although some families may be limited to inexpensive trips. The frequency of travel and the magnitude of travel expenditures increase rapidly as income increases. All travel surveys, whether conducted by the Census Bureau, TIA, market research firms, or the media, show a direct relationship between family income and the incidence of travel. The greater the income, the more likely a household will travel. The affluent spend more on just about

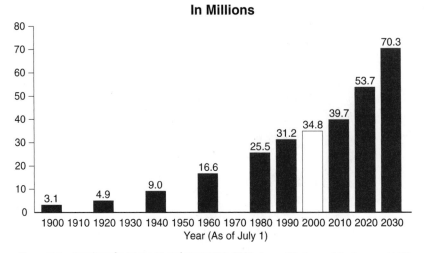

Figure 11.1 **Number of persons 65 and over, 1900–2030.** *Source: U.S. Bureau of the Census and AARP.*

everything, but spending on travel is particularly strong. The value placed on time increases with household income, which is one of the reasons air travel attracts the higher-income consumer.

How the travel dollar is spent obviously depends on income. When the income of the population is divided into fifths, less than 33 percent of the lowest fifth report an expenditure for travel, whereas 85 percent of those in the top fifth report a travel expenditure. Almost half of all consumer spending for vacation and pleasure trips comes from households in the top fifth of the income scale. The affluent spend more on lodging, all-expense-paid tours, food, and shopping, but transportation expenditures are a smaller share of their total travel outlays than with those at the bottom of the income scale—32 percent versus 43 percent. This results from the fact that it is more difficult to economize on transportation than on food, lodging, and miscellaneous expenses.[3]

If current trends continue, the U.S. population will become wealthier. The Bureau of the Census reports that real median household income was $43,318 in 2003. Per capita income was $23,276. In addition to a rise in real wage rates, an exceedingly important factor was the growth in dual wage earners. The increase in the number of women who work outside the home has been dramatic and has boosted household income. The U.S. Census Bureau estimates that 68.6 percent of wives worked in 2003 compared with less than 45 percent in 1975. Married-couple families with both parents employed is just over 64 percent. As incomes increase, it bodes well for travel, but with husbands and wives both working, it may be more difficult to find time for travel and vacation. It is believed that this is one of the

[3]Fabian Linden, "The Business of Vacation Traveling," *Across the Board*, Vol. 27, No. 4, pp. 72–75, April 1980.

reasons for the trend toward shorter and more frequent vacations.

Travel expenditures historically have been income elastic; consequently, as per capita real incomes continue to rise, consumers should spend an increasing proportion of their incomes on travel. Besides making more trips in the future, increasing numbers of consumers can be expected to choose air travel over other modes of travel. Income and education are closely correlated. We discuss this relationship below.

Education

Another factor deserving attention from tourism managers is education, because it tends to broaden peoples' interests and thus stimulate travel. People with college educations take more pleasure trips than do those with high school edu-

The front porch of the Chalfonte seaside summer hotel, Cape May, New Jersey, invites the tourist to rock and relax. *Photo courtesy of the Chalfonte.*

cations, and those with high school educations take more trips than do those with grade school educations. Educators are forecasting continued increases in the average educational level, which would result in a continued positive impact on pleasure travel.

Studies uniformly show that well-educated individuals account for the most travel and the most dollars spent for vacation and pleasure trips. Only about 50 percent of the homes where the household head did not earn a high school diploma report an expenditure for vacation trips. Where the head holds a high school diploma, about 65 percent report vacation expenditures; where the head has some college, 75 percent spend on vacations; and where the head has a degree, 85 percent report vacation expenditures. Income accompanies education as an important factor. In the approximately 35 percent of the homes where the head of the household has had some college, approximately 55 percent of the expenditures for vacation travel are made. Where the head has more than four years of college, vacation expenditures run two to three times the U.S. average. There appears to be no question that increased education levels heighten the propensity to travel; and with expanding higher education levels within the population, air travel should also expand.

The nation's educational level continues to rise. Fifty years ago, a high school diploma was nearly as rare a credential as a four-year college degree is today. As of 2002, 84.1 percent of all adults 25 years of age and older had completed four years

TABLE 11.1   **PHYSICAL OR MENTAL CONDITIONS LIMITING TRAVEL**

CONDITION	NUMBER OF CONDITIONS	PERCENTAGE OF RESPONDENTS
Heart condition	20	33
Crutches	6	10
Old age	5	8
Wheelchair	3	5
Stroke victim	3	5
Recent major surgery	3	5
Diabetes	3	5
Leg braces	2	3
Blindness	2	3
Other[a]	15	23
	62	100
		($n = 60$)

[a]For example, phobia of mountains, mental retardation, pregnancy, bad leg, dizziness, sprained back, flu, and stomach virus.

of high school. The proportion of the population completing college has also increased considerably. In 1960, only 9.7 percent of men and 5.8 percent of women had completed college. In 2002 the proportion of persons 25 and over completing four years of college or more grew, so that 28.5 percent of men and 25.1 percent of women were college graduates. Today, the majority of college students (56.6 percent) are women.[4] Education is closely correlated with income and occupation, so the rising level of education should help to increase the demand for travel.

Travel and the Handicapped

In the United States alone, there are about 50 million physically **handicapped** people—more than twice the total population of Australia.[5] This group constitutes an excellent potential market for travel if the facilities and arrangements are suitable for their use and enjoyment. Woodside and Etzel made a study of the degree to which physical and mental conditions restricted travel activities by households and how households with one or more handicapped persons were likely to adjust their vacation travel behavior.[6]

Findings in Table 11.1 indicate that many of the physical or mental conditions that limit travel (such as heart condition or diabetes) are unobservable by other

[4]U.S. Bureau of the Census, *Statistical Abstract of the United States: 2003*, 123rd ed., Washington, D.C.: U.S. Government Printing Office, 2003, pp. 151–54.

[5]John J. Burnett and Heather B. Baker, "Assessing the Travel-Related Behaviors of the Mobility-Disabled Consumer," *Journal of Travel Research*, Vol. 40, No. 1, pp. 4–11, August 2001.

[6]Arch G. Woodside and Michael J. Etzel, "Impact of Physical and Mental Handicaps on Vacation Travel Behavior," *Journal of Travel Research*, Vol. 18, No. 3, pp. 9–11, Winter 1980.

TABLE 11.2   **NUMBER OF NIGHTS AWAY FROM HOME (AS A PERCENTAGE OF TOTAL)**

	Travel Parties	
NIGHTS	WITH HANDICAPPED PERSONS, %	WITHOUT HANDICAPPED PERSONS, %
1–3	37	42
4–6	24	31
7–9	15	15
10–12	5	5
13–15	7	3
16 or more	12	4
Number of respondents	60	530

travelers or by employees of tourist facilities. But this high percentage of disabled persons creates a substantial potential for emergency situations, and the planning and management of travel equipment and facilities must aim for a major reduction or elimination of such possibilities.

The effect of the presence of handicapped persons in a family on lengths of stays is summarized in Table 11.2. The number of nights away from home differed considerably between those traveling with handicapped persons and those traveling without handicapped persons.

Many households reported little difficulty in using accommodations, because of careful planning before making the trip. The majority of difficulties encountered seemed to be at recreational facilities.

In a later study by Burnett and Baker, they found that the disabled represent the largest and fastest-growing market segment. These consumers, while not wealthy, have adequate resources to travel several times per year, especially for the purpose of vacations, family visits, and medical care. It is necessary to recognize that as is the case with any consumer group, much is to be learned if the group is considered as being made up of segments, rather than being homogeneous. Historically, individuals with disabilities have been categorized by either their medical conditions or their level of self-sufficiency. Severe, moderate, or minor are the common disability classifications. Of the three subgroups, the more severe the mobility disability, the more special attention is needed. The severely disabled are seeking a quiet and peaceful destination that allows them to be independent and that provides easy access. Travel suppliers should know that the moderately and severely disabled use only two modes of transportation: car or van and air. Mobility-disabled consumers are very loyal to destination hotels, motels, and resorts that are sensitive to their needs while not being patronizing.[7]

[7]Burnett and Baker, pp. 6–11.

Americans with Disabilities Act

Substantial improvements have been made by the tourist industry to serve this segment of the market over the years. Activity accelerated with the enactment of the Americans with Disabilities Act (ADA) on July 26, 1990. ADA contains five titles, or sections: Employment, Public Services, Public Accommodations and Services Operated by Private Entities, Telecommunications, and Miscellaneous Provisions. Included in these titles are mandates for accessible public transit and complementary paratransit; accessible intercity (Amtrak) and commuter rail; accessible stations; accessible public accommodation (private entities), including inns, hotels, motels, restaurants, bars, theaters, concert halls, auditoriums, convention centers, all kinds of stores, service establishments, offices, terminals and depots, museums, libraries, galleries, schools, and so on; and telecommunications relay services for hearing- and speech-impaired persons.

Although the act is not specifically a travel law, travel agencies, lodging establishments, motorcoach operators, museums, and restaurants fall into the broad

The American with Disabilities Act (ADA) now makes it easier for handicapped persons to enjoy travel. *Copyright ©2001 Amtrak. Photo provided as a courtesy by Amtrak.*

category of public accommodations that are required to make their facilities accessible to disabled persons. As the U.S. Justice Department and Transportation Department issue final regulations and firms comply, easier travel for the disabled will result.

The Society for Accessible Travel and Hospitality

The Society of Accessible Travel and Hospitality (SATH), founded in 1976, is an educational, nonprofit membership organization whose mission is to raise awareness of the needs of all travelers with disabilities, remove physical and attitudinal barriers to free access, and expand travel opportunities in the United States and abroad. Members include travel professionals, consumers with disabilities, and other individuals and corporations who support this mission.

SATH (formerly Society for Advancement of Travel for the Handicapped) has a well-established record in representing the interests of persons with disabilities. SATH participated in the writing of the regulations for the Americans with Disabilities Act and the Air Carriers Access Act, as well as Resolutions 700 and 1700 of the International Air Transport Association. A Code of Conduct toward travelers with disabilities written by SATH was adopted by the World Tourism Organization in 1991. SATH has also lobbied for legislative change in the European Community and assisted numerous governments to develop national access guidelines.

To raise awareness and provide detailed training on how to serve and market to travelers with disabilities, SATH organizes conferences and provides speakers and panels for other industry associations such as American Society of Travel Agents (ASTA), National Tourism Association, International Institute for Peace Through Tourism, and Travel Industry Association of America (TIA). SATH has sponsored the World Congress for Travelers with Disabilities and the Mature since 1977. It also sponsors Travelers with Disabilities Awareness Week, created in 1990 by SATH founder, Murray Vidockler, CTC, to commemorate the ADA.

Since its inception, SATH has served as a clearinghouse for access information. SATH's travel magazine, *Open World,* features inspiring articles by travelers with disabilities and updates on destinations, cruises, web sites, legislation and more. The SATH web site (**http://www.sath.org**) is geared to consumers.

EMERGENCE OF GROUP TRAVEL PATTERNS

Travel Clubs

Travel clubs are groups of people, sometimes with a common interest (if only in travel), who have formed travel organizations for their mutual benefit. For example, some purchase an aircraft and then arrange trips for their members. Others join international membership clubs such as Club Méditerranée, which owns resort properties in many countries and provides package-type holidays at usually modest cost.

Low-Priced Group Travel

Many tour companies cater to common-interest groups, such as the members of a religious group or professional or work group. A tour is arranged, often at reasonable cost, and is promoted to members of the group.

Public Carrier Group Rates and Arrangements

Airlines and other public carriers make special rates available for groups; a common number is 15 at discounted rates. A free ticket is issued to the group's escort or leader. Chartering all or part of a public transportation vehicle, aircraft, or ship is also a special effort on the part of the carrier to accommodate travel groups.

Incentive Tours

One of the fastest-growing group arrangements is that of incentive tours provided by a company to members who are successful in achieving some objective, usually a sales goal. Spouses are often included on these tours. At the destination, the group is sometimes asked to review new products and receive some company indoctrination.

Special-Interest Tours

Special-interest group travel is another segment growing in importance. Tours are arranged for those interested in agriculture, archaeology, architecture, art, bird-watching, business, castles and palaces, ethnic studies, fall foliage, festivals, fishing, flower arranging, gardening, gems and minerals, golf, history, hunting, industry, literature, music, nature, opera, photography, professional interests, psychic research, safaris, skiing, scuba diving, social studies, sports, study, theater, and wine, to name a few examples. Social and fraternal organizations also are traveling more in groups. Some private clubs are taking group trips. Some are extensive

Special hobbies and interests such as fishing provide another strong motivation for travel, either individually or in groups. *Photo courtesy of South Dakota Deprtment of Tourism.*

trips around the world or trips lasting up to sixty days. Women's groups, social groups, youth groups, alumni, and professional societies commonly take extended trips together as a group. Preconvention and postconvention trips are also popular.

SOCIAL (SUBSIDIZED) TOURISM

Although there is as yet no agreed definition of **social tourism,** there has been considerable study of the question. W. Hunziker at the Second Congress of Social Tourism held at Vienna and Salzburg in 1959 proposed the following definition: "Social tourism is a type of tourism practiced by low income groups, and which is rendered possible and facilitated by entirely separate and therefore easily recognizable services." Another definition, that of M. Andre Poplimont, is as follows: "Social tourism is a type of tourism practiced by those who would not be able to meet the cost without social intervention, that is, without the assistance of an association to which the individual belongs."

From these definitions and from the reports of the three International Congresses on Social Tourism, it is clear that certain elements may be described. First is the idea of "limited means." Second, social tourism is subsidized by the states, local authorities, employers, trade unions, clubs, or other associations to which the worker belongs. Third, it involves travel outside the normal place of residence, preferably to a different environment that is usually within their own country or sometimes to a country nearby.

Holidays with Pay

Paid holidays are now established all over the world, and in most countries a minimum duration (one, two, or three weeks) is specified either by law or by collective agreement. Some, however, consider this institution only a first stage, and they believe that attention should now be turned to the way in which these holidays are used. Great subjects of discussion by twentieth-century sociologists are: (1) the use of the increased leisure time now available to workers, and (2) the cultural and educational development that such leisure time makes possible.

Large numbers of workers are obliged to spend their holidays at home, partly because of their lack of means or tourist experience and partly because of lack of information, transport difficulties, or shortage of suitable accommodation. Organized social tourism, if efficiently managed, can overcome most of these problems: finance through subsidies and savings schemes, experience and information through contacts elsewhere in the country concerned or abroad, transportation through package deals with carriers, and accommodation through contracts with resorts. Thus, organizations can bring tourism within the reach of many who would otherwise be unable to travel. There will be some, however, who for reasons of age, health, family responsibility, or disinclination are unwilling to join in such holidays even when all arrangements are made for them.

Determination of Needs

Some countries carry out research in this field. In Belgium, almost 60 percent of the respondents to an inquiry preferred a continuous stay to moving from place to place, but this preference was more marked among older people than among younger ones. In the Netherlands, another inquiry revealed that about a million holidaymakers preferred not to rely on the hospitality of relatives if other facilities within their means were provided. It was evident that existing facilities of this kind were inadequate.

It was also found that the tendency to take holidays away from home was increasing and that more attention should be given to the educational and cultural aspects of tourism. Studies in France and Italy have found orders of preference among the countryside, the seaside, the mountains, health resorts, and other places; and in Sweden and Italy, inquiries have been carried out into the types of accommodations favored.

Examples of Social Tourism

Leysin, in Switzerland, is one of the best-known examples of holiday centers for social tourism. Originally a famous health resort, advances in medicine meant that its clientele would gradually diminish; but with the cooperation of certain organizations, including the Caisse Suisse de Voyage, the resort was adapted to attract a new type of tourist. A small golf course, a swimming pool, tennis courts, and arrangements for skiing were established, and sanatoria and hotels were converted to meet the new demands. A publicity campaign was begun, and in its first year, over two thousand tourists arrived and spent more than fifty thousand bed-nights in the resort.

Camping and staying at hostels are popular with younger tourists and also with families. In recent years there has been a considerable development of RV camps, particularly in Great Britain. Camping has the advantage of being one of the least expensive forms of holiday and makes possible more mobility. Financial aid is given to camps by the state in France and other countries. In Greece, camps are operated by some large industrial firms for the benefit of their employees, and in most countries they are run by camping clubs and youth associations.

In 1999, the French government set up an official state-funded agency to help French tourist resorts fill vacant beds with up to one thousand unemployed or otherwise struggling citizens. Supporters claim that the right to leisure is as important a human value as the right to housing, education, and medical care.

Provision of Information

In the development of social tourism, other problems arise, but these are largely common to tourism in general. The provision of information, however, deserves brief mention here, because many of the beneficiaries of social tourism will have little knowledge of the special attractions of different resorts. In some countries, government authorities, trade unions, national tourist organizations, and other bodies have given attention to this question. In the United States, for example, there are tourist information offices in the large cities, and publications are issued advising workers how they can spend their holidays. In Canada, bulletins are sent to the trade union offices and other organizations.

To date, most progress has been made in domestic tourism only; and although many workers are already traveling abroad, there is great opportunity for joint action between the official travel organizations of different states. Proposals have been made in some regions as how best to promote foreign travel by the lower-income groups, and the Argentine national tourist organization has invited the correspondent bodies in other South American states to arrange programs on a reciprocal basis.

SUMMARY OF THE PRINCIPAL SOCIAL EFFECTS OF TOURISM

1. The vacation and special business trips a person takes are often among life's most vivid memories.
2. For families, vacation trips taken together are among the highlights of the year's activities.
3. The presence of visitors in a particular area can affect the living patterns of local people. The extent to which a local population is affected depends on the diversity of the mixing groups, including factors such as obvious differences in wealth, habits, appearance, and behavior.
4. On a national basis, people of a particular country can have their lives changed by tourism, particularly if there are large numbers of tourists in proportion to the indigenous population. Visitors may influence ways of dressing, consumption patterns, desire for products used by tourists, sexual freedoms, and a broadening outlook on the world.
5. For both hosts and guests, the most satisfying relationships are formed when they can meet and interact socially at a gathering such as a reception, a tea, or a cultural event; in "people-to-people" programs (home visitation); or in life-seeing tourism (a structured learning-leisure program).
6. Tourism's effects on crime are negligible, but tourists can become easy victims of crime. Hosts must help them avoid dangerous places and areas.
7. Resentment of visitors by local (indigenous) people can occur. There may be conflicts over the use (or abuse) of local facilities and resources. Consumer prices may rise during the "tourist season."
8. Extensive tourism development can bring about undesirable social effects such as increased prostitution, gambling, drunkenness, rowdyism, unwanted noise, congestion, and other excesses.
9. Domestic and international tourism increases for people in a country that has a rising standard of living, a population age distribution favoring young adults or young marrieds with no children, and an increasing population of older, affluent adults.
10. People living in cities are more interested in travel than those living in small towns or rural areas.

11. Wealthy people and those in higher social classes are greatly inclined to travel.

12. Increase in the educational level in a population brings about an increase in travel.

13. Catering to handicapped persons substantially increases markets.

14. Group travel and tours are popular ways to travel.

15. Social tourism is a form of travel wherein the cost is subsidized by the traveler's trade union, government, public carrier, hotel, or association.

16. Travelers thus assisted are in low-income groups or older age groups, or they are workers in organizations authorized to receive such subsidies or vacation bonuses.

THE INTERNATIONAL TOURIST

International travel largely emanates from countries with a comparatively high standard of living, with high rates of economic growth, and with social systems characterized by declining inequality of incomes and a sizeable urban population. In addition, these international travelers come from countries where large-scale industry and commerce comprise the foundations of the economy and where the communications and information environment is dominated by the mass media. The international market is largely made up of middle-income people, including the more prosperous minority of the working class, who normally live in large cities and earn their living in managerial, professional, white-collar, supervisory, and skilled occupations.

There are four extremes relating to the preferences of the international tourist: (1) complete relaxation to constant activity, (2) traveling close to one's home environment to a totally strange environment, (3) complete dependence on group travel to traveling alone, and (4) order to disorder. These extremes are not completely separate, and most travelers may have any number of combinations on any given trip. For example, a traveler may take a peaceful river cruise and then enjoy a strenuous swim in a quiet pool.

Relaxation versus Activity

Historically, the first wave of mass international travel (the interwar and postwar years) occurred at a time when there was a sharp differentiation between work and leisure and when the workweek for most people, including the middle class, was long and exhausting. Under these circumstances, it was not surprising that the demand concentrated on holidays that offered relaxation, recuperation, and rest. Essentially they provided an opportunity for winding down and getting fit for the next 49 weeks of arduous activity. Since then, the balance between work and leisure has shifted sharply in favor of the latter. Usually the weekend is free, and the annual holiday leave for some workers has been lengthened. In other words, over the past decades people have become used to greater slices of leisure time. Relaxation is possible throughout the year, and there is less need to use a holiday exclusively for this purpose.

With the arrival of year-round leisure, there seems to be a surfeit of opportunities for relaxation, so that increasingly the people have started to use their non-holiday leisure time to acquire and exercise new activity skills: sailing, climbing, sports, horseback riding. It is reasonable to forecast that the balance between leisure and work will continue to move in the direction of leisure and that the relative demand for activity-oriented travel will increase.

Familiarity versus Novelty

Most people, when they make their first venture abroad, tend to seek familiarity rather than novelty: people speaking the visitors' language, providing the meals and beverages they are accustomed to, using the same traffic conventions, and so on. Having found a destination where the traveler feels at home, this sort of tourist, at least for the first few ventures abroad, will be a "repeater," going back time and again to the same place. Not until more experience is gained will the traveler want to get away from a normal environment—to mix with people who speak differently, eat differently, dress differently.

A great deal of international travel is conducted to experience the novel. A striking example is the well-known floating market in Bangkok. *Photo courtesy of the Tourism Authority of Thailand.*

In the Western world the general change in social conditions seems to be in the direction of speeding up the readiness for novelty. Where previously the social climate and rigid structure of society had reinforced a negative attitude to change, we now find increasingly a positive attitude to change. People accept and seek innovation in industry, education, family life, the arts, social relationships, and the like.

In particular, in countries with high living standards, manufacturers faced with quickly saturated markets concentrate on developing new products and encouraging the consumer to show greater psychological flexibility. More and more markets are dependent on the systematic organization of rapid change in fashion to sustain and expand. With the blurring of class differences and rising standards of living, travel demand will likely reflect this climate and express fragmentation of the total market as people move away from the traditional resorts to a succession of new places.

Dependence versus Autonomy

A widely accepted analysis of modern industrial society is based on the concept of alienation in work. Briefly, this view states that most people are inevitably employed in work that, though perhaps well paid, is not intrinsically rewarding and satisfying and that from this frustration results, among other things, a general sense of powerlessness, a withdrawal from political and social activities, and the pursuit of status symbols. In the field of leisure, this work alienation should lead to a demand for passive, time-killing holidays or for holidays where the main gratification is the achievement of easily recognized status. Fundamental absence of significance in work, in other words, would lead to holidays during which the same sense of powerlessness and dependence would prevail—organized holiday camps, organized package trips, mass entertainment, and so forth.

In fact, very little empirical research has substantiated this description of an industrialized society. Indeed, the data available suggest the contrary—that many industrial workers, backed by strong trade unions and state-created full employment, feel that as workers they wield considerable power. Certainly, industry and social organization is moving in the direction of providing work that is intrinsically rewarding and satisfying, which should enhance life for today's workers, leading to a sense of personal autonomy in all aspects of their lives, including their leisure time. They are likely to seek holidays during which they feel independent and in control of what they do and how they do it. One would expect that for some time ahead, economic and social circumstances should generate a greater proportion of autonomous participants in the total demand for travel.

Order versus Disorder

Until recently in most Western societies, the training of children has been based on control and conformity, defined and enforced by an all-embracing circle of adult authority figures: parents, teachers, police officers, clergy, employers, civil authorities. With such a background, it is not surprising that most tourists sought holidays that reinforced this indoctrination: set meals at fixed times, guidebooks that told them the "right" places to visit, and resorts where their fellow tourists were tidy, well behaved, "properly" dressed, and so on. They avoided situations where their sense of orderliness might be embarrassed or offended.

More recently, child-rearing practices have changed in the direction of greater permissiveness, and the traditional incarnations of authority have lost much of their Victorian impressiveness. The newer generation of tourists no longer feels inhibited about what to wear and how to behave when on holiday; differences of others, opportunities for unplanned action, and freedom from institutionalized regulations are distinctive characteristics of the contemporary traveler.

Summing up, then, one would predict that because of deep and persisting social and economic changes in modern Western society, the demand for travel will be based less on the goals of relaxation, familiarity, dependence, and order and increasingly on activity, novelty, autonomy, and informality. One should not, of course, ignore the fact that, since international travel is a rapidly growing market, each year's total consumers will always include a minority who value familiarity, dependency, and order.

BARRIERS TO TRAVEL

While travel has become a popular social phenomenon, there are a number of reasons why people do not travel extensively, or do not travel at all. The reasons, products of psychological analysis, are not meant to be ultimate answers as to why people travel where they do. We can, however, look at the more concrete reasons why those studied did not go on a trip during a certain period of time. For most of these studies, barriers to travel fall into six broad categories:

1. **Cost.** Consumers operate within monetary constraints, and travel must compete with other allocations of funds. Saying that travel is too expensive is an indirect way of saying that travel is not important, but, even allowing this interpretation, costs are a principal reason for staying home.
2. **Lack of time.** Many people cannot leave their businesses, jobs, or professions for vacation purposes.
3. **Health limitations.** Poor health and physical limitations keep many persons at home. Also the fear of contracting AIDS, SARS, Norwalk flu, bird flu, Legionnaires' disease, food poisoning, and so on keeps people from traveling. For many, health has become a major tourism safety issue.
4. **Family stage.** Parents of young children often do not travel because of family obligations and inconveniences in traveling with children. Widows and singles sometimes do not travel because of the lack of a traveling companion.
5. **Lack of interest.** Unawareness of travel destinations that would bring pleasurable satisfaction is a major barrier.
6. **Fear and safety.** Things unknown are often feared, and in travel, much is often not familiar to the would-be traveler. Wars, unrest, and negative publicity about an area will create doubt and fear in the mind of the prospective traveler. Terrorism has reared its ugly head in the last decade and is a deterrent to travel.

When motivation to travel is sufficiently powerful, the barriers may be overcome, but these forces may still influence means of travel and destinations selected.

Although travelers may be able to overcome the first four variables listed, tourism marketers need to modify the fifth barrier—lack of interest. This is a challenge for tourism marketing managers. To illustrate just how widespread this barrier is, the following approach was taken where the cost barrier was eliminated. The respondents were asked this incomplete sentence: "Mr. and Mrs. Brown were offered an expense-free tour of the United States, but they didn't want to go because . . ." Forty-two percent of the respondents said that the Browns wanted to go on the trip but couldn't because of job reasons, poor health, age, or responsibilities for children. However, 26 percent indicated that the Browns did not want to go on the trip at all; they would rather stay home, or they did not like to travel, or they were afraid to travel. It is evident that in spite of widespread desires to travel, some people would rather stay home. For others, a weak desire to travel is compounded by nervousness or fear of what the experience may bring. Such a reluctance to travel runs counter to the tide, but this segment is too large a group to be overlooked. With the proper motivational tools, a significant percentage of this untapped group of potential travelers might be convinced that there are places or things of interest outside the world in which they are now existing.

When analyzing some of the psychological reasons contributing to the lack of interest in travel, at least some are related to conflicts between exploration and safety needs. A person's home is safe and is a place thoroughly known, and he or she is not required to maintain a facade there. On the other hand, the familiarity of home can also produce boredom and the need to explore. A person is thus possessed of two very strong drives, *safety* and *exploration,* and he or she needs to reduce this conflict.

One way to do this is by traveling in areas that the person knows well. He or she may go to the same cottage at the same lake with the same people that he or she has known for years. Thus, a new experience that may threaten the need for safety is avoided, but this approach reduces the exploration need by the persons leaving home and traveling to a different place even though it is familiar.

SUMMARY

Sociologists are interested in tourism because travel profoundly affects individuals and families who travel, inducing behavioral changes. The new insights, understandings, and appreciations that travel brings are enlightening and educational.

A person who travels to a strange environment encounters problems that must be resolved. How well the traveler solves these problems will largely determine the degree of the trip's success. In planning a trip the traveler must decide how much cultural distance (from the home environment) he or she desires. Tourists differ greatly in this regard.

In this chapter we have described various social phenomena related to mass tourism. Included are social tourism, international travel behavior extremes, and barriers to travel. Your understanding of these can help to provide a basis for determining tourist volume policy. Consideration must be given to the likely influence that masses of tourists will have on their hosts. Furthermore, applying the procedures explained in this chapter should minimize the negative sociological influences and enhance the positive effects of large numbers of tourists on their host society. Although tourism expenditures have a negligible effect on crime, tourists are potential targets for crime. It is essential that they be protected as much as possible.

ABOUT THE READING

This reading contains a brief excerpt from an article by the distinguished sociologist Erik Cohen. In his classic article, "Toward a Sociology of International Tourism," *Social Research*, Vol. 39, No. 1 (Spring 1972), he classified into a topology four tourist roles. It was one of the early attempts to develop a classification of international tourists. Once understood, the classifications became very useful criteria for making decisions about who one would wish to attract as tourists and what kinds of supply components are appropriate for each type of tourist. While many other typologies have been developed and put forward, Dr. Cohen's continues to enjoy citation and use.

READING 11.1

Erik Cohen's Classification of International Tourists

There is a continuum of possible combinations of novelty and familiarity. This continuum is, to my mind, the basic underlying variable for the sociological analysis of the phenomenon of modern tourism. The division of the continuum into a number of typical combinations of novelty and familiarity leads to a typology of tourist experiences and roles. I will propose here a typology of four tourist roles.

The Organized Mass Tourist: The organized mass tourist is the least adventurous and remains largely confined to his "environmental bubble" throughout his trip. The guided tour, conducted in an air-conditioned bus, traveling at a high speed through a steaming countryside, represents the prototype of the organized mass tourist. This tourist type buys a package tour as if it were just another commodity in the modern mass market. The itinerary of his trip is fixed in advance, and all his stops are well-prepared and guided; he makes almost no decisions for himself and stays almost exclusively in the microenvironment of his home country. Familiarity is at a maximum, novelty at a minimum.

The Individual Mass Tourist: This type of tourist role is similar to the previous one, except that the tour is not entirely preplanned, the tourist has a certain amount of control over his time and itinerary and is not bound to a group. However, all of his major arrangements are still made through a tourist agency. His excursions do not bring him much further afield than do those of the organized mass tourist. He, too, does his experiencing from within the "environmental bubble" of his home country and ventures out of it only occasionally—and even then, only into well-charted territory. Familiarity is still dominant, but somewhat less so than in the preceding type; the experience of novelty is somewhat greater, though it is often of the routine kind.

The Explorer: This type of tourist arranges his trip alone; he tries to get off the beaten track as much as possible, but he nevertheless looks for comfortable accommodations and reliable means of transportation. He tries to associate with the people he visits and to speak their language. The explorer dares to leave his "environmental bubble" much more than the previous two types, but he is still careful to be able to step back into it when the going becomes too rough. Though novelty dominates, the tourist does not immerse himself completely in his host society, but retains some of the basic routines and comforts of his native way of life.

The Drifter: This type of tourist ventures furthest away from the beaten track and from the accustomed ways of life of his home country. He shuns any kind of connection with the tourist establishment, and considers the ordinary tourist experience phony. He tends to make it wholly on his own, living with the people and often taking odd jobs to keep himself going. He tries to live the way the people he visits live, and to share their shelter, foods, and habits, keeping only the most basic and essential of his old customs. The drifter has no fixed itinerary or timetable and no well-defined goals of travel. He is almost wholly immersed in his host culture. Novelty is here at its highest, familiarity disappears almost completely.

The first two tourist types I will call *institutionalized* tourist roles; they are dealt with in a routine way by the tourist establishment—the complex of travel agencies, travel companies, hotel chains, etc., which cater to the tourist trade. The last two types I will call *noninstitutionalized* tourist roles, in that they are open roles, at best only very loosely attached to the tourist establishment.

KEY CONCEPTS

contrasting cultures and cultural distance
democratization of travel
effects of travel experiences
group travel arrangements
handicapped travelers
income
negative social effects on host society

population changes and travel interests
resentment toward visitors
social tourism
sociology
standardization of facilities
strangeness versus familiarity
tourism and crime

travel patterns change with age, family
travel preferences of international tourists
world as a global village

Internet Sites

The Internet sites mentioned in this chapter are repeated here for convenience, plus some selected additional sites. For more information, visit these sites. Be aware that Internet addresses change frequently, so if a site cannot be accessed, use a search engine. Also use a search engine to locate many additional relevant sites.

AARP
http://www.aarp.org

Access-Able Travel Source
http://www.access-able.com

American Association of People with Disabilities
http://www.aapd-dc.org

American Sociological Association
http://www.asanet.org

Americans With Disabilities Act (ADA)
http://www.usdoj.gov/crt/ada

Annals of Tourism Research
http://www.elsevier.com

Centers for Disease Control
http://www.cdc.gov/travel

Club Med
http://www.clubmed.com

The Disability Resource
http://www.disabilityresource.com

International Bureau of Social Tourism (BITS)
http://www.bits-int.org

The International Center for Disability
Resources on the Internet
http://www.icdri.org

The National Theatre Workshop of the
Handicapped
http://www.ntwh.org

Open Doors Organization
http://www.opendoorsnfp.org

Rural Sociological Society
http://www.ruralsociology.org

Society of Accessible Travel and
Hospitality (SATH)
http://www.sath.org

Travel Industry Association of
America
http://www.tia.org

United Nations Environment
Programme (UNEP)
http://www.uneptie.org/pc/tourism

U.S. Census Bureau
http://www.census.gov

VSA arts
http://www.vsarts.org

World Travel Organization
http://www.world-tourism.org

Internet Exercises

Site Name: Open Doors Organization
URL: http://www.opendoorsnfp.org
Background Information: The Open Doors
Organization (ODO) was founded in 2000 for the
purpose of creating a society in which all persons with
disabilities have the same consumer opportunities as
those without. They aspire to teach businesses to succeed in the disability market, while simultaneously
empowering the disability community.

Exercises
1. How large is the disabled traveler market in dollars
according to the ODO study? How much is spent on
air travel and accommodations?
2. What corporate programs are offered?
3. What community programs are offered?
4. What youth programs are offered?

QUESTIONS FOR REVIEW AND DISCUSSION

1. As a manager of a resort hotel popular with families, what social and/or educational activities
would you offer your guests?
2. You have decided to take a trip to a country
whose culture is very much different from your
own. Would you participate in a group tour or go
alone? Why?
3. Would a child's learning experience during a trip
to another part of his or her country be comparable to school learning for that period of time?
In what ways might parents maximize the educational benefits of such a trip?
4. Describe how a hotel's food and beverage manager might avoid the "universal waiter uniform"
image.

5. Discuss the effects of television news coverage of
global and national events on tourism.
6. Give some examples of how tourism suppliers accommodate handicapped travelers. How important is this segment of the market?
7. Is there a potential for increased social tourism in
your country?
8. How might the four extremes relating to the preferences of present-day international tourists affect
a resort hotel's social and recreational program?
Give some specific examples.
9. How do your travel interests differ from your parents'? From your grandparents'?
10. Do you feel governments have a responsibility for
encouraging and supporting social tourism?

CASE PROBLEMS

1. Alfred K. is a widower, 67 years old. He has not had an opportunity to travel much, but now as a retiree he has the time and money to take extensive trips. As a travel counselor, what kinds of travel products would you recommend?

2. Sadie W. is president of her church missionary society. She has observed that many visitors to her fairly small city in England are interested in the local history. Her church is a magnificent cathedral, the construction of which began in the year 1083. Mrs. W. and her colleagues believe that missionary work begins at home. By what methods could her group reach and become acquainted with the cathedral visitors?

3. A U.S. group tour conductor wishes to maximize the mutual social benefits of a trip to an underdeveloped country. Describe possible kinds of social contacts that would be beneficial to the hosts and to the members of the tour group.

4. A popular beach resort hotel is located in a tropical country that, unfortunately, has a high crime rate. One section of the city nearby has some "South Seas" atmosphere gambling casinos. Many guests would like to visit them. How might the hotel's staff control this situation?

5. Nadia P. is minister of tourism for a small West African country. This country has become a very popular winter destination for Scandinavians. The tourists seem to be mainly interested in the beaches, which are among the finest in the world. However, it is customary for these visitors to wear very scanty clothing, especially when swimming. In fact, nude swimming is occasionally practiced. About 90 percent of the indigenous population of the host country are Muslims. The appearance and sometimes behavior of the visitors, especially when shopping and otherwise contacting local citizens, often seems improper to their hosts. Tourism is increasing each year. The economic benefits are considerable and are very much needed. However, the social problem is becoming more acute. What should Ms. P. do about this?

SELECTED REFERENCES

Aspostolopoulos, Yorghos, Stella Leivadi, and Andrew Yiannakis. *The Sociology of Tourism: Theoretical and Empirical Investigations.* Oxford, U.K.: Routledge, 2001.

Börocz, J. *Leisure Migration: A Sociological Study on Tourism.* Oxford, UK: Pergamon Press, 1996.

Clift, S., and P. Grabowski (eds). *Tourism and Health: Risks, Research, and Responses.* London: Pinter, 1997.

Cohen, Erik. "Authenticity, Equity and Sustainability in Tourism." *Journal of Sustainable Tourism*, Vol. 10, No. 4, pp. 267–276, 2002.

Cohen, Erik. *Contemporary Tourism: Diversity and Change.* Oxford, UK: Butterworth-Heinemann, 2004.

Cohen, Erik. "Traditions in Qualitative Sociology of Tourism." *Journal of Travel Research*, Vol. 15, No. 1, pp. 29–46, 1988.

Dann, Graham M. S. *The Language of Tourism: A Sociolinguistic Perspective.* Wallingford, UK: CAB International, 1996.

Dann, Graham, and Erik Cohen. "Sociology and Tourism." *Annals of Tourism Research*, Vol. 18, No. 1, pp. 155–169, 1991.

deKadt, Emanuel. "Social Planning for Tourism in the Developing Countries." *Annals of Tourism Research*, Vol. 6, No. 1, pp. 36–48. Special issue on Sociology of Tourism, January–March 1979.

Farrell, Bryan H. *The Social and Economic Impact of Tourism on Pacific Communities.* Santa Cruz: Center for South Pacific Studies, University of California at Santa Cruz, June 1977.

Hiller, Harry H. "Toward an Urban Sociology of Mega-Events." *Research in Urban Sociology*, Vol. 15, pp. 181–205, 2000.

Jurowski, Claudia, Muzaffer Uysal, and Daniel R. Williams. "A Theoretical Analysis of Host Community Resident Reactions to Tourism." *Journal of Travel Research*, Vol. 36, No. 2, pp. 3–11, Fall 1997.

MacCannell, Dean. *The Tourist: A New Theory of the Leisure Class.* New York: Schocken Books, 1976.

Milman, Ady, and Abraham Pizam. "Social Impacts of Tourism in Central Florida." *Annals of Tourism Research*, Vol. 15, No. 2, pp. 191–205, 1998.

Pizam, Abraham, and Peter Tarlow. "Special Issue on War, Terrorism, Tourism." *Journal of Travel Research*, Vol. 38, No. 1, pp. 4–65, August 1999.

Pizam, Abraham, Peter E. Tarlow, and Jonathon Bloom. "Making Tourists Feel Safe: Whose Responsibility Is It?" *Journal of Travel Research*, Vol. 36, No. 1, pp. 23–28, Summer 1997.

Pizam, Abraham, and Y. Mansfield (eds). *Tourism, Crime, and International Security Issues.* New York: Wiley, 1995.

Richter, Linda K. "International Tourism and Its Global Public Health Consequences." *Journal of Travel Research*, Vol. 41, No. 4, pp. 340–347, May 2003.

Ryan, Chris, and Rachel Kinder. "Sex, Tourism, and Sex Tourism: Fulfilling Similar Needs?" *Tourism Management*, Vol. 17, No. 7, pp. 507–518, November 1996.

Smith, Valene L., and Maryann Brent. *Hosts and Guests Revisited: Tourism Issues of the 21st Century.*

Elmsford, NY: Cognizant Communications, 2001.

Teuscher, Hans. "Social Tourism for All: The Swiss Travel Saving Fund." *Tourism Management*, Vol. 4, No. 3, pp. 216–219, September 1983.

Travel Industry Association of America. *The Mature Traveler.* Washington, DC: TIA, 2000.

Travel Industry Association of America. *The Minority Traveler.* Washington, DC: TIA, 2003.

Turner, Louis, and John Ash. *The Golden Hordes.* London: Constable, 1975.

Ury, John. *The Tourist Gaze.* London: Sage Publications, 2002.

Wilks, Jeff, and Stephen Page. *Managing Tourist Health and Safety in the New Millennium.* Oxford, UK: Butterworth-Heinemann, 2003.

Wyllie, Robert W. *Tourism and Society: A Guide to Problems and Issues.* State College, PA: Venture Publishing, 2001.

Tourism Supply, Demand, Policy, Planning, and Development

Hotel facilities built to accommodate visitors to Ayers Rock (seen in distance), one of Australia's most famous landmarks.

TOURISM COMPONENTS AND SUPPLY

CHAPTER 12

Learning Objectives

- Know the four major supply components that any tourist area must possess.
- Become familiar with the newer forms of accommodations: condominium apartments and time-sharing arrangements.
- Be able to use the mathematical formula to calculate the number of guest rooms needed for the estimated future demand.
- Develop the ability to perform a task analysis in order to match supply components with anticipated demand.
- Discover methods of adjusting supply components in accordance with fluctuating demand levels.

The eye takes in the spectacular colors at a street celebration in **Singapore**. *Copyright © PhotoDisc, Inc.*

INTRODUCTION

Considering that tourism is a composite of activities, services, and industries that deliver a travel experience, it is important to identify and categorize its supply components. The quality and quantity of these determine tourism's success in any area.

In Chapter 1 (Figure 1.2) you observed that tourism was a complex phenomenon—the composite of activities, policies, services, and industries involving many players that deliver the travel experience. The purpose of this chapter is to look at just one segment of the tourism phenomenon by examining the physical supply side of tourism. It is important for a tourist area to identify and categorize its sup-

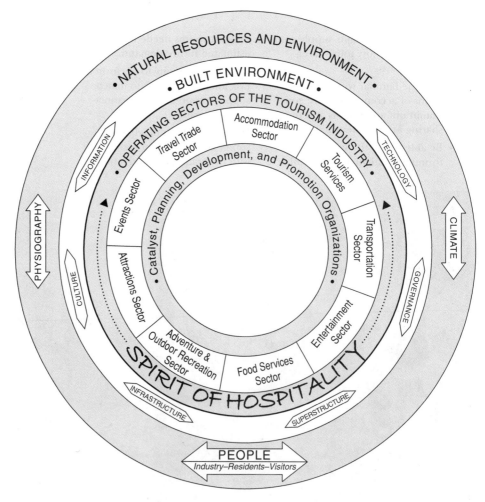

Figure 12.1   Components of tourism supply.

ply components and compare them with the competition because the quality and quantity of supply components are a critical factor in determining tourism's success. Figure 12.1 extracts the supply components from Figure 1.2 and provides the basis for discussion in this chapter. However, it is important to recognize that no segment operates in a vacuum and that supply is interrelated to all other aspects of tourism. It must be matched with demand (see Chapter 13). It is also an important part of policy considerations (see Chapter 15).

SUPPLY COMPONENTS

Tourism **supply components** are classified into four broad categories for discussion in this chapter.

1. *Natural resources and environment.* This category constitutes the fundamental measure of supply—the **natural resources** that any area has available for the use and enjoyment of visitors. Basic elements in this category include air and climate, physiography of the region, landforms, terrain, flora, fauna, bodies of water, beaches, natural beauty, and water supply for drinking, sanitation, and similar uses.

2. *Built environment.* This includes the infrastructure and superstructure discussed in Chapter 1. This component has been developed within or upon the natural environment. One of the most basic elements of the built environment is the **infrastructure** of the region, which consists of all underground and surface developmental construction such as water supply systems, sewage disposal systems, gas lines, electrical lines, drainage systems, roads, communications networks, and many commercial facilities. The tourism **superstructure** includes facilities constructed primarily to support visitation and visitor activities. Primary examples are airports, railroads, roads, drives, parking lots, parks, marinas and dock facilities, bus and train station facilities, resorts, hotels, motels, restaurants, shopping centers, places of entertainment, museums, stores, and similar structures. For the most part, the operating sectors of the industry are part of the built environment and provide much of the superstructure or facilitate access to the physical supply.

3. *Operating Sectors.* The operating sectors of the tourism industry represent what many of the general public perceive as "tourism." First and foremost, the transportation sector comprised of airlines, cruise lines, motorcoach companies, taxis, limousines, automobiles, aerial tramways, and so on typify the movement of people in travel (see Chapter 5). Because nothing happens until someone leaves home, transportation is a critical component. Without transportation, the tourist would be unable to reach and enjoy the natural and built environment. Tourists need a place to stay and be fed, so the accommodation sector and the food service sector are important supply components (see Chapter 6). Attractions are the reason people travel. Without

attractions (see Chapter 8) drawing tourists to destinations, there would be little need for all other tourism services such as transportation, lodging, food, distribution, and so on.

4. *Spirit of hospitality and cultural resources.* Pervading all of the foregoing physical elements of the built infrastructure and superstructures is the social foundation of the destination—its culture, which consists of the language, customs, and religions of the residents of the region, as well as their work- and leisure-related behaviors. It is the people and the cultural wealth of an area that make possible the successful hosting of tourists. Examples are the tourist business employees' welcoming spirit aloha in Hawaii, attitude of the residents toward visitors, courtesy, friendliness, sincere interest, willingness to serve and to get better acquainted with visitors, and other manifestations of warmth and friendliness. In addition, the cultural resources of any area are included here: fine arts, literature, history, music, dramatic art, dancing, shopping, sports, and other activities.

A wide range of tourist resources is created by combining cultural resources. Such examples would be sports events and facilities, traditional or national festivals, games, and pageants.

NATURAL RESOURCES

A great variety of combinations of natural resource factors can create environments attractive to tourism development. Thus, no general statements can be formulated. Probably the most noticeable factors are the pronounced seasonal variations of temperature zones and the changes in demand for recreational use of such areas. To even out demand, the more multiple-use possibilities, the better. For example, it is more desirable that an area be used for golf, riding, fishing, hunting, snow skiing, snowmobiling, mushroom hunting, sailing and other water sports, nature study, and artistic appreciation such as painting and photography than for hunting alone. The wider the appeal throughout the year, the greater the likelihood of success.

Another highly important consideration is that of location. As a rule, the closer an area is to its likely markets, the more desirable it is and the more likely to have a high demand. User-oriented areas (e.g., golf courses) should be close to their users. By contrast, an area of superb natural beauty such as a U.S. national park could be several thousand miles from major market areas and yet have very satisfactory levels of demand.

Productivity of the natural resources of the area for tourism is a function of the application of labor and management. The amounts and proportions of these inputs will determine the quality and quantity of the output. The terrain, vegetation, and beaches of the natural resources will be affected by the intensity of use. Taking such concentrations of use under consideration and planning accordingly for per-

Delicate Arch in Arches National Park, Utah, is an example of how the beauty of natural resources attract tourists. *Photo courtesy of the Utah Travel Council.*

manent aesthetic appreciation will help to maintain the quality of the natural resources for the enjoyment of present and future users.

The quality of the natural resources must be maintained to sustain tourism demand. Proper levels of quality must be considered when planning, and the maintenance of quality standards after construction is completed is absolutely necessary for continued satisfaction of the visitor. In fact, tourism is very sensitive to the quality of recreational use of natural resources, and unless high standards are maintained, a depreciation of the demand will inevitably result. Thus, ecological and environmental considerations are vital.

BUILT ENVIRONMENT

Another supply component is the built environment that has been created by humans. It includes the infrastructure and superstructure of the destination.

Infrastructure and Superstructure

The ground and service installations described as infrastructure are of paramount importance to successful tourism. These installations must be adequate. For example, the diameters of the pipes in various utility systems should be ample for any future increase in use. Electrical installations, water supply systems, communications installations, waste disposal, and similar service facilities should be planned with a long-term viewpoint so that they can accommodate future expansion. Airport runways should be built to adequate standards for use by the newest group of jets so that future costly modifications will not be necessary.

Hotel or lodging structures are among the most important parts of the superstructure. The goal should be to produce an architectural design and quality of construction that will result in a distinctive permanent environment. A boxlike hotel typical of any modern city is not considered appropriate for a seaside resort dominated by palms and other tropical vegetation, nor is it likely to attract tourists.

An example of the built environment is the Pepsi Center in Denver, Colorado. This sports and entertainment venue illustrates how corporate sponsorship has become important in the marketplace. *Photo by Randy Brown; courtesy of the Denver Metro Convention and Visitors Bureau.*

Attractive lodging is an important tourism supply component. *Photo courtesy of Sunset Beach Resort and Spa, Montego Bay, Jamaica.*

A tourist is often more attracted by a facility designed in conformance with local architecture as a part of the local landscape than by the modernistic hotel that might be found at home. Attention must be given to this subject because people often travel to immerse themselves in an environment totally different from their own. Modern amenities such as air-conditioning, central heating, and plumbing, however, should be used in buildings otherwise characteristic of a particular region.

Interior design should also be stimulating and attractive. Lodging structures need local decor and atmosphere as well as comfort. To minimize the expense of obsolescence, high-quality materials and furnishings and first-rate maintenance are necessary. Infrastructure is expensive and requires considerable time to construct.

Auto Traveler Services

In developed countries, automobile transportation is most common. As the economy of a country develops, the usual pattern progresses from walking, to using horses or other working animals, to bicycles, to motorcycles, and finally to small and then larger automobiles, augmented by public transport. Roads should be hard, all-weather surfaced, be properly graded and drained, and be built to international standards for safe use. Small, inadequate roads will only have to be torn up and replaced with better and more adequate systems.

Auxiliary services, such as gasoline stations, roadside eating facilities, motels, roadside parks, roadside picnic facilities, rest parks that have toilet facilities, scenic turnouts, marked points of interest within easy access of the road, and auto repair and service facilities are all needed for successful auto tourism. The number and spacing of essential services depend on the nature of the area, but a spacing of about one hour's driving distance is recommended.

Roadside Parks

Auto tourists use and enjoy roadside parks, picnic tables, rest areas, scenic turnouts, and similar roadside facilities. These facilities are sometimes abused by inconsiderate motorists who litter the area with their trash. Thus, the rule "If you can't maintain it, don't build it" is a cardinal principle of tourism development, and regular maintenance to keep the park in an orderly condition is essential. If the parks are not properly maintained, the tourist is disappointed and the investment in the park is largely wasted.

Some states provide deluxe roadside parks with a fine information building, free refreshments, tourist hosts and hostesses, and rest rooms. These parks are equipped with supplies of folders, maps, pictures, and other amenities for a refreshing, informative stop.

OPERATING SECTORS

Accommodations

For successful tourism, **accommodations** must be available in sufficient quantity to match the demand of the travelers who arrive at the destination. Given access to the destination, accommodations should precede any other type of development; their importance cannot be overemphasized.

Hotels vary tremendously in their physical facilities, level of maintenance and cleanliness, and services provided. Unless all of these factors are at satisfactory levels, tourism cannot succeed. The hotels must provide the physical facilities, price ranges, locations, and services that meet the expectations, wants, and needs of the travelers. Should the quality of facilities and services drop, demand will fall off—a serious blow to the tourism industry in the area.

Types of Accommodations

Hotels
Hotels are of several types: commercial, resort, motor, airport, and residential. In relation to tourism, residential hotels are probably not important, although there are usually some rooms available to tourists in most residential hotels. The primary type is the resort hotel situated in attractive surroundings and usually accompanied by a large mix of services, including entertainment and recreational activities for

The personal greeting of guests conveys a feeling of warmth and professionalism at the Sheraton New York Hotel and Towers. *Photo courtesy of Sheraton Hotels of New York.*

the traveler and vacationer. The commercial hotel is usually a downtown structure located conveniently for the business traveler, convention attendee, and vacationer.

The demand for accommodations varies according to the price guests are willing to pay, services required, and similar considerations. Many successful tourism areas have no multistoried, expensive, contemporary-looking hotels. For example, a bungalow-type accommodation constructed with native materials, built to modern standards of comfort and safety, and kept immaculately clean will be acceptable to a large segment of the market.

The motor hotel is of primary importance for tourists traveling by car and is of major importance in the United States, Canada, and Mexico. Suitable accommodations should be available for all segments of the market. American companies such as Marriott, Ramada, Hilton, and Choice now offer accommodations under different names that are aimed at specific price levels of the market. Thus, they compete for various segments of the travel market. Expensive hotel accommodations may be demanded by those who "want the best" and are willing and able to pay accordingly. On the other hand, youth tourism and adults unable or unwilling to pay for top-level accommodations should have facilities available such as hostels, pensions, and bed and breakfasts. Camping or RV facilities are often needed.

Other types of accommodations include marina hotels, airport hotels, gambling resort hotels, and rustic cabins in wilderness areas. All accommodations should be harmonious with one another.

Certain places are known as expensive destination areas, and travelers expect to find higher-quality accommodations there. Conversely, other areas are expected to be inexpensive, and the high-priced hotel would be out of place in such a locality.

Condominium Apartments

Individual buyers of condominium units typically use the apartment for their own enjoyment, or they rent it to tourists for all or part of the year. This form of accommodation has become increasingly important and, in some resort areas, constitutes considerable competition to the resort hotels. Real estate management firms often manage such apartments or groups of condos within a building or complex and thus serve as agents for the owners. They rent the condos as managers of the group, charging a fee for this service to the absent owner. Such arrangements can be made through a local travel agent in the prospective traveler's home city. The agent will book the reservation through the real estate management firm.

Timesharing

Timesharing is a technique for the multiple ownership and/or use of resort and recreational properties. Timesharing has been applied to hotels, motels, condominiums, town houses, single-family detached homes, campgrounds, and even boats and yachts. It involves both new construction and conversion of existing structures, along with properties devoted solely to timesharing and projects that integrate timesharing and nontimesharing properties. While most programs may be classified as either ownership or nonownership (right to use), there are wide variations in program and legal format.

The attraction of timesharing is simple: It permits purchasers to own or have occupancy rights at a resort accommodation for a period of time each year for a fraction of the purchasing price of the entire unit. Timeshare owners pay for exactly what they plan on using, and when they leave they don't have to think about where they'll be vacationing next year. Another option or advantage of timesharing is the exchange program. The exchange system affords vacation flexibility by allowing owners to trade or swap their timeshares for other locations and times. Finally, a well-designed timeshare program can be a hedge against inflation in resort accommodations.

The benefits of timesharing are substantially borne out by the high degree of consumer satisfaction it has achieved. In a survey of approximately ten thousand timeshare buyers, conducted by the National Timesharing Council, 86.3 percent of the respondents said they were "very satisfied" or "satisfied" with their purchase. About 40 percent indicated that they were interested in purchasing additional timeshares. Additional information on timesharing is available from the American Resort Development Association, **http://www.arda.org.** Also see the discussion in Chapter 6.

Hotel Management

The management of a hotel should ideally be the same group that was involved in the planning and construction of the hotel. To do otherwise is unadvisable because the hotel business is very competitive, and any efficiency that can be built into the design or layout of the hotel as recommended by an experienced management group helps to ensure a better chance of success. For best results, the manager should be a graduate of a hotel school so there is a proper depth of understanding and appreciation of the industry as well as training for the job.

All decisions pertaining to the management of the hotel should begin with the customers and guests. What is the likely reaction to each management decision? Implementation of such a policy favors success for the hotel as the policy is most likely to produce a high measure of guest satisfaction.

Success in hotel management also depends on organization and the functioning of each department. Each department head should be considered a manager of his or her own department. The goals of each should affect and support the overall goals of the hotel. The personal goals of each employee should contribute to and buttress the goals of the department. Each employee should be taught high standards of service, sanitation, and personal conduct, essential for the success of the hotel.

Thorough training sessions must be conducted for new employees, and recurring training should be provided for all employees. A wide selection of home study courses (also suitable for group use) is available, in English, from the Educational Institute of the American Hotel and Lodging Association, 800 Magnolia Avenue, Suite 1800, Orlando, Florida 32803; Web site **http://www.ei-ahla.org.**

Assistance in training staff and managers can also be obtained from colleges and universities, state departments of education and public instruction, trade associations, and private management institutes or associations as well as from resources from within the organization or from larger affiliates or chain staff personnel.

Local Charm

A principal appeal of travel is the enjoyment of people of other cultures, and guests will inevitably become acquainted with the staff of the hotel. In fact, at a resort hotel, the guest probably gets to know his or her waiter or waitress better than anyone else in the hotel or local area.

Tourists expect all hotel personnel to serve them with courtesy and efficiency. Thus, all hotel employees should be indoctrinated into the importance of this relationship and its success-building potential. The use of local costumes, the retention of unsophisticated charm, and the practice of friendliness and cleanliness are integral to achieving good hotel management.

Inspection

The most common types of hotel inspection relate to water supplies, sewage and waste disposal, general cleanliness, kitchen and food storage, and safety. Such inspection can be accomplished by local-, area-, or state-level authorities. Inspections of these conditions should be made no less than annually, and semiannually would be preferred.

Inspection to prevent fires is also important. Rigid inspections of electrical systems, heating systems, ventilating systems, air-conditioning systems, fuel storage, elevators, and storage areas are all important. Cleanliness and orderliness are essential ingredients in the prevention of fires. Fire prevention systems such as automatic sprinklers or similar warning devices should be inspected, and installation of fire prevention devices should be encouraged, if not required.

Regulations

Regulations of hotels take many forms depending on local conditions and requirements. Regulations often relate to fairness and minimum standards of wages, hours, and ages of employees. Others relate to the licensing for selling alcoholic beverages; various tax structures for hotels; the disposal of wastes; hours of operation for public eating and drinking facilities; registration of guests; the importation of various food and drink items; equipment, unemployment, and disability insurance and other staff benefits; passport identification; zoning and building regulations; and fair employment and civil rights regulations. Many states regulate the sale of alcoholic beverages and the licensing of serving establishments, usually via a special agency.

Hotel Classification

Hotels are classified using a number of different systems. Then, too, many tourist countries have no classification system whatsoever. Many in the industry prefer the five-star rating system, which grades hotels according to specific criteria (usually by the national tourist organization) from the highest (five stars) to the most modest accommodations (one star) suitable for travelers. Countries such as Spain also classify nonhotel accommodations, such as pensions. Criteria used for star ratings are public rooms, bathrooms, climatization, telephone, bar, dining rooms, and other characteristics.

Other classifications are deluxe, superior, and good; or superdeluxe, and first-class reasonable. Still another classification is A, B, C, D, or E. Because many classification

Accommodations vary tremendously from luxury properties to charming hostels, such as this one in Galway, Ireland. *Photo by the author.*

schemes are confusing or not useful, a uniform worldwide classification truly indicative of the grades of hotels in any country would be a real plus to tourism. Of course, differences in general standards of development in various countries would be understood. A five-star hotel in a highly developed country would likely be more deluxe than would a five-star hotel in a less developed area.

Promotion through Referral and Franchise Groups

A substantial number of U.S. hotels and motels belong to some kind of an endorsing or referral association. Examples are Best Western, American Automobile Association (AAA), and Preferred Hotels. The main purpose of group membership is to obtain substantial numbers of reservations from other properties in the group and from the association's computerized reservation system.

Accommodations firms can also hold a franchise, such as Holiday Inns or Hilton Hotels. All members of the franchise encourage their guests to make free reservations at another property in the group. Franchise companies operate sales offices (called hotel rep firms) in major cities and also provide national and international reservations services. All of this effort is aimed at increasing members' annual volume of reservations.

Types of Transportation

All factors concerning transportation should be considered in developing tourism, beginning with taxis, limousines, and bus service from the place of lodging to the departure terminals. Such services must be adequate and economical.

Air

As described in Chapter 5, the airline industry dominates public intercity transportation systems, capturing over 92 percent of the common-carrier passenger mile market. Thus, planners looking to improve tourism must evaluate the adequacy of air transportation. Flight frequencies as well as size and type of aircraft are important. Air service from important origins for tourists is, of course, essential.

Airport facilities must be adequate. Major problems frequently encountered are the accessibility to

Transportation takes many forms around the world. Some are familiar and others are unique. This device carries foot-weary tourists around Melaka, Malaysia, in comfort. *Photo by the author.*

the airport and the loading-unloading parking space sequence. Newly built airports seem to have solved these to a considerable degree and have also reduced walking distances because of design improvements. There is also frequent shuttle bus service for interline passengers.

Motorcoach

Motorcoaches intended for tour use should have large windows, air-conditioning, comfortable seats, and rest room facilities. Springs or other suspension systems in the coaches should be designed so that the joggling of passengers is kept to a minimum or eliminated. Multilingual guide service or multilingual tape recording facilities with earphones for each passenger are useful in communities or on tours where an interpretation of the points of interest is desirable.

Personnel assigned to buses should be selected for suitable temperament, courtesy, and spirit of hospitality. For example, if a bus is staffed by a driver and an interpreter, the interpreter can assist passengers on and off the bus as well as inform them of local environment, particularly attractions of interest. Interpreters or guides should be trained and educated for this duty. Too often, the interpretation of points of interest is superficial (and inaccurate). A program of certification for guides should be conducted by a special school or provided in the curriculum of an institution of higher learning. In such a program, competent instructors should educate potential guides in the history, archaeology, ethnology, culture, and economic system of the area in which the tour is being conducted. Competency in the various languages commonly encountered with tourists is also an essential qualification.

Ship and Boat

Water travel is a major part of tourism and contributes considerably to the development of travel on land and by air. Forms of water travel include cruise ship, passenger travel on freighters, ferryboats, river stern-wheelers, chartered boats and yachts, houseboats, and smaller family boats and canoes.

Cruise ships and other large vessels need convenient piers and good land-air transportation connections for their passengers. Smaller boats need docks and loading-unloading ramps for easy accessibility to water. Charter boat operators must have

Cruise sailing is a special component of the cruise market. The *Wind Spirit* is shown here under full sail. *Photo by Harvey Lloyd; courtesy of Windstar Cruises.*

reliable weather forecasting and ready availability of needed supplies and repair services. Where rental canoes are popular, delivery and pickup services are often necessary, as are campgrounds in wilderness areas where canoeists can stay overnight. Persons owning their own boats appreciate good public-access points for launching.

Rail

Travelers worldwide often prefer rail travel, particularly because of its safety record and the convenience and comfort of viewing the scenery from an air-conditioned car. Also, the frequent schedules of trains in many countries appeal to travelers. The recent advent of high-speed trains further enhances their appeal. Some trains have stewardesses or hostesses, which travelers seem to appreciate.

Rail allows travelers the opportunity of viewing scenery as they travel in a comfortable atmosphere. *Copyright ©2001 Amtrak. Photo provided as a courtesy by Amtrak.*

Adequate taxi, limousine, or bus service from the railroad station to hotels and downtown points is essential. Such transportation service must be frequent enough to get the traveler to the destination promptly. Conversely, the traveler should be able to get to the railroad station in ample time to make connections with the train as well.

Taxis

Adequate taxi and limousine services are essential in a tourist area. Ideally, taxis should have removable and washable seat covers so the car always presents a clean appearance to the passenger. Also, to make the best impression, the taxi driver should dismount from the driver's seat and open the door for the passenger. He or she also should assist in stowing the luggage in the trunk or elsewhere in the cab and be courteous at all times.

Taxi drivers who are multilingual are highly desirable and, in fact, essential if tourism is to be an important element of the economy of the location. Training taxi drivers in foreign languages should be no more difficult than training tourist guides or front-desk clerks. Where taxi drivers have no foreign language ability, hotels may provide written directions for the tourist to give to the driver concerning the destination and the return to the hotel at the end of the excursion.

SPIRIT OF HOSPITALITY AND CULTURAL RESOURCES

The development of **hospitality resources** is perhaps the most important factor in tourism. The finest physical facilities will be worthless if the tourist feels unwelcome. For example, we suggest having a welcoming sign and a special reception area for visitors at airports and other entry points. A favorable attitude toward the visitor can be created through programs of public information and propaganda. Public relations and publicity designed to convince local citizens of the importance of tourism are helpful. Courses at tourist hospitality schools for all persons who have direct contact with visitors are useful. In these schools, store clerks, gasoline station attendants, hotel clerks, and other persons who are directly in contact with the visitor are given indoctrination on the importance of tourism to their community and are taught the location of important points of interest. Other parts of the program include the importance of

The growing popularity of "heritage tourism" has created a desire to preserve and enjoy early railway equipment.
Photo courtesy of Utah Travel Council.

appearance and good grooming, greeting of visitors, providing information, and being helpful, gracious, friendly, and cooperative.

Cultural programs such as "Meet the Danes" (home visitation arrangements) help greatly in this respect. Adequate training of personnel by tourist hospitality businesses can also create the desired hospitable attitude.

Activities Tourists Enjoy Most

One of the most important functions of a tourism promotion organization is to ascertain what activities visitors would enjoy. When substantial data are accumulated, the findings should be reported to those who accommodate and entertain. Thus, they are guided into more successful methods and programs. Table 12.1 shows some tourists' favorite things.

The best method of obtaining this information is by interviewing both the visitors and their hosts. Questionnaires can also be placed in guests' rooms. Public contact employees can be instructed to inquire politely as to guests' interests and

TABLE 12.1	TOURISTS' FAVORITE THINGS: WHAT EUROPEAN-BOUND TRAVELERS PLAN TO DO	
ACTIVITY		PERCENT CITING IT
Dining at restaurants		86.2
Shopping		76.9
Visiting a historical site		67.5
Visiting a small town		53.6
Sight-seeing in a city		51.8
Touring the countryside		47.0
Visiting an art gallery/museum		40.1
Visiting a cultural heritage site		38.3
Visiting a nightclub/dancing		21.4
Taking a guided tour		21.0
Attending a concert/play		20.2
Visiting an ethnic heritage site		13.3
Participating in water sports/sunbathing		10.7
Visiting an amusement park		8.1
Visiting a national park		6.7
Taking a cruise		6.4
Camping/hiking		4.9
Playing golf/tennis		4.9
Visiting a casino		4.8
Attending a sports event		3.8
Skiing		2.9
Participating in an ecological excursion		2.5
Hunting/fishing		1.4

Source: Travel Weekly, European Travel Commission, and Tourism Industries, U.S. Department of Commerce.

entertainment preferences. Careful recording and thorough analysis of these data will result in findings of real value. When those responsible for attracting and hosting visitors provide the requested entertainment activities, the community will likely be a preferred destination area. There is no better advertising than a satisfied visitor (see Chapter 18).

Shopping

Shopping is an important tourist activity and thus an essential element in tourism supply because it affects the success of the tourist destination area. The most important single element in shopping is the authenticity of the products offered for sale as they relate to the local area. A product that is supposedly a "native handicraft" should be that. If it is an import, the purchaser may be disappointed if he or she expected an authentic, locally made item.

Tourists who are shopping are particularly interested in handicraft items that are typical or indigenous to the particular locale or region. Of course, they are also interested in essential items such as toothpaste, but our discussion here is confined to purchases that tourists make as souvenirs or special gifts.

Tourists can be encouraged to spend more money on shopping if displays are high quality, imaginative, and attractive. Hotels are excellent places for shops; and if these shops are exquisitely furnished and stocked, the tourist is attracted to the shop and is more likely to make purchases.

Native Marketplaces

Another shopping experience concerns the local market or so-called native marketplace. Such areas are rich in ethnicity and have much local color. They are popular with visitors, even though the visitor may not understand the language and may have trouble making a purchase. Although many persons in native shopping places do not understand any foreign languages, the sign language of bargaining is fairly universal.

Shops and Clerks

Shopkeepers and clerks themselves should be amiable and courteous. Furthermore, the shopkeeper should not be so anxious to close a sale that the tourist is pressured. A tourist who is courteously served in a store and who makes a good purchase will tell friends back home. Thus, future business can be developed in this way. Salespeople should also take the time to explain the value of the item and relate something of its history that would be otherwise unknown to the purchaser. Of course, this information should be accurate and truthful.

Salespersons must have sufficient language ability to conduct conversations with the visitors. The most common language is English, but a knowledge of other languages that are commonly spoken by tourists who visit a particular area is a necessary qualification of clerks who serve these visitors. Salespersons must be patient and understanding and try to help the prospective purchaser cheerfully at all times.

The many colors and varieties of products in foreign markets make shopping a unique and enjoyable experience for visitors. *Copyright © PhotoDisc, Inc.*

Prices and Unethical Practices

One of the most important considerations in shopping is the pricing of the goods. Probably resented more than any other single factor of tourism is higher prices for tourists than for local residents. Because many shoppers compare prices from one store to another, prices should be as consistent as possible and in line with costs.

If the shopkeeper resorts to unethical methods of selling, such as deception, selling imitation goods or products of inferior quality, refusing to exchange damaged goods, or shortchanging or short-weighting, the seller is hurting the tourist trade and should be prosecuted by local authorities.

Entertainment, Recreation, and Other Activities

The recreation and other activities engaged in by tourists at their destination comprise a major component of tourism. Thus, considerable thought and effort should be devoted to the type of activities that visitors are likely to enjoy.

Entertainment

The most satisfying entertainment for visitors is native to the area. In any country, there are expressions of the culture in the music, dance, drama, poetry, literature, motion pictures, television, ceremonies, festivals, exhibits, shows, meetings, food and beverage services, and tours (or local excursions) that portray the best the area has to offer.

Not all forms of entertainment can be successfully described or illustrated in tourist promotional literature. One of the best ways to bring these entertainment opportunities to the attention of the visitor is with a social director whose desk is in the lobby of hotels, resorts, and other forms of accommodation so that the visitor can readily find out what is going on and make arrangements to attend. In European hotels, this desk is traditionally staffed by the concierge, who provides an amazing amount of information concerning all types of entertainment and activities available. An appropriate substitute is a knowledgeable person at the front desk to provide information concerning recreation and entertainment.

Bulletin board displays or posters and verbal announcements of outstanding events made in the dining room or other areas where guests gather can also provide entertainment information. A local newspaper that features articles concerning everyday as well as special entertainment events and opportunities is a valuable method of distributing information. These newspapers or bulletins are presently provided in popular vacation destination areas such as Miami Beach and Honolulu, but the idea is not widespread. In metropolitan centers, a weekly magazine is normally provided to hotel guests to give current information on entertainment, recreational, and cultural opportunities in the city.

Special Events

Entertainment can be provided very effectively as a special promotional event to attract visitors during an off-season. One of the best examples of this is Aloha Festivals, which was inaugurated in Hawaii as Aloha Week in the mid-1940s to bolster tourist traffic in the fall. This festival is enthusiastically supported by local tourism interests and is very successful in attracting tourists. Musicians, dancers, exhibits, floral displays, and special programs are assembled and give the visitor an unusual opportunity to enjoy the beauty and excitement of cultural expression that this state offers. Once created, such events become annual and typically grow in visitors and importance. Expositions and festivals are very attractive to visitors and deserve adequate promotion.

Museums and Art Galleries

Museums and art galleries are another major attraction for tourists. They provide some of the highlights in many of the world's most important tourist destinations such as New York, Washington, D.C., Chicago, Paris, London, Madrid, Rome, Singapore, Tokyo, Buenos Aires, Mexico City, and many others. The quality and magnitude of these institutions are an important consideration for attracting and satisfying tourists.

Sports

Golf and sports such as tennis, surfing, swimming, mountain climbing, skiing, hunting, fishing, hiking, prospecting, or any other outdoor sports activity require properly publicized facilities and services. Guides, equipment, charter boats, and other services needed to enjoy these sports must be readily available at fair prices. Convenience and accessibility are key factors in this type of entertainment.

MATCHING SUPPLY WITH DEMAND

Providing an ample tourism supply to meet anticipated demand is a challenge for the tourism planner or manager. Supply functions are always constrained by demand. The following formula can be used to calculate the number of hotel rooms (or other types of lodging) required:

$$\text{Room demand per night} = \frac{\text{no. tourists} \times \% \text{ staying in hotels} \times \text{average length of stay}}{365 \times \text{average no. persons per room}}$$
(100% occupancy)

$$R = \frac{T \times P \times L}{S \times N}$$

where

    R = room demand per night, at 100 percent occupancy
    T = number of tourists
    P = percentage staying in hotels
    L = average length of stay
    S = number of days per year open for business
    N = average number of persons per room (obtained from hoteliers); total number of guest nights divided by the number of guests, during any period of time
    O = hotel occupancy used for estimating; for 70 percent occupancy, divide number of rooms needed at 100 percent occupancy by 70 percent

Illustration of application of the formula:

    T = 1,560,000 visitors
    P = 98% staying in hotels
    L = 9 days
    S = 365 days per year open for business
    N = 1.69 persons per room
    O = 70% occupancy

$$R = \frac{1,560,000 \times 0.98 \times 9}{365 \times 1.69} = \frac{13,759,200}{616.85} = 22,306 \text{ (rooms needed at 100\% occupancy)}$$

$$= \frac{22,306}{0.70} \text{ (as more rooms will be needed at 70\% occupancy than at 100\%)}$$

$$= 31,866 \text{ rooms needed}$$

Infrastructure factors in supply will be determined largely by the number of guest rooms as well as restaurants, stores, and similar installations. Infrastructure appropriate to the size of the development is an engineering problem and is readily ascertained as the plans are developed. Transportation equipment is generally supplied by commercial firms as well as publicly owned or quasi-public transportation facilities and services.

Regarding hospitality resources, the recruiting and training of staff for the various elements of supply is a critical one. The traveler generally enjoys being served by unsophisticated local persons who have had proper training and possess a hospitable attitude. Such persons may be recruited through government and private employment agencies as well as through direct advertisement to the public. Newly hired employees must be indoctrinated in the importance of tourism, how it affects their own personal welfare as well as that of their community, the importance of proper service to the visitors, and how their economic welfare is closely related to their performance.

Museums, art exhibits, festivals, craft shows, and similar cultural resources are usually created by community cooperation and the willing assistance of talented people. A chamber of commerce or tourism body is the best mechanism for organizing the creation of these hospitality resources.

Task Analysis

The procedure used in matching supply with demand is called a task analysis. Suggested steps are as follows:

1. Identification of the present demand
   a. By mode of transportation and by seasons of the year
   b. For various forms of tourism such as activities, attendance at attractions, and similar categories
   c. For special events such as conventions, celebrations, fairs
   d. Group and tour visitors
   e. Family and individual visitors
   f. Business visitors
2. A quantitative and qualitative inventory of the existing supply
3. The adequacy of present supply with present demand
   a. Natural resources
   b. Infrastructure
   c. Transportation and equipment
   d. Hospitality and cultural resources
4. Examination of present markets and the socioeconomic trends
   a. Geographic market segmentation and orientation
   b. Demographic market segmentation and orientation
      i. Population age, sex, occupation, family life stages, income, and similar data
      ii. Leisure time and work patterns
   c. Psychographic market segmentation
      i. Motivations, interests, hobbies, employment orientation, skills, professional interests
      ii. Propensity to travel, responsiveness to advertising
5. Forecast of tourism demand
   a. Computer systems simulation method
   b. Trend analysis

   c. Simple regression—linear least squares
   d. Multiple regression—linear least squares
   e. Executive judgment or Delphi method
6. Matching supply with anticipated demand
   a. If adequate, no further action necessary
   b. If inadequate, inauguration of planning and development procedures

To perform the task analysis, certain skills are required, with statistical research techniques employed to identify and quantify the present demand. Suggestions for doing this are provided in Chapter 13.

When making a quantitative and qualitative inventory of the existing supply, the aid of specialists and experts is usually needed. For example, the adequacy of the present supply in relation to present demand requires the work of tourism specialists such as travel agents, tour company and hotel executives, tourism promotion people, ground operators (companies that provide baggage transfers, taxi services, local tours, and similar services), shopkeepers, and perhaps a sample of the tourists themselves.

Examining the present markets and the socioeconomic trends that will affect future markets requires specialized market research activities. These should include determination of market characteristics, development of market potentials, market share analysis, sales analysis, competitive destination studies, potentials of the existing and possibly new markets, short-range forecasting, and studies of travel business trends. A number of sophisticated techniques are now available. The engagement of a reputable market research firm is one way to obtain this information.

Forecasting tourism demand is a perilous business. However, a well-structured statistical analysis coupled with executive judgment is most likely the best approach to this difficult problem. See Chapter 13 for several methods for accomplishing this.

Finally, matching supply with the anticipated demand must be done by knowledgeable planners. A tourism development plan within the master plan is recommended. Supply items are essentially rigid. They are elaborate and expensive and, thus, cannot be expanded rapidly. An exception would be transportation equipment. Additional sections of planes, buses, trains, or cars could be assembled quite rapidly to meet an unusually high demand situation.

Peaks and Valleys

The foregoing discussion dealt with matching supply and demand in a long-run context. Another important consideration is that of fluctuations in demand in the short run (**seasonality**) and the resulting **peaks and valleys of demand.** This is a vexing problem.

The reason for this is simply that tourism is a service, and services cannot be placed in inventory. If a 400-room hotel rents (sells) 350 rooms on a particular night, it cannot place the other 50 rooms in inventory, for sale the following night. Regardless of how many rooms went unoccupied in the past, a 400-room property can rent no more than 400 rooms on any given night. By way of contrast, consider the case of some tangible good, say, television sets. If some television sets are not sold in one month, the storekeeper can keep them in inventory and sell them the next month. Of course, the storage charges, interest payments, and other expenses incurred in inventorying a particular item reduce the item's economic value. But in tourism, the economic value of unsold items such as the 50 hotel rooms mentioned is exactly zero.

Thus, it should be clear that while in most cases, firms selling tangible goods can deal with demand fluctuation through the inventory process, this option is not available to firms providing travel services. In the travel industry, an effort must be made to reduce seasonal fluctuations as much as possible. Because of the high economic cost involved, no effort should be spared in attempting to limit the amount of seasonal variations in demand. Nor can the problem be dealt with by simply selecting an appropriate supply level. The following charts illustrate various supply situations associated with fluctuating demand levels.

Suppose that the demand for a particular destination exhibits the seasonal pattern depicted in Figure 12.2a. If no action is taken to "level off" the demand, then three possible levels of supply can be considered. In Figure 12.2b, the level of supply is provided so that demand in the peak season is fully satisfied. This implies that tourists coming to the destination in the peak season will be accommodated comfortably and without overcrowding. However, during the slack season, the destination will suffer from extremely low occupancy levels, with obvious implications for profitability. If, on the other hand, the supply is set at a low level (Figure 12.2c), the facilities during the peak season will be overcrowded enough to detract from the tourist experience. Visitor satisfaction will be at a low level, and the future of such a resort area will be doubtful. Last, if supply is set in between the level of demand during the peak season and the off-season (Figure 12.2d), the problems are somewhat mitigated. Nevertheless, low occupancy will result during low demand periods, and overcrowding will result in peak periods; neither is desirable. To maximize customer satisfaction and to utilize the facilities year-round, some action must be taken. Two strategies for dealing with this situation are as follows:

1. **Multiple use.** This involves supplementing peak-season attractions of a destination with other attractions that would create demand for travel to that destination during off-season periods. In effect, the peak season for the destination is extended. Examples of such efforts abound. In Michigan, for example, the current demand for off-season travel (during the fall, winter, and spring) has been successfully increased and sustained at much higher levels than in the past. While Michigan was once viewed primarily as a summer destination, the development and promotion of winter sports in resort areas, foliage tours, and superb salmon fishing in the fall and spring have created new markets for these off-season periods. Festivals, special celebrations, conventions, and sports activities sponsored and promoted during off-seasons are other examples of multiple-use strategies.

2. **Price differential.** This technique, as contrasted with the multiple-use strategy, creates new markets for the off-season periods by employing price differentials as a strong tool to shift demand away from the peak season in favor of

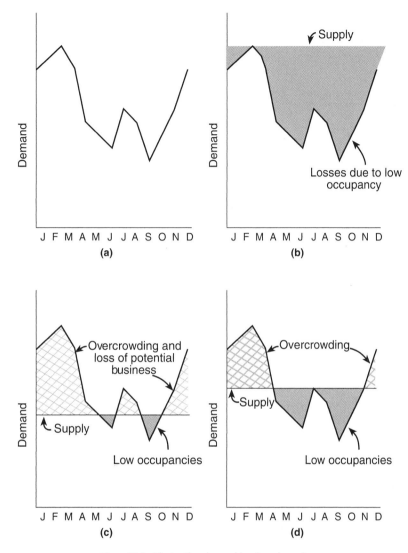

Figure 12.2 Fluctuating demand levels and supply.

the off-season. Florida and destinations in the Caribbean have used this strategy rather effectively. The prices in these destinations during the off-seasons are considerably less than during the peak seasons. In addition, the development of promotional fares by airlines and other carriers, along with the expansion of the number, timing, and variety of price-discounted tours, have helped to stimulate demand in the off-season. Increased efficiency and effectiveness of promotional campaigns and better marketing also tend to offset the traditional seasonal patterns of demand. Yield management techniques used in the airline and lodging industries are very effective in using price differentials to match supply and demand.

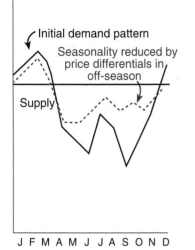

Figure 12.3 Reducing seasonality through price differentials.

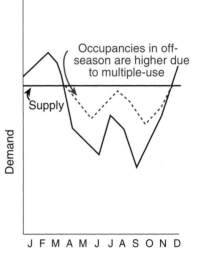

Figure 12.4 Reducing seasonality through multiple use.

In addition to these strategies implemented by destination areas, some trends in the employment and leisure patterns of Western societies contribute further to the leveling of demand between off-seasons and peak seasons. The staggering of holidays, the increasing popularity of three-day weekends with a holiday on Friday or Monday, and the splitting of vacations between various seasons of the year all lend themselves to leveling the demand for travel. Once the demand is evened out, the destination is then able to maximize customer satisfaction during the peak season and during the off-season. Also, facilities are utilized at a considerably higher level than previously. The importance of boosting off-season demand and, therefore, utilization level is further underscored by the fact that in most tourist service businesses, fixed costs are quite high in relation to operating costs. This implies that increasing total yearly revenue, even modestly, produces proportionally larger profits. There may be some softening of demand during the peak season due to those who might switch to the off-season because of the lower prices (see Figure 12.3). However, this is believed to be minimal. When off-season demand is boosted by the multiple-use strategy, peak-season demand is unaffected. Therefore, overall demand for the entire year will be substantially higher (see Figure 12.4).

SUMMARY

Certain broad classifications of supply components must be provided by any area that is attractive to tourists. The components consist of natural resources, the built environment, operating sectors, and the spirit of hospitality and cultural resources.

These factors may be combined in many ways to create the environment, facilities, and services that the planners hope will attract and please the customers.

Creation of supply components necessarily involves financing—a critical element. Ideally, all the supply components perfectly match the demand at any given time. However, this is unrealistic. Too much supply means unused facilities, which is uneconomic. Too little supply results in overcrowding with resultant depreciation of the vacation experience. A moderate supply level is recommended.

Supply can be matched with demand using a mathematical formula. When confronted with a supply problem, the proper level of supply to meet the anticipated demand can be estimated by using the formula provided in this chapter. The process is refined and completed by a six-step task analysis.

KEY CONCEPTS

accommodations
cultural resources
entertainment, recreation, and
   other activities
hospitality resources
hotel management

infrastructure
multiple use
natural resources
peaks and valleys of demand
price differentials
seasonality

shopping
superstructure
supply components
task analysis
timesharing
transportation

Internet Sites

The Internet sites mentioned in this chapter are repeated here for convenience, plus some selected additional sites. For more information, visit these sites. Be aware that Internet addresses change frequently, so if a site cannot be accessed, use a search engine. Also use a search engine to locate many additional relevant sites.

Airport Council International
http://www.aci.aero

Air Transport Association of America
http://www.airlines.org

American Automobile Association
http://www.aaa.com

American Hotel and Lodging
   Association
http://www.ahla.com

American Public Transportation
   Association
http://www.apta.com

American Resort Development
   Association
http://www.arda.org

Cruise Lines International Association
http://www.cruising.org

Federal Highway Administration
http://www.fhwa.dot.gov

Fodor's Guidebooks
http://www.fodors.com

International Air Transport
   Association
http://www.iata.org

International Association of
Amusement Parks and
Attractions
http://www.iaapa.org

International Civil Aviation
Organization
http://www.icao.org

International Road Federation
http://www.irfnet.org

Lonely Planet Online
http://www.lonelyplanet.com

National Park Service
http://www.nps.gov

National Restaurant Association
http://www.restaurant.org

Tourist Railway Association
http://www.train.org

Internet Exercises

Activity 1
Site Name: Fodor's Travel Publications
URL: http://www.fodors.com
Background Information: Fodor's Travel Publications, a subsidiary of Random House, is the largest publisher of English-language travel information in the world. Fodor's now publishes 14 guidebook series and more than 290 books on destinations around the world.

Exercise
1. Using the four major supply components your textbook indicates that any tourist area must possess, discuss how the Fodor's web site addresses each of these areas for the potential tourist.

Activity 2
Site Name: Lonely Planet Online
URL: http://www.lonelyplanet.com
Background Information: Lonely Planet publishes some of the world's best guidebooks for independent travelers. Their books are known worldwide for reliable, insightful travel information, maps, photos, and background historical and cultural information.

Exercise
1. Choose a destination or use one provided by the instructor. How does this site address the four components of travel for the potential tourist to this destination?

QUESTIONS FOR REVIEW AND DISCUSSION

1. In planning supply components for a development in an entirely new area, which one of the four components should be considered first? Last? Why?
2. When a gorgeous new hotel is opened for business, are the attractive physical facilities more important than the quality and training of the staff?
3. As a resort hotel manager, do you believe your guests need to be educated about environmental protection? Do you need to educate your staff?
4. In a poor, developing country, a world-class hotel uses about half of the community's water supply. This requires rationing of water by the local people, which creates resentment. Suggest a partial solution to this problem.

5. For new developments, should the access roads be supplied by a government agency, the developer, or both? If both, who should supply what?
6. What might be appropriate costumes and uniforms for waiters and waitresses in various localities?
7. A motor hotel manager states, "I can't sell any souvenirs that cost over $5." How could this situation be improved?
8. The sports director of a large resort hotel has been instructed to upgrade the hotel's physical fitness program. Provide some suggestions as to how this might be done.
9. Is changing the prices of hotel rooms, meals, and entertainment the best way to mitigate fluctuating levels of demand? Are there nonprice methods? Could combinations of methods be used?

CASE PROBLEMS

1. To maintain and hopefully enhance the appeal and quality of its area's natural resources, the city council has decided that it needs to enact protective laws to help ensure its future tourism success. What specific laws and regulations might these be?

2. Resort City is anxious to attract more tourists. The chamber of commerce has been successful in attracting several new tourist firms to the community. These firms plan to develop new hotels, lodges, shops, and restaurants. However, an influential member of the chamber of commerce expresses the viewpoint that the community should enact some strict zoning and building code laws before these construction projects get under way. The prospective developers and many other members of the chamber disagree. What do you think should be done to resolve this situation, and why?

3. A destination tourism organization (DMO) is seeking ways in which to improve the proficiency of accommodations booking. It is exploring the possibility of installing a computer-based accommodations information system. This system provides data comparisons between similar operations considering size, location, and countrywide averages. What do you see as advantages for implementing such a system? How might the system be implemented in your destination?

SELECTED REFERENCES

Arbel, Avner, and Abraham Pizam. "Some Determinants of Urban Hotel Location: The Tourist Inclinations." *Journal of Travel Research,* Vol. 15, No. 3, pp. 18–22, Winter 1977.

Bonn, Mark A., H. Leslie Furr, and Muzaffer Uysal. "Seasonal Variation of Coastal Resort Visitors: Hilton Head Island." *Journal of Travel Research,* Vol. 31, No. 1, pp. 50–56, Summer 1992.

Carter, R. W., G. S. Baxter, and M. Hockings. "Resource Management in Tourism Research: A New Direction?" *Journal of Sustainable Tourism,* Vol. 9, No. 4, pp. 265–280, 2001.

Clawson, Marion, and Jack L. Knetsch. *Economics of Outdoor Recreation.* Baltimore: Johns Hopkins Press, 1966.

Maguire, Patricia A. "Tourism Supply: A U.S. Perspective." *Tourist Review,* No. 3, pp. 2–6, July–September 1990.

Manning-Shaw, Janet. "The Channel Tunnel." *Tourism Management,* Vol. 12, No. 1, pp. 5–7, March 1991.

McCool, Stephen F. "Recreation Use Limits: Issues for the Tourism Industry." *Journal of Travel Research,* Vol. 17, No. 2, pp. 2–7, Fall 1978.

Moulin, Claude. "Appreciating the Built Environment through Cultural Tourism." *Tourist Review,* No. 2, pp. 7–13, 1996.

Pearce, Douglas G. "Islands and Coastal Tourism: Demand and Supply. Perspectives from Samoa, Sarawak and New Zealand." *Tourism,* Vol. 49, No. 3, pp. 255–266, 2001.

Qu, Hailin, Ping Xa, and Amy Tan. "A Simultaneous Equations Model of the Hotel Room Supply and Demand in Hong Kong." *International Journal of Hospitality Management,* Vol. 21, No. 4, pp. 455–462, 2002.

Smith, Darren L., and Nancy V. Kniskern (eds). *The Traveler's Sourcebook.* Detroit: Omnigraphics, 1997.

Smith, Stephen L. "Room for Rooms: A Procedure for the Estimation of Potential Expansion of Tourist Accommodations." *Journal of Travel Research,* Vol. 15, No. 4, pp. 26–29, Spring 1977.

Waddell, Joseph M. "Hotel Capacity: How Many Rooms to Build?" *Cornell Hotel and Restaurant Administration Quarterly,* Vol. 18, No. 2, pp. 35–47, August 1977.

World Bank. *Tourism Supply in the Caribbean Region.* Washington, DC: World Bank, November 1974.

MEASURING AND FORECASTING DEMAND

CHAPTER 13

Learning Objectives

- Understand the concept of demand and its application and importance in tourism development planning.
- Understand the factors determining the magnitude and fluctuations of demand.

- Become able to apply various methods to measure and forecast demand.

Travelers enjoy the speed of the Très Grand Vitesse train to Paris.
Copyright © Corbis Digital Stock.

INTRODUCTION

Economists define demand as a schedule of the amount of any product or service that people are willing and able to buy at each specific price in a set of possible prices during some specified period of time. Thus there exists at any one time a definite relationship between the market price and the quantity demanded.

WHY DEMAND IS IMPORTANT

The amount of demand for travel to a particular destination is of great concern to anyone involved in tourism. Vital demand data include: (1) how many visitors arrived, (2) by what means of transportation, (3) how long they stayed and in what type of accommodations, and (4) how much money was spent. There are various measures of demand; some are much easier to obtain and are usually of more general interest than are others. Techniques also exist for making forecasts of future demand. Such estimates are of great interest to anyone planning future tourism developments. The availability of financing will depend largely on reliable forecasts of the future gross sales or revenues from the project to determine if the proposal will be financially feasible.

Marketing and sales promotion programs are, of course, aimed at increasing demand. Sometimes this effort focuses on increasing demand at certain times of the year or to a particular market. But the basic purpose is the same—to increase demand.

DEMAND TO A DESTINATION

In somewhat more specific terms, the demand for travel to a particular destination will be a function of the person's propensity to travel and the reciprocal of the resistance of the link between origin and destination areas. Thus,

$$D = f(\text{propensity, resistance})$$

where D is demand.

Propensity can be thought of as a person's predisposition to travel—in other words, how willing the person is to travel, what types of travel experiences he or she prefers, and what types of destinations are considered. A person's propensity to travel will, quite obviously, be determined largely by his or her psychographic profile and travel motivation, as discussed in previous chapters. In addition, a person's socioeconomic status will have an important bearing on propensity. It follows that to estimate a person's propensity to travel, we must understand both psychographic and demographic variables concerning the person. Propensity is *directly* related to demand.

Resistance, on the other hand, relates to the relative attractiveness of various destinations. This factor is, in turn, a function of several other variables, such as economic distance, cultural distance, the cost of tourist services at destination, the quality of service at destination, effectiveness of advertising and promotion, and seasonality. Resistance is inversely related to demand.

Economic Distance

Economic distance relates to the time and cost involved in traveling from the origin to the destination area and back. The higher the economic distance, the higher the resistance for that destination and, consequently, the lower the demand. It follows, conversely, that between any origin and destination point, if the travel time or travel cost can be reduced, demand will increase. Many excellent examples of this are available, such as the introduction of the jet plane in 1959 and the introduction of the wide-bodied jets in the late 1960s. They first cut travel time between California and Hawaii, for example, from twelve hours to five hours, and demand grew dramatically. A similar surge in demand was experienced with the introduction of the wide-bodied planes for transatlantic flights. The introduction of these planes cut the travel cost by almost 50 percent between the United States and most countries on the European continent.

Cultural Distance

Cultural distance refers to the extent to which the culture of the area from which the tourist originates differs from the culture of the host region. In general, the greater the cultural distance, the greater will be the resistance. In some cases, however, the relationship might be the opposite. For example, the higher the cultural distance between particular origin and destination areas, the more an allocentric person may wish to travel to that destination, to experience this extreme difference.

Cost of Services

The higher the **cost of services** at a destination, the higher the resistance to travel to that destination

Many tourists seek familiarity, while others seek new cultural experiences where they can mingle with the population and enjoy local food from a vendor, such as this one in Morocco. *Photo by the author.*

will be and, therefore, the lower the demand. This variable captures the familiar inverse relationship between the price of a good or service and demand for it.

Quality of Service

Clearly, the higher the **quality of service** at a destination, the lower the resistance will be for travel to that destination. Although the relationship between quality of service and demand is straightforward enough, a difficulty arises in the interpretation and evaluation of *quality*. Evaluation of quality is a highly personal matter, and what is quality to one tourist is not necessarily quality to another. Second, if a tourist does not have previous travel experience at a destination, can the tourist accurately judge the quality of services there? In such a case, the tourist must select a destination based on what the quality of service is *perceived* to be. Often, due to misleading advertisements or inaccurate input from others, the tourist's perception of the quality of service may not be realized at the destination. Such a situation has serious implications for establishing a repeat clientele, which is an important ingredient for success in the tourist business. Consequently, a destination area must be meticulous in projecting an accurate image.

Seasonality

The effect of **seasonality** on demand is quite apparent. The relative attractiveness of a given destination will depend on the time of year for which a vacation is planned. For a ski resort, for example, the demand will be at the highest level during the winter months. Resistance is at a minimum in this season.

The following illustrates the relationship between propensity, resistance, and demand, in terms of these variables as just described:

Demand = f (propensity, resistance)

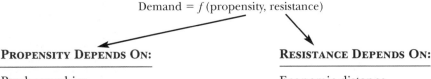

PROPENSITY DEPENDS ON:	**RESISTANCE DEPENDS ON:**
Psychographics	Economic distance
Demographics (socioeconomic status)	Cultural distance
Marketing effectiveness	Cost of tourist services
	Quality of service
	Seasonality

MEASURING DEMAND

Demand is strongly affected and limited by the supply. If the supply aspects are not taken into consideration when using demand figures, planners might be led into the false assumption that in a particular area, the supply should be increased to meet the demand when, in actuality, the increased supply may be needed much more elsewhere.

There are several measures of actual demand:

1. Visitor arrivals
2. Visitor-days or visitor-nights
3. Amount spent

Visitor Arrivals

Simply counting the number of people who arrive at a destination is a measure of demand, although not a particularly adequate one. However, when visitors arrive by ship or aircraft, for example, to an island, quite accurate data are obtainable. Those who are en route to someplace else should not be included in the arrival data. **Visitor arrivals** are the easiest type of data to obtain, especially if public transportation is the principal mode used. Regular reporting of visitor arrivals is of value in measuring broad changes in demand. Variation in the number of arrivals month by month is quite significant because it indicates the rise and fall of demand during the course of a year.

Arrival data become more of a problem if a large proportion of visitors arrive by private automobile on many major highways. In this case, a sampling method is employed, sometimes involving a tourist information center. Those stopping at the center are asked to fill out a card with data about their trip. The total number of visitors is then estimated, based on the sample obtained.

Visitors coming through seaports should be classified according to the United Nations' definition of tourists and excursionists. Excursionists remain in an area for less than twenty-four hours, whereas tourists stay twenty-four hours or longer. Arrival statistics should not include those who enter the country illegally, air travelers who do not leave the airport transit area, or analogous cases.

Visitor-Days or Visitor-Nights

Data on **visitor-days** and **visitor-nights** are much more valuable to

Tourists seek out famous sights such as the Leaning Tower of Pisa in Italy and create visitor-days and visitor-nights, which are a convenient way of measuring travel demand. *Copyright © Corbis Digital Stock.*

tourism planners than are data on the number of arrivals. To calculate the former, the number of visitors is multiplied by their average length of stay. Public park planners and beach managers are interested in visitor-day figures. Hotel and other accommodations people want data on visitor-nights. When such data are obtained, it is not difficult to make an estimate of the likely expenditures made per visitor per day or night. But these expenditure figures are at best only estimates and need to be used carefully. Data on visitor-days and visitor-nights are of great benefit to planners who work on public facilities for tourists, such as utility systems, parking, and recreation areas. Similarly, private developers planning new hotels or other accommodations or services want and need visitor-night information. Thus visitor-days and/or visitor-nights are the most practical data to obtain and are useful to tourism people.

$$D = \text{no. of visitors} \times \text{avg. no. of days or nights at destination}$$

Amount Spent

Amount spent is the most meaningful measure of demand, if it is determined accurately. However, it is the *most* difficult measure to obtain. Statistics of this type tend to be hidden or partially forgotten by the visitor. Thus, they are not as accurate as desired. However, to members of legislatures and the public, total tourist expenditures are the most easily understood and the most impressive.

The most common method of estimating tourist expenditures is to multiply visitor-days or visitor-nights by the average per-day or per-night expenditure. Thus,

$$D(\$) = \text{no. of visitor-days or visitor-nights} \times \text{avg. expenditures per day/night}$$

Total expenditures in an area consist of the visitor-day and visitor-night total expenditures over a specified period of time.

Measuring Tourism Expenditures through Tax Collections

Many states have a **sales and use tax** on consumer items. These tax collections provide a statistical base for calculating tourist expenditures. Suppose that a state has a 4 percent use tax on hotel and motel rooms. If we know what percentage of the average tourist dollar is spent for lodging, we could make an estimate of how much is spent on lodging and total expenditures, as illustrated in the following hypothetical example:

Rooms tax collections = $5 million

Rooms use tax rate = 4 percent

Total lodging spending = $5 million ÷ 0.04 = $125 million

Lodging expenditures = 25 percent of total spending

Total expenditures = $125 million ÷ 0.25 = $500 million (visitor-nights)

Estimated spending of those not using commercial lodging
+ visitor-day spending = $600 million

Total $D(\$)$ = $500 million + $600 million = $1.1 billion

Research in Measuring Demand

Considerable interest exists in improving methods of measuring current demand. Tourism is a labor-intensive service industry. As such, it is looked upon by state governments as a promising business to relieve unemployment. But one of the main problems is to determine its present financial dimensions.

Official tourism organizations are typically charged with the responsibility of undertaking research to measure economic impact and current demand. In this task they are assisted greatly by the Travel Industry Association of America. Details on research are provided in Chapter 18. The next research task is to make an estimate of what the future demand might be should certain steps be taken by the destination area.

PROJECTION METHODOLOGY

Several statistical methods or econometric analyses can be used to project demand. All require a degree of statistical or mathematical sophistication, familiarity with computers, and a clear understanding of the purpose (and limitations) of such projections. Listed are several such methods with brief explanations. (For a more complete review, see the references at the end of this chapter.)

Trend Analysis Method

The trend analysis method involves the interpretation of historical demand data. For instance, if a record of the number of tourist arrivals in an area on an annual basis is available, then demand for future years can be projected using this information. The first step is to plot the available data on a graph: time (in years) against the tourist arrivals. Once this has been done, a linear trend can be established which best captures the changes in demand levels in the past. Demand projections for future years can now be made by extending the trend line up to the relevant year and reading the demand estimate off the graph. Figure 13.1 illustrates this procedure. The points represent the levels of demand for the six-year period for which data are available.

A linear trend in demand levels can then be determined (say, line *AB*). If a demand projection for year 10 were needed, the trend line *AB* can be extended to a point such as *C*. Finally, the projected demand level in year 10 can be determined to be approximately 180,000 arrivals, as shown in Figure 13.1.

The advantage of using trend analysis is that the data needed are rather basic and easy to obtain. Only one data series is required: visitor arrivals, or some other measure of demand on a quarterly or on an annual basis for the past few years. In

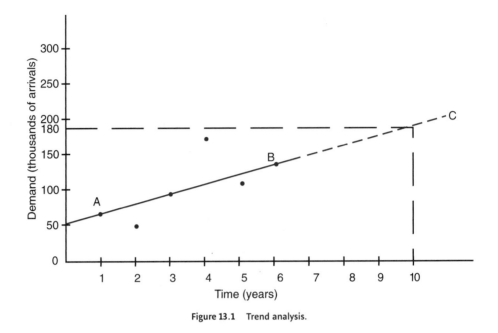

Figure 13.1   Trend analysis.

addition, the method is simple and does not require a great deal of mathematical sophistication. Characteristically, however, the simplicity of the model is to a large extent a trade-off for the usefulness of the results. For instance, the future demand estimates obtained in this manner should be interpreted with a great deal of caution. There are several reasons for this. First, trend analysis does not "explain" demand in any way. In other words, if demand changes from year to year, we would expect this to be because of changes in the components of demand (propensity and resistance, as discussed earlier in this chapter). Trend analysis does not acknowledge the influence that these variables have on demand levels and, therefore, cannot explain why it changed. Second, to *extrapolate* from a linear trend (extending the trend line *AB* to point *C*) is to assume that past growth trends will continue without change. Such an assumption is tentative at best. Estimates based on a constant growth rate tend to become very unrealistic in rather short periods of time, due to the nature of compounding.

Simple Regression: Linear Least Squares Method

In simple regression, information on demand levels for past years is plotted against one important determinant of demand, say, income or prices. Then, through the application of a statistical technique called **least squares** regression, a straight line is used to "explain" the relationship between demand and the particular variable being considered (such as income levels of tourists). Consider, for example, the hypothetical data in Table 13.1 for demand levels for ten years and the income levels of tourists for these same years.

TABLE 13.1	**DEMAND AND INCOME DATA**	
YEAR	NUMBER OF TOURIST ARRIVALS (THOUSANDS)	PER CAPITA INCOME OF TOURISTS (DOLLARS)
1	75	6,300
2	90	7,200
3	100	7,000
4	105	7,400
5	95	6,800
6	110	7,500
7	105	7,500
8	100	7,200
9	110	7,600
10	120	7,900

By plotting the pairs of arrivals and income data on a graph, we obtain a relationship between income and travel demand, illustrated in Figure 13.2. The points represent the annual observations, and the line *AB* represents the line of "best fit." It is obtained by the least squares method. We can now obtain demand projections from this method based on what we expect income levels to be in the future. Suppose we wish to estimate demand for year 15. In this year, income is projected to be $8,300 per capita. As shown in the figure, the estimate of demand for this income level is 128,000.

Because income is a major determinant of demand, simple regression "explains" demand to some extent. It is superior to trend analysis for this reason. Besides, the methodology is still relatively simple and can be presented visually. Data needed for this method are relatively easy to collect, when compared to the data needs of the two following projections methods.

Multiple Regression: Linear Least Squares Method

The major drawback of simple regression is that only one variable can be considered at a time. In reality, demand is affected by all the factors that influence propensity and resistance, as discussed earlier. It may not be feasible to include all these variables at one time, but it is certainly practical to isolate a few that are particularly relevant to determining demand and deal with these in one model. Multiple regression is one way to do this. It is essentially the same as simple regression, except that now more than one variable can be used to explain demand. Through a mathematical formula, a relationship is established between demand and the variables that we have chosen to consider in the model. For example, suppose that we had data on the prices of tourist services at a destination in addition to the incomes of the tourists. We could then regress demand on these two variables (income and prices) and obtain a mathematical relationship between them. To estimate future demand, projected income and price levels for the relevant year can simply be substituted into the mathematical formula. The resulting estimate of

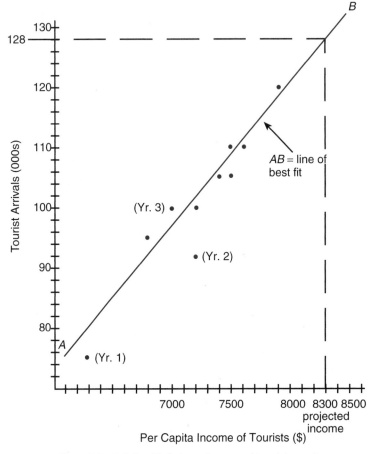

Figure 13.2   Relationship between income and travel demand.

demand will be more reliable than will one obtained by the simple regression method, because the former incorporates the *combined* effect of income and price on demand.

Indeed, the analysis is not restricted to these two variables alone. Conceptually, any number of variables can be used to explain and predict demand levels. But there are some practical limitations. As the number of "explanatory" variables increases, the calculations become increasingly complex. In addition, the costs involved in collecting the additional data and solving the mathematics of the technique are considerable. In some instances, the incremental reliability of the estimates may not justify these expenses, because estimates are after all only estimates, and not certain to materialize—no matter how comprehensively they may be calculated.

In addition to the expense involved, another drawback of multiple regression is that the relationships cannot be depicted graphically, as the results of the two earlier methods can be. The reason is, of course, that we get into multidimensional

Cruise travel is forecasted to continue to be the fastest-growing sector of the travel industry. This forecast is based on survey research, past trends, demographics, customer satisfaction, marketing efforts, and new ships joining the fleet. *Photo by Andy Newman; courtesy of Carnival Cruise Lines.*

planes. Up to three dimensions can be depicted visually, but beyond that it becomes impossible.

Computer Simulations and Models

Another projection method is to build a computer model that will simulate tourist demand. Typically, the demand for tourism to a particular area is a function of factors such as levels of income of tourists, the cost of travel from the tourists' homes to the destination, price levels, competition, currency exchange rates, and distance or journey time. These relationships are usually identified using multiple regression, as discussed above.

Simulation models include a complex set of equations that will usually combine both the trend-line extrapolation methods and the regression-technique models into a more comprehensive systems simulation. Relationships between many variables are specified through interrelated equations. Simulation models rely on historical data for input and model calibration. Once a model gives reasonably accurate distributions for past years, it can be used to predict probable future distributions.

Simulation models require specially trained personnel with a high degree of technical expertise to set up original model and data processing programs.

Knowledge of time-series, cross-sectional, and causal relationships and change processes is required. Also, powerful computing resources and high data precision are necessary. These are serious problems that have to be faced by any tourism organization that might consider using this approach. Simulation forecasting is best suited for a problem that is complex with known and quantifiable relationships and some feedback effects. It is also suitable for long forecast horizons.

Executive Judgment (Delphi) Method

Mathematical and statistical models are most useful and often produce accurate results. However, the combined experience of tourism executives is also valuable. The **Delphi method,** in essence, consists of a systematic survey of such experts. A series of questions is asked, and then the results, as a consensus, are reached.

Mathematical statistical tools cannot incorporate the influences of variables not explicitly included in the model. For example, under multiple regression, income and travel prices were the only two variables used to predict demand. However, other factors such as the political situation, fuel situation, changes in taste, amounts of leisure, and the effectiveness of promotion campaigns obviously have an impact on demand levels. By the Delphi method, the combined effects of all such factors are carefully considered from the base of the executive's experience. For estimating tourism demand, then, *a combination of various mathematical statistical methods and the Delphi method* is believed to produce the most reliable demand estimates in any given situation.

SUMMARY

Demand, without doubt, is the fundamental measure of any area's success in attracting visitors. All planning activities are ultimately intended to increase or control demand. Marketing programs are aimed at increasing demand, sometimes at certain periods during the year, and/or to attract particularly identified market segments.

Understanding demand requires a knowledge of its definition, what comprises demand, what affects the levels of demand, and how future demand can be identified and estimated. Thus, use of demand data is essential in any tourist business situation.

Development of a destination area, whether by public authority, private developers, or both, requires demand data that are as accurate as possible. Providing such data is one of the most important responsibilities of an official tourism organization. Similar data are provided by research organizations and consulting firms, usually when commissioned to make feasibility studies. Any development proposal must have ample estimates of expected demand before any financing can be committed.

Becoming familiar with methods of measuring or estimating present and future demand, as described in this chapter, should enable you to produce such data. With the current high cost of land and construction, reasonably accurate demand statistics are of paramount importance.

KEY CONCEPTS

amount spent
arrivals
computer
   simulation
cost of services
cultural distance
demand
economic distance

executive judgment (Delphi
   method)
linear least squares method
multiple regression
projection methodology
propensity
quality of service
resistance

sales and use tax
seasonality
simple regression
tax collections
trend analysis
visitor-days
visitor-nights
visitors

Internet Sites

The Internet sites mentioned in this chapter are repeated here for convenience, plus some selected additional sites. For more information, visit these sites. Be aware that Internet addresses change frequently, so if a site cannot be accessed, use a search engine. Also use a search engine to locate many additional relevant sites.

**Office of Travel and Tourism
   Industries**
http://www.tinet.ita.doc.gov

**Organization for Economic
   Cooperation and Development**
http://www.oecd.org

Tourism Australia
http://www.tourismaustralia.com

**Travel Industry Association of
   America**
http://www.tia.org

World Tourism Organization
http://www.world-tourism.org

World Travel and Tourism Council
http://www.wttc.org

Internet Exercises

Activity 1
Site Name: Office of Travel and Tourism Industries
URL: http://www.tinet.ita.doc.gov
Background Information: The Office of Travel and Tourism Industries functions as the U.S. federal tourism office. A core responsibility is to collect, analyze, and disseminate international travel and tourism statistics for the U.S. Travel and Tourism Statistical System.

Exercise
1. What statistical data are available at this Web site that would help a tourism professional determine the demand for travel and tourism?

Activity 2
Site Name: STAT-USA/Internet
URL: http://www.stat-usa.gov
Background Information: STAT-USA/Internet, a service of the U.S. Department of Commerce, is a site for the U.S. business, economic, and trade community, providing authoritative information from the federal government.

Exercises
1. What information does the National Trade Data Bank (NTDB) provide?
2. What publications are available to the public from this organization?

QUESTIONS FOR REVIEW AND DISCUSSION

1. Why are demand data so important? Give examples. By whom are demand data used?
2. Explain why resistance to make a trip is inversely related to demand. Are there situations with which you are familiar? Explain.
3. Describe in detail the three factors that determine propensity to travel. Create an example using all three of these major elements.
4. What determines the degree of resistance to travel experiences? Considering the five factors described in this chapter, give an example involving: (1) an irresistible travel offer, and (2) a seasonal travel product.
5. Using the three measures of demand presented, describe a situation in which each one of these would be the most meaningful.
6. A state tourism director wants to convince the legislature to increase the promotion budget for the next fiscal year. What measure of demand should be used? How might these data be obtained?
7. How much faith should be placed in mathematical models of demand projection? What characteristics of input data affect the degree of reliability?
8. A national lodging chain is planning expansion. What are the best methods for estimating future demand?
9. How valuable is trend analysis?
10. What is the Delphi method?

CASE PROBLEMS

1. Assume that the federal government has imposed an increase in the gasoline tax of fifty cents per gallon, effective in three months. How might a motel franchise headquarters organization estimate the effect on demand that this new tax would have for their member motels, which are located in all parts of the country? How could a restaurant chain organization operating turnpike food services make such an estimate? How could a regional airline?
2. Byron C. is director of development for a major hotel systems firm. His company has formulated a new concept in resort-type overnight and longer-stay accommodations. The new suites will possess an exciting array of electronic entertainment features, including a large screen, stereo sound, movies, compact discs, and cassette players. Understandably, these suites are quite expensive to build. Thus, reasonably accurate demand forecasts are essential. Byron C. has tentatively selected your city as a location for the first of these new suite concepts. As executive vice president of your city's convention and visitors bureau, what method would you use to assist Mr. C. in making these crucial demand estimates?

SELECTED REFERENCES

Crouch, Geoffrey I. "A Meta-Analysis of Tourism Demand." *Annals of Tourism Research*, Vol. 22, No. 1, pp. 103–118, Summer 1995.

Crouch, Geoffrey I. "The Study of International Tourism Demand." *Journal of Travel Research*, Vol. 32, No. 4, pp. 41–53, Spring 1994.

Crouch, Geoffrey I. "The Study of International Tourism Demand: A Review of Findings." *Journal of Travel Research*, Vol. 33, No. 1, pp. 12–23, Summer 1994.

Edwards, Anthony. *Asia-Pacific Travel Forecasts to 2005.* London: Economist Intelligence Unit, 1995.

Faulkner, Bill, and Peter Valerio. "An Integrative Approach to Tourism Demand Forecasting." *Tourism Management*, Vol. 16, No. 1, pp. 29–37, February 1995.

Frechtling, Douglas C. *Forecasting Tourism Demand: Methods and Strategies.* Oxford, UK: Butterworth-Heinemann, 2001.

Lim, Christine. "An Economic Classification and Review of International Tourism Demand Models." *Tourism Economics*, Vol. 3, No. 1, pp. 69–82, March 1997.

Morley, Clive L. "A Comparison of Three Models for Estimating Tourism Demand Models." *Tourism Economics,* Vol. 2, No. 3, pp. 223–235, September 1996.

Morley, Clive L. "An Evaluation of the Use of Ordinary Least Squares for Estimating Tourism Demand Models." *Journal of Travel Research,* Vol. 35, No. 4, pp. 69–74, Spring 1997.

Moutinho, Luiz, and Stephen F. Witt. "Forecasting the Tourism Environment Using a Consensus Approach." *Journal of Travel Research,* Vol. 33, No. 4, pp. 46–50, Spring 1995.

Schwartz, Zvi, and Stephen Hiemstra. "Improving the Accuracy of Hotel Reservations Forecasting: Curves Similarity Approach." *Journal of Travel Research,* Vol. 36, No. 1, pp. 3–14, Summer 1997.

Sheldon, Pauline J. "The Demand for Incentive Travel: An Empirical Study." *Journal of Travel Research,* Vol. 33, No. 4, pp. 23–28, Spring 1995.

Song, Haiyan, and Stephen F. Witt. "Tourism Forecasting: The General-to-Scientific Approach." *Journal of Travel Research,* Vol. 42, No. 1, pp. 65–74, August 2003.

Song, Haiyan, and Stephen F. Witt. *Tourism Demand Modelling and Forecasting: Modern Econometric Approaches.* Amsterdam: Pergamon, 2000.

Travel Industry Association of America. *2005 Outlook for Travel and Tourism.* Washington, DC: TIA, 2005.

Travel Industry Association of America. *Economic Review of Travel in America.* Washington, DC: TIA, 2004.

Travel Industry Association of America. *Japan Travel Demand: Trends & Insights.* Washington, DC: TIA, 2004.

Travel Industry Association of America. *UK Travel Demand: Trends & Insights.* Washington, DC: TIA, 2004.

Travel Industry Publishing Company. *Travel Industry World Yearbook.* Spencertown, NY: TIPC, annual.

Turner, L., N. Kulendran, and H. Fernando. "The Use of Composite National Indicators for Tourism Forecasting." *Tourism Economics,* Vol. 3, No. 4, pp. 309–318, 1997.

Turner, Lindsay W., and Stephen F. Witt. "Forecasting Tourism Using Univariate and Multivariate Structural Time Series Models." *Tourism Economics,* Vol. 7, No. 2, pp. 135–147, 2001.

Uysal, Muzaffer, and John L. Crompton. "An Overview of Approaches Used to Forecast Tourism Demand." *Journal of Travel Research,* Vol. 23, No. 3, pp. 7–15, Spring 1985.

Witt, Stephen F., and Christine A. Martin. "Econometric Model for Forecasting International Tourism Demand." *Journal of Travel Research,* Vol. 25, No. 3, pp. 23–30, Winter 1987.

Witt, Stephen F., and Christine A. Witt. *Modeling and Forecasting Demand in Tourism.* London: Academic Press, 1992.

World Tourism Organization. *Tourism: 2020 Vision.* Madrid: WTO, 2001.

Zalatan, Antoine. *Forecasting Methods in Sports and Recreation.* Toronto: Thompson Educational Publishing, 1994.

TOURISM'S ECONOMIC IMPACT

CHAPTER 14

Learning Objectives

- Know the economic generators and impact of tourism.
- Perceive the economic importance of tourism in various regions of the world.
- Know about tourism satellite accounts.

- Understand multipliers.
- Know about balance of payments.
- Comprehend elasticity and inelasticity.

The bustling Nakamise shopping lane of Sensoji Temple. *Photo courtesy of the Japan Information Center.*

INTRODUCTION

Tourism is a powerful economic force providing employment, foreign exchange, income, and tax revenue. The generators of **economic impact** for a city, a state, a province, a country, or a destination area are visitors, their expenditures, and the multiplier effect. The economic impact of tourism spending is a function of the numbers of domestic and international visitors and their expenditures (see Chapter 1). Because of the economic importance of tourism, the World Tourism Organization (WTO) maintains statistics by region and country on tourism arrivals (visitors) and both tourism expenditures (what a country spends) and receipts (what a country receives from visitor expenditures). Tourism destinations are becoming increasingly competitive as more and more destinations look at tourism to become the new economic generator replacing declining activity in agriculture, mining, and manufacturing.

The economic impact of tourism was dramatically demonstrated by the events of September 11, 2001. As a consequence of pervasive anxiety caused by these events, people cut back on their travel; economic forecasts were put on hold; airline, lodging, tour operators, and travel agent revenue declined; and widespread layoffs occurred throughout the industry. We realized very directly and in a personal manner the real economic impact of tourism. However, over the long run, it is believed that travel will recover and the 2020 forecasts will be realized.

TOURISM'S ECONOMIC IMPACT: AN INTERNATIONAL PERSPECTIVE

Negative factors such as the Iraq conflict, terrorism, SARS, and a weak economy made 2003 another difficult year for international tourism. SARS brought the steady growth of Asia and the Pacific to an abrupt halt in April and May, and while tourists quickly started to return after the virus was contained, the region could not make up the losses in the remainder of the year. The war and the economy dampened tourism demand in other key regions. According to WTO preliminary results, the total number of international arrivals reached 694.0 million in 2003, a decrease of 1.2 percent from 2002 (see Table 14.1).

Europe is the main tourist receiving region, followed by Asia and the Pacific, and the Americas. In 2003, Europe accounted for almost 58 percent of the arrivals, Asia and the Pacific 17.2 percent, and the Americas 16.2 percent.

International arrivals were most impacted by the unexpected drop of 12 million (−9.3 percent) in Asia and the Pacific due to the SARS panic. The Americas recorded a decrease of 2.5 million (−2.5 percent), while Europe was basically flat, recording an increase of 0.4 percent. The Middle East and Africa were the surprise regions in 2003 as they recorded healthy increases in tourism arrivals of 10 percent and 5 percent respectively.

Table 14.2 shows international tourism receipts by region in U.S. dollars. An initial analysis of this data shows that international receipts increased by $40.2 billion,

TABLE 14.1   **INTERNATIONAL TOURIST ARRIVALS**

	Arrivals (million)		Change Rate (%)	Market Share (%)
	2002	2003	2003[a]/2002	2003
World	**702.6**	**694.0**	**−1.2**	**100**
Africa	29.1	30.5	4.9	4.4
Americas	114.9	112.4	−2.1	16.2
Asia and the Pacific	131.3	119.1	−9.3	17.2
Europe	399.8	401.5	0.4	57.8
Middle East	27.6	30.4	10.3	4.4

[a]Data as collected in WTO database, January 2004.

Source: WTO World Tourism Barometer, World Tourism Organization, Vol. 2, No. 1, January 2004.

and measured in U.S. dollars every region recorded an increase in receipts except Asia and the Pacific. The series has always been reported in U.S. dollars; however, in this case, it does not present as accurate a picture as it should and illustrates the impact exchange rates can have.

When one examines the increase of receipts from $474.2 billion in 2002 to $514.4 billion in 2003, it should be taken into account that this is largely because of the strong depreciation of the U.S. dollar versus many other currencies, especially the euro. In 2003, a euro bought almost 20 percent more U.S. dollar than in 2002. Thus, receipts earned in euro destinations, which account for over a quarter of worldwide receipts, when expressed in dollar terms, are magnified. Consequently, expressing worldwide receipts in a currency other than the U.S. dollar would present a different picture. WTO has computed worldwide receipts in euros and found that worldwide receipts decreased by 50 billion from euro 502 billion in 2002 to euro 455 billion in 2003. WTO states that a way to compensate for this distortion caused by exchange rates is to express the evolution of receipts in weighted local currencies. At the same time, it is preferable to take inflation into account by

TABLE 14.2   **INTERNATIONAL TOURIST RECEIPTS**

	(US$ billion)		Change Rate (%)	Market Share (%)	Receipts per Arrival 2003
	2002	2003[a]	2003/2002	2003	(US$)
World	**474.2**	**514.4**	**9.2**	**100**	**740**
Africa	11.8	14.0	8.4	2.7	460
Americas	114.3	115.8	9.8	22.5	1030
Asia and the Pacific	94.7	88.6	−6.4	17.2	740
Europe	240.5	281.9	8.5	54.8	700
Middle East	13.0	14.1	9.2	2.7	460

Source: WTO World Tourism Barometer, World Tourism Organization, Vol. 2, No. 2, June 2004.

[a]Data as collected in WTO database, June 2004.

using constant prices instead of current prices. Calculated this way, international tourism receipts were estimated to have decreased by about 2 percent in 2003, while 2002 was still just positive at 0.3 percent.

When one reviews the period 1996 to 2000, they find that international tourism receipts grew faster than arrivals. In the last three years, receipts have grown at a lower rate, reflecting unsettled times and a slow economy. In difficult times, travelers are resourceful and will keep traveling, but will economize by traveling with friends, taking shorter trips, staying in less expensive accommodations, eating out less, and so on. All of these actions reduce tourism receipts.

Looking at the market share figures in Table 14.2, one sees that Europe dominates (54.8 percent) just as with arrivals (57.8 percent). The Americas' share is 22.5 percent and Asia and the Pacific share is 17.2 percent. The shares of Africa and the Middle East were both at 2.7 percent.

Receipts per arrivals averaged $740. The Americas averaged the highest receipts per arrival at $1,030, followed by Asia and the Pacific at the average of $740, Europe with $700, and Africa and the Middle East both at $460.

Expectations for 2004 and Beyond

Prospects for 2005 and the future appear to be very positive as short-term data confirm the upward trend in arrivals that started in late 2003. Asia and the Pacific is showing a strong rebound from 2003. United States international arrivals are recording monthly double-digit increases. Business travel is showing signs of recovery. Low-cost airlines are continuing to increase their capacity and expand their coverage. As expected 2004 saw a return to growth in the travel industry with a record 760 million international arrivals for a 10 percent increase over 2003. However, rising oil prices are a major concern.

Tourism 2020 Vision is the World Tourism Organization's long-term forecast and assessment of the development of tourism through the first twenty years of the new millennium. An essential outcome of *Tourism 2020 Vision* are quantitative forecasts covering a 25-year period, with 1995 as the base year and forecasts for 2000, 2010, and 2020.

WTO's *Tourism 2020 Vision* forecasts that international arrivals are expected to reach over 1.56 billion by the year 2020. Of these worldwide arrivals in 2020, 1.18 billion will be intraregional and 377 million will be long-haul travelers.

The total tourist arrivals by region shows that by 2020 the top three receiving regions will be Europe (717 million tourists), East Asia and the Pacific (397 million), and the Americas (282 million), followed by Africa, the Middle East, and South Asia.

East Asia and the Pacific, South Asia, the Middle East, and Africa are forecasted to record growth at rates of over 5 percent, compared to the world average of 4.1 percent. The more mature regions of Europe and the Americas are anticipated to show lower-than-average growth rates.

Europe will maintain the highest share of world arrivals, although there will be a decline from 60 percent in 1995 to 46 percent in 2020. By 2010, the Americas will lose its number-two position to the East Asia and Pacific region, which will receive

25 percent of world arrivals in 2020, with the Americas decreasing from 19 percent in 1995 to 18 percent in 2020.

Long-haul travel worldwide will grow faster, at 5.4 percent per year over the period 1995–2020, than intraregional travel, at 3.8 percent. Consequently, the ratio between intraregional and long-haul travel will shift from around 82:18 in 1995 to close to 76:24 in 2020.

COMPARING INTERNATIONAL AND DOMESTIC EXPENDITURES

Despite the importance of international tourism (that is, tourists traveling outside of their country of residence), for many (if not most) countries, domestic tourism (tourists traveling in their country of residence) is even more important. As shown in Table 14.2, the World Tourism Organization (WTO) estimated (based on preliminary figures) that international travel involved receipts of US$514.4 billion in 2003. In contrast, the World Travel and Tourism Council estimated that in 2004, both international and domestic travel together generated about US$3,133.2 billion. As can be seen from these estimates of the magnitude of international and domestic travel, the latter is much greater than the former. This fact surprises many people who primarily think of tourism as being exotic, international travel.

In the United States the travel industry received $545.5 billion from domestic and international travelers (including international passenger fares) in 2002. Of this total international visitors spent $83.5 billion traveling in the United States for 15.3 percent of the total. Domestic travel expenditures were $462.0 billion for 84.7 percent of the total.

Employment

The World Travel and Tourism Council estimates that in 2005 employment in the travel and tourism economy was 221,568,000 jobs or 8.3 percent of total employment, which is 1 in every 12.0 jobs. By 2015, this should grow to 269,556,000 jobs, 8.9 percent of total employment or 1 in every 11.2 jobs. The 74,223,000 travel and tourism industry jobs accounted for 2.8 percent of total employment in 2005 and are forecast to rise to 85,521,000 jobs or 2.8 percent of the total by 2015.

Tourism provides both direct and indirect employment. Firms such as hotels, restaurants, airlines, cruise lines, and resorts provide direct employment because their employees are in contact with tourists and provide the tourist experience. Employees of firms providing goods and services to the direct employment firms, such as aircraft manufacturers, construction firms, and restaurant suppliers, create indirect employment.

The impact of this can be illustrated using a United States example. In 2003, the TIA published its annual study, *Tourism Works for America,* which contains employment estimates. Table 14.3, which illustrates employment by sector, shows that in 2002, travel and tourism directly generated nearly 7.2 million jobs in the U.S. economy.

TABLE 14.3   **DIRECT TRAVEL-GENERATED EMPLOYMENT BY INDUSTRY CATEGORY, 2002**

(Employees in thousands)

	2002	PERCENT OF TOTAL	PERCENT CHANGE FROM 2001
Public transportation	990.4	15.8	−8.9
Auto transportation	251.8	4.0	−1.8
Lodging	1,165.1	18.6	−4.0
Food service	2,346.9	37.5	−1.4
Entertainment/recreation	987.1	15.8	−4.6
General retail	331.7	5.3	−3.4
Travel planning	183.3	2.9	−12.8
Total	**6,255.8**	**100.0**	**−4.1**
Generated by international visitors[a]	908.9		−5.0
Grand Total	**7,164.7**		**−4.2**

[a]Data on employment generated by international visitor spending not available by category.

Source: Travel Industry Association of America, and Office of Travel and Tourism Industries.

Travelers in the United States produce secondary impacts over and above that of their original expenditures. These secondary outputs (sales) and earnings (wage and salary income) supported by this "indirect" and "induced" spending add an additional 9.7 million jobs to the U.S. economy. With the almost 6.3 million jobs in 2002 generated directly by domestic travel spending, and the 900,000 employment opportunities generated by international travel to the United States, total U.S. employment created by the travel and tourism industry was 16.9 million in 2002.

The complexity of accurately measuring the vast economic impacts of the tourism industry has created a movement to link tourism expenditure accounting with that used for the national system of accounting in most countries. Earlier attempts to include tourism in the standard industry classification (SIC) codes proved unsuccessful because of the diversity and overlapping nature of many tourism expenditures. In order to overcome these difficulties, a system of tourism satellite accounting has been proposed and implemented. The Tourism Satellite Account (TSA) is discussed later in the chapter.

OPTIMIZATION

Economics is concerned with the attainment of an **optimum** return from the use of scarce resources. Whether it is a person seeking psychological benefit from travel, or a business interested in providing tourists goods and services at a profit, or a host community government viewing tourism in terms of the economic benefits resulting from tourist expenditures, the principle is the same. Economic agents seek to allocate the limited supply of tourism resources (both physical and financial) as they seek to meet the demands of tourists. The demands are the result of their physical/functional needs (which, as a rule are limited) and their psychological wants (which can be virtually unlimited).

Optimizing the tourist experience is both a managerial and a personal challenge. In this instance, the hotel guests appear to be optimizing at the personal level. *Photo courtesy of Gaylord Opryland.*

As such, the problem that economics attempts to solve is how to achieve an economical optimal allocation of scarce tourism resources, when facing the constantly shifting demand (generated by physical needs and psychological wants) for these resources.

Goals

As indicated, at least three major goals can be identified in tourism:

1. Maximize the amount of psychological experience for tourists.
2. Maximize profits for firms providing goods and services to tourists.
3. Maximize the **direct** (primary) and **indirect** (secondary) benefits of tourist expenditures on a community or region.

These goals are often compatible; maximizing psychological experience creates happy clientele, which causes them to return, to spend money, and to make everyone in the industry and the region satisfied. In certain situations, they can also be incompatible. A short-run profit-maximizing goal may cause the development of facilities beyond the capacity of the site, thus leading to overuse and a decline in psychological enjoyment. Extreme emphasis on tourism as an element in economic development might have the same result. There can also be clashes between the use of resources for tourism and for other kinds of development.

Constraints

The second half of the optimizing situation is occupied by those factors that place obstacles in the way of goal attainment. We assume that it is desirable to have unlimited amounts of psychological enjoyment, profits, and local impacts. But that is not possible, because something always gets in the way. Tourism, being extremely broad and diverse, must deal with a large number of constraints. To make an analysis of relationships, it will be necessary to classify them.

Demand
Every firm providing goods and services to tourists is constrained by the **demand** functions of its customers. These relate quantity purchased to price, wealth, and income.

Supply of Attractive Resources
Possibly one of the most important constraints faced by the industry as a whole is the limited amount of resources available for tourist enjoyment. This is particularly true when geographic distribution of these sites is considered. Some areas are simply better attractions for tourists than others are.

Technical and Environmental Constraints
Each particular site or situation has certain technical and environmental constraints. They involve such things as the relationship between sewage effluent disposal and the environment, numbers of fish and numbers of fishermen, number of people who can walk in a given area without causing unacceptable damage, number of elephants supportable on a wildlife range, impact on lions' behavior of tourists observing them from a car, number of campsites possible in a given area without harming the environment, and so on.

Time Constraints
The amount of vacation time available limits what the vacationer can do. The length of the tourist season influences profitability of tourist-oriented businesses and the impact of tourist expenditures on the local economy.

Indivisibilities
Many times it is necessary to deal either with all of something or with nothing. It is not possible to fly half an airplane, even though the seats are only half filled. It may not be profitable to build a hotel under a given size. A road has to be built all the way from one point to another.

Legal Constraints

Several types of legal constraints affect tourism. Activities of the government tourist bureau might be one. Laws concerning environmental problems could be another. Zoning and building codes may influence the construction of facilities. Laws concerning contractual relations may limit activities.

Self-Imposed Constraints

Conflicting goals need to be reconciled, which leads to self-imposed constraints. The conflicts may arise within a firm or among firms, government agencies, and so on, that are seeking to develop a particular area or concept.

Lack of Knowledge

Many activities are limited because little is known about particular situations. Businesspeople are used to living with a certain amount of uncertainty, but there are inevitable limits to the amount they are willing to countenance. Ignorance influences governmental operations as well.

Limits on Supportive Resources

There are always limits to the amount of money, managerial talent, workers, construction materials, social capital, and so on. And these, in turn, limit chances to provide psychological enjoyment, take advantage of profit-making opportunities, or develop local attractions.

Many times these individual constraints interact, creating compound constraints on given activities.

Optimizing the Experience

Maximization of the tourist experience is subject to a number of constraints and is manifested in the demand function. Demand for tourist experience is peculiar in the sense that the product being purchased is not easy to identify directly and is frequently purchased sight unseen.

The tourist is particularly constrained by time and budget. To optimize the experience, it is necessary to determine the combination of destinations preferred and then the possibilities within the money and time constraints. This explains some of the popularity of package tours, where both time and cost can be known in advance. There are some exceptions. Retired persons and young people often have time but limited resources. A few people have neither constraint.

Optimizing Returns to Businesses

Because goods and services provided to tourists are really inputs to the process of producing the experience, demand for them is derived from demand for tourism as a whole. Some goods and services are complementary, and their demand is interrelated in a positive fashion. Others are substitutes and are characterized by limited area competition.

Packaged tours have the characteristic of putting all parts and services together, so they become complementary. Competition occurs among tours. Tour operators can maximize profits by selling tours of different value and costs, in order to cater to as many people as possible along the demand curve. The number of people to be accommodated can be determined from the marginal cost of the tour and the marginal revenue to be derived from a given price level.

Goods and services sold to tourists are subject to severe peaking in demand. That is, the heaviest tourist season is usually limited. During that period, demand is intense and must be met with facilities that are excess in the off-season. This means that investment necessary to provide the excess capacity must be paid for from revenues received during the peak period. During off-peak periods, only variable cost is of interest, but because demand is low, some capacity will not be utilized.

As owners of the facilities, firms are concerned with providing adequate long-run capacity and with choosing those investments that will give optimum returns. In the tourist industry, a number of interrelationships must be considered. Sometimes, low benefit-cost investments are made so that higher-yielding investments can succeed. Consequently, it is not always true that investors choose the highest-yielding opportunities.

Generally, it is considered the long-run business of the firm to remove constraints on operations. But tourism has a number of constraints to expansion. These include demand for the tourist experience and environmental constraints.

Optimizing for the Local Economy

Tourism affects a region during periods of intense investment activity and afterward when the investments are producing. The effects depend on linkages among economic units. Money spent for investment will go to construction and a few other industrial sectors. These will have links to economic units varying from households to manufacturing plants. Money spent by tourists will also be introduced through a few sectors that will also be linked to the economy.

North Americans traveling in Morocco spend money in the country and bring travel experiences home with them. By doing so, these tourists create export income for Morocco. *Photo by the author.*

The **multiplier** effects in both cases are dependent upon the strength of the linkages. The multiplier reflects the amount of new economic activity generated as basic income circulates through the economy. Some sectors have strong links to other sectors in an economy and a large multiplier effect. Others have weak links and small multipliers. It is possible to have a thriving tourist industry and abject poverty in the local populace if there are no links. For example, linkages will be strong and the income multiplier high if the year-round resorts in a particular destination area hire all local labor; buy their flowers, fruit, vegetables, and poultry products from local farmers; hire local entertainers; and buy furnishings for guest rooms from local manufacturers. Linkages would be weak if most of these goods and services were imported from another state or country.

Tourism Exports and Imports

The host region is defined loosely as a county, a state, or a nation, depending on the level at which the problem is being considered. For a county-level government, the income of the county is of primary interest. A state government would perceive the maximization of the combined income of the entire state to be its objective, and so on.

Regardless of which definition of host region is being considered, expenditures in this area by tourists coming from another region represent injections into the area's economy.

Japanese tourists traveling to the United States presumably earned their income in Japan. When spending money in the United States as tourists, they are "injecting" money into our economy that wasn't here before. As such, expenditures by foreigners in this country (for travel purposes) represent tourism **exports** for the United States. This may be somewhat confusing because we are accustomed to thinking of something leaving the country as an export. When we export computers or cars, for example, these commodities are sent out of the United States. In the example of the Japanese tourists, the tourists are coming into this country. So how is it an export? There seems to be a contradiction in terminology. As the astute student would note, however, when tourists come into this country, they are purchasing travel experiences. When they leave, they take these experiences back with them. Thus, we have exported travel experiences, which are, after all, what tourism is all about.

Figure 14.1 clarifies this concept. When U.S. tourists travel to Japan and spend money there, this becomes a tourism **import** to the U.S. economy. Japanese money spent in the United States is a tourism import for the Japanese economy.

In tourism exports, the flows of tourists and payments are in the same direction, whereas in commodity exports, the two flows are in opposite directions. Therein lies the confusion. However, if one were to look at the *direction of payment flow* to determine what is an export, there is no contradiction between the two cases. When payment flows into the United States, something has been exported—travel experiences, for instance, or commodities. Both payment flows are in the same direction.

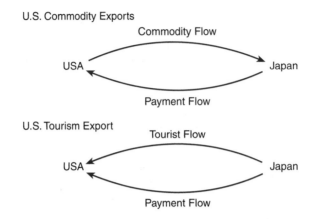

Figure 14.1   Economic comparison: Commodity flows and tourist flows.

Balance-of-Payments Effects

Tourism is one of the world's largest international industries. As such, it has a noticeable impact on the **balance of payments** of many nations. We have heard much about the balance-of-payments problems of the United States, and, indeed, tourism imports do affect the balance of payments and economic conditions generally. We define tourism imports as those expenditures made by American tourists in foreign countries. An easy way to remember this is to ask, "Who got the money?" If, for example, Great Britain received American funds, it makes no difference whether an American bought some English china or an American tourist visited England.

Our balance-of-payments situation directly affects the gross national product of the United States (Y). The formula is

$$Y = C + I + G + (X - M)$$

where
Y = gross national product
C = consumer expenditures
I = investments
G = government expenditures
X = exports
M = imports

By looking at the formula, we can see that if imports (M) exceed exports (X), then the difference ($X - M$) will be a negative number, and Y will thus be smaller. Thus, it is advantageous to us in our American economy to attract more visitor spending in the United States. These "tourism exports" are like credits and help our economy. It is economically better to have foreign visitors come to the United States than it is to have U.S. citizens travel abroad. However, this should be tempered with the realization that the situation is not entirely positive or negative.

Expenditures by U.S. tourists abroad make possible purchasing power in foreign countries for those countries to buy American-made products. For example, most airlines of the world use American-made equipment. Purchase of these aircraft, parts, supplies, repair services, and so forth makes an important contribution to the export trade of the United States; thus, we cannot charge the U.S. international traveler with a total negative balance of payments. The purpose of the foregoing discussion is simply to point out the relationships.

Tourism exports become very desirable as far as the gross national product and the prosperity of the country are concerned. Efforts on the part of national tourism offices to attract foreign visitors have a great impact on the balance-of-payments situation. Business firms that serve the foreign visitor, provide desired services, and stimulate sales materially help our national economy. However, during periods when the U.S. dollar is high against foreign currencies, a dampening effect occurs on our tourism exports because this situation is seen as unfavorable by prospective foreign visitors. Conversely, if the dollar is low, more foreign tourists will visit the United States. This increases our tourism exports, improves our balance of payments, and raises the gross national product. These same relationships of comparable currency values exist between any country that exports tourism and the countries of its tourists' origin.

In 1998 the value of the Canadian dollar was low in comparison to the U.S. dollar and illustrated this principle. The number of Americans visiting Canada to take advantage of the exchange rate increased dramatically. This contributed positively to Canada's balance of payments.

Investment Stimulation

The tourist industry has a unique structure. It is characterized by and, in fact, is an agglomeration of a large number of very small units, covering a variety of different service trades—the small restaurants, motels, guest houses, laundries, arts and crafts shops, and others. Thus, investment in infrastructure and sometimes expensive superstructure by the government stimulates investment in numerous smaller businesses. Because of the small size of these businesses, capital requirements are relatively low and investment generally proceeds at a rapid pace. In this respect, too, governments view tourism rather favorably. The initial investment in tourism brings forth a large investment in supporting and tertiary industries. This also includes large investments in major hotels, restaurants, shopping centers, marinas, airports, and so on.

Tourism Increases Tax Revenue

Tourists must pay **taxes** like most other people. Because they come from other regions or countries, their expenditures represent an increased tax base for the host government. In addition to the usual sales tax, tourists sometimes pay taxes in less direct ways. Airport taxes, exit fees, customs duty, and charges assessed for granting visas are just a few examples of commonly used methods of taxing tourists. The wisdom of imposing such special taxes on tourists is questionable, because it merely serves to reduce demand. In some countries, for instance, the room rate at a hotel can be different for tourists (generally higher) than for residents. This is a questionable practice, because it leaves the tourist with a feeling that he has been "taken." Apart from these special cases, the usual taxes collected from both tourists and residents increase because of tourism expenditures.

Is tourism, then, a panacea for all the economic woes of a region or country? It has been claimed that tourism increases incomes, employment, investment, tax revenues, and so forth, so it might indeed appear to be one. However, constraints limit the extent to which governments can maximize the benefit from these aspects of tourism. These constraints are of two types: social and economic. The social constraints have already been discussed. The economic constraints are in the form of potential economic costs that the tourism industry may impose. These merit further scrutiny to gain a better understanding of the government's optimization problem.

Inflationary Pressure

Tourists inject money (earned elsewhere) into the destination economy. While this increases the income of the region (as discussed earlier), it also might cause **inflationary pressures.** Tourists typically have a higher expenditure capability than the residents do—either because tourists have higher incomes or because they have saved for the trip and are inclined to "splurge" while on vacation. Hence, they are able to somewhat bid up the prices of such commodities as food, transportation, and arts and crafts. This causes inflationary pressures, which can be detrimental to the economic welfare of residents of the host community. This is particularly true when inflation affects the prices of essentials such as food, clothing, transportation, and housing. Land prices have been known to escalate rapidly in tourist destination areas. The prices that foreigners are willing to pay for "vacation homes" in the area can decrease the demand for "first homes" by residents.

Lundberg[1] notes that as the tourist industry developed in an area, land prices rose sharply. In a particular underdeveloped area, the amount of investment in land constituted just 1 percent of the total investment for a hotel project. By contrast, this ratio increased to 20 percent in an area where tourism was already overdeveloped. With such increases in land prices, it can be expected that local residents (with their lower incomes) are effectively "chased out" of the housing market in a tourism-developing section.

ECONOMIC MULTIPLIERS

Direct Effect

In addition to the direct impact of tourism expenditures on an area, there are also indirect impacts. The indirect or **multiplier** impact comes into play as visitor spend-

---

[1]Donald E. Lundberg, "Caribbean Tourism," *Cornell Hotel and Restaurant Administration Quarterly,* Vol. 14, No. 4, pp. 30–45, February 1974.

ing circulates and recirculates. The direct effects are the easiest to understand because they result from the visitor spending money in tourist enterprises and providing a living for the owners and managers and creating jobs for employees.

Indirect Effect

This visitor expenditure gives rise to an income that, in turn, leads to a chain of expenditure-income-expenditure, and so on, until leakages bring the chain to a halt. Consequently, the impact of the initial income derived from the tourist's expenditure is usually greater than the initial income, because subsequent rounds of spending are related to it. For example, a skier purchases a lift ticket for $40. This money received by the ski area will be used to pay the wages of the lift operators. The lift operator spends the money on groceries; the grocer uses the money to pay part of his rent to the local landlady; the landlady uses it to pay for her dry cleaning; the dry cleaner spends it in a restaurant for a dinner; the restaurant owner spends it for steaks shipped in from Kansas City; and the cycle stops as the money is lost to the local economy. This last transaction is known as *leakage* from the economy. The combination of the direct and indirect effects of an expenditure pattern determines the impact. In a typical situation, not all of the income generated in each round of expenditure is respent. Some portion tends to be saved, and some portion tends to be spent outside the local economy. The greater the proportion of income spent locally, the greater will be the multiplier.

The degree to which a local area is able to retain tourist income depends on how self-sufficient the local economy is. If the local economy is able to produce the goods and services tourists buy, the greater will be the multiplier effect. The more goods that have to be imported from outside the region, the smaller the multiplier will be.

From the discussion, it is clear that when a tourist's spending injects funds into the economy of a host area, an economic effect occurs that is a specified number of times what was originally spent. Initially, this effect is thought of as an *income multiplier,* as tourist expenditures become income directly and indirectly to local people. However, there are additional economic phenomena. Increased

The money spent by tourists circulates and recirculates, creating an economic multiplier. *Photo courtesy of Gaylord Opryland.*

spending necessitates more jobs, which results in an *employment multiplier.* Because money changes hands a number of times during a year, there is a transactions multiplier. This is of particular interest to governmental tax officials where sales taxes are imposed. As business grows in a tourist destination area, more infrastructure and superstructure are constructed. This results in a *capital multiplier.* Examples are provided here of how an employment multiplier and an income multiplier were determined.

Employment Multiplier

The employment multiplier varies from region to region depending on its economic base. In a study entitled *Recreation as an Industry,* by Robert R. Nathan Associates, county employment multipliers calculated for the Appalachian region provide a good illustration of what typical multipliers are and how they work.[2]

The multipliers estimated in this study were based on county employment data. They represent the approximate measure of the direct and indirect employment associated with each addition of direct employment to the export sector of a county. Multipliers were estimated for 375 counties and three independent cities. The smallest multiplier was 1.13, and the highest was 2.63. Thus, the county with the smallest multiplier value would provide other employment opportunities for approximately 0.13 person for each person directly employed in servicing export demand, and the county with the highest multiplier value would provide other employment opportunities for approximately 1.63 persons for each person directly employed in servicing export demand. In general, county employment multipliers vary directly with the population or total employment size of the counties: As county population size grows, so does the multiplier value. This relationship is as might be expected, insofar as import leakages would tend to be less where diversity of occupations is greater, and diversity is positively associated with county population or total employment.

Income Multiplier

Jobs mean income, which stimulates the economy of the area in which the development occurs. How much stimulation occurs depends on several factors. The management of a hotel, for example, takes two actions with the revenue earned: It spends parts of the money on goods and services, and it saves part of such funds. Economists refer to such actions as marginal propensity to consume (MPC) and marginal propensity to save (MPS)—removing funds from the local economy. Such removal of these marginal (extra) funds can be made in two ways: (1) they can be saved and not loaned to another spender, or (2) they can be used to purchase imports. In either case, so doing removes the funds and thus does not stimulate the local economy.

Economic research is needed in a tourist destination area to determine what these income relationships are. If the results of such economic research were made

---

[2]Robert R. Nathan Associates and Resource Planning Associates, *Recreation as an Industry* p. 57, Washington, DC: 1966.

available, many beneficial results might be possible. For example, governmental bodies might be more inclined to appropriate additional funds for tourism promotion to their areas if they knew more about the income that was generated by tourist expenditures. Also, improved and added developments of facilities to serve tourists might be more forthcoming if prospective investors could have more factual data upon which to base decisions.

To understand the multiplier, we must first make some approximation as to what portion of the tourist dollars received in a community is spent (consumed) and what portion is saved (leakage). To illustrate this, suppose that we had a total of $1,000 of tourist spending in a community and that there was an MPC of 1/2. The expenditure pattern might go through seven transactions in a year. These are illustrated in Table 14.4. The other formula for the multiplier is 1/MPS. This is a

TABLE 14.4 **FORMULA FOR THE MULTIPLIER**

$$\text{Multiplier} = \frac{1}{1 - MPC}$$

where

$M =$ marginal (extra)
$P =$ propensity (inclination)
$C =$ consume (spending, MPC)
$S =$ savings (money out of circulation, MPS)

Suppose $1,000 of tourist expenditure and an MPC of $\frac{1}{2}$. Then

$1,000.00
+
$500.00 $\qquad \frac{1}{2} \times 1,000$
+
250.00 $\qquad \left(\frac{1}{2}\right)^{2} \times 1,000$
+
125.00 $\qquad \left(\frac{1}{2}\right)^{3} \times 1,000$
+
62.50 $\qquad \left(\frac{1}{2}\right)^{4} \times 1,000$
+
31.25 $\qquad \left(\frac{1}{2}\right)^{5} \times 1,000$
+
15.63 $\qquad \left(\frac{1}{2}\right)^{6} \times 1,000$
+
7.81 $\qquad \left(\frac{1}{2}\right)^{7} \times 1,000$
. . .

$2000.00 (approx.)

Multiply: $\dfrac{1}{1 - \frac{1}{2}} \times \$1,000$, or $2 \times \$1,000 = \$2,000$

Thus, the original $1,000 of tourist expenditure becomes $2,000 of income to the community.

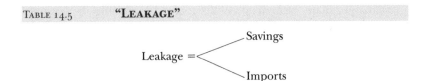

TABLE 14.5   **"LEAKAGE"**

$$\text{Leakage} = \begin{cases} \text{Savings} \\ \text{Imports} \end{cases}$$

where

Savings = not loaned to another spender
Imports = spending on tourism needs in sources outside country (state)

$$\text{Multiplier} = \frac{1}{MPS}$$

Suppose the *MPS* is $\frac{1}{3}$. Then

$$\text{Multiplier} = \frac{1}{\frac{1}{3}} = 3$$

simpler formula, because it is the reciprocal of the marginal propensity to save. If the marginal propensity to save were 1/3, the multiplier would be 3. This is shown in Table 14.5.

Leakage, as defined, is a combination of savings and imports. If we spend the money outside our country for imports, obviously it does not stimulate the economy locally. If it is put into some form of savings that are not loaned to another spender within a year, it has the same effect as imports—not stimulating the economy. Thus, to get the maximum benefits economically from tourist expenditures, we should introduce as much of the tourist funds as possible into the local economy for goods and services rather than save the proceeds or buy a large amount of imports.

Here, also, more economic research is needed. Some studies have indicated that the multiplier might be as high as 3 in some areas, but economic research in other localities indicates that it may be more typically lower than this.

Economic Benefits Widely Distributed

Using a conceptual approach, you should realize that tourism is characterized by the existence of a large number of very small businesses that support and are ancillary to the industry. The receipts from tourism quickly filter down to an extremely broad cross section of the population, so that the entire community shares the economic benefits. Table 14.6, based on a partially hypothetical example, illustrates how quickly tourism receipts seep through the economy and the diversity of the businesses that benefit from tourism. As the table indicates, the tourism dollar is shared by over seventy distinguishable types of enterprises in just two rounds of spending.

TABLE 14.6	**DISTRIBUTION OF TOURISM EXPENDITURES**		
VISITORS SPEND FOR	**TRAVEL INDUSTRY SPENDS FOR**	**ULTIMATE BENEFICIARIES**	
Lodging	Wages and salaries	Accountants	Government
Food	Tips, gratuities	Advertising and public	Education
Beverages	Payroll taxes	relations	Health
Entertainment	Commissions	Appliance stores	Roads and railroads
Clothing, etc.	Music and entertainment	Architects	Utilities
Gifts and souvenirs	Administrative and general	Arts and crafts	Development and
Photography	expenses	producers	others
Personal care	Legal and professional	Attorneys	Greengrocers
Drugs and cosmetics	services	Automobile agencies	Grocery stores
Internal transportation	Purchases of food,	Bakers	Financiers
Tours and sight-seeing	beverages, etc.	Banks	Furniture stores
Miscellaneous	Purchases of goods sold	Beach accessories	Importers
	Purchases of materials and	Butchers	Insurance agencies
	supplies	Carpenters	Landlords
	Repairs and maintenance	Cashiers	Laundries
	Advertising, promotion,	Charities	Manufacturing agents
	and publicity	Chemists	Managers
	Utilities—electricity, gas,	Clerks	Motion picture theaters
	water, etc.	Clothing stores	Newspapers, radio, etc.
	Transportation	Clubs	Nightclubs
	Licenses	Confectioners	Office equipment
	Insurance premiums	Contractors	suppliers
	Rental of premises and	Cooks	Painters
	equipment	Cultural organizations	Pastoralists
	Interest and principal	Dairies	Plumbers
	payments of borrowed	Dentists	Porters
	funds	Department stores	Printers, sign painters
	Income and other taxes	Doctors	Publishers
	Replacement of capital	Dry cleaning	Real estate brokers and
	assets	establishments	developers
	Return to investors	Electricians	Resorts
		Engineers	Restaurants
		Farmers	Room maids
		Fishermen	Shareholders
		Freight forwarders	Sporting events
		Garages and auto	Transportation
		repairs	Travel brokers
		Gardeners	Taxi, limo services
		Gas stations	Unions
		Gift shops	Wholesale
			establishments

Source: Pannell Kerr Forster and Belt Collins and Associates.

Structural Changes

In countries that primarily rely on a single industry, such as agriculture, the introduction of tourism has often led to a decrease in the agricultural base of the country. Agriculture is an extremely low productivity industry in the developing countries. The promise of much higher wages in the tourism industry draws people away from farming. Agricultural output declines as a result, just when the demand for food increases because of the influx of tourists. The inflationary pressure on food prices is further aggravated and can lead to considerable social upheaval. In the mid-1970s, some Caribbean countries experienced a wave of protests and even direct attacks on tourists, as the resident population expressed its dissatisfaction over rising prices.

Another major implication of the structural change is that instead of diversifying its economic base, the country's tourism sector merely "cannibalizes" its other major economic sector. Diversity is the foundation of economic stability. When one sector (or industry) experiences a slump, another sector booms, thus reducing the probability of a severe depression and, indeed, reducing its impact if a depression does occur. Thus, tourism, instead of diversifying an economy, sometimes replaces agriculture as a "subsistence" sector.

Dependence on Tourism

Permitting tourism to become the subsistence industry is not desirable for a number of reasons. First, tourism is by its very nature subject to considerable seasonality. While seasonal fluctuations in demand can sometimes be reduced, they cannot be eliminated. Thus, when tourism is the primary industry in an area, the off-season periods inevitably result in serious unemployment problems. Such areas find that the seasonal character of tourism leaves severe economic and social effects on the host region.

Another very important reason relates to the source of demand for tourism. The demand for tourism depends largely on the income and the tastes of tourists, both of which are beyond the control of the host region. When the American economy goes through a slump, demand for travel to a foreign destination by Americans will fall off. A destination area can do precious little, in this case, to increase the level of demand. If the tastes of the people in the tourist-generating area change—that is, they decide to travel to a new destination—tourism in the old area will decline, causing economic and social problems. Again, the destination can do little or nothing to avoid this. In fact, as Plog[3] points out, there is reason to believe that such a decline in an area's popularity may be largely inevitable. Quite clearly, then, tourism should not be allowed to grow to an extent that the destination area becomes totally dependent on it.

---

[3]Stanley C. Plog, "Why Destination Areas Rise and Fall in Popularity," *Cornell Hotel and Restaurant Administration Quarterly*, Vol. 14, No. 4, pp. 55–58, February 1974.

Seasonal fluctuations in tourism result in an uneven source of revenue. During the winter months, skiers enjoy the powder snow of Aspen, Colorado, and make a significant contribution to the Colorado economy. *Photo courtesy of the Aspen Skiing Company.*

In other words, total dependence on a single industrial sector is undesirable. If it cannot be avoided, then dependence on domestic agriculture is in many ways preferable to dependence on tourism. The country has presumably adapted itself economically and socially to dependence on agriculture over several centuries. The demand for agricultural output is also unlikely to suffer from a secular decline, because people must eat. Also, it is the residents, not foreigners as in tourism, who directly benefit from agricultural production.

Investment Priorities

Sometimes, governments of developing countries take an overly optimistic view of tourism. They undertake aggressive investment programs to develop tourism, assigning it top priority in their development plans. In extreme cases, such an approach can lead to the neglect of more fundamental investment needs of the country. For example, funds can be channeled into tourism development at the cost of education, health, and other social services—aspects of the social well-being of the population that should be of primary concern for a developing country. Not only is undue glamorization of tourism unwise because it usurps this position, but such a strategy only speeds up the process of dependence on tourism, which, as discussed earlier, is itself undesirable. Moreover, investment in tourism at the cost of health and education programs also slows down the rate at which the local population is assimilated into the modern market economy of the country. Under certain circumstances, it may actually retard development rather than enhance it.

The conclusion is that although tourism has tremendous potential as a tool in economic development, it is no panacea. Governments should attempt to optimize (not maximize) the benefits that tourism provides, being ever mindful of the costs that it can impose. It should be noted also that the probability and the intensity of the economic costs of tourism are greater for developing nations (or regions) than for wealthy ones. Wealthy nations, by definition, possess robust economies that can more easily absorb the cost of tourism. Typically, such economies are well diversified, and government investment programs are not so central to development efforts.

The social benefits and costs of tourism should be viewed similarly. While the host community seeks to maximize the benefits, it must weigh these against the social costs. The social costs are likewise higher in both probability and magnitude when tourism is being considered for development in an area that still possesses a traditional social structure.

Quantity Demanded and Price Elasticity

For some products, even a large change in price over a certain range of the demand curve results in only a small change in quantity demanded. In this case, demand is not very responsive to price (Table 14.7). For other products, or for the same product over a different range of prices, a relatively small change in price elicits a much larger relative change in quantity demanded. Demand can be classified as inelastic or elastic on the basis of the relative responsiveness of quantity demanded to changes in price. Specifically, price elasticity of demand may be defined as the percentage change in demand resulting from a given percentage change in price. Most tourism products are price elastic. During 1992, when U.S. airlines began offering half fares, the number of air travelers increased to record-high levels.

Income Elasticity of Demand

As income rises, more travel is demanded at any given price. Thus, the relationship between income and demand is positive. The responsiveness of demand to changes in income is called **income elasticity** of demand. It is defined as the percentage

TABLE 14.7	**RELATIONSHIPS BETWEEN PRICE ELASTICITY AND TOTAL REVENUE (TR)**		
	ELASTIC DEMAND ($\|\epsilon p\| > 1$)	UNITARY ELASTICITY ($\|\epsilon p\| = 1$)	INELASTIC DEMAND ($\|\epsilon p\| < 1$)
Price rises	TR falls	No change	TR rises
Price falls	TR rises	No change	TR falls

change in quantity demanded in response to a given percentage change in income, price remaining unchanged.

MORE ADVANCED ECONOMIC CONCEPTS RELATED TO TOURISM

As can be seen from the beginning of this chapter, tourism makes a major economic contribution to the world economy. Despite this economic significance, tourism managers have for some time been met with complaints such as "All the hype about tourism's contribution to economic growth and job creation is a gross exaggeration." As well, members of the industry itself want to be sure that the economic impact figures are indeed accurate so that they can better plan their investments and improve their productivity and performance.

In an attempt to ensure the accuracy and reliability of the measures of tourism's economic impact, the World Tourism Organization (WTO) in collaboration with the World Travel and Tourism Council (WTTC), and with the support of the Canadian Tourism Commission (CTC), have undertaken to develop a tourism accounting system that is not only rigorous, but consistent with the national accounts of every country. This system has been named Tourism Satellite Account.

Tourism Satellite Account

What Is Tourism Satellite Account?
A Tourism Satellite Account (TSA) is a system developed by the United Nations to measure the size of economic sectors that are not defined as industries in national accounts. Tourism, for example, is an amalgam of industries such as transportation, accommodation, food and beverage services, recreation, and entertainment and travel agencies.

Tourism is a unique phenomenon as it is defined by the consumption of the visitor. Visitors buy goods and services associated with both tourism and non-tourism alike. The key from a measurement standpoint is to associate their purchases to the total supply of these goods and services within a country.

The TSA is a new statistical instrument designed to measure these goods and services according to international standards of concepts, classifications, and definitions that will allow for valid comparisons with other industries and eventually from country to country and between groups of countries. Such measures will also be comparable with other internationally recognized economic statistics.

In addition, a TSA possesses the following characteristics. It:

- Provides credible data on the impact of tourism and the associated employment

- Is a standard framework for organizing statistical data on tourism

- Is a new international standard endorsed by the U.N. Statistical Commission

- Is a powerful instrument for designing economic policies related to tourism development

- Provides data on tourism's impact on a nation's balance of payments

- Provides information on tourism human resource characteristics

While it may be obvious, it is useful to stress why a TSA is needed. In brief, there is an acute shortage of information on the increasing role of tourism in national economies worldwide, hence the need for reliable data relative to the importance and magnitude of tourism, using the same concepts, definitions, and measurement approaches as other industries. With the TSA, governments, entrepreneurs, and citizens will be better equipped for designing public policies and business strategies for tourism and for evaluating their effectiveness and efficiency.

Development of a TSA framework has been fueled by the recognition that its implementation will serve to increase and improve knowledge of tourism's importance relative to overall economic activity in a given country. It will also provide an instrument for designing more efficient policies relating to tourism and its employment aspects; and it will create awareness among the various players directly and indirectly involved with tourism of the economic importance of this activity, and by extension its role in all the industries involved in the production of goods and services demanded by visitors.

The Nature of a TSA

A TSA is characterized by the manner in which it seeks to balance measures of tourism demand versus supply. Tourism measurements, in order to be credible and comparable with other industries in a country's economy, must follow concepts and definitions consistent with internationally accepted macroeconomic guidelines, such as the System of National Accounts.

The fundamental structure of the TSA therefore relies on the balance existing within an economy between, on one hand, the demand for goods and services generated by visitors and by other consumers and, on the other hand, the overall supply of these goods and services. The idea is to analyze in detail all aspects of demand for goods and services that are associated with tourism within the economy, and to measure the relationship with the supply of such goods and services within the same economy. More specifically, a TSA measures:

- Tourism's contribution to gross domestic product (GDP)

- Tourism's ranking compared to other economic sectors

- The number of jobs created by tourism in an economy

- The amount of tourism investment

- Tax revenues generated by tourism industries

- Tourism consumption

- Tourism's impact on a nation's balance of payments

- Characteristics of tourism human resources

Because of its comprehensive nature, a TSA provides decision makers with a valuable tool for planning and policy making. In particular, it provides them with reliable data of tourism's impact on the economy and employment. As well, it permits the measurement of both domestic and nonresident tourism—and the employment associated with each. A TSA, however, can do much more. Following are some examples.

A TSA can provide information on how much tourism is worth to the national economy, and how it compares to other industries and other countries. By demonstrating and using the size of tourism, tourism officials and private-sector businesses will have more influence on policy makers at all levels of government. As well, it can make clear which industries benefit from tourism and by how much—in particular, industries not traditionally associated with tourism. For instance, business enterprises can identify the role tourism plays in their success and develop business strategies accordingly.

A TSA is able to provide information regarding how much tax revenue is generated by tourism. This information is useful in convincing municipal, provincial, or federal levels of government to invest further in tourism.

In addition, it provides data on visitor demand and how this demand is met by domestic supply. A TSA enables the establishment of a tourism economic impact model, which can be used to estimate the effect on the economy and on employment of various tourism expenditure shocks. Such an impact model provides a better understanding of tourism employment and where each industry ranks compared to other tourism industries.

It should be emphasized that the ongoing development of TSAs as national promotion tools has been a process dating back to at least 1993. The most recent focus of this development was a major international TSA conference held in Vancouver, Canada, in 2001. This and other conferences have brought together the following organizations: World Tourism Organization (WTO), World Travel and Tourism Council (WTTC), Organization for Economic Cooperation and Development (OECD), United Nations (UN), Eurostat, and a number of government statistical agencies, national tourism administrators, and central banks.

The above collaboration demonstrates the general principle that in order to develop a national TSA, it is essential to involve a number of key actors within a country. The most significant of these are:

- National statistical offices, national tourism administrations (NTAs), central banks, and associations of national tourism enterprises

- Information-producing units such as tourism enterprises and establishments, and other public departments

- Users of the tourism information that is generated, the NTAs themselves, the units responsible for preparing the national accounts and the balance of payments, and others

- The participation and collaboration of tourism enterprises and, more specifically, their corresponding national associations

Sources of Data Used in a TSA

Canada, as an Example

The data used in the calculation of a TSA in Canada come from a diverse number of surveys produced by Statistics Canada. The preparation of tourism demand estimates involve several surveys that record information on tourism consumption of Canadians traveling in and outside Canada and nonresidents traveling to Canada. These include:

- Canadian Travel Survey

- International Travel Survey of Canadian Residents

- Canadian Resident Questionnaire for same-day automobile travel between the United States and Canada

- United States Resident Questionnaire for same-day automobile travel between the United States and Canada

- Government Travel Survey of U.S. visitors to Canada

- Government Travel Survey of visitors to Canada

Much of the information for the supply-side estimates are drawn from the worksheets used in the making of the input-output tables by industry, commodity, and employment of the System of National Accounts. Data from reference publications, and relevant business surveys and administrative data, are used to obtain as much detail as possible on revenues generated from the sale of tourism commodities.

In conclusion, a TSA recognizes that tourism is not an industry in the traditional sense—that is, identified in the System of National Accounts—because industries are classified according to the goods and services they produce (e.g., forestry), while tourism is a consumption-based concept that depends on the status of the customer. Furthermore, tourists buy many of the same products as other consumers, including items not normally associated with tourism—clothes, groceries—while Canadians at home buy tourism goods and services for nontourism reasons—restaurant meals, postcards, recreational services.

The TSA brings together these diverse aspects of tourism by providing a tourism dimension to the framework of the System of National Accounts. It makes it possible to separate and examine the demand and supply sides of tourism within an integrated system that describes the production and demand aspects of the whole economy.

The recognition of these factors has led to the situation where more than ten countries have a TSA and more than thirty are in the process of developing a TSA. These include Austria, Canada, Chile, the Dominican Republic, France, Mexico, New Zealand, Norway, Singapore, Sweden, the United States, Spain, and Italy.

SUMMARY

Domestic and international tourism are major economic strengths to many of the world's countries, states, cities, and rural areas. Thus, those who live there are affected by the economic results of tourist spending. This chapter explained why these resulting effects vary greatly and what brings about a large measure of benefits or possible detriments to a community. The main economic phenomena described are various multipliers, balance of payments, investments, tax consideration, employment, economic impact generators, travel expenditures, dependence on tourism, price and income elasticity as related to buying travel experiences, and optimization. The chapter also discussed a new method of measuring tourism economic impact, satellite accounting.

Many people do not understand or appreciate the economics of tourism. The following list summarizes the principal economic effects.

1. Expenditures by foreign visitors in one's country become exports (mainly of services). The economic effects are the same as those derived from exporting tangible goods. If there is a favorable exchange rate (foreign currency buying appreciably more of one's own country's currency), the country that has the devalued currency will experience a higher demand for visitor services than before devaluation.

2. If citizens of one country spend money in foreign countries, these expenditures become imports for the tourists' originating country.

3. Sums of the values of national exports and imports are used when calculating a nation's balance of payments. A positive balance results when exports exceed imports, thus increasing a nation's gross national product (GNP).

4. Tourism developments typically require large investments of capital. Thus, local economies where the developments take place are stimulated by such investments.

5. Tourists pay various kinds of taxes directly and indirectly while visiting an area. Thus, tax revenues are increased for all levels of government.

6. Because tourists usually spend more per day at a destination than they do while at home, these extra expenditures may cause inflationary pressures and rising prices for consumer goods in the destination area.

7. Tourism expenditures injected into the economy produce an income multiplier for local people. This is because of the diversity of expenditures made by those receiving tourist payments. Tourist receipts are used to buy a wide variety of goods and services over a year's time. The money turnover creates additional local income.

8. The amount of income multiplication, however, will depend on how much leakage takes place. Leakages are a combination of (1) imported goods and services purchased by tourism suppliers, and (2) savings made of tourist receipts not loaned to another spender within one year of receipt. Thus, the more tourist goods that are supplied locally, the higher will be the multiplier.

9. Income multiplication caused by tourist expenditures necessitates hiring more people. Thus, they also affect an employment multiplier.

10. As increased spending produces more financial transactions, they create a transactions multiplier. These are of particular interest to governments that have a sales or value-added tax on such transactions.

11. As a tourist area grows, more capital is invested in new facilities. This results in a capital multiplier.

12. It is an unwise policy for a society to place too much dependency on tourism as a subsistence industry.

13. Although tourism often has an excellent potential in economic development, it is not a panacea for economic ills. Its economic benefits should be optimized rather than maximized.

14. We believe that tourism products are mainly price elastic, meaning that as prices rise, the quantity demanded tends to drop.

15. In general, we believe that tourism is income elastic. This means that as family income rises, or a particular market's income rises, and tourism prices do not rise proportionally, the demand for travel to that particular area will increase.

KEY CONCEPTS

balance of payments
demand
direct impact
economic impact
employment
exports and imports

income elasticity
indirect impact
inflationary pressure
leakage
multipliers
optimization

price elasticity
price inelasticity
tax revenue
tourism satellite account

Internet Sites

The Internet sites mentioned in this chapter are repeated here for convenience, plus some selected additional sites. For more information, visit these sites. Be aware that Internet addresses change frequently, so if a site cannot be accessed, use a search engine. Also use a search engine to locate many additional relevant sites.

Asia-Pacific Economic Cooperation
http://www.apecsec.org.sg

Canadian Tourism Commission
http://www.canadatourism.com

Economist Intelligence Unit
http://www.eiu.com

Organization for Economic Cooperation and Development
http://www.oecd.org

World Tourism Organization
http://www.world-tourism.org

World Travel and Tourism Council
http://www.wttc.org

Internet Exercises

Site Name: World Travel and Tourism Council
URL: http://www.wttc.org
Background Information: The World Travel and Tourism Council (WTTC) is the global business leaders forum for travel and tourism. Its central goal is to work with governments to realize the full economic impact of the world's largest generator of wealth and jobs—travel and tourism.

Exercises

1. Review the economic research for a particular region selected by either you or your instructor. What are the economic forecasts for that region?

2. What are the overall tourism forecasts worldwide?
3. What do the statistical data reveal about the United States?
4. What are the regional statistics for the region where you live?
5. What are the employment projections?

QUESTIONS FOR REVIEW AND DISCUSSION

1. What is meant by *optimization*?
2. Discuss how an airline executive might use tourism economics relating to passenger load-factors, ticket prices, discounts, frequent-flyer programs, joint fares, and flight frequencies.
3. Selecting one form of public transportation, enumerate the economic constraints that affect this business.
4. A full-service restaurant is considering having an elaborate buffet dinner three nights a week. What constraints are likely to bear on this consideration?
5. Define tourism exports and imports in terms of national economies.
6. Explain how international tourism could assist in reducing the current sizeable U.S. trade deficit. How could it increase the deficit?

7. Give several reasons why a hotel's purchasing director should be familiar with the income multiplier phenomenon.
8. Trace how tourist expenditures in a community provide financial support to the public library.
9. Enumerate various methods by which a tourist-dependent community can at least partially overcome seasonality of tourism demand.
10. Why is a tourism satellite account considered to be the best way to measure tourism's impact on the economy?

CASE PROBLEMS

1. Mr. and Mrs. Henry B. are considering taking their first trip abroad. Deciding to buy a group tour, they find that some countries in which they are interested seem to offer a much better value than do others. Assuming that the ingredients of the tours being considered are very similar, what factors are likely to account for this price difference?
2. A western U.S. state is quite popular with tourists, hosting about 6 million visitors per year. The state's director of sales and use taxes has recently advised the governor that a special 5 percent hotel and motel rooms tax should be added to the present 4 percent use tax, making a 9 percent total rooms tax. Currently, the state's budget is in the red. Thus, an increase in revenue is badly needed. What economic advice should the governor seek?

SELECTED REFERENCES

Braun, Bradley M. "The Economic Contribution of Conventions: The Case of Orlando, Florida." *Journal of Travel Research*, Vol. 30, No. 3, pp. 32–37, Winter 1992.

Cannon, Thomas. "Relationship of Demographics and Trip Characteristics to Visitor Spending: An Analysis of Sports Travel Visitors Across Time." *Tourism Economics—Special Issue: Measuring the Economic Impact of Tourism*, Vol. 8, No. 3, pp. 263–271, 2002.

Deply, Lisa, and Ming Li. "The Art and Science of Conducting Economic Impact Studies." *Journal of Vacation Marketing*, Vol. 4, No. 3, pp. 230–254, 1998.

Dwyer, Larry, Peter Forsyth, and Ray Spurr. "Evaluating Tourism's Economic Effects: New and Old Approaches." *Tourism Management*, Vol. 25, No. 1, pp. 307–318, June 2004.

Dwyer, Larry, and Peter Forsyth. "Economic Impacts of Cruise Tourism in Australia." *Journal of Tourism Studies*, Vol. 7, No. 2, pp. 36–45, December 1996.

Dwyer, Larry, Peter Forsyth, John Madden, and Ray Spurr. "Economic Impacts of Inbound Tourism under Different Assumptions Regarding the Macroeconomy." *Current Issues in Tourism*, Vol. 3, No. 4, pp. 325–363, 2000.

Dwyer, Larry, Robert Mellor, Nina Mistilis, and Trevor Mules. "Forecasting the Economic Impacts of Events and Conventions." *Event Management*, Vol. 6, No. 3, pp. 191–204, 2000.

Faulkner, Bill, Laurence Chalip, Graham Brown, Leo Jago, Roger March, and Arch Woodside. "Monitoring the Tourism Impacts of the Sydney 2000 Olympics." *Event Management*, Vol. 6, No. 4, pp. 231–246, 2001.

Frechtling, Douglas C. and Endre Horvath. "Estimating the Multiplier Effects of Tourism Expenditures on a Local Economy Through a Regional Input-Output Model." *Journal of Travel Research*, Vol. 37, No. 4, pp. 324–332, 1999.

Ioannides, D., and K. G. Debbage (eds). *The Economic Geography of the Tourist Industry: A Supply-Side Analysis*. London: Routledge, 1998.

Mak, James. *Tourism and the Economy: Understanding the Economics of Tourism*. Honolulu: University of Hawaii Press, 2004.

Nirdstrom, Jonas. "Tourism Satellite Account for Sweden 1992–93." *Tourism Economics*, Vol. 2, No. 1, pp. 13–42, March 1996.

Smith, Stephen. "The Tourism Satellite Account: Perspectives of Canadian Tourism Associations and Organizations." *Tourism Economics*, Vol. 1, No. 3, pp. 225–244, September 1995.

Tourism Works for America Council, Travel Industry Association of America. *Tourism Works for America 2004*, 13th ed. Washington, DC: TIA, annual.

Travel Industry Association of America. *Economic Review of Travel in America: 2004 Edition*. Washington, DC: TIA, 2004.

Travel Industry Association of America. *Impact of Travel on State Economies 2004*. Washington, DC: TIA, 2004.

Travel Industry Association of America. *A Portrait of Travel Industry Employment in the U.S. Economy*. Washington, DC: TIA, 1999.

Vanhove, Norbert. *The Economics of Tourism Destinations*. Oxford, UK: Butterworth-Heinemann, 2004.

Wagner, John E. "Estimating the Economic Impacts of Tourism." *Annals of Tourism Research*, Vol. 24, No. 3, pp. 592–608, July 1997.

Wanhill, Stephen. "The Measurement of Tourism Income Multipliers." *Tourism Management*, Vol. 15, No. 4, pp. 281–283, August 1994.

World Tourism Organization. *Compendium of Tourism Statistics*. Madrid: WTO, 2004.

World Tourism Organization. *Enzo Paci Papers on Measuring the Economic Significance of Tourism*, Vol. 1. Madrid: WTO, 2001.

World Tourism Organization. *The Tourism Satellite Account as an Ongoing Process: Past, Present, and Future Developments*. Madrid: WTO, 2001.

World Tourism Organization. *Tourism Satellite Account: Recommended Methodological Framework*. Madrid: WTO, 2001.

World Tourism Organization. *Travel and Tourism Barometer*. Madrid: WTO, 2004.

TOURISM POLICY: STRUCTURE, CONTENT, AND PROCESS

CHAPTER 15

Learning Objectives

- Demonstrate the critical importance of tourism policy to the competitiveness and sustainability of a tourism destination.
- Outline the structure and content of a typical policy framework for a tourism destination.
- Describe a process for the formulation of a destination tourism policy.

Developing new tourism destinations and successfully maintaining existing ones requires a policy that combines competitiveness and sustainability. No trip to Sydney is complete without a tour of the Opera House, one the world's most daring and beautiful examples of twentieth-century architecture.

Copyright © Corbis Digital Stock.

INTRODUCTION

This chapter addresses an important dimension of tourism—one that is being increasingly recognized for the impact it can have on the long-term success of a tourism destination. Although the concept of "master planning" has been around for some time, the need for high-level strategic planning involving the explicit definition of major policies reflecting an ongoing consensus among all the stakeholders within a tourism destination is the outgrowth of social changes in which all citizens are demanding a greater level of participation in the formulation of policies and programs and in development that affects their daily lives.

Tourism has not escaped the pressure of this social change. As a consequence, this chapter plays several important roles in enhancing our understanding of tourism in future years. It also discusses two other global forces that all tourism destinations must now face: (1) the growing competition from both established and emerging destinations, and (2) the pressure to maintain the ecological integrity of regions affected by tourism. These two pressures together have led to the overall need to strive to build "**competitive** and **sustainable**" destinations (see Figure 15.1).

The impacts of September 11, 2001, illustrate the underlying significance to tourism of carefully formulating effective policies well in advance of unanticipated events. They also demonstrate the high degree of interdependence between tourism policy and a broad range of national and local policies. Some of the most obvious examples include policies regarding airline security, immigration and visitation, money laundering, and emergency health procedures. An area that has been neglected in the past may now receive greater attention.

The chapter starts by defining tourism policy and its overall purpose. It then demonstrates the broad scope of stakeholders who are affected by tourism policy,

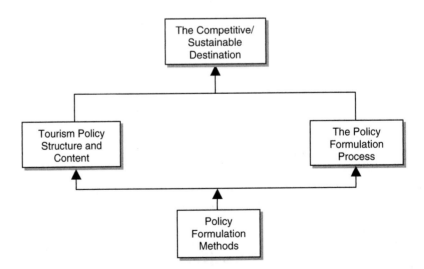

Figure 15.1 The competitive/sustainable tourist destination: A managerial framework.

whether good or bad. Subsequent discussion focuses on the specific functions of tourism policy and describes the many areas that must be addressed by a comprehensive tourism policy.

TOURISM POLICY: A DEFINITION

Tourism policy can be defined as a set of regulations, rules, guidelines, directives, and development/promotion objectives and strategies that provide a framework within which the collective and individual decisions directly affecting long-term tourism development and the daily activities within a destination are taken.

The Purpose of Tourism Policy

A tourism destination hosts visitors in order to provide its stakeholders (see Figure 15.2) with a broad range of economic and social benefits, most typically employment and income. This employment and income allow stakeholders to reside in and to enjoy the quality of the region. Tourism policy seeks to ensure that visitors are hosted in a way that maximizes the benefits to stakeholders while minimizing the negative effects, costs, and impacts associated with ensuring the success of the destination. In effect, tourism policy seeks to provide high-quality visitor experiences that are profitable to destination stakeholders while ensuring that the destination is not compromised in terms of its environmental, social, and cultural integrity.

Why Is Tourism Policy Important?

The area of tourism policy is often overlooked in terms of its importance in ensuring the success of a tourism destination. Perhaps its most important role is to ensure that a given destination has a clear idea as to where it is going or what it is seeking to become in the long term. In parallel, it must strive to create a climate in which collaboration among

Very few attractions are as striking as the North American pronghorn antelope. Developing policies to promote tourism while ensuring the protection of wildlife demands commitment on the part of planners and sensitivity on the part of tourists. *Photo courtesy of Wyoming Division of Tourism.*

◄ Residents of the "host" destination
◄ Local/municipal/regional/provincial/national governments
◄ Local/regional/national environmental groups
◄ Local visitors/excursionists
◄ Remote visitors/tourists
◄ Tourism industry sectors:
  • *Accommodation*
  • *Attractions*
  • *Adventure and outdoor recreation*
  • *Entertainment*
  • *Events*
  • *Food services*
  • *Tourism visitor services*
  • *Transportation*
  • *Travel trade*
◄ Destination management organization (DMO)
◄ Culture/heritage groups
◄ Social/health/education groups

Figure 15.2 Examples of the many "stakeholders" in tourism within a given destination/region.

the many stakeholders in tourism is both supported and facilitated. In more specific terms, tourism policy fulfills the following functions:

1. It defines the rules of the game—the terms under which tourism operators must function.
2. It sets out activities and behaviors that are acceptable for visitors.
3. It provides a common direction and guidance for all tourism stakeholders within a destination.
4. It facilitates consensus around specific strategies and objectives for a given destination.
5. It provides a framework for public/private discussions on the role and contributions of the tourism sector to the economy and to society in general.
6. It allows tourism to interface more effectively with other sectors of the economy.

In light of the foregoing, it is important to keep in mind that tourism policy affects the extent to which all the day-to-day operational activities of tourism—such as marketing, event development, attraction operations, and visitor reception programs—are successful. As such, it is not just a theoretical concept; it has very real implications in day-to-day practice.

Areas Addressed by Tourism Policy

In general terms, a formal tourism policy for a given destination will address (at the national level) such areas as:

1. The roles of tourism within the overall socioeconomic development of the destination region
2. The type of destination that will most effectively fulfill the desired roles
3. Taxation—types and levels
4. Financing for the tourism sector—sources and terms
5. The nature and direction of product development and maintenance
6. Transportation access and infrastructure
7. Regulatory practices (e.g., airlines, travel agencies)
8. Environmental practices and restrictions
9. Industry image, credibility
10. Community relationships
11. Human resources and labor supply
12. Union and labor legislation
13. Technology
14. Marketing practices
15. Foreign travel rules

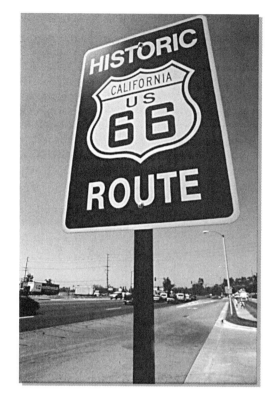

Prior to the national transportation policy creating the interstate highway system, many family summer vacations were enjoyed traveling on the legendary Route 66, which has been immortalized by song and television.

Photo by Robert Holmes; courtesy of the California Division of Tourism.

THE FOCUS OF TOURISM POLICY: THE COMPETITIVE/SUSTAINABLE DESTINATION

In a complex world of many jurisdictions, it is important to explicitly identify the geographic area to which a tourism policy applies. We refer to the "generic" entity in question as the **tourism destination.** A tourism destination, in its simplest terms, is a particular geographic region within which the visitor enjoys various types of travel experiences.

Types and Levels of Tourism Destinations

Tourism destinations are most commonly defined in formal terms by recognized political jurisdictions such as:

1. A nation or country
2. A macro region, consisting of several countries (e.g., Europe) or other groupings that either transcend national borders (e.g., the European Riviera) or reflect economic trade zones (e.g., NAFTA and the Americas)
3. A province or state within a country
4. A localized region within a country, such as western Canada or the U.S. northwest or southeast
5. A city or town
6. A unique locale, such as a national park, a historic site, or a memorial that is in itself sufficiently significant to attract visitors (e.g., substantive and readily identifiable institutions such as Walt Disney World in Orlando, the Hermitage in St. Petersburg, and St. Peter's Basilica in Rome; these may, in themselves, exert sufficient drawing power to be classified as destinations)

THE MAJOR PARAMETERS OF TOURISM DESTINATION MANAGEMENT (TDM)

While the task of tourism destination management (TDM) is a complex, multidimensional challenge, when all the rhetoric is stripped away there are two primary parameters that must be satisfied if the destination is to be successful. These are competitiveness and sustainability. Either alone is not sufficient; they are both essential and mutually supportive.

The **competitiveness** of a destination refers to its ability to compete effectively and profitably in the tourism marketplace. **Sustainability** pertains to the ability of a destination to maintain the quality of its physical, social, cultural, and environmental resources while it competes in the marketplace. A major concern in this regard is to avoid the false appearance of economic profitability, a profitability that is derived from the subtle, often invisible (in the short run) depletion of the destination's "natural capital." Conversely, sustainability may be viewed as encouraging "natural capital investment"—that is, refraining from current consumption in order to protect the environment, and the restoration of natural stocks (those that are renewable), thus ensuring the availability of such resources for future consumption.[1]

We can see that, when viewed in the above light, successful TDM involves traditional economic/business management skills balanced with environmental management capabilities (Figure 15.3). The economic business skills required are

---

[1]Thomas Prugh et al., *National Capital and Human Economic Survival,* Solomons, MD: ISSE Press, 1995.

COMPETITIVENESS *[Resource Deployment]* Business/Economic Management Skills	SUSTAINABILITY *[Resource Stewardship]* Environmental Management Capabilities

• Marketing
• Financial Management
• Operations Management
• Human Resources Management
• Information Management
• Organization Management
• Strategic Planning
• Project/Development
  Management
	• Waste Management
	• Water Quality Management
	• Air Quality Management
	• Wildlife Management
	• Forest/Plant Management
	• Visitor Management
	• Resident/Community
	  Management
	• Commemorative Integrity
	• Recycling
	• Site Protection

Information Management	
Destination Monitoring	**Destination Research**

Figure 15.3   Some elements of successful total tourism destination management (TTDM).

those related to effective resource development and deployment. They include strategic planning for destination development (see Chapter 16), the marketing of the destination (see Chapter 19), the management of the human resources necessary to deliver quality visitor experiences, the management of the financial resources/investment required to support development, and the ability to develop the organizational capacity to coordinate and ensure the delivery of essential services.

The environmental management capabilities are those that are critical to effective destination stewardship. Traditionally, these have included the knowledge and skills essential for ensuring the protection of air and water, forest and plants, and wildlife management.

More recently, the concept of stewardship has been expanded to encompass management practices designed to both maintain and enhance the commemorative, social, and cultural integrity of the destination. It also involves the ability to effectively manage the human presence within the boundaries of the destination. This human presence has two main components: visitor management and resident/community management.

Finally, the tasks of resource deployment and resource stewardship are linked by the shared need for a **tourism destination management information system** (TDMIS) to support policy formulation, strategic planning, day-to-day decision making, and overall performance evaluations. Information management has, in turn, two major components. The monitoring component provides stakeholders, and particularly the destination management organization (DMO), with an ongoing assessment of destination performance across a broad range of indicator variables. These indicator variables should be carefully chosen so as to be representative of the overall health of the destination in terms of both competitiveness and sustainability. Monitoring also includes an environmental scan component that seeks to identify unusual or emerging trends and forces that have the potential to significantly affect the competitiveness or sustainability of a destination.

The research component of the TDMIS is normally structured to play several distinct roles. One of these is to provide research for policy formulation. Policy research is characterized by analysis of the overall destination situation. It is undertaken with a view to providing information that assists in developing well-defined but broad guidelines that serve to establish priorities to direct the activities of the destination.[2] More specifically, policy research seeks to gather and interpret macro-level data related to present values and the evolution of trends of major economic, social, technological, and political factors that bear on the success of the destination.

A Model of the Competitive/Sustainable Destination

Regardless of the size or scope of a destination, it is useful to view it from a holistic perspective in which the structure and management processes are explicitly defined and examined. One framework that attempts to do this has been developed by Ritchie and Crouch.[3] From the standpoint of this model, the purpose of tourism policy is to ensure a common, agreed-upon purpose for tourism and to establish the broad parameters for planning and coordinating the efforts of all tourism stakeholders, those whose well-being relates in some way to the success of tourism in the destination. This model is shown and described in detail in Chapter 16.

A Warning: Tourism Destination and Tourism Policy Do Not Exist in a Vacuum

In all of the foregoing discussions, it needs to be kept in mind that tourism policies are but part of the social, economic, and political policies that govern and direct the functioning of the overall society within which tourism exists and functions.

In brief, a number of more general policies (regulations, rules, directives, objectives, strategies) are controlled by governments, as well as other industry sectors

---

[2]J. R. Brent Ritchie and C. R. Goeldner (eds.), *Travel, Tourism, and Hospitality Research: A Handbook for Managers and Researchers,* 2d ed., New York: Wiley, 1994.

[3]J. R. Brent Ritchie and Geoffrey I. Crouch, *The Competitive Destination: A Sustainable Tourism Perspective,* Oxfordshire, UK: CABI Publishing, 2003.

and organizations, and these policies may have a significant effect on the success of tourism and tourism destinations. These include:

- Taxation—affects costs and thus profitability

- Interest rate policy—affects costs and thus profitability

- Bilateral air agreements—determine foreign visitor access

- Environmental policy—limits growth and access to attractive but sensitive areas

- Customs and immigration policy—can facilitate or hinder international visitation

- Communications policy—can restrict use of certain advertising media

- Minimum wage policy—can affect labor markets

- Welfare policy—can influence nature and behavior of workforce

- Education policy—can affect quality of workforce

- Cultural policy—can affect preservation and promotion of national heritage

The White House tourism conference in the United States was a major tourism event where policy recommendations were made and are still being implemented. *Photo courtesy of the Washington, D.C., Convention and Visitors Association.*

- Foreign investment policy/regulations—can affect availability of investment capital

- Local zoning policy/bylaws—can restrict or encourage tourism facility development

- National/provincial/local policy pertaining to funding support for major public facilities (e.g., stadiums, convention centers, museums, parks)—can drastically affect destination attractiveness

- Infrastructure policy—can make destination safer for visitors, or restrict resident travel to foreign destinations

- Currency/exchange-rate policies—directly affect destination cost competitiveness

- Legal system—determines consumer/visitor protection legislation (e.g., liability for failing to deliver advertised facilities/tours/experiences)

To summarize, a whole range of social, economic, legal, and technological policies greatly affects the appeal, attractiveness, competitiveness, and sustainability of a tourism destination. Some are under the control of the tourism sector (such as visitor satisfaction, guarantee policy, truth-in-advertising policy), but the great majority are not. Thus, the challenge facing tourism managers is to try to influence global policies where they can, and adapt to them as effectively as possible where they cannot.

The Many Influences on Tourism Policy

As stressed above, tourism does not exist in a vacuum. It can function smoothly only if it shares, cooperates, and dialogues effectively with many other sectors of society and of the economy (Figure 15.4). Many of these sectors have little understanding of, or explicit interest in, tourism in the region—unless, of course, visitor activity somehow appears to detract from the functioning or well-being of another sector. Conflicts between tourism and other sectors most commonly arise when there is competition for a shared resource base (e.g., the extractive industries), where there is a common need for specific individuals or types of individuals (e.g., entertainment, technology, education), or where there may exist a divergence of philosophical views (e.g., the environment, transportation sectors).

Each of these interfaces can pose either a threat or an opportunity for tourism. The environmental sector and the extractive industries have traditionally viewed tourism as a competing force; the technology, entertainment, and transportation sectors most often perceive tourism as an ally or business opportunity.

In order to dialogue and to present its case effectively at each interface, the tourism sector must be as capable, as well trained, and as well prepared as the professionals of any specific sector at any given point in time. Otherwise, tourism risks being undermined and weakened. Consequently, it may miss a critical market opportunity or may fail to establish an innovative alliance or partnership. All too often, tourism's lack of sophistication and preparedness has resulted in government

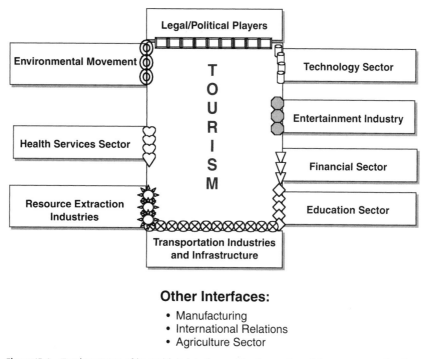

Other Interfaces:
- Manufacturing
- International Relations
- Agriculture Sector

Figure 15.4 Tourism: Some of its multiple interfaces with other sectors of the economy and society.

decisions and policies that significantly weaken its ability to compete, or to do so more profitably. In certain cases, the tourism sector has never been aware of the extent to which it has been disadvantaged by its naïveté or by a failure to proactively and adequately prepare its case. This can be particularly disastrous in public forums where both the issue at hand and the industry's long-term credibility can be lost.

The Multidisciplinary Nature of Tourism and Tourism Policy

As explained in Chapter 1, tourism is, by its very nature, a multidisciplinary phenomenon (see Figure 1.3). The tourism experience is impacted by a range of economic, psychological, societal, technological, legal, and political forces.[4,5] It follows that, in order to formulate policies that accommodate or address these multiple forces, those involved must appreciate the complexities of each discipline and their interactions in any given situation. The disciplines of psychology, economics,

---

[4]J. Jafari and J. R. Brent Ritchie, "Toward a Framework for Tourism Education: Problems and Prospect," *Annals of Tourism Research,* Vol. 8, No. 1, pp. 13–34, 1981.
[5]C. Echtner and T. B. Jamal, "The Disciplinary Dilemma of Tourism Studies," *Annals of Tourism Research,* Vol. 24, No. 4, pp. 868–883, October 1997.

sociology, and law are but some of the disciplines that can enhance our understanding of international marketing. The environmental sciences, political science, and the behavioral sciences are essential to the formulation of national park policy that defines the levels and types of tourism that are appropriate and desirable.

Some Other Characteristics of Tourism Policy

In addition to the multidisciplinary nature of tourism policy, it also possesses several other essential characteristics:

1. It must focus on macro-level policies—that is, be concerned with societal views of the direction that tourism development should take at the subnational, national, and even transnational level.
2. It must be designed to formulate policies having a long time perspective.
3. It must concentrate on how critical and limited resources can best respond to perceived needs and opportunities in a changing environment.
4. It must recognize the intellectual nature of the process of policy formulation. As such, it must incorporate tacit knowledge and personal experience as important sources of information, in addition to more conventional methods of research and study.
5. It must encourage and stimulate organized creativity so as to avoid policies based on stereotyped or outmoded perceptions.
6. It must be constructed to permit and facilitate a continuing dynamic social process requiring inputs from multiple sources.
7. It must break down the traditional boundaries between industry sectors in tourism.
8. It must relate policies of the tourism subsystem to those of the total socioeconomic system of a nation or region of which it is a part.
9. It must acknowledge the destination roles of both competition and cooperation and seek to identify situations where each is appropriate. The judicious application of either or both in tourism policy has given rise to use of the term "coopetition."[6]

TOURISM POLICY: STRUCTURE, CONTENT, AND PROCESS

In discussing tourism policy, it is helpful to clearly distinguish among the overall structure of a policy and the specific policy content found within that structure. In the same vein, readers must distinguish between: (1) the static concepts of policy structure and content, and (2) the dynamic concept of policy formulation. Structure and context define the "what" of tourism policy; the process of policy

---

[6]David L. Edgell and R. Todd Haenisch, *Competition: Global Tourism beyond the Millennium.* Kansas City: International Policy Publishing, 1995, p. 2.

formulation describes the "how" of defining the structure of a destination's policy and determining the content of policy found within that structure. In tourism, the process, or the "how," provides the following:

- An overview of the different stages or steps involved in the policy formulation process

- A review of the various possible methodologies that might be used within, or across, the stages of policy formulation

The Structure of Tourism Policy

While no single model can define the content of tourism destination policy, Figure 15.5 provides one framework for tourism policy (i.e., a set of guidelines for successful destination development and operations).

Total System and Tourism Macro Policy

Macro policy, or what some have referred to as "megapolicy," involves determination of the premises, assumptions, and main guidelines to be followed by specific policies. They are a kind of master policy, clearly distinct from detailed discrete

State governments are an important seat of tourism policy formation. Shown here is the state capitol building in Richmond, Virginia. *Photo courtesy of Washington, D.C., and the Capital Region.*

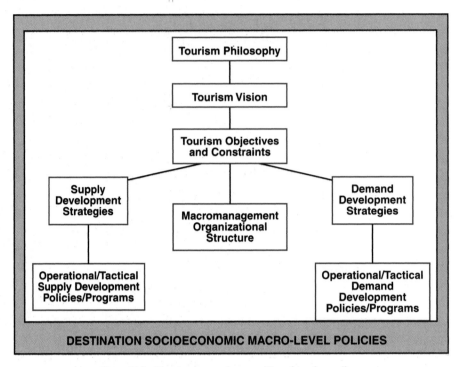

Figure 15.5 The structure and composition of tourism policy.

policies.[7] In this regard, tourism policy is viewed as being directly based upon and derived from the policies that direct the total socioeconomic system of the nation or region in which the tourism subsystem is located. In fact, it is the general content of these total system policies that provides much of the basis upon which to derive the tourism philosophy of the destination region in question.

Tourism Philosophy

An explicit tourism philosophy is an essential foundation on which to develop a coherent policy. In general, a philosophy may be defined as a system for guiding life—a body of principles of conduct, beliefs, or traditions—or the broad general principles of a particular subject or field of activity. Adapting this general definition for present purposes, a tourism philosophy may be defined as a general principle or set of principles that indicates the beliefs and values of members of a society concerning how tourism shall serve the population of a country or region, and that acts as a guide for evaluating the utility of tourism-related activities.

It is important to stress the critical role that the values of destination residents exert in determining the context of tourism policy. In effect, the values of residents

[7] Y. Dror, *Design for Policy Sciences,* New York: American Elsevier, 1971.

provide the foundation on which the policy and its various components rest. In the end, tourism policies that do not reflect the values of the destination stakeholders, or hosts, will inevitably fail to gain ongoing popular or political support. Policies that do not maintain long-term political support are doomed to failure.

The philosophical distinction sometimes made between value-driven and market-driven destinations, while conceptually appealing, is in practice somewhat ambiguous. No destination can be competitive unless it succeeds in appealing to profitable segments of the market over the long term. By the same token, no destination can be sustainable unless, while it generates economic rewards, it also succeeds in maintaining the value-driven legitimacy required by a democratic society.

The Destination Vision

Although a tourism philosophy sets out the overall nature of tourism in a destination, it is the **destination vision** that provides the more functional and more inspirational portrait of the ideal future that the destination hopes to bring about in some defined future (usually five, ten, twenty, or fifty years).

Visions can take many different forms. Some are very concise (the equivalent of a corporate mission statement); others are much more extensive and idealistic. Typically, however, a destination vision is structured as shown in Figure 15.6.

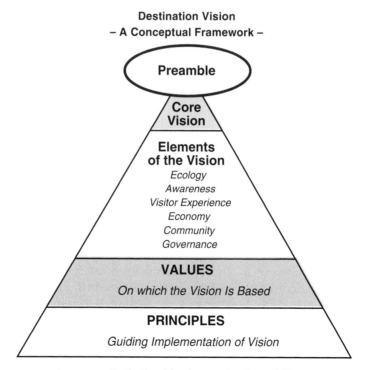

Figure 15.6   **Destination vision framework.**   *Source: Ritchie, 1996.*

The **preamble** sector of a vision sets the tone and provides the context and rationale for the vision being developed. The **core vision,** as the name implies, attempts to capture the overall essence of the ideal future for the destination in question. The values component of the vision statement seeks to provide an understanding of the deeply held enduring beliefs of the stakeholders formulating the vision. It is these values that effectively drive—or provide a foundation—for the vision statements that are enunciated by individuals. One cannot understand or appreciate a vision without understanding and appreciating the values on which it is based.

The **elements** of the vision are the means by which the essence or idealism of the vision (the core vision) is linked to the reality of the destination. In effect, they provide the means by which operational components of the vision can be defined. The nature of these components is dependent upon the specific destination in question. In the example in Figure 15.6, the core vision for a Canadian national park gave rise to six vision elements.

Finally, once the core vision and its elements have been agreed upon, it is frequently useful to provide a statement of principles designed to provide guidance as to how the vision and its elements should be interpreted and implemented.

Crafting versus Formulating a Strategic Vision

The preparation of a destination vision is a stimulating, intellectual process that often attracts and should involve the relevant stakeholders of a destination. There is, however, a significant difference between formulating and crafting the vision. Policy formulation is a term reflecting a traditional approach to strategic planning that can be described as prescriptive in orientation. This terminology implies that strategy formulation is a process of conceptual design, of formal planning, and of analytical positioning. The essence of this model is that it is by nature structured, logical, and somewhat mechanical. It emphasizes that strategy formulation should be a controlled, conscious process of thought for which ultimate responsibility lies with the chief executive officer of the entity involved in strategy development. The outcome of this process is a simple, unique, and explicit "best" strategy for a given situation.

At the other end of the spectrum is what Mintzberg defines as the crafting of strategy. Under this conceptualization, crafting a strategy is a dynamic, evolving process in which strategies take form as a result of learning over a period of time, as opposed to being formulated at a fixed point in time. He emphasizes that the crafting of strategy reflects an ongoing iterative process of thinking and acting—and then thinking some more. One idea leads to another until a new pattern forms. As such, strategies can form as well as be formulated. A strategy can emerge in response to an evolving situation, or it can be brought about deliberately, through a process of formulation followed by implementation. Crafting strategy requires dedication, experience, involvement with the material, the personal touch, mastery of detail, a sense of harmony, and integration.[8]

---

[8]H. Mintzberg, "Crafting Strategy," *Harvard Business Review,* pp. 66–75, July–August 1987.

In brief, the process of "strategic visioning"—or simply "visioning"—like the crafting of strategy, is seen as a dynamic, interactive phenomenon.[9]

Tourism Objectives and Constraints

Component three of a tourism policy consists of a statement of the objectives of the tourism system. Objectives are defined as operational statement(s) of the specific results sought by the tourism system within a given time frame. The objectives of the tourism system should possess a number of important characteristics. First, because the objectives are formulated in light of the tourism vision, their achievement should clearly contribute to the fulfillment of this vision. Second, in order that the objectives can be qualified as operational, it is essential that managers are able to measure the extent to which desired results have or have not been attained. This implies that we must have some explicit means of quantifying appropriate performance standards. Third, we must ensure that the measures selected with respect to each objective are indeed valid indicators of the desired results; that is, they must measure what we truly want to achieve. Fourth, in the common situation where the tourism system has multiple objectives, it is advisable to indicate an order or priority among objectives. This indication of relative importance provides a basis for decision making should different strategies or programs for achieving the objective be in conflict. Fifth, the objectives must be related to a given time period as is directly stated in the above definition. Finally, the objectives that are stated must be reasonable. While they should serve to offer a real challenge, goals that are virtually impossible to attain quickly become a negative rather than a positive source of motivation.

One further remark concerning the formal statement of objectives is in order. Objectives identify those events or results that we wish to bring about. The word *objective* implies that the results are positive entities, such as a certain number of visitors, but this is not necessarily so. In fact, the managers of a tourism system may seek goals with respect to what they do not want to happen as a consequence of their activities. Examples include the avoidance of environmental and cultural pollution. These types of results could be stated as specific objectives of the tourism system. While very important, their essentially negative nature provides little incentive for management action. An alternative and more satisfactory manner of dealing with effects that one wishes to avoid is to express them in the form of constraints. A common approach to formally stating constraints on system activities is to specify, where possible, the maximum level of each undesirable outcome (e.g., pollution) that can be tolerated as a result of tourism activity. Even where it is difficult to quantify the tolerable levels of undesirable outcomes, constraints can be formulated so as to at least provide explicit indications as to the type of outcomes to be minimized or avoided.

---

[9]F. Westley and H. Mintzberg, "Visionary Leadership and Strategic Management," *Strategic Management Journal*, Vol. 10, pp. 17–32, 1989.

THE PROCESS OF TOURISM POLICY FORMULATION

Discussion to this point in the chapter has focused on the structure and content of tourism policy. In this section, attention is directed toward understanding the process by which the structure and content of policy, as presented in Figure 15.5, may be developed. This process is conceptualized as containing distinct stages grouped into four main phases (Figure 15.7). These phases are identified as the definitional phase, the analytical phase, the operational phase, and the implementation phase.

Definitional Phase

The definitional phase of tourism policy formulation is concerned with the development of explicit statements that define the content and direction of the overall tourism system in question. As shown in Figure 15.7, these statements deal with four different topics. The definition of the destination tourism system represents the critical first step in the process of policy formulation.

Figure 1.3 in Chapter 1 provides one model that might be useful as the basic framework for defining a tourism system. It views the tourism system as being constructed of two major components, namely, the operating sectors and the planning/catalyst organizations. These in turn contain various subcomponents that form the basis for identifying and classifying the individual organizations and actors (the stakeholders) that make up a given tourism system. It is essential that each region develop such a model that is generally accepted by the policy makers con-

Definitional Phase	Analytical Phase	Operational Phase	Implementation Phase
Definition of tourism destination system	*Internal Analysis* • Review of existing policies and programs • Resource audit • Strategic impact analysis	Identification of strategic conclusions	Implementation of strategy for destination development, promotion, and stewardship
Explication of a tourism philosophy		Implications of conclusions for supply and demand development	Allocation of responsibilities for recommendation implementation
Crafting of a destination vision	*External Analysis* • Macro level analysis of current and future demand	Policy/program recommendations	Identification of sources of funding to support competitive initiatives and stewardship programs
Objectives and constraints	• Micro level analysis of current and future demand and behaviors • Review of competitive and supportive tourism development and promotion policies		Specification of timing for recommendation implementation
			Monitoring and evaluation of the results

Figure 15.7 The process of tourism policy, strategy formulation, and implementation.

cerned. Once agreed to, this model should become a constant frame of reference for discussion and decision making.

The remaining three components of the definitional phase (Figure 15.7) involve the explication of a tourism philosophy, the formulation of a destination vision, and the determination of tourism objectives and constraints for the destination. Previous discussion has described the content of these policy components.

Analytical Phase

The analytical phase of tourism policy development, while perhaps less stressful than the previous one from a managerial standpoint, involves considerably greater amounts of effort. The definitional phase requires fundamental, value-based decisions concerning the nature and direction of tourism development in a region. The analytical phase accepts these decisions as a given and proceeds to carry out the extensive collection and assessment of information needed to identify and assess the desirability of alternative means of attaining the destination vision and to achieve the goals defined by the vision.

The overall process of analysis is best viewed as being composed of two major subprocesses: (1) an internal or supply-oriented analysis, and (2) an external or demand-oriented analysis.

The internal/supply analysis consists of a thorough review and analysis (frequently termed an "audit") of two major elements. The first element relates to existing policies and programs for the development of the various components of tourism supply. These policies/programs must be critically reviewed to determine the extent to which they are both consistent with, and effective in, developing the type of tourism facilities and services that are likely to achieve the goals of the region, given the nature of demand facing that region. As can be quickly seen, this statement implies a direct interaction between the supply analysis and the demand analysis. In effect, the analytical phase involves parallel, iterative forms of analysis that must constantly be related one to the other.

A second element of the supply analysis is termed a resource audit. A resource audit should be conducted with two goals in mind. First, it should provide a comprehensive cataloguing of the quantity and distribution of tourism facilities and services within the tourism system. Such information is basic to an understanding of the current state of affairs of supply development. Second, the resource audit should provide some assessment of the quality of existing facilities and services. Again, the execution of the audit to assess the adequacy of the quantity, distribution, and quality of supply can only be meaningful if it is eventually related to the analysis of demand. There are no absolute measures of desirability in terms of supply; *only those that relate to a given demand at a given point in time for a given market segment are relevant.*

The third form of internal analysis is a strategic impact analysis. This analysis seeks to provide policy makers with well-defined benchmarks as to the extent to which tourism is currently impacting the destination in economic, ecological, social, and cultural terms. Economic benchmarks have traditionally been the most requested forms of impact analysis because both managers and politicians seek to measure and understand both the level of tourism receipts and the incomes and employment they create.

The external/demand analysis is composed of three distinct types of analytical activity. The first involves macro-level analysis of data that describes and defines the overall nature and structure of current tourism demand as well as those markets having a potential for future demand. This form of analysis relies heavily on aggregate statistics measuring the flows of tourists and travel-related expenditures within a region; it must not, however, limit itself to such historical data. In addition, macro-level analysis must be future-oriented and attempt to constantly monitor the environment in order to identify shifts or trends in social, political, or technological factors that might significantly affect the region's success in its field of tourism.

The second type of external/demand analysis is termed micro-level analysis. Here, rather than focusing on aggregate trends in tourism demand, attention is directed toward gaining an understanding of the motivations and behavior of the different segments of the total tourism market. The purpose of gaining this understanding is to provide those responsible for supply development with the information needed to design facilities and services that will appeal most to each of the various demand segments. In addition, such data facilitates the task of those responsible for the promotion of existing facilities and services.

The final component of external/demand analysis involves a review and evaluation of competitive and supportive tourism development and promotion policies and programs. Competitive analysis is a common form of managerial investigation. In this case, it is designed to produce a clear picture concerning the identity, strength, and strategies of those tourism destinations most likely to be appealing to the same segments of demand as those of interest to the tourism region in question. Such information is essential if a region is to effectively counter the efforts of such competitors from the standpoint of both supply development and demand modification.

Operational Phase

Once the various types of analysis have been carried out, policy makers must move to develop specific strategies and action plans that can be implemented. As shown in Figure 15.7, this operational phase is envisaged to contain three conceptually different types of activity; in reality, these different activities are executed almost simultaneously.

The identification of strategic conclusions flows directly out of the analytical phase, and its goal is to synthesize the large amounts of information obtained into a limited number of major conclusions. In addition to specifying the major findings from each type of internal and external analysis, this process also must attempt to provide conclusions that assess the impact of the trade-offs that inevitably are made when attempting to match supply and demand.

The strategic conclusions themselves may be viewed as reasonably factual information; that is, they are the result of a logical process of analysis that would give rise to generally similar findings irrespective of the investigator. In contrast, the drawing of "implications of the conclusions for supply-and-demand development strategies" involves a high degree of judgment on the part of the individuals involved. The goal of this process is to attempt to assess the significance of each conclusion for tourism in the region. While the actual conclusions may be clear, the implications of these facts for the kind of policies and programs needed to deal with them involves a considerable level of interpretive skills derived from both experience and a creative mind.

The subsequent stage of the policy formulation process is the identification of specific "policy/program recommendations for supply/demand development." For present purposes, this rather complex activity has been oversimplified in reality; a range of policy options would normally be developed that attempt to respond to alternative implications or alternative scenarios. Some judgment would then be exercised as to which implications or scenarios are most likely to occur. Policy/program recommendations most appropriate to the most likely scenario events would probably, although not necessarily, be adopted.

Implementation Phase

Finally, for a destination tourism policy to truly succeed, it is essential to include an implementation phase. At a minimum, such a strategy must: (1) identify the

The presentation of national treasures is an integral part of tourism policy. In this photo, the great Buddha in Taiwan is but one of the kinds of treasure that policy formulation in tourism must address. *Copyright © Corbis Digital Stock.*

individual groups or organizations that will assume responsibility for each major dimension of the policy realization, (2) establish initial estimates of the financial requirements, and (3) provide preliminary timelines for the launching of all major facilities, events, and programs that support the destination vision. The specifics of implementation are the object of tourism planning. These specifics are examined in detail in Chapter 16.

TRANSLATING POLICY INTO REALITY

It must be emphasized that once overall supply-and-demand development strategies have been enunciated and appropriate organizational structures put in place, these strategies must be translated into specific policies and programs of an operational nature. At this level, the management process becomes one of detailed planning and implementation of the many tasks necessary to provide the individual tourist with the satisfying yet challenging experience that he or she is seeking. While detailed discussion of tourism planning is beyond the scope of this chapter, the need to effectively translate strategic ideas into real-world actions cannot be too strongly stressed. Without effective execution, even the most brilliant policies will prove of little value.

An example illustrating the need to translate policy into reality is crisis management. Today, every tourism organization needs crisis management policies and plans that work. A discussion of crisis management follows.

FORMULATING POLICY TO DEAL WITH CRISES

Despite the best efforts to formulate tourism policies that support destination development, to plan and execute the development of an attractive tourism destination, and to effectively manage a tourism destination, sometimes the unthinkable happens. The September 11, 2001, terrorist bombing of the twin towers in New York and the Pentagon in Washington, D.C.; the 2002 bombing of a tourist-filled night club in Bali, Indonesia; the 2004 bombing of the commuter trains in Madrid, Spain; and the 2003 failure of the electrical grid in eastern North America all created sudden disruptions in the normally smooth functioning of tourism. Other less sudden but more widespread happenings such as the Iraq war, the 2003 outbreaks of SARS (severe acute respiratory syndrome) in China and Canada, the outbreak of foot-and-mouth disease in the United Kingdom, the forest fires in the western United States, threat of the bird flu, and the tsunami, all affected people's desire and ability to travel, and thus the well-being of tourism destinations around the world.

While the above crises were not all directly related to the tourism sector, their widespread repercussions created situations that seriously affected or interfered with people's willingness to travel, or the smooth functioning of the tourism system. They were thus the root cause of crises that tourism managers needed to understand or to take account of in their ongoing management of tourism destinations.

In an effort to help improve our formal understanding of the nature of "crisis management" related to both unthinkable happenings and major events having global repercussions, Mitroff and Anagnos divide crisis-causing events into seven general types and/or categories of risk:

1. Economic crises, such as labor strikes, labor shortage, market crashes, major declines in stock prices, and fluctuations or declines in major earnings
2. Informational crises, such as a loss of proprietary and confidential information, tampering with computer records, or the loss of key computer information with regard to customers and suppliers
3. Physical crises, such as loss of key equipment, plants, and material suppliers; breakdowns of key equipment and industrial plants; loss of key facilities; and major plant disruptions
4. Human resource crises, such as loss of key executives, loss of key personnel, increased absenteeism, increased vandalism, an increased number of accidents, and a rise in workplace violence
5. Reputation crises, such as slander, gossip, rumors, damage to corporate reputation, and tampering with corporate logos
6. Crises resulting from psychopathic acts, such as product tampering, kidnapping, hostage taking, terrorism, and workplace violence
7. Natural disasters, such as earthquakes, fires, floods, explosions, typhoons, and hurricanes[10]

They further stress that, although the major categories of crises share many similarities, there can be substantial differences in the impact they have on an organization. More specifically, a crisis brought about by a natural disaster will probably affect a destination very differently from one caused by the loss of a key executive. Given this reality, Mitroff and Anagnos suggest that the best management approach is to develop policies to prepare for at least one crisis in each of the categories. Unfortunately, they note that the majority of organizations do much less, in that they tend to consider at most one or two categories. For example, most companies prepare for natural disasters. Organizations that do broaden their preparations for crises other than natural disasters often do so only for "core" or "normal" disasters that are specific to their particular industry.

Dealing with Crises

The best method of crisis management is preparation before a crisis occurs—first implementing effort to prevent the crisis from occurring at all, and then developing the ability to react immediately and effectively should an outbreak or incident arise. This means a disaster (crisis) plan must be developed.

---

[10]I. I. Mitroff and G. Anagnos, *Managing Crises before They Happen: What Every Executive and Manager Needs to Know about Crisis Management,* New York: Amacom, 2001.

Good crisis management requires policies to deal with each stage of a crisis situation if a destination is to prevent or minimize a crisis. First, one needs detection policies. This requires a monitoring system of the macroenvironment to make sure one is detecting problems and anticipating tomorrow rather than reacting to yesterday. The second requirement is for prevention or minimization policies. This involves such areas as legislation, law enforcement, security devices, and safety and security training for employees. The third need is for readiness policies that require leadership for crisis coordination, emergency response, assistance for families, internal and external communications, information dissemination, and media relations. Fourth, response policies, which include effective emergency response and answering the public call for information, should be put in place. Telling the truth is a vital crisis management policy. Finally, recovery policies to enable a return to normalcy are a high priority. These include the rebuilding process, information dissemination, publicity, public relations, and marketing.

The concern of the World Tourism Organization (WTO) about crises resulted in their creating the WTO Recovery Committeee. This committeee has published *Crisis Guidelines for the Tourism Industry,* which offers a one-step reference document suggesting specific actions to take before, during, and immediately after a crisis to get tourists returning to a destination as quickly as possible. The publication is available on WTO's Web site **(http://www.world-tourism.org).**

SUMMARY

This chapter points out that (1) tourism policy is needed for destinations at all levels and for all types of political jurisdictions, (2) in all cases, competitiveness and sustainability must be the primary goal of policy, and (3) the effective pursuit of each of these goals requires a different set of skills and capabilities. With this background firmly in place, the chapter then fulfills one major role.

This role is to provide a framework describing the structure and composition of a formal tourism policy. The primary components discussed are the philosophy for tourism and the formulation of a long-term vision for the destination. This vision provides important guidance for the definition of specific objectives for a tourism destination, as well as for identifying any constraints that must be observed as tourism is developed. These objectives, in turn, provide a basis for formulating long-term development strategies for the region. Next, the chapter focuses on the process of policy formulation, which includes the definitional phase, the analytical phase, the operational phase, and the implementation phase. The chapter concludes with an example discussing crisis management.

ABOUT THE READING

This reading is the World Tourism Organization's *Global Code of Ethics for Tourism.* This publication should be required reading for tourism policy makers, and they should incorporate the ethical principles into policy.

READING 15.1

Global Code of Ethics for Tourism
World Tourism Organization

1. Tourism's Contribution to Mutual Understanding and Respect between Peoples and Societies

1. The understanding and promotion of the ethical values common to humanity, with an attitude of tolerance and respect for the diversity of religious, philosophical, and moral beliefs, are both the foundation and the consequence of responsible tourism; stakeholders in tourism development and tourists themselves should observe the social and cultural traditions and practices of all peoples, including those of minorities and indigenous peoples and to recognize their worth.

2. Tourism activities should be conducted in harmony with the attributes and traditions of the host regions and countries and in respect for their laws, practices, and customs.

3. The host communities, on the one hand, and local professionals, on the other, should acquaint themselves with and respect the tourists who visit them and find out about their lifestyles, tastes, and expectations. The education and training imparted to professionals contribute to a hospitable welcome.

4. It is the task of the public authorities to provide protection for tourists and visitors and their belongings. They must pay particular attention to the safety of foreign tourists owing to the particular vulnerability they may have. They should facilitate the introduction of specific means of information, prevention, security, insurance, and assistance consistent with their needs. Any attacks, assaults, kidnappings, or threats against tourists or workers in the tourism industry, as well as the willful destruction of tourism facilities or of elements of cultural or natural heritage should be severely condemned and punished in accordance with their respective national laws.

5. When traveling, tourists and visitors should not commit any criminal act or any act considered criminal by the laws of the country visited and abstain from any conduct felt to be offensive or injurious by the local populations or likely to damage the local environment. They should refrain from all trafficking in illicit drugs, arms, antiques, protected species, and products and substances that are dangerous or prohibited by national regulations.

6. Tourists and visitors have the responsibility to acquaint themselves, even before their departure, with the characteristics of the countries they are preparing to visit. They must be aware of the health and security risks inherent in any travel outside their usual environment and behave in such a way as to minimize those risks.

2. Tourism as a Vehicle for Individual and Collective Fulfillment

1. Tourism, the activity most frequently associated with rest and relaxation, sport, and access to culture and nature, should be planned and practiced as a privileged means of individual and collective fulfillment. When practiced with a sufficiently open mind, it is an irreplaceable factor of self-education, mutual tolerance, and for learning about the legitimate differences between peoples and cultures and their diversity.

2. Tourism activities should respect the equality of men and women. They should promote human rights and, more particularly, the individual rights of the most vulnerable groups, notably children, the elderly, the handicapped, ethnic minorities, and indigenous peoples.

3. The exploitation of human beings in any form, particularly sexual, especially when applied to children, conflicts with the fundamental aims of tourism and is the negation of tourism. As such, in accordance with international law, it should be energetically combated with the cooperation of all the states concerned and penalized without concession by the national legislation of both the countries visited and the countries of the perpetrators of these acts, even when they are carried out abroad.

4. Travel for purposes of religion, health, education, and cultural or linguistic exchanges are particularly beneficial forms of tourism, which deserve encouragement.

5. The introduction into curricula of education about the value of tourist exchanges, their economic, social, and cultural benefits, and also their risks, should be encouraged.

3. Tourism, a Factor of Sustainable Development

1. All the stakeholders in tourism development should safeguard the natural environment with a view to achieving sound, continuous, and sustainable economic growth geared to satisfying equitably the needs and aspirations of present and future generations.

2. All forms of tourism development that are conducive to saving rare and precious resources, in particular water and energy, as well as avoiding so far as possible waste production, should be given priority and encouraged by national, regional, and local public authorities.

3. The staggering in time and space of tourist and visitor flows, particularly those resulting from paid leave and school holidays, and a more even distribution of holidays should be sought so as to reduce the pressure of tourism activity on the environment and enhance its beneficial impact on the tourism industry and the local economy.

4. Tourism infrastructure should be designed and tourism activities programmed in such a way as to protect the natural heritage composed of ecosystems and biodiversity and to preserve endangered species of wildlife. The stakeholders in tourism development, and especially professionals, should agree to the imposition of limitations or constraints on their activities when these are exercised in particularly sensitive areas—desert, polar, or high mountain regions, coastal areas, tropical forests, or wetlands—propitious to the creation of nature reserves or protected areas.

5. Nature tourism and ecotourism are recognized as being particularly conducive to enriching and enhancing the standing of tourism, provided they respect the natural heritage and local populations and are in keeping with the carrying capacity of the sites.

4. Tourism, a User of the Cultural Heritage of Mankind and a Contributor to Its Enhancement

1. Tourism resources belong to the common heritage of mankind. The communities in whose territories they are situated have particular rights and obligations to them.

2. Tourism policies and activities should be conducted with respect for the artistic, archaeological, and cultural heritage, which they should protect and pass on to future generations. Particular care should be devoted to preserving and upgrading monuments, shrines, and museums as well as archaeological and historic sites, which must be widely open to tourist visits. Encouragement should be given to public access to privately owned cultural property and monuments, with respect for the rights of their owners, as well as to religious buildings, without prejudice to normal needs of worship.

3. Financial resources derived from visits to cultural sites and monuments should, at least in part, be used for the upkeep, safeguarding, development, and embellishment of this heritage.

4. Tourism activity should be planned in such a way as to allow traditional cultural products, crafts, and folklore to survive and flourish, rather than causing them to degenerate and become standardized.

5. Tourism, a Beneficial Activity for Host Countries and Communities

1. Local populations should be associated with tourism activities and share equitably in the economic, social, and cultural benefits they generate, and particularly in the creation of direct and indirect jobs resulting from them.

2. Tourism policies should be applied in such a way as to help to raise the standard of living of the populations of the regions visited and meet their needs. The planning and architectural approach to and operation of tourism resorts and accommodation should aim to integrate them, to the extent possible, in the local economic and social fabric. Where skills are equal, priority should be given to local manpower.

3. Special attention should be paid to the specific problems of coastal areas and island territories and to vulnerable rural or mountain regions, for which tourism often represents a rare opportunity for development in the face of the decline of traditional economic activities.

4. Tourism professionals, particularly investors, governed by the regulations laid down by the

public authorities, should carry out studies of the impact of their development projects on the environment and natural surroundings. They should also deliver, with the greatest transparency and objectivity, information on their future programs and their foreseeable repercussions and foster dialogue on their contents with the populations concerned.

6. Obligations of Stakeholders in Tourism Development

1. Tourism professionals have an obligation to provide tourists with objective and honest information on their places of destination and on the conditions of travel, hospitality, and stays. They should ensure that the contractual clauses proposed to their customers are readily understandable as to the nature, price, and quality of the services they commit themselves to providing and the financial compensation payable by them in the event of a unilateral breach of contract on their part.

2. Tourism professionals, insofar as it depends on them, should show concern, in cooperation with the public authorities, for the security and safety, accident prevention, health protection, and food safety of those who seek their services. Likewise, they should ensure the existence of suitable systems of insurance and assistance. They should accept the reporting obligations prescribed by national regulations and pay fair compensation in the event of failure to observe their contractual obligations.

3. Tourism professionals, so far as this depends on them, should contribute to the cultural and spiritual fulfillment of tourists and allow them, during their travels, to practice their religions.

4. The public authorities of the generating states and the host countries, in cooperation with the professionals concerned and their associations, should ensure that the necessary mechanisms are in place for the repatriation of tourists in the event of the bankruptcy of the enterprise that organized their travel.

5. Governments have the right—and the duty—especially in a crisis, to inform their nationals of the difficult circumstances or even the dangers they may encounter during their travels abroad.

It is their responsibility, however, to issue such information without prejudicing in an unjustified or exaggerated manner the tourism industry of the host countries and the interests of their own operators. The contents of travel advisories should therefore be discussed beforehand with the authorities of the host countries and the professionals concerned. Recommendations formulated should be strictly proportionate to the gravity of the situations encountered and confined to the geographical areas where the insecurity has arisen. Such advisories should be qualified or cancelled as soon as a return to normality permits.

6. The press, and particularly the specialized travel press and the other media, including modern means of electronic communication, should issue honest and balanced information on events and situations that could influence the flow of tourists. They should also provide accurate and reliable information to the consumers of tourism services. The new communication and electronic commerce technologies should also be developed and used for this purpose. As is the case for the media, they should not in any way promote sex tourism.

7. Right to Tourism

1. The prospect of direct and personal access to the discovery and enjoyment of the planet's resources constitutes a right equally open to all the world's inhabitants. The increasingly extensive participation in national and international tourism should be regarded as one of the best possible expressions of the sustained growth of free time, and obstacles should not be placed in its way.

2. The universal right to tourism must be regarded as the corollary of the right to rest and leisure, including reasonable limitation of working hours and periodic holidays with pay, guaranteed by Article 24 of the Universal Declaration of Human Rights and Article 7.d of the International Covenant on Economic, Social, and Cultural Rights.

3. Social tourism, and in particular associative tourism, which facilitates widespread access to leisure, travel, and holidays, should be developed with the support of the public authorities.

4. Family, youth, student, and senior tourism and tourism for people with disabilities should be encouraged and facilitated.

8. Liberty of Tourist Movements

1. Tourists and visitors should benefit, in compliance with international law and national legislation, from the liberty to move within their countries and from one state to another, in accordance with Article 13 of the Universal Declaration of Human Rights. They should have access to places of transit and stay and to tourism and cultural sites without being subject to excessive formalities or discrimination.

2. Tourists and visitors should have access to all available forms of communication, internal or external. They should benefit from prompt and easy access to local administrative, legal, and health services. They should be free to contact the consular representatives of their countries of origin in compliance with the diplomatic conventions in force.

3. Tourists and visitors should benefit from the same rights as the citizens of the country visited concerning the confidentiality of the personal data and information concerning them, especially when these are stored electronically.

4. Administrative procedures relating to border crossings whether they fall within the competence of states or result from international agreements, such as visas or health and customs formalities, should be adapted, so far as possible, so as to facilitate to the maximum freedom of travel and widespread access to international tourism. Agreements between groups of countries to harmonize and simplify these procedures should be encouraged. Specific taxes and levies penalizing the tourism industry and undermining its competitiveness should be gradually phased out or corrected.

5. So far as the economic situation of the countries from which they come permits, travelers should have access to allowances of convertible currencies needed for their travels.

9. Rights of the Workers and Entrepreneurs in the Tourism Industry

1. The fundamental rights of salaried and self-employed workers in the tourism industry and related activities should be guaranteed under the supervision of the national and local administrations, both of their states of origin and of the host countries with particular care, given the specific constraints linked in particular to the seasonality of their activity, the global dimension of their industry, and the flexibility often required of them by the nature of their work.

2. Salaried and self-employed workers in the tourism industry and related activities have the right and the duty to acquire appropriate initial and continuous training. They should be given adequate social protection. Job insecurity should be limited so far as possible. And a specific status, with particular regard to their social welfare, should be offered to seasonal workers in the sector.

3. Any natural or legal person, provided he, she, or it has the necessary abilities and skills, should be entitled to develop a professional activity in the field of tourism under existing national laws. Entrepreneurs and investors—especially in the area of small and medium-size enterprises—should be entitled to free access to the tourism sector with a minimum of legal or administrative restrictions.

4. Exchanges of experience offered to executives and workers, whether salaried or not, from different countries contributes to foster the development of the world tourism industry. These movements should be facilitated so far as possible in compliance with the applicable national laws and international conventions.

5. As an irreplaceable factor of solidarity in the development and dynamic growth of international exchanges, multinational enterprises of the tourism industry should not exploit the dominant positions they sometimes occupy. They should avoid becoming the vehicles of cultural and social models artificially imposed on the host communities. In exchange for their freedom to invest and trade, which should be fully recognized, they should involve themselves in local development, avoiding, by the excessive repatriation of their profits or their induced imports, a reduction of their contribution to the economies in which they are established.

6. Partnership and the establishment of balanced relations between enterprises of generating and receiving countries contribute to the sustainable

development of tourism and an equitable distribution of the benefits of its growth.

10. Implementation of the Principles of the *Global Code of Ethics for Tourism*

1. The public and private stakeholders in tourism development should cooperate in the implementation of these principles and monitor their effective application.
2. The stakeholders in tourism development should recognize the role of international institutions, among which the World Tourism Organization ranks first, and nongovernmental organizations with competence in the field of tourism promotion and development, the protection of human rights, the environment or health, with due respect for the general principles of international law.
3. The same stakeholders should demonstrate their intention to refer any disputes concerning the application or interpretation of the Global Code of Ethics for Tourism for conciliation to an impartial third body known as the World Committee on Tourism Ethics.

KEY CONCEPTS

competitive destinations
content of tourism policy
core vision
destination positioning
destination vision
elements of the vision
implementation strategy

multidisciplinary tourism
    policy
policy formulation
preamble sector
principles
structure of tourism policy
sustainable destinations

total system policy
tourism constraints
tourism destination management
    information system
    (TDMIS)
tourism objective
tourism policy

Internet Sites

The Internet sites mentioned in this chapter are repeated here for convenience, plus some selected additional sites. For more information, visit these sites. Be aware that Internet addresses change frequently, so if a site cannot be accessed, use a search engine. Also use a search engine to locate many additional relevant sites.

Asia Pacific Economic Corporation
http://www.apecsec.org.sg

Australian Tourist Commission
http://atc.net.au

British Tourist Authority
http://www.visitbritain.com

California Tourism Policy Act
http://www.gocalif.ca.gov (type "policy act" into the site's search feature)

Canadian Tourism Commission
http://www.canadatourism.com

Caribbean Tourism Organisation
http://www.doitcaribbean.com

Centre for Tourism Policy and Research
http://www.sfu.ca/~dossa

European Travel Commission
http://www.visiteurope.com

European Union
http://www.europa.eu.int

German National Tourist Board
http://www.germany-tourism.de

India Tourism Policy Initiatives
http://www.tourismofindia.com/misc/
tourismpolicy.htm

International Air Transport Association
http://www.iata.org

International Association of Convention and Visitor Bureaus
http://www.iacvb.org

International Civil Aviation Organization
http://www.icao.org

International Labour Organization
http://www.ilo.org

Office of Travel and Tourism Industries (U.S.)
http://tinet.ita.doc.gov

Organization of American States
http://www.oas.org

Organization for Economic Cooperation and Development
http://www.oecd.org

Pacific Asia Travel Association
http://www.pata.org

Tourism Offices Worldwide Directory
http://www.towd.com

Travel Industry Association of America
http://www.tia.org

UNESCO
http://www.unesco.org

United Nations
http://www.un.org

World Tourism Organization
http://www.world-tourism.org

World Travel and Tourism Council
http://www.wttc.org

▸ Internet Exercises

Activity 1
Site Name: Tourism Policy in Turkey
URL: http://www.turizm.net/economy/touris~1.htm
Background Information: In 1983, the government of Turkey amended its tourism policy to encourage Turkish and foreign investment companies to participate more effectively in the development of Turkey's tourism sector.

Exercise
1. Compare the Turkish tourism policy with the elements of a good tourism policy as described in the textbook. What similarities and differences can you find?

Activity 2
Site Name: Western States Tourism Policy Council (WSTPC)
URL: http://www.wstpc.org
Background Information: The mission of the Western States Tourism Policy Council is to foster and encourage a positive environment for travel and tourism by serving as a forum to identify, research, analyze, and advocate travel and tourism related issues of public policy and opinion in the Western United States.

Exercises
1. Using information from the site, list the objectives of WSTPC.
2. Identify the policy position papers published by WSTPC.

QUESTIONS FOR REVIEW AND DISCUSSION

1. What is a tourism policy, and why is it important for a tourism destination to have a formal policy?
2. Why might a major stakeholder not wish to participate in the policy process?
3. How might tourism policy differ from countries, states/provinces, and cities? Why might it differ?
4. How would you identify and choose the stakeholders who should be involved in the formulation of a tourism policy for a region? Is there anyone who you feel should be excluded from the process?
5. What are the implications of no involvement in policy formulation by a major stakeholder?
6. What is the difference between a tourism policy and a tourism strategy?
7. Who should be "in charge" of policy formulation?
8. What are the most important interfaces of tourism policy; that is, which other sectors of the economy and society need to be aware of tourism policy or might have a significant impact on the success of tourism policy?
9. What do you see as the major barriers to successful policy formulation for tourism?
10. Must there be total consensus by all stakeholders on the content of a region's tourism policy? If not, how would you determine if there was adequate support for the different components of a policy?
11. How frequently should the policy formulation process take place for a destination? Why?
12. Why is a vision especially important for policy formulation? How long into the future should a vision attempt to define an ideal future?
13. Implementation of policy recommendations is often a problem. What do you see as the major barriers to the implementation of policy? Why do they exist? How might these barriers be overcome?

SELECTED REFERENCES

Andriotis, Konstantinos. "Tourism Planning and Development in Crete: Recent Tourism Policies and their Efficacy." *Journal of Sustainable Tourism*, Vol. 9, No. 4, pp. 298–316, 2001.

Becherel, Lionel. "The WTO Policy and Strategy Course." *TedQual*, Vol. 4, No. 2, pp. 16–20, 2001.

Beirman, David. *Restoring Tourism Destinations in Crisis*. Oxfordshire, UK: CABI Publishing, 2003.

Blake, Adam, and M. Thea Sinclair. "Tourism Crisis Management: U.S. Response to September 11." *Annals of Tourism Research*, Vol. 30, No. 4, pp. 813–832, 2003.

Bramwell, Bill, and Bernard Lane (eds). *Tourism, Collaboration, and Partnership: Politics, Practice, and Sustainability*. Clevedon, UK: Channel View Publications, 2000.

Briassoulis, Helen, and Jan van der Straaten (eds). *Tourism and the Environment: Regional, Economic, Cultural, and Policy Issues*, rev. 2d ed. Boston: Kluwer Academic Publishers, 2000.

Buckley, Ralf. "Pay to Play in Park: An Australian Policy Perspective on Visitor Fees in Public Protected Areas." *Journal of Sustainable Tourism*, Vol. 11, No. 1, pp. 56–73, 2003.

Datzira-Masip, Jordi. "Tourism Policy in Spain: An Overview." *Tourist Review*, Vol. 53, No. 1, pp. 41–50, 1998.

Deegan, J., and D. A. Dineen. *Tourism Policy and Performance: The Irish Experience*. London: ITBP, 1997.

Edgell, Sr., David L. *Tourism Policy: The Next Millennium*. Champaign, IL: Sagamore Publishing, 1999.

Faulkner, Bill. "A Model for the Evaluation of National Tourism Destination Marketing Programs." *Journal of Travel Research*, Vol. 35, No. 3, pp. 23–32, Winter 1997.

Glaesser, Dirk. *Crisis Management in the Tourism Industry*. Oxford, UK: Butterworth-Heinemann, 2003.

Hall, D. *Tourism and Transition: Governance, Transformation and Development*. Oxfordshire, UK: CABI Publishing, 2004.

Hollinshead, Keith. "Policy in Paradise: The History of Incremental Politics in the Tourism of Island-State Fiji." *Tourism*, Vol. 49, No. 4, pp. 327–348, 2001.

International Association of Scientific Experts in Tourism (eds). Future-Oriented Tourism Policy: A Contribution to the Strategic Development of Places. *Proceedings of 49th Annual Congress of the International Association of Scientific Experts in Tourism,* Portoroz, Slovenia. St. Gallen, Switzerland: AIEST, University of St. Gallen, 1999.

Kerr, William R. *Tourism Public Policy and the Strategic Management of Failure.* Oxford, UK: Elsevier, 2003.

Lewis, Robert C. *Cases in Hospitality Strategy and Policy.* New York: Wiley, 1998.

Parker, Steven. "Collaboration on Tourism Policy Making: Environmental and Commercial Sustainability on Bonaire, NA." *Journal of Sustainable Tourism,* Vol. 7, No. 3–4, pp. 240–259, 1999.

Parker, Steven. "Ecotourism, Environmental Policy, and Development." In Soden and Steel (eds), *Handbook of Global Environmental Policy and Administration,* pp. 315–345. New York: Marcel Dekker, 1999.

Ritchie, J. R. Brent, and Geoffrey I. Crouch. *The Competitive Destination: A Sustainable Tourism Perspective.* Oxfordshire, UK: CABI Publishing, 2003.

Ritchie, J. R. Brent. "Interest Based Formulation of Tourism Policy for Environmentally Sensitive Destinations." In Bill Bramwell and Bernard Lane (eds.), *Tourism, Collaboration, and Partnership: Politics, Practice, and Sustainability,* pp. 44–77.

Clevedon, UK: Channel View Publications, 2000.

Ritchie, J. R. Brent. "Policy Formulation at the Tourism/Environment Interface: Insights and Recommendations from the Banff-Bow Valley Study." *Journal of Travel Research,* Vol. 38, No. 2, pp. 100–110, 1999.

Soteriou, E. C., and C. Roberts. "The Strategic Planning Process in National Tourism Organizations." *Journal of Travel Research,* Vol. 37, pp. 21–29, August 1998.

Suder, Gabriele G. S. *Terrorism and the International Business Environment.* Cheltenham, UK: Edward Elgar Publishing, 2004.

Vanhove, Norbert. "Tourism Policy between Competitiveness and Sustainability: The Case of Bruges." *Tourist Review,* Vol. 57, No. 3, pp. 34–40, 2002.

Veal, A. J. *Leisure and Tourism Policy and Planning.* Oxfordshire, UK: CABI Publishing, 2002.

Wilkinson, Paul F. *Tourism Policy and Planning: Case Studies from the Commonwealth Caribbean.* Elmsford, NY: Cognizant Communication Corporation, 1997.

World Tourism Organization. *Co-operation and Partnership in Tourism: A Global Perspective,* Madrid: WTO, 2003.

World Tourism Organization. "India Introduces New Tourism Policy." *WTO News,* Vol. 2, No. 10, 2002.

TOURISM PLANNING, DEVELOPMENT, AND SOCIAL CONSIDERATIONS

Learning Objectives

- Identify the factors that determine the success of a tourism destination.

- Relate tourism planning to tourism policy.

- Discover what the goals of tourism development should be.

- Recognize that some serious barriers to tourism development must be overcome if a desired growth is to occur.

- Learn the political and economic aspects of development, including those related to developing countries.

- Appreciate the importance of architectural design and concern for heritage preservation, local handicrafts, and use of indigenous materials in creating tourist facilities.

Good planning is necessary for a luxury resort to come together and work for management, guests, and the surrounding community. *Photo courtesy of the Phoenician.*

CHAPTER 16

INTRODUCTION

Planning follows the policy formulation process described in Chapter 15. Tourism planners and managers need to use this process as a framework for the planning and development of a destination. Good policy and sound planning needs to be conducted to ensure that a destination will be both competitive and sustainable. This chapter presents a model for destination competitivness and sustainability, the need for tourism policy and planning to be integrated, steps in the planning process, and development issues.

PLANNING FOR A COMPETITIVE/SUSTAINABLE DESTINATION

Good tourism planning must be based on a sound understanding of those factors that fundamentally determine the success of a tourism destination. One framework that graphically identifies these factors is given in Figure 16.1. As shown, the framework includes nine major components, each of which contains a number of subcomponents.

1. **The Core Resources and Attractors:** The fundamental reasons why prospective visitors choose one destination over another. These factors fall into seven categories: physiography and climate, culture and history, market ties, mix of activities, special events, entertainment, and the tourism superstructure.

2. **Supporting Factors and Resources:** Whereas the core resources and attractors of a destination constitute the primary motivations for inbound tourism, the supporting factors and resources, as the term implies, provide a functional foundation that facilitate tourism and enhance its contribution to destination well-being. These factors are physical infrastructure, accessibility, resident/industry hospitality, the entrepreneurial efforts of tourism operators, political support for tourism, and facilitating resources such as a trained and welcoming customs/immigration staff.

3. **Qualifying and Amplifying Determinants:** The potential success of a destination is conditioned or limited by a number of factors. This group of factors might alternatively be labeled **situational conditioners** because their impact on the success of a tourism destination are to define its scale, limit, or potential. These qualifiers and amplifiers moderate or magnify destination success by filtering the influence of the other core groups of factors. They may be so important as to represent a ceiling to tourism demand or potential, but are largely beyond the control of the tourism sector alone.

4. **Destination Policy, Planning, and Development:** While, unfortunately, not all destinations have a formal tourism policy, a strategic or policy-driven framework for the planning and development of a destination, with particular economic, social, and other societal goals as the intended outcome, can help ensure that the tourism development that does occur promotes a successful

The Ritchie/Crouch Model of

DESTINATION COMPETITIVENESS & SUSTAINABILITY

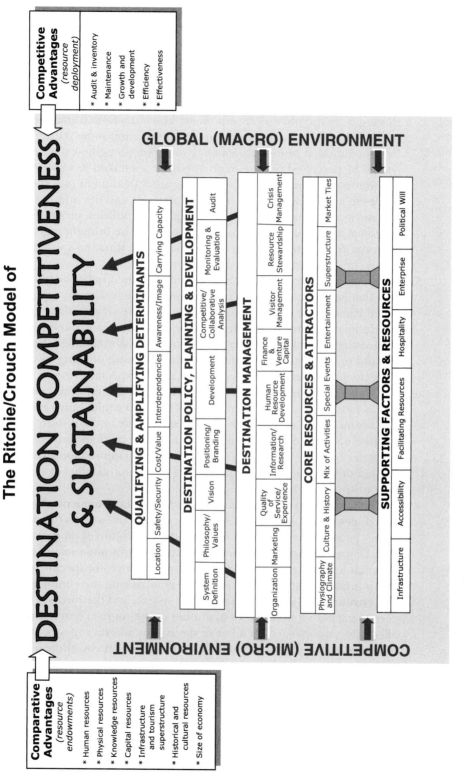

Comparative Advantages
(resource endowments)

* Human resources
* Physical resources
* Knowledge resources
* Capital resources
* Infrastructure and tourism superstructure
* Historical and cultural resources
* Size of economy

Competitive Advantages
(resource deployment)

* Audit & inventory
* Maintenance
* Growth and development
* Efficiency
* Effectiveness

GLOBAL (MACRO) ENVIRONMENT

COMPETITIVE (MICRO) ENVIRONMENT

QUALIFYING & AMPLIFYING DETERMINANTS

| Location | Safety/Security | Cost/Value | Interdependencies | Awareness/Image | Carrying Capacity |

DESTINATION POLICY, PLANNING & DEVELOPMENT

| System Definition | Philosophy/Values | Vision | Positioning/Branding | Development | Competitive/Collaborative Analysis | Monitoring & Evaluation | Audit |

DESTINATION MANAGEMENT

| Organization | Marketing | Quality of Service/Experience | Information/Research | Human Resource Development | Finance & Venture Capital | Visitor Management | Resource Stewardship | Crisis Management |

CORE RESOURCES & ATTRACTORS

| Physiography and Climate | Culture & History | Mix of Activities | Special Events | Entertainment | Superstructure | Market Ties |

SUPPORTING FACTORS & RESOURCES

| Infrastructure | Accessibility | Facilitating Resources | Hospitality | Enterprise | Political Will |

Figure 16.1   The Ritchie/Crouch model of destination competitiveness and sustainability.

437

and sustainable destination while meeting the quality-of-life aspirations of those who reside in the destination. This core component is comprised of eight subcomponents: a formal *definition* of the tourism system; an explication of a *philosophy* of tourism—or how tourism should serve the community; flowing from the philosophy is a *vision,* which is a formal statement describing the ideal future state of the tourism destination some 20, 50, 100 years into the future; a *positioning/branding strategy* defining how the destination should be perceived relative to competitors; a detailed *development* plan; a *competitive/collaborative analysis* providing an evaluation of how the destination relates to and compares with other destinations and the international tourism system; the *monitoring and evaluation* of policies, programs, and their outcome; and finally, all the foregoing needs to be brought together into a rigorous *destination audit,* which identifies the destination's strengths, weaknesses, problems, challenges, and opportunities.

5. **Destination Management:** This component of the model focuses on the activities that implement the policy and planning framework on a daily, operational basis. These nine activities involve effective *organization, marketing* of the destination, ensuring a high-quality *visitor experience,* gathering and disseminating *information, human resource development,* obtaining adequate financing and venture capital, effective *visitor management,* ongoing resource *stewardship,* and being prepared to manage unexpected crises.

6., 7. **Comparative versus Competitive Advantage:** An important characteristic of this model is the distinction it makes between comparative and competitive advantages of destinations. The former refers to the resources with which the destination is endowed, and which enhance its chances of success, while the latter refers to the effectiveness with which a destination's resources are utilized or deployed, thus enhancing its relative probability of success relative to competing destinations.

8., 9. **Global (Macro) versus Competitive (Micro) Environment:** A final important dimension of the Ritchie/Crouch (R/C) framework is the distinction it makes between the impact of macro versus micro forces on destination success. Global/macro forces refer to the vast array of phenomena that broadly affect all human activities, and which are therefore not specific to the travel and tourism industry in their effect. By comparison, the competitive, or micro, environment is part of the tourism system, and the forces it contains concern the actions and activities of entities in the tourism system that directly affect the goals of each member of the system, whether they be individual tourism firms or the collection of organizations that constitute a destination.

THE NATURE OF TOURISM PLANNING

Tourism planning seeks to provide a detailed, "on the ground" outline as to how each of the factors affecting the success of a tourism destination should be developed. Good tourism planning goes far beyond schemes to maximize profit. While profitable development brings positive economic and social benefits to the community, it also carries inevitable drawbacks. Therefore, developers must incorporate ways to enhance human welfare and happiness. These include insistence on quality architectural, landscape, and environmental design; planning for transportation; and energy conservation and education.

If such diverse goals are to be achieved, planners must implement a model that will guide their thinking by incorporating each aspect (including various political aspects) into a master plan. These include zoning, road maintenance, water and sewage treatment systems, and promotional expenses. An official body, financed through tourist earnings, is useful in keeping abreast of socioeconomic activities in the industry as well as dealing with other problems such as stabilizing prices, forecasting demand, keeping an inventory of potential national tourist resources, and arranging publicity campaigns.

Resort development also necessitates working out financial arrangements that will not only enable the developer to take out loans for construction but also to be granted reduced or forgiven taxes for a period of time in order to improve the venture's financial success.

RELATING TOURISM PLANNING TO TOURISM POLICY

The previous chapter provides an understanding of the role of tourism policy in providing a set of guidelines for the development and promotion of a tourism destination. It also describes the structure and content of a formal tourism policy, as well as the process of policy formulation.

Because tourism policy formulation and tourism planning are very directly related to each other, it is important to distinguish between the two, to identify their similarities and their differences in a tourism context. Their similarities are:

1. They both deal with the future development of a tourism destination or region.
2. They both emphasize the strategic dimensions of managerial action, although planning must also address a number of tactical concerns.

Their differences are:

1. Policy formulation is definitely "big picture," while much of planning is characterized by an attention to detail.
2. Policy formulation is a creative, intellectual process, while planning is generally a more constrained practical exercise.
3. Policy, particularly its visioning component, has a very long-term strategic emphasis, while planning tends to be more restrictive in its time horizon. A one-year planning cycle is not uncommon, although three- to five-year plans are a possibility. In contrast, destination visions may have a five-, ten-, fifty-, or even a hundred-year time horizon.

4. Policy formulation must allow for as-yet-unseen circumstances and technologies to be considered. In contrast, planning tends to assume current conditions and technologies, with some allowances for predictable (i.e., evolutionary) change.

5. Policy formulation tends to emphasize a systematic determination of "what" should be done in long-term tourism development, while planning tends to emphasize the "how" for the achievement of specific destination goals.

The reader should keep these distinctions in mind when reviewing the rest of this chapter. While policy formulation and planning appear to have certain commonalties, they are, in effect, quite distinct processes. Failure to acknowledge this reality has been quite limiting in the past.

It should be noted that the definitions and distinctions related to policy, strategy, goals, objectives, and planning are ongoing sources of debate in the management literature. Different scholars and managers frequently debate the exact meaning of these terminologies. While the debate is not inconsequential, it should not stand in the way of creative thinking or managerial action.

Integrating Policy and Planning

Although policy formulation and destination planning are different types of processes, they must nevertheless be seen as integrated components of an ongoing process of destination management. This need is reflected in Table 16.1 on pages 446–448. In examining Table 16.1, keep in mind that the ultimate goal of the planning process is to identify the exact nature and timing of the specific actions and activities that must be carried out in efforts to ensure that all the factors that influence destination success (see Figure 16.1) are made as effective as possible. To reiterate, policy provides the guidelines for the development of tourism facilities, events, and programs, while planning stipulates the details and timing of the specific actions/activities to develop each component, subcomponent, and element of the R/C model of destination competitiveness/success. In doing so, it is essential that both processes be fully integrated so as to avoid both waste and duplication.

WHY TOURISM PLANNING IS NECESSARY

The decision to develop tourism or expand present tourism development in a community, a region, or a country must be studied carefully. The socioeconomic benefits from tourism are powerful. Tourism development looks attractive to both developed and underdeveloped countries with the right preconditions—some combination of natural, scenic, historical, archaeological, cultural, and climate attractions. Tourism is a growth industry, and while that growth may show some slowing in the short run, the long-run prospects are good. The expected continued growth is based on continually rising per capita incomes, lower travel costs, increased leisure time, and changes in consumers' tastes and preferences toward travel, recreation, and leisure goods and services. Many advocates look at tourism as a panacea for solving an area's development problems. This view is unrealistic because benefits may be accompanied by detrimental consequences. A review of some advantages and disadvantages from Chapter 1 arising from tourism development will indicate why careful planning is necessary. Major arguments for tourism are that it:

1. Provides employment opportunities, both skilled and unskilled, because it is a labor-intensive industry
2. Generates a supply of needed foreign exchange
3. Increases incomes
4. Creates increased gross national product
5. Requires the development of an infrastructure that will also help stimulate local commerce and industry
6. Justifies environmental protection and improvement
7. Increases governmental revenues
8. Helps to diversify the economy
9. Creates a favorable worldwide image for the destination
10. Facilitates the process of modernization by education of youth and society and changing values
11. Provides tourist and recreational facilities that may be used by a local population who could not otherwise afford to develop facilities
12. Gives foreigners an opportunity to be favorably impressed by a little-known country or region

Some disadvantages of tourism are that it:

1. Develops excess demand
2. Creates leakages so great that economic benefits do not accrue
3. Diverts funds from more promising forms of economic development
4. Creates social problems from income differences, social differences, introduction of prostitution, gambling, crime, and so on
5. Degrades the natural physical environment
6. Degrades the cultural environment
7. Poses the difficulties of seasonality
8. Increases vulnerability to economic and political changes
9. Adds to inflation of land values and the price of local goods and services

Consequently, tourism is not always a panacea. On the contrary, overdevelopment can generate soil and water pollution and even people pollution, if there are too many visitors at the same place at the same time. Consider automobile and bus traffic congestion, inadequate parking, hotels dwarfing the scale of historic districts, and the displacement of the local community-serving businesses by tourist-serving firms, leading to degradation, rather than improvement, of the quality of life.

Furthermore, too many visitors can have a harmful impact on life in the host country and on the visitors themselves. A beautiful landscape can suffer through thoughtless and unwise land development and construction methods. And customers and crafts can be vulgarized by overemphasis on quantity and cheapness. These responsibilities cannot really be blamed on tourism, but rather on overcommercialization. Tourism is one of the world's greatest and most significant social and economic forces. But government officials and businesspeople must weigh the economic benefits against the possible future degradation of human and natural resources.

Tropical island resorts require good planning to integrate facilities and protect the environment. *Photo courtesy of the Abaco Beach Resort and Boat Harbour.*

Tourism development must be guided by carefully planned policy, a policy not built on balance sheets and profit and loss statements alone, but on the ideals and principles of human welfare and happiness. Social problems cannot be solved without a strong and growing economy that tourism can help to create. Sound development policy can have the happy result of a growing tourist business, along with the preservation of the natural and cultural resources that attracted the visitors in the first place.

Planning is critical to having sustainable development and protecting the environment. For that reason the next chapter has been devoted to tourism and the environment to expand the discussion on how to have development and, hopefully, both protect and enhance the environment.

Viewed comprehensively, the relationship between tourism and the community, state, regions, and countries requires consideration of many difficult issues: the quality of architecture, landscape, and environmental design; environmental reclamation and amenity; natural conservation; land-use management; financial strategies for long-term economic development; employment; transportation; energy conservation; education, information, and interpretation systems; and more.

These are the reasons why sound tourism planning is essential. Planning can ensure that tourist development has the ability to realize the advantages of tourism and reduce the disadvantages.

THE PLANNING PROCESS

Proper planning of the physical, legal, promotional, financial, economic, market, management, social, and environmental aspects will help to deliver the benefits of tourism development—and it can be carried out much more effectively when fully integrated with the process of policy formulation.

Good planning defines the desired result and works in a systematic manner to achieve success. The following steps briefly describe a logical sequence.

1. **Define the system.** What is the scale, size, market, character, and purpose? Formulate objectives. Without a set of objectives, the development concept has no direction. The objectives must be comprehensive and specific and should include a timetable for completion.
2. **Gathering data.** Fact finding, or research, provides basic data that are essential to developing the plan. Examples of data gathering are preparing a fact book, making market surveys, undertaking site and infrastructure surveys, and analyzing existing facilities and competition.

Denver International Airport exemplifies good planning for traveler convenience. The modern terminal building has separate drop-off levels for passengers arriving in private and commercial vehicles, close-in parking, and trains to shuttle passengers from the terminal to three concourses. *Photo courtesy of Denver International Airport.*

3. **Analyze and interpret.** Once collected, the many fragments of information must be interpreted so the facts gathered will have meaning. This step leads to a set of conclusions and recommendations that leads to making or conceptualizing a preliminary plan.

4. **Create the preliminary plan.** Based on the previous steps, alternatives are considered and alternative physical solutions are drawn up and tested. Frequently, scale models are developed to illustrate the land-use plans; sketches are prepared to show the image the development will project; financial plans are drafted from the market information, site surveys, and the layout plan to show the investment needed in each phase of the project and the cash flow expected; and legal requirements are met.

5. **Approve the plan.** The parties involved can now look at plans, drawings, scale models, estimates of costs, and estimates of profits and know what will be involved and what the chances for success or failure will be. While a great deal of money may have been spent up to this point, the sum is a relatively small amount compared to the expenditures that will be required once the plan is approved and master planning and implementation begin.

6. **Create the final plan.** This phase typically includes a definition of land use; plans for infrastructure facilities such as roads, airports, bike paths, horse trails, pedestrian walkways, sewage, water, and utilities; architectural standards; landscape plans; zoning and other land-use regulations; and economic analysis, market analysis, and financial programming.

7. **Implement the plan.** Implementation carries out the plan and creates an operational tourism development. It also follows up and evaluates. Good planning provides mechanisms that give continuing feedback on the tourism project and the levels of consumer satisfaction achieved.

Good planning should eliminate problems and provide user satisfaction. The final user is the judge in determining how successful the planning process has been.

Figure 16.2 provides a graphical summary of the above tourism planning and development process and illustrates the increasingly detailed nature of the process as we move from stage to stage. The advantage of utilizing such a model is that it requires the planner to view the total picture and guides the thinking process. While no model can depict all interrelated facts of a planning process or eliminate all guesswork, such a model deserves inclusion in the initial phases of planning as a tool that helps to order, coordinate, and control the process.

Table 16.1 shows an integrated approach to planning. Again it serves as a guide to asking the right questions and making sure that the process is complete. It also illustrates that there are a number of approaches to tourism planning. There is no single magic approach.

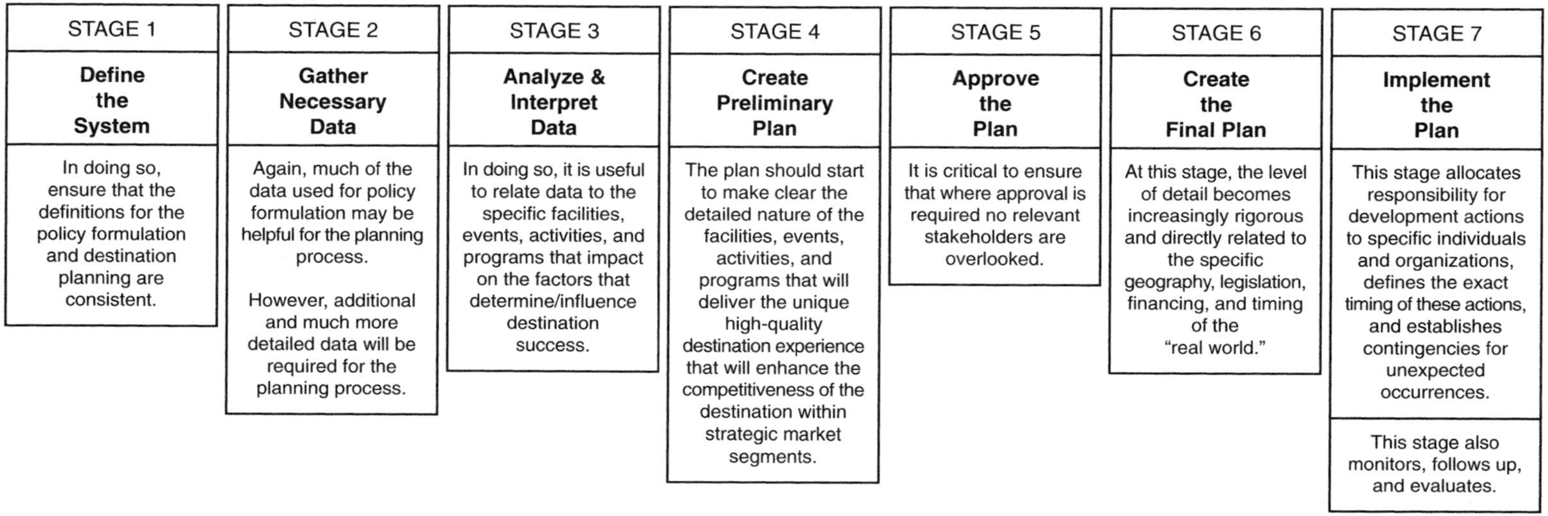

STAGE 1	STAGE 2	STAGE 3	STAGE 4	STAGE 5	STAGE 6	STAGE 7
Define the System	**Gather Necessary Data**	**Analyze & Interpret Data**	**Create Preliminary Plan**	**Approve the Plan**	**Create the Final Plan**	**Implement the Plan**
In doing so, ensure that the definitions for the policy formulation and destination planning are consistent.	Again, much of the data used for policy formulation may be helpful for the planning process. However, additional and much more detailed data will be required for the planning process.	In doing so, it is useful to relate data to the specific facilities, events, activities, and programs that impact on the factors that determine/influence destination success.	The plan should start to make clear the detailed nature of the facilities, events, activities, and programs that will deliver the unique high-quality destination experience that will enhance the competitiveness of the destination within strategic market segments.	It is critical to ensure that where approval is required no relevant stakeholders are overlooked.	At this stage, the level of detail becomes increasingly rigorous and directly related to the specific geography, legislation, financing, and timing of the "real world."	This stage allocates responsibility for development actions to specific individuals and organizations, defines the exact timing of these actions, and establishes contingencies for unexpected occurrences. This stage also monitors, follows up, and evaluates.

Figure 16.2 An overview of the tourism planning process.

445

TABLE 16.1   TOURISM PLANNING: AN INTEGRATED APPROACH

PLANNING ACTIVITY	ORGANIZATIONAL DEVELOPMENT	COMMUNITY INVOLVEMENT	TOURISM PRODUCT DEVELOPMENT	TOURISM PRODUCT MARKETING
		Where Are We Today?		
1. Gather information.	Evaluate existing group composition. Identify potential representatives that could or should be involved.	Identify both tourism and nontourism interests that may be affected by the proposed tourism development. Determine key issues and concerns of the various stakeholders.	Conduct an inventory and assessment of the area's tourism resources, services, and infrastructure. Estimate existing levels of use and carrying capacity.	Profile the existing markets in terms of geographic origin, demographics, family life cycle, spending patterns, needs, and interests.
		Where Do We Want to Go?		
2. Identify community values.	Tourism organization members express community values by answering questions related to quality of life now and in the future.	Community representatives express their values by answering questions related to quality of life now and in the future.	Values expressed by the tourism organization and community representatives begin to form the foundation upon which future tourism development and resource allocation decisions will be based.	Values expressed by the tourism organization and community representatives begin to form the foundation upon which future tourism marketing decisions will be based.
3. Create a vision.	Tourism organization members create an image of how the community should look, feel, and be, now and in the future.	Community representatives create an image of how the community should look, feel, and be, now and in the future.	The descriptive "story" about future development and quality of life in the community further strengthens the foundation and guides tourism development and resource allocation decisions.	The descriptive "story" about future development and quality of life in the community further strengthens the foundation and guides tourism marketing decisions.
4. Identify concerns and opportunities.	Tourism organization members brainstorm a list of concerns and opportunities that the group or community may be facing. Similar ideas are combined and narrowed down to	Community representatives brainstorm a list of concerns and opportunities the community may be facing. Similar ideas are combined and narrowed down to reflect (1) those related	The major concerns and opportunities will provide direction for tourism development initiatives. Ideas expressed should be revisited as more concrete plans for developing or enhancing	The major concerns and opportunities will provide direction for tourism development initiatives. Ideas expressed should be revisited as more concrete plans for

Where Do We Want to Go? (Continued)

	reflect (1) those related to tourism, and (2) those the tourism organization *should* handle.	to tourism and (2) those that can be addressed by the tourism organization or through tourism initiatives.	tourism attractions, services, and infrastructure are being considered.	marketing tourism resources and services are being considered.
5. Develop a mission.	Tourism organization members articulate their purpose for existing and determine who they are serving. It is important to recognize not only the visitor; but also community needs during this activity.	The tourism organization's mission serves as a vehicle to inform the community about the group's purpose for existing.	The mission, along with the values, vision, concerns, and opportunities help guide the tourism development effort.	The mission, along with the values, vision, concerns, and opportunities help guide the tourism marketing effort.
6. Develop goals.	Based on the tourism organization's values, vision, concerns, opportunities, and mission, *goals* relative to the structure and administration of the organization are developed.	Goals related to community education and involvement in the tourism development effort are developed. Most likely, goals will center on ways to involve the public in the planning process.	Based on the expressed values, vision, concerns, opportunities, and mission, goals for the physical development and/or enhancement of tourism resources, traveler services, and infrastructure are developed.	Based on the plans for tourism product development and/or enhancement, goals for tourism marketing are developed.

How Are We Going to Get There?

7. Develop objectives.	Tourism organization members develop action-oriented statements that propose how to achieve each *organizational* goal. The number of objectives for each goal will vary depending on the group's stage of development and available human, physical, and financial resources.	Tourism organization members develop action-oriented statements that propose how to achieve each *community education and involvement* goal. The number of objectives for each goal will vary depending on the community's level of interest and involvement in the tourism initiatives, and the available human, physical, and financial resources.	Tourism organization members develop action-oriented statements that propose how to achieve each *tourism product development* goal. The number of objectives for each goal will vary depending on the community's stage of development, the quantity and quality of existing tourism resources, services, and infrastructure, and available human, physical, and financial resources.	Tourism organization members develop action-oriented statements that propose how to achieve each *tourism product marketing* goal. The number of objectives for each goal will vary depending on the quantity and quality of existing tourism marketing activities and available human, physical, and financial resources.

(continued)

TABLE 16.1   TOURISM PLANNING: AN INTEGRATED APPROACH

PLANNING ACTIVITY	ORGANIZATIONAL DEVELOPMENT	COMMUNITY INVOLVEMENT	TOURISM PRODUCT DEVELOPMENT	TOURISM PRODUCT MARKETING
How Are We Going to Get There? (Continued)				
8. Develop actions.	Tourism organization members define strategies and tactics that outline specifically how each *organizational development* objective will be achieved. This includes exploring funding and technical assistance alternatives, identifying timelines, and assigning tasks.	Tourism organization members define strategies and tactics that outline specifically how each *community education and involvement* objective will be achieved. This includes exploring funding and technical assistance alternatives, identifying timelines, and assigning tasks.	Tourism organization members define strategies and tactics that outline specifically how each *tourism product development objective* will be achieved. This includes exploring funding and technical assistance alternatives, identifying timelines, and assigning tasks.	Tourism organization members define strategies and tactics that outline specifically how each *tourism marketing* objective will be achieved. This includes exploring funding and technical assistance alternatives, identifying timelines, and assigning tasks.
How Did We Do?				
9. Evaluate progress.	Organization members conduct a periodic review of the organization's activities and progress. A report is written and copies submitted to appropriate governing bodies, funding agencies, and the general public.	Organization members conduct a periodic review of key public involvement activities. A report is written and copies submitted to appropriate governing bodies, funding agencies, and the general public.	Organization members conduct a periodic review of tourism product development and implementation activities and progress. A report is written and copies submitted to appropriate governing bodies, funding agencies, and the general public.	Organization members conduct a periodic review of tourism product marketing activities and progress. A report is written and copies submitted to appropriate governing bodies, funding agencies, and the general public.
10. Update and modify plan.	Based on new information or changing circumstances, revisions to the organizational development plan are made.	Based on new information or changing circumstances, revisions to the plan for community involvement are made.	Based on new information or changing circumstances, revisions to the plan for tourism product development are made.	Based on new information or changing circumstances, revisions to the plan for tourism marketing are made.

Source: Jonelle Nuckolls and Patrick Long, *Organizing Resources for Tourism Development in Rural Areas,* Boulder: University of Colorado, 1993.

GOALS OF TOURISM DEVELOPMENT

Tourism development should aim at:

1. Providing a framework for raising the living standard of the people through the economic benefits of tourism
2. Developing an infrastructure and providing recreation facilities for visitors and residents alike
3. Ensuring types of development within visitor centers and resorts that are appropriate to the purposes of those areas
4. Establishing a development program consistent with the cultural, social, and economic philosophy of the government and the people of the host country or area
5. Optimizing visitor satisfaction

Obstacles to Development of Supply

The first **obstacle** to overcome in turning potential supply into actual supply is the lack or inadequacy of transportation and access routes to the tourist nucleus or center. It is, of course, not enough to get there. The tourist should also be induced to stay. To this end, another basic obstacle to the development of actual supply should be overcome: the lack or shortage of accommodation.

Tourists inevitably require a series of goods and services. Some may be found on the spot and may be economically flexible enough to adapt to the fluctuations of demand. The infrastructure capacity must meet maximum demand. Financing can be a major obstacle. Finally, we cannot overlook the need for sufficiently trained and hospitable personnel.

Internal Obstacles
Internal obstacles found within the destination area can be corrected or eliminated by direct, voluntary means. They may occur in incoming as well as outgoing or internal tourism.

As tourism in all its forms absorbs consumer goods, prices in this field tend to be extremely sensitive to movements in the prices of goods. The rising price of tourism has the same effect as a decrease in the income of the potential tourist. Consequently, when considering costs and planning a holiday, the tourist will choose to go—if the value is the same—where money goes the furthest.

Another major obstacle is the attitude of government and business leaders in the destination area. If this leadership is resistant or even passive toward tourism, development will lag.

POLITICAL ASPECTS OF TOURISM DEVELOPMENT

Like any significant element of an area's economy, political aspects can and often do have major influences on the creation, operation, and survival of tourism projects. Many examples can be cited. One is the land-use regulations (zoning) for commercial or public tourism developments, which can be emotionally and politically sensitive topics. Another is the degree of involvement of governmental agencies in creating and maintaining tourism infrastructure. A third is the type and extent of publicity, advertising, and other promotional efforts.

Land Use (Zoning)

Zoning ordinances specify the legal types of **land use.** But the final determination of the land use and the administration of the zoning ordinances are typically assigned to a publicly employed zoning administrator and a politically appointed or elected zoning board. Thus, the government decides how land is to be used, and it also rules on any request for changes in the zoning districts or rezoning to accommodate a nonconforming proposed development.

Attitudes of these public bodies toward tourism development will be influenced by the general public's perception (if any) of the desirability of a specific development. Creating a favorable public image is the responsibility of the developer and the managers of all tourism supply components. The public tourism promotion organization bears responsibility as well. If the public feels that tourism is desirable, rational zoning regulations and administration should result. Furthermore, if principles of tourism planning and development, as presented in this chapter, are faithfully implemented, the result should be well-planned projects. These will be accepted in the community as welcome sources of employment and tax revenues.

Creation and Maintenance of Infrastructure

Any tourism development will need **infrastructure.** Whether this is provided by government agencies or the private developer, or both, is basically a political question. What troubles many local people is that their taxes are spent in part to provide roads, water systems, sewers, airports, marinas, parks, and other infrastructure that they perceive as benefiting mainly tourism. Is this fair or desirable from their point of view? Those having a common concern in tourism must realize that it is their responsibility to convince the public that such expenditures by government are desirable and do benefit the local economy. One way to achieve this understanding is through an intelligent lobbying effort. Another approach is to address service clubs, social organizations, and school groups. A third method shows how much money was spent by tourists or convention delegates.

Maintenance policies are also a vital factor in successful tourism development. Any element of infrastructure, once created, needs maintenance. The level of this maintenance can greatly affect successful tourism. An example is the promptness and adequacy of snow removal from public roads servicing ski resorts. Another is the quality and adequacy of public water and sewage systems. Many other examples could be given. Political influence to obtain good maintenance can be brought to bear by hotel and motel associations, chambers of commerce, convention and visitors bureaus, and promotion groups. Such efforts can be very effective, because public service agencies tend to be receptive if the demands are frequent and forceful.

Government and private industry must interact cooperatively if tourism development is to be successful. Political friction can develop when government officials think that private industry should do more to help itself and businesspeople believe that the government should do more to assist them. A knowledgeable outside consulting firm can study the situation and make recommendations in the best interests of both factions.

Promotional Efforts

Publicly funded promotional programs are an essential part of the industry. However, the level or degree of participation in such publicity is largely a political process. To convince lawmakers and local political decision makers of the desirability of tourism, produce accurate data on the economic impact of tourism spending. An "investment" concept is the preferred way to view government programs. Pointing out industry diversification in the economy is another good approach. Other benefits cited could be employment, income multipliers, additional investments, and preservation and enhancement of local industries, crafts, and the arts, as well as building local pride and recognition.

Lobbying efforts need to be convincing and persistent. Organizations representing tourism must have both moral and monetary support in sufficient measure to bring about successful political influence. Nothing succeeds like success. If tourism booms, the politicians can well take pride in their important contribution. We repeat: As in all other aspects of the tourist business, cooperation pays!

DEVELOPMENT OF TOURIST POTENTIAL

Official Tourism Body

A **tourism body** or **organization** (referred to as the Destination Management Organization, or DMO) should be created to keep abreast of socioeconomic developments in the various market countries or areas to provide a reasonably early forecast of the size, type, and structure of probable tourism demand. It would be equally useful to have a report on developments in the tourist industry of supplying centers or areas and on activities and projects undertaken to promote development.

Because tourism is such a complex phenomenon, distinct ministerial departments are responsible for finding solutions to developmental problems.

The stabilization of general and tourist prices should be a constant objective, because rising prices automatically reduce the volume of demand. Land speculation should be discouraged.

The inventory of potential national tourist resources (parks, attractions, recreational facilities, and so on) should be kept up to date and extended so that these resources may be duly incorporated into actual tourist trade in accordance with quantity and quality forecasts of demand.

Tax pressures that directly affect operating costs also influence prices. Because of the export value of tourism, a fiscal policy similar to that applied to the conventional or classical export trade should be devised.

Publicity campaigns should be organized and implemented every year according to the forecasts. These should be to the point, detailed, and constructive and should zero in on socioeconomic developments and activities in the market. Financing to cover this activity should be obtained from annual tourist earnings and other identifiable funds at a rate of not less than 1 percent and perhaps not more than 4 percent of total earnings. Customs facilities should be as lenient as possible while ensuring control and maintenance of order and avoiding fraud or other crimes.

For their own benefit, host countries should make the tourists' sojourn as agreeable as possible. But proof that tourists have the financial means to cover the costs of their stay may be desired.

The seasonal nature of mass tourism causes congestion in the use of services required by tourists. Some services, such as accommodation, cannot adapt easily to seasonal fluctuation. On the other hand, some, such as transportation and communications, can adapt. Government provision of public services is important for development.

Transportation

Because of transportation's role in tourist development, the following measures are recommended.

1. Continual, detailed study of transport used for tourism with a view toward planning necessary improvements and extensions.

Transportation is an important component of tourism planning. Union Station in Washington, D.C., is an outstanding example of good planning. This beautiful facility accommodates rail service, metro service, dining, and shopping in a pleasant atmosphere. *Photo courtesy of Washington, D.C., and the Capital Region, U.S.A.*

2. Establishing a national or international plan of roads relevant to tourism, building new roads if necessary, improving those in a deficient state, and improving road sign systems. Such activities should be included in the general road plans with priorities according to economic necessity and the significance of road transport in tourism.

3. Improving rail transport (where needed) for travelers on lines between the boundary and the main tourist centers and regions as well as short-distance services in these regions of maximum tourist influx.

4. Improving road frontier posts, extending their capacity to ensure smoother crossings, organizing easier movement of in- and outgoing tourist flows. Crossing the frontier is always either the prologue or the epilogue to any journey between countries and is therefore important for the favorable impression the tourist will retain.

5. Providing adequate airport services and installations to meet demand. The rapid progress of technology in air transport makes reasonable forecasts possible.

6. Planning for ports and marinas equipped for tourism.

7. Extending car services (with and without drivers) for tourists who arrive by air or sea.

Accommodations

Accommodations must be properly placed in the regional plan. Hotels are permanent structures and grace the landscape for a long time. Planning considerations are vital. Figure 16.3 shows a specific site development plan.

One of the first considerations to be made by any planning body should be where hotels will be located. This can be accomplished by using zoning laws. Hotels are commonly allowed in "commercial" zones. Also to be decided is the number of hotel rooms needed in relation to the anticipated demand. Then to be considered is a provision for expansion of hotels as demand increases.

One consideration in hotel planning is intelligent spacing of hotels in a given area. Hotels spaced too close together tend to have a mutual value-reducing effect. Views are cut off or inhibited, and structures are lowered in value.

Also important is the ratio of the number of persons on the beach to the number of rooms in the hotel. Research in the Department of Natural Resources of the state of Michigan indicates that the optimum capacity of an average-size ocean or Great Lakes beach is approximately 1,000 persons for each 400 lineal feet of beach. Typically, about 50 percent of those vacationers in a resort or beach area will actually be on the beach; and of this group, 25 percent will be in the water and 75 percent will be on the beach.

Another consideration is the topography. In rolling or hilly country, more accommodations can be placed close together without a feeling of interference with one another than in a flat area. Also, the type of vegetative cover affects the density of the accommodations. A heavy, thick cover tends to obscure the view, and more accommodations can be successfully placed in a limited area than if the vegetation is sparse or absent entirely (see Figure 16.4).

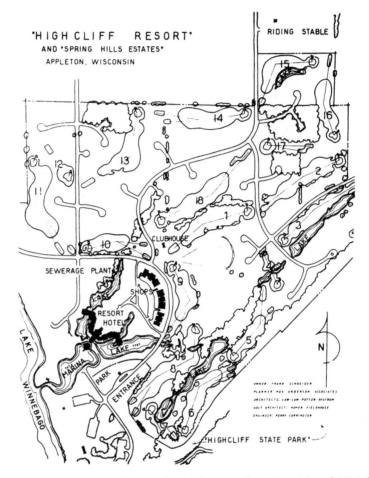

"HIGH CLIFF RESORT"
AND "SPRING HILLS ESTATES"
APPLETON, WISCONSIN

RIDING STABLE

CLUBHOUSE

SEWERAGE PLANT

SHOPS

RESORT
HOTEL

LAKE
WINNEBAGO

MARINA

PARK
ENTRANCE

LAKE

N

"HIGHCLIFF STATE PARK"

Figure 16.3   Example of "planning for private tourism development adjacent to a state park." Note integration of infrastructure and recreational facilities. *Source:* Recreational Land Developemnet, Wisconsin Department of Natural Resources, Division of Resource Development, Bureau of Recreation.

Clustering accommodations in reasonably close proximity, surrounded by extensive natural areas, is recognized as superior planning, as opposed to spreading out accommodations over a wide area. The beauty of the natural environment can be more fully appreciated in such an arrangement.

Before any investment in hotels and similar lodging facilities is made, the traveling and vacation habits of the prospective guests should be studied to tailor the facilities to the requirements and desires of guests. This is extremely important and conforms to the "market orientation" concept in which major decisions on investment begin with the desires of the potential customers. Another factor is the harmony required between the various elements of the travel plan, the local environment, and infrastructure.

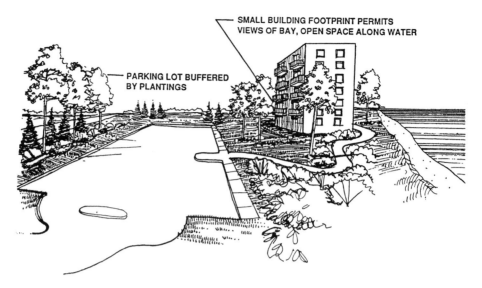

Figure 16.4 *"Better approach" planning principles of "buffering and minimizing building site space to open scenic views." Source: Grand Traverse Bay Region Development Guidelines.*

Finally, when resort development is to be limited (and it usually is), it is best to select the most desirable location and create a hotel of real distinction at this site. Then, later, if proper planning and promotion have been accomplished, expansion to other nearby sites can be achieved. Distinctive design of other hotel sites will encourage the visitor to enjoy the variety, architectural appeals, and other satisfactions inherent in each resort hotel.

Financing

Possible procedures for financing construction include a mortgage guarantee plan and direct loans from a variety of sources.

Mortgage Guarantee Plan

Under a mortgage guarantee plan, the government would guarantee mortgage loans up to 80 percent of the approved and appraised value of the land, building, furnishings, and equipment when the resort is completed. The approved mortgage would carry interest at prevailing mortgage rates and would require a schedule of amortization for the full retirement of the loan in not more than perhaps thirty years.

A guarantee fund would be established that at all times would be maintained at 20 percent of the total outstanding principal amount of mortgages guaranteed under this plan. The guarantee fund would be managed by trustees who would make any payments of interest and principal certified to them by the agency in charge of the mortgage loan plan. This agency would supervise the status of all approved loans and would investigate the facts and situations whenever it might become necessary to rely upon the guarantee fund to make the required interest and amortization payments. In such cases, an assignment of assets and income would be taken from the resort in default, which would have to be made up from subsequent earnings before any other use could be made of it.

Under this plan, the investor in the resort project would secure a mortgage loan from a lending institution or issue bonds or mortgage certificates to one or more sources of the borrowed capital. With the guarantee of payments of interest and principal and the existence of the guarantee fund for that purpose, mortgage loans under this plan should be attractive to lending institutions and other sources of borrowed capital.

Hotel accommodations should be planned to blend in and enhance the surrounding environment so tourists will want to visit. The Loretto Inn, Sante Fe, New Mexico, sits at the end of the Santa Fe Trail and blends in with its surroundings. *Photo courtesy of Corbis Digital Stock.*

With an approved resort development project and a guaranteed mortgage loan equivalent to 80 percent of the total financing required for land, building, furniture, and equipment, 20 percent of the cost could be invested as equity risk capital. The ability to finance on this basis would provide incentive to those directly interested in the business, as well as other investors, to participate in new resort development projects.

Financing Procedures

A group interested in building a resort must convince the local city, regional, or national authorities that the resort should be built. The next step is to obtain a suitable site designated for construction under a previously completed tourist development plan for the area. A third-party feasibility study should be undertaken.

To indicate that this group is seriously interested in building a resort, architects, engineers, consultants, and other specialists should be contacted during the planning phase. The organization that is to operate the resort should be the same group that builds the hotel. An important planning ingredient is the recommendation of experienced resort managers concerning design and layout of the project.

The next step is to obtain construction capital either from local sources or from government or foreign sources. Also, capital must be secured for equipment, supplies, and services, including opening expenses and pre-break-even expenses. Government aid in obtaining imported supplies and equipment is often necessary. Governmental consideration should be given for reduction or elimination of taxes for an adequate length of time to help ensure the financial success of the resort venture. Elimination of import duties on materials needed to build and run resorts is also desirable.

SUMMARY

This chapter opens with the presentation of a model that identifies and explains those factors that fundamentally determine the competitiveness, sustainability, and success of tourism destinations. It then examines the nature and necessity of tourism planning and development, as well as the distinct characteristics of each process. Subsequently, discussion focuses on the importance of relating policy to planning with a view to achieving a meaningful integration of the two processes.

The quality of tourism planning and development will determine the ultimate success and longevity of any destination area. Thus, time, effort, and resources devoted to planning are essential investments.

Thoughtful planners have formulated the goals for tourism development, and these should be guiding principles everywhere. Obstacles must be overcome by sound planning augmented by political means, if growth is desired. This is often accomplished by the official tourism body. Tourism development should be a part of the overall regional or urban land-use development plan.

Tourism developments almost always involve both government and private developers. Each sector can best contribute certain parts of a project. Government typically provides the infrastructure, such as roads, water supply, sewers, public transportation terminals, and parks. Private developers supply superstructure, such as hotels, restaurants, recreation facilities, and shopping areas.

Government can also help considerably in making financing available. The private sector must deem an investment in a tourist facility attractive from the standpoint of financial return and risk before funds will be committed.

KEY CONCEPTS

architectural recommendations	obstacles to development	preservation and
creating infrastructure	official tourism body	environmentalism
goals of tourism development	planning process	transportation
heritage preservation	policy formulation	zoning
land use	political aspects	

Internet Sites

The Internet sites mentioned in this chapter are repeated here for convenience, plus some selected additional sites. For more information, visit these sites. Be aware that Internet addresses change frequently, so if a site cannot be accessed, use a search engine. Also use a search engine to locate many additional relevant sites.

Business Enterprises for Sustainable Travel
http://www.sustainabletravel.org

Canadian Tourism Commission
http://www.canadatourism.com

Community Tourism Planning and Design
http://www.community-tourism.net

European Union
http://www.europa.eu.int

Institute of Destination Architects & Designers
http://www.IDAD.org

International Civil Aviation Organization
http://www.icao.org

Leisure, Recreation, and Tourism Abstracts
http://www.leisuretourism.com

Organization of American States
http://www.oas.org

Organization for Economic Cooperation and Development
http://www.oecd.org

Pacific Asia Travel Association
http://www.pata.org

Travel Industry Association of America
http://www.tia.org

UNESCO
http://www.unesco.org

United Nations
http://www.un.org

World Tourism Organization
http://www.world-tourism.org

World Travel and Tourism Council
http://www.wttc.org

Internet Exercises

Activity 1
Site Name: The International Ecotourism Society (TIES)
URL: http://www.ecotourism.org
Background Information: The International Ecotourism Society identifies key issues in the field of ecotourism that require international attention each year.

Exercise
1. What criteria does the International Ecotourism Society use to determine which issues to address?

Activity 2
Site Name: Alaska Wilderness Recreation and Tourism Association
URL: http://www.awrta.org
Background Information: The Alaska Wilderness Recreation and Tourism Association (AWRTA) is a nonprofit trade association that promotes the recognition and protection of Alaska's wilderness.

Exercises
1. What guidelines has AWRTA established for businesses to follow when planning for tourism?
2. What planning issues are currently being addressed by AWRTA?

Activity 3
Site Name: Cyburbia
URL: http://www.cyburbia.org
Background Information: Cyburbia contains a comprehensive directory of Internet resources relevant to planning, architecture, urbanism, and other topics related to the built environment. Cyburbia also contains information regarding architecture- and planning-related mailing lists and Usenet newsgroups, and it hosts interactive message areas.

Exercise
1. Surf this Web site and identify current issues facing the tourism industry. How do these issues coincide with those discussed in the textbook?

Questions for Review and Discussion

1. What are the factors that determine the success of a tourism destination that the tourism manager can control?
2. What is destination competitivness?
3. Basically, what is the purpose of planning?
4. Discuss the importance of transportation to tourism development.
5. Discuss the most important factors that would influence the success of a newly built resort.
6. Why is tourism developmental planning so necessary?
7. What are some of the most significant relationships between a large-size resort development and its nearby community?
8. Referring to the previous question, if the community is a rather small one, should any input be solicited from residents of the community before major remodeling or new construction is undertaken?
9. What goals should guide the land-use plan of a small lakeshore village that is popular with summer visitors?
10. Provide some descriptions of the importance of infrastructure to the following: ski resort, summer campground, fishing pier, public marina, shopping center, resort apartment condominium project.
11. From planning to completed project, name the principal individuals and organizations that would be involved.
12. Do you agree with the statement that if a community's government and business leaders are resistant or passive toward tourism, development will lag?
13. Currently, heritage preservation is a popular trend. Is it a desirable one?
14. Would you encourage tourism development if your community and area were already very prosperous ones?
15. Enumerate various kinds of environmental pollution that unwise developments can create.
16. How could greater emphasis be placed on the importance of a development process in which meticulous attention is given to the environment to create a harmonious combination of natural assets and human-made facilities?

Case Problems

1. A real estate developer, aware of a growing demand for a lakeshore resort condominium, planned for 126 apartments plus a 56-slip marina. Upon submission of his plan, the township planning board informed him that only one apartment and one boat slip would be allowed for each 100 feet of lakeshore. Because he did not own that much lakeshore, plans were redrawn to construct the planned development back from the lakeshore. Access to the lake would be provided via a canal, using one of the lakeshore lots—a "keyhole" plan. This proposal was also rejected. The developer then sued the township board to force approval. What should the court or judge decide?

2. You have accepted a United Nations Development Program assignment in tourism to a small Central American country. Your first task is to make financial calculations concerning the economic feasibility for a resort development. What factors do you consider when beginning this process? Assuming your findings result in a favorable conclusion, what would your next step be?

3. Hotels built in a boxlike manner are cheaper to construct and maintain than those with more elaborate designs. Hotel companies normally aim to maximize profits. Thus, should all hotels be built in that manner?

SELECTED REFERENCES

Ashworth, G. J., and J. E. Tunbridge. *The Tourist-Historic City: Retrospect and Prospect of Managing the Heritage City.* Amsterdam: Pergamon, 2000.

Brown, Frances, and Derek Hall (eds.). *Tourism in Peripheral Areas: Case Studies.* Buffalo, NY: Channel View Publications, 2000.

Canestrell, Elio, and Paolo Costa. "Tourist Carrying Capacity: A Fuzzy Approach." *Annals of Tourism Research,* Vol. 18, No. 2, pp. 295–311, 1991.

Chon, Kaye S. (ed.). *Tourism in Southeast Asia: A New Direction.* New York: Haworth Hospitality Press, 2000.

Cooper, C., and S. Wanhill (eds). *Tourism Development: Environmental and Community Issues.* New York: Wiley, 1997.

de Kadt, Emanuel (ed.). *Tourism—Passport to Development?* New York: Published for the World Bank and UNESCO by Oxford University Press, 1979.

Dieke, Peter U. C. *The Political Economy of Tourism Development in Africa.* New York: Cognizant Communication Corporation, 2000.

Dorwood, Sherry. *Design for Mountain Communities.* New York: Van Nostrand Reinhold, 1990.

Dowling, Ross K. "Tourism Planning: People and the Environment in Western Australia." *Journal of Travel Research,* Vol. 31, No. 4, pp. 52–58, Spring 1993.

Gartner, William C. *Tourism Development: Principles, Processes, and Policies.* New York: Van Nostrand Reinhold, 1996.

Go, Frank M., and Carson L. Jenkins (eds). *Tourism and Economic Development in Asia and Australia.* London: Cassell, 1997.

Godde, P. M., M. F. Price, and F. M. Zimmermann. *Tourism and Development in Mountain Regions.* New York: CABI Publishing, 2000.

Godfrey, Kerry, and Jackie Clarke. *The Tourism Development Handbook: A Practical Approach to Planning and Marketing.* London: Continuum International Publishing Group, 2000.

Gunn, Clare A., and Turgut Var. *Tourism Planning,* 4th ed. London: Taylor and Francis, 2002.

Gunn, Clare A. *Vacationscape: Developing Tourist Areas,* 3d ed. Washington, DC: Taylor and Francis, 1997.

Hall, C. Michael. *Tourism Planning: Policies, Processes and Relationships.* New York: Longman, 1999.

Inskeep, Edward. *Tourism Planning: An Integrated and Sustainable Development Approach.* New York: Wiley, 1997.

Lewis, James B. "A Rural Tourism Development Model." *Tourism Analysis,* Vol. 2, No. 2, pp. 91–106, 1998.

Mill, Robert Christie. *Resorts: Management and Operation.* New York: Wiley, 2001.

Muirhead, Desmond, and Guy L. Rando. *Golf Course Development and Real Estate.* Washington, DC: Urban Land Institute, 1994.

Murphy, Peter, and Ann Murphy. *Strategic Management for Tourism Communities.* Clevedon, UK: Channel View, 2004.

Nuckolls, Jonelle, and Patrick Long. *Organizing Resources for Tourism Development in Rural Areas.* Boulder: University of Colorado, 1993.

Pearce, Douglas. *Tourist Development,* 2d ed. New York: Wiley, 1989.

Pearce, Douglas G. "Tourism Development in Paris: Public Intervention." *Annals of Tourism Research,* Vol. 25, No. 2, pp. 457–476, April 1998.

Phillips, Patrick. *Developing with Recreational Amenities.* Washington, DC: Urban Land Institute, 1986.

Richter, Linda K. *Land Reform and Tourism Development.* Cambridge, MA: Schenkman, 1982.

Sandiford, Peter John, and John Ap. "The Role of Ethnographic Techniques in Tourism Planning." *Journal of Travel Research,* Vol. 37, No. 1, pp. 3–11, August 1998.

Singh, TejVir, and Shalini Singh (eds). *Tourism Development in Critical Environments.* New York: Cognizant Communication Corporation, 1999.

Tooman, L. Alex. "Tourism and Development." *Journal of Travel Research,* Vol. 35, No. 5, pp. 33–40, Winter 1997.

Tourism Center. *Community Tourism Development.* St. Paul: University of Minnesota Extension Service, 2001.

TOURISM AND THE ENVIRONMENT

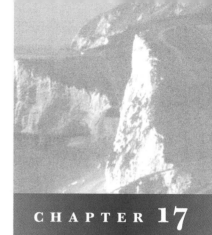

CHAPTER 17

Learning Objectives

- Recognize the worldwide importance of natural resource conservation and sustainable tourism development.
- Learn how ecotourism can benefit local people.
- Understand the dangers and limitations of ecotourism.
- Understand tourist codes of ethics and guidelines.
- Learn current environmental practices of tourism organizations and suppliers.
- Learn how to maintain natural destinations.

The cliffs that make up the Dorsey Heritage Coast are a popular natural attraction in England.
Photo courtesy of the British Tourist Authority.

INTRODUCTION

As tourism moves further into the twenty-first century, the enterprise will have to make the environment a priority. Because tourism is now the world's largest industry, the environment is taking center stage in tourism development. Tourism is not only a powerful economic force but a factor in the physical environment as well. Because more attention will be paid to the environment in the future, projects that are economically feasible but not environmentally desirable will remain unbuilt. The environment is the core of the tourism product. Profitability in tourism depends on maintaining the attractiveness of the destination people want to see and experience.

Tourism has the power to enhance the environment, to provide funds for conservation, to preserve culture and history, to set sustainable use limits, and to protect natural attractions. It also has the power to destroy. If tourism is not properly planned and implemented, it can destroy vegetation, create overcrowding, litter trekking areas, pollute beaches, result in overbuilding, eliminate open space, create sewage problems, cause housing problems, and ignore the needs and structure of the host community.

It is being recognized that tourism must preserve and protect the environment and natural attractions so that people will continue to travel, and must set use limits so that sites will be truly sustainable. The problem is how to do this. Concepts such as ecotourism, nature tourism, sustainable development, carrying capacity, and alternative tourism have been proposed and are examined in this chapter. Also, we look at the industry's efforts to be environmentally responsible.

DOES TOURISM THREATEN THE ENVIRONMENT? THE WTTC POSITION

Before addressing how tourism can best respond to the negative impacts on the environment, it is useful to explore the extent to which these impacts are significant. The World Travel and Tourism Council has issued a position statement[1] in which it examines these issues and presents its case in support of tourism.

The very preparation of the position paper indicates the seriousness that the WTTC accords to the environmental issue. In its report, the WTTC argues:

> the causes of environmental problems are much debated; their effects cannot yet be predicted with any certainty. There are those who doubt even the existence of some problems. Nonetheless, it is clear that the world's environment is being altered by human activity, and that, without remedial action, the results may be catastrophic.

---

[1]WTO, *Round Table on Planning for Sustainable Tourism Development*, 10th General Assembly, Bali, Indonesia: World Tourism Organization, 1993

WTTC subsequently proceeds to examine the key environmental issues under five headings:

- Global warming

- Depletion of the ozone layer

- Acid rain

- Depletion and pollution of water resources

- Depletion and pollution of land resources

In examining the possible implications for tourism, the WTTC expresses particular concern with respect to the depletion and pollution of land resources. It states:

> the long-term implications of resource depletion are obviously extremely serious. Even over the next few decades the Travel & Tourism industry could find that:
>
> - Political instability or increased competition for land could lead to loss of potential new tourism destinations and degradation of existing destinations.
>
> - Loss of landscape and wildlife could cause a decrease in customer satisfaction with tourism products and hence lower propensity to travel to some destinations.
>
> - Higher fuel prices could lead to operational price increases and corresponding decreases in the number of travelers in this price-sensitive market.

WTTC further notes:

> ultimately whole segments of tourism are threatened by the disappearance of habitats and species. The World Wide Fund for Nature estimates that of the $55 billion earned by Travel & Tourism in developing countries in 1988, some

The beach at Coral Bay in Cyprus has been awarded the Blue Flag, an exclusive eco-label awarded to more than 2,900 beaches and marinas across Europe, South Africa, and the Caribbean in 2004. The Blue Flag Campaign is owned and run by the independent, nonprofit organization Foundation for Environmental Education (FEE).
Courtesy of International Blue Flag Coordination.

$12 billion was due to ecotourism. Ecotourism—that is, tourism with the specific intention of enjoying wildlife or undeveloped natural land-scapes—is a rapidly growing sector. In some destinations, such as the Galápagos Islands, the wildlife of the area is the major attraction. However, even where the tourist's primary aim is not to see wildlife, the opportunity to do so once or twice during the trip may influence the choice of destination. The ecotourism market cannot be sustained with-out quality environments. The industry itself can implement careful man-agement of existing destinations, but new destinations may be destroyed by other less sustainable forms of activity, such as commercial logging, preventing this market from reaching its full capacity.

As one might realistically anticipate, the WTTC response to the question "Does the world's largest industry have the world's largest impact on the environment?" is as follows:

The simple answer is no. However, as environmental concern becomes more and more widespread, Travel & Tourism must expect to be increas-ingly questioned about how it will meet its environmental obligations. Existing patterns of economic activity, and the global consumption and pollution of natural resources, are not sustainable at current rates. Travel & Tourism, at 6 percent of GDP, is a vital component of economic activ-ity, and must play its part in tackling environmental issues.

The effects of environmental damage will not be distributed according to any sense of justice. All regions and industries will be affected by emerging environmental problems. In addition to being the world's largest industry, Travel & Tourism has perhaps the most powerful incen-tive to secure a clean and healthy environment. For leisure travel, at least, visits are made by choice. There is declining consumer desire to visit polluted environments now and such preferences are predicted to be more significant over the next decade.

All industries, from agriculture and automotive to manufacturers of washing machines and refrigeration equipment, are having to respond to exactly the same environmental pressures as Travel & Tourism. Many are further along the road to improved practice. But, as the examples of good practice in the following sections illustrate, Travel & Tourism com-panies are increasingly developing systems and programmes to manage their environmental impact.

In addition to presenting its defense of tourism's case, the WTTC also presents a positive vision of travel and tourism and the environment. Its vision comprises the following elements:

- Travel and tourism is an integral aspect of modern societies.

- Global awareness of environmental damage is developing rapidly.

- The resources of the world's largest industry can and must be harnessed to achieve environmental goals.

- The industry has the potential to influence billions of customers per year and to use its leverage to achieve beneficial environmental effects.

- The customer challenge will exert a growing pressure to achieve environmental improvements.

- Environmental lobbies will add pressure to develop good environmental practice.

- Self-regulation must be developed rapidly and effectively and used to influence the development of appropriate and workable regulations.

- Corporate environmental mission statements are a vital first step toward self-regulation.

- Environmental leadership must come from the major international companies.

SUSTAINABLE DEVELOPMENT

The concept of **sustainable development** has achieved prominence and acceptance in recent years; hopefully, it will permeate all levels of economic development and tourism development, from local to global, in the future. It has become popular because it is an approach that holds out the promise of maintaining a standard of living somewhat similar to that which we possess today while recognizing that we cannot continue to exploit the global environment as we have in the past. While other sectors of the economy are undoubtedly the greatest focus of concern, tourism is increasingly being brought under the microscope regarding its role in contributing to the long-term well-being of the planet. So far, tourism has not attracted the cries of alarm that have accompanied major oil spills, the depletion of nonrenewable resources, or the destruction of the ozone layer. To date, the criticisms directed at tourism from an impact of development standpoint have tended to focus on the deterioration of natural and cultural environments that tourism can cause. Clearly, the foregoing is a much too simplistic assessment of tourism and its impacts (both positive and negative) on our total environment. Because of its pervasive and diverse nature, tourism affects, and is affected by, many factors relating to our social and economic well-being. The use of nonrenewable petroleum is perhaps the best single example; tourism depends heavily on the fuel that is burned to transport travelers both around the block and around the world. As such, any policies that affect the use of petroleum-based fuels will affect the tourism sector.

This point, the interdependency of tourism with other sectors, is being emphasized because any effort to deal with the topic in isolation would be naive and futile. Once this is recognized, however, it is also true that tourism does have major responsibility to contribute to the debate (and the subsequent action) concerning sustainable development.

We Are All Responsible

If it is to work, sustainable development must become a normal way of thinking and acting by a majority of the global community. It cannot be the exclusive purview of the enlightened segments of a society or of an industry. It cannot be something we practice on Sunday. It cannot be only the burden of the less privileged members of the local or the world community. And it cannot be the concern of only those nations and regions whose population growth is under control. In brief, if sustainable development is to be an effective model for the future, it must be a workable approach to ensuring that we can replace what we consume and that in the process of consumption we do not create by-products that pollute or destroy the ecosystem on which future generations depend.

In discussing the responsibility for sustainable development in the field of tourism, four main areas need to be addressed:

1. The premises on which sustainable development policy in tourism should be based
2. The most critical areas of sustainable development as applied to tourism
3. How responsibility for sustainable development in tourism should be allocated
4. An agenda of suggested sustainable development actions for the tourism sector

Some Premises of Sustainable Development in Tourism

The concept of sustainable development is not new. Although the words are more modern and more widely accepted, there have always been similar causes. The concepts of conservation, preservation, and environmental protection have always had as their goal the desire to prevent the destruction of desirable natural conditions and species. What is perhaps new is the insertion into the equation of a recognition that the human race seeks economic, social, and cultural development—and that any attempt to prevent such development on a strictly ideological basis is unlikely to gain widespread acceptance. In parallel, there is also the recognition that demographic, economic, social, and cultural growth that is consumptive and/or destructive cannot continue unabated without serious impacts on the natural environment on which we depend for life itself.

This said, we need to enunciate several key premises on which sustainable development policy, as it applies to tourism, should be based. These premises are simply statements that need to be kept clearly in mind as we in the tourism industry attempt to wrestle with the concept of sustainable development and how it can best be applied to tourism.

Polar bears are only one of the many natural wonders luring visitors to cold-weather climates. The world's cold regions are rich in wildlife, and ecotours to Alaska, northern Canada, and even regions in the Antarctic are popular with travelers. These are areas where great care must be taken to protect the environment and the wildlife. *Copyright © Corbis Digital Stock.*

The Premise of Interdependency

As implied above, tourism as a sector affects, and is affected by, a whole range of social and economic activities. We first need to identify the most important of these interdependencies. We then need to work with those individuals, groups, and organizations that have responsibility for and a commitment to sustainable development in the sectors affected by these interdependencies.

The Premise of Multidisciplinarity

In seeking to implement initiatives to support sustainable development, it will be essential to draw on the ideas and experience of a broad range of disciplines. Indeed, as we have realized for some time now, a true understanding of the phenomenon of tourism is not possible using the thinking and the tools of a single discipline. Similarly, an understanding and implementation of actions to realize sustainable development in tourism will, by necessity, involve the seeking and acceptance of concepts, methodologies, and approaches of individuals from many fields.

For example, natural resource managers have developed carrying-capacity limits so that natural attractions will not be overwhelmed by visitors. Carrying capacity is defined as the maximum amount of development, use, growth, or change that a site can endure without an unacceptable alteration in the physical environment, the community's social fabric, and the local economy and without an unacceptable decline in the quality of experience by the visitor. Thus, for sustainable development, one needs to call on experts in many fields: botanists, ornithologists, zoologists, and foresters, to name a few.

The Premise of Previous Experience

It is always difficult to accept that there is nothing new under the sun, or at least not much. When it comes to sustainable development, we certainly do not know everything, but we do know a lot as to what may work and what may not work. For example, much useful research knowledge was gained from the energy crisis of the 1970s concerning how various segments of the population reacted to a range of alternative approaches to reduce consumer energy use. The recent presence of drought in some western states provided experience in water conservation.

The Premise That Nature Is Better

Perhaps one of the most important premises of the sustainable development movement is that the natural state is generally preferred to the developed state. This is, of course, one of the areas that provides the greatest room for both apparent agreement and mutual deception on the part of individuals and groups that have substantially different views. This important problem aside, it would seem that adherents to the sustainable development lifestyle generally believe that the natural ecosystem is preferable to artificially built environments or settlements. The compelling argument—that the balance of nature is sounder than the imbalance of civilization—has considerable merit. At the same time, the educated world is only too well aware of certain of the excesses and cruelties of nature, as well as the continuous changes that occur in nature over long periods of time. As a result, there is still room for a legitimate questioning of this premise and its universality.

The Premise of Politics and Power

The premise of politics and power has been left until the last because it is both the easiest and the most difficult to deal with. As the world has evolved over the past several centuries, we have seen the growing disparity that has developed between the have and the have-not nations. Today, we find ourselves in a situation where a relatively few advanced nations having small populations possess most of the world's wealth and consume most of its resources. At the other end of the spectrum, we find the poorer countries with rapidly growing populations. By any logic, a long-term projection of this situation and associated trends would lead to the conclusion that the present equilibrium is far from being sustainable. Thus, in our discussions of sustainable development for tourism, we need to keep in mind constantly the question "Sustainable for whom?"

Sustainable Development and Tourism: The Critical Areas

Now that at least some of the critical premises underlying sustainable development have been identified explicitly, it may be useful to define those areas in tourism that merit our consideration. Four such areas are presented for discussion.

Defining the Relevant Population/Community

Let's take the last premise discussed above and focus on the question of sustainable development for whom? As professionals in the field, we need to know if we are to take a global, macro perspective in our discussions of tourism and sustainable development or whether we should restrict our thinking to a more local focus. While recognizing that there is a need for global thinking, we also need to recognize that we may need to restrict the allocation of our energies to those jurisdictions where we have the power to act and to make a difference.

In any event, the principle being enunciated here is that, as professionals, we need to define our sphere of interest and action. The impacts and populations of relevance may be quite different for each sphere, and, consequently, so may our likely actions.

Defining the Time Horizon

While sustainable developments as a concept implies forever, this may be impractical to deal with and can even lead to a feeling of helplessness. There is some merit in seeking to develop programs that are sustainable in perpetuity, but such programs may require huge amounts of resources and considerable time for their implementation. It may be wiser and more effective to undertake a less demanding series of phased programs that initiate movement in desired directions rather than delaying action until longer-term programs can be put in place.

Defining the Dimensions of Sustainability

The concept of sustainability is relevant in practical terms only when we define what is to be sustained. From a tourism perspective, discussions on sustainability may pertain to the environment, cultural identity, economic well-being, or social stability. Individuals responsible for, or interested in, each of these areas taken separately may very legitimately focus on their area of concern and attempt to achieve sustainability in relation to some acceptable ongoing carrying capacity of the destination.

However, from an overall destination management perspective, the task becomes much more complex. Here, the challenge becomes one of attempting to balance the sustainability of economic, cultural, social, and environmental systems. While one hopes for compatibility in the pursuit of sustainability within and across these systems, such is not always possible. Often, the reason for such incompatibility is a divergence of the values from which the goal of sustainability is being pursued.

Defining the Values That Underlie Sustainable Development

Regardless of the way in which the values of a society are determined, they will ultimately determine the policies that emerge with regard to sustainable development. Whether these policies are the result of compromise or consensus is the concern of the political entity involved. In the end, however, the political process and the power of different political units will determine the level and form that sustainability will take. Those of us in the tourism sector have traditionally ignored this reality, and we are weaker for it.

Allocating Responsibility

It should be apparent from the nature of the foregoing discussion that the allocation of responsibility for tourism-related sustainability issues and decisions will not be a neat and tidy exercise. The highly interdependent, multidisciplinary, multisector, and political nature of the decisions does not allow for simplistic answers. However, as long as this caveat is taken seriously, it may be possible to provide some guidelines as to how the process might be conducted and how the prime agents might be assigned to different areas of responsibility.

The Concept of Shared Responsibility

Society is no longer (if it ever was) contained in neat boxes. Rather, at best, it may be viewed as consisting of very ill-defined clusters that change shape constantly as they interface with one another. To complicate matters, a particular citizen may belong to more than one cluster (and indeed probably does) and may change his or her perspective as he or she assumes different roles in society. For example, as a wage earner we may have one perspective, as a parent another, and as a member of a particular religious group, yet another. In the end, however, each

person must reach a weighted position with respect to any given issue.

From the standpoint of the tourism sector, the reality is that all questions related to the nature and extent of tourism development must be supported by the community at large. This means that whatever direction tourism development takes in a community, region, or country, it must have the support of the majority of citizens who are affected by it. This means very simply that the perceived benefits from tourism must be seen to outweigh the total costs (economic, environmental, cultural, social) associated with it.

All this said, it then becomes necessary to propose an operational allocation of responsibility that remains true to the democratic model and the concept of resident-responsive tourism. See Table 17.1 for a proposed allocation of responsibilities.

Unspoiled tropical rain forests, such as this one in Washington state, are of great interest to ecotourists.
Copyright © Corbis Digital Stock.

TABLE 17.1	SUSTAINABLE DEVELOPMENT (SD) IN TOURISM: A POSSIBLE ALLOCATION OF RESPONSIBILITY	
LEVEL/ORGANIZATION	**RESPONSIBILITIES**	
Host community/region	Defining the tourism philosophy and vision for the community/region Establishing social, physical, and cultural carrying capacity for the host community/region	
Destination management/ community organization	Coordination of implementation of community SD plan for tourism Monitoring of levels and impact of tourism in the community/region	
Individual tourism firms and operators	Fair contribution to implementation of SD plan for tourism Observance of regulations, guidelines, and practices for SD	
Host community/region	Encouragement/acceptance of tourism within parameters of SD plan	
Visitors/tourists	Acceptance of responsibility for minimal self-education with respect to values of host region Acceptance and observance of terms and conditions of host community SD plan for tourism	

An Agenda for Action

Once a framework for the allocation of responsibility has been agreed upon, it becomes imperative to establish an agenda and a process for implementation. While the total community bears the ultimate responsibility for this agenda, it is suggested that in practice the destination management organization should assume a leadership role in developing the action agenda and should serve as a catalyst for generating the process that brings about its implementation. Examples of the kind of activities involved in this process include:

- Coordinating the development of a tourism philosophy and vision for the community/region

- Specifying the major goals of the community/region with respect to tourism

- Obtaining consensus concerning the social, physical, and cultural carrying capacity of the community/region in question

- Identifying the specific action initiatives necessary to meet the tourism development objectives while respecting the destination's carrying capacities

- Gaining agreement on the measures to be used in monitoring the impacts of tourism in the community/region

- Gathering and disseminating information concerning the impacts of tourism on the community/region

Based on these findings, it is suggested that an action agenda to support a sustainable development program for tourism might include the following elements:

- Maximum total visitation levels to a community/region

- An obligatory tax to support tourism infrastructure planning, development, and maintenance

- Community-supported legislation to protect and preserve unique resources and heritage sites

- Community and industry consensus concerning architectural and signage standards

- Support for standards and certification programs that encourage staff development and the delivery of high-quality service

Tourism has long been touted as a "renewable industry" that is to be greatly preferred over the traditional "smokestack industries" of the manufacturing age. However, we have learned that tourism can engender its own forms of degradation to the environment and to a society unless it is carefully planned and managed.

The concept of sustainable development is an approach by which efforts are made to balance the benefits or outputs of an industry with the investments and restrictions required to ensure that the industry can continue to exist without depleting or destroying the resource base on which it depends. In the tourism sector, this implies caring for the natural and built environments in a way that will ensure their continuing viability and well-being. Although we in the tourism sector are starting to understand what this implies, there is much that remains to be learned. The industry needs to identify an action agenda and allocate responsibility for its implementation so that we can move toward the goal of a truly sustainable tourism system.

View of Triplet Falls in Australia. It is this kind of pristine beauty that those responsible for tourism must constantly seek to preserve for the enjoyment of future generations. *Courtesy of Digital Vision.*

Acknowledgment and acceptance of the importance of achieving sustainable tourism has given rise to the concept of *ecotourism*. Indeed, in the tourism world the terms *sustainable tourism* and *ecotourism* tend to be used interchangeably. While they certainly are strongly related, each contains a particular nuance that many regard as significant. In our view, the concept of ecotourism conveys a greater concern for the fundamental obligation of all travelers to avoid harming, and indeed to protect, all sites that they visit. As such, ecotourism is highly value-laden in an intrinsic sense; that is, individual travelers must accept responsibility for their behavior and its impact. In contrast, the term *sustainable tourism* conveys a more functional societal obligation to ensure the conditions necessary to maintain the physical environment in a "preserved state" for future generations. These conditions are not simply economic and political dimensions—a recognition that desirable values and good intentions must be supported by hard cash and tough decisions.

ECOTOURISM: COMMON TERMS USED

Ecotourism, geotourism, nature tourism, green tourism, low-impact tourism, adventure travel, alternative tourism, environmental preservation, symbiotic development, responsible tourism, soft tourism, appropriate tourism, quality tourism, new tourism, sustainable development, and *sustainable tourism* all are monikers for similar types of tourist activities and developments. Of all the terms, **ecotourism** and **sustainability** are most frequently used. The principle of both is to sustain or even enhance the quality and attractiveness of the natural environment.

Definitions of ecotourism abound. Conservation International states, "Ecotourism is responsible travel that promotes conservation of nature and sustains the well-being of local people."

Dianne Brouse[2] defines ecotourism as responsible travel in which the visitor is aware of and takes into account the effects of his or her actions on both the host culture and the environment.

The International Ecotourism Society (TIES) defines ecotourism as "responsible travel to natural areas that conserves the environment and improves the well-being of local people." This means that those who implement and participate in ecotourism activities should adhere to the following principles:

- Minimize impact

- Build environmental and cultural awareness and respect

- Provide positive experiences for both visitors and hosts

- Provide direct financial benefits for conservation

- Provide financial benefits and empowerment for local people

---

[2]Dianne Brouse, "Socially Responsible Travel," *Transitions Abroad*, p. 23, January–February 1992.

- Raise sensitivity to host countries' political, environmental, and social climate

- Support international human rights and labor agreements

The Travel Industry Associations of Canada (TIAC) felt that a nationally accepted definition of ecotourism was needed to assist this growing industry segment and to protect the reputation of Canadian tourism. TIAC launched extensive consultations with the industry in 2002 and 2003. This led to the final definition: Ecotourism is a segment of sustainable tourism that offers experiences that enable visitors to discover natural areas while preserving their integrity, and to understand, through interpretation and education, the natural and cultural sense of place. It fosters respect toward the environment, reflects sustainable business practices, creates socioeconomic benefits for communities/regions, and recognizes and respects local and indigenous cultures, traditions, and values.

The definition of ecotourism adopted by Ecotourism Australia is: "Ecotourism is ecologically sustainable tourism with a primary focus on experiencing natural areas that fosters environmental and cultural understanding, appreciation, and conservation."

Other definitions reported in the Travel Industry Association of America's study *Tourism and the Environment* are as follows:

- Ecotourism is environmentally friendly travel that emphasizes seeing and saving natural habitat and archaeological treasures.

- Ecotourism is a tool for conservation.

- Broadly defined, ecotourism involves more than conservation. It is a form of travel that responds to a region's ecological, social, and economic needs. It also provides an alternative to mass tourism. It encompasses all aspects of travel—from airlines to hotels to ground transportation to tour operators. That is, each component of the ecotourism product is environmentally sensitive.

- As a form of travel, ecotourism nurtures understanding of the environment's culture and natural history, fosters the ecosystem's integrity, and produces economic opportunities and conservation gains.

National Geographic has created the term *geotourism*, which it defines as tourism that sustains or enhances the geographical character of the place being visited—its environment, culture, aesthetics, heritage, and the well-being of its residents. This definition tries to describe all aspects of sustainability in travel.

In a study sponsored by *National Geographic Traveler,* the Travel Industry Association of America (TIA) has documented the strong feelings U.S. travelers have about preserving the natural environment as well as history and culture. The report, called *Geotourism: The New Trend in Travel,* showed that more than three-quarters of American travelers feel it is important that their visits not damage the environment. And 62 percent say its important to learn about other cultures when they travel. Furthermore, 38 percent of travelers say they would pay more to use a travel company

Adventure travel is a rapidly growing market, and one of the most popular activities is whitewater rafting. All tourists and especially these rafters on the Stanislaus River in California have a responsibility to leave only footprints and promote conservation. *Photo by Robert Holmes; courtesy of the California Division of Tourism.*

that strives to protect and preserve the environment. Visit the National Geographic Sustainable Tourism Resource Center Web site at **http://www.nationalgeographic. com/travel/sustainable.**

If the definitions above sound like a case of the best of all possible worlds for the traveler, the destination, and the locals, to a degree it is. The problem is living up to the promises of the definitions and making ecotourism a reality. Otherwise, ecotourism becomes a paradox, bringing visitors to fragile environments and ruining them rather than preserving them. In fact, many people quarrel with the word *ecotourism.* If you consider the two parts of the word *ecotourism—ecology* and *tourism*—the inconsistencies are apparent. *Ecology* is defined as the science of the relationships between organisms and environment. When *tourism* is connected to it, a foreign entity is introduced and nature's relationships are changed. Ecotourism does not work when ecotours are so popular that they destroy the very environment they seek to protect.

A number of organizations participate in **debt for nature swaps,** which are a rather unique method of financing new or enlarging existing natural areas. The World Wildlife Fund and Conservation International arrange to pay off a country's debt, in part, and at a discount, in exchange for protecting certain areas. These areas are usually new national parks possessing superb scenic and natural history resources, or the country involved promises to enlarge existing parks, wildlife refuges, or forests. Such plans have already succeeded in Latin American and Asia. An example is an agreement between Bolivia and Conservation International. This pact provides that in return for $650,000 of Bolivia's outstanding debt purchased by Conservation International, Bolivia will provide a 3.7-million-acre expansion of the Beni Biosphere Reserve in the heart of the Amazon rain forest. Over a decade or so, the cumulative effect of this kind of imaginative program in countries rich in natural resources for ecotourism will be to possess very attractive destinations for the ecotourist. Similar programs in other parts of the world are also taking place.

Benefits and Importance of Ecotourism

- Provides jobs and income for **local** people

- Makes possible funds for purchasing and improving protected or natural areas to attract more ecotourists in the future

- Provides environmental education for visitors

- Encourages heritage and **environmental preservation** and enhancement (the creation of new or enlarged national and state parks, forest preserves, biosphere reserves, recreation areas, beaches, marine and underwater trails, and attractions)

Third World countries host many ecotourists. In Brazil, nature travel has become the country's largest new source of revenue. In south-central Africa, Rwanda's ecotourism is the third largest source of foreign exchange earnings. Much of this is generated by visitors to the Mountain Gorilla Project begun in the 1970s. The success of this project has convinced the national government to preserve and protect the critical habitat of the gorilla. It has also brought about support for other parks and reserves in that country.

In Costa Rica, 60 percent of visitors are interested in seeing the national park system, which comprises 11 percent of the country's land area. If biological and private reserves are added, the protected areas total 23 percent of the nation.

Dangers and Limitations of Ecotourism

A low-density rural population is typically found at ecotourism destinations. Most of these people depend on the use of the natural environment for their livelihood. Introduce tourism and there is the danger that tourism consumes resources and has the ability to overconsume. If an ecotour operator does not hire locals to perform services needed by the tour group and use local supplies, the financial benefits of ecotourism are not shared with the local population. This results in the local population and the tourists competing for scarce natural resources, which is unhealthy for the environment. To be successful as tour operators, it is imperative that the locals be involved. If not, their pressing need for survival will doubtless prevail, and this is very likely to damage the very natural attractions that first lured the visitors there.

Another problem is that scientific knowledge of visitor impacts on remote areas, nature areas, wilderness areas, and other relatively undisturbed natural areas in most countries is rather poor or nonexistent. Thus tourism and land management decisions are made in the absence of good science. Once tourism starts there is great pressure to allow more visitors. Consequently, the destinations face the danger of becoming overvisited. Carrying capacities need to be determined and enforced.

Finally, tourism is a multifaceted industry and thus is almost impossible to control. What starts out as well-planned ecotourism can turn into too popular an adventure and overwhelm the destination. To prevent this from happening, the basics of sustainable tourism must be practiced.

Translating Idealism into Sustainable Ecotourism

The idealism of ecotourism must be translated into reality. To do so, experts in the field and practicing managers have identified a number of indicators. These indicators focus on what managers need to know most to reduce their risk of inadvertently making decisions that may damage the natural and cultural environments on which the tourism industry depends. These include measures of:

- The general relationship between tourism and the environment

Paos Volcano National Park in Costa Rica is a popular natural attraction. In addition to the giant volcano crater, the park also possesses abundant wildlife and unusual vegetation. *Photo by Richard Mills; courtesy of International Expeditions, Inc.*

- The effects of environmental factors on tourism

- The impacts of the tourism industry on the environment

In effect, indicators seek to identify specific cause-effect relationships between tourism and the environment. Through their measurement and use, managers can more effectively do the following:

- Identify emerging issues, allowing prevention or mitigation

- Identify impacts, allowing action before they cause problems

- Support sustainable tourism development, identifying limits and opportunities

- Promote management accountability, developing responsible decision making built on knowledge

Two types of indicators are of value to tourism managers:

1. *Core indicators of sustainable tourism* that have been developed for general application to all destinations.
2. *Destination-specific indicators* applicable to particular ecosystems or types of tourism. These indicators fall into two categories:

   - *Supplementary ecosystem-specific indicators* for application to particular ecosystems (e.g., coastal areas, parks and protected areas, or mountainous regions).

   - *Site-specific indicators* that are developed uniquely for the particular site. These indicators reflect important factors of the site, which may not be adequately covered by the core and supplementary ecosystem-specific indicator sets, but are nonetheless needed for management of the particular site.

Examples of indices developed by an expert task force for the World Tourism Organization are given in Table 17.2. By identifying desirable levels of each indicator for a particular destination or site and then working toward meeting these ideals, managers can put in place a process that will ensure sustainability to the greatest extent possible.

It should be noted in reviewing these sets of indicators that they do not address environments or ecological goals alone. There are also indicators that seek to ensure desirable levels of visitor satisfaction and local resident satisfaction as well as satisfactory levels of contributions to the local economy. The use of the indicators helps ensure the economic means to support sustainable ecotourism as well as public (and thus political) support for tourism with a destination.

2002: The International Year of Ecotourism

Ecotourism activities have been expanding rapidly over the past two decades worldwide, and further growth is expected in the future. Recognizing its global impor-

TABLE 17.2	**CORE INDICATORS OF SUSTAINABLE TOURISM**
INDICATOR	SPECIFIC MEASURES
Site protection	Category of site protection according to IUCN[a] index
Stress	Tourist numbers visiting site (per annum/peak month)
Use intensity	Intensity of use in peak period (persons/hectare)
Social impact	Ratio of tourists to locals (peak period and over time)
Development control	Existence of environmental review procedure or formal controls over development of site and use densities
Waste management	Percentage of sewage from site receiving treatment (additional indicators may include structural limits of other infrastructural capacity on-site, such as water supply)
Planning process	Existence of organized regional plan for tourist destination region (including tourism component)
Critical ecosystems	Number of rare/endangered species
Consumer satisfaction	Level of satisfaction by visitors (questionnaire-based)
Local satisfaction	Level of satisfaction by locals (questionnaire-based)
Tourism contribution to local economy	Proportion of total economic activity generated by tourism only
COMPOSITE INDICES[b]	SPECIFIC MEASURES
Carrying capacity	Composite early warning measure of key factors affecting the ability of the site to support different levels of tourism
Site stress	Composite measure of levels of impact on the site (its natural and cultural attributes due to tourism and other sector cumulative stresses)
Attractivity	Qualitative measure of those site attributes that make it attractive to tourism and can change over time

[a]IUCN, International Union for the Conservation of Nature and Natural Resources.

[b]The composite indices are largely composed of site-specific variables. Consequently, the identification and evaluation of the indicators composing these indices require on-site direction from an appropriately trained and experienced observer. In the future, based on the experiences in designing composite indicators for specific sites, it may be possible to derive these indices in a more systematic fashion. See the case studies for Villa Gesell and Peninsula Valdes for application of these indices.

Source: World Tourism Organization.

tance, the United Nations designated the year 2002 as the International Year of Ecotourism, and its Commission on Sustainable Development requested international agencies, governments, and the private sector to undertake supportive activities.

In the framework of the U.N. International Year of Ecotourism, 2002, under the aegis of the United Nations Environment Programme (UNEP) and the World Tourism Organization (WTO), over one thousand participants from 132 countries, from the public, private, and nongovernmental sectors met at the landmark World Ecotourism Summit, held in Québec City, Canada, May 19–22, 2002.

The Québec Summit represented the culmination of 18 preparatory meetings held in 2001 and 2002, involving over 3,000 representatives from national and local governments including the tourism, environment, and other administrations; private ecotourism business and their trade associations; nongovernmental organizations;

academic institutions and consultants; intergovernmental organizations; and indigenous and local communities.

The Summit produced the Québec Declaration on Ecotourism, which contained general statements on ecotourism principles and practices and concluded with forty-nine recommendations, which they proposed to governments, the private sector, nongovernmental organizations, community-based associations, academic and research institutions, intergovernmental organizations, international financial institutions, development assistance agencies, and indigenous and local communities. The declaration was the main outcome of the World Ecotourism Summit and can be found on the Web sites of both the UNEP and the WTO, along with the Final Report of the Summit. (See Internet sites at the end of the chapter.)

Three major conclusions were the outcome of the International Year of Ecotourism. These were:

1. Ecotourism is established as a politically valuable concept. Over fifty countries have developed special policies and strategies focused on ecotourism at a national level. The concept of ecotourism proved its relevance as it positions natural and cultural diversity as a tourism asset. It also stresses the participation of host communities and mandates the educational value of leisure experience.
2. Ecotourism has received mixed reviews. Concrete evidence shows that, if managed in a sustainable manner, ecotourism helps conserve biodiversity, alleviates poverty in rural areas, and can provide benefits to local and indigenous communities situated near, or in, officially protected areas. Evidence also suggests that "greenwashing" exists and the term *ecotourism* has been abused.
3. Tourism is now acknowledged as a global economic driver. The main challenge for the future is to apply the principles of ecotourism/sustainable tourism to all forms of tourism development.

CURRENT TOURISM INDUSTRY PRACTICES

It is fortunate that a concern for the environment has become a major trend that is still gathering momentum. Environmentalism is now a major international and national force with the development of the green movement and other concerned groups. Protection of the environment has been embraced by the tourism industry. Recognition is a start and progress is under way.

Individual Tourists' Responsibilities

If ecologically sustainable tourism is to become a reality, it will require efforts by all the players in the tourism arena, starting with the tourists themselves. Tourists have responsibilities and must be educated as to their obligations and responsibilities to contribute to socially and environmentally responsible tourism. Tourists must first be brought into the process as clients (guests) for the tourist destination and second as persons coresponsible for maintaining the destination.

Several codes of ethics, guidelines, and "ten commandments" for tourist behavior have been developed. Again, they are a start in the process of educating the tourist. Two examples are presented here. The first, and one of the most publicized, was produced by the American Society of Travel Agents (ASTA).

ASTA's Ten Commandments on Ecotourism

Whether on business or leisure travel:

1. *Respect the frailty of the earth.* Realize that unless all are willing to help in its preservation, unique and beautiful destinations may not be here for future generations to enjoy.
2. *Leave only footprints.* Take only photographs. Leave no graffiti. Do not litter. Do not take away "souvenirs" from historic sites and natural areas.
3. To make your travels more meaningful, *educate yourself about the geography, customs, manners, and cultures of the region you visit.* Take time to listen to the people. Encourage local conservation efforts.
4. *Respect the privacy and dignity of others.* Inquire before photographing people.
5. *Do not buy products made from endangered plants or animals, such as ivory, tortoise-shell, animal skins, and feathers.* Read "Know Before You Go," the U.S. Customs list of products that cannot be imported.
6. *Always follow designated trails.* Do not disturb animals, plants, or their natural habitats.
7. Learn about and *support conservation-oriented programs and organizations* working to preserve the environment.
8. Whenever possible, *walk or utilize environmentally sound methods of transportation.* Encourage drivers of public vehicles to stop engines when parked.
9. *Patronize those* (hotels, airlines, resorts, cruise lines, tour operators, and suppliers) *who advance energy and environmental conservation;* water and air quality; recycling; safe management of waste and toxic materials, noise abatement; community involvement; and also patronize those who provide experienced, well-trained staff *dedicated to strong principles of conservation.*
10. Ask your ASTA travel agent to *identify those organizations that subscribe to the ASTA Environmental Guidelines* for air, land, and sea travel. ASTA has recommended that these organizations adopt their own environmental codes to cover special sites and ecosystems.

Code of Ethics for Tourists

A high-quality tourism experience depends on the conservation of our natural resources, the protection of our environment, and the preservation of our cultural heritage. The Canadian tourism industry has developed and adopted a **Code of**

Ethics and Practices to achieve these objectives. Tourists are encouraged to consider the following guidelines.

1. Enjoy our diverse natural and cultural heritage and help us to protect and preserve it.
2. Assist us in our conservation efforts through the efficient use of resources, including energy and water.
3. Experience the friendliness of our people and the welcoming spirit of our communities. Help us to preserve these attributes by respecting our traditions, customs, and local regulations.
4. Avoid activities that threaten wildlife or plant populations or that may be potentially damaging to our natural environment.
5. Select tourism products and services that demonstrate social, cultural, and environmental sensitivity.

Although the codes above are illustrative of the work being done, it should be recognized that other organizations are also active. The National Audubon Society has been a leader, publishing their *Travel Ethic for Environmentally Responsible Travel* in

1989. Save Our Planet published *Guidelines for Low-Impact Vacations* in 1990. The Center for Responsible Tourism in San Anselmo, California, has also developed a *Tourist Code of Ethics*.

Codes and guidelines are fine, but the next step is making tourists aware of the codes and educating them to follow the important guidelines so they will become responsible travelers.

Travel Organizations' Efforts

Efforts to increase environmental protection are being made by major tourism organizations such as the World Tourism Organization (WTO), World Travel and Tourism Council (WTTC), Tour Operators Initiative, Business Enterprises for Sustainable Travel (BEST), Pacific Asia Travel Association (PATA), Tourism Industry Association of Canada (TIAC), and the Travel Industry Association of America (TIA).

Ecotourists discover a dramatically different perspective of the world of nature when they proceed along the rain forest canopy walkway at the Amazon Center for Environmental Education and Research. *Photo by Richard Mills; courtesy of International Expeditions, Inc.*

As evidenced by its 1982 statement, WTO has been an advocate of protecting the environment for years: "The satisfaction of tourism requirements must not be prejudicial to the social and economic interests of the population in the tourist areas, to the environment, or above all, to natural resources which are fundamental attractions of tourism." Today, WTO has an environmental committee because it has recognized the need to understand and manage the link between tourism and the environment. The WTO Environment Committee is developing a set of internationally acceptable indicators. A set of indicators will help tourism planners and managers prevent problems and protect the resource base.

The Tour Operators Initiative for Sustainable Tourism Development has the mission to advance the sustainable development and management of tourism, and to encourage tour operators to make a corporate commitment to sustainable development. In carrying out this mission, the initiative addresses ways to minimize adverse impacts on, and to generate benefits for environment, culture, and communities in tourism destinations through the design and operation of tours and of the conduct of tour operators' business activities.

The initiative has been developed by tour operators for tour operators with the support of the United Nations Environment Programme (UNEP), the United Nations Educational, Scientific and Cultural Organization (UNESCO), and the World Tourism Organization (WTO), who are also full members of the initiative.

Under this international umbrella, tour operators who are members of the initiative will be able to respond to international agendas while creating a platform to develop ideas and projects to address the environmental, social, economic, and cultural aspects of sustainable development within the tourism sector.

Business Enterprises for Sustainable Travel (BEST) has the objective to serve as a leading source of knowledge on innovative travel and tourism practices that advance business, community, and travelers' interests and that also support the economic and social sustainability of destinations.

BEST's major areas of activity are education programs, a showcase of case studies, and a resource center. BEST program activities involve university-level education, travelers' philanthropy, and community tourism. The aim of their web site is to showcase and share good practice information.

BEST was started in 1999 with a grant from the Ford Foundation and served as an incubator for a variety of activities aimed at encouraging the adoption of sustainable practices, stimulating the demand for such practices by travelers and helping communities start pilot programs. Their case studies are especially noteworthy and feature such organizations as the Punta Cana Resort and Club, Turtle Island Fiji, Aspen Skiing Company, Ka'anapali Beach Hotel, Conservation Corporation Africa, BAA, and Lindblad Expeditions.

Regional organizations such as PATA and APEC have also developed codes for environmentally responsible tourism. The APEC/PATA code for sustainable tourism lists guidelines that their member organizations are to follow with respect to tourism's environmental relationships.

The APEC/PATA code urges association and chapter members and APEC member economies to:

Conserve the natural environment, ecosystems, and biodiversity
- Ensure that community attitudes, local customs, and cultural values, and the role of women and children, are understood in the planning and implementation of all tourism-related projects

- Contribute to the conservation of any habitat of flora and fauna affected by tourism

- Encourage relevant authorities to identify areas worthy of conservation and to determine the level of development, if any, that would be compatible in or adjacent to those areas

- Include enhancement and corrective actions at tourism sites to conserve wildlife and natural ecosystems

Respect and support local traditions, cultures, and communities
- Ensure that community attitudes, local customs, and cultural values, and the role of women and children are understood in the planning and implementation of all tourism-related projects

- Provide opportunities for the wider community to take part in discussions on tourism planning issues where these affect the tourism industry and the community

- Encourage relevant authorities to identify cultural heritage worthy of conservation and to determine the level of development, if any, that would be compatible in or adjacent to those areas

- Contribute to the identity and pride of local communities through providing quality tourism products and services sensitive to those communities

Maintain environmental management systems
- Ensure that environmental assessment is an integral step in planning for a tourism project

- Encourage regular environmental audits of practices throughout the tourism industry to promote desirable changes to those practices

- Establish detailed environmental policies and indicators, and/or guidelines for the various sectors of the tourism industry

- Incorporate environmentally sensitive design and construction solutions in any building or landscaping for tourism purposes

Conserve and reduce energy, waste, and pollutants
- Foster environmentally responsible practices for:
  1. reducing pollutants and greenhouse gases
  2. conserving water and protecting water quality
  3. managing efficiently waste and energy

4. controlling noise levels
5. promoting the use of recyclable and biodegradable materials

Encourage a tourism commitment to environments and cultures
- Encourage those involved in tourism to comply with local, regional, and national planning policies and to participate in the planning process

- Foster, in both management and staff of all tourism projects and activities, an awareness of environmental and cultural values

- Encourage all those who provide services to tourism enterprises to participate through environmentally and socially responsible actions

- Support environmental and cultural awareness through tourism marketing

Educate and inform others about local environments and cultures
- Support the inclusion of environmental and cultural values in tourism education, training, and planning

- Enhance the appreciation and understanding by tourists of natural environments and cultural sensitivities through the provision of accurate information and appropriate interpretation

- Encourage and support research on the environmental and cultural impacts of tourism

Cooperate with others to sustain environments and cultures
- Cooperate with other individuals and organizations to advance environmental improvements and sustainable development practices, including establishing indicators and monitoring

- Comply with all international conventions and national, state, and local laws that safeguard natural environments and cultural sensitivities

National organization codes have also been developed, with the TIAC leading the way. The TIAC has created not just one code, but a series of ethical codes for the tourism industry as a whole, for tourists, and for specific sectors of its membership, such as accommodation, food services, tour operators, and government bodies. A particularly distinguishing feature of the TIAC codes is that they extend beyond just protection of the environment guidelines and incorporate the philosophy of sustainable development, which includes all facets of development—social, cultural, and economic. For those seeking more information or a copy of TIAC's Code of Ethics for Tourists, Code of Ethics for the Industry, or Guidelines of Tourist Industry Associations, contact the Tourism Industry Association of Canada, 130 Albert Street, Ottawa, Ontario, Canada K1P 5G4.

The United Nations itself, within its UNEP (United Nations Environment Programme), has demonstrated its interest and concern in the topic. In a 1995 report,[3]

---

[3]UNEP, *Environmental Codes of Conduct for Tourism,* Paris: United Nations Environment Programme, 1995.

the organization carried out a review of a range of environmental codes of conduct for the tourism industry. Following this review, they concluded that such codes must be positive, specific, and action-oriented. If codes are too vague, they have no bite and signatories commit themselves to very little when adopting them. Real change requires real codes, with real objectives.

Although codes must be tailored specifically to the situation they confront, most have several features in common. These are:

- The need to make an overall commitment to the physical and human environment, to accept responsibility for environmental damage and take corrective action where necessary, and to promote and reward outstanding environmental performance

- The need to develop policies and strategies that take account of land-use planning regulations and the need to protect some areas from further development

- The need to develop management policies that enhance beneficial and minimize adverse impacts on the environment

- The need to cooperate with other firms, sectors, and countries

It is important that codes are not developed in isolation. All codes should be the result of partnerships with other businesses, with tourists themselves, or with potential host communities, as appropriate.

Secondly, codes are nothing more than words on paper if they are not implemented. It is essential to consider the implementation and monitoring of codes from the very beginning, even at the time when they are being drafted. While many organizations have already prepared codes, far fewer have given serious thought to implementation and monitoring. Those that have, however, have developed interesting packages of measures that comprise the following:

- Publicity and dissemination campaigns

- Publications of all types

- The provision of expert services to signatories of the code

- The provision of networks to improve communications between participants

- The organization of conferences and seminars for the exchange of ideas

- The provision of awards for outstanding environmental behavior

- The organization of demonstration projects to set examples for others to follow

To be most efficient, measures such as publications, seminars, and conferences must be practical in orientation and directed at specific audiences.

Individual Firm Efforts

A third set of environmental codes focuses on individual companies. These codes tend to be quite technical and operations-oriented, covering the day-to-day management practices of businesses such as airlines, accommodations, cruise lines, ski resorts, golf resorts, theme parks, tour operators, and others. What distinguishes these codes from those discussed previously is their effort to integrate the best business practices with sound environmental management. Companies such as Fairmont Hotels and Resorts (formerly Canadian Pacific Hotels and Resorts), Sheraton, Ramada International Hotels and Resorts, Marriott International, British Airways, American Airlines, United Air Lines, US Airways, Avis Rent-A-Car System, Busch Entertainment Corporation, Anheuser-Busch, Universal Studios, Walt Disney Company, and American Express have focused on recycling, reusing, energy conservation, water conservation, community involvement, and community environmental obligations to employees and guests.[4]

Inter-Continental Hotels has produced and distributed a three-hundred-page manual for its properties worldwide with guidelines on waste management, product purchasing, air quality, energy conservation, noise pollution, fuel storage, asbestos, pesticides, herbicides, and water.[5]

Hyatt Hotels and Resorts has implemented an international recycling program that saves the organization more than $3 million annually. Hyatt's commitment is not only to recycle, but also to close the recycling loop by establishing a market for recycled products. This is important when you consider that a typical Hyatt guest room generates 383 pounds of garbage annually, according to the consulting firm International Recycleco.

Under Hyatt's new plan, the same guest room will generate an average of only 37 pounds of nonrecyclable garbage annually, saving the company $2 million in annual waste-hauling costs. Under design is a trash container for guest rooms to encourage separation of paper, plastics, and aluminum.

With the help of its recycling consultant, the Hyatt Regency Chicago is now operating its own miniature materials-recovery facility (MRF). The MRF processes nine different items, including leftover soap, and cuts the annual disposal costs in half. The program has saved the hotel money by retrieving hotel items discarded by mistake, including linens, silverware, and coffeepots.

In addition, all new Hyatt Hotels in the United States will be designed with recycling centers. Hotels outside the United States will implement programs in accordance with local guidelines and availability of environmentally friendly products.[6]

---

[4]Suzanne Hawkes and Peter Williams, *The Greening of Tourism*, Burnaby, BC: Centre for Tourism Policy and Research, Simon Fraser University, 1993; and U.S. Travel Data Center, *Tourism and the Environment*, Washington, DC: Travel Industry Association of America, 1992.
[5]Wimberly Allison Tong & Goo, *Do Not Disturb*, Newport Beach, CA: WAT&G, n.d.
[6]Ibid.

Environmentally responsible tourism can be achieved through the combined efforts of private operators, travel organizations, and individuals. *Photo by The Inn By The Sea, Cape Elizabeth, Maine.*

Sheraton has several programs. They select products such as cleaning solvents and containers for their conservation and recyclability. Their "Going Green" program invites guests at Sheraton Hotels in Africa and the Indian Ocean region to add a dollar to their final bill. Sheraton then matches this amount in local currency and contributes the money to local conservation projects that the World Society for the Protection of Animals has identified.[7]

United Airlines recycles aluminum used aboard its aircraft and food containers up to thirty or forty times. It has also reduced the amount of water carried on board and is replacing its fleet with quieter, more fuel-efficient aircraft.[8]

Sea World Orlando operates a beached-animal rescue and rehabilitation program that aids sick, injured, or orphaned manatees, dolphins, whales, otters, sea turtles, and birds.[9]

---

[7]Ibid.
[8]Ibid.
[9]Ibid.

A Closing Note

This chapter concludes with a statement by Ken Brown, chairman of Mauna Lani Resorts, Inc., in Hawaii. It epitomizes the attitude that developers need to be sensitive to the environment. Brown has orchestrated one of the most highly acclaimed destination resorts in the world, so his views bear careful study. Brown states, "Developers must not act like elephants at a picnic." He reminds us, "We should not only be sensitive to the environment, we should also add something to the life of the people—something aesthetic, physically beautiful, socially and economically enriching. We need to examine our actions and ask, "Is this really benefiting the community?"

Brown's convictions about environmental responsibility run deep. "I am absolutely convinced that environmental concerns are ethical and moral issues." Acknowledging the high economic cost of environmentally responsive development, Brown expresses confidence in its long-range profitability. He has been inspired by the late Noboru Gotoh, Japanese industrialist, Tokyu Group chairman, and Mauna Lani developer, whose motto, "For the Betterment of Mankind," set exacting standards for Mauna Lani.[10]

Summary

Responsible citizens of the world have cause to realize that all of humankind's activities must be increasingly examined in a very critical manner with respect to their impact or their sustainability of this planet. Tourism is only one of these activities, but it is an extremely important one. It follows that tourism must understand and accept those limitations that are essential to maintaining a high quality of life for all species.

The main concept of ecotourism is responsible travel to natural areas that conserves the environment and sustains the well-being of local people. From the tourists' viewpoint, ecotourism is typically the gratification provided by a unique experience in an undisturbed natural environment, viewing flora, fauna, birds, animals, landforms, scenery, and natural beauty.

Benefits of ecotourism include providing jobs, helping preserve more areas, educating, and encouraging heritage and environmental enhancement. Benefits to the local people are maximized by hiring as many locals as possible and obtaining supplies and services locally.

Carrying capacity for visitors must be determined. It is defined as the maximum number of daily visitors that the area can receive without damaging its attractive features. Enforcement of this limit, along with good management and maintenance, is essential.

---

[10]Wimberly Allison Tong & Goo, *Do Not Disturb.*

Sustainable tourism development is development that has been carefully planned and managed. It is the antithesis of tourism that has developed for short-term gains. Because of the expected continuing growth of tourism, sustainable development is the approach that will be needed. Because of the pressure on the world's resources, it is the only sensible approach.

No business sector has greater reason to promote and enforce environmental and business ethics codes than tourism. The environment is the resource base for tourism, and without protection, the natural attraction that brought the tourist in the first place will be lost. As a result, a number of codes for tourists, the tourism industry, and the environment have emerged. If the codes developed by the American Society of Travel Agents, World Travel and Tourism Council, Pacific Asia Travel Association, the Tourism Industry Association of Canada, and other organizations are followed, the possibility of truly sustainable tourism can be a reality.

KEY CONCEPTS

ASTA's ten commandments
benefits of ecotourism
carrying capacity
code of ethics
debt for nature swap
ecotourism

ecotourism development
environmental preservation
land-use planning
local populations and benefits
PATA code for environmentally
    responsible tourism

principles for implementing
    sustainable tourism
sustainable development
sustainable tourism

Internet Sites

The Internet sites mentioned in this chapter are repeated here for convenience, plus some selected additional sites. For more information, visit these sites. Be aware that Internet addresses change frequently, so if a site cannot be accessed, use a search engine. Also use a search engine to locate many additional relevant sites.

American Society of Travel Agents
http://www.astanet.com

Blue Flag
http://www.blueflag.org

Business Enterprises for Sustainable Travel (BEST)
http://www.sustainabletravel.org

Conservation International
http://www.conservation.org

Earth Pledge Foundation
http://www.earthpledge.org

Earthwatch Institute
http://www.earthwatch.org

Eco-Source Network
http://www.ecosourcenetwork.
    com

Ecotourism Australia
http://www.ecotourism.org.au

The Ecotravel Center
http://www.ecotour.org

ecoVenture
http://www.ecoventure.org

Environment Australia
http://www.erin.gov.au

Gateway Antarctic
http://www.anta.canterbury.ac.nz

Gorilla100.com
http://www.gorilla100.com

Green Globe 21
http://www.greenglobe.org

GreenNet
http://www.gn.apc.org

International Council of Tourism Partners
http://www.tourismpartners.org

The International Ecotourism Society
http://www.ecotourism.org

Journal of Sustainable Tourism
http://www.multilingual-matters.com

The Mountain Gorilla Conservation Fund
http://www.mgcf.net

The Nature Conservancy
http://www.nature.org/aboutus/travel/ecotourism

Pacific Asia Travel Association
http://www.pata.org

Planeta
http://www.planeta.com

Sustainable Tourism CRC
http://www.crctourism.com.au

Sustainable Tourism Resource Center
http://www.nationalgeographic.com/travel/sustainable

Swedish Ecotourism Society
http://www.ekoturism.org

Tour Operators Initiative
http://www.toinitiative.org

Travelers Conservation Foundation
http://www.tconline.org

United Nations Environment Programme
http://www.unep.org

World Conservation Monitoring Centre
http://www.unep-wcmc.org

World Conservation Union (IUCN)
http://www.iucn.org

World Heritage
http://www.unesco.org

World Tourism Organization
http://www.world-tourism.org

World Travel and Tourism Council
http://www.wttc.org

World Wide Web Resources: Environment
http://www.uky.edu/Subject/environment.htm

World Wildlife Fund
http://www.wwf.org

Internet Exercises

Site Name: Ecotourism Australia
URL: http://www.ecotourism.org.au
Background Information: Ecotourism Australia was formed in 1991 as an incorporated nonprofit organization and is the peak national body for the ecotourism industry.

Exercises
1. Describe the vision of Ecotourism Australia.
2. Describe its nature and ecotourism accreditation program.
3. Discuss its EcoGuide Certification Program.
4. What other activities does the association engage in?

Site Name: United Nations Environment Programme
URL: http://www.unep.org
Background Information: UNEP provides leadership and encourages partnerships in caring for the environment by inspiring, informing, and enabling nations and people to improve their quality of life without compromising that of future generations.

Exercises
1. What publications does UNEP have on ecotourism and sustainable tourism?
2. What kind of information can you find in their *Tourism Focus Newsletter?*
3. How does UNEP define ecotourism?
4. What does UNEP say about the environmental impacts of tourism?

QUESTIONS FOR REVIEW AND DISCUSSION

1. What exactly is ecotourism? Why are there so many different terms for this idea?
2. Why has this concept become so popular?
3. Give some examples of the resources necessary for an ecotourism destination.
4. Are resources other than natural ones involved? Are these meaningful? Explain.
5. Describe the role of local people in ecotourism, in sustainable development.
6. Why are preservation planning principles so important?
7. What should be the goals of ecotourism for a tour company? For the ecotourist? For the local population? For the local government? For a conservation organization?
8. Differentiate ecotourism policy in developing and developed countries.
9. Identify the principal limitations to ecotourism.
10. Referring to question 9, state some ways that these limitations might be ameliorated.
11. Why is capacity so important?
12. Why is it important to identify the values on which tourism development is based?
13. Of what use are "principles" in implementing recommendations to achieve sustainable tourism?

CASE PROBLEMS

1. Bonnie S., CTC, is an agency travel counselor. She has decided that her agency's market area has a good potential to sell more ecotours. How should Bonnie proceed to identify prospective buyers of such tours?
2. As director of Ecuador's national park system, Ernesto B. has become increasingly concerned about the overuse of Galápagos National Park. He worries that the current popularity of the park—about 65,000 tourists each year—may actually be sowing the seeds of destruction. This situation may be inducing a disastrous future drop in visitor numbers. Outline some steps that he might take to:
   • Ascertain the present quality of the visitor experience.
   • Remedy some aspects of overuse of the park, to ensure future success.
3. Nathan M. is the local managing director of a tour company specializing in ecotourism. His company operates big-game and bird photo safaris in Tan-zania. He has decided that his firm would be more socially responsible if his tours (by minibus) would obtain practically all needs from local sources. Give some examples of how he might do this and describe the benefits that would accrue locally. (When discussing, include both economic and social benefits.)
4. Upon graduation, you have secured a job as tourism specialist with the World Wildlife Fund. Your first assignment is to be a team member charged with helping to formulate plans for some kind of wildlife protection area in Zambia. This country is located in south-central Africa. Their government is considering a new national park and has requested expert assistance from the fund. The president of the fund has made it very clear to the team that such plans must also aim to improve living standards for the local population. These standards, at present, are grievously low. Most local people are subsistence farmers. They occasionally shoot big-game animals that damage their crops,

and also for meat. After extensive field study, a particularly attractive area has been found in which the scenery is spectacular, the climate very pleasant, the natural history resources outstanding, and the local people friendly and hospitable. Thus the proposed park seems to have an excellent potential for attracting substantial numbers of ecotourists. Propose some conceptual ideas as to how this challenge can be met successfully.

5. A very vocal environmental group has recently voiced harsh criticism of the state's tourism business. They claim that the industry rapidly consumes valuable natural resources, provides mostly low-paying unskilled employment, and degrades the culture of the main tourist centers. As the state's tourism director, how would you answer these charges?

6. Referring to case 5, the same environmental group has succeeded in convincing the state's attorney general that all roadside billboards be eliminated. The various state hotel, motel, restaurant, attractions, and tourist promotion organizations vehemently oppose such legislation. Can you think of some kind of compromising plan that might satisfy both of these opposing groups?

SELECTED REFERENCES

Aronsson, Lars. *The Development of Sustainable Tourism.* London: Continuum International Publishing Group, 2000.

Blamey, Russell K. "Ecotourism: The Search for an Operational Definition." *Journal of Sustainable Tourism,* Vol. 5, No. 2, pp. 109–122, 1997.

Bramwell, B., and A. Fearn. "Visitor Attitudes to a Policy Instrument for Visitor Funding of Conservation in a Tourist Area." *Journal of Travel Research,* Vol. 35, No. 2, pp. 29–33, Fall 1996.

Bramwell, Bill, and Bernard Lane. "Tourism and Sustainable Development in an Economic Downturn." *Journal of Sustainable Tourism,* Vol. 11, No. 1, pp. 1–2, 2003.

Bramwell, Bill, and Bernard Lane (eds.). *Tourism, Collaboration, and Partnership: Politics, Practice, and Sustainability.* Clevedon, UK: Channel View Publications, 2003.

Buckley, Ralf. *Case Studies in Ecotourism.* Oxfordshire, UK: CABI Publishing, 2003.

D'Amore, Louis J. "A Code of Ethics and Guidelines for Socially and Environmentally Responsible Tourism." *Journal of Travel Research,* Vol. 31, No. 3, pp. 64–66, Winter 1993.

Fennell, D. A. *Ecotourism Programme Planning.* Oxfordshire, UK: CABI Publishing, 2002.

Font, Xavier, and R. C. Buckley. *Tourism Ecolabelling: Certification and Promotion of Sustainable Management.* Oxfordshire, UK: CABI Publishing, 2001.

Garrod, Brian, and Julie C. Wilson. *Marine Ecotourism.* Clevedon, UK: Channel View Publications, 2003.

Harrill, Rich. *Guide to Best Practices in Tourism and Destination Management.* Lansing, MI: Educational Institute of the American Hotel and Lodging Association, 2003.

Harris, Rob, Tony Griffin, and Peter Williams. *Sustainable Tourism.* Oxford, UK: Butterworth-Heinemann, 2002.

Hvenegaard, Glen T. "Using Tourist Typologies for Ecotourism Research." *Journal of Ecotourism,* Vol. 1, No. 1, pp. 7–18, 2002.

Luck, Michael, and Torsten Kirstges. *Global Ecotourism Policies and Case Studies.* Clevedon, UK: Channel View Publications, 2003.

Malloy, David Cruise, and David A. Fennel. "Ecotourism and Ethics: Moral Development and Organizational Cultures." *Journal of Travel Research,* Vol. 36, No. 4, pp. 47–56, Spring 1998.

McCool, S. F., and R. N. Moisey (eds.). *Tourism, Recreation, and Sustainability: Linking Culture and the Environment.* Oxfordshire, UK: CABI Publishing, 2001.

Mowforth, Martin, and Ian Munt. *Tourism and Sustainability: New Tourism in the Third World.* London: Routledge, 2003.

Ritchie, J. R. Brent, and Geoffrey I. Crouch. *The Competitive Destination: A Sustainable Tourism Perspective.* Oxfordshire, UK: CABI Publishing, 2003.

Singh, Sagar. *Shades of Green: Ecotourism for Sustainability.* New Delhi: The Energy and Resources Institute, 2004.

Sirakaya, Ercan, and Robert W. McLellan. "Modeling Tour Operators' Voluntary Compliance with Ecotourism Principles: A Behavioral Approach." *Journal of Travel Research,* Vol. 36, No. 3, pp. 42–55, Winter 1998.

Travel Industry Association of America. *Geotourism: The New Trend in Travel.* Washington, DC: TIA, 2003.

United Nations Environment Programme. *Environmental Codes of Conduct for Tourism.* Paris: UNEP, 1995.

Weaver, David B. *Ecotourism in the Less Developed World.* Oxfordshire, UK: CABI Publishing, 1998.

Weaver, David B. (ed). *The Encyclopedia of Ecotourism.* Oxfordshire, UK, CABI Publishing, 2001.

Wight, Pamela A. "Ecotourism: Ethics or Eco-sell?" *Journal of Travel Research,* Vol. 31, No. 3, pp. 3–9, Winter 1993.

Wight, Pamela A. "North American Ecotourism Markets: Motivations, Preferences, and Destinations." *Journal of Travel Research,* Vol. 35, No. 1, pp. 3–10, Summer 1996.

Wight, Pamela A. "North American Ecotourists: Mar-ket Profile and Trip Characteristics." *Journal of Travel Research,* Vol. 34, No. 4, pp. 2–10, Spring 1996.

World Tourism Organization. *The British Ecotourism Market.* Madrid: WTO, 2001.

World Tourism Organization. *The Canadian Ecotourism Market.* Madrid: WTO, 2002.

World Tourism Organization. *The French Ecotourism Market.* Madrid: WTO, 2002.

World Tourism Organization. *The German Ecotourism Market.* Madrid: WTO, 2002.

World Tourism Organization. *Guide for Local Authorities on Developing Sustainable Tourism.* Madrid: WTO, 1998.

World Tourism Organization. *The Italian Ecotourism Market.* Madrid: WTO, 2002.

World Tourism Organization. *The Spanish Ecotourism Market.* Madrid: WTO, 2002.

World Tourism Organization. *Sustainable Development of Ecotourism: A Compilation of Good Practices in SMEs.* Madrid, Spain: WTO, 2003.

World Tourism Organization. *Sustainable Tourism in Protected Areas: Guidelines for Planning and Management.* Madrid: WTO, 2003.

World Tourism Organization. *The U.S. Ecotourism Market.* Madrid: WTO, 2002.

World Tourism Organization. *Voluntary Initiatives for Sustainable Tourism.* Madrid: WTO, 2002.

World Tourism Organization. *The World Ecotourism Summit: Final Report.* Madrid: WTO, 2002.

Essentials of Tourism Research and Marketing

Will tomorrow's customers be different from todays'? *Photo by Tom Johnson, courtesy of Verde Canyon Railroad.*

Travel and Tourism Research

CHAPTER 18

Learning Objectives

- Recognize the role and scope of travel research.
- Learn the travel research process.
- Study secondary data and how it can be used.
- Understand the methods of collecting primary data.
- Know who does travel research.

The information derived from travel and tourism research helps private firms and public agencies make informed decisions on complex tourism development issues. *Copyright © PhotoDisc, Inc.*

INTRODUCTION

Information is the basis for decision making, and it is the task of travel research to gather and analyze data to help travel managers make decisions. Travel research is the systematic, impartial designing and conducting of investigations to solve travel problems. Examples of travel research are:

- United Air Lines investigating consumer attitudes and behaviors to enable the airline to better serve the flying public

- Marriott Hotels, Resorts, and Suites studying the leisure travel market

- The Aspen Skiing Company conducting a market profile study to understand its customers

- Travel Industry Association of America (TIA) measuring the economic impact of travel in the United States

Although travel research does not make decisions, it does help travel decision makers operate more effectively. Managers can plan, operate, and control more efficiently when they have the facts. Thus research, which reduces the risk in **decision making,** can have a great impact on the success or failure of a tourism enterprise.

ILLUSTRATIVE USES OF TRAVEL RESEARCH

Some of the **uses** or **functions** of travel research are as follows:

1. **To delineate significant problems.** The constant pressure of day-to-day business operations leaves the travel executive with little time to focus on problem areas that handicap operations. The isolation of causes and problems that create inefficiency is often one of the most important single contributions that travel research makes to management.

2. **To keep an organization or a business in touch with its markets.** Travel research identifies trends, interprets markets, and tracks changes in markets so that policies can be developed that are aimed in the right direction and are based on facts rather than on hunches or opinions. Research reduces the risk of unanticipated changes in markets. In a way, research is insurance against these changes to make sure that a business does not stick with a product until it becomes obsolete.

3. **To reduce waste.** Research has always been effective in measuring methods of operation to eliminate those methods that are inefficient and to concentrate on those that are the most effective. Automation of travel makes this use even more important. The energy crisis led to research that has produced dramatic savings in aircraft fuel requirements.

4. **To develop new sources of profit.** Research can lead to the discovery of new markets, new products, and new uses for established products. Research can

show the lodging industry the types of rooms and the type of lodging facilities that should be offered to meet customers' needs.

5. **To aid in sales promotion.** Many times the results of research are interesting not only to the firm but also to the public and can be used in advertising and promotion. This is particularly true of consumer attitude research, as well as research where consumers are asked to rank products and services.

6. **To create goodwill.** Consumers react favorably to travel research; they feel that the company that is involved in research really cares about them and is trying to create a product or service that will meet their needs.

THE STATE OF THE ART

Travel research today runs from the primitive to the sophisticated—from simple fact gathering to complex, mathematical models. For those who really wish to dig into the subject, several references are worth noting. The most important is *Travel, Tourism, and Hospitality Research: A Handbook for Managers and Researchers* (Wiley, 1994); the second is *Tourism Analysis* (Longman, 1995); the third is the *Journal of Travel Research* (Sage Publications); and the fourth is *Annals of Tourism Research* (Pergamon Press).

Measurement is a critical element in research activity, and the lack of standard or precise definitions has hampered the development of travel research. Without definitions, measurement cannot be taken and data cannot be generated and compared from study to study. Economic projections or analytical findings made by sophisticated models or pure intuition must be based on some kind of data. Without a quantitative record of past experiences, only individual, isolated studies making a limited contribution to the state of the art are possible. That is basically where we stand in the area of travel research at the present time. Giant strides are being made, improving travel research by adopting techniques developed by other disciplines and utilizing new and more sophisticated techniques; however, the existing body of literature largely consists of individual isolated studies utilizing different definitions that were set up to solve only the immediate problem at hand. Fortunately, some researchers are now using an approach termed **meta-analysis,** in which an attempt is made to extract the common findings from a broad range of studies on a related topic.

THE TRAVEL RESEARCH PROCESS

The key to good travel research is to define the problem and work through it in a systematic procedural manner to a final solution. The purpose of this section is to describe briefly the basic procedures that will produce a good research result:

1. **Identify the problem.** First, the problem must be defined or identified. Then you are in a position to proceed in a systematic manner.

One of the first things to do in examining a tourism problem is to review and discuss the problem with a research firm representative. Here, Suzanne Cook, Senior Vice President Research and Technology, Travel Industry Association of America is visiting with Terry Berggren, Destination Research Manager, Ruf Strategic Solutions. *Photo courtesy of the Travel and Tourism Research Association.*

2. **Conduct a situation analysis.** In this step you gather and digest all the information available and pertinent to the problem. The purpose is to become familiar with all the available information to make sure that you are not repeating someone else's work or that you have not overlooked information that will provide a ready solution to the problem. The situation analysis is an exhaustive search of all the data pertinent to the company, the product, the industry, the market, the competition, advertising, customers, suppliers, technology, the economy, the political climate, and similar matters. Knowledge of this background information will help you to sort out the likely causes of the problem and will lead to more efficient, productive research. The organization will get the most from the research result when you understand the organization's internal environment and its goals, strategies, desires, resources, and constraints. In addition to a trip to the library, the Internet is an ideal tool to use in conducting the situation analysis.

3. **Conduct an informal investigation.** After getting background information from available sources, you will talk informally with consumers, distributors, and key people in the industry to get an even better feel for the problem. During both the situation analysis and informal investigation, you should be developing hypotheses that can be tested. The establishment of hypotheses is one

of the foundations of conducting research and is a valuable step in the problem-solving process. A hypothesis is a supposition, a tentative proposal, or a possible solution to a problem. In some ways it could be likened to a diagnosis. If your automobile quit running on the interstate, you might hypothesize that: (1) you were out of gas, (2) the fuel pump had failed, or (3) you had filter problems. An investigation would enable you to accept or reject these hypotheses.

4. **Develop a formal research design.** Once adequate background information has been developed and the problem has been defined against this background, it is time to develop the specific procedure or design for carrying out the total investigation or research project. This step is the heart of the research process. Here you have to develop the hypotheses that will be tested and determine the types and sources of data that are to be obtained. Are secondary sources available, or will it be necessary to conduct primary research? If primary research has to be conducted, then it is necessary to develop the sample, the questionnaires, or other data-collection forms and any instruction sheets and coding methods and tabulation forms. Finally, it is necessary to conduct a pilot study to test all of the foregoing elements. The results are then written up in a detailed plan that serves as a guide that any knowledgeable researcher should be able to follow and conduct the research satisfactorily.

5. **Collect the data.** If the data are available from secondary sources, then collecting the data becomes primarily desk research. However, if primary data are collected, this step involves actual fieldwork in conducting survey research, observational research, or experimental research. The success of data gathering depends on the quality of field supervision, the caliber of the interviewers or field investigators, and the training of investigators.

6. **Tabulate and analyze.** Once the data have been collected, they must be coded, tabulated, and analyzed. Both this step and the previous one must be done with great care; it is possible for a multitude of errors to creep into the research process if collection, tabulation, and analysis are not done properly. For example, if one is going to use the survey method, then interviewers must be properly selected, trained, and supervised. Obviously, if instead of following the carefully laid out sample, the interviewers simply fill out questionnaires themselves, the data will not be useful. In today's environment, it is likely that tabulation will take place on the computer. A number of excellent packages are available for this purpose. One of the most used is SPSS, the Statistical Package for the Social Sciences.

7. **Interpret.** Tabulation results in stacks of computer printout, with a series of statistical conclusions. These data must now be interpreted in terms of the best action or policy for the firm or organization to follow—a series of specific recommendations of action. This reduction of the interpretation to recommendations is one of the most difficult tasks in the research process.

8. **Write the report.** Presentation of the results of the research is extremely important. Unless the data are written up in a manner that will encourage management to read them and act upon them, all of the labor in the research

process is lost. Consequently, emphasis should be put on this step in the research process to produce a report that will be clearly understood with recommendations that will be accepted.

9. **Follow up.** Follow up means precisely that. A study sitting on the shelf gathering dust accomplishes nothing. While many people will consider the researcher's task to be done once the final report or presentation has been made, the work is not completed until the results of the survey are put into action. Research is an investment, and an ultimate test of the value of any research is the extent to which its recommendations are actually implemented and results achieved. It is the task of the researcher to follow up to make the previous investment of time and money worthwhile.

SOURCES OF INFORMATION

Primary data, secondary data, or both may be used in a research investigation. Primary data are original data gathered for the specific purpose of solving the travel research problem that confronts you. In contrast, secondary data have already been collected for some other purpose and are available for use by simply visiting the library or other such repositories of secondary data. When researchers conduct a survey of cruise passengers to determine their attitudes and opinions, they are collecting primary data. When they access Census Bureau information on travel agents, they are using a secondary source.

The situation analysis step of the travel research process is emphasized because it focuses on the use of secondary sources; however, their use is not confined to this step. One of the biggest mistakes in travel research is to rush out and collect primary data without exhausting secondary source information. Only later do you discover that you have duplicated previous research when existing sources could have provided information to solve your problem for a fraction of the cost. Only after exhausting secondary sources and finding that you still lack sufficient data to solve your problem should you turn to primary sources.

Secondary Data

In the last ten years there has been a virtual explosion of information related to tourism, travel, recreation, and leisure. A competent researcher must be well acquainted with these sources and how to find them. The Internet is a source that contains a wealth of information.

If you are fortunate enough to find secondary sources of information, you can save yourself a great deal of time and money. Low cost is clearly the greatest advantage of secondary data. When **secondary data** sources are available, it is not necessary to construct and print questionnaires, hire interviewers, pay transportation costs, pay coders, pay data inputters, and pay programmers; thus, it is easy to see the cost advantage of utilizing secondary data. Secondary data can also be collected much more quickly than can primary data. With an original research project, it typically takes a minimum of sixty to ninety days or more to collect data; secondary data could be collected in a library within a few days.

Secondary data are not without disadvantages; for example, many times the information does not fit the problem for which you need information. Another problem is timeliness; many secondary sources become outdated. For example, the Census of Population and Housing is conducted every ten years; as we get to the end of that time period, the data are not very useful.

Evaluating Secondary Data

While it is not expected that everyone will be a research expert, everyone should be able to evaluate or appraise secondary data. Any study, no matter how interesting, must be subjected to evaluation: "Is it a valid study? Can I use the results to make decisions?" On such occasions the researcher must evaluate the secondary data and determine whether they are usable.

The following criteria may be used to appraise the value of information obtained from secondary sources:

1. **The organizations supplying the data.** What amount of time went into the study? Who conducted the study? What experience did the personnel have? What was the financial capacity of the company? What was the cost of the study? An experienced research firm will put the proper time and effort into a study to yield results, whereas a novice or inexperienced organization may not.

2. **The authority under which the data are gathered.** For example, data collected by the Internal Revenue Service (IRS) are likely to be much better than data collected by a business firm. Data that are required by law, such as census data, are much more dependable than is information from other sources.

D. K. Shifflet and Associates, Ltd., is one of the many firms available to conduct travel and tourism research studies and consult with clients. The firm has been providing research and consulting services to clients for over twenty years. Jim Caldwell serves as Vice President Marketing and Sales. *Photo courtesy of the Travel and Tourism Research Association.*

3. **Freedom from bias.** One should always look at the nature of the organization furnishing the data. Would you expect a study sponsored by airlines to praise the bus industry for providing the lowest-cost transportation on a per-mile basis in the United States?

4. **The extent to which the rules of sampling have been rigidly upheld.** What is the adequacy of the sample? Adequacy is frequently difficult to evaluate because deficiencies in the sampling process can be hidden. One indication of adequacy is the sponsor's willingness to talk about the sample. Will the sponsor release sampling details? Are the procedures well-known, acceptable methods?

5. **The nature of the unit in which the data are expressed.** Here even simple concepts are difficult to define. In defining the term *house,* how do you handle such things as duplexes, triplexes, mobile homes, and apartment houses? Make sure that good operational definitions have been used throughout the research so there will be no problems in understanding it. Research results that are full of terms such as *occasionally* and *frequently* are not likely to be useful; these terms have different meanings to different people.

6. **The accuracy of the data.** Examine the data carefully for any inconsistencies and inquire into the way in which the data were acquired, edited, and tabulated. If at all possible, check the data against known data from other sources that are accurate. For example, check the demographics in a study against known census data.

7. **Pertinency to the problem.** You must be concerned with fit. You may have a very good study, but if it does not pertain to the problem at hand, it is not worth anything to you. The relevance of secondary data to the problem must stand up; otherwise, the study cannot be used.

8. **Careful work.** Throughout your evaluation, always look for evidence of careful work. Are tables constructed properly? Do all totals add up to the right figures or to 100 percent? Are conclusions supported by the data? Is there any evidence of conflicting data? Is the information presented in a well-organized, systematic manner?

Primary Data

When it is not possible to get the information you need from secondary sources, it is necessary to turn to primary sources—original, firsthand sources of information. If you need information on travelers' attitudes, you would then go to that population and sample it. As stated earlier, you should collect primary data only after exhausting all reasonable secondary sources of information.

Once you have determined that you are going to collect primary data, then you must choose what method of gathering primary data you are going to use. The most widely used means of collecting primary information is the survey method. Other methods are the observational method and the experimental method. It is not uncommon to find one or more of these methods used in gathering data. These basic methods are discussed in the next section.

BASIC RESEARCH METHODS

Focus Groups

It has been said the **focus group** may be the worst form of market research—except for all others. Because of this reality, focus-group interviewing is a popular form of market research in tourism. Its primary purpose is exploratory: either to establish the parameters for subsequent survey research or to delve into the motivations and behaviors of travelers.

A focus group is a form of qualitative research that brings together a small number of individuals (usually about 8 to 12) for an in-depth discussion regarding the topic of interest to the client. Typical topics include the most-desirable/least-desirable characteristics of a planned attraction or service, reaction to a planned advertising theme or program, or the probable public reaction to developments in an environmentally sensitive region.

Focus-group participants are chosen to represent a cross section of the population having a likely interest or stake in the area to be studied. However, because they are not selected scientifically (usually availability and willingness to participate play a major role in focus-group composition), great care must be taken in extrapolating the findings of focus-group sessions to the general population. In addition, because the session facilitator can significantly influence the nature of the discussion, it is essential that the facilitator be well trained and very familiar with the underlying goals of the focus group.

Despite these cautions and concerns, focus-group interviewing remains one of the most insightful and valuable ways of gaining a true understanding of the factors affecting complex managerial situations and decisions.

The Survey Method

If we look at the methods of collecting travel research data, we will find that the **survey method** is the most frequently used. The survey method, also frequently referred to as the questionnaire technique, gathers information by asking questions. The survey method includes factual surveys, opinion surveys, or interpretative surveys, all of which can be conducted by personal interviews, mail, or telephone techniques.

Factual Surveys
A quick look at the types of surveys will reveal that factual surveys are by far the most beneficial. "In what recreational activities did you participate last week?" is a question for which the respondent should be able to give accurate information. While excellent results are usually achieved with factual surveys, all findings are still subject to certain errors, such as errors of memory and ability to generalize or the desire to make a good impression. Nonetheless, factual surveys tend to produce excellent results.

Sampling is a critical element of research. ASDE Inc. provides sampling and related services to research professionals making Survey Sampler, which draws sample numbers through a random digit dialing methodology, available to clients doing phone surveys. Randa Bell, Marketing Director, serves client needs. *Photo courtesy of the Travel and Tourism Research Association.*

Opinion Surveys

In these surveys, the respondent is asked to express an opinion or make an evaluation or appraisal. For example, a respondent could be asked whether tour package A or B was the most attractive or which travel ad is the best. This kind of opinion information can be invaluable. In studies of a ski resort conducted by the University of Colorado, vacationer respondents were asked to rate the performance of the resort's employees as excellent, good, average, or needs improvement. The ratings allowed resort management to take action where necessary. Opinion surveys tend to produce excellent results if they are properly constructed.

Interpretive Surveys

On interpretive studies the respondent acts as an interpreter as well as a reporter. Subjects are asked why they chose a certain course of action—why they participated in a particular recreation activity the previous week (as well as what activity), why they flew on a particular airline, why they chose a particular vacation destination, why they chose a particular lodging establishment.

While respondents can reply accurately to what questions, they often have difficulty replying to why questions. Therefore, while interpretive research may give you a feel for consumer behavior, the results tend to be limited. It is much better to utilize motivational and psychological research techniques, which are better suited for obtaining this information.

In summary, try to get factual or opinion data via the survey method and utilize in-depth interviewing or psychological research techniques to get "reason why" data.

It was mentioned earlier that surveys can be conducted by personal interviews, telephone, or mail. The purpose of a survey is to gather data by interviewing a limited number of people (sample) who represent a larger group. Reviewing the basic survey methods, one finds the following advantages and disadvantages.

Personal Interviews

Personal interviews are much more flexible than either mail or telephone surveys because the interviewer can adapt to the situation and the respondent. The interviewer can alter questions to make sure that the respondent understands them or probe if the respondent does not respond with a satisfactory answer. Typically, one can obtain much more information by personal interview than by telephone or mail surveys, which by necessity must be relatively short. Personal interviewers can observe the situation as well as ask questions. For example, an interviewer in a home can record data on the person's socioeconomic status, which would not be possible without this observation. The personal interview method permits the best sample control of all the survey techniques.

A major limitation of the personal interview method is its relatively high cost. It tends to be the most expensive of the three survey methods. It also takes a considerable amount of time to conduct, and there is always the possibility of personal interviewer bias. There is also the issue of working couples today, which means it is difficult to find respondents at home.

Telephone Surveys

Surveys in which respondents are interviewed over the telephone are usually conducted much more rapidly and at less cost than are personal interviews. The shortcomings of telephone surveys are that they are less flexible than personal interviews, and of necessity they are brief. While a further limitation of phone surveys is that not everyone has a telephone, those with telephones tend to have the market potential to travel or buy tourism products. Consequently, this limitation is not very serious for travel research. Speed and low cost tend to be the primary advantages of telephone interviews. Computer-assisted telephone interviewing using random dialing is growing at a rapid pace.

The survey questionnaire is entered into computer memory. The interviewer reads the questions from the computer screen and records the respondent's answers into computer memory by using a keyboard or by simply touching a sensitive screen. Because the data are recorded immediately, these systems tend to be faster and less expensive than traditional methods.

Mail Surveys

Mail surveys have the potential of being the lowest-cost method of research. As would be expected, mail surveys involve mailing the questionnaire to carefully

CAREY AMERICAN LIMOUSINE Colorado Springs Shuttle Service

Please take a moment to respond to the following questions. This information will be used to evaluate areas of service to afford you quality service for your next trip. Thank you.

1. Was the vehicle on time? Yes _____ No _____ (Delay time: _____ Reason given   )
2. What was the condition of the equipment? Clean _____ Average _____ Unkempt _____
3. Was your driver courteous? Yes _____ No _____
4. How was your service? Excellent _____ Fair _____ Poor _____ (Why?   )
5. Was it easy to make your reservation? Yes _____ No _____ (Why?   )
6. Where did you find out about our company? Travel agent _____ Advertisement _____ (Referred by   )
7. Was the scheduled time convenient for you? Very _____ Acceptable _____ Inconvenient _____
8. Were you traveling on Business _____ Pleasure _____
9. Will you recommend our service to others? Yes _____ (Name & Address   ) No _____

Comments

Name

Address:

City: _____ State: _____ Zip: _____

COLORADO TRANSPORTATION GROUP

If you represent a company or travel agency, please include that information:

Telephone (   )

Figure 18.1 A sample mail questionnaire.

selected sample respondents and requesting them to return the completed questionnaires (see Figure 18.1). This survey approach has a great advantage when large geographical areas must be covered and when it would be difficult to reach respondents. Other advantages of this approach are that personal interview bias is absent and the respondent can fill out the questionnaire at his or her convenience.

The greatest problem in conducting a mail survey is having a good list and getting an adequate response. If a large percentage of the target population fails to respond, you will have to question whether those who did not respond are different from those who have replied and whether this introduces bias. Length is another consideration in mail questionnaires. While they can be longer than telephone surveys, they still must be reasonably short. Another limitation of mail surveys is that questions must be worded carefully and simply so that respondents will not be confused. While questions may be very clear to the person who wrote them, they can be very unclear to the respondent.

Using the Internet for Survey Research
The Internet has become increasingly pervasive in all aspects of life today—and the field of research is no exception. In an ongoing effort to reduce the cost and

increase the effectiveness of survey research, many researchers have turned to the Internet. In general, the results of this move to online survey research have been impressive, to the point where web-based research may even be the mode of choice for a large percentage of studies.

Despite its appeal, Web-based survey research does have certain shortcomings that need to be kept in mind when contemplating its use. One of the industry's current top concerns relates to growing consumer distaste for any unsolicited marketing messages, whether they come from researchers or not. This reality makes it increasingly more difficult for research organizations to recruit participants for both surveys and focus groups.

Another problem is that because Internet-based research is so easy and inexpensive to conduct, a lot of inexperienced, poorly qualified individuals are carrying out their own surveys online. Because it is easy to author a survey online and e-mail it out, research has gone through a damaging period during which untrained people have conducted surveys using unprofessional sampling or consolidation of results, and as a consequence have derived unreliable results.

Despite the above problems, there is little doubt that the use of online surveys, primarily because of their economic efficiency, will continue to grow and to improve in quality.

Electronic Devices

A relatively new way of conducting survey research is the use of computer-type electronic devices to ask the consumer questions and immediately record and tabulate the results. This equipment can be placed in a hotel lobby, mall, or other high-traffic location and attract consumers to record responses to questions. Use of these machines is a low-cost method of getting consumer information because the questions are self-administered, saving the cost of interviewers, and the results are tabulated automatically. A disadvantage is that children, who like to play with such machines, may distort the results. The prediction that such devices will become increasingly popular in the future has yet to materialize.

Observational Method

The **observational method** relies upon the direct observation of physical phenomena in the gathering of data. Observing some action of the respondent is obviously much more objective and accurate than is utilizing the survey method. Under the observational method, information can be gathered by either personal or mechanical observation. Mechanical recorders on highways count the number of cars that pass and the time that they pass. Automatic counters at attractions observe and count the number of visitors.

Advantages of the observational method are that it tends to be accurate and it can record consumer behavior. It also reduces interviewer bias. Disadvantages are that it is much more costly than the survey method and it is not possible to employ in many cases. Finally, the observational method shows what people are doing but does not tell you why they are doing it. It cannot delve into motives, attitudes, or opinions. If the why is important, this would not be a good method to use.

Davidson-Peterson Associates, Inc., is one of the leading and most experienced firms conducting travel and tourism research in the United States. *Photo courtesy of the Travel and Tourism Research Association.*

Experimental Method

The experimental method of gathering primary data involves setting up a test, a model, or an experiment to simulate the real world. The essentials of the **experimental method** are the measurement of variations within one or more activities while all other conditions and variables are being controlled. The experimental method is very hard to use in tourism research because of the difficulty of holding variables constant. Tourism researchers have no physical laboratory in which to work. However, it is possible for resort areas to run advertising experiments or pricing experiments or to develop simulation models to aid in decision making. Such test marketing is being conducted successfully; and as time passes, we will see the experimental method being used more and more.

WHO DOES TRAVEL RESEARCH?

Many organizations use and conduct travel research. The types of firms and organizations that engage in travel research include government, educational institutions, consultants, trade associations, advertising agencies, media, hotels and motels, airlines and other carriers, attractions, and food service organizations.

Government

The federal government has been a major producer of travel research over the years. The Office of Travel and Tourism Industries, in the U.S. Department of Commerce, conducts studies on international visitors, focusing on both marketing information and economic impact. State and local governments also employ travel research to assist in making marketing and public policy decisions. Examples are studies of highway users, the value of fishing and hunting, the economic impact of tourism in various geographic areas, inventories of tourism facilities and services, tourism planning procedures, and visitor characteristics studies. In other countries, research inaugurated by the official tourism organization of a state or country often has very significant ramifications for tourism development and promotion. Research done in Australia, Canada, Mexico, England, Spain, France, Poland, and Croatia has been outstanding.

Educational Institutions

Universities conduct many travel research studies. The chief advantage is that the studies are usually conducted without bias by trained professionals. Many of the studies have contributed greatly to the improvement of travel research methods. Institutions of higher learning, particularly universities with departments of hotel and restaurant management, hospitality management, and tourism, have a vital need for such information. Such educational organizations are concerned with the teaching of tourism or related subjects and need the most-current available research findings to do an effective teaching job. Research is also needed by such academic departments as geography, fisheries and wildlife, resource development, park and recreation resources, and forestry. All these departments have an interest in the effect on the environment because of the use of the natural landscape for recreation and tourism.

Many departments of universities are qualified to accomplish pure research or applied research in tourism. Bureaus of business and economic research are often active in this field. An example is the research accomplished by the Business Research Division of the University of Colorado at Boulder. This organization has published many tourism research findings, bibliographies, and ski industry studies. Departments of universities that can be helpful include psychology, sociology, economics, engineering, landscape architecture and urban planning, management, hotel and restaurant administration, theater, home economics, human ecology, forestry, botany, zoology, history, geography, and anthropology.

Consultants

Numerous organizations specialize in conducting travel research on a fee basis for airlines, hotels, restaurants, ski areas, travel agents, resorts, and others. Consultants offer the service of giving advice in the planning, design, interpretation, and application of travel research. They will also provide the service of conducting all or a part of a field investigation for their clients.

TNS, Plog Research, formerly Plog/NFO, is a strong supporter of the *Journal of Travel Research* **and well known for their transportation, travel, and hospitality research. Shown here are Stephan Mayer, Senior Project Director, and Richard Cain, Vice President and Account Executive for TNS.** *Photo courtesy of the Travel and Tourism Research Association.*

The primary advantage of consultants or consulting firms is that they are well-trained, experienced specialists who have gained their experience by making studies for many different clients. They also provide an objective outsider's point of view, and they have adequate facilities to undertake almost any job. The disadvantage of consultants is that of any outsider: the lack of intimate knowledge of the internal problems of the client's business; however, management can provide this ingredient. Many travel firms with their own research departments find it advantageous to use consultants or a combination of their own internal staff and consultants.

Many well-known firms specialize in travel research. A few of these are Opinion Research Corporation; Davidson-Peterson Associates; Economics Research Associates; Gallup Organization; Arthur D. Little; Midwest Research Institute; TNS Plog Research; Yesawich, Pepperdine, Brown, and Russell; SDR, Inc.; Ipsos-Reid (formerly the Angus Reid Group); Leisure Trends; D. K. Shifflet and Associates; Longwoods International; Menlo Consulting Group; IPK International; Dean Runyan Associates; Ruf Strategic Solutions; Smith Travel Research; and Simmons Market Research Bureau.

An example of a syndicated service is one offered by the Menlo Consulting Group in Palo Alto, California, called TravelStyles, which provides research on the

U.S. market for international travel. It is a source of information on travel trends, market segments, and the changing preferences of Americans who travel outside the country.

Trade Associations

Extensive travel research is conducted by trade associations. The trade association often provides facilities for carrying on a continuous research service for its members, particularly in the area of industry statistics. Many associations have excellent Internet sites and make their data available to the public.

Advertising Agencies

Today, advertising agencies typically maintain extensive research departments for both their own and their clients' needs. The agency must have basic facts if it is to develop an effective advertising campaign for its travel client in today's rapidly changing world. Advertising agencies that have been leaders in travel research are Ogilvy and Mather Worldwide; J. Walter Thompson; BBDO Worldwide; Foote, Cone and Belding; Leo Burnett; and DDB Needham Worldwide.

Media

Trade journals often conduct outstanding tourism research. *Travel Weekly*'s annual issue on the U.S. Travel Industry is an example of good media research. Consumer magazines have also been active producers of travel research. *Time, U.S. News and World Report, Newsweek, Better Homes and Gardens, National Geographic, New Yorker, Sunset, Southern Living, Sports Illustrated,* and *Travel Holiday* are all known for their travel research.

Hotels and Motels

Hotels and motels constantly use current research findings concerning their markets, trends in transportation, new construction materials, management methods, use of electronic data processing, human relations techniques, employee management, advertising, food and beverage supplies and services, and myriad other related information.

Airlines and Other Carriers

Airlines and other carriers offer services designed for the business and vacation traveler. Because of their needs and the importance of research to their operations, airlines and other carriers will usually have their own market research departments to conduct ongoing studies of their customers and the market. They are also frequent employers of outside consultants.

Attractions

The most ambitious private attractions in the country are the major theme parks, and research has played a major role in the success of these enterprises. That research has run the gamut from feasibility studies to management research. Walt Disney's thinking still dominates the industry. The Disney formula of immaculate grounds, clean and attractive personnel, high-quality shops, tidy rest rooms, and clean restaurants are still the consumers' preference today. Research shows that if attractions are not clean, they are not likely to be successful.

Food Service

Much of the pioneering work in the use of research by restaurants has been done by franchises and chains because what will work in one location will typically work in others, resulting in a large payoff from funds invested in research. All travel firms, whether they are restaurants, airlines, hotels, or other hospitality enterprises, need to be in touch with their markets and find new and better ways of marketing to sell seats, increase load factors, and achieve favorable occupancy ratios.

TRAVEL AND TOURISM RESEARCH ASSOCIATION

The Travel and Tourism Research Association (TTRA) is an international organization of travel research and marketing professionals devoted to improving the quality, value, scope, and acceptability of travel research and marketing information. The association is the world's largest travel research organization, and its members represent all aspects of the travel industry, including airlines, hotels, attractions, transportation companies, media, advertising agencies, government, travel agencies, consulting firms, universities, students, and so on.

TTRA's mission is to be the global leader in advocating standards and promoting the application of high-quality travel and tourism research, planning, management, and marketing information, with the following specific objectives:

- To serve as an international forum for the exchange of ideas and information among travel and tourism researchers, marketers, planners, and managers

- To encourage the professional development of travel and tourism researchers, marketers, planners, and managers

- To facilitate global cooperation between producers and users of travel and tourism research

- To promote and disseminate high-quality, credible, and effective research to the travel and tourism industry

- To foster the development of travel and tourism research and related curricula in institutes of higher education

- To advocate the effective use of research in the decision-making process of professionals in the travel and tourism industry

TTRA has chapters in Europe, Canada, and within the United States in the central states, Florida, Texas, the western states, the Southeast, Hawaii, the south-central states, and the northeast. TTRA contributes to the publication of the *Journal of Travel Research,* the TTRA newsletter, annual conference proceedings, and other special publications. TTRA has an extensive awards program that recognizes excellence and encourages professional development of researchers, marketers, planners, and students involved in the travel and tourism industry. Those wishing further information on TTRA should visit the association's Web site at **http://www.ttra.com.**

Summary

Travel research provides the information base for effective decision making by tourism managers. Availability of adequate facts allows managers to develop policy, plan, operate, and control more efficiently and decreases risk in the decision-making process.

Useful travel research depends on precise identification of the problem; a thorough situation analysis supplemented by an informal investigation of the problem; careful research design; and meticulous collection, tabulation, and analysis of the data. The researcher must also present a readable written report with appropriate recommendations for action and then follow up to ensure that the recommendations are actually implemented so that results can be achieved.

The research itself may use secondary (preexisting) data or require collection of primary data (original research). Primary data may be gathered by survey—personal interview, mail, or telephone surveys—or by the observational and experimental methods. Numerous organizations and agencies use and conduct travel research. The Travel and Tourism Research Association is the world's largest tourism research organization.

Key Concepts

basic research methods	measurement	Travel and Tourism Research
decision making	meta-analysis	Association
experimental method	observational method	travel research process
feasibility studies	primary data	uses of travel research
focus groups	secondary data	
information surveys	sources of information	

Internet Sites

The Internet sites mentioned in this chapter are repeated here for convenience, plus some selected additional sites. For more information, visit these sites. Be aware that Internet addresses change frequently, so if a site cannot be accessed, use a search engine. Also use a search engine to locate many additional relevant sites.

Annals of Tourism Research
http://www.elsevier.com

The Big Picture
http://www.travelbigpicture.com

CAB International
http://www.cabi.org

Canadian Tourism Commission
http://www.canadatourism.com

Canadian Tourism Research Institute
http://www.conferenceboard.ca/ctri

Centre International de Recherches et d'Etudes Touristiques
http://www.ciret-tourism.com

eRTR Review of Tourism Research
http://www.ertr.tamu.edu

Journal of Travel Research
http://www.sagepub.com

National Laboratory for Tourism and eCommerce
http://tourism.temple.edu

Office of Travel and Tourism Industries
http://tinet.ita.doc.gov

Tourism Laboratory for Economic and Social Behavior Research
http://www.tourism.uiuc.edu

Tourism Recreation Research
http://www.trrworld.com

Tourism Research Australia
http://www.tourism.australia.com/Research

Tourism Research Links
http://www.waksberg.com

Travel and Tourism Research Association
http://www.ttra.com

Travel Industry Association of America
http://www.tia.org

World Tourism Education and Research Centre
http://www.haskayne.ucalgary.ca/research/centres/wterc

World Tourism Organization
http://www.world-tourism.org

World Travel and Tourism Council
http://www.wttc.org

Internet Exercise

Site Name: National Laboratory for Tourism and eCommerce

URL: http://tourism.temple.edu

Background Information: The primary mission of the National Laboratory for Tourism and eCommerce is to foster quality inter- and multidisciplinary research in the varied aspects of tourism.

Exercise

1. Discuss how the laboratory supports its research mission.

QUESTIONS FOR REVIEW AND DISCUSSION

1. What does a situation analysis cover?
2. What problems can travel research solve?
3. When should you use primary data? Secondary data?
4. What are the basic research methods?
5. What are the strengths and weaknesses of focus groups?
6. Why would you choose survey research over focus groups?
7. Why are research findings so important to intelligent decision making?
8. If you were director of a major city's convention and visitors bureau, how would you use travel research?
9. As a consultant, you are researching the feasibility of a new resort hotel project. What procedures would you use, step by step?
10. How would a resort developer use a consultant's report when the report is completed? Once the resort is built, does the manager need further research?
11. What methods could be used by a state tourist office to survey out-of-state visitors?
12. Should a state tourist office conduct its own research or hire an outside supplier? Why?

SELECTED REFERENCES

Baker, Kenneth G., G. C. Hozier, Jr., and R. D. Rogers. "Marketing Research and Methodology and the Tourism Industry: A Nontechnical Discussion." *Journal of Travel Research*, Vol. 32, No. 3, pp. 3–7, Winter 1994.

Breen, Helen, Adrian Bull, and Maree Walo. "A Comparison of Survey Methods to Estimate Visitor Expenditure at a Local Event." *Tourism Management*, Vol. 22, No. 5, pp. 473–479, October 2001.

Bruner, Gordon C., II, and Paul J. Hensel. *Marketing Scales Handbook: A Compilation of Multi-Item Measures.* Chicago: American Marketing Association, 2001.

Crompton, John L., and Shu Tian-Cole. "An Analysis of 13 Tourism Surveys: Are Three Waves of Data Collection Necessary?" *Journal of Travel Research*, Vol. 39, No. 4, pp. 356–368, May 2001.

Dann, Graham, Dennison Nash, and Philip Pearce. "Methodology in Tourism Research." *Annals of Tourism Research*, Vol. 15, No. 1, pp. 1–28, 1988.

International Association of Scientific Experts in Tourism. *Tourism Research: Achievements, Failures, and Unresolved Puzzles.* St-Gallen, Switzerland: AIEST, 1994.

Litvin, Stephen, and Goh Hwai Kar. "E-Surveying for Tourism Research: Legitimate Tool or a Researcher's Fantasy?" *Journal of Travel Research*, Vol. 39, No. 3, pp. 308–314, February 2001.

Page, Stephen (ed.). *Advances in Tourism Research,* series. Oxford, UK: Elsevier Science, 2000.

Pearce, Philip L. "Recent Research in Tourist Behaviour." *Asia Pacific Journal of Tourism Research,* Vol. 1, No. 1, pp. 7–17, 1996.

Ritchie, B. W., P. Burns, and C. Palmer. *Tourism Research Methods: Integrating Theory with Practice.* Oxfordshire, UK: CABI Publishing, 2005.

Ritchie, J. R. Brent, and Charles R. Goeldner (eds.). *Travel, Tourism, and Hospitality Research: A Handbook for Managers and Researchers,* 2d ed. New York: Wiley, 1994.

Seaton, A. V. "Unobtrusive Observational Measures as a Qualitative Extension of Visitor Surveys at Festivals and Events: Mass Observation Revisited." *Journal of Travel Research,* Vol. 35, No. 4, pp. 25–30, Spring 1997.

Smith, Stephen L. J. *Tourism Analysis: A Handbook,* 2d ed. Essex, UK: Longman, 1995.

Sturman, Michael (ed). "Special-Focus Issue on Research." *Cornell Hotel and Restaurant Administration Quarterly,* Vol. 44, No. 2, pp. 9–152, April 2003.

Travel Industry Publishing Company. *Travel Industry World Yearbook.* Spencertown, NY: TIPC, 2001.

Van Hoof, Hubert B., and Marja J. Verbeeten. "Tourism Research Inquiries: The Response of the State Office of Tourism." *Journal of Travel Research,* Vol. 35, No. 4, pp. 75–76, Spring 1997.

Walle, Alf H. "Quantitative versus Qualitative Tourism Research." *Annals of Tourism Research,* Vol. 24, No. 3, pp. 524–536, July 1997.

Williams, Peter W., P. Bascombe, N. Brenner, and D. Green. "Using the Internet for Tourism Research: 'Information Highway' or 'Dirt Road'?" *Journal of Travel Research,* Vol. 34, No. 4, pp. 63–70, Spring 1996.

World Tourism Organization. *Collection and Compilation of Tourism Statistics: Technical Manual No. 4.* Madrid: WTO, 1995.

World Tourism Organization. *Collection of Domestic Tourism Statistics: Technical Manual No. 3.* Madrid: WTO, 1995.

World Tourism Organization. *Collection of Tourism Expenditure Statistics: Technical Manual No. 2.* Madrid: WTO, 1995.

Yaman, H. Ruhi, and Robin N. Shaw. "Assessing Marketing Research Use in Tourism with the USER Instrument." *Journal of Travel Research,* Vol. 36, No. 3, pp. 70–78, Winter 1998.

Yaman, H. Ruhi, and Robin N. Shaw. "The Conduct of Marketing Research in Tourism." *Journal of Travel Research,* Vol. 36, No. 4, pp. 25–32, Spring 1998.

TOURISM MARKETING

CHAPTER 19

Learning Objectives

- Become familiar with the marketing mix and be able to formulate the best mix for a particular travel product.

- Appreciate the importance of the relationship between the marketing concept and product planning and development.

- Understand the vital relationship between pricing and marketing.

- Know about distribution systems and how this marketing principle can best be applied to a variety of travel products.

- Be able to do market segmentation to plan a marketing program for the business you are the most interested in.

- Demonstrate the linkage between tourism policy and tourism marketing.

The Statue of Liberty is an internationally recognized tourism icon that greatly enhances market awareness of New York City—and the entire United States—as a travel destination. *Photo courtesy of New York Sate Division of Tourism.*

INTRODUCTION

Tourism marketing is:

- The State of New York creating a tourism promotion fund, developing a marketing plan, and creating an advertising campaign around the theme "I Love New York"

- Marriott International segmenting its lodging product into many brands

- United Air Lines offering different classes of service, supersaver fares, and Mileage Plus; advertising the "friendly skies"; developing a logo; adding new routes and schedules; using their own reservation system and travel agents; and working with tour groups

- Using the Internet as a new medium

Marketing includes all of the above and much more. Marketing has been defined in a variety of ways. The American Marketing Association defines it as "an organizational function and a set of processes for creating, communicating, and delivering value to customers and for managing customer relationships in ways that benefit the organization and its stakeholders." Others have stated that marketing is the delivery of the standard of living to society. You are no doubt acquainted with the old adage "nothing happens until somebody sells something."

Most people have little idea what marketing is all about and would probably say that it has something to do with selling or advertising. However, marketing is a very broad concept, of which advertising and selling are only two facets. Marketing is goal oriented, strategic, and directed. It both precedes and follows selling and advertising activities. Marketing is the total picture in getting goods and services from the producer to the user.

Unfortunately, the term *marketing* often conjures up unfavorable images of used-car salespeople, TV furniture advertisers, high-pressure selling, and gimmicks, leading to the perception of marketing in terms of stereotypes. In fact, marketing plays a critical role in all organizations whether they are nonprofit educational institutions, tourist resorts, or manufacturers. The role of marketing is to match the right product or service with the right market or audience.

Marketing is an inevitable aspect of tourism management. Marketing can be done effectively and well, with sophistication, or it can be done poorly in a loud, crass, intrusive manner. The goal of this chapter is to discuss the basic elements of marketing so that it can be done effectively, with style, and with a favorable economic impact.

MARKETING CONCEPT

The heart of good marketing management today is the **marketing concept,** or a **consumer orientation.** Tourism organizations that practice the marketing concept find out what the consumer wants and then produce a product that will satisfy those wants at a profit. The marketing concept requires that management thinking be directed toward profits rather than sales volume.

Assume that you are going to develop a new major resort area. This is a difficult exercise in planning that requires that the designs that are developed be based on how consumers view the product. One of the first steps is to employ the marketing concept and do research to understand the consumers' (the market's) needs, desires, and wants. Designers of products and consumers of products often perceive them differently. Architects, for example, may see a hotel in terms of such things as space utilization, engineering problems, and design lines or as a monument; consumers may see the hotel as a bundle of benefits—as being attractive, as offering full service and outstanding food, as having recreational facilities, and so on. Once consumer views are determined, the task is to formulate strategic marketing plans that match the resort and its market. In today's competitive environment where consumers have choices, firms need to employ the marketing concept.

THE MARKETING MIX

The marketing program combines a number of elements into a workable whole—a viable, strategic plan. The tourism marketing manager must constantly search for the right **marketing mix**—the right combination of elements that will produce a profit. The marketing mix is composed of every factor that influences the marketing effort.

1. **Timing.** Holidays, high season, low season, upward trend in the business cycle, and so on, must all be considered.
2. **Brands.** The consumer needs help in remembering your product. Names, trademarks, labels, logos, and other identification marks all assist the consumer in identifying and recalling information about your product.
3. **Packaging.** Although tourism services do not require a physical package, packaging is still an important factor. For example, transportation, lodging, amenities, and recreation activities can be packaged and sold together or separately. Family plans or single plans are other forms of packaging.
4. **Pricing.** Pricing affects not only sales volume but also the image of the product. A multitude of pricing options exist, ranging from discount prices to premium prices.
5. **Channels of distribution.** The product must be accessible to the consumer. Direct selling, retail travel agents, wholesale tour operators, or a combination of these methods all comprise distribution channels that must be developed.
6. **Product.** The physical attributes of the product help to determine its position against the competition and provide guidelines on how to best compete.
7. **Image.** The consumer's perception of the product depends to a great extent on the important factors of reputation and quality.

8. **Advertising.** Paid promotion is critical, and the questions of when, where, and how to promote must be carefully considered.
9. **Selling.** Internal and external selling are essential components for success, and various sales techniques must be incorporated in the marketing plan.
10. **Public relations.** Even the most carefully drawn marketing plan will fail without good relations with the visitors, the community, suppliers, and employees.
11. **Service quality.** Outstanding service is necessary to have satisfied customers and repeat business.
12. **Research.** Developing the right tourism marketing mix depends in large part on research.

The preceding list makes it obvious that the marketing manager's job is a complex one. Using knowledge of the consumer market and the competition, the marketing manager must come up with the proper marketing mix for the resort, attraction, or other organization. The marketing manager's job begins with planning to allow direction and control of the foregoing factors.

The many elements in the marketing mix have been defined most frequently as "**the four Ps,**" a term popularized by E. Jerome McCarthy, coauthor of *Basic Marketing*[1] and *Essentials of Marketing*.[2] While the four Ps are an oversimplification, they do provide a neat, simple framework in which to look at marketing and put together a marketing program. The four Ps are **product, place, promotion,** and **price.** The product includes not only the actual physical attributes of the product but also product planning, product development, breadth of the line, branding, and packaging. Planning the product should consider all these aspects in order to come up with the "right" product.

Place is really concerned with distribution. What agencies, channels, and institutions can be linked together most effectively to give the consumer easy access to the purchase of your product? Where is the "right" place to market your product?

Promotion communicates the benefits of the product to the potential customers and includes not only advertising but also sales promotion, public relations, and personal selling. The "right" promotional mix will use each of these promotional techniques as needed for effective communication.

Price is a critical variable in the marketing mix. The "right" price must both satisfy customers and meet your profit objectives.

Mill and Morrison[3] have added another "three Ps" that they believe are particularly relevant to tourism. *Programming* involves special activities, events, or other types of programs to increase customer spending or to give added appeal to a package or other tourism service. As noted in Chapter 15, tourism policy views programs as a strategic consolidation of a range of different activities designed to ensure a clear focus for development and marketing efforts.

---

[1]William D. Perreault, Jr., and E. Jerome McCarthy, *Basic Marketing*, 14th ed., Boston: McGraw-Hill, 2002.
[2]E. Jerome McCarthy and William D. Perreault, Jr., *Essentials of Marketing*, 6th ed., Burr Ridge, IL: Irwin, 1994.
[3]Robert C. Mill and Alastair M. Morrison, *The Tourism System*, 4th ed. Dubuque, IA: Kendall/Hunt, 2002.

Tourism icons, such as the Golden Gate Bridge in San Francisco, can be used to promote travel to a given location. Not all icons are bridges or statues, however. For example, the Southern Belle of Mississippi is an enduring symbol of southern hospitality. *Golden Gate Bridge photo by Robert Holmes; courtesy of the California Division of Tourism. Southern Belle photo courtesy of the Mississippi Department of Community Development/Division of Tourism Development.*

The second of the additional three Ps concerns *people*. This P is intended to stress that tourism is a "people business"—that we must not lose sight of the importance of providing travel experiences that are sensitive to the human side of the visitor as well as to the functional requirements.

The final P is defined as *partnership*. This highlights the high degree of interdependency among all destination stakeholders, as well as the need for alliances and working relationships that build a cooperation—sometimes with competitors as well as colleagues. Edgell's concept of coopetition, discussed in Chapter 15, captures the value of partnership in a unique way.

Product Branding

A fundamental concept in traditional marketing is that of the product **brand:** "a distinguishing name and/or a symbol (such as a logo, trademark, or package design) intended to identify the goods or services of one seller, or groups of sellers, and to differentiate those goods or services from competitors who would attempt to provide products that appear to be identical."[4]

---

[4]D. A. Aaker, *Managing Brand Equity: Capitalizing on the Value of a Brand Name*, New York: Free Press, 1991.

"Virginia Is for Lovers" is a destination branding tagline that has proven to be very succesful, demonstrating the value of sticking with a successful theme over the long term. *Photo courtesy of Washington, D.C., and the Capital Region, USA.*

Recently, tourism marketers have been attempting to "brand" their destinations. While the approach has considerable potential, the transference of its application from traditional products and services to the tourism setting is not without its difficulties.

One particularly useful transference of branding from products to tourism destinations postulates that "place branding" performs four main functions.[5] First, destination brands serve as "communicators," where brands represent a mark of ownership and a means of destination differentiation that is manifested in legally protected names, logos, and trademarks. Second, they provide an image for the destinations, which is characterized by a set of associations or attributes to which consumers attach personal value. Third, brands serve as "value enhancers" that create brand equity for the destination in the form of improved streams of future income. Finally, a destination brand can be viewed as possessing a personality that enables it to form a relationship with the visitor.

---

[5]Graham Hankinson, "Relational Network Brands: Towards a Conceptual Model of Place Brands." *Journal of Vacation Marketing*, Vol.10, No. 2, pp. 109–121, 2004.

Product Planning and Development

The objective of most firms is to develop a profitable and continuing business. To achieve this objective, companies must provide products and services that satisfy consumer needs, thereby assuring themselves of repeat business. **Product planning** is an essential component in developing a profitable, continuing business and has frequently been referred to as the "five rights"—planning to have the right product, at the right place, at the right time, at the right price, in the right quantities.

A product is much more than a combination of raw materials. It is actually a bundle of satisfactions and benefits for the consumer. Product planning must therefore be approached from the consumer's point of view. Creating the right service or product is not easy: Consumer needs, wants, and desires are constantly changing, and competitive forces typically carry products through a **life cycle,** so that a product that is successful at one point declines and "dies" at a later time.

Figure 19.1 shows the phases that a new product goes through from inception to decline: (1) introduction, (2) growth, (3) maturity, (4) saturation, and (5) decline. Because of the rapidly changing consumer lifestyles and technological changes, the life cycle for products and services has become shorter, but the product life cycle remains a useful concept for strategic planning. Each stage of the product life cycle has certain marketing requirements.

Introduction
The introductory phase of the product's life cycle requires high promotional expenditures and visibility (the most productive time to advertise a product or

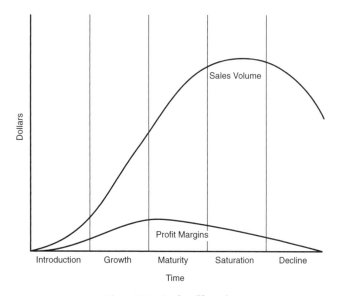

Figure 19.1   Product life cycle.

service is when it is new). Operations in this period are characterized by high cost, relatively low sales volume, and an advertising program aimed at stimulating primary demand; in this stage of the life cycle, there will be a high percentage of failures.

Growth

In the growth period, the product or service is being accepted by consumers. Market acceptance means that both sales and profits rise at a rapid rate, frequently making the market attractive to competitors. Promotional expenditures remain high, but the promotional emphasis is on selective buying motives by trade name rather than on primary motives to try the product. During the growth stage, the number of outlets handling the product or service usually increases. More competitors enter the marketplace, but economies of scale are realized and prices may decline some.

Maturity

The mature product is well established in the marketplace. Sales may still be increasing, but at a much slower rate; they are leveling off. At this stage of the product's life cycle, many outlets are selling the product or service; they are very competitive, especially with respect to price, and firms are trying to determine ways to hold on to their share of the market. The ski resort is an excellent example of a mature product. After years of spectacular growth, sales are now leveling off, and the resorts are looking for ways to hold market share and diversify.

Saturation

In the saturation stage, sales volume reaches its peak: The product or service has penetrated the marketplace to the greatest degree possible. Mass production and new technology have lowered the price to make it available to almost everyone.

Decline

Many products stay at the saturation stage for years. However, for most products, obsolescence sets in, and new products are introduced to replace old ones. In the decline stage, demand obviously drops, advertising expenditures are lower, and there is usually a smaller number of competitors. While it is possible for a product to do very well in this stage of the product life cycle, there is not a great deal of comfort in getting a larger share of a declining market. Hot springs resorts are a good example of a tourist product in the decline stage. These facilities, at their peak in the 1920s, are no longer the consumer's idea of an "in" place to go.

Pricing

One of the most important marketing decisions is the **pricing** decision. Price determines how consumers perceive the product and strongly affects other elements of the marketing mix.

Firms have a choice of three strategies in pricing their products. First, they may decide to sell their product at the market price, which is the same price that everyone else charges. They then compete on nonprice terms. Selling at a price equal to competitors' tends to prevent price cutting and protect margins, and customers are not driven away by price. However, because there is no price individuality, there can be no price demand stimulation.

Second, firms may decide to price below the current market price. Firms that adopt such a discount policy are trying to create the reputation of having the lowest prices and underselling all competitors. To be successful, such firms must make sure that demand is elastic; otherwise, they will gain only at the expense of their competitors and start a price war. This pricing strategy is more successful when it is based on the elimination of services. Motel 6, for example, took its name from its original $6-a-night charge and built its network on a no-frills philosophy. Today it is one of the top budget chains in the United States.

The third approach is to charge above-market prices. Premium pricing strategy must be coupled with the best service in the industry and other features and amenities to make this higher price attractive. Such an approach emphasizes quality, which many consumers think is a function of price; provides higher margins; generates more revenue for promotion; and makes better service possible. However, premium pricing reduces volume, raises overhead costs, and encourages substitution. Nevertheless, numerous tourism firms successfully use this approach, including the Ritz-Carlton (winner of the U.S. Malcolm Baldrige National Quality Award in 1992 and 1999), Fairmont, Hyatt, Marriott, and Westin hotels.

Some firms choose to employ two or three pricing strategies and develop a product to appeal to consumers in each market segment. The lodging industry began employing this strategy in the last decade. Ramada, Choice, Marriott, Hilton, and others have developed products to appeal to a broad range of market segments.

The tourism marketing manager must consider the following factors that influence price policies.

Southwest Airlines is well known for its low airfares, but they also have a reputation for going out of their way to deliver fun service to keep customers happy. *Photo courtesy of Southwest Airlines.*

1. **Product quality.** The quality of the product really determines the price-value relationship. It is common sense that a product that offers greater utility and fills more consumer needs than a competitive product can command a higher price.

2. **Product distinctiveness.** A staple or standard product with no distinctive features offers little or no opportunity for price control. However, a novel and different product may be able to command higher prices. The Hyatt Corporation, for example, features lobby atriums; this attractive novelty combined with excellent service and facilities makes it possible for the Hyatt Hotels to command higher prices.

3. **Extent of the competition.** A product that is comparable to competitors' products must be priced with the competitors' prices in mind. The product's price to some extent determines its position in the market.

4. **Method of distribution.** The price of the product must include adequate margins for tour operators, travel agents, or the company's own sales force.

5. **Character of the market.** It is necessary to consider the type and number of possible consumers. If there is a small number of consumers, then the price must be high enough to compensate for a limited market. However, one must also consider the ability of consumers to buy and their buying habits.

6. **Cost of the product and service.** It should be obvious that price must exceed cost over the long run or else the business will not survive. Both cost and market conditions should serve as guides to pricing.

7. **Cost of distribution.** Distribution costs must also be included in the pricing equation. Unfortunately, in many cases they are much more difficult to estimate than other costs.

8. **Margin of profit desired.** The profit margin built into the price of the product must be more than returns realized on more conventional investments in order to compensate for the risk involved in the enterprise.

9. **Seasonality.** Most tourism products are affected by seasonality because of school-year patterns and vacation habits; consequently, the seasonal aspects must be considered in developing prices.

10. **Special promotional prices.** Many times it is good strategy to offer introductory prices and special one-time price offers to acquaint consumers with your product. However, these must be carefully planned so that they fill the proper intent and do not become a regular discount price.

11. **Psychological considerations.** Throughout our economy we see psychological pricing employed, usually using prices that are set in odd amounts such as 19¢, 99¢, $19.95, or $29.99. Consumers respond well to odd pricing, and there seems to be something particularly magical about prices that end in nine.

Price Skimming

When a new product or service is introduced, two pricing philosophies prevail: **price skimming** and **penetration pricing.** A price-skimming strategy sets the price as high as possible. No attempt is made to appeal to the entire market. The price is set to appeal only to the top of the market; consequently, this approach is frequently called skimming the cream. The strategy is to sell the product to as many consumers as possible at this price level; then, as either buyer resistance or direct competition develops, the seller will lower prices step by step. This approach typically results in higher profits and more rapid repayment of development and promotion costs. It also tends to invite competition. Skimming is appropriate when the product or service has the following characteristics: (1) price inelasticity, (2) no close substitutes, (3) high promotion elasticity, and (4) distinct market segments based on price.

Penetration Pricing

The opposite approach to price skimming is market penetration, in which the seller attempts to establish the price of the product as low as possible to penetrate the market as completely as possible. A low price makes the product available to as many income levels as possible, and the sellers are likely to establish a large market share quickly. When penetration pricing is used, this introductory price tends to become the permanent price of the product. It results in a slower recovery of fixed costs and requires a greater volume to break even. The factors that would recommend a penetration-pricing approach would be: (1) high price elasticity, (2) large savings from high-volume production (economies of scale), and (3) an easy fit of the product into consumer purchasing patterns.

Place (Distribution)

Another difficult decision for the marketing manager concerns what distribution channel or channels will be used. The distribution decisions affect the other elements of the marketing mix, and in the best marketing mix all aspects will be compatible with one another. Chapter 7 contains a description of the travel distribution system.

Channels of distribution are selected by: (1) analyzing the product, (2) determining the nature and extent of the market, (3) analyzing the channels by sales, costs, and profits, (4) determining the cooperation you can expect from the channel, (5) determining the assistance you will have to give to the channel, and (6) determining the number of outlets to be used. For example, if you want intensive distribution, exposing your product to maximum sale, you will use many travel agents. In contrast, with an exclusive distribution policy, you would sell your product through one or a few agents who would have the sole right to sell your product or service in a given area.

Promotion

The aim of **promotion** activities is to create demand for a product or service. *Promotion* is a broad term that includes advertising, personal selling, public relations, publicity, and sales promotion activities such as familiarization tours, giveaways, trade shows, point of purchase, and store displays.

To sell the product, it is necessary to: (1) attract attention, (2) create interest, (3) create a desire, and (4) get action. Either personal selling or advertising can carry out all of these steps in the selling process; however, the two used together tend to be much more powerful. Advertising is ideally suited to attract attention and create interest in the products and services. Personal selling is best suited to creating desire and conviction on the part of the customer and to closing the sale. Advertising and personal selling are even more effective when supplemented by publicity and sales promotion activities. Familiarization tours (or "famtours," as they are commonly called) are a form of promotion of particular importance in the travel industry. Travel agents and other persons who influence travel decisions are invited on a "famtour" in order to become more knowledgeable about the destination.

Advertising

Advertising has been defined as any nonpersonal presentation of goods, ideas, or services by an identified sponsor. In travel marketing, these paid public messages are designed to describe or present a destination area in such a way as to attract consumers. This can be done through the use of the major advertising media such as newspapers, magazines, direct mail, television, outdoor, or radio. Effective advertising gains the attention of the prospective visitor, holds the attention so the message can be communicated, and makes a lasting positive impression on the prospect's mind.

Each advertising medium has advantages and disadvantages. A key decision in developing promotional strategy is to select the right medium to maximize advertising expenditure. To assist in media selection, turn to Standard Rate and Data Service (SRDS), 1700 Higgins Road, Des Plaines, IL 60018. SRDS publications contain advertising rates and other media information required to make intelligent decisions. The advantages and disadvantages of the major media are as follows.

Newspapers

Newspapers give comprehensive coverage of a local market area, are lower in cost than other media, are published frequently, are flexible (short lead time) and timely, have a wide audience, and get a quick response. Most newspapers have travel sections. The major disadvantages are low printing quality and short life.

Direct Mail

Although mail costs have increased rapidly, direct mail is one of the most important advertising methods for tourism enterprises. It is the most personal and selective of all the media; consequently, it is the most effective medium in minimizing waste circulation. Direct mail gets the message directly to the consumers that one wishes to contact. Direct-mail advertising is self-testing when it asks for a response.

The critical problem with direct mail is obtaining and maintaining the right mailing lists. Many types of lists are commercially available through firms specializing in this activity. (One source of such information is Standard Rate and Data Service.)

For the tourism industry, previous visitors comprise the most important mailing-list sources. However, names and addresses must be correct, and the lists must be kept in ready-to-use form, such as address plates or on a computer. Other good sources of prospects are the inquiry lists.

Internet

Although a relatively recent arrival on the advertising scene, Web sites have very rapidly established themselves as one of the most pervasive and most powerful means of directly communicating with individuals in the marketplace. They are particularly valuable to small and medium-size tourism operators, who in the past had difficulty conveying information regarding their products and services to their many potential customers. Care must be taken, however, to ensure a well-designed Web site. Because of the ease of access to Web sites, many firms assume that a simple listing of products and services is adequate. This is far from true. The growing sophistication of Web site marketers means that both innovation and functionality must be carefully built into a Web site for it to be successful.

Frontier Airlines, a regional low-cost carrier headquartered in Denver, provides an excellent case study on creative advertising and branding. Frontier's planes are unique in that they have animals painted on their tails. With this part of branding in place, Frontier launched an advertising campaign focusing on Frontier being "a whole different animal." The multimedia campaign covers TV, radio, print, and the Web. The constant message of Frontier is: Affordable fares; newer, more comfortable planes; wider seats; expanded legroom; and DIRECTV service. Try the airline with the animals on its tails. *Ad courtesy of Frontier Airlines.*

Television

Television presents both an audio and a visual message and comes as close to approximating personal selling as a mass medium can. Television requires minimal exertion on the part of listeners and is very versatile. However, television is not a flexible medium; commercials have a short life; and advertising on television is expensive relative to the costs of using other media. Nevertheless, despite television's expense, many destinations are using television and finding it very cost effective.

Magazines

The major advantage of magazines is their print and graphic quality. Other advantages are secondary readership, long life, prestige, and favorable cost per thousand circulation. Many special-interest magazines reach specialized market segments effectively, making it possible to target markets. Regional editions allow further selectivity, with a minimum of waste circulation. Some of the unfavorable characteristics of magazines are that they require long lead times and that changes cannot be made readily. Magazines also reach the market less frequently than do newspapers, radio, and television.

Radio

Radio has the advantage of outstanding flexibility and relatively low cost. While the warmth of the human voice adds a personal touch to the selling message, radio has the disadvantage that it presents only an audio message. Tourists driving in their automobiles are typically radio listeners, and many attractions find radio an excellent medium.

Outdoor Advertising

Outdoor advertising has been used with great success by many tourism organizations. It is a flexible, low-cost medium that reaches virtually the whole population. It has made the Wall Drug Store in Wall, South Dakota, world famous. Outdoor advertising has the disadvantage that the message must be short; however, it does reach travelers. An additional problem is highway signing laws, which are making it more difficult to advertise tourism attractions.

Using an Advertising Agency

While promotion managers must know the fundamentals of marketing, advertising, personal selling, and public relations, the specialized skill and experience of an **advertising agency** can greatly increase business—and can do it profitably. An advertising agency will do the following:

This outdoor sign at Ayers Rock Resort in Australia features the resort's logo, reinforcing a branded image in the consumer's mind. *Photo by the author.*

1. Work with ideas in copy and layout. *Copy* is the term used to describe written messages; *layout* refers to the arrangement of copy, art, and pictures.
2. Advise on the choice of media to convey advertising messages, devising an organized and carefully worked-out plan using newspapers, magazines, radio, TV, guidebooks, posters, direct mail, postcards, folders, or other advertising media.
3. Conduct market analysis and research so that advertising efforts can be directed to the best prospects.
4. Assist in planning and carrying out a public relations program.

The advertising program must be planned objectively by setting forth specific, achievable goals. The advertising agency can help to establish such goals. When seeking the services of an advertising agency, look at the agency's experience in promoting tourism, and check the agency's past advertising campaigns and clients to determine the campaign's effectiveness.

The Advertising Budget

No magic formula exists for setting the advertising budget. How much to spend is always a perplexing question. Commonly used methods include a percentage of last year's sales, a percentage of potential sales, or the industry percentage. These methods are all flawed because advertising should create sales and cause things to happen, not react to what has happened in the past or in other companies. Consequently, the best method of setting advertising budgets is to determine the objectives to be performed and allocate the proper amount to reach these objectives.

Promoting a new tourist destination area will require more money than will promoting one with an established clientele. The specific amount to budget for advertising and sales promotion will depend on each situation. However, as a general rule, most resorts spend about 3 percent of sales on media advertising and about 3 percent on other sales promotion activities.

No matter what expenditures are, efforts should be made to coordinate the promotion program so it is consistent with the product offered and consumer expectations will be met. Word of mouth is the least expensive, most convincing form of personal advertising. A friendly and capable host encourages this type of communication. Visitors who are treated as very important persons will not only come back, they will recommend the area to their friends. All facilities, services, hospitality, and pricing policies must be directed to this one goal—a happy, satisfied visitor.

Research

Successful tourism marketing depends in large part on research. Tourism promotion efforts undirected by research are largely wasted effort. Unless the following characteristics are known, advertising expenditures cannot be productive.

1. Who are the present visitors, and where do they live?
2. What do you know about their likes and dislikes?
3. Who are your potential customers, and where do they live?
4. What are their travel and vacation preferences and interests?

5. What are your visitors' travel destination preferences?
6. What are your visitors' preferences for shopping and entertainment?
7. What is your competitive situation?
8. What are the trends in competition?
9. What are the likely future trends in your share of the market?
10. What are the prospects for increasing demand for your area?
11. What kind(s) of marketing program(s) do you need?
12. How will these programs be implemented?

Carefully review questions of this kind; adequate answers to them are obtained only through research.

Market research can be classified into three main categories: geographic market orientation (where present and potential visitors reside), demographic market orientation (age, sex, levels of education, income, population distribution, family status, and similar data), and psychographic market orientation (motivations, interest, hobbies, responsiveness to advertising, and propensity to travel). Guidance of the subsequent marketing program will rest largely on the results of such research, and the success of the marketing upon the adequacy of the research. See Chapter 18 for methods of conducting tourism research.

Personal Selling

Personal selling is the most-used and oldest method of creating demand. Because it is adaptable to the prospect, it is the most compelling and effective type of selling. In contrast to advertising, which is the impersonal component in the promotional mix, personal selling consists of individual, personal communication. The U.S. economy depends on salespeople; there are over 13 million people working in sales compared to about 500,000 working in advertising. In many companies, personal selling is the largest operating expense item, ranging from about 8 to 15 percent of sales. Expenditures for salespeoples' compensation, expenses, training, and supervision and the cost of operating sales offices make management of the sales force an important task.

Personal selling is so widely used because it offers maximum flexibility. Sales representatives tailor their presentation to each individual customer. They can tell which approaches are working and which are not and adjust accordingly. Prospects can be identified so target market customers are approached and efforts are not wasted.

Counterbalancing these advantages is the fact that personal selling is the most expensive means of making contact with prospects, and productivity gains are unlikely. Another limitation is that it is not always possible to hire the caliber of person needed for the sales job.

Because of the importance of personal selling, all staff should be sales-minded. They must be trained to offer sales suggestions to prospects when opportunities present themselves. This includes expert selling on the telephone; the telephone

The Avis "Preferred Service" is but one part of the firm's marketing programs built on their very successful slogan, "We try harder." This photo shows an Avis employee putting the marketing program into action. *Photo courtesy of Cendant Car Rental Group.*

receptionist, for example, can create a favorable image for a resort. Inquiries can often be the opening for a polite and skillful sales effort. Obviously, an unfriendly manner can discourage customers and sales.

Public Relations

Public relations may be defined as an attitude—a "social conscience" that places first priority on the public interest when making any decisions. Public relations permeate an entire organization, covering relations with many publics: visitors, the community, employees, and suppliers.

Acceptance of any tourist destination by the public is of utmost importance. No business is more concerned with human relations than is tourism, and all public interests must be served. Serving one group at the expense of another is not sound public relations. Furthermore, each individual business manager and the group he or she represents must be respected and have the confidence of the community. There is no difference between a personal reputation and a business reputation.

Favorable public relations within the firm emphasize respect for people. Employees must have reasonable security in their jobs and be treated with consideration. Externally, tourism employees have a powerful influence on the public as they represent the owners in the public's eye. Employees should be trained to be courteous, respectful, and helpful to guests. Little things make a big difference, and the attitude of employees can make or break a public relations effort.

Considerations for the public relations effort include being aware of public attitudes toward present policies; ask some of the visitors for feedback. Communication is the lifeblood of good relations. In publicizing the firm, first do good things and then tell the public about them. Above all, give the public factual information about your area. False information is detrimental; you must describe conditions as they exist.

Service Quality

Service quality is the customers' perception of the service component of a product. Service quality is an important element of the marketing mix and in building and delivering a competitive advantage in tourism.

Outstanding service quality leads to customer satisfaction, which leads to repeat business. Customer satisfaction and loyalty are the keys to repeat business and long-term profitability. Keeping customers satisfied is everybody's job in an organization. Employees should strive to exceed customer expectations.

Since in tourism, there are many service transactions over the course of a trip, or a vacation, it is increasingly useful to introduce the concept of the quality of the experience (QOE) in tourism—where the tourism experience consists of a complex chain of service transactions and visitor participation in a broad range of activities and events. Using this framework, the goal of the tourism managers is to provide the visitor with a holistic combination of services, activities, and events from which he/she derives a high level of satisfaction.

Unfortunately, because the experience chain involves such a diverse mix of services, activities, and events, a great number of the links in the chain are outside of the control—or even the influence—of any single manager. As such, it is important to develop management structures and processes that can assist in coordinating and enhancing the quality of the various services, activities, and events of the experience chain. It is here where the Destination Management Organization (DMO) plays a critical role.

Internet Marketing

The **Internet** has become pervasive in tourism marketing today. It is being used by the tourism industry to perform multiple tasks and impact a number of areas of the marketing mix. Direct e-mail marketing, advertising, customer service, relationship marketing, providing information, distribution and sales, and research are all tasks being performed by the Internet. The Internet provides the same capabilities found in direct mail and telemarketing, it provides a new advertising medium, it can provide interaction with the customer, and it has the ability to deliver a message 24 hours a day, 7 days a week, 365 days a year. A large segment of consumers are looking to the Internet for information, research, trip planning, and even booking trips; therefore, the Internet will continue to grow as an important marketing tool.

MARKET SEGMENTATION

The strategy of **market segmentation** recognizes that few vacation destination areas are universally acceptable and desired. Therefore, rather than dissipate promotion resources by trying to please all travelers, you should aim the promotional efforts specifically to the wants and needs of likely prospects. One of the early steps in marketing tourism, then, is to divide the present and potential market on the basis of meaningful characteristics and concentrate promotion, product, and pricing efforts on serving the most prominent portions of the market—the target markets.

An effective market strategy will determine exactly what the target markets will be and attempt to reach only those markets. The target market is that segment of a total potential market to which the tourism attraction would be most salable. Target markets are defined geographically, demographically (age, income, education, race, nationality, family size, family life cycle, gender, religion, occupation), or psychographically (values, motivations, interests, attitudes, desires) (see Figure 19.2).

Once target markets have been determined, appropriate media are chosen to reach these markets. For example, if tennis players are a target market, advertising in tennis magazines would give comprehensive coverage of this market. This "rifle approach" allows you to zero in exactly on the market in which you are interested. In contrast, a "shotgun approach" would be to advertise in *Time* magazine, which would reach only a small number of your target market and result in large waste circulation.

Market segmentation must be employed in the marketing programs if a shotgun approach is to be avoided. Every tourism attraction can appeal to a multitude of market segments, and market segments can overlap a great deal. The marketing manager must look at market segments and determine which ones offer the most promising potential for his or her services. An excellent example of target marketing to a particular segment is provided by Courtyard by Marriott. The moderate price and attractive rooms were designed to appeal to the business traveler. Marriott has been very successful in attracting this market segment.

Tourist resorts typically segment in a variety of ways. One of the most common is geographic. Here, the segments tend to be destination visitors (those visitors traveling long distances to vacation at the resort), regional visitors (those who live within the region of the resort and can arrive within four hours' driving time), and local residents.

Proximity of the destination area to the market is an important factor. Generally, the nearer the tourist destination is to its major market, the more likely

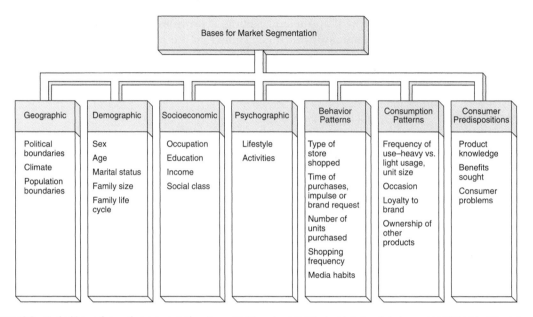

Figure 19.2   Typical bases for market segmentation. *Source: W. Zikmund and M. D'Amico,* Marketing, *3rd ed., copyright ©1984, John Wiley & Sons, Inc., New York; adapted by permission of Prentice-Hall, Englewood Cliffs, N.J., from Philip Kotler,* Principles of Marketing, *copyright ©1980, p. 297.*

it is to attract large numbers of visitors. For example, Bob-Lo Island is just a few miles from Detroit and may be reached by excursion boat. As might be expected, this vacation destination receives many times the number of visitors from the greater Detroit area than does Bermuda or the Bahamas.

It follows, then, that the prime target area for promotion of any given tourist destination area will be that area of greatest population density nearest the vacation area. In the United States, the best concentration of markets for tourism promotion are the metropolitan statistical areas (MSAs), formerly called standard metropolitan statistical areas (SMSAs). These are defined by the U.S. Bureau of the Census as a county or group of contiguous counties containing at least one city of fifty thousand inhabitants or more. An authoritative source of market data concerning these areas is found in the *Survey of Buying Power* published by *Sales and Marketing Management Magazine,* 770 Broadway, New York, NY 10003.

Demographics also provide good segmentation variables. Demographics are the social statistics of our society. Age groups are an excellent example.

Psychographic Market Segmentation

Several models have been developed to classify people according to **psychographic** types. One such early model was developed by Stanley C. Plog, who classified the

Camp Carnival kid's program features morning-till-night activities. These guests are obviously taking advantage and enjoying the many facilities available. Carnival is successfully appealing to the families-with-children market. *Photo courtesy of Carnival Cruise Lines.*

U.S. population along a psychographic continuum, ranging from the psychocentric at one extreme to the allocentric at the other.[6]

The term **psychocentric** is derived from *psyche-* or *self-*centered, meaning the centering of one's thought or concerns on the small problem areas of one's life. Such a person tends to be self-inhibited and nonadventuresome. **Allocentric,** on the other hand, derives from the root word *allo,* meaning "varied in form." An allocentric person is thus one whose interest patterns are focused on varied activities. Such a person is outgoing and self-confident and is characterized by a considerable degree of adventure and a willingness to reach out and experiment with life. Travel becomes a way for the allocentric to express inquisitiveness and satisfy curiosity. Table 19.1 shows personality and travel characteristics of psychocentrics and allocentrics.

---

[6]Stanley C. Plog, "Why Destination Areas Rise and Fall in Popularity," *Cornell Hotel and Restaurant Administration Quarterly,* Vol. 14, No. 4 pp. 55–58, February 1974; Stanley C. Plog, *Leisure Travel: Making It a Growth Market . . . Again!* (New York: Wiley, 1991); and Stanley C. Plog, "Why Destination Areas Rise and Fall in Popularity," *Cornell Hotel and Restaurant Administration Quarterly,* Vol. 42, No. 3 pp. 13–24, June 2001.

TABLE 19.1	PERSONALITY AND TRAVEL-RELATED CHARACTERISTICS OF PSYCHOCENTRICS AND ALLOCENTRICS	
PYCHOCENTRICS/"DEPENDABLES"	**ALLOCENTRICS/"VENTURERS"**
Intellectually restricted	Intellectually curious
Low risk-taking	Moderate risk-taking
Withhold income	Use disposable income
Use well-known brands	Try new products
Territory bound	Exploring/searching
Sense of powerlessness	Feel in control
Free-floating anxiety/nervousness	Relatively anxiety-free
Nonactive lifestyle	Interested/involved
Nonadventurous	Adventurous
Lacking in confidence	Self-confident
Prefer the familiar in travel destination	Prefer nontouristy areas
Like commonplace activities at travel destinations	Enjoy sense of discovery and delight in new experiences, before others have visited the area
Prefer sun-and-fun spots, including considerable relaxation	Prefer novel and different destinations
Low activity level	High activity level
Prefer destinations they can drive to	Prefer flying to destinations
Prefer heavy tourist development (lots of hotels, family-type restaurants, tourist shops, etc.)	Tour accommodations should include adequate-to-good hotels and food, not necessarily modern or chain-type hotels, and few "tourist-type" attractions
Prefer familiar atmosphere (hamburger stands, familiar-type entertainment, absence of foreign atmosphere)	Enjoy meeting and dealing with people from a strange or foreign culture
Complete tour packaging appropriate, with heavy scheduling of activities	Tour arrangements should include basics (transportation and hotels) and allow considerable freedom and flexibility
Travel less	Travel more frequently
Spend more of income on material goods and impulse buys	Spend more of income on travel
Little interest in events or activities in other countries	Inquisitive, curious about the world and its peoples
Naive, nondemanding, passive traveler	Demanding, sophisticated, active traveler
Want structured, routinized travel	Want much spontaneity in trips
Expect foreigners to speak in English	Will learn language or foreign phrases before and during travels
Want standard accommodations and conventional (American) meals	Seek off-the-beaten-path, little-known local hotels, restaurants
Buy souvenirs, trinkets, common items	Buy native arts/crafts
Prefer returning to same and familiar places	Want different destinations for each trip
Enjoy crowds	Prefer small numbers of people

Source: Stanley C. Plog. *Leisure Travel: Making It a Growth Market . . . Again!,* New York: Wiley, 1991.

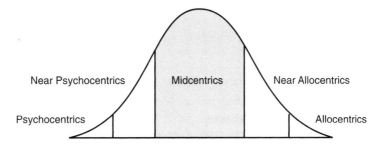

Figure 19.3 **U.S. population distribution by psychographic type.** *Source: Stanley C. Plog, "Why Destinations Areas Rise and Fall in Popularity." Cornell Hotel and Restaurant Administration Quarterly No. 3, pp. 13–24, June 2001.*

Plog modified his model of destination preferences based on more recent research (1995).[7] According to Plog's findings, *Dependables* prefer a life that is more structured, stable, and predictable. These individuals would rather follow a set pattern or routine in order to be able to plan their lives. *Venturers* tend to go more places more often. Leisure travel occupies a central place in their lives, and they eagerly seek out new, exotic, and/or unknown places. Venturers are more likely to fly to their destinations, and they shun guided tours in favor of exploration. *Centrics* comprise the largest group, as one would expect. It is easier to move Centrics, because they possess characteristics of both Dependables and Venturers, and they tend to react favorably to destinations, activities, and events that appeal to travelers on either end of the lifestyle continuum. Both Plog's early work and current work is summarized here.

Plog found that the U.S. population was normally distributed along a continuum between these two extreme types. This is illustrated in Figure 19.3. Other groups have been identified between the allocentrics and psychocentrics. Most people fall in the midcentric classification.

A new dimension was added with the establishment of an energy versus lethargy scale. It was determined that this dimension was not correlated, making it possible to place individuals into four quadrants based on how they scored on the two scales. The four quadrants were high-energy allocentrics, low-energy allocentrics, high-energy psychocentrics, and low-energy psychocentrics. High-energy allocentrics have an insatiable desire to be active on trips, exploring and learning what is new and exciting at a destination. Low-energy allocentrics would travel at a more leisurely pace, be more intellectual, and delve into culture, history, and local customs. At the other end of the continuum, the low-energy psychocentrics were most likely to stay at home.

Through further research, Plog identified the travel preferences of psychocentrics and allocentrics. These are summarized in Figure 19.4. In studying the population on the basis of income level, Plog discovered another interesting relationship. At the lower end of the income spectrum, he discovered a heavy loading of psychocentrics.

---

[7]Stanley C. Plog, *Vacation Places Rated*, Redondo Beach, CA: Fielding Worldwide, Inc., 1995.

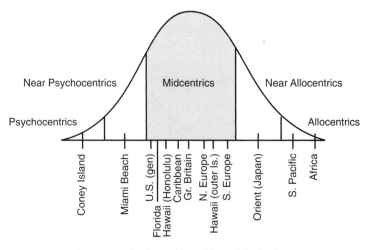

Figure 19.4   Psychographic positions of destinations.

People at the upper end of the income levels were found to be predominantly allocentric. However, for the broad spectrum in between—for most of America—interrelations are only slightly positive. This finding has several implications.

It is evident that at extremely low levels of family income, travel patterns may be determined largely by the income constraints. Regardless of the psychographic type, a person at the low end of the income spectrum may be compelled to take what Plog considers to be psychocentric-type vacations. College students are a good example of this. They may be allocentric by nature but cannot afford an allocentric-type vacation because such vacations are generally very expensive (a trip to Antarctica or a mountain-climbing expedition in Nepal). They travel, instead, to nearby destinations, spend less money, and participate in familiar activities. Therefore, it may be erroneous to conclude that a person with a low income is likely to be psychocentric. The severe income constraint may distort the person's classification in terms of psychographics.

Having defined types of destinations and types of tourists, one is tempted to link these two classifications directly, as Plog has done. Plog superimposed a list of destinations on the population distribution curve, suggesting that allocentrics would travel to such destinations as Africa or the Orient. Psychocentrics, on the other hand, would vacation in nearby destinations (such as Cedar Point theme park for a psychocentric from Toledo, Ohio). The intervening psychocentric types are similarly identified with particular destinations (refer to Figure 19.4).

Such a direct linkage between the classification of tourists and of destinations does not consider the important fact that people travel with different motivations on different occasions. A wealthy allocentric may indeed travel to Africa on an annual vacation, but may also take weekend trips to a typically psychocentric destination during other times of the year. Similarly, though probably not as likely, psychocentrics could conceivably vacation in essentially allocentric destinations (with the exception of people with extremely low incomes). For instance, a psychocentric may travel to a remote area under the security provided by traveling with a group of similar tourists, which, being escorted at all times, may persuade a psychocentric to travel, say, to Asia.

What, then, is the link between the types of tourists and the types of destinations? To develop such a linkage, which will provide a method for predicting travel patterns, two things must be realized. First, as already pointed out, a tourist may travel for different reasons from one trip to the next. Second, a given destination can provide a variety of travel experiences, suitable to a wide range of tourists, depending on the manner in which the trip is planned. The only way in which a systematic linkage can be developed between the types of destinations and the types of tourists is to consider each trip in isolation and examine the motivations that have prompted the trip.

Plog first developed his model in 1972, over thirty years ago, and it has been widely cited in tourism literature since that time. It was one of

Couples on a honeymoon or celebrating an anniversary remain a popular target market for resorts and cruise lines, which have developed marketing campaigns promoting the romance of travel and the thrill of visiting exotic destinations. *Photo courtesy of Carnival Cruise Lines.*

the first attempts to provide a framework within which to analyze tourist behavior. The world has changed considerably since Plog introduced his model. For example, today there are fewer countries that are considered exotic. Also, there are now other ways to look at tourists, such as through lifestyle analysis or benefit segmentation. Plog's pioneering efforts, however, should not be overlooked. His model still provides a way to examine travel and think about developments using current market conditions.

MARKETING PLANNING: THE TOURISM MARKETING PLAN

To this point, the chapter has examined a broad range of fundamental marketing concepts and attempted to give selected examples of their utilization in a tourism context.

In order to make these concepts truly valuable from a tourism standpoint, they must be applied in a comprehensive, integrated manner. The process of application is known as **marketing planning.** The end result of this process is the marketing plan.

The **marketing plan** for a destination or firm is one of the most important working documents that exists. It serves to translate the many ideals of tourism policy into an active process for attracting visitors and providing the range of experiences they seek from a destination.

The California Tourism Marketing Plan

While tourism marketing plans can take different forms, an exemplary state tourism office plan is that of California. Their operational plan was first created in 1998 following the passage of the California Tourism Policy Act and has been updated annually because marketing plans are by nature "living" documents that change over time. The California plan conveys good comprehensive marketing planning.

One of the distinctive characteristics of the California Tourism Marketing Plan (CTMP) is the fact that it actually flows from a policy framework. The California Tourism Policy Act (CTPA) first provides a philosophical foundation for tourism development and marketing in one of the most significant tourism destinations in the world. It subsequently asserts the need for an effective marketing program (CTMP) to realize the ideals and goals of its philosophical foundation. Furthermore, it also sets out an organizational policy (in the form of the California Travel and Tourism Commission) to support implementation of its marketing goals. Finally, it takes the all-important step of providing for a funding policy (private assessments) to support the operations of the commission. To examine the California Tourism Marketing Plan and the California Policy Act, go to **http://www.gocalif.ca.gov** and in the search feature type "marketing plan" or "policy act."

JOINT MARKETING EFFORTS

In the majority of cases, a tourism organization will want to market its product and services individually; however, in other cases, joint cooperative efforts will be the most profitable. Typically, these efforts are launched through associations or government agencies. Colorado Ski Country USA and the Utah Ski and Snowboard Association are groups that jointly promote the services of their members, many of whom are in competition with each other. Publishing posters and directories, answering inquiries, and providing snow reports promote the industry in the most cost-effective way. In addition to these joint marketing efforts, the areas have their own individual marketing programs. They may also work with other private firms such as airlines, rental car companies, and credit card firms to stretch their marketing dollars.

Experience to date has shown that tourism promotion on a country or state basis is best accomplished by a cooperative effort of private industry and government. Joint promotion by private interests and official government tourist organizations is an effective and efficient procedure. One of the examples of the pooling of private and government funds is the Hawaii Visitors and Convention Bureau, an independent nonprofit organization that conducts tourism promotion under contract with the Hawaii Tourism Authority (HTA).

In some states, specific "matching funds" are provided by a government tourism agency for tourist promotion, such as the provision of a portion of advertising costs of a private regional tourist promotion association. Various combinations of matched funds are possible, depending on the amount of funds available and the provisions of the legislation that authorizes such expenditures of public funds. The Pennsylvania Tourism, Film, and Economic Development Marketing Office operates one of the largest matching-grants fund programs in the United States.

Private firms also find joint marketing efforts to be profitable. For example, in 2003, Universal Parks and Resorts entered into a ten year marketing partnership with Coca-Cola. The partnership, first made in 1999, designates Atlanta-based Coke as Universal theme parks' official soft drink. The new agreement expands that to include Minute Maid as the parks' official juice. Coca-Cola and Universal plan a cross-brand promotional strategy targeted to teens and young adults as well as themed beverage attractions in Universal's parks.

SUMMARY

Marketing can be defined as the performance of business activities that direct the flow of goods and services from the producer to the consumer or user. Such activities are vital to tourist businesses. The finest, most satisfying tourist facility would be unprofitable without marketing. People have to be informed about a travel destination and become interested in going there before a market can be created.

Basic to the marketing effort are the marketing concept, the marketing mix, product planning and development, pricing, branding, distribution channels, promotion, market research, personal selling, public relations, and market segmentation.

Joint marketing efforts among official tourism organizations, public carriers, and providers of accommodations or even with nearby competing destination areas are strategically sound and typically successful.

A destination and organization's marketing plan defines the approach by which prospective visitors are identified and selectively attracted through promotion and other marketing tools outlined in a destination or organization's marketing plan.

KEY CONCEPTS

advertising	marketing concept	product planning and development
advertising agency	marketing mix	promotion
allocentric	marketing plan	psychocentric
branding	marketing planning	psychographics
channels of distribution	market research	public relations
consumer orientation	place	segmentation
four Ps	pricing	selling
joint marketing efforts	product	Survey of Buying Power
marketing	product life cycle	target market

Internet Sites

The Internet sites mentioned in this chapter are repeated here for convenience, plus some selected additional sites. For more information, visit these sites. Be aware that Internet addresses change frequently, so if a site cannot be accessed, use a search engine. Also use a search engine to locate many additional relevant sites.

Advertising Age
http://www.adage.com

American Marketing Association
http://www.marketingpower.com

Association of Travel Marketing Executives
http://www.atme.org

California Tourism
http://www.gocalif.ca.gov

Chartered Institute of Marketing/ Travel Industry Group (CIMTIG)
http://www.cimtig.org

Journal of Travel and Tourism Marketing
http://www.haworthpressinc.com/ web/JTTM

SRDS Media Solutions
http://www.srds.com

Sales and Marketing Management
http://www.salesandmarketing. com

Internet Exercises

Site Name: Switzerland Tourism
URL: http://www.schweizferien.ch
Background Information: Information regarding tourism in Switzerland.
Site Name: Welcome to Lago di Garda
URL: http://gardalake.it
Background Information: Tourism information on Lake Garda, Italy.

Site Name: Tourism New Zealand
URL: http://www.newzealand.com
Background Information: The Tourism New Zealand Web site is an introduction to tourism in New Zealand and how a visit can be a fantastic experience.
Site Name: Egypt's Tourism Net
URL: http://www.tourism.egypt.net

Background Information: Egypt's Tourism Net provides searchable directories of Egypt's hotels, restaurants, cruise lines, travel agents, transportation companies, and tourist attractions.

Site Name: Queen Victoria Market, Australia

URL: http://www.qvm.com.au

Background Information: The Queen Victoria Market is more than just Melbourne's shopping mecca; it is a historic landmark, a tourist attraction, and an institution for Melbournians.

Site Name: Travel Alaska

URL: http://www.travelalaska.com

Background Information: Travel Alaska provides vacation-planning information.

Site Name: Genuine Nebraska

URL: http://visitnebraska.org

Background Information: This Web site offers extensive, database-driven information about places to go and things to see and do in Nebraska.

Site Name: Wyoming Travel and Tourism

URL: http://www.wyomingtourism.org

Background Information: This guide has been created with one goal: to help you find information about Wyoming quickly and efficiently.

Site Name: Delaware Tourism Office

URL: http://www.visitdelaware.net

Background Information: The official site of the Delaware Tourism Office, with information on visiting Delaware.

Exercises

Choose three state and three international tourism sites from the list above.

1. Which sites have the most powerful marketing concept in each category?
2. What characterizes the sites you have chosen?
3. What marketing concepts do these sites employ?
4. What is your opinion of using the Internet as a channel of distribution for advertising? Why?
5. How do the U.S. sites compare with the international sites?

QUESTIONS FOR REVIEW AND DISCUSSION

1. What is the marketing concept?
2. Do you regard the concept of consumer-oriented marketing as a step forward? Why or why not?
3. What are the stages in a product life cycle? What are the marketing implications of each stage?
4. What are the key factors a tourism marketing manager must consider in setting price?
5. Discuss the conditions when penetration pricing should be used. Price skimming?
6. Discuss how a tourism firm's pricing strategy may influence the promotional program.
7. How are channels of distribution selected? Using an example, explain.
8. How does the branding of a tourism destination differ from the branding of: (a) a tube of toothpaste, (b) an automobile, (c) a computer, (d) a fast-food restaurant, and (e) a hotel?
9. What does branding a tourism destination really mean?
10. The cost of running an ad on the back cover of *Time* magazine is more expensive than is hiring a salesperson for a year. As the marketing manager for a leading hotel chain, you have just been told by the president of the company to eliminate ads and hire more salespeople. You feel that this would be a serious mistake. What would you do to change the president's mind?
11. What are some examples of realistic objectives of a tourism marketing program? Use a resort hotel, a motorcoach company, and a tour company.
12. Explain the statement "tourism promotion efforts undirected by research are largely a waste of effort." Do you agree?
13. What are the advantages of marketing vacation packages?
14. Give an example of a vacation package that might be marketed in your area. How would you market it? To whom?
15. Why is marketing planning so important?
16. What value do you see in market segmentation? Give an example.
17. As the planner of a new wing on your resort hotel, how does product planning and development in a marketing context apply?
18. You are a restaurant manager in a popular year-round resort area. How do you decide on the price levels of your meals?

19. As president of your local convention and visitors bureau, propose a joint marketing scheme that would have surefire results.

20. As a resort hotel manager, would you always advertise your destination area along with your individual resort property? Explain why or why not.

CASE PROBLEM

A Midwest lakeshore community is economically depressed. By 2005, industrial employment had fallen to 50 percent of its 1990 level. Tourism seems to be a logical industry to expand. The county has 25 miles of beautiful Lake Michigan sandy beaches and is adjacent to a 1.5-million-acre national forest. The forest has many fine rivers and inland lakes, offering bountiful year-round recreation. This area is only about a five-hour drive from Chicago or Detroit and has thrice-daily air service from Chicago.

The chamber of commerce has virtually no budget for tourism promotion. State law authorizes an added 2 percent local tourism promotion tax to the 4 percent state rooms tax. However, enacting the added tax must be approved by local lodging establishments. Vote is apportioned by number of rooms owned. Managers of the two larger resorts are in favor of the tax, but they suspect that the many smaller motel owners will not approve the tax. Added tourism is greatly needed to stimulate the local economy. How can this impasse be resolved?

SELECTED REFERENCES

Aaker, D. A. *Managing Brand Equity: Capitalizing on the Value of a Brand Name.* New York: Free Press, 1991.

Abbey, James R. *Hospitality Sales and Advertising,* 4th ed. Lansing, MI: Educational Institute of the American Hotel and Lodging Association, 2003.

Augustyn, Marcjanna, and Samuel K. Ho. "Service Quality and Tourism." *Journal of Travel Research,* Vol. 37, No. 1, pp. 71–75, August 1998.

Berry, Leonard L. *On Great Service: A Framework for Action.* New York: Free Press, 1995.

Bonn, Mark A., and Richard R. Brand. "Identifying Market Potential: The Application of Brand Development Indexing to Pleasure Travel." *Journal of Travel Research,* Vol. 34, No. 2, pp. 31–35, Fall 1995.

Bowen, John, James Makens, and Stowe Shoemaker. *Casino Marketing.* New York: Wiley, 1999.

Bowie, David, and Francis Buttle. *Hospitality Marketing: An Introduction.* Oxford, UK: Butterworth-Heinemann, 2004.

Butterfield, David W., Kenneth R. Deal, and Atif A. Kubursi. "Measuring the Returns to Tourism Advertising." *Journal of Travel Research,* Vol. 37, No. 1, pp. 12–20, August 1998.

Dev, Chekitan S., Saul Klein, and Reed A. Fisher. "A Market-Based Approach for Partner Selection in Marketing Alliances." *Journal of Travel Research,* Vol. 35, No. 1, pp. 11–17, Summer 1996.

Fodness, Dale, and Brian Murray. "A Typology of Tourist Information Search Strategies." *Journal of Travel Research,* Vol. 37, No. 2, pp. 108–119, November 1998.

Fuchs, Matthias, and Klaus Weiermair. "Destination Benchmarking: An Indicator-Systems' Potential for Exploring Guest Satisfaction." *Journal of Travel Research,* Vol. 42, No. 3, pp. 212–225, February 2004.

Hankinson, Graham. "Relational Network Brands: Towards a Conceptual Model of Place Brands." *Journal of Vacation Marketing,* Vol. 10, No. 2, pp. 109–121, 2004.

Harrill, Rich. *Fundamentals of Destination Management and Marketing.* Lansing, MI: Educational Institute of the American Hotel and Lodging Association, 2005.

Heath, Ernie, and Geoffrey Wall. *Marketing Tourism Destinations: A Strategic Planning Approach.* New York: Wiley, 1992.

Holloway, C. J., and C. Robinson. *Marketing for Tourism,* 3d ed. Essex, UK: Longman, 1995.

Horner, S., and J. Swarbrooke. *Marketing Tourism Hospitality and Leisure in Europe.* London: ITBP, 1996.

Hudson, Simon. *Marketing for Tourism and Hospitality: A Canadian Perspective.* Toronto: Thomson/ Nelson, 2005.

Hudson, Simon, Paul Hudson, and Graham A. Miller. "The Measurment of Service Quality in the Tour Operating Sector: A Methodological Comparison." *Journal of Travel Research*, Vol. 42, No. 3, pp. 305–312, February 2004.

Hsu, Cathy, and Tom Powers. *Marketing Hospitality.* New York: Wiley, 2002.

Kotler, Philip, Donald H. Haider, and Irving Rein. *Marketing Places.* New York: Free Press, 1993.

Kotler, Philip, John Bowen, and James Makens. *Marketing for Hospitality and Tourism,* 3d ed. Upper Saddle River, NJ: Prentice Hall, 2003.

Lewis, Robert C. *Cases in Hospitality Marketing and Management,* 2d ed. New York: Wiley, 1997.

Lewis, Robert C., Richard E. Chambers, and Harsha E. Chacko. *Marketing Leadership in Hospitality: Foundations and Practices,* 2d ed. New York: Wiley, 1995.

Lumsdon, I. *Tourism Marketing.* London: ITBP, 1997.

Messmer, Donald J., and Robert R. Johnson. "Inquiry Conversion and Travel Advertising Effectiveness." *Journal of Travel Research*, Vol. 31, No. 4, pp. 14–21, Spring 1993.

Middleton, Victor T. C. and Jackie Clark. *Marketing in Travel and Tourism,* 3d ed. Oxford, UK: Butterworth Heinemann, 2001.

Mill, R. C., and A. M. Morrison. *The Tourism System: An Introductory Text,* 4d ed. Dubuque, IA: Kendall/Hunt, 2002.

Morgan, Nigel, and Annette Pritchard. *Tourism, Promotion, and Power.* New York: Wiley, 1998.

Morgan, Nigel, Annette Pritchard, and Roger Pride. *Destination Branding: Creating the Unique Destination Proposition.* Oxford, UK: Butterworth Heinemann, 2004.

Morrison, Alastair M. *Hospitality and Travel Marketing,* 3d ed. Albany, NY: Thomson Learning, 2002.

Novelli, Marina. *Niche Tourism: Contemporary Issues, Trends, and Cases.* Oxford, UK: Butterworth Heinemann, 2004.

Nykiel, Ronald A. *Marketing in the Hospitality Industry,* 4d ed. Lansing, MI: Educational Institute of the American Hotel and Lodging Association, 2003.

O'Neill, John W. "Effective Municipal and Convention Operations and Marketing Strategies: The Cases of Boston, San Antonio, and San Francisco." *Journal of Travel and Tourism Marketing,* Vol. 7, No. 3, pp. 95–125, 1998.

Otto, Julie E., and J. R. Brent Ritchie. "The Service Experience in Tourism." *Tourism Management,* Vol. 17, No. 3, pp. 165–174, May 1996.

Perdue, Richard R. "Target Market Selection and Marketing Strategy: The Colorado Downhill Skiing Industry." *Journal of Travel Research,* Vol. 34, No. 4, pp. 39–46, Spring 1996.

Petrick, James F. "The Roles of Quality, Values, and Satisfaction in Predicting Cruise Passengers' Behavioral Intentions." *Journal of Travel Research,* Vol. 42, No. 4, pp. 397–407, May 2004.

Plog, Stanley C. *Leisure Travel: A Marketing Handbook.* Upper Saddle River, NJ: Prentice Hall, 2004.

Razo, Ivo. *Heads in Beds: Hospitality and Tourism Marketing.* Upper Saddle River, NJ: Prentice Hall, 2005.

Reich, Allen Z. *Marketing Management for the Hospitality Industry: A Strategic Approach.* New York: Wiley, 1997.

Selin, Steven W., and Nancy A. Myers. "Tourism Marketing Alliances: Member Satisfaction and Effectiveness Attributes of a Regional Initiative." *Journal of Travel and Tourism Marketing,* Vol. 7, No. 3, pp. 79–94, 1998.

Travel Industry Association of America. *Domestic Travel Report.* Washington, DC: TIA, 2004.

Travel Industry Association of America. *Geotourism: The New Trend in Travel.* Washington, DC: TIA, 2003.

Travel Industry Association of America. *The Historical/Cultural Traveler.* Washington, DC: TIA, 2003.

Travel Industry Association of America. *The Minority Traveler.* Washington, DC: TIA, 2003.

Travel Industry Association of America. *The Shopping Traveler.* Washington, DC: TIA, 2001.

Vladimir, Andy, and Bob Dickinson. *The Complete 21st Century Travel Marketing Handbook.* Upper Saddle River, NJ: Prentice Hall, 2005.

Walle, A. H. "Tourism and the Internet: Opportunities for Direct Marketing." *Journal of Travel Research,* Vol. 35, No. 1, pp. 72–77, Summer 1996.

Williams, Anna Graf. *Hospitality Cases in Marketing and Operations.* Upper Saddle River, NJ: Prentice Hall, 1997.

Williams, Peter, Alison Gill, and Neil Chura. "Branding Mountain Destinations: The Battle for

'Placefulness.' " *Tourism Review,* Vol. 59, No. 1, pp. 6–15, 2004.

Woodside, Arch G. "Measuring Advertising Effectiveness in Destination Marketing Strategies." *Journal of Travel Research,* Vol. 29, No. 2, pp. 3–8, Fall 1990.

World Tourism Organization. *Shining in the Media Spotlight: A Communications Handbook for Tourism Professionals.* Madrid: WTO, 2002.

World Tourism Organization. *Tourism Market Trends: The World.* Madrid: WTO, 2002.

PART 6

Tourism Prospects

A mariachi band entertains visitors to Mexico City. *Photo courtesy of the Mexican Government Tourism Office.*

TOURISM'S FUTURE

CHAPTER **20**

Learning Objectives

- Examine forecasts concerning the growth of international tourism.
- Identify the major global forces that are shaping the tourism of tomorrow.

- Understand the impacts, both positive and negative, that these forces are likely to have on tourism markets and on the ability of destinations to respond to the demands of these markets.

New technology has brought high-speed trains that move passengers efficiently, helping to solve transportation and environmental problems. Shown here is Japan Railway's Shinkansen super express. *Photo courtesy of the Japan Information Center.*

INTRODUCTION

According to most forecasts, the future of tourism continues to be full of promise. Projections concerning the levels of arrivals, receipts, and growth in employment for most destinations have all painted a fairly rosy picture. For the most part, the contents of this chapter reflect the general optimism that pervades the travel industry.

Over and above this optimism, what is especially important about this chapter is its attempt first to define some of the more specific dimensions of future opportunities. In addition, it seeks to indicate how the travel product may need to evolve in response to these opportunities.

Finally, we also wish to sound a cautious note. As shown by the 1998 Asian economic crisis, even the most dynamic of economies can turn sour. On top of this, the events of September 11, 2001, had a devastating impact on travel. As well, SARS drastically impacted Asian and Canadian travel. While we continue to be optimistic that long-term stability and growth will return to these regions, the lessons of history are that we must learn to manage effectively in bad times as well as good. So while readers should prepare for the optimistic future trends this chapter presents, they should also ask themselves, "What if?" How might the travel industry take advantage of periods of lower economic growth? How might the travel industry be a catalyst for other sectors of the economy? As we said at the beginning of this text— bon voyage!

TOURISM IN THE THIRD MILLENNIUM

The purpose of this book has been to provide the student with a basic understanding of the principles, practices, and philosophies of tourism as they relate to the industry of today. To understand the present, it has, of course, been necessary to review the evolution and historical development of the field. Clearly, the tourism industry of today is the product of many forces that have shaped both its structure and the manner in which it functions. As has been pointed out on several occasions, the growth and development of tourism has been particularly rapid over the past half century. As noted by the World Tourism Organization:[1]

- Since 1950, when international travel started to become accessible to the general public, tourist activity has risen from 25 million to 760 million arrivals in 2005. International tourism receipts have risen from US$2.1 billion to US$514 billion in 2003.

- International tourism receipts grew faster than world trade in the 1980s and now constitute a higher proportion of the value of world exports than all

---

[1]World Tourism Organization, *Tourism 2020 Vision: A New Forecast from the World Tourism Organization,* Madrid: WTO, 1997.

sectors other than crude petroleum/petroleum products and motor vehicles/parts/accessories.

The result is that tourism in the late 1990s was a very large and dynamic sector of the economy. Because of the rapid growth and change of the past, one might be inclined to believe that tourism has now reached a mature phase of its development in which the rate of change and expansion will decrease.

On the other hand, a realistic assessment of the probable future suggests that tourism is likely to continue to grow and develop much more rapidly and more dynamically than many other sectors for many years to come.

THE WORLD OF TOURISM IN 2020

Forecasts, 2005–2020

As shown in Table 20.1, international tourist arrivals are forecast to top 1 billion in 2010, and reach 1.6 billion in 2020. These volumes rep-

The concierge at the Sheraton Hotel in Casablanca, Morocco, offers important information and service to make the customer's travel experience more rewarding. The continued growth of international travel will add more than forty-eight million new jobs around the world in the next decade. *Photo by the author.*

resent an overall average annual rate of growth between 1995 and 2020 of 4.3 percent, with no slackening of growth over the period (i.e., 1995–2000, 4.2 percent per annum [p.a.]; 2000–2010, 4.2 percent p.a.; 2010–20, 4.4 percent p.a.).

- Europe will remain the largest receiving region, though its below-global-average rate of increase will result in a decline in market share from 59 percent to 45 percent. East Asia and the Pacific, increasing at 7.0 percent per annum, will pass the Americas as historically the second largest receiving region, holding a 27 percent market share in 2020 against 18 percent by the Americas. The respective shares of Africa, the Middle East, and South Asia will all record some increase to 5 percent, 4 percent, and 1 percent by 2020.

- Most significantly, WTTC research shows that some 269.5 million people around the globe will be employed in jobs that exist because of demand generated by travel and tourism by 2015.

	Tourist Arrivals (millions)	
TABLE 20.1 **FORECASTS OF INTERNATIONAL TOURIST ARRIVALS WORLDWIDE AND BY REGION 2010–2020**		
REGIONS	2010	2020
Europe	527	717
East Asia/Pacific	231	438
Americas	195	284
Africa	46	75
Middle East	37	69
South Asia	11	19
World	**1,047**	**1,602**

Source: World Tourism Organization.

The bottom line is that travel and tourism is driving, directly and indirectly, more than 10 percent of employment today, globally, regionally, and nationally.

THE NATURE OF FUTURE GROWTH

As we have seen, tourism is expected to continue to grow. However, the nature of this growth and development will in many ways be quite different from that of the previous five decades. As has become abundantly clear over the past several years, the period of the 1990s proved itself to be dramatically different from that of the previous three decades. As a global community we are living through widespread changes whose scope and significance are barely perceptible at this point in time. Yet somehow, we know that what has come to be known as the "New World Order" of the post-Cold War era is evolving in some very fundamental ways as we have passed the magical year 2000 and moved into the third millennium of Western history. And even though the Cold War now belongs to history, the reality of war is still with us. The war in Iraq, and the ongoing war on terrorism have more than replaced the Cold War as a negative influence on people's desire and willingness to venture far from home. Until the threat of war is diminished, tourism managers will have to develop a comprehensive destination policy, strategy, and management framework that adapts to and accommodates the reality of the long-term war on terrorism.

Some of the dimensions of this adaptation and accommodation are already recognizable, and indeed, some are even predictable. Others are but as yet stirrings of anxiety or discontent. These stirrings are possibly the most disconcerting for the mature adults of the so-called developed nations—adults whose well-being and prosperity have improved constantly over their lifetime. For perhaps the first time, the fundamental changes occurring around them threaten to leap out of control and to undermine the foundations of their secure and attractive lifestyles. Others, in less fortunate circumstances, see these same changes as possibly the only glimmer of hope for what they view as a more equitable distribution of all the opportunities that life has to offer. Ironically, they may see these same changes as irrevocably condemning themselves to a life of endless poverty.

LEISURE, TOURISM, AND SOCIETY IN THE THIRD MILLENNIUM

A significant component of the high-quality lifestyle that characterized the last half of the twentieth century was access to, as well as the use of, increasing amounts of leisure time. Although the extent of this increase in leisure time has been questioned for decades,[2] there is little doubt that in aggregate terms the populations of the developed Western nations have had greater and more broadly based access to recreation and travel opportunities than has any previous society. As a result, tourism has grown to the point where it can now claim to be the "world's largest industry."[3] While traditionally those in the tourism sector have lamented the lack of recognition received by the industry from both governments and the public, this situation is changing dramatically—in many cases, to the chagrin of the tourism establishment. Suddenly, tourism is being blamed for the destruction of cultures, degradation of the environment, and homogenization of lifestyles. In brief, because of its growing economic and social importance, tourism has suddenly found itself thrust into the mainstream of societal concerns—this at a time when all aspects of society are being questioned as to their value, their continued relevance, and, perhaps above all, their sustainability over the long term.

It is against this background of global societal change that several leading organizations and individuals having a strong interest in the future of tourism have attempted to understand the important forces of change in the world and their likely implications for the future of tourism. A review and analysis of the conclusions of these efforts indicates that the tourism of tomorrow will face a number of constraints and limitations that cannot be ignored. These "new realities" will force tourism policy makers and the tourism industry to alter dramatically the way it both develops and operates. They will also require that tourists themselves alter their demands and their behaviors. These changes that are now imposing themselves are, however, by no means entirely negative. Many can be viewed as corrections to the bad judgments and excesses of the past. Others represent opportunities for innovative and exciting new products and experiences. These "new horizons" in tourism may well prove more rewarding, and certainly more sustainable, than those of the past.

---

[2]Juliet B. Schor, *The Overworked American: The Unexpected Decline of Leisure,* New York: Basic Books, 1991.
[3]World Travel and Tourism Council, *Travel and Tourism: A New Economic Perspective,* Brussels: WTTC, 1993.

NEW REALITIES—NEW HORIZONS: FORCES IMPACTING THE FUTURE OF TOURISM

Tourism has had an illustrious past since the 1950s and currently has a dynamic present. It is not surprising that its future is equally optimistic, if not more so. Despite this optimism, a large number of major influences will significantly alter the nature and shape of tourism in the coming years and decades. These influences will present tourism managers with a number of new realities difficult to overcome or adapt to. At the same time, they will also present new horizons that open up many new opportunities for growth and enhancement of the tourism experience.

The specific forces that influence tourism are, of course, constantly changing. Some of the most influential for the present and into the foreseeable future are described below.

Economic

Despite the current economic situation, tourism can optimistically anticipate continued moderate-to-good overall rates of global economic growth of the traditional economies, but with an emerging importance of certain economies such as China, India, Brazil, Indonesia, and Russia. While history may very well prove us wrong in the longer term, the foreseeable future indicates that competitive economic forces will continue to triumph over ideologies. Over the past several decades, we have seen throughout the world the emergence of what appear to be overpowering pressures to adopt the model of the market economy. As part of this model, we have seen movements to deregulation, to privatization, to regional economic integration, and to a greater role for the global, or transnational, corporation. Whether these movements represent winds of change or a lasting restructuring of our economic system, remains to be seen. However, for the moment, the direction of the tide is unquestionable.

Space tourism has already arrived. Dennis Tito has the distinction of being the first tourist to go into space. Others have been visiting land-based space attractions for years. The Kennedy Space Center and space shuttle launches continue to draw thousands of visitors.
Photo courtesy of Kennedy Space Center Visitors Complex.

In parallel, we are seeing a rapidly growing adoption of the concept of private-sector branding by tourism destinations all over the world. It remains to be seen whether this rush to "brandification" will prove cost effective. In the meantime, no one seems to want to risk being left out.

It is clear that 2004, somewhat surprisingly, will go into history as a very strong year for tourism. The World Tourism Organization reported at the World Travel Market that according to an initial projection, the number of international tourist arrivals is heading for a new all-time record, as growth for the entire year is estimated to reach around 10 percent. In summary, after three years with an accumulated growth of less than 1 percent, international tourism is seen as firmly on its way to convincingly bounce back in 2004 and the future.

Political

Historians will long debate exactly why the period 1989–1991 was the specific point in time that saw such a dramatic spread of the democratic movement. The record will show that few individuals (experts or ordinary people) foresaw the rapid transformations of the political systems that occurred in eastern and central Europe during this period. Of course, all is not as simple as it seems. Many other forces were at work that allowed this rather focused eruption of democracy to occur. Indeed, as will be argued later, this very visible political shift was only symptomatic of a much more fundamental and underlying desire by people all over the world to participate more directly in the governing processes that affect their lives. From a tourism perspective, these forces have led to the very powerful concept of resident-responsive tourism. No longer can it be assumed that the residents of a tourism destination or region will automatically accept all (or any) forms of tourism development that the industry proposes or attempts to impose. Tourism development in the third millennium will actively have to seek the support of the communities it affects most directly. To do this, those responsible for tourism will have to involve the residents of a growing percentage of destinations in the assessments of the costs and benefits associated with all forms of proposed (and even existing) facilities and activities. Unless a consensus is reached that the net benefits to the community are positive, it is questionable that tourism development in the coming years will have the support necessary to proceed.

The rather surprising rebound in tourism in the Middle East region in 2004 has indicated that the efforts of the United States-led military coalition—which sought to install and strengthen a democratic government in Iraq—although perhaps not visibly successful in political terms, has not dampened the flow of domestic travelers within the region. WTO figures for the Middle East show a 20 percent increase in arrivals for 2004, making tourism one of the most dynamic economic sectors of the region.

The Continued Growth of "Super-Europe"

As of May 2004, the European Union nearly doubled in geographic size, and vastly expanded its cultural and linguistic scope, with the long-awaited addition of 10 new member countries (Cyprus, the Czech Republic, Estonia, Hungary, Latvia, Lithuania, Malta, Poland, Slovakia, and Slovenia). Although none of these new members are unknown to U.S. travel agents, they do vary in their level of familiarity. However, since it will be years before the new entrants will be permitted to adopt the euro or to share open borders with the other 15 countries, the impact on travel agents selling them will not be substantial for some time.

A Decline in the Meganation: The Rise of the City-State

As noted above, the increasing importance of regional trading blocs, such as the new "borderless Europe," is now a reality. The North American Free Trade Agreement has created another similar bloc. In response to these two initiatives, the Asian nations are moving toward an equivalent arrangement. Also, one can anticipate some similar form of free trade agreement in South America at some point in the future.

Although it is too early yet to reach firm conclusions regarding the changes that free movement of labor will bring to the social fabric of Europe, it does seem reasonable to anticipate that despite attachment to the concept of "national sovereignty," the importance of each existing individual nation-state will slowly decline. Indeed, one of the major goals of European integration is to arrive at common standards, a common currency, and a more common political system based on common values. At first glance, one might argue that the creation of the new Europe will result in another meganation. In strictly pragmatic terms, this may be the case. Certainly, the effective elimination of borders will greatly facilitate travel flows. At the same time, it will, over time, greatly reduce national distinctiveness and thus the appeal of a particular country as a unique travel destination.

Although speculative at this point, some evidence exists that as a reaction to the decline of national identities, major metropolitan centers—or city-states—will rise in importance. These city-states, it is argued, may become the focal point both for economic development and for individual identity. Of direct relevance to tourism is the possibility that the new city-states may also become the primary basis for tourism destination development and promotion. Indeed, it can be argued that cities such as London, Rome, New York, and Beijing have already achieved such a status.

Socioenvironmental Awareness

Perhaps as the result of greater media reporting on major global problems, concern for the environment continues to occupy center stage in tourism. This tourism reality is, however, a reflection of a much broader societal realization that the world's population—all of it—must get serious about the health of our planet. Indeed, the recent ratification by Russia of the Kyoto Agreement represents nearly the final step in the move toward its global acceptance, and its ultimate implementation. This implementation of "Kyoto" makes it abundantly clear that spaceship Earth has a limited capacity to sustain life as we know it—and that action needs to be taken to change the behavior of the world's population. As such, policy makers in tourism must now acknowledge that development in the future will have to be compatible with the environment. At the same time, however, many believe that tourism is among the better alternatives for land use. While such compatibility is laudable, it must also be stressed that other areas exist where compatibility between tourism and the environment is perhaps not so obvious. For example, the use of fossil fuels for transportation and their polluting effect cannot be denied. As a consequence, the sustainability of tourism in the long term is in doubt unless alternative nonpolluting energy sources become available.

Technology will continue to penetrate all sectors of the tourism industry in both operations and attractions. Shown here is the Rose Center for Earth and Space in New York City. This 333,500-square-foot center uses cutting-edge technology on a grand scale to make complex, abstract concepts of astronomy and earth sciences accessible and comprehensible to the public. *Photo by Denis Finnin © American Museum of Natural History.*

Technology: Toward "Land of the Free, Home of the Bar Code"[4]

As WTO has noted, the world in the year 2020 will be characterized by the penetration of technology into all aspects of life. It will become increasingly possible to live one's life without exposure to other people, with automated service being the norm, and with full access to, and exchange of, information on everything being possible from one's own home. Even the emergence of space tourism will be, by definition, an activity that is undertaken largely in isolation. In consequence, people will crave the human touch, and tourism will be a principal means through which they seek to achieve this.

In brief, while tourism has traditionally been characterized as a "people industry," it is now coming face to face with the realities of the massive advances in technology that have occurred over the past several decades. During this period, industries that are less dependent on the human interactions that characterize the tourism sector have adapted labor-saving technology with a vengeance. As a consequence, these industries have been able to improve wage levels and enhance career opportunities for employees while keeping costs under control.

---

[4]Daniel Franklin (ed.), *The World in 2004*. London: The Economist, 2004.

On the other hand, the travel industry has been one of the most successful in utilizing the Internet to market its products. Both large and small firms have enhanced their ability to reach the consumer with their promotional messages; they have also surpassed other sectors in actually selling their product electronically.

The quote "Land of the Free, Home of the Bar Code," in the above subhead, from the *Economist*, highlights another area where technology is having, and will continue to have, a pervasive impact on controlling the movement of travelers across certain international or interregional borders. As of October 2004, all foreign visitors to America must have either a machine-readable passport or a visa. In addition, the new American visas will be required to contain biometric data in the form of fingerprints and a digital image of the traveler's face. Eventually it is envisaged that this kind of data will be required on all passports, since such documents are hard to fake and can be scanned into security databases. The drawback is that the full program, called US VIST, could cost from $3 billion to $10 billion to set up, and could in the end deter visitation rather than facilitate it. As well, there continue to be doubts over the reliability of biometric passports, largely due to the fact that, according to the *Economist*, "the lighting when photos are taken makes it hard for the technology to work, or because it is very hard for people to behave in exactly the way the technology needs them to behave."

While the foregoing reflects a willingness on the part of governments to invest in technology to improve the efficiency of the travel system, many components of the travel industry have generally preferred to keep wages low, thus avoiding the need for technological innovation, particularly in the actual delivery of services. Although technology has been used extensively in a supporting role to enhance performance and effectiveness (e.g., computerized reservation system, air control technology), there has been a great reluctance to replace human service providers with technologically driven alternatives (such as the banks did when replacing human tellers with automatic teller machines). Similarly, aside from fast-food restaurants, there has been relatively little focused effort to undertake a major rethinking or redesign of travel-related facilities and support systems so as to substantially reduce personnel requirements or to enhance the productivity of employees. While some "tinkering" has occurred in selected areas and sectors, we have not yet seen many of the benefits from technology that are possible. Until technology is adapted more widely, it will be difficult for the travel industry to make new travel experiences available to a mass audience and to do so at prices that are affordable by much of the population.

On the other side of the coin—and this is the dilemma—the introduction of technology is viewed as a "job killer." Indeed, a common conclusion is that both skilled and not-so-skilled personnel in the labor force could be replaced by various forms of technology. While some argue that the increased use of capital and technology will require highly skilled labor, others argue that technology (particularly computer technology) may, in fact, increase the demand for a less-skilled labor force.

Hotels of the Future

Should space tourism become a reality, travelers will need somewhere to stay—so why not an "inflatable space hotel," a proposal of Robert Bigelow, the owner of the Budget Suites of America hotel chain. The "Genesis Pathfinder," as Bigelow has named his project, is a one-third-scale inflatable, the launch of which is planned for November 2005. If all proceeds smoothly, a full-scale inflatable code-named Nautilus should head into space in 2006. Bigelow Aerospace states on its Web site that the program will "make the difference between space stations being only government-available, or having space stations affordable for general business ownership."

Other more modest yet still future-oriented conceptualizations of the "hotel of the future," have been set out by founder of **futurist.com,** Glen Hiemstra. He believes that three things will define the future of hotels: robotics, nanotechnology, and biometric security such as retina scans. "Robotics will be the most significant technology to affect the hotel industry in the future," says Hiemstra. He envisions a hotel where robots can do the majority of the cleaning and check-in, and safes will become automated by devices like retina scans. "But the really far-out science fiction scenario is with nanotechnology." (In short, nanotechnology is the ability to manipulate and manufacture things at the molecular level). "In 2025 or 2030, we might be able to have rooms reconfigure themselves to suit whatever guests want, whether it's a king-sized bed and a couch, or a single bed and a desk."

But swinging back to the present day, where is most of the hotel innovation taking place? Howard J. Wolff, of the international design firm Wimberly, Allison, Tong & Goo (WATG), which counts Claridge's hotel in London and the Mansion at the MGM Grand in Las Vegas as clients, laughs and says, "The bed . . . Starwood thought about what people wanted from their hotel room and when it comes down to it, it's a comfortable place to sleep, which is why they spent their money developing the Heavenly Bed." (Starwood Hotel and Resort Worldwide's Westin Hotel subsidiary developed the Heavenly Bed, a custom-made mattress set by Simmons with 900 individual coils, which hotel guests can purchase for $2,565).

The Continuing Evolution of Air Travel

In the ongoing race to be number one in aircraft manufacturing, Airbus has recently edged out Boeing as the top commercial jet maker. The Airbus A380 will be ready to take off sometime in 2006—and 179 orders have already been secured for what is touted as currently the world's largest passenger plane (with seating capacity of 555). Boeing, in contrast, believes the future need will be for smaller aircraft. Its 787 Dreamliner, said to be the super-efficient plane of tomorrow, will have three configurations flying between 6,500 and 15,700 kilometers and with passenger capacities of 217 to 289.

While all of the above is occurring in the realm of product development, the future of air travel is also likely to see a continuation of the growth of low cost, reduced service air carriers. Airlines such as Southwest Airlines (U.S.), Ryan Air (Ireland), EasyJet (U.K.), and WestJet (Canada) pose an ongoing threat to the traditional full-service airlines.

The Final Frontier?
Space Tourism

Human curiosity about the stars predates travel and tourism as we know it today, so it is not surprising that travel into space should be gaining in popularity. In this regard, Brown identifies a number of studies demonstrating public interest in space tourism.[5] Despite this interest, the prohibitively expensive cost of space travel makes it clear that not too many of us are likely to be getting a "moon-tan" in the near future. Nevertheless, the continued interest in space tourism indicates that the concept should not be totally dismissed. The fact that the $10 million "X Prize" (for two suborbital flights in space) has now been won, plus the establishment of the space tourism company Virgin Galactica by Virgin Group Chairman Richard Branson, are both clear signals. In the words of leading space tourism researcher Geoffrey Crouch, "there is a strong possibility that a viable, commercial space tourism industry is poised for growth through the 21st century."[6] In fact, Space Adventures is a privately owned space experiences company headquartered in Arlington, Virginia, with an office in Moscow. Their goal is to open the space frontier to everyone and promote private space exploration by building a series of successful, privately funded space-flight missions.

Space Adventures, Ltd., which positions itself as the world's leading space experience company, seeks to be a unifying force for a generation of space explorers. Space Adventures, the only company to have launched two private space explorers—American businessman Dennis Tito in 2001 and South African Mark Shuttleworth in 2002—to the International Space Station, launched a Soyuz rocket from Baikonur Cosmodrome in Kazakhstan. *Courtesy of Space Adventures.*

[5]Frances Brown, "The Final Frontier? Tourism in Space," *Tourism Recreation Research*, Vol. 29, No. 1, pp. 37–43, 2004.
[6]Geoffrey I. Crouch, "Space Tourism through the 21st Century," *Proceedings of the Tourism: State of the Art II Conference,* June 27–30, 2004, Glasgow, Scotland.

Terrorism and Crisis Management Becomes Integral to Travel and Tourism

The announcement of Schedules for Terrorism Awareness Training Courses, developed by the Department of Homeland Security, directed toward stadiums and arenas, is but one more clear indication that terrorism—and the need to counter it, have become an integral part of our daily lives.

As discussed earlier, nowhere is the significance of the reality of terrorism more important than in tourism. Because we, in the tourism industry, are encouraging the members of any population to travel on a discretionary basis, we have a special obligation to do all we can to take every step possible to provide travelers with security.

Why do terrorists attack tourism centers? According to the *Futurist,*[7] terrorists seek out tourist destinations for four primary reasons:

1. First, an attack on a tourism center is an attack on a nation's entire economy—a fact that further emphasizes the economic significance of tourism.
2. Second, tourism is highly media-oriented—terrorism seeks publicity, and tourist attractions like sporting events and festivals are likely to have media already at the site.
3. Third, tourist attractions such as museums, historic sites, and beautiful scenery represent the spirit and essence of a nation.
4. Finally, tourist spots provide terrorists with relative anonymity. Police and security professionals rarely know the identities or motivations of visitors at sites and events.

As a consequence of the foregoing, increasing security will be a must for airlines, hotels, restaurants, and other tourism services. Furthermore, security experts in the travel industry must address the possibility of a "suicide disease carrier" seeking to infect an entire population.

The tourism industry must, however, go beyond mere security management and put in place a crisis management system that is capable of dealing with a wide range of catastrophes. Examples of recent tourism-related crises include:

- Britain: foot-and-mouth disease in cattle

- Cuba, Haiti, and Florida: the advent of successive major hurricanes

- China: SARS

- Bali: nightclub bombing

- Egypt: Luxor killings of tourists

- Thailand: avian (bird) flu and the threat of its spreading to humans

- Asia: tsunami

---

[7]Edward Cornish (ed.). *The Futurist,* Bethesda, MD: World Future Society (online: **http://www.wfs.org/futurist.htm**), 2002.

Terrorism affecting tourism has become so serious that costly efforts to develop missile warning systems and expendable decoys to protect commercial aircraft against shoulder-fired missile attacks are now under development.

Will Outsourcing Take the Service out of Customer Service?

A highly visible and highly contentious phenomenon of the past decade has been the "outsourcing" of certain services to lower-wage areas of the world. While the trend started in the manufacturing sector, it subsequently spread to the services sector of the economy, and selected tourism/hospitality services have been caught up in this offspring of global restructuring. A common example is destination call services that respond to visitor enquiries for information. Another relates to the follow-up requests for reservations.

Cost reduction, the primary motivation for outsourcing, can provide substantial improvements in the profitability of tourism firms. Travelocity, for example, has said that it expected to save $10 million in 2004 by outsourcing 300 jobs to India over the following year.

The ongoing concern in the continuing outsourcing debate pertains to the trade-off between cost savings and quality of customer service.

THE TOURIST OF THE FUTURE

The foregoing sections have dwelled on how technology may definitely alter tourism facilities, products, and services—and, indeed, the travel experience itself. In the meantime, the tourist who seeks to enjoy the experiences offered will also be changing. What changes can we expect?

Emergence of the Knowledge-Based Society and Workforce

One consequence of the above-noted rise of technology is that certain of the developed nations have already entered an era in which one of their greatest competitive advantages is the information or knowledge they possess, rather than their ownership of natural resources or their access to cheap labor. Assuming that such a trend continues and expands to other countries, it behooves the tourism industry to examine how the travel behavior of people in a knowledge-based society might differ from that of people from a manufacturing or more traditional service-based setting.

If the world's leading economies are any indication of trends in this regard, we can expect travelers from knowledge-based economies to be more experienced, more discerning, and more demanding—in brief, more sophisticated. In particular, we can expect that they will be seeking more individualized experiences, often characterized as **special-interest travel.** Such travelers "are more interested in enriching their lives through experiences rather than hands-off entertainment. They seek authentic, interactive, highly involved, quality travel experiences, focusing on in-depth coverage of the special interest topic or destination at hand."[8]

Pushing the limits even further, certain individuals and groups are now espousing the potential of **virtual reality** (VR) as a replacement for travel.[9] This technology represents perhaps the outer limits of the knowledge-based industries in that it purports to provide simulated experiences that conceptually are equivalent to the real thing. It is asserted that someday (supposedly not too far away), by merely strapping on the necessary technology, people will be able to "experience" a destination without actually visiting it. While it is easy for the traveler of today to dismiss such an idea as sheer fantasy, it does seem logical that such an approach would (if truly feasible) find ready acceptance among members of a knowledge-based society. It goes without saying that, if successful, "virtual-reality tourism" would have profound impacts on the travel industry as we know it.

At the same time as we espouse the potential of VR, we must acknowledge that the implementation of the concept has lagged behind its promise for some time now. It is currently argued by its proponents that VR should become feasible and affordable around 2010–2015. But, even if it does, one must question whether humans will find that the virtual experience is truly an attractive substitute for the reality of travel.

Demographic Shifts

Although very little in the social sciences is truly predictable, there is one notable exception: the demographics of the world's present population. In this regard, the forces of change that will drive and shape the face of the next generation are already evident. The populations of the developed Western world are aging and will decline in relative size. At the same time, the populations of the developing world continue to explode. While in the short term such changes may present opportunities for the tourism industry, they also raise some fundamental long-term questions. These questions concern not only the distribution of the income and wealth on which travel depends, but also the geographic distribution of the world's population.

The above-noted aging of the populations of tourist originating countries will bring about a number of significant changes in the choice of destinations and in the travel behavior of individuals. Just a few selected examples of such changes are:

• Leisurely, rather than highly programmed, vacations will increase.

• More grandparents will be traveling with children.

---

[8]Robert J. Forbes and Maree S. Forbes, "Special Interest Travel," *World Travel and Tourism Review*, Vol. 2, Wallingford, UK: CAB International, 1992.
[9]Travel and Tourism Research Association, "Examining the Dynamics of New Partnerships, Strategies, and Products," newsletter, Boise, ID: TTRA, 1992.

- Convenience will be paramount; airport delays due to increased security and overcrowded facilities will result in a trend away from short flights.[10]

- Many individuals will tend to turn inward toward family and friends (cocooning) as they seek protection in a hostile world.

- Concern for health and medical travel facilities will be driven by both physiological and psychological needs of older travelers.

- Travelers will seek "home hotels" where they can easily find most things they need, including shoes, clothing, and other necessities—so as to minimize the luggage they require.

- Educational hotels will meet the growing desire of tourists both to learn and to acquire new skills.[11]

- Since nearly half of all households in America are now headed by persons who are not married, this will increasingly change the need for travel facilities, events, and activities that were designed and developed to meet the needs of the traditional family vacation.

- The evolving ethnic composition of the North American population is changing the choice and travel behavior of tourists. In the United States, one in three Americans will belong to an ethnic minority by 2020. At the present, non-Hispanic whites comprise 73 percent of America's population, but this is a shrinking share. By 2020, blacks will comprise 14 percent of the U.S. population. Hispanics (now 11 percent) will grow to 16 percent of the total population by 2020.[12]

The Long-Predicted "Chinese Elephant" Is Starting to Become a Tourism Reality

Chinese government travel restrictions on its population are continuing to be relaxed—to the point where 2005 may be the year when mainland Chinese really start to see the world. Travel industry experts forecast that the number of Chinese outbound travelers will continue to grow by at least 20 percent each year. However, strict U.S. visa rules have made the U.S. a destination that has not seen a dramatic increase in Chinese visitors.

It should be noted that in addition to their numbers, the Chinese bring with them growing disposable incomes. In 2002, Chinese international travelers spent $15.4 billion, an average of $1,200 per person.

---

[10]Peter E. Tarlow, "Tourism in the Twenty-First Century," *Futurist,* Vol. 36, No. 5, pp. 48–51, September–October 2002–2003.

[11]Ivanka Avelini Holjevac, "A Vision of Tourism and the Hotel Industry in the 21st Century," *International Journal of Hospitality Management,* Vol. 22, No. 2, pp. 129–134, 2003.

[12]Robert A. Dunn, *Demographic Trends and Facilities Modernization in the Corps of Engineer Recreation Program: Draft Study Plan.* Vicksburg, MS: U.S. Army Engineer Research and Development Center, Waterways Experiment Station, 2000.

Diversity within a Homogeneous World

Despite the fact that the popularity of Coca-Cola and McDonald's contributes to the trend to "sameness" around the world, there are strong counter pressures to maintain individual and cultural distinctiveness. A visit to any major city in the world demonstrates how information, economic pressures, and the tendency to imitate has left the world "less different" than it was a century, even decades, ago. It seems, however, that the human entity, while recognizing the pragmatic value of sameness, is determined at the same time to make every effort to preserve and enhance unique identity. Whether or not the culture that spawned the Bolshoi Ballet is threatened by the arrival of McDonald's restaurants remains to be seen. However, if the determination of those who are facing this issue is any indication, the existence of cultural diversity within a global society is a reality whose time has come.

The Quest for Stability and Security

After literally decades of economic growth and relative stability, many highly successful and valued persons are suddenly facing the prospect of decreasing economic well-being—and in many cases, even unemployment. This was not how it was supposed to turn out. We have seen, in response to this threat, a strong reluctance to spend, even by those who have the resources. Although the resulting increase in saving rates may provide the investments necessary for modernization and long-term economic growth, the more immediate impacts on leisure and tourism spending are already being felt.

In the area of physical (as opposed to economic) security, we have known for some time that risk of physical danger is certain to diminish the prospects of a given tourism destination or travel-related firm. War in the Middle East has affected tourism both locally and worldwide. Terrorism aimed at U.S. air carriers has diverted traffic to competitors. Concern for health is of increasing importance, particularly for older travelers. In a different but related vein, the growing threat of AIDS and other diseases has added yet another dimension of concern, only this time for younger segments of the population. We note without exaggeration that the wise tourist visiting certain regions of the world now seeks a traveling companion having a compatible blood type in case a blood transfusion is required. Such concern and attention to detail with respect to health care while traveling should not be dismissed as an aberration of the few.

The events of September 11, 2001, have vividly reinforced the critical significance of safety and security to people's desire to travel and thus to the well-being of the tourism industry. It follows that a primary goal of all sectors of the industry, as well as its government partners, must be to restore a pervading sense of confidence to travelers regarding all aspects of the travel experience.

Pressures for Mass Migration

While those in the developed world try to preserve their level of well-being, many millions in developing nations seek to better their lives. As fading borders increasingly facilitate population movements within trading blocs, there will be those who will first request, and then demand, the right for such freedom of movement to be extended. The day is not far off when freedom of movement of all peoples of the world may be termed a "basic human right." Although this certainly does not mean that this right will be granted, it will undoubtedly be asserted. Clearly, the implications of this still weak but emerging pressure go far beyond the concerns of those in the leisure and tourism field. This said, however, it is very clear that should such pressures succeed in even a modest way, the entire landscape of leisure and tourism could change dramatically.

The Arrival of "Perpetual Tourism"

While the poor of the world are seeking new permanent homes in order to better their lives, a select segment of the world's wealthy are always on holidays—to the extent in some cases that they have no permanent residence. These persons are, in affect, "perpetual tourists." While the most widespread example involves those who use recreational vehicles (RVs) as their home, the most extreme and most luxurious lifestyle in this category are those who live on cruise ships. Although the motivation for such a cruise lifestyle is generally thought to be the pursuit of pleasure, there is often a functional motivation as well, namely the desire to avoid taxation of personal income.

The Emergence of Extreme/Adventure/Disaster or "Dark" Tourism

Yet another extreme form of tourism that has been recognized more recently is where individuals undertake to visit locations of mass destruction where local uprisings, or even wars, create a unique type of destination experience that some travelers find exciting. In the same vein, major disasters such as floods, earthquakes, tornadoes, and hurricanes—despite or perhaps because of the danger they create—draw visitors to the disaster site. While by their nature these events are inherently difficult to plan for, it is not uncommon to see entrepreneurs selling T-shirts that make it possible for visitors to make everyone aware that they visited the site of the event/disaster or even mass killings (such as Auschwitz).

Change from a "Service" to an "Experience" Economy

Another fundamental change that has been occurring is what Pine and Gilmore[13] refer to as the creation of the experience economy. This change is seen as part of an ongoing evolution from the product and service economies of the past. In such an economy, consumers seek a quality experience from an investment of their time and money. In many ways, tourism has been an important force underlying the cre-

---

[13]B. Joseph Pine II and James H. Gilmore, *The Experience Economy: Work Is Theatre and Every Business a Stage,* Boston, MA: Harvard Business School Press, 1999.

ation of the experience economy. As Otto and Ritchie[14] have demonstrated, travelers seek a quality "experience chain" that links together the many service components of a complex travel experience. The challenge facing the tourism industry is to ensure not only high-quality links in the experience chain, but an enjoyable, hassle-free passage from one link to another. Since each of the links is often managed by a different owner/operator, it is difficult to maintain a continuously high experience across the links. Because of this, destination management organizations (DMOs)—a role often assumed by convention and visitors bureaus (CVBs)—have become increasingly critical to the success of the destination visitation experience, as they seek to coordinate the many service/experience providers at a destination.

The Evolution of Leisure Time and Leisure Itself

While all of the foregoing forces are at work changing the nature of tourism, the underlying essence of tourism, leisure time, is itself undergoing major transformation.[15] Although the amount of actual leisure time is not expected to increase significantly in most developed countries over the short term with respect to paid or public holidays, one important related change is taking place. This change involves the development of more flexible working patterns in many countries, together with a restructuring and delayering that are likely to lead to more individualized working patterns, with longer, less predictable working hours for many. This will accelerate the trend toward late booking and increase the importance of easy and efficient services for vacation selection and purchase. It will also, in all likelihood, lead to increased flexibility of work through the week and through the year, together with the growth of long-haul travel that will spread vacations more evenly through the year.

Competition for Leisure Time

A WTO study[16] has found that the amount of leisure time available varies widely among the countries included in the study. The proportion of that time that is spent on tourism will depend upon the attractiveness of the products that the industry offers. As standards of living rise, so the range of leisure-time options broadens. People lead fuller lives and have more hobbies and interests. Many of these are focused in or near the home, which is increasingly a relaxation and entertainment center. Towns and cities around the world invest heavily to become more pleasant places to invest in and to live in. So shopping, cultural, restaurant, leisure, and pleasure facilities proliferate, often on single sites so that people on tight schedules can save time, yet spend on a variety of activities and attractions.

---

[14]Julie E. Otto and J. R. Brent Ritchie, "The Service Experience in Tourism," *Tourism Management,* Vol. 17, No. 3, May 1996, pp. 165–174.
[15]World Tourism Organization, *Changes in Leisure Time: The Impact on Tourism,* Madrid: WTO Business Council, 1999.
[16]Ibid.

At the same time, for many people, changes in the employment market are making time as precious as money. In addition, increasingly knowledgeable and experienced consumers seek more value and individuality from their purchases, whether of goods or services.

THE CHANGING NATURE OF TOURISM PRODUCTS

To meet contemporary vacation needs, tourism products must compete with the pressures on consumers' leisure time and the widening range of leisure opportunities near to home, as well as with second homes and timeshare. There are also those attractions that offer alternatives to overseas travel, for example Center Parcs, which provide weatherproof centers for family water-recreation vacations in northern Europe, and Disney's Animal Kingdom, which re-creates the Serengeti in Florida. Many theme parks offer day trips and short breaks from major urban centers.

A fundamental competitive advantage of leisure investments of this kind is that they offer easy, convenient access. This must add to the vital interest of the tourism industry in pressing governments to ensure the quality of transport services. Congestion, delay, and unreliable transport deter travel.

An analysis of the views of the industry on growth prospects suggests that already the following range of products is well adapted to the changing market:

- Beach and other resorts that provide a range of activities and attractions in a good environment, are easy to reach, are pleasant to be in, and have good communications to home and office

- Cities with good transport links, user-friendly airports, and an attractive environment offering culture, entertainment, and good shopping, which can be enjoyed during a short break

- "Get away from it all" destinations, offering an excellent environment, whether for total relaxation and tranquility or for the pursuit of cultural, physical, or environment interests; also with excellent communications with home and office

- Theme parks that are conveniently located, with good transport links, and offer a full range of entertainment and activities to be enjoyed by all the family over a short break

- Cruises, many of which are getting shorter and more affordable, are floating resorts that offer a full range of entertainment and leisure options to satisfy the whole family

Products with distinctive appeal to the young include activity vacations, particularly diving, skiing, trekking, and soft adventure. These interests provide an indication of the probable vacation preferences of this market as it grows older and comes under greater time pressures.

While technology often takes the spotlight when talking about the future, it is equally important to take action to protect our environment, our heritage, and our animals for future generations. *Photo courtesy of Digital Vision.*

Vacations with particular appeal to those traveling independently include special-interest vacations, coach touring, event-related tourism, and cultural and health-related vacations. These products are suited to individuals vacationing independently, whether to avoid the difficulties of synchronizing vacation time with other family members, or in an increasingly differentiated market, simply using their leisure time to pursue individual interests.

Vacations with particular appeal to the retired include winter sun, cruises, special-interest, cultural, coach-touring, walking, and health-related products.

Time and Money

The broadening of income differentials that has accompanied the pressure on leisure time in many countries means that increasingly income is inversely related to available time. So, those in the working population who are best able to afford vacations have the greatest difficulty in finding time to get away, especially for more than a short break. The challenge for the industry is to create compellingly attractive products that can be enjoyed within the purchaser's time constraints.

Reflecting this response from the industry, in addition to the general expectation that the greatest growth will be in short breaks, also shows that there is an expectation of increased demand for tailored vacations. Opportunities exist for luxury and exotic breaks, but also for high-quality domestic or same-region or time-zone products that minimize traveling time as a proportion of the break and avoid jet lag.

Those with more time but with lower incomes will be concerned with affordability. This may be reflected in the growth anticipated by the industry in fully inclusive vacations, which make it easier for people to budget for their vacation before leaving home.

For all those affected by the increased flexibility of employment and greater work pressure, opportunities to select and book vacations at the last minute are important. This may stimulate direct bookings and use of the Internet, but is also an opportunity for travel agents who can provide fast, efficient service.

Income differentials are also widening among the retired, and the gap between highly priced and cheaper products aimed at this market is likely to increase. The retired who are financially secure, with relatively high incomes, form the core of outbound tourism growth in many countries and have the greatest potential for more frequent travel. A wide range of products attracts this market, but it is discerning, increasingly seeks tailored products, and has plenty of non-travel-related interests, which make many reluctant to be away from home too often or too long.

The retired with less substantial incomes are likely to become even more cost and value conscious, particularly in countries facing significant changes in pension arrangement, but are an important market, especially for destinations where living costs compare favorably with those at home and where long winter sun vacations are affordable.

In view of the importance of the retired market, more research on their travel interests would be helpful, focusing particularly on willingness to take extended vacations and to travel in the shoulder months and out of season.

The older retired greatly appreciate ease of travel arrangements, not having to handle baggage, and having medical services at hand. Cruises meet these requirements well, offer security, and largely eliminate the effort that would otherwise be involved in visiting several cities or other attractions within a short period. Generally, however, as the retired grow older, the propensity to travel gets lower. The challenge to tourism marketing is to change, or at least defer, this. Since populations are growing only slowly or stagnating in many of the established major tourism markets, particularly Japan and most of the European countries, the retired market is an increasingly important opportunity for growth and merits continuing close attention.

SUMMARY

Social and economic trends in developed countries seem to favor long-term growth in both domestic and international travel demand. More long-term leisure, increased disposable income, higher levels of education, and more awareness of other countries and peoples are significant factors influencing a growing market for travel. The movement toward an experience economy is another fundamental change from which tourism can benefit if it plans and adapts appropriately.

Technological trends are also favorable. Transportation equipment is now more efficient and more comfortable; hotel and motel accommodations have become more complete, attractive, convenient, and comfortable; and new developments have given much more attention to environmental considerations.

Tourism is believed to have a positive effect on world peace. As people travel from place to place with a sincere desire to learn more about their global neighbors, knowledge and understanding grow. Then at least a start has been made in improving world communication, which seems so important in building bridges of mutual appreciation, respect, and friendship.

We trust that you are now ready to contribute your part toward making this world a bit more experiential, as well as more prosperous and peaceful through tourism.

KEY CONCEPTS

city-state
concern for safety
cultural diversity
demographic changes
environmental sensitivity
experience economy
global forces of change

high-tech/high-touch
   interface
knowledge-based society
lifestyle diversity
market economy
need for stability
population migration

resident-responsive tourism
space tourism
special-interest tourism
spread of democracy
value-system changes
virtual reality

Internet Sites

The Internet sites mentioned in this chapter are repeated here for convenience, plus some selected additional sites. For more information, visit these sites. Be aware that Internet addresses change frequently, so if a site cannot be accessed, use a search engine. Also use a search engine to locate many additional relevant sites.

World Tourism Organization
http://www.world-tourism.org

World Travel and Tourism Council
http://www.wttc.org

Internet Exercises

Site Name: World Travel and Tourism Council
URL: http://www.wttc.org
Background Information: The World Travel and Tourism Council (WTTC) is the global business leaders' forum for travel and tourism. Its members are chief executives from all sectors of the travel and tourism industry.

Exercises
1. Visit the annual forecast (TSA Research) on the WTTC site and examine the worldwide employment forecast for the current year and the ten-year projection.
2. Do the same for the United States.
3. Do the same for the European Union.
Site Name: Space Adventures
URL: http://spaceadventures.com
Background Information: Space Adventures is a privately owned space experiences company headquartered in Arlington, Virginia, with an office in Moscow. Their goal is to open the space frontier to everyone and promote private space exploration by building a series of successful, privately funded spaceflight missions.

Exercises
1. Visit the site and determine their role in assisting the world's first two space tourists, Dennis Tito and Mark Shuttleworth.
2. Examine the space tourism opportunities that are available today.
Site Name: Virgin Galactica
URL: http://virgingalactica.com
Background Information: Virgin Galactica is a company established by the Richard Branson Group to undertake the challenge of developing space tourism for everyone.

Exercises
1. What do you see as the future of space tourism?
2. What do you see as the different roles between Space Adventures and Virgin Galactica?

QUESTIONS FOR REVIEW AND DISCUSSION

1. What might be an obstacle to the optimistic projections of increased international tourism forecast in this chapter?
2. Intelligent, creative, sensitive tourism developments can actually improve the environment and heighten the appeal of an area. Give examples of how this might happen.
3. Can tourism enhance and improve a destination area's cultural and hospitality resources? Provide actual or hypothetical examples.
4. What is the expected trend in health-oriented accommodations and programs? Food services?

5. What are the realistic prospects for a four-day workweek?
6. Does early retirement appeal to most workers?
7. How can tourism interests obtain a growing share of leisure market expenditures?
8. What do you think the future of space tourism will be?
9. Would you or anyone you know pay $100,000 to travel in space? What would you pay?

SELECTED REFERENCES

Crouch, Geoffrey I. "The Market for Space Tourism: Early Indications." *Journal of Travel Research*, Vol. 40, No. 2, pp. 213–219, 2001.

Faulkner, Bill, Eric Laws, and Gianna Moscardo. *Tourism in the 21st Century: Learning from Experience*. London: Continuum International Publishing Group, 2000.

Foot, David K., and Daniel Stoffman. *Boom Bust and Echo: Profiting from the Demographic Shift in the 21st Century*, rev. ed. Toronto, Canada: Stoddart Publishing, 2001.

Lockwood, Andrew, and S. Medlik. *Tourism and Hospitality in the 21st Century*. Oxford, UK: Butterworth-Heinemann, 2001.

Mueller, Hansruedi. "Long-Haul Tourism 2005: Delphi Study." *Journal of Vacation Marketing,* Vol. 4, No. 2, pp. 193–201, April 1998.

Schor, Juliet B. *The Overworked American: The Unexpected Decline of Leisure.* New York: Basic Books, 1991.

Weiermair, Klaus, and Christine Mathies. *The Tourism and Leisure Industry: Shaping the Future.* Binghamton, NY: Haworth Hospitality Press, 2004.

World Tourism Organization. *Tourism 2020 Vision: A New Forecast from the World Tourism Organization.* Madrid: WTO, 1997.

World Tourism Organization Business Council. *Public-Private Sector Cooperation: Enhancing Tourism Competitiveness.* Madrid: WTOBC, 2001.

GLOSSARY

A

Accommodation Facilities for the lodging of visitors to a destination. The most common forms are hotels, motels, campgrounds, bed and breakfasts (B&Bs), dormitories, hostels, and the homes of friends and relatives.

Adventure travel A form of travel in which the perception (and often the reality) of heightened risk creates a special appeal to certain segments of the travel market. Examples include white-water rafting and mountaineering.

Affinity group A group bound together by a common interest or affinity. Where charters are concerned, this common bond makes them eligible for charter flights. Persons must have been members of the group for six months or longer. Where a group configuration on a flight is concerned, the minimum number of persons to which the term would apply may be any number determined by a carrier rule-making body. They must travel together, on the departure and return flight, but they can travel independently where ground arrangements are concerned.

Agreement, bilateral An agreement regulating commercial air services between two countries.

Agreement, multilateral An agreement regulating commercial air services between three or more countries.

Airline Reporting Corporation (ARC) A corporation set up by the domestic airlines that is concerned with travel agent appointments and operations.

Air Transport Association of America (ATA or ATAA) The authoritative trade association maintained by domestic airlines.

Alliance An association to further the common interests of the parties involved.

American plan A room rate that includes breakfast, lunch, and dinner.

Attractions Facilities developed especially to provide residents and visitors with entertainment, activity, learning, socializing, and other forms of stimulation that make a region or destination a desirable and enjoyable place.

B

Balance of payments or trade Practical definition of an economic concept. Each nation is assumed to be one tremendous business doing business with other big businesses. When a business (country) sells (exports) more than it buys (imports), there is a positive balance of payments. When a country buys (imports) more than it sells (exports), there is a negative balance of trade. Tourism is a part of balance of trade classified under services.

Built environment The components or activities within a tourism destination that have been created by humans. These include the infrastructure and superstructure of the destination, as well as the culture of its people, the information and technology they use, the culture they have developed, and the system of governance that regulates their behaviors.

C

Cabotage The ability of an air carrier to carry passengers exclusively between two points in a foreign country.

Capacity The number of flights multiplied by the number of aircraft seats flown.

Carrier A public transportation company, such as air or steamship line, railroad, truck, bus, monorail, and so on.

Carrier-participating A carrier over whose routes one or more sections of carriage under the air waybill or ticket is undertaken or performed.

Carrying capacity The amount of tourism a destination can handle.

Charter The bulk purchase of any carrier's equipment (or part thereof) for passengers or freight.

Legally, charter transportation is arranged for time, voyage, or mileage.

Charter flight A flight booked exclusively for the use of a specific group of people who generally belong to the same organization or who are being "treated" to the flight by a single host. Charter flights are generally much cheaper than regularly scheduled line services. They may be carried out by scheduled or supplemental carriers.

Clients Those persons who patronize travel agencies.

Climate The meteorological conditions, including temperature, precipitation, and wind, that prevail at, or within, a tourism region.

Code sharing An agreement between two airlines that allows the first carrier to use the airline designation code on a flight operated by the second carrier.

Concierge This is a wonderful European invention. Depending on the hotel, the concierge is a superintendent of service, source of information, and/or link between the guest and city or area.

Conservation Management of human use of the environment to yield the greatest sustainable benefit to present generations while maintaining its potential to meet the needs and aspirations of future generations.

Consolidator A travel firm that makes available airplane tickets, cruise tickets, and sometimes other travel products at discount prices. These are usually sold to retail travel agencies but are also sometimes sold directly to the public.

Consortium A privately owned firm (not owned by its members as is a cooperative) that maintains a list of preferred suppliers. This list is made available to members, resulting in superior commissions earned.

Continental breakfast A beverage, roll, and jam. Sometimes fruit juice is added. In Spain, Holland, and Norway, cheese, meat, or fish is sometimes included.

Continental plan A hotel rate that includes a continental breakfast.

Cooperative A membership group of retail travel agencies that offers advantages to each agency member, such as lower prices on wholesale tour offerings, educational opportunities, problem solving, and other aids.

Coupon flight The portion of the passenger ticket and baggage check or excess baggage ticket that indicates particular places between which the coupon is good for carriage.

Culture The totality of socially transmitted behavior patterns, arts, beliefs, institutions, and all other products of human work and thought that are characteristic of the destination population.

D

Destination The ultimate stopping place according to the contract of carriage. Can also be defined as a place offering at least 1,500 rooms to tourists.

Destination Management Organization (DMO) Organization responsible for coordination, leadership, and promotion of a destination and its stakeholders, thus enabling it to provide tourists with an enjoyable and memorable visitation experience.

Development Modification of the environment to whatever degree and the application of human, financial, living, and nonliving resources to satisfy human needs and improve the quality of human life.

Domestic independent travel (DIT) A tour constructed to meet the specific desire of a client within a single country.

E

E-commerce The transaction of commercial dealings (advertising and promotion, sales, billing, payment, and customer servicing) by electronic means rather than through traditional "paper" channels.

Entertainment Performances, shows, or activities that attract and hold the attention of visitors. A successful destination will seek to integrate the travel, hospitality, and entertainment dimensions of tourism.

Environment All aspects of the surroundings of human beings, including cultural, natural, and manmade, whether affecting human beings as individuals or in social groupings.

Eurailpass A special pass sold overseas for unlimited first-class rail travel in fifteen European countries for varying numbers of days. Youth and children's passes are also available.

European plan A hotel rate that includes only lodging, no food.

Events Includes a broad range of "occurrences," "happenings," and "activities" that are designed around various themes, with a view to creating or enhancing interest in the destination. Local festivals and megaevents (such as the Olympic Games and world expositions) have proven to be most effective.

Excursionist A traveler who spends less than twenty-four hours at a destination.

F

Familiarization tour A tour with free or reduced-rate arrangements for travel agents or public carrier employees that is intended to stimulate them to sell travel or tours as experienced on the "famtour."

Federal Aviation Administration (U.S.) A governmental regulatory agency concerned with airport operation, air safety, licensing of flight personnel, and other aviation matters.

Flag carrier An international airline often owned and/or operated by the government of its home country.

Flight, connecting A flight that requires a change of aircraft and flight number en route to a destination.

Flight, direct A flight that may make intermediary stops en route to a destination.

Flight, nonstop A flight that travels to a destination without any intermediary stops.

Food services Facilities that provide food and meals to visitors to a destination. The most common forms are restaurants, fast-food outlets, snack bars, cafeterias, food fairs, and the homes of friends and relatives.

Foreign independent travel (FIT) An individually designed tour by an individual or family rather than a predesigned package tour.

Frequent-flyer plan Program where bonuses are offered by the airlines to passengers who accumulate travel mileage.

G

Governance The system that defines the organizations, the processes, and the complex of political institutions, laws, and customs through which power and authority within a destination are exercised.

Ground arrangements All those services provided by a tour operator after reaching the first destination. Also referred to as land arrangements.

Group inclusive tour (GIT) A tour that includes group air and ground arrangements for a minimum of fifteen persons. They may or may not stay together

as a group for both the land and air portions of the trip.

H

Hub and spoke A system that feeds connecting passengers into major gateway airports from short-haul or point-to-point downline routes.

I

Incentive tour A tour arranged especially for employees or agents of a company as a reward for achievement, usually sales. Spouses are typically included on the trip.

Inclusive tour A travel plan for which prearranged transportation, wholly by air or partly by air and partly by surface, together with ground facilities (such as meals, hotels, and so on) are sold for a total price.

Information Knowledge obtained from investigation, study, or instruction.

Infrastructure The facilities, equipment, and installations needed for the basic functioning and daily lives of the residents of a region. These include communication systems, water and sewage facilities, public protection, health, transportation, and education systems.

International Air Transport Association (IATA) The authoritative trade association maintained by international and overseas airlines.

Internet service providers Companies that provide domain space for others on computer servers they own, companies that provide travel information that they develop, and companies that provide a combination of the two.

M

Modified American plan A room rate that includes a full American breakfast and lunch or dinner, usually dinner.

O

Open jaw A pairing of two or more nearby destinations that allows a passenger to arrive at one airport and depart from a second.

Open skies An agreement between two or more nations that allows its air carriers to fly unrestricted within each other's borders; the United States and the Netherlands recently signed an open skies pact.

P

Package A prepaid tour that includes transportation, lodging, and other ingredients, usually meals, transfers, sight-seeing, or car rentals. May be varied, but typically includes at least three ingredients sold at a fixed price.

Passport Issued by national governments to their own citizens as verification of their citizenship. It is also a permit to leave one's own country and return.

Pension A French word widely used throughout Europe meaning guesthouse or boardinghouse.

People Those humans who reside in, or visit, a tourism destination.

Physiography The physical geography of a tourism destination.

R

Reception agency A tour operator or travel agency specializing in foreign visitors. American Adventure Tours is such a company.

Retail travel agency Mostly in the United States. Travel agents sell carriers' tickets and wholesalers' or operators' tours. In perspective, retail agents are commissioned or subagents.

Revalidation The authorized stamping or writing on the passenger ticket showing that it has been officially altered by the carrier.

Run-of-the-house A hotel term to guarantee a firm price that applies to any room in the house. Often a hotel will provide a superior room, if available, in an effort to please the guest and the tour operator.

S

Spa A hotel or resort providing hot springs or baths and other health-enhancing facilities and services.

Superstructure The equipment and facilities needed to meet the particular needs of the visitors to a region. These include accommodation and food services, visitor information and services, tourism attractions, special events, supplementary transportation, and special education and training programs for front-line staff and industry managers.

Supplier An industry term meaning any form of transportation, accommodations, and other travel services used by a travel agency or tour operator to fulfill the needs of travelers.

T

Tariffs The published fares, rates, charges, and/or related conditions of carriage of a carrier.

Technology The entire body of methods and materials used to achieve commercial, industrial, or societal objectives.

Timeshare Concept of dividing the ownership and use of a lodging property among investors.

Tour-basing fare A reduced, round-trip fare available on specified dates, and between specified times, only to passengers who purchase preplanned, prepaid tour arrangements prior to their departure to specified areas.

Tourism (1) The entire world industry of travel, hotels, transportation, and all other components, including promotion, that serves the needs and wants of travelers. Tourism today has been given new meaning and is primarily a term of economics referring to an industry. (2) Within a nation (political subdivision or transportation-centered economic area of contiguous nations), the sum total of tourist expenditures within their borders is referred to as the nation's tourism or tourist industry and is thus ranked with other national industries. More important than just the total monetary product value of tourism is its role in the balance of trade. Here tourism earnings from foreigners truly represent an export industry. Tourism is an "invisible" export.

Tourist A person who travels from place to place for nonwork reasons. By U.N. definition, a tourist is someone who stays for more than one night and less than a year. Business and convention travel is included. This thinking is dominated by balance-of-trade concepts. Military personnel, diplomats, immigrants, and resident students are not tourists.

Tour operator A company that specializes in the planning and operation of prepaid, preplanned vacations and makes these available to the public, usually through travel agents.

Tour organizer An individual, usually not professionally connected with the travel industry, who organizes tours for special groups of people, such as teachers, church leaders, farmers, and the like.

Tour package A travel plan that includes several elements of a vacation, such as transportation, accommodations, and sightseeing.

Tour wholesaler A company that plans, markets, and (usually) operates tours. Marketing is always through intermediaries such as retail travel agents, an association, a club, or a tour organizer—never directly to the public as is sometimes done by tour operators. The wholesaler would not operate the tour if, for example, it was functioning as a wholesaler in the United States for tours operated by a foreign firm. In industry jargon, tour operator and tour wholesaler are synonymous.

Transportation The act or process of carrying or moving people or goods, or both, from one location to another.

Travel (see Tourism) Often interchangeable with *tourism*. Actually, this term should represent all direct elements of travel. Included in the term *travel* are transportation, vacations, resorts, and any other direct passenger elements, including but not limited to national parks, attractions, and auto use for any of the above purposes. To make a journey from one place to another.

Travel industry services Includes those organizations, firms, and individuals that provide a diverse range of services that enable and facilitate travel, as well as make it more convenient and less risky. Examples include computer support services, financial services, insurance, information, and interpretation.

Travel trade Includes those organizations, firms, and individuals that provide various elements of the total travel experience.

V

Vacation ownership A term often used to describe resort timesharing.

Visa Document issued by a foreign government permitting nationals of another country to visit or travel. The visa is usually stamped on pages provided in one's passport but may also be a document fastened to the passport.

Y

Yield management The use of pricing and inventory controls, based upon historical data, to maximize profits by offering varying fares over time for the same product.

Selected Tourism Abbreviations
▼

AAA	American Automobile Association
ABA	American Bus Association
ABC	Advanced Booking Charter
AHLA	American Hotel and Lodging Association
AIEST	International Association of Scientific Experts in Tourism
AIT	Académie Internationale du Tourisme
ATME	Association of Travel Marketing Executives
Amtrak	National Railroad Passenger Corporation
AP	American Plan
APEC	Asia-Pacific Economic Cooperation
APEX	Advance Purchase Excursion Fare
ARC	Airlines Reporting Corporation
ARDA	American Resort and Development Association
ARTA	Association of Retail Travel Agents
ASTA	American Society of Travel Agents
ATA	Air Transport Association of America
BIT	Bulk Inclusive Tour
BTA	British Tourist Authority
CHRIE	Council on Hotel, Restaurant, and Institutional Education
CITC	Canadian Institute of Travel Counselors
CLIA	Cruise Lines International Association
COTAL	Confederation of Tourist Organizations of Latin America
CRS	Computerized Reservations System
CTC	Canadian Tourism Commission
CTC	Certified Travel Counselor
CTO	Caribbean Tourism Organization
DIT	Domestic Independent Tours
DMO	Destination Management Organization
DOT	U.S. Government Department of Transportation
ECOSOC	Economic and Social Council of the United Nations
EP	European Plan

ETC	European Travel Commission	NARVPC	National Association of RV Parks and Campgrounds
FAA (U.S.)	Federal Aviation Administration		
FHA	Federal Highway Administration	NCA	National Council of Attractions
FIT	Foreign Independent Tour	NRA	National Restaurant Association
GIT	Group Inclusive Tour	NRPA	National Recreation and Park Association
HSMAI	Hospitality Sales and Marketing Association International		
		NTA	National Tour Association
IAAPA	International Association of Amusement Parks and Attractions	OAG	Official Airline Guide
		OAS	Organization of American States
IACVB	International Association of Convention and Visitor Bureaus	OECD	Organization for Economic Cooperation and Development
IAF	International Automobile Federation	OTTI	Office of Travel and Tourism Industries (U.S.)
IAST	International Academy for the Study of Tourism	PAII	Professional Association of Innkeepers International
IATA	International Air Transport Association	PATA	Pacific Asia Travel Association
		RAA	Regional Airline Association
IATAN	International Airlines Travel Agent Network	RPM	Revenue Passenger Miles
		RTF	Rural Tourism Foundation
ICAO	International Civil Aviation Organization	RVIA	Recreation Vehicle Industry Association
ICC	Interstate Commerce Commission		
ICCL	International Council of Cruise Lines	SATW	Society of American Travel Writers
ICSC	International Council of Shopping Centers	SITE	Society of Incentive and Travel Executives
IFWTO	International Federation of Women's Travel Organizations	S&R	Sell and Report
		TIA	Travel Industry Association of America
IH&RA	International Hotel and Restaurant Association	TIAC	Tourism Industry Association of Canada
IIPT	International Institute for Peace through Tourism	TTRA	Travel and Tourism Research Association
IIT	Inclusive Independent Tour	UFTAA	Universal Federation of Travel Agents' Association
ILO	International Labor Organization		
ISMP	International Society of Meeting Planners	UNDP	United Nations Development Programme
ISTTE	International Society of Travel and Tourism Educators	UNESCO	United Nations Educational, Scientific, and Cultural Organization
IT	Inclusive Tour		
ITC	Inclusive Tour Charter	USTOA	United States Tour Operators Association
IYHF	International Youth Hostel Federation		
		WATA	World Association of Travel Agencies
MAP	Modified American Plan	WHO	World Health Organization
MCO	Miscellaneous Charges Order	WTAO	World Touring and Automobile Organization
MPI	Meeting Professionals International		
NACOA	National Association of Cruise Oriented Agencies	WTO	World Tourism Organization
		WTTC	World Travel and Tourism Council
NAPVO	National Association of Passenger Vessel Owners	WWW	World Wide Web

INDEX